5. Develop and strengthen writing as needed by planning, revising, editing, rewriting ~~~ approach.

6. Use technology, including the Internet, to produce and publish writing and ~~~ collaborate with others.

Research to Build and Present Knowledge

7. Conduct short as well as more sustained research projects based on focuse~~~ demonstrating understanding of the subject under investigation. | **9, 13**

8. Gather relevant information from multiple print and digital sources, assess the credibility and accuracy of each source, and integrate the information while avoiding plagiarism. | **6, 8, 9** Icons throughout

9. Draw evidence from literary or informational texts to support analysis, reflection, and research. | **8, 9**

Range of Writing

10. Write routinely over extended time frames (time for research, reflection, and revision) and shorter time frames (a single sitting or a day or two) for a range of tasks, purposes, and audiences. | **3, 4, 5, 6, 7, 8, 9, 12, 13**

College and Career Readiness Anchor Standards for Speaking and Listening	Chapters
Comprehension and Collaboration	
1. Prepare for and participate effectively in a range of conversations and collaborations with diverse partners, building on others' ideas and expressing their own clearly and persuasively.	**4, 8** Icons throughout
2. Integrate and evaluate information presented in diverse media and formats, including visually, quantitatively, and orally.	**9** Icons throughout
3. Evaluate a speaker's point of view, reasoning, and use of evidence and rhetoric.	**8, 9** Icons throughout
Presentation of Knowledge and Ideas	
4. Present information, findings, and supporting evidence such that listeners can follow the line of reasoning and the organization, development, and style are appropriate to task, purpose, and audience.	**6, 8, 9** Icons throughout
5. Make strategic use of digital media and visual displays of data to express information and enhance understanding of presentations.	**9** Icons throughout
6. Adapt speech to a variety of contexts and communicative tasks, demonstrating command of formal English when indicated or appropriate.	**5, 6** Icons throughout

College and Career Readiness Anchor Standards for Language	Chapters
Conventions of Standard English	
1. Demonstrate command of the conventions of standard English grammar and usage when writing or speaking.	**5**
2. Demonstrate command of the conventions of standard English capitalization, punctuation, and spelling when writing.	**5**
Knowledge of Language	
3. Apply knowledge of language to understand how language functions in different contexts, to make effective choices for meaning or style, and to comprehend more fully when reading or listening.	**4, 5, 8, 9**
Vocabulary Acquisition and Use	
4. Determine or clarify the meaning of unknown and multiple-meaning words and phrases by using context clues, analyzing meaningful word parts, and consulting general and specialized reference materials, as appropriate.	**5, 7**
5. Demonstrate understanding of word relationships and nuances in word meanings.	**4, 5, 7, 8**
6. Acquire and use accurately a range of general academic and domain-specific words and phrases sufficient for reading, writing, speaking, and listening at the college and career readiness level; demonstrate independence in gathering vocabulary knowledge when encountering an unknown term important to comprehension or expression.	**5, 7, 9**

Developing Literacy
Reading and Writing
To, With, and By Children

Timothy G. Morrison
Brigham Young University

Brad Wilcox
Brigham Young University

PEARSON

Boston   Columbus   Indianapolis   New York   San Francisco   Upper Saddle River
Amsterdam   Cape Town   Dubai   London   Madrid   Milan   Munich   Paris   Montreal   Toronto
Delhi   Mexico City   São Paulo   Sydney   Hong Kong   Seoul   Singapore   Taipei   Tokyo

To Carol and Debi

Vice President, Editor in Chief: Aurora Martínez Ramos
Editor: Erin K.L. Grelak
Editorial Assistant: Michelle Hochberg
Executive Marketing Manager: Krista Clark
Production Editor: Karen Mason
Production Coordination, Editorial Services, and Text Design: Electronic Publishing Services Inc., NYC
Art Rendering and Electronic Page Makeup: Jouve
Cover Designer: Jenny Hart
Cover, Chapter Opener, and Creative Feature Illustrations: Steve Morrison
Photos: Gian Rosborough and Jill Shumway

Library of Congress Cataloging-in-Publication Data

Morrison, Timothy (Timothy G.) author.
  Developing literacy : reading and writing to, with, and by children / Timothy G. Morrison & Brad Wilcox.
    pages cm
Includes bibliographical references and index.
ISBN-13: 978-0-13-501961-0
ISBN-10: 0-13-501961-3
1. Reading (Elementary)   I. Wilcox, Brad, 1959- author.   II. Title.
LB1573.M664 2013
372.4—dc23
                                            2012015735

ISBN 10: 0-13-501961-3
ISBN 13: 978-0-13-501961-0

About the Authors

Timothy G. Morrison and Brad Wilcox are associate professors in the Department of Teacher Education at Brigham Young University, where they teach undergraduate and graduate courses in reading, language arts, and children's literature. They both earned their BA and MEd degrees at Brigham Young University. Tim received his PhD at the University of Illinois at Urbana–Champaign, and Brad earned his PhD at the University of Wyoming. Prior to joining the faculty at BYU, Tim served as a faculty member at Boise State University and California State University–Fresno.

Early in his career, Tim taught grades four, five, and six in Pocatello, Idaho and third grade in Springville, Utah; Brad previously taught sixth grade in Provo, Utah. More recently, they have both done extensive consulting throughout the United States, as well as in Central America, Australia, and Europe. They both have directed BYU's New Zealand Study Abroad Program, living in Auckland, where they taught and supervised teacher candidates in practicum settings.

Their research and professional writing focuses on literacy, teacher education, children's literature, and education in international settings. They have served as editors for the professional publications of the Association of Literacy Educators and Researchers and have published articles in many professional journals, including *Literacy Research and Instruction*, *Reading Psychology*, *The Journal of Adolescent and Adult Literacy*, and *The Reading Teacher*.

Tim and his wife, Carol, are the parents of three grown sons and have four grandchildren. Brad and his wife, Debi, have four children and three grandchildren.

Contents

Preface   xiii

part one foundations of literacy   1

Chapter 1   Understanding Literacy Contexts   1

HISTORICAL OVERVIEW   2
Colonial Period   2
Early American History   3
Early 1900s   4
Late 1900s   6
2000s   7

LITERACY THEORIES   9
Bottom-Up   9
Top-Down   10
Interactive   10
SUMMARY   11
SELF-CHECK   12
MyEducationLab™   12

Chapter 2   Understanding the Needs of All Learners   13

CULTURE   15
LANGUAGE MINORITIES   20
Second Language Acquisition   20
    Pre-production   20 • Early
    Production   20 • Speech
    Emergence   20 • Intermediate
    Fluency   21 • Advanced Fluency   21
School Assistance   21
    Special Services   21 • Instructional Support   22

POVERTY   23
URBAN AND RURAL EDUCATION   24
Urban   24
Rural   25
LEARNING DISABILITIES   26
SUMMARY   28
SELF-CHECK   29
MyEducationLab™   29

Chapter 3   Teaching for Learning   30

IMPACT OF TEACHERS   32
Learning and Teaching   32
Key Behaviors of Effective Teaching   33
    Variety   34 • Clarity   34 • Task
    Orientation   34 • Engagement   35 • Success
    Rate   35
COMPONENTS OF LITERACY   36
Elements of Reading   36
    Phonological Awareness   36 • Phonics   37
    Vocabulary   37 • Fluency   38
    Comprehension   38
Traits of Writing   39
    Voice   40 • Organization   41 • Ideas   41
    Conventions   42 • Word Choice   42 • Sentence

    Fluency   42 • Presentation   42
Linking Reading and Writing   43
LEARNERS' PROCESSES   43
Reading Process   44
    Prereading   44 • Reading   45
    Responding   45 • Exploring   45 • Applying   46
Writing Process   46
    Prewriting   47 • Drafting   47 • Seeking a
    Response   49 • Revising   49 • Editing   50
    Publishing   51
Linking Reading and Writing   51
INSTRUCTION   52
Approaches   53

Core Literacy Programs   53 • Reading and Writing
Workshops   54 • Literature Units   54
Self-Regulated Strategy Development   55 • Genre
Writing   56
Essential Elements   57
    Time to Learn   57 • Time to Do   58 • Time to
    Share   59
MOTIVATION AND LITERACY   60

Perceived Requirements   60
Perceived Expectations   60
Sincere Desires   61
Progressing Through Levels   61
SUMMARY   62
SELF-CHECK   62
MyEducationLab™   63

part two components of literacy 64

Chapter 4   Emergent Literacy   64

ORAL LANGUAGE DEVELOPMENT   65
Phonology   65
Semantics   66
Syntax   66
Pragmatics   67
Schema Theory   67
    Insufficient Text Clues   68 • Limited
    Schema   68 • Mismatched Schema   69
LITERACY DEVELOPMENT   69
Emergent   69
Beginning   69
Fluent   70

AWARENESS OF SOUNDS AND LETTERS   70
Recognition of Language Sounds   71
    Phonemic Awareness   71 • Phonological
    Awareness   71 • Word Play   72
Written Language Development   73
    Developmental Stages   75 • Developmental
    Journal Writing   75
Combining Spoken and Written Language   78
    Picture Books   78 • Language Experience
    Approach (LEA)   79
SUMMARY   82
SELF-CHECK   82
MyEducationLab™   82

Chapter 5   Beginning Reading and Writing   83

WORD IDENTIFICATION   84
Phonics   84
Useful Generalizations   86 • Instruction   88
Word Families   90
    Instruction   91 • Word Games   92
Sight Words   94
    High Frequency Words   95 • Instruction   95
Putting It All Together   96
**CONVENTIONS OF WRITTEN
    LANGUAGE   99**

Concepts about Print   99
Spelling   101
Handwriting   102
Grammar   103
Interactive Writing   104
SUMMARY   107
SELF-CHECK   107
MyEducationLab™   107

Chapter 6   Fluency   108

COMPONENTS OF FLUENCY   109
SKILLS AND STRATEGIES   110
Rate and Accuracy   110
    Repeated Reading   110 • Neurological
    Impress   112 • Echo Reading   112
Expression   112

Readers' Theater   113 • Puppet
Shows   113
ORAL READING   116
Group Reading   116
Assessment   117
Transition to Silent Reading   117

WRITTEN LANGUAGE   118
Sentence Fluency   118
   Timed Writing   119 • Conferencing for
   Content   119
Voice   120

Class Book   121 • Classroom Post Office   124
SUMMARY   124
SELF-CHECK   125
MyEducationLab™   125

Chapter 7   Vocabulary   126

VOCABULARY AND READING   127
Size   128
Word Collections   129
Guiding Principles   131
   Experience   131 • Environment   131
   Exposure   132 • Engagement   132
Types of Words   133
Instruction   136
   Key Word Prediction   136 • Five-Step
   Approach   137 • Semantic Mapping   140

VOCABULARY AND WRITING   141
Word Choice   142
   Precise Language   142 • Powerful
   Language   144
Poetry   146
SUMMARY   148
SELF-CHECK   148
MyEducationLab™   148

Chapter 8   Creating Meaning   149

FOUNDATIONAL MEANING-MAKING
   ABILITIES   150
CREATING MEANING THROUGH
   READING   151
Reading Comprehension Strategies   151
   Organizational Strategies   152 • Identifying Main
   Ideas   153 • Inferential Strategies   160 •
   Metacognitive Strategies   173
Multiple Strategies   175

CREATING MEANING THROUGH
   WRITING   177
Ideas   177
   Life Maps   178 • Shared Stories   178 • Writers'
   Notebooks   179
Organization   180
   Audience   180 • Forms of Writing   182
SUMMARY   185
SELF-CHECK   186
MyEducationLab™   186

Chapter 9   Integrating Literacy with Content Areas   187

READING IN CONTENT AREAS   188
Expository Text Structure   188
   Description   189 • Sequence   190
   Comparison   190 • Cause and Effect   190
   Problem and Solution   190
Expository Text Features   190
   Print Features   190 • Organizational Aids   191
   Graphic Aids   192
Study Strategies   192
   SQ3R   193 • Mnemonic Devices   194
   KWL   195
Study Guides   197
   Graphic Organizers   197 • Anticipation Guides   198
   Internet Inquiries   200 • Games   201

WRITING IN CONTENT AREAS   203
Writing without Revision   203
   Learning Logs   204 • Think-Write-Share   205 •
   Note Taking/Note Making   206
Writing with Revision   206
   Shared Writing   207 • Small Groups   208
Expository Text   209
   Reports   210 • Alphabet Books   212
Argumentative Writing   214
   Persuasive Papers   214 • Advertisements   217
SUMMARY   217
SELF-CHECK   218
MyEducationLab™   218

part three literacy assessment and instruction 219

Chapter 10 Assessing for Learning 219

TYPES OF ASSESSMENT 220
Summative 220
  Norm-Referenced 221 • Criterion-Referenced 221
Formative 222
  Response to Intervention (RtI) 223 • Assessment
  for Learning 224
Performance-Based 225
  Performances 226 • Portfolios 226
  Projects 227
READING ASSESSMENT 227
Individual Methods 228
  Running Records 228 • Informal Reading
  Inventories 230

Student-Text Matching 231
  Readability Formulas 231 • Cloze Procedure 232
  Range of Text Complexity 234
WRITING ASSESSMENT 235
Large-Scale 235
Classroom 236
  Ongoing Assistance 236 • Judging Student
  Writing 237
INFORMING INSTRUCTION 239
SUMMARY 240
SELF-CHECK 241
MyEducationLab™ 241

Chapter 11 Reading and Writing to Children 242

READING TO CHILDREN 244
Importance of Reading Aloud 245
  Motivation 245 • Vocabulary 246 • Language
  and Print Concepts 246 • Attention Span 247
Read Aloud Techniques 248
  Expression 248 • Illustrations 249
  Questions 249
Book Selection 250
  Narrative 252 • Informational 252 • Poetic 252
WRITING TO CHILDREN 253
Methods 253

Personal Notes 254 • Morning
Messages 254 • Instructions 255 • Classroom
Labels 256 • Dialogue Journals 257
Models 258
  Author Visits 258 • Teacher
  Modeling 258 • Author's Craft 259
SUMMARY 260
SELF-CHECK 260
MyEducationLab™ 260

Chapter 12 Reading and Writing with Children—Whole Class 261

READING WITH CHILDREN—WHOLE
  CLASS 262
Shared Reading within Various Instructional
  Approaches 262
  Core Literacy Programs 263 • Reading
  Workshop 263 • Literature Units 264
Reading Process 265
  Before Reading 266 • During Reading 268 •
  After Reading 271
WRITING WITH CHILDREN—WHOLE
  CLASS 276

Shared Writing within Various Instructional
  Approaches 277
  Core Literacy Programs 277 • Writing
  Workshop 277 • Self-Regulated Strategy
  Development 277 • Genre Writing 278
Writing Process 278
  Before Writing 279 • Advance Planning 279
  During Writing 282 • After Writing 285
SUMMARY 289
SELF-CHECK 289
MyEducationLab™ 289

Chapter 13   Reading and Writing with Children—Small Groups   290

READING WITH CHILDREN—SMALL
    GROUPS   291
Core Literacy Programs   292
    Primary Grade Groups   292 • Intermediate Grade
    Groups   295 • Facilitating   296
Reading Workshop   297
    Organizing   298 • Working   298
    Facilitating   299
Literature Discussion Groups   299
    Organizing   300 • Working   300 • Facilitating   302

WRITING WITH CHILDREN—SMALL
    GROUPS   303
Core Literacy Programs   303
    Primary Grade Groups   303 • Intermediate Grade
    Groups   305
Writing Workshop   305
    Organizing   306 • Working   306 • Facilitating   310
Formula Writing   311
    Organizing   312 • Working   313 • Facilitating   313
SUMMARY   314
SELF-CHECK   314
MyEducationLab™   314

Chapter 14   Reading and Writing by Children   315

READING BY CHILDREN   316
Classroom Libraries   317
    Creating a Classroom Library   318 • Using a
    Classroom Library   319
Teacher Support and Encouragement   323
    Teacher Modeling   323 • Interacting
    with Students   324 • Lending
    Libraries   324 • Incentive Programs   325

WRITING BY CHILDREN   326
Journals   327
    Regular Time   328 • Choice of Topic   328
Technology   330
SUMMARY   331
SELF-CHECK   332
MyEducationLab™   332

Glossary   333

References   339

Name Index   354

Subject Index   358

Credits   363

"Try This"

Try This for Professional Development

Try This for Teaching

Chapter 1 • Understanding Literacy Contexts
History of Literacy Timeline   9
Exploring Literacy Theories   11

Chapter 2 • Understanding the Needs of All Learners
Respond to a Teacher   15
Create Your Own Culture Grams   16
Transnational and Community
   Exploration   19
Modeled Talk   23
Literacy Autobiography   28

Chapter 3 • Teaching for Learning
Thank a Teacher   32
Cross-age Tutoring   35
Songs and Sounds   37
Authors to Emulate   39
Six Traits Acronym   43
Writing Process Plus   52
Window Lesson Plan   57
Levels of Motivation   61

Chapter 4 • Emergent Literacy
Interview with an English
   Learner
Word Play Around the School   73
Plastic-Covered Pages   79
Class Thank-You Note   81

Chapter 5 • Beginning Reading and Writing
Alphabet Name Book   85
Enhance Your Phonics
   Knowledge   86
Logo Language   90
Word Family Wall   91
Hink Pink   92
I'm Thinking of a Word   94
Making Words   94
Word Hunt   96
Model Cursive Writing   103
Elkonin Boxes   106

Chapter 6 • Fluency
Repeated Reading   111
Neurological Impress   111
Echo Reading   112
Explore Expressive Reading
   Assessments   113
Readers' Theater   114
Books for Multiple Voices   114
Joke Books   114
Puppet Shows   115
Fill in the Blank   115
Fluency Phones   116
Turn Down the Volume   117
Timed Writing   119
Conferencing for Content (Sentence
   Fluency)   120

A Shift in Focus   120
Class Book   123
Classroom Post Office   124

Chapter 7 • Vocabulary
Increase Affirmations   129
Word Wall Activities   131
Vocabulary Role Play   132
Four Es Evaluation   133
Fist to Five   134
Word Scavenger Hunt   135
Key Word Prediction   137
Contextual Redefinition   138
RIVET   138
Five-Step Approach   139
Semantic Mapping   141
Reporting Back   141
Synonym Stacking   143
Good and Better   143
Use Your Senses   145
Samples of Sensory Writing   145
Throw Out Your First Thought   146
Telephone Number Poem   147

Chapter 8 • Creating Meaning
Many Ways to Teach Meaning
   Making   151
Key Word Notes   154
Create a Title   154
Comprehension Process
   Motions   154

Read-Talk-Write 155
TwitterTalk 156
Best Book 156
Story Maps 157
A Book in 30 Minutes 157
Argument Chart 160
Read with Purpose 161
Point of View 161
Modeling Predictions 163
Reading Detectives 164
Venn Diagram 165
"So What?" and "Aha!"
    Connections 165
Arrow Connections 167
Bridge Connections 167
Character Clues 170
Musical Images 170
A Play in Your Mind 170
Mind Illustrations 171
Talking About Thinking 172
Questioning the Author 173
Clicking and Clunking 174
Think-Alouds 175
Teaching Beyond the Test 177
Life Maps 178
Shared Stories 179
Writers' Notebooks 179
Picture Word Inductive Model 181
Create a Title 181
Pen Pals 182
Writing Frames 184
Memoir 184
Class Newspapers 185

Chapter 9 • Integrating Literacy
with Content Areas
Textbook Scavenger Hunt 192
SQ3R 194
Are You Sure? 196
Reversing the Trend 197
Create Your Own Graphic
    Organizers 199
Create Your Own Anticipation
    Guide 200
Internet Inquiry 200
WebQuests Across the Grades 201
Survivor Whiteboard Game 202

Learning Logs 205
Think-Write-Share 206
Collaborative Book 207
Put It in Your Own Words 208
Put Yourself in the Writing 210
Class ABC Books 212
Opinion Writing 214
Create Travel Brochures 217

Chapter 10 • Assessing for
Learning
Test Wiseness 222
Prep for Praxis 223
Review of RtI Assessments 224
CAFEÉ 225
Create Your Own Rubric 227
Attend to Genre Prompts 235
"Fix It" 237
AUTHORS: A Quality Writing
    Checklist 238
Publishing Deadlines 239

Chapter 11 • Reading and Writing
to Children
Read-Aloud Memories 245
Where Else Do You Hear These
    Words? 246
Information for Parents 247
Recorded Books 248
Lines, Between the Lines, and
    Beyond the Lines 249
Caption Read-Alouds 253
Notes for Everyone 254
Fill-in-the-Blank Morning
    Message 255
Reading Around the Room 256
Dialogue Journals 257
Successful Author Visits 258

Chapter 12 • Reading and Writing
with Children—Whole Class
Share Your Advice 264
Realia 267
Role Play 267
Verify and Clarify 268
Back-and-Forth Reading 270
Dyad Reading 271
Eight Ws 273
Student Survey 274

Answering Game 274
Reading Logs 276
Artistic Prompts 280
Hunting for LIONS 281
Word Banks 282
Spelling in Context 283
Individual Whiteboards 284
Four Ps of Reflection 286
Reflect on Your Teaching 286
Interactive Editing 287
Adapting Instruction 288

Chapter 13 • Reading and
Writing with Children—Small
Groups
Exploring Newspapers 297
Preparing to Read 298
Language Arts Workshop 299
Voting for Books 300
Group Responses 302
Instructional Moves During Small
    Groups 302
Clothespin Organization 306
Journals to Projects 308
WRITE: Conferencing Tips 308
Visit the Writing Center 309
Enlisting Readers 310
Final Draft Workstation 311
Phone Conferences 312

Chapter 14 • Reading and Writing
by Children
Examine the NRP (2000) 317
Book Exchanges 319
Just What the Doctor Ordered 319
Readers in a Box 321
Rain Gutter Display 321
Two Books Are Better than
    One 322
Book Talks 324
Scaffolded Silent Reading
    (ScSR) 325
Lending Library 325
Genre Wheel 326
Traveling Tales 328
Three-Word Journal 330
Taking a Stand? 330
Emails and Attachments 331

Preface

In effective elementary classrooms that produce high language arts achievement, children are highly engaged because skills and strategies are taught with rich opportunities for application to real reading and writing experiences. Teachers provide positive literacy models and scaffolded support as they work with students. They also allow students to work independently (Pressley, Gaskins, Solic, & Collins, 2006).

Such schools are not always the norm. As we work with teachers and teacher candidates in literacy, we frequently see fragmented implementation of aspects of a comprehensive literacy program, but rarely do we see all those parts put together into a meaningful whole. One teacher may closely follow a basal reading program. Another may use technology to motivate independent reading. Still others are so focused on phonics that they overlook vocabulary. And then there are teachers who are so anxious to get their students ready for the tests that they overlook the need for more authentic motivation. Some teachers say they know what they *should* be doing, but they just don't have the time to do it. They say they have too many other demands placed on them. Still others do not know how to begin organizing time and resources to present a balanced program. This discrepancy among teachers can be seen at times within the same school building. Children in a high-quality, literacy rich classroom one year can make great progress but slow their growth and lose their enthusiasm in a different classroom the following year (Jacob, Lefgren, & Sims, 2010).

Purpose

We wrote this book to give a comprehensive view of all the elements that are essential to develop effective literacy and provide the necessary **gradual release of responsibility** from teachers to students (Mooney, 1990; Mooney & Young, 2006; Pearson & Gallagher, 1983). Like the oft-repeated story of the blind man and the elephant, many literacy educators focus on the trunk, the legs, or the tail. What today's students need are more teachers who see the whole elephant—the big picture—and consistently implement what they know.

When we observe preservice teachers and their mentors, we also notice that writing is sometimes overlooked. A high number of students are not developing the competencies they need in writing (Persky, Daane, & Jin, 2003). Most teachers are concerned about reading success, as they should be, but some do not see writing as an important component in literacy growth. In this text, reading and writing are both treated in each chapter, rather than as separate chapters. We hope that you will see interconnections between the two and teach both reading and writing in your literacy curriculum. Ideally, writing leads to reading, and reading leads to writing. In fact, on close examination writing *is* reading, because authors are composing meaning; and reading *is* writing, because readers are also composing meaning. Competent readers and writers usually engage in these meaning-making processes interactively (Fitzgerald & Shanahan, 2000).

Using This Book

This book is organized into three main parts: Part I, Foundations of Literacy; Part II, Components of Literacy; and Part III, Literacy Assessment and Instruction. The ordering of the parts will help you understand *why* and *who* you are teaching, then *what* you are teaching, and finally *how* you are teaching. In Part II, Components of Literacy, we present the five essential elements of literacy in the same order that they are outlined by the National Reading Panel (2000).

Throughout the book, you will notice connections with the **Common Core State Standards**, which have been printed on the inside covers, along with **International Reading Association Standards**. There is no question that these standards greatly influence our schools, and you need to be aware of them and feel confident using them as a guide as you meet individual needs of children. You will also find "Try This" boxes, which include activities and ideas for immediate practice and practical application of the concepts you are learning. Some "Try This" boxes encourage professional development. We have also included samples of teacher and student work.

Rather than having specific chapters on speaking and listening, language conventions, **English language learners**, struggling students, and **new literacies**, we have chosen to integrate these important issues throughout the text. Icons in the margins will help you recognize where these connections have been made:

Each chapter begins with a chapter outline followed by a personal experience. We hope these vignettes provide realistic contexts for the upcoming chapters, but most of all we hope they will give you a chance to see us as real teachers who have worked in classrooms with children. Each chapter concludes with a brief summary and a Self-Check exercise to help you remember key content.

As you progress through your career, you will move through phases of development much like children move in their literacy development. Just as you receive knowledge and mentoring and gain greater expertise, so do children in their listening, speaking, reading, and writing. Just as you learn to reflect on your practice, children also develop habits of reflection. Both you and your students are developing. That's why we didn't title this book *Teaching Literacy* or *Learning Literacy*, but rather we put the focus on the word *developing*.

As former elementary teachers ourselves, we realize the importance of literacy in the lives of children, and we also realize the challenges that are inherent in teaching. We are passionate about facing these challenges and have devoted our professional lives to promoting literacy and making a positive difference. Thanks for being part of our dream!

Supplements

The following supplements comprise an outstanding array of resources that facilitate learning about literacy instruction. For more information, ask your local Pearson representative. For technology support, please contact technical support directly at 1-800-677-6337 or online at 247.pearsoned.com.

Instructor's Resource Manual and Test Bank

For each chapter, the instructor's resource manual features activities and resources for instructors to use in the classroom. Answers to the Self-Check questions for each chapter from the text are also included. In addition, the Test Bank includes multiple choice, essential terms, and short answer items. Page references to the main text, suggested answers, and skill types have been added to each question to help instructors create and evaluate student tests. This supplement has been written completely by the text authors. (Available for download from the Instructor Resource Center at **www.pearsonhighered.com/irc**.)

Pearson MyTest

The Test Bank is available as a downloadable file and can be printed by the user through our computerized testing system, MyTest, a powerful assessment generation program that helps instructors easily create and print quizzes and exams. Questions and tests are authored online, allowing ultimate flexibility and the ability to efficiently create and print assessments anytime, anywhere! Instructors can access Pearson MyTest and their test bank files by going to **www.pearsonmytest.com** to log in, register, or request access. Features of Pearson MyTest include:

Premium assessment content.

- Draw from a rich library of assessments that complement your Pearson textbook and your course's learning objectives.
- Edit questions or tests to fit your specific teaching needs.

Instructor-friendly resources.

- Easily create and store your own questions, including images, diagrams, and charts using simple drag-and-drop and Word-like controls.
- Use additional information provided by Pearson, such as the question's difficulty level or learning objective, to help you quickly build your test.

Time-saving enhancements.

- Add headers or footers and easily scramble questions and answer choices—all from one simple toolbar.
- Quickly create multiple versions of your test or answer key, and when ready, simply save to Microsoft Word or PDF format and print!
- Export your exams for import to Blackboard 6.0, CE (WebCT), or Vista (WebCT)!

PowerPoint™ Presentation

Designed for teachers using the text, the PowerPoint™ Presentation consists of a series of slides that can be shown as is or used to make handouts or overhead transparencies. The presentation highlights key concepts and major topics for each chapter. (Available for download from the Instructor Resource Center at **www.pearsonhighered.com/irc**.)

MyEducationLab™

Proven to **engage students**, provide **trusted content**, and **improve results**, Pearson MyLabs have helped over 8 million registered students reach true understanding in their courses. **MyEducationLab** engages students with real-life teaching situations through dynamic videos, case studies, and student artifacts. Student progress is assessed, and a personalized study plan is created based on the student's unique results. Automatic grading and reporting keeps educators informed to quickly address gaps and improve student performance. All of the activities and exercises in MyEducationLab are built around essential learning outcomes for teachers and are mapped to professional teaching standards.

In *Preparing Teachers for a Changing World*, Linda Darling-Hammond and her colleagues point out that grounding teacher education in real classrooms—among real teachers and students and among actual examples of students' and teachers' work—is an important, and perhaps even an essential, part of training teachers for the complexities of teaching in today's classrooms.

In the MyEducationLab for this course, you will find the following features and resources.

Study Plan Specific to Your Text.   MyEducationLab gives students the opportunity to test themselves on key concepts and skills, track their own progress through the course, and access personalized Study Plan activities.

The customized Study Plan—with enriching activities—is generated based on the results from student pretests. Study Plans tag incorrect questions from the pretest to the appropriate textbook learning outcome, helping students focus on the topics they need help with. Personalized Study Plan activities may include eBook reading assignments and review, practice, and enrichment activities.

After students complete the enrichment activities, they take a posttest to see the concepts they've mastered or the areas where they may need extra help.

MyEducationLab then reports the Study Plan results to the instructor. Based on these reports, the instructor can adapt course material to suit the needs of individual students or the entire class.

Connection to National Standards.   Now it is easier than ever to see how coursework is connected to national standards. Each topic, activity, and exercise on MyEducationLab lists intended learning outcomes connected to either the Common Core State Standards for Language Arts or the IRA Standards for Reading Professionals.

Assignments and Activities.   Designed to enhance your understanding of concepts covered in class, these assignable exercises show concepts in action (through videos, cases, and/or student and teacher artifacts). They help you deepen content knowledge and synthesize and apply concepts and strategies you read about in the book. (Correct answers for these assignments are available to the instructor only.)

Building Teaching Skills and Dispositions.   These unique learning units help users practice and strengthen skills that are essential to effective teaching. After presenting the steps involved in a core teaching process, you are given an opportunity to practice applying this skill through videos, student and teacher artifacts, and/or case studies of authentic classrooms. Providing multiple opportunities to practice a single teaching concept, each activity encourages a deeper understanding and application of concepts, as well as the use of critical thinking skills. After practice, students take a quiz that is reported to the instructor gradebook.

Lesson Plan Builder.   The **Lesson Plan Builder** is an effective and easy-to-use tool that you can use to create, update, and share quality lesson plans. The software also makes it easy to integrate state content standards into any lesson plan.

Iris Center Resources.   The IRIS Center at Vanderbilt University (iris.peabody .vanderbilt.edu), funded by the U.S. Department of Education's Office of Special Education Programs (OSEP), develops training enhancement materials for preservice and practicing teachers. The Center works with experts from across the country to create challenge-based interactive modules, case study units, and podcasts that provide research-validated information about working with students in inclusive settings. In your MyEducationLab course, we have integrated this content where appropriate.

A+RISE Activities.   A+RISE activities provide practice in targeting instruction. A+RISE®, developed by three-time Teacher of the Year and administrator Evelyn Arroyo, provides quick, research-based strategies that get to the "how" of targeting instruction and making content accessible for all students, including English language learners.

A+RISE® Standards2Strategy™ is an innovative and interactive online resource that offers new teachers in grades K–12 just-in-time, research-based instructional strategies that:

- Meet the linguistic needs of ELLs as they learn content
- Differentiate instruction for all grades and abilities
- Offer reading and writing techniques, cooperative learning, use of linguistic and nonlinguistic representations, scaffolding, teacher modeling, higher order thinking, and alternative classroom ELL assessment
- Provide support to help teachers be effective through the integration of listening, speaking, reading, and writing along with the content curriculum
- Improve student achievement
- Are aligned to Common Core Elementary Language Arts standards (for the literacy strategies) and to English language proficiency standards in WIDA, Texas, California, and Florida.

Course Resources.   The Course Resources section of MyEducationLab is designed to help you put together an effective lesson plan, prepare for and begin your career, navigate your first year of teaching, and understand key educational standards, policies, and laws.

It includes the following:

The **Grammar Tutorial** provides content extracted in part from *The Praxis Series*™ *Online Tutorial for the Pre-Professional Skills Test: Writing*. Online quizzes built around specific elements of grammar help users strengthen their understanding and proper usage of the English language in writing. Definitions and examples of grammatical concepts are followed by practice exercises to provide the background information and usage examples needed to refresh understandings of grammar and then apply that knowledge to make it more permanent.

Children's and Young Adult Literature Database offers information on thousands of quality literature titles, helping students choose appropriate literature and integrate the best titles into language arts instruction.

The **Preparing a Portfolio** module provides guidelines for creating a high-quality teaching portfolio.

Beginning Your Career offers tips, advice, and other valuable information on:

* Resume Writing and Interviewing: Includes expert advice on how to write impressive resumes and prepare for job interviews.
* Your First Year of Teaching: Provides practical tips to set up a first classroom, manage student behavior, and more easily organize for instruction and assessment.
* Law and Public Policies: Details specific directives and requirements you need to understand under the No Child Left Behind Act and the Individuals with Disabilities Education Improvement Act of 2004.

The **Certification and Licensure** section is designed to help you pass your licensure exam by giving you access to state test requirements, overviews of what tests cover, and sample test items. The Certification and Licensure section includes the following:

* **State Certification Test Requirements**: Here you can click on a state name link to see a list of state certification tests.
* You can click on the **Licensure Exams** you need to take to find:
  * Basic information about each test
  * Descriptions of what is covered on each test
  * Sample test questions with explanations of correct answers.

* **National Evaluation Series**™ by Pearson: Here, students can see the tests in the NES, learn what is covered on each exam, and access sample test items with descriptions and rationales of correct answers. You can also purchase interactive online tutorials developed by Pearson Evaluation Systems and the Pearson Teacher Education and Development group.
* **ETS Online Praxis Tutorials:** Here you can purchase interactive online tutorials developed by ETS and by the Pearson Teacher Education and Development group. Tutorials are available for the Praxis I exams and for select Praxis II exams.

Visit **www.myeducationlab.com** for a demonstration of this exciting new online teaching resource.

CourseSmart eBook and other eBook Options Available

CourseSmart is an exciting choice for purchasing this book. As an alternative to purchasing the printed book, you may purchase an electronic version of the same content via CourseSmart for a PC or Mac and for Android devices, or an iPad, iPhone, and iPod Touch with CourseSmart Apps. With a CourseSmart eBook, you can read the text, search through it, make notes online, and bookmark important passages for later review. For more information or to purchase access to the CourseSmart eBook for this text, visit **http://www.coursesmart.com**.

Look for availability of alternative eBook platforms and accessibility for a variety of devices on **www.mypearsonstore.com** by inserting the ISBN of this text (0-13-501961-3) and searching for access codes that will allow you to choose your most convenient online usage.

Acknowledgments

We are grateful for devoted parents who fostered our love of literacy and learning: Dorothy Beckstead and Ray T. and Val C. Wilcox. We also appreciate our teachers over the years and caring mentors whose words and examples encouraged us to seek further education. Thanks to Bill Hartman, Bill Dickson, Ed Peterson, Peter Crawley, Hal and Barbara Jones, Robert E. and Helen Wells, and Gerald J. and LuAnn S. Day in particular.

We acknowledge the powerful influence of our doctoral chairs, P. David Pearson and Louise Jackson. Other professional colleagues have made rich contributions to our lives and we thank them: Penny Dyer, Bill Kirtland, Roger Stewart, Norma Decker, Jim Jacobs, Mike Tunnell, Nancy Livingston, Eula E. Monroe, Beverly R. Cutler, D. Ray Retuzel, Lisa Cutler, and Russell T. Osguthorpe.

Without the support of students, colleagues, and administrators at Brigham Young University, and educators within the BYU/Public School Partnership it would have been impossible for us to complete this book. Sharon Black deserves special recognition for her expertise and insights as she assisted in revising and editing the manuscript. We also appreciate the help of Heather Krieger and Nora Ballantyne, and the patience and love of our wives and families.

We found the input of our reviewers to be invaluable. Thanks to: Janice Abrams, Carlow University; Martha Adam Colwell, Framingham State University; Julie Ellison Justice, University of North Carolina at Chapel Hill; Dianna Cherie Roberts, Bloomsburg University of Pennsylvania; Tammy Weiss Schimmel, The University of Tampa; and Laurie Stowell, California State University, San Marcos.

Thanks also to our friends at Pearson, especially Erin Grelak, whose encouragement and guidance have been incredible. We feel fortunate to have a beautiful cover and inside illustrations created by Steve Morrison. They truly capture the essence of the book. Finally, thanks to caring educators everywhere who make a positive difference for children.

Understanding Literacy Contexts

Chapter Outline

HISTORICAL OVERVIEW
Colonial Period
Early American History
Early 1900s
Late 1900s
2000s
LITERACY THEORIES
Bottom-Up
Top-Down
Interactive
SUMMARY

When I was in graduate school, I came across several books that expanded my thinking about teaching, learning, language, and literacy. One of these books, first published in 1908, was *The Psychology and Pedagogy of Reading,* by Edmund Burke Huey. In the book Huey wrote of the wonder of the written word. Consider how just because something is written, people give it more credibility. Huey challenged us to learn about processes that take place in our minds so we can better understand the act of reading: "And so to completely analyze what we do when we read would almost be the acme of a psychologist's achievements, for it would be to describe very many of the most intricate workings of the human mind and to unravel the tangled story of the most remarkable specific performance that civilization has learned in all its history" (p. 38). Even though that book had been written years ago, I realized its contents were still relevant to me. I determined to strive harder to understand how the human mind works, how language works, and how children learn so I could make more informed choices as a teacher.

—Tim

An enslaved man on a Southern plantation was required to work from sunrise to sunset six days a week. However, the plantation owner offered to pay him a few coins for working on his one day off. The enslaved man eagerly accepted this opportunity, for he had secret plans to save those coins and buy his freedom. He had heard of a free man who would forge release papers for a price. When he had finally saved enough, he bought his ticket for freedom and escaped. When the inevitable happened and someone asked to see his papers, he did not panic. He confidently presented his forged papers and was confused when he was promptly arrested and returned to the plantation. Because he could not read, he had no idea that he had paid a forger who could not write. His hard-earned coins had bought him nothing but a page of scribbles. His hopes were dashed. His open window was closed forever.

Throughout history, reading and writing have always opened windows for those who possessed these life-changing skills. Literacy has always meant the difference between bondage and freedom in one form or another.

It is no different today. Reading and writing are processes that are almost indispensable in our society. In order to be successful in school, at work, or even in many leisure activities, one must be able to read and write. Your career as a teacher of literacy will permit you to open windows of opportunity for your students. You will give them a ticket to freedom that will be real and will last forever.

To become successful as a teacher of literacy, you should familiarize yourself with literacy contexts that will anchor your teaching. Durkin (2004) repeatedly said, "The most important question teachers can ask themselves is '*Why* am I doing what I'm doing?'" (p. 31; emphasis in original). To answer that question, you need to know something about the history of literacy instruction and the application of learning theories. Instead of being a teacher who is satisfied with teaching a lesson because it is the next one in the book or because you have found a cute new activity to try, you will teach with purpose behind your instruction.

H istorical Overview

Understanding what has happened in the past helps you understand the present and prepare for the future. Most instructional approaches, materials, and trends you see in education have been used before. This brief history of American reading and writing instruction provides an important overview of the significant events, individuals, and publications that have shaped instruction during the colonial period, early American history, the early 1900s, the late 1900s, and the period from 2000 to the present.

Colonial Period

Figure 1.1
Sample Hornbook

Parents provided much of the reading and writing instruction for children living in the American colonies. Many of the first colonists came from England, so the instructional materials and texts they used had been published there. The most common teaching tool for reading was the **hornbook**, a small paddle with a sheet of paper placed beneath a thin piece of clear horn from an animal (see Figure 1.1). Hornbooks were used for children's reading instruction from the mid-1400s to the early 1700s.

Hornbooks were most commonly made of wood, but were also shaped from pewter, ivory, silver, and even gingerbread (Smith, 2002). Each small piece of paper contained similar elements, as well as different lessons. The alphabet was written at the top of the page, usually in both upper- and lowercase manuscript letters. Next came a series of common vowel-consonant combinations (such as *ab*, *et*, and *in*) and a verse from the Bible. Children named the letters of the alphabet, read the short letter combinations, then read the scripture orally, as a parent or older sibling listened and made corrections.

The first American-produced reading book, *The New England Primer*, was published in 1683 (Heartman, 1727; see Figure 1.2). A **primer** is an instructional tool for teaching reading to emerging and beginning readers. This small bound book emphasized initial learning of the alphabet and included short reading texts as well. Reflecting the culture of the people at that time, the content of the reading selections was religious.

One of the major reasons people learned to read during this period was to nourish themselves spiritually. Each lesson in *The New England Primer* ended with a type of catechism, which was a question-and-answer section reviewing the major content of the lesson. Although some public schools had been established by the late seventeenth century, most education occurred at home, especially for girls. *The New England Primer* sold over six million copies in 22 editions. Many families and schools in early America used this book to teach children to read.

In the colonial period, writing was not emphasized for females and was only taught to males who were planning to enter an occupation that specifically required writing. For most boys, to be able to write their names was considered sufficient. Little attention was paid to composing original prose, but neat penmanship was emphasized. Young boys worked on slates with chalk since paper and ink were expensive. Young women often stitched the alphabet and scripture verses on samplers. However, their skills with a needle were emphasized over their writing abilities.

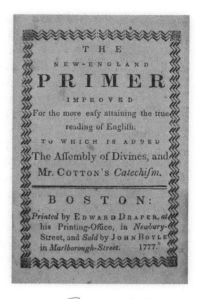

Figure 1.2

New England Primer

Early American History

Noah Webster's *American Spelling Book* (1798), also called the Blue-back Speller for its distinctive color, was an American book. It unified spelling and pronunciation patterns distinctive to the new country. For example, the traditional British spelling of the word *colour* was changed to the American form *color*. In addition to emphasizing the alphabet, this book included exercises and rules for pronunciation and enunciation, highlighting the prominence of oral reading that would be maintained for over a century. While some selections were religious, many took a patriotic stance. Following publication of Webster's book came others that focused on spelling as a means of learning to read.

When schools became graded (first grade, second grade, etc.), materials were written to accommodate groups of children. Though not the first to grade reading materials for children, McGuffey's readers, which appeared in 1836, are the best known (see Figure 1.3). They were popular through the 1800s (McGuffey, 1866). The books in McGuffey's series do not match grade levels as you now know them. The grades indicated the order in which to use the books, regardless of the age of the learner.

McGuffey's readers sold more than 120 million copies, making them the most influential set of reading books in their era. These readers were referred to as **eclectic**, reflecting emphasis on both alphabetic and whole word instructional methods. The religious and moralistic content echoed the sentiments of

Figure 1.3

McGuffey's Reader

the country. As was the case with all materials published to this time, the readers contained limited direction for teachers. The books emphasized oral reading performance and memorization, with much less attention given to issues of reading comprehension. What little instruction was offered to teachers centered mostly on how to help children with **elocution**, speaking clearly with a conventional accent.

Early in American history, writing did not receive much more attention than it had in the colonial period. Handwriting was stressed, with great value placed on beautiful penmanship. However, in 1873 Harvard added a composition class as an entry requirement. This spurred more focus on the content of student writing, not just on transcription (North, 1987). Personal journals and correspondence provided meaningful contexts in which most people learned to write and continued to improve their writing, although writing for these purposes was not usually stressed in schools. Spelling bees were common because of the influence of the many spelling books published during this period, but spellings of words varied widely from book to book. Punctuation was not a major focus for teachers or authors; rather it was considered the job of typesetters who prepared manuscripts for publication.

Early 1900s

Major shifts in reading education occurred in the early 1900s for a variety of reasons. Changes in educational philosophy exemplified by Dewey (1916) and Skinner (1954), along with the emergence of scientific approaches to reading (Huey, 1908), led to changes in the ways reading was taught. Some began to emphasize the individual in the development of reading ability, but the **behaviorist movement**, which stressed the study of observed human behaviors, quickly became the guiding philosophy of thought and practice in education. Emphasis shifted from oral to silent reading. Researchers considered such issues as when reading instruction should begin and how vocabulary should be controlled in reading materials. Development of reading tests, teachers' manuals, and reading clinics characterized this period. Gray (1927) emphasized the whole word approach to beginning reading instruction, which led to the creation of the Dick and Jane series. These books were used for decades to teach young students how to read (see Figure 1.4). Instead of explicitly teaching phonics generalizations, Gray used words that were familiar to young readers and repeated them ("look, look" and "run, run, run"), so they could be recognized by sight.

This whole word approach was used from the 1930s through the 1950s in the United States. Then a significant event in history brought that era in reading instruction to an abrupt halt—on October 4, 1957, the launching of the Russian satellite *Sputnik* captured the attention of the world. Because Americans had not been first in the "space race," people called for changes in American schools. Blue-ribbon panels were formed to investigate how to improve the education system.

This led to a number of changes in the 1950s and 1960s in the way reading was taught. It was a period of experimentation, during which some researchers encouraged more emphasis on phonics instruction (Flesch, 1955), while others suggested various other alternatives (Bloomfield, 1942; Fries, 1963). The minimal pairs contrast

Look, Jane.
See me go.
See Sally and me go.
Go, go, go.

19

Figure 1.4

Page from the Dick and Jane Reader, *Happy Days with Our Friends*

(Source: Montgomery, Bauer, & Gray, 1948, p. 19; reprinted by permission of Pearson Education, Inc.)

approach allowed for decoding words without isolating individual speech sounds. For example, instead of teaching children to read the word *cat* by segmenting and then blending three distinct sounds, linguists suggested helping them to recognize the word family –*at* and then adding the initial /k/. This approach had been used earlier and is still used today.

Another experimental method introduced during this period was individualized reading instruction. Programmed reading (Buchanan, 1966) was one popular method that focused on phonics instruction and moved students through graded materials at their own pace rather than as a class. Students took placement tests that allowed them to begin the program at different places based on their scores. The booklets provided a way for students to check themselves. After completing several pages, students took a test to see how well they had mastered the material and then either proceeded on or practiced the material more before retaking the test.

One program developed during this time was designed to help children deal with complexities of the English spelling system. Since the English language does not have a match between speech sounds and written symbols, the **initial teaching alphabet**, better known as ITA (Mazurkiewicz & Tanyzer, 1966), was developed with 44 symbols that exactly matched the 44 sounds used in English pronunciation—no exceptions. Figure 1.5 shows uppercase above lowercase ITA symbols. Students knew that the same symbol represented the same sound each time. For example, when students saw the symbol *i*, they knew that the short sound was being represented, as in the word *insect*. But when they saw the symbol *ie*, they knew that the long sound was being used, as in *ice*.

The DISTAR program (Direct Instruction System for Teaching Arithmetic and Reading), now called reading mastery, has been used widely since its introduction in the 1960s by Engelmann and Bruner (1988). The developers of this program believed that phonics should be taught using a **synthetic approach**: Each sound in a word should be isolated and then blended to identify the word. For example, if a child saw the word *cat*, she should say the three sounds /k/, /a/, and /t/ individually and then blend them together to decode the entire word. Children were placed in small groups and taught phonics principles with one hundred percent mastery expected for each lesson. The group did not go on until all students had mastered the material in one lesson. Though they moved slowly, students came away understanding letter-sound relationships. However, the program was criticized for focusing too strongly on only one aspect of reading—phonics—and minimizing other essential elements such as vocabulary and comprehension.

Writing instruction was emphasized about the same time as Joseph Dixon, an American entrepreneur, developed an inexpensive way to produce pencils (Petroski, 1990). More attention was placed on composition than in the past, but students were still expected to complete an error-free final draft in one sitting, with little expectation of revision. The prevailing approach to writing instruction was to give students a topic and allow limited time to write to that prompt. The compositions were then read, corrected, and graded by the teachers. The grade often reflected students' spelling and handwriting proficiency more than the content. However, Dewey (1916) and Piaget (1926) provided theoretical underpinnings that helped people begin to view writing differently.

Figure 1.5

Initial Teaching Alphabet

Late 1900s

In 1967 Jeanne Chall published her book *Learning to Read: The Great Debate*, in which she reviewed a number of studies about early reading instruction. She found that children who were initially taught some form of phonics performed better than peers who were not. Since many educators had become dissatisfied with whole word methods, her book was widely accepted. Also at this time, the federally funded First Grade Studies (Bond & Dykstra, 1967) were completed. Some 20 different researchers conducted independent studies at various locations around the United States to identify which of the many experimental instructional approaches for reading were most effective. The results led to many suggestions for change and improvement, but one major finding showed that approaches that focused on phonics were superior to those that did not. Armed with this information, most publishers included phonics instruction in all materials provided to teachers. Also at this time, programs were developed that were targeted to meet the needs of children of color and of poverty, as well as children with learning disabilities.

Individualized instruction and mastery learning were popular in the 1970s. Some districts used open school models in which a small number of teachers oversaw large numbers of students. For example, four teachers would work with the same 120 students from several grade levels, grouping them for instruction based on the students' abilities rather than their ages. Many times this open model also meant open space, where teachers worked with students in large, nontraditional classrooms with spaces partitioned for small groups.

During the 1970s and 1980s, constructivist thought gained prominence over behaviorist beliefs. Instead of focusing solely on observed behavior, the **constructivist movement** began to examine how the human mind works. Constructivism is a theory of knowledge that humans create understanding and meaning based on their experiences and ideas. Many researchers began to acknowledge that when children were reading, they were creating meaning and not just repeating what they had heard or decoding what they had seen. Chomsky (1965) postulated that children are born with the ability to create language in their minds—that they work out patterns of oral language and generalize them to other forms. They say words and phrases that they have never heard before because they are trying out their understanding of how language works. Chomsky's work revolutionized thinking in linguistics and influenced thinking in related fields like literacy. Work in psychology and linguistics led to new fields of study like cognitive science, artificial intelligence, psycholinguistics, and sociolinguistics. Educators began to see connections between oral language and learning to read and write. They also acknowledged that students used language for social purposes, such as discussing a book they were reading or sharing their writing with others. Researchers at the federally funded Center for the Study of Reading, housed at the University of Illinois, studied how these ideas related to vocabulary and comprehension in reading instruction. Their work led to the development of instructional methods that went beyond decoding.

One movement that was heavily influenced by constructivist thought was whole language. Following the example of educators in Australia and New Zealand particularly, U.S. teachers began a grassroots effort to align reading instruction with five principles closely related to Cambourne's (1988) conditions of learning. First, instead of dividing language into separate subjects like reading, writing, spelling, and handwriting, Cambourne said that all of the language arts should be taught simultaneously and throughout the school day in all of the subject areas. A second principle was that texts and tasks in literacy learning should be authentic. Instead of using basal reading passages that had been written for instructional purposes, teachers began to use literature that had been written for children. Third, the role of students as passive learners who soaked in what their teachers gave them changed dramatically; Cambourne saw students as active learners who created understanding and composed their own writing. Fourth, the view of the teacher's role began to shift from the "sage on the stage" to the "guide on the side." Teachers became facilitators of learning, coaches who supported their students in their own learning. Last, student-centered assessment emerged. Instead of relying on large-scale standardized tests, teachers began to use measures that showed how individual students had changed over a brief instructional period.

The whole language movement in the United States has been considered among the most influential educational movements in the twentieth century (De Carlo, 1995), but its impact was confined mostly to a span of about 10 years, from the late 1980s to the late 1990s. Its demise was caused by a variety of factors related to the temper of the times. Because it was largely a grassroots effort, there was little central control over the movement. This led to a variety of definitions of whole language. Some educators defined the term as a personal guiding philosophy of education and others considered it as a set of guidelines. For example, some felt that the use of phonics instruction was not consistent with principles of whole language, whereas others believed that phonics was one of many appropriate means of language instruction in whole language classrooms. The whole language label was no longer used, but the principles associated with the movement continued to influence education. By the late 1990s, policy decisions and in some cases state legislation mandated more focus on word identification and explicit instruction (Allington, 2002a).

Writing instruction also changed dramatically during this period. The English translation of Vygotsky's *Thought and Language* (1962) confirmed many of Piaget's theories and had an impact on both reading and writing. Unlike Piaget, Vygotsky believed that cognitive growth was the product of language use and that students use language to organize their thinking as well as express it. Rogers (1969) wrote *Freedom to Learn*, in which he claimed that teachers should teach children how to learn rather than just what to learn. He tied self-expression to self-discovery. In a more practical vein, Murray (1968), Emig (1971), and Elbow (1973) provided an insider's view of the process authors use as they write. Graves (1983), Calkins (1986), and Atwell (1987) guided teachers to teach writing in a **workshop format**, during which students learned writing skills, engaged in authentic writing activities, and shared their writing with others.

Beliefs about writing included the idea that writers need regular periods of time to explore their own topics and purposes and subsequently to seek response to their writing. They need to learn mechanics in context, see adults who write, read widely on their own, and feel safe to take a risk. Qualities of effective writing were defined by Diederich (1974) and expanded by educators in Oregon and Montana. These definitions became known as the "six traits" and were used as a widespread method of first assessing and later teaching writing (Education Northwest, 2011).

Although typewriters were used in the early 1900s, keyboarding was a skill mastered by only a few. During the late 1900s, keyboarding became essential with the emergence of personal computers and word-processing programs that shortened the time necessary to complete the writing process. Revision could be done with cutting and pasting, and spelling and grammar checking programs made editing easier. Penmanship, a long-standing hallmark of writing instruction, was no longer stressed as it had been in the past.

New Literacies

2000s

The whole language movement was followed quickly by greater federal involvement in education generally and in literacy instruction specifically. The Report of the National Reading Panel (2000) focused heavily on empirical research in education for children with disabilities. The term "scientifically based reading research" was used repeatedly in calls for "gold standard research" that would be experimental or quasi-experimental. Other methodologies were discounted. This reliance on evidence-based instruction was apparent in the No Child Left Behind and Reading First federal legislation in the early 2000s, and was pervasive in the field of literacy education through the late 2000s and into the 2010s. The Common Core State Standards led to rigorous literacy instruction nationally. The state of literacy instruction in the 2000s can be characterized with the words *assessment*, *accountability*, and *evidence-based instruction*.

Common Core State Standards

Significant demographic changes in the United States have led to increased focus on teaching English language learners (ELLs). Teachers have learned ways to accommodate and accelerate the learning of these students. Similarly, accommodations and scaffolding of instruction for students with learning disabilities have become more widespread in regular education classrooms through response to intervention (RtI). Although some teachers had been accommodating for individual needs and differentiating instruction for years, increased emphasis on teaching ELLs and helping struggling students has led to increased efforts by many teachers.

English Language Learners

New technologies challenged the ideas of what reading is, what writing is, and what text is (Coiro, Knobel, Lankshear, & Leu, 2008). When a computer novice who is trying to install software reads the technical words in an instruction manual over the telephone to a computer support person who interprets the wording, who is really reading? If a teacher writes the words that a child dictates, who is really writing? Must a text always come in the form of a book with pages or lines on a screen? What about a painting, a ballet, a mathematical equation, or a musical score—are they also texts? What does it mean to create or to read such texts? Although foundational skills such as understanding letter-sound relationships, grammar, and conventions of written language are essential in reading and writing words in nearly any context, many differences exist in the reading demands of various types of text. For example, reading on the Internet involves the use of strategies that require readers to select sites to read, to choose what portions of a site to read, and to determine what parts of a site to dismiss.

Struggling Learners/ RtI

A student and teacher working at a computer.

During the 2000s, instruction in and opportunities for student writing decreased (Applebee & Langer, 2006). The National Commission on Writing in America's Schools and Colleges (2003) called writing "the neglected 'R'" (p. 9). In a national survey, fourth through sixth grade teachers reported that they taught writing for only 15 minutes a day (Gilbert & Graham, 2010), and most of their writing activities did not include expectations for students to revise or edit their work. This decline may have been due in part to the focus on reading instruction and assessment of reading skills and the pressure for school performance on standardized tests (Brandt, 2001). Writing was not part of the national testing movement.

New Literacies

The writing process that had influenced the field for decades began to be affected because of the focus of the Common Core State Standards on three genres of writing—narrative, informational, and argumentative. Some educators are beginning to experiment with new approaches to writing instruction to help children succeed with these genres.

Outside of school, the availability of technology, including the Internet, allowed students to engage in reading and writing for their own purposes. Educators who initially

Common Core State Standards

viewed technologies such as emailing, texting, blogging, and social networking skeptically soon accepted these technologies and sought ways to utilize them as motivating contexts for increased literacy learning (Richardson, 2010).

New Literacies

Literacy Theories

Along with understanding historical contexts, it is important to see how reading and writing have been viewed through a theoretical lens. Many theorists have attempted to describe the reading process in order to better understand the complex exertions of the mind (Huey, 1908) in order to increase understanding and to improve instruction. Three major literacy theories have resulted from these efforts—bottom-up, top-down, and interactive. The following explanations are brief and simple; they are presented as an overview.

Bottom-Up

The **bottom-up theory** outlines a linear process that proceeds from perceiving letters to understanding sentences. Gough (1972) wrote about what he thought would transpire during one second of elapsed time of reading. In this model Gough explained that the eye views the page of text and sends information to the brain for letter-by-letter processing. The mind ties this visual information to the speech sounds associated with the letters. A mental lexicon then determines which letter/sound combinations go together and identifies the word. The words are finally combined in sequence, and semantic and syntactic rules are applied to them so that sentences can be understood.

This approach to explaining the reading process is called bottom-up because the factors that are lowest on the scale of making meaning (letters, sounds, and individual words) build sequentially to comprehension. Some refer to this theory as an outside-in model; that is, information that is outside the mind is used first before sense can be made inside the head. In their model LaBerge and Samuels (1974) emphasized the importance of developing automatic word identification as a means of combining subskills to reach comprehension.

In writing, bottom-up models maintain that when children begin to write, they must first learn how to form the letters, then learn how to spell words, and finally learn how to create sentences and paragraphs. Knowledge of grammar would also precede meaningful composition.

In bottom-up theory the parts add up to the whole. This theory is evidenced in phonics-first programs, reading readiness materials, and letter-of-the-week instructional approaches. Practically, the theory could be described as memorizing notes before playing music, mastering strokes before swimming, and proving proficiency at dribbling in preparation for a basketball game.

Top-Down

At about the time Gough was promoting the bottom-up model of reading, others (Goodman, 1967; Smith, 1971) were exploring a theory influenced by Chomsky's (1965) ideas in linguistics that individuals acquire oral language ability as they try to make meaning by inferring rules of language. The **top-down theory** of reading begins with powerful meaning-making processes such as using semantic and syntactic information, and only later in the process employs visual information like association of letters and sounds. In fact, Goodman (1967) suggested that syntactic and semantic information can be used to make accurate predictions or guesses in identifying individual words, and that the letters are used only to confirm those predictions. For example, when reading the sentence "I saw a cow at the farm," the reader would not need to process all of the letters in the word *farm*. If all of the preceding words had been identified, noting only the initial letter *f* would be necessary for the reader to predict *farm* to be the word. Because higher-level information sources are used first, this linear process theory is commonly referred to as top-down. Others refer to it as an inside-out model.

In writing, top-down theories argue that children begin to write by first focusing on meaning, then organizing their thoughts, then recording their ideas as best they can, and finally attending to conventions of print so their ideas can be accessible to others.

In this theory the whole motivates the natural learning of parts. This theory is evidenced in writing to read programs, emergent literacy practices, and holistic literature-based approaches. In practice, the theory could be described as learning notes in the context of music, developing strokes in the swimming pool, and improving dribbling while playing basketball.

Interactive

The third literacy theory is usually called **interactive**. Although many educators see this as simply a combination of bottom-up and top-down theories, or a meeting in the middle of two extremes, the relationship is not that simple. This theory proposes the notion of parallel processing. Rumelhart (1976) argued that cognitive processing is not linear in either a bottom-up or a top-down direction. Rather, he explained that multiple information sources interact simultaneously on the visual information that the eye sends to the brain. When perceptual processes forward the letters to the mind, syntactic, semantic, orthographic, and lexical information sources work simultaneously to identify the meaning of the symbols. The fast rate of reading indicates that multiple information sources are working together to create meaning.

Stanovich (1984) described an interactive model of reading that included the idea of **compensation**; that is, when one of the information sources is weaker, the strengths of the others can compensate. For example, if a child is weak in using letter/sound knowledge or if the text presents words that are difficult to immediately identify, the syntactic and semantic sources can provide more information to identify the words.

Exploring Literacy Theories

- List the key features, unique contributions, and limitations of the theories described.
- Identify classroom applications associated with each theory (e.g., methods, materials, and teacher roles).
- Think of something you have learned in a bottom-up, top-down, or an interactive way (e.g., piano lessons, baseball practice, computers, speaking a foreign language, and cooking). Analyze the process

you went through and how that process has affected your motivation to continue learning in this area.

Variations

Explore broader learning theories, such as behaviorism (Skinner, 1974), contructivism (Piaget, 1969; Smith, 1971), and sociolinguistics (Vygotsky, 1978). List the key features, unique contributions, and limitations for each.

Another interactive model of reading, proposed by Rosenblatt (2004), is referred to as a transaction between readers and authors, who create meaning together. She explained that meaning does not lie in the text or even in the author's intent. It is created when the reader and the writer work together as readers bring themselves to the writer's words. This theory also acknowledges the stances that readers can take as they read text: aesthetic and efferent. An **aesthetic stance** means the reader is paying attention to feelings, images, and emotions that are evoked by the text. Reading aesthetically allows readers to get lost in a story and care about characters. An **efferent stance** refers to taking meaning from the text. Efferent reading focuses on learning information. It is reading to remember and to be able to use facts and insights to enrich understanding. Students can also take a **critical stance** by evaluating authors' words and analyzing the support given for their positions. Reading critically raises questions about whose voices are represented and whose are missing in the text. It examines the text from multiple perspectives and helps readers avoid being manipulated (McLaughlin & DeVoogd, 2004).

In writing, interactive theories would argue that children combine the use of skills and expression of thoughts to create meaningful text. Meaning can be created during the act of writing. If writers feel inadequate in spelling, their strengths in creative ideas can make up for this weakness; they may even invent new words for people or places. Writers consciously decide their own purposes for writing and deliberately take stances to help a reader enjoy a story, to convey information, or to persuade others.

In this theory the whole becomes greater than the sum of its parts. This theory is evidenced in balanced literacy programs, process writing practices, and integrated literacy approaches. In broad practical terms, the theory could be described as notes so related with music, strokes so connected to swimming, and dribbling so intertwined with other moves in basketball that the parts cannot be separated from the whole.

Summary

To assist in the development of children's literacy, you should know about the history of reading and writing instruction in the United States. This context will help you understand the progress educators have made and the way certain activities and processes have come into use today. As you become familiar with the many ways to consider what counts as text and what reading and writing really are, you can assist young people to deal with the variety of literacy demands in our current society.

As you become familiar with the context provided by theories of language processing, you will be able to evaluate instructional programs and materials. You will want to be sure that the ways you teach reading and writing are consistent and align with your beliefs and philosophy of language instruction.

Within these literacy contexts, you will discover the foundations required to better understand the needs of all students and help them develop as learners and reach their potential as human beings. Young children have dreams and desires. Literacy opens the windows that allow them to pursue those dreams and desires. You can help children develop into learners and lovers of literacy throughout their lives.

Self-Check

1. Describe the major areas of focus in early American reading and writing instruction.

2. Explain what process dominated reading instruction during the early to mid 1900s.

3. Indicate some of the innovations in reading instruction that were used in the early 1960s.

4. Explain how new literacies can influence the language learning of children.

5. Why is it important to understand history?

6. Explain the bottom-up and top-down theories of reading.

7. Explain how bottom-up and top-down theories of reading are different from interactive theory.

8. Compare aesthetic, efferent, and critical stances in reading and writing.

MyEducationLab™

Go to the Topic, Media/Digital Literacy, in the MyEducation Lab (www.myeducationlab.com) for your course, where you can:

- Find learning outcomes for Media/Digital Literacy along with the national standards that connect to these outcomes.

- Complete Assignments and Activities that can help you more deeply understand the chapter content.

- Apply and practice your understanding of the core teaching skills identified in the chapter with the Building Teaching Skills and Dispositions learning units.

- Examine challenging situations and cases presented in the IRIS Center Resources.

- Check your comprehension on the content covered in the chapter by going to the Study Plan in the Book

Resources for your text. Here you will be able to take a chapter quiz, receive feedback on your answers, and then access Review, Practice, and Enrichment activities to enhance your understanding of chapter content (optional).

- Visit **A+RISE** Standards2Strategy™, an innovative and interactive online resource that offers new teachers in grades K–12 just-in-time, research-based instructional strategies that meet the linguistic needs of ELLs as they learn content, differentiate instruction for all grades and abilities, and are aligned to Common Core Elementary Language Arts Standards (for the literacy strategies) and to English language proficiency standards in WIDA, Texas, California, and Florida.

chapter 2

Understanding the Needs of All Learners

Chapter Outline

CULTURE
LANGUAGE MINORITIES
   Second Language Acquisition
   School Assistance
POVERTY
URBAN AND RURAL EDUCATION
   Urban
   Rural
LEARNING DISABILITIES
SUMMARY

About three weeks after school had started, a new student was assigned to my third-grade class. Sisimone was a nine-year-old boy who had just arrived in the United States from Laos because his father was preparing to attend the local university. Sisimone had been well educated in Loas as a young boy, but he had not learned the English language there. Despite his limited ability with English, Sisimone was anxious to get to know his new classmates and was eager to learn. He loved to play soccer during recess, and he even learned how to play American football and kickball. I had never before had a student who was so new to the language, so I was at a loss as to what to do. After talking to other teachers, I decided to seat Sisimone close to the front of the classroom next to Carl, with whom Sisimone liked to play. I encouraged Carl to try to help him as best he could. My wife and I created word cards that we placed throughout the classroom to label various objects, like the wall clock, the door, desks, chairs, and so on. I also met regularly with Sisimone to teach him about letters and sounds and words. During whole class instruction, I would stop periodically to simplify things for Sisimone. He loved to come to the front of the class and show us how to spell words in his language. "Sisimone already knows one language, and he is learning a new one," I explained to the other students. Sisimone made quick progress in learning how to communicate on the playground and in the classroom. In a few short months he was able to carry on short conversations and ask questions during lessons. However, I noticed that he had much more difficulty when dealing with the increased demands of content area subjects. Unfortunately for us, Sismone's time in our class came to an end in March when his family found a different apartment and moved away. We had a going-away party and were sad to see him leave. We had all learned as much by having Sisimone in our class as he had learned from us.

—Tim

Most teachers enter the profession because they love children. Working with children can be exhilarating, but it can also be frustrating. One first-year teacher complained to his wife, "I feel like every day is a roller coaster ride with so many highs and lows. I wish things would just even out." His wife, a nurse, replied, "When they hook you up to a heart monitor, you don't want a straight line. That's the bad news. The up and down lines are what let you know you're alive." Truly, working with children takes you to extremes, but that is what lets you know that you are participating, not just observing; living, not just existing.

Children often bring a fresh perspective that is delightful. One sixth-grader came to school late one day—about four hours late. His teacher asked, "Where have you been?" He replied, "I'm sorry, but this morning I got this thing stuck in my nose and I couldn't get it out. My mom had to take me to the emergency room, and they finally got it. But they didn't know if they got everything, so they took an x-ray of my head, but there was nothing there!"

A student teacher met with her university supervisor for a debriefing session after she had taught a lesson. A kindergartner interrupted them and declared, "I can't find my coat!" The student teacher replied, "It's right there on the hook." The child responded, "That's not mine." The adults immediately joined the child in searching the classroom and playground for the lost coat. Finally the student teacher asked, "Are you sure that's not your coat on the hook?" The child emphatically responded, "No! Mine had snow on it."

Despite challenges, children's fresh perspectives bring joy to teaching. As a teacher, you will have students in your classes who come from various backgrounds. Some will be from wealthy families; others will come from homes of poverty. Some will be very proficient in English; others will come from homes where other languages or variant dialects of English are spoken. There will also be physical, ethnic, cultural, and cognitive differences. A brief review of cultural issues, language minority matters, poverty concerns, urban and rural education themes, and learning disabilities will help you understand variations. This knowledge will give you a strong foundation from which you can respond to student needs appropriately and effectively.

Try This for Professional Development   **Respond to a Teacher**

Teaching isn't always easy. Consider this letter written by a first-grade teacher during the first month of school:

My Dear Friends,

Oh my, teaching first grade is crazy. The first week of school I spent most of my time thinking there was no way I was going to make it through the week, let alone a year. It took me days to finally answer my phone, I was afraid I would cry if I talked to any of my friends.

I miss going to the bathroom. I have found everything I hoped I would—my students think I am the prettiest, smartest teacher in the world. I get hugs and one student tells me I look like a princess. However, I get asked 20 times a day when it is time to go home, I have a few students who spend most of their day rolling around on the floor, tapping their pencils, and making odd/irritating noises with various body parts. I literally peel one crying child off of her mother every morning and secretly hope one boy will go on a very long vacation. I say "shhhh" 500 times a day even though I know it is totally ineffective and inappropriate.

However, the children are so wonderful. They make me laugh and I am amazed at the growth I have seen in just 2 weeks. Yesterday all of the boys decided they could read Magic Treehouse books and wanted to take one home. I had one of the boys read to me today—of course he could only read a few words. I think that is pretty good for a 6 year old. It's so great to have a child ask you if it would be ok if he read a book. Almost all of the children are reading and returning the books I send home with them each day.

If I had to make a decision tonight—it would be easier to work at the gas station on the corner next year, where I could drink Dr. Pepper, eat candy corn, and go to the bathroom whenever I want. But I know things will get easier and that what I'm doing matters.

- In what ways do you relate to this teacher?
- Tell how you would respond to this teacher.
- Reflect on your personal choice to become a teacher.

Culture

Culture consists of "the vast structure of behaviors, ideas, attitudes, values, habits, beliefs, customs, language, rituals, ceremonies, and practices peculiar to a particular group of people" (Nobles, 1990, p. 5). This definition of culture can apply to large groups of people as well as to smaller groups. Sometimes people even refer to individual families as cultural groups.

Cultures vary significantly. In one culture being quiet and reserved may be valued, whereas being louder and more aggressive may be viewed positively in another

Children from multiple ethnicities and cultures at school.

Struggling Learners/ RtI

English Language Learners

culture. One culture may highlight competition; another may place value on cooperation and group efforts. Being aware of cultural differences of students in your class enables you to help your students feel more comfortable and better able to learn (Au, 2000).

You should expect to have students from a variety of cultures in your classroom. In the United States, many teachers are culturally different from their students. At times this mismatch can cause fear and insecurity that can affect performance (Jackson, 2001). Perhaps you have heard of an **achievement gap** in the United States. This refers to disparity in scores on achievement tests among groups of students from different cultures, races/ ethnicities, and income levels. Those students who are not in the mainstream culture generally score lower on large-scale tests. Although many factors contributing to these differences are outside your control, there are some things you can do to close or at least reduce that gap for your students (Levine, 2000).

One of the first steps you can take is to recognize the cultural capital, or funds of knowledge, children bring with them to school (Gonzales, Moll, & Amanti, 2005; Sullivan, 2001). **Cultural capital** refers to the knowledge, accomplishments, and qualifications that an individual has within a given social circle. You might hear some people make disparaging remarks about children and refer to their cultures as deficient or deviant. On the other extreme, you might hear people say, "I don't see color, I just see children." Both responses are inappropriate. You need to view culture as a significant element of education. Use the cultural capital that students possess to improve learning in your classroom. One resource to find out more about cultures around the world is a compilation of brief articles called CultureGrams, available online (online .culturegrams.com/kids/index.php/). Each is concise, accurate, and often more up to date than print sources. There is also a kids' edition of CultureGrams designed for elementary school children. Although this site is for subscribers, the free demonstration

---

Try This for Teaching **Create Your Own Culture Grams**

- Discuss what children already know about a country of interest (e.g., food, holidays, dress).
- Following a pattern such as those found at online.culturegrams.com/kids/index.php/ or in encyclopedias or other resources, assign children to create their own brief report about that country.
- Students can provide facts, a map, and a flag and then choose several categories (e.g., history, greeting, customs, education, and climate) to expand on.
- Students can explore the sample pages (e.g., hear the name of the country pronounced or the

national anthem, a timeline history, and see photos of favorite foods and sports) and create something similar for their country.
- Have students compare and contrast multiple countries.

Variations for ELLs

- Invite a guest who is from or has visited another country to share the culture of that country with the class.
- Compare the United States with a foreign country.

and sample pages found under New Reports can provide a pattern to follow as students create their own culture grams for peers or for younger students.

When you have children from minority cultures in your class, it may not be wise to place them in a fishbowl by asking them to explain their differences. They may be trying desperately to fit in. Instead, allow all students to study various cultures in school and share what they learn with the rest of the class. One effective way to do this is through books. Figure 2.1 lists some favorite multicultural books for children. Be sure to seek out books that portray the cultures of children in your class so you can add to this list. Be careful that racial or cultural stereotypes are not portrayed in the literature. Cultural details need to be accurately presented. Not only will children gravitate to those books that tie to their culture but they can be encouraged to discuss the meaning of the books and expand their vocabularies by reading and talking about them. For example, children could study the Harlem Renaissance, a cultural movement in the early 1900s in New York City. Using the book *Harlem Stomp! A Cultural History of the Harlem Renaissance* (Hill, 2009), individuals or small groups of students could study and report on various aspects of the movement, including art, poetry, literature, music, people, and places.

New Literacies

English Language Learners

Figure 2.1   Favorite Multicultural Books

Author	Title	Culture/Country
Aardema, Verna	*Bringing the Rain to Kapiti Plain*	Kenya
Alexander, Lloyd	*The Fortune-Tellers*	Cameroon
Ancona, George	*Pablo Remembers: The Fiesta of the Day of the Dead*	Latino
Andrews-Goebel, Nancy	*The Pot That Juan Built*	Latino
Bunting, Eve	*Smoky Night*	Urban U.S.
Cofer, Judith Ortiz	*An Island Like You: Stories of the Barrio*	Latino
Demi	*The Empty Pot*	China
de Paola, Tomie	*Legend of the Bluebonnet*	Native American
Donaldson, Julia	*The Magic Paintbrush*	China
Dorros, Arthrur	*Abuela*	Latino
Farmer, Nancy	*A Girl Named Disaster*	Mozambique
Feelings, Muriel	*Moja Means One: Swahili Counting Book*	Kenya
Filipovic, Zlata	*Zlata's Diary: A Child's Life in Sarajevo*	Bosnia and Herzegovina
Fletcher, Susan	*Shadow Spinner*	Middle East
Fox, Mem	*Possum Magic*	Australia
Friedman, Ina R.	*How My Parents Learned to Eat*	Asian-American
Fritz, Jean	*The Double Life of Pocahontas*	Native American/England
Goble, Paul	*The Girl Who Loved Wild Horses*	Native American

(continued)

Figure 2.1   *(Continued)*

Author	Title	Culture/Country
Grifalconi, Ann	*Osa's Pride*	Africa
Hamilton, Virginia	*Her Stories: African American Folktales, Fairy Tales and True Tales*	African-American
Heide, Florence Parry	*The Day of Ahmed's Secret*	Middle East
Hill, Laban Carrick	*Harlem Stomp! A Cultural History of the Harlem Renaissance*	Urban U.S.
Ho, Mingfong	*Hush! A Thai Lullaby*	Thailand
Kimmel, Eric A.	*The Greatest of All: A Japanese Folktale*	Japan
Kimmel, Eric A.	*The Three Princes*	Middle East
King, Martin Luther, Jr.	*I Have a Dream*	African-American
Martin, Rafe	*The Rough-Face Girl*	Native American
McDermott, Gerald	*Raven: A Trickster Tale from the Pacific Northwest*	Native American
McKissack, Patricia C. and Frederick L.	*Christmas in the Big House, Christmas in the Quarters*	African-American
Miles, Miska	*Annie and the Old One*	Native American
Munsch, Robert	*A Promise Is a Promise*	Native American
Myers, Walter Dean	*Slam*	Urban U.S.
Nelson, Kadir	*He's Got the Whole World in His Hands*	African-American
Oppenheim, Shulamith Levey	*The Hundreth Name*	Middle East
Polacco, Patricia	*The Keeping Quilt*	Russia
Polacco, Patricia	*Pink and Say*	African-American
Ringgold, Faith	*Tar Beach*	Urban U.S.
Salisbury, Graham	*Under the Blood-Red Sun*	Asian-American
San Souci, Robert D.	*A Weave of Words*	Armenia
Say, Allen	*El Chino*	Asian-American
Say, Allen	*Grandfather's Journey*	Asian-American
Snyder, Diane	*The Boy of the Three-Year Nap*	Asian-American
Soto, Gary	*Snapshots from the Wedding*	Latino
Soto, Gary	*Too Many Tamales*	Latino
Steptoe, John	*Mufaro's Beautiful Daughters*	Zimbabwe
Taylor, Mildred	*Roll of Thunder, Hear My Cry*	African-American
Tunnell, Mike and George Chilcoat	*The Children of Topaz*	Asian-American

Author	Title	Culture/Country
Uchida, Yoshiko	*The Bracelet*	Asian-American
Volavkova, Hana	*I Never Saw Another Butterfly*	Czechoslovakia
Wisniewski, David	*Golem*	Czechoslovakia
Wyndham, Robert	*Chinese Mother Goose Rhymes*	China
Yashima, Taro	*Crow Boy*	Japan
Young, Ed	*Lon Po Po*	China

You should make yourself aware of reading materials and authors that your students will identify with. For example, one author who is very appealing to many African-American young people is Walter Dean Myers, an African American who frequently sets his stories in inner cities and uses black characters to direct the action. Allen Say is a Japanese-American author and illustrator who often depicts events in the lives of Japanese-American characters.

In addition to using multicultural websites and books, you can make learning relevant to your students by investigating what is motivating and engaging to them. For example, when working with African-American students, you may recognize that rhythm, repetition, and recitation are recurring learning patterns for many (Mann, 2001). These principles can influence your teaching across the school day. For example, you can use songs and chants to teach about speech sounds. A repetitive piece with physical movements can help students learn states and their capitals. Help children learn meanings of words by feeling the rhythm and repetitive pattern of definitions you write together. Recite them with your students with animated emphasis: "*Ancestral* means pertaining to our ancestors, those in our families from whom we are descended" and "To *admonish* means to mildly caution someone and give . . . advice" (Mann, 2001, p. 25). Example sentences that you create can often reinforce the meanings of the words: "Last summer we traveled back home to our *ancestral* country" and "He *admonished* me for driving too fast" (Mann, 2001, p. 25).

Speaking/Listening

Try This for Professional Development

Transnational and Community Exploration

- Visit a location in your community that is considered to be mainstream or most typical.
- Also visit a place in your community that could be described as an immigrant community.
- In both locations, gather evidence of literacy practices and materials as well as literacy opportunities and access.
- Compare and contrast the two areas, detailing similarities and differences between them in terms of literacy.

Variations

- Reach out to a class in another area and compare your two communities.
- Be sensitive to how different cultures are depicted in movies, books, and TV programs.

Language Minorities

Language differences of students in schools often accompany cultural differences. The number of students in U.S. schools who come from minority language backgrounds has increased, exceeding 11 million in grades K through 12 in 2011 (National Center for Educational Statistics, 2011a). Because of this growth, your class will probably include students who are not proficient in English. In order to assist them, you need to know how second language is acquired and what school assistance is available.

Second Language Acquisition

English Language Learners

Acquiring a second language (L2) is similar to developing a first or primary language (L1) (Haynes & Zacarian, 2010). As with first language acquisition, development of another language takes time, up to about 10 years. In general, English learners (ELLs) progress through five stages of language development: pre-production, early production, speech emergence, intermediate fluency, and advanced fluency (Krashen & Terrell, 1983).

Pre-Production.   As children acquire English as a second language, many may experience a period when they simply do not speak much, commonly referred to as the **silent period**. Although children may not produce much oral language at this time, they are still acquiring language. They may have an L2 listening/speaking vocabulary of up to 500 words and may feel comfortable repeating words and sentences they hear. Take time to explain words and concepts to them so their receptive vocabularies can grow. They could benefit from having a friend or a buddy assigned to them who may or may not speak their L1 (Echevarria, Vogt, & Short, 2008).

Early Production.   During this stage, which can last for about six months, students will be able to speak in one- or two-word phrases. They are still acquiring new words and may have developed a listening/speaking vocabulary of over 1,000 words. They can use language to serve different purposes, like asking and answering questions and taking turns in conversations. Many students at this stage will benefit from your use of objects and illustrations. Listening activities and small group work are particularly helpful for them. You should use graphic organizers and charts to help them learn content (Grabe, 2009). Ask other students to support and encourage these L2 learners. Remind them that when they were learning language as little children, they made lots of mistakes as they progressed.

Speech Emergence.   At this stage, L2 students can speak in short sentences. Although they may be able to communicate in brief conversations, grammatical miscues are often evident. Many teachers have found that rather than correcting a mistake in grammar, they can simply repeat the sentence using conventional form. For example, when a child said, "I runned real fast," one teacher said, "I'm so happy that you ran fast." When a child said, "Me and Jose went to a movie," the teacher responded, "My husband and I like to go to movies too." In this way students heard a correct model without constantly feeling corrected.

During speech emergence, students' oral language vocabulary may have grown to about 3,000 words, and they also may be able to write many of them. Choral reading and journals are especially helpful. Many students will remain at the speech emergence phase one year or more before they progress further (Haynes & Zacarian, 2010).

Intermediate Fluency.   Some students require three years or more to achieve intermediate levels of language proficiency. Students at this phase have added more words to their listening, speaking, reading, and writing vocabularies. They are also using more complex language structures in their speech and writing. Many are more successful in school subjects like mathematics and science that are less dependent on language proficiency than other subjects. They are feeling more confident, and they may be willing to ask more questions for help. This stage may last for months and even years.

You can help children continue their progress by making sure that some of their reading materials are at appropriate levels. You can also offer plenty of opportunities for speaking and listening, such as sharing about books they have read or stories they have written. Children benefit greatly by having a safe place to practice before presenting in front of peers. In writing, emphasize the drafting step of the writing process (Herrell & Jordan, 2011). In reading, offer children time to rehearse a text before being expected to read aloud.

English Language
Learners

Advanced Fluency.   At the beginning of this final stage, students are able to converse fluently in most informal settings. At the end of this phase, students have reached near native language ability. The duration of this stage is usually about four to nine or more years (Haynes & Zacarian, 2010). Throughout this stage students will need ongoing support from you and from classmates, especially in content areas that require advanced language proficiency.

Cummins (2008) explained two terms to describe the language development of L2 learners. When individuals who are acquiring English develop the ability to converse in casual conversation and can carry out many functions of everyday life using simple oral language, we say that they have developed **basic interpersonal communication skills (BICS)**. BICS capabilities are generally acquired in students' first three years after arrival in the United States. However, it takes much longer to develop **cognitive academic language proficiency (CALP)**. CALP abilities are those required to succeed in the demands of academic learning in schools. In these settings the vocabulary load and language complexity require much more advanced language proficiency than BICS demands. As with L1 acquisition, the rate at which students progress to BICS and on to CALP will vary, and individual differences are expected. You cannot assume that because children can carry on a conversation with you that they have the language capacity to succeed in all the reading and writing tasks required for success in your classroom. These students benefit from being involved in group work before they must produce independently.

School Assistance

Facing a classroom of students who speak many different primary languages can seem overwhelming; however, you are not without support. Many schools and districts provide special services including pull-out ESL, newcomer, and bilingual immersion programs (Duff, 2005). Programs and resources are also available to teach you strategies that make a difference for L2 students in your own classroom (Herrell & Jordan, 2011; Echevarria, Vogt, & Short, 2008). You have the responsibility to refer language minority students for special services and to provide instructional support in your classroom.

Special Services.   Identify students who may qualify for English language services by closely observing children whose first language is not English. Your conversations and observations will help you determine what general level of English proficiency they have.

English Language
Learners

If you find children who are unable to communicate well or who are in a silent period of their second language (L2) development for too long, communicate with an ELL specialist in your school or district who can help you match the needs of your student with the services available.

There are several commonly used tests to determine students' levels of English language proficiency. The LAS Links (ctb.com/ctb.com/control/ctbProductViewAction?p=products&productId=800) assesses listening, speaking, reading, and writing in a 30-minute session. The Woodcock-Muñoz Language Survey (www.riverpub.com/products/WMLS-R-NU-IIP/) is similar but does not measure speaking, and it takes about one hour to administer. The Batería III Woodcock-Muñoz (www.riversidepublishing.com/products/bateriaIII/details.html) is the Spanish-language version of the Woodcock-Johnson test that assesses multiple aspects of language, mathematics, and general intellectual ability. To test vocabulary and conceptual understanding, try the Spanish-language version of the Peabody Picture Vocabulary Test (PPVT) called the TVIP (Test de Vocabulario en Imagenes Peabody; www.pearsonassessments.com/HAIWEB/Cultures/en-us/Productdetail.htm?Pid=PAa2600&Mode=summary).

Based on results of such tests, students may be placed for part of each day in a class designed for ELLs and taught by those who have specific education and experience in this area. Instruction in that setting is designed to help the student master concepts as well as skills in English to help him or her become more successful in your regular classroom.

English Language Learners

Speaking/Listening

Instructional Support.   The most successful teachers of English do not always focus on teaching English—they teach students science, mathematics, reading, and writing. They view English as a means to those ends. Some teachers say, "Good teaching for ELLs is good teaching for all children." Although this is true, you will find you must vary the amount and intensity of certain aspects of good instruction to make a difference with ELLs. **Sheltered instruction** involves adjusting how much you are teaching vocabulary, connecting content to students' prior knowledge, and using visuals and real objects to help students learn the content of the curriculum as they acquire English.

One version of sheltered instruction is the sheltered instruction observation protocol (SIOP®), a framework for creating lessons to assist ELLs. Among the activities suggested are language experience, cooperative learning, and text structure instruction. Total Physical Response (TPR) is a related approach to L2 acquisition in which a teacher shows objects related to the lesson, demonstrates actions, and asks students to respond to commands using physical movement.

You can help L2 students acquire English more effectively by focusing on authentic language interactions with them more than attending to specific features of language like phonics, spelling, and punctuation. Use whole texts—stories, books, songs, poems, and articles—rather than isolated words and sentences. Speak clearly and stress key content words. Use fewer idioms and avoid slang and figurative language. Make judicious use of gestures and facial expressions. Take advantage of appropriate pictures, objects, videos, and hands-on activities (Herrell & Jordan, 2011).

Teacher using a prop during instruction.

Modeled Talk

- Along with verbal directions, provide students with additional support.
- Offer assistance through written directions that you track as you read them to students. Visuals that support the writing make the directions even more clear. For example, if the written direction tells students to cut two circles out of a piece of paper, add a drawing of two circles.
- Props can support both verbal and written directions. For example, cut two circles from a piece of paper as you speak about doing so.

- Gestures that you make as you speak can also be helpful. For example, pantomime cutting a circle out of a piece of paper as you talk about it.

(Herrell & Jordan, 2011)

Variation for ELLs

- Help other students learn the importance of physical demonstrations by setting aside a half hour during which all students can communicate only through gestures, facial expressions, pointing, and pantomiming. Discuss their experiences.

Poverty

Poverty in U.S. schools has always been an issue, but its influences on achievement for children have only been studied in recent decades (Korbin, 1992; Kozol, 2006). Inequalities in public education across the country as well as within individual school districts are being documented and addressed. Some schools in a given district are newer, better maintained, and equipped with the latest books and supplies, but other schools are rundown, with broken equipment and shabby surroundings. Beyond the physical differences, teacher morale is often worse in the lower income areas. Many teachers want to transfer to more affluent schools; thus newer and more inexperienced teachers are left working in schools in the lower income areas.

Poverty is not a simple concept. It involves more than the amount of money a family earns. Opportunity and access to benefits like hospital care, public utilities, libraries, and safety also define poverty (Connell, 1994). Poverty is often related to other issues that affect learning, including high transience, malnutrition, violence, and nontraditional families. To address problems of poverty and inequality, compensatory programs like the War on Poverty initiatives of the 1960s were created. **Title I** is part of the Elementary and Secondary Education Act first passed in 1965 and reau-

Poverty setting.

thorized consistently since. This federal program provides financial assistance to school districts with a high percentage of students from low-income families, providing funds for initiatives and resources to help at-risk children succeed at school. More recently the No Child Left Behind (2001) legislation also has attempted to address some of these challenges. Unfortunately, children of poverty still struggle and are still falling behind (National Assessment of Educational Progress, 2005). The overall achievement gap between children of wealth and poverty remains high (Alexander, Entwisle, & Olson, 2011).

Poverty affects children's literacy development (Snow, Barnes, Chandler, Goodman, & Hemphill, 1991). The reading achievement of students at all income levels improves during the school year, but reading skills diminish over the long summer break more for children of poverty than for their wealthier peers.

The enormity of the problem can seem daunting to you as a teacher, and large-scale solutions go far beyond your sphere. But within your classroom and school, you can take action to help all children learn to read and write. Mraz and Rasinski (2007) remind us to not underestimate the importance of reading aloud to our children, encouraging them to write notes to others, asking them questions about what they are reading, and modeling for them various strategies for decoding unfamiliar words. Additionally, be aware of children in your class who come from difficult life situations and make adjustments for them. For example, you may not want to require students to complete homework that requires a computer and printer. Also, do not assume that all of your students have access to a public library.

Struggling Learners/
RtI

U rban and Rural Education

Issues of culture, language, and poverty are applicable in both urban and rural schools. Students from both areas perform equivalently on standardized achievement tests (USDA Economic Research Service, 2011). However, teachers in these settings face different challenges and opportunities.

Urban

An **urban** setting is one with a population of over 250,000 (National Center for Educational Statistics, 2011b). Many urban students face funding inequality, high teacher and student mobility, and limited access to literacy resources in their communities (Cooper, 2004; Teale & Gambrell, 2007). Urban schools generally have larger enrollments than schools in other areas. Urban teachers frequently have fewer resources available to them, and they exert less control over the curriculum that they are required to teach. Urban teachers are more likely to serve low-income students, who are more likely to be exposed to safety and health risks and less likely to have access to regular medical care. Teacher absenteeism, a possible indicator of low morale, is more prevalent in urban schools than in suburban or rural schools (Lippman, Burns, & McArthur, 1996).

Much has been done to help children who live in urban areas through teacher professional development efforts (Au, 2006; Au, Hirata, & Raphael, 2005; Taylor, Pearson, Clark, & Walpole, 2000; Taylor, Pearson, Peterson, & Rodriguez, 2003, 2005). Individual classroom teachers who act as professionals by seeing needs and meeting them make a greater difference than those who implement a program with absolute fidelity (Teale & Gambrell, 2007). When teachers implement high-quality literacy instruction and are involved in ongoing professional development, children's scores on large-scale assessments increase, even for students who live in highly impacted areas.

Urban setting.

Many urban students are street smart and will be able to apply relevant schemata to the topics they are reading and writing about. However, many of them have not traveled a great deal outside their city or neighborhood, so their acquaintance with other parts of the United States and different regions of the world may be limited. You may find yourself in the position of needing to build background knowledge for these students to help them better understand what they read. A related challenge may be to interest them in reading passages that stretch them beyond their experiences (Flood & Anders, 2005).

Urban students need to be able to write on topics that interest them, and they need to write to authentic audiences so that their voices can be validated. *The Freedom Writers Diary* (The Freedom Writers, 1999) recounts the experience of Erin Gruwell, a first-year high school teacher in southern California who was trying to reach urban students. Having no success in interesting them in books and skills that she was supposed to cover, she invited them to start keeping their own diaries. The students came alive as they documented the violence, homelessness, racism, illness, and abuse that surrounded them. Learning became personal as it was driven by a need to express as well as to receive.

Rural

A **rural** community is at least five miles from an urbanized center (National Center for Educational Statistics, 2011b); however, some are much farther. Some people love the peace and tranquility of rural settings; others feel out of touch.

A basic principle of education in the United States is that equal educational opportunity should be provided for all children. Although schools are a critical part of any rural community, providing some kinds of educational opportunities can be particularly challenging in rural areas due to isolation, limited resources, and school and class size (Schafft & Jackson, 2010). Students who live in rural areas may be challenged in their access to literacy opportunities. Some may live great distances from a public library and may depend on a bookmobile or online sources to obtain access to reading materials. In some remote areas Internet, telephone, and TV services are limited. People may have to travel great distances to shop for supplies and to obtain medical services. Despite such drawbacks, many rural schools have the advantage of closer ties among teachers, parents, and students that can lead to a supportive learning environment.

Rural setting.

All school districts are expected to maintain necessary services regardless of location, including facilities, staff, transportation and food services. However, the cost for a small school district to provide these services is greater than for a larger district. Rural schools face many challenges in acquiring the financial and human resources necessary to offer the quality of education students need. Some rural school districts have more difficulty attracting and retaining qualified teachers and administrators. In many places it is difficult to provide after school programs because of the costs of transporting students in sparsely populated areas. Some of the challenges of education in rural areas are felt more acutely in the secondary grades (for example, there may be fewer opportunities for students to participate in team sports and advanced placement courses, and there may be less technical equipment and fewer labs available).

If you are an elementary teacher in a rural area, you have the responsibility of providing high-quality literacy experiences and opportunities for your students.

New Literacies

Be prepared to create more of your own resources than your peers in larger school districts. Get to know your students so you can judge the match between text demands and their prior knowledge and experiences. Where there are mismatches, be prepared to provide information to build students' background knowledge. Also be aware of any language dialects in your region that may affect children's acquisition of letter-sound knowledge. You may need to alter your phonics instruction to prevent confusion for your students. In rural settings you will continually need to remind students of the larger world in which they live.

In the book *October Sky* (Hickam, 2000), Homer Hickam, a NASA engineer, tells of a teacher in his rural coal mining community who instilled in him a love of learning and helped him see potential he was unable to see himself. Although some resources in that rural community were limited, Homer's teacher was able to help him see that his possibilities were unlimited.

Learning Disabilities

Professionals in the field of special education are dedicated to working with children who struggle with challenges such as deafness, autism, dyslexia, and attention deficit disorder, to name a few. In your classroom, you will probably have children who have been classified as having learning disabilities. A **learning disability** is defined as an auditory, visual, neurological, or perceptual disability that interferes with a child's ability to learn. About 5 to 10 percent of children are identified as having a learning disability at some time during their school years (Hallahan & Kauffman, 2000). The most common learning disabilities affect reading and spelling, with writing and math disabilities less common.

The Learning Disabilities Association of America (2011) lists four major categories of disabilities. The first, *input*, refers to processing difficulties related to getting information into the brain. Students may struggle with auditory or visual perception or both. The second, *organization*, deals with making sense of information after it is in the brain. Some students may struggle with sequencing, and others have difficulties with abstraction. The third category, *memory*, is concerned with storing and retrieving information. Children may struggle to hold information in their short-term memory long enough to be combined with their long-term memory. The fourth category, *output*, focuses on getting information from the brain. Some students deal with a variety of language disabilities; others have motor difficulties; and some others must cope with a combination of the two.

Until recently children were identified as having a disability when discrepancies were found between their performance on measures of intelligence and their achievement scores in specific areas. This discrepancy model has been replaced with a new approach that identifies children as having a learning disability when they do not respond appropriately to effective instruction (Fletcher, Coulter, Reschly, & Vaughn, 2004). This change in the field of special education has led to the emergence of the **response to intervention** or **RtI** movement.

Struggling Learners/ RtI

The essential components of RtI revolve around making decisions based on data (National Center on Response to Intervention, 2011). Teachers initially screen their students to identify needs. Then they organize their classrooms to allow for differentiated or tiered instruction. Finally, the teacher monitors progress. Following RtI guidelines, screening is done with approved tests. Effective instruction is delivered to all students in the *first tier*. While the rest of the class works independently, the teacher works with students who need additional help in small groups; this constitutes *tier two*. *Tier three* provides special education instruction for individuals who need a greater level of support. Progress of students is monitored in all three tiers, which informs teachers' next steps.

Figure 2.2   Favorite Books Dealing with Disabilities

Author	Title
Bezzant. Pat	*Angie*
Bloor, Edward	*Tangerine*
Byars, Betsy	*Summer of the Swans*
Charlip, Remy & Miller, Mary Beth	*Handtalk Birthday*
Corcoran, Barbara	*A Dance to Still Music*
Little, Jean	*Listen for the Singing*
Maguire, Gregory	*Missing Sisters*
Martin, Ann M.	*A Corner of the Universe*
St. George, Judith	*Dear Dr. Bell . . . Your Friend, Helen Keller*
Wolff, Virginia Euwer	*Probably Still Nick Swansen*
Wright, Betty Ren	*The Dollhouse Murders*

Although RtI is firmly established throughout the United States, some researchers challenge its basic principles. There are concerns about both the task of defining and measuring what is expected of students and the validity of the assessment measures used to screen, diagnose, and monitor student achievement (Goodman, 2006). Teachers' professional judgment and interactions with students on a daily basis should be recognized as additional sources of information about children. There is also controversy around the issue of knowing when students have responded adequately (Tierney & Thome, 2006). Additionally, some people question the viability of labeling children as learning disabled when their difficulties may be related more to the impact of factors like poverty, second language acquisition, or ineffective instruction than to innate difficulties.

Despite the controversy, you should expect to have children in your class who experience particular difficulties in learning to read and write. In working with such children you must be prepared to modify your instruction and make appropriate accommodations. Some may need extra time to complete assignments, and others may need the assistance of a buddy or a tutor. You can work with small groups or with individuals while the rest of the class is busy with other work (Ortiz, 2004). Along with modifying instruction, you can help children become familiar with books about those who have mental or physical challenges. Figure 2.2 lists a few favorite books about children with disabilities.

Struggling learners experience difficulty mastering a range of aspects of in language learning. Two in particular are phonological awareness and vocabulary development.

Many young learning disabled students have difficulty developing phonological awareness. Typical students require 5 to 12 hours of phonological awareness instruction (National Reading Panel, 2000), but some of your students will require much more. You should be prepared

Struggling Learners/
RtI

Speaking/Listening

Students engaged in a project.

- Think about your own literacy development from birth to the present.
- Get additional information from parents, siblings, grandparents, and others.
- Make a timeline of significant individuals, events, places, and so forth that contributed to your growth as a reader and writer, noting how they have influenced your view of literacy.
- Include both positive and negative examples of writing and reading (DeGroot, 2010).

- Write or prepare a presentation about your literacy development.

Variations

- Talk to a parent, grandparent, or other person not of your generation about his or her literacy development and compare that story with yours.
- Encourage your students to write their own literacy autobiographies.

Struggling Learners/ RtI

with many songs, chants, and games that stress the sounds that make up words in spoken language (Yopp & Yopp, 2010).

Vocabulary development is crucial for all children, but especially for the learning disabled. Resist the urge to use traditional approaches like giving students a list of words and requiring them to find those words in the dictionary, write definitions, and compose sentences using them. Johnson and Pearson (1984) described the inadequacy of this approach. They ventured that if students looked up the meaning of the word *exasperated*, they would probably choose the shortest definition, *vexed*, and write the sentence "He was exasperated." After the student had completed this activity, you would know that he was able to locate the word in the dictionary, find the shortest definition, and apply his knowledge of syntax to use the word correctly in a sentence. What you would not know, however, is whether the student understood the meaning of the word. Instead of using ineffective activities, focus on usable, meaningful words found in the context of wide reading. Utilize a combination of approaches to teach words and link them to a conceptual framework. Provide multiple opportunities to use new words (Marzano, 2004).

Summary

Cultural diversity will almost certainly characterize your classroom. View this diversity of background as a strength, and use your children's cultural capital to advance their learning. Become aware of the backgrounds of your students so you can understand and appreciate their cultural heritage.

Poverty is a multidimensional issue that goes beyond the amount of money available to individuals and families. As much as possible in your classroom, identify children of poverty and modify instruction and assignments to help them feel success. Awareness of individuals' backgrounds and circumstances will give you insights into accommodations you can provide.

Children who live in urban surroundings and those from rural areas all face challenges not encountered by their peers who live in the suburbs and other more affluent areas. Many students in urban settings face challenges including financial inequality, high teacher and student mobility, and limited access to literacy resources in their communities. Students who live in rural areas also face the challenge of limited access to literacy opportunities. They may live in remote areas that have inadequate Internet, telephone, and TV service, and they may have to travel great distances to shop for supplies and to obtain medical services.

You will also work with children who have various learning disabilities. Become aware of the types of learning disabilities represented in your class and determine what accommodations you can make in your teaching to help the children learn the content of the curriculum. Work with the specialists in your school or district to identify children with special needs who will require additional services. Organize your classroom to provide interventions that will assist struggling learners.

Although working with the diversity of students in your classroom can be challenging, the satisfaction of providing all students with excellent instruction and materials is great. Don't forget what probably attracted you to education in the first place—a love of children. Actively seek ways to understand the needs of all learners and act as an advocate for them.

Self-Check

1. What is meant by the terms *cultural capital* or *funds of knowledge*? How can you use your students' cultural capital to advantage in helping them learn and develop?

2. Outline the common steps of second language acquisition.

3. Describe differences between the acronyms *BICS* and *CALP* as they relate to second language acquisition.

4. What are some specific steps you can take to assist students who are acquiring English as a second language?

5. Describe aspects of poverty other than low income.

6. What are some specific challenges faced by teachers in urban and rural settings?

7. How are students with learning disabilities identified today? Compare that process with the traditional method of identification.

8. Explain some strategies you can try as a classroom teacher to help students with learning disabilities.

MyEducationLab™

Go to the Topic, English Language Learners, in the **My EducationLab** (www.myeducationlab.com) for your course, where you can:

- Find learning outcomes for English Language Learners along with the national standards that connect to these outcomes.

- Complete Assignments and Activities that can help you more deeply understand the chapter content.

- Apply and practice your understanding of the core teaching skills identified in the chapter with the Building Teaching Skills and Dispositions learning units.

- Examine challenging situations and cases presented in the IRIS Center Resources.

- Check your comprehension on the content covered in the chapter by going to the Study Plan in the Book

Resources for your text. Here you will be able to take a chapter quiz, receive feedback on your answers, and then access Review, Practice, and Enrichment activities to enhance your understanding of chapter content (optional).

- Visit **A+RISE** Standards2 Strategy™, an innovative and interactive online resource that offers new teachers in grades K–12 just-in-time, research-based instructional strategies that meet the linguistic needs of ELLs as they learn content, differentiate instruction for all grades and abilities, and are aligned to Common Core Elementary Language Arts Standards (for the literacy strategies) and to English language proficiency standards in WIDA, Texas, California, and Florida.

chapter 3

Teaching for Learning

Chapter Outline

IMPACT OF TEACHERS
Learning and Teaching
Key Behaviors of Effective Teaching
COMPONENTS OF LITERACY
Elements of Reading
Traits of Writing
Linking Reading and Writing
LEARNERS' PROCESSES
Reading Process
Writing Process
Linking Reading and Writing
INSTRUCTION
Approaches
Essential Elements
MOTIVATION AND LITERACY
Perceived Requirements
Perceived Expectations
Sincere Desires
Progressing Through Levels
SUMMARY

Soon after I began teaching at the university level, I was observing a student teacher who was teaching a lesson in an elementary classroom. I arrived at the predetermined time. She handed me a copy of her lesson plan and explained her objective. She was well prepared and seemed confident. I sat toward the back of the room and pulled out my notebook. She gathered the children and began. Her presentation was flawless—almost as if she had practiced it before a mirror. She hit every step outlined on her plan. Had she been the only one in the room the lesson would have been considered a complete success. But she wasn't the only one in the room. There were also about 28 children there who were completely uninterested and uninvolved. Some were bored and staring out the window. Others were poking each other and making faces at friends across the room. Still others were beginning to become a little disruptive. Unaware of the students, the student teacher continued with her well-planned lesson as if someone had pushed play on a DVD and left it running in front of the students whether or not they paid attention. When I later met privately with the student teacher, she broke down in tears. "What happened?" I asked gently. She sobbed, "I don't know. I was so well prepared. I worked so hard. It would have been perfect if it weren't for those pesky kids." I had to laugh. She was right. Teaching would be a breeze if it weren't for all those students muddying things up! As the student teacher and I conferred, I tried to help her see that our goal as educators is not just getting through lesson plans, but getting through to learners.

—Brad

As children learn to read and write, they progress through developmental phases. As you develop as a teacher, you will also go through phases (Clark & Cutler, 1990; Witherell & Erickson, 1978). At first it is common to focus on yourself—on sheer survival. Your mind will be filled with questions such as "Does my hair look okay? Will the students like me? Will I be able to control the class?" With experience you will begin to focus more on your task. You will ask yourself "Am I covering the core curriculum? Are my examples clear? Will I be able to get through everything I need to get done?" Finally, you will focus on the impact you are having in the lives of students. That doesn't mean you will stop combing your hair and planning your lessons, but those things will be done with an eye toward making an impact. Your questions will become "How will I know that my students have learned what I have taught them? What will they know and do that they did not before? How can I help them become all that they can be? Do they know I truly care about them?" When teachers begin to focus on impact, they are never the same again. They interact differently with children. They plan and prepare differently. They boldly invite students to change. They stop searching for excuses and start finding solutions. They teach for learning and never tire of learning about teaching.

Regrettably, not enough teachers have reached that level yet. In *A Place Called School*, Goodlad (1984) reported the results of an eight-year study of American schools. He reported that only 75 percent of class time was devoted to instruction, and the majority of that time was filled with teachers talking and telling, as if teaching consisted of nothing else. Students were rarely asked to do anything more than listen. They made few decisions about their own learning. Tests and quizzes stressed recall of specific information and measured narrow skills. Results were not used to inform or improve instruction. The findings shocked educators and motivated many of them to reconsider how schools and teacher preparation programs should be structured. Many years have passed since then, and although educators at some schools and universities have made great strides, others have not (Allington, 2002b).

You can be a teacher who makes a positive difference. Keep that focus, and it will motivate you to understand learning and teaching and to incorporate key behaviors of effective teaching as you help students learn elements of reading and traits of writing.

Combine this with understanding learners' processes and you will have the foundation necessary to select and adapt appropriate models of instruction in order to foster literacy, motivate students, and make an impact.

Impact of Teachers

Booker T. Washington, 1858 or 59 to 1915.

Booker T. Washington was born into slavery. When the Civil War ended and he and his family were declared free, they made their way to West Virginia to start a new life. Though he was only a young boy, Washington worked with his brother and stepfather shoveling salt into barrels. At night he was exhausted, but he still dreamed of learning to read and gaining an education. At that point in history, it was nearly impossible for him to attend school, and yet a few caring teachers, seeing his desire and potential, were willing to break away from the rules, traditions, and prejudices of the past. With great effort, Washington (1901) did obtain an education and went on to become one of the greatest teachers the country has ever known. Reminiscing about his own teachers, he wrote, "What a rare set of human beings they were! They worked for the students night and day, in season and out of season. They seemed happy only when they were helping the students in some manner" (p. 32). Later he reflected on his own teaching: "Without regard to pay and with little thought of it, I taught anyone who wanted to learn anything that I could teach him. I was supremely happy in the opportunity of being able to assist somebody else" (p. 40). Where would the world be without a teacher named Booker T. Washington? Where would Booker T. Washington have been without those who taught him?

With those questions in mind, the following words of David O. McKay (1934) do not seem overstated: "I think it must be apparent to every thinking mind that the noblest of all professions is that of teaching, and that upon the effectiveness of that teaching hangs the destiny of nations" (p. 722).

Learning and Teaching

Definitions of words like *learning* and *teaching* can be quite complex because both acts are dynamic and multifaceted (Gagne, 1985; Krathwohl, 1989; Scardamalia & Bereiter, 2006). Although studying complexities can be important and illuminating, there is also a place for simplicity. Asking children "What is learning?" led to

---

Try This for Professional Development   **Thank a Teacher**

- Consider teachers who have had an impact on your life.
- Find a way to contact one of these teachers. (Social networking and Internet directories can be helpful). If the teacher has passed away, try contacting family members.
- Write an email or letter expressing gratitude and detailing specific reasons that the teacher's influence was felt so strongly, and

let that person know about your desire to become a teacher.

- Send the message.

Variations

- Locate books or articles about teachers who made a difference (e.g., *Thank You, Mr. Falker,* Polacco, 2001; "In Praise of Teachers," Medoff, 1987; *A Place for Us,* Gage, 2004).

some interesting responses: "Learning is something that happens inside that affects everything outside," "Learning is a choice you have to make," "Learning is making changes." Osguthorpe and Osguthorpe (2009) presented a simple and straightforward definition of learning: "Doing something you've never done before" (p. 38). They pointed out that although this definition emphasizes what learners do, it also includes the knowledge and motivation that led to the doing and the dispositions that follow it. Learning is a transformative process.

What is teaching? Children provided these answers: "Making learning fun," "Helping students learn," "Inspiring others." These children did not see teachers as merely disseminators of knowledge. They realized that teaching includes much more. Osguthorpe and Osguthorpe (2009) wrote that a teacher is someone with high expectations who simply will not let a student be "satisfied with the present, just the way it is, with no improvement at all" (p. 4). They claimed "a teacher's primary role is to design the environment in which students can thrive—to design ways to help students take risks, to stretch themselves, to try new things, to do something they've never done before" (p. 42).

Professionals have a knowledge base that sets them apart. They use that knowledge to make decisions, to see needs, and to meet those needs. They reflect on their decisions and present alternatives when their first attempts don't work. Teachers are professionals. That is why your teacher preparation cannot be conducted in a six-week correspondence course. You are not simply mastering a series of skills that you implement over and over. You are being prepared at a college or university because you must learn to think clearly, act courageously, and take responsibility. You are being prepared to make a positive difference.

Key Behaviors of Effective Teaching

Good teaching is defined differently. For one person a good teacher is one who is friendly and doesn't require a lot. For another a good teacher is hard and demanding. Many parents request teachers for their children because they want a good one, but those requests vary greatly. Lower income parents tend to request disciplinarians who are skills-focused instructors, whereas higher income parents seek passionate motivators who can instill a love of learning (Jacob & Lefgren, 2007).

Through the centuries the general definition of good teaching has evolved. In early American history, a good teacher was a good person. Communities sought out men and women of integrity—hard-working citizens who would be positive role models for children. In addition, good teachers were sometimes judged by how well they filled the lamps, cleaned the chimneys, and whittled tips for the students' pens.

Later these early definitions of good teaching gave way to acknowledging teachers' experiences and achievements. Teachers with degrees, high test scores, and high grade point averages were valued and sought after. The more years teachers had taught, the better they were considered to be, and the more they were paid. Good teachers were also considered to be those who came on time, got along with people, and volunteered for recess duty.

Today the definition of good teaching includes the impact of specific teacher behaviors on the cognitive and affective behaviors of their students (Ruddell, 2008). Borich (2006) identified what he called "key behaviors"—key because they are essential for effective teaching: variety, clarity, task orientation, engagement in the learning process, and high success rate. Of course, these are only some of many positive attributes and skills that you must acquire in your quest to be effective, but these five behaviors create a foundation on which to build and are summarized in Figure 3.1.

[Handwritten marginal note: While teaching be a WARM demander!]

Figure 3.1 Key Behaviors of Effective Teachers

Variety	Variability and flexibility are present in your teaching.
Clarity	Your presentations and instructions are easy to interpret and follow.
Task Orientation	You begin with the end in mind. You are goal-oriented and achievement-oriented in your teaching.
Engagement	Your students are on task and highly involved.
Success Rate	You control the level of difficulty at which material is presented so students can succeed.

Source: Borich, 2006.

Variety.   A cook said, "It may be potatoes every night, but there are lots of ways to serve potatoes!" The same could be said about the elements of curriculum that teachers are expected to help students master. **Variety** refers to variability and flexibility during lessons. Using a variety of instructional materials and techniques increases student attention and achievement (Brophy & Good, 1986).

You can vary the types of feedback you give students and the type of questions you ask. You can change the classroom environment often and switch between explicit and implicit forms of teaching. You can invite student participation and give children more responsibility for their own learning.

When one teacher saw that the students would soon be reading about ancient Rome, he asked them to bring sheets to school that they threw over their shoulders in order to make togas. This brought a little variety to the activity and went over well with the students.

Struggling Learners/
RtI

Clarity.   Perhaps you have had a teacher who has spoken over your head or used vague, ambiguous, or indefinite language. You probably felt lost and confused. Did the teacher use overly complicated sentences? Perhaps you wanted to raise your hand and ask for clarification but were hesitant. You probably don't remember much of what you were supposed to be learning.

When you teach, make clarity your goal. Teaching with **clarity** means that your presentations, expectations, and instructions are easy to understand and easy to follow. One teacher found that posting a written objective on the board during a lesson helped her students stay focused on the main point even if the class discussion drifted into other topics. This simple practice helped her teach with clarity.

English Language
Learners

Task Orientation.   **Task orientation** refers to teachers being goal oriented and achievement oriented regarding students. It means you start with the end in mind. You know the final destination for your students, and you chart a course to get there. You don't waste a lot of time with procedural matters. Something that simple can have a direct effect on achievement (Fisher et al., 1978).

"I didn't want to be accused of teaching to the test," said one new teacher. However, she realized the value in becoming highly conversant with the content likely to appear on the test to ensure that the learning experiences she orchestrated in her classroom could prepare students to do well. This teacher gathered her students at the beginning of the year and set goals as a class. She reminded them of the goals and helped them stick steadfastly to them when they were tempted to become distracted. "It is not to say we didn't celebrate birthdays or acknowledge holidays, but we kept our eyes on where we needed to be by the end of the year and maintained a business-like pace," this teacher said. This teacher was task oriented.

Engagement.

Engagement refers to the amount of time devoted to learning when students are actually on task and involved. Many flight attendants are task oriented and dutifully present their required safety information, but how many passengers listen? How involved are their learners? In a classroom it is easy to spot students who are not engaged if they are misbehaving, but there are also more subtle ways that students can check out.

One teacher found that if she had a system in place for pupils to attend to personal and procedural needs without having to ask permission, things went more smoothly in her classroom. She also found that if she moved around the room and didn't sit at her desk or teach invariably from the front, students were less bored. She found that the more she invited students to read, write, and speak themselves as well as listen to her, the more involved they became. "I thought that by giving them more time to work on their own I was opening the door for trouble and behavior problems," she explained. "Actually, the opposite was true. The more engaged the students were, the better they behaved."

Students engaged in a project.

Success Rate.

Bowling isn't always a lot of fun for young children. They think it is impossible to knock down pins. Their balls always end up in the gutter. Smart parents and teachers usually let children start with bumper pads to keep balls in the lane. In this way the children experience enough success that they maintain interest in the game and are willing to practice until they no longer need the bumper pads. The same holds true when

Struggling Learners/ RtI

Try This for Teaching   Cross-Age Tutoring

- One way to engage children is to offer them the opportunity to be tutored one-on-one by an older child or to encourage them to tutor a younger child.

- Tutoring can be an established arrangement throughout the year, or it can be temporary.

- Older students often benefit from training sessions to help them feel confident in working with younger children.

- Younger students can read their writing to older students and receive feedback.

- Younger students can read to older students and receive assistance.

- Older students can read to younger students and write for them.

(Schneider & Barone, 1997)

Variations for ELLs

- Try having older students interview younger students about their likes and dislikes and then write a story or informational article including that information.

- Older students can help younger children learn how to navigate the Internet or learn how to use other technology tools.

- Older students can play educational games with partners or help them complete assigned projects.

- You can ask younger students to tell how an older student could help them learn.

- You can also ask older students to come up with their own ideas for engaging their tutees based on their experiences.

New Literacies

Speaking/Listening

English Language
Learners

it comes to providing training wheels for a child learning to ride a bike. Helping children experience a moderate-to-high **success rate** means that you control the level of difficulty at which material is presented so that children can taste success. This will increase retention, achievement scores, and positive attitudes (Wyne & Stuck, 1982). In a classroom it may mean isolating only one skill for a mini-lesson or completing tasks together as a class before requiring students to work independently. It may mean overlooking handwriting and spelling errors in rough drafts and journal entries that are not shared in public.

Components of Literacy

The key behaviors of effective teaching are general and can relate to all aspects of teaching. Effective literacy teachers combine their knowledge of good teaching with knowledge of the components of reading and writing.

Most people agree that reading and writing are basics in education that cannot be overlooked. Formerly people saw teaching these basics as being the responsibility of only primary grade teachers, but today every teacher is considered a literacy teacher—even middle school and high school teachers are beginning to see themselves as teachers of literacy (Biancarosa & Snow, 2004). What exactly do you teach when you teach literacy? It is important for you to know the elements of reading, traits of writing, and ways reading and writing are interconnected.

Elements of Reading

The National Reading Panel (2000) outlined **elements of reading,** five areas that are central to the teaching of reading. Their report is not complete—they excluded certain elements, such as oral language development, motivation, and writing, which should have been included. Nevertheless, their results provide common ground on which educators can begin. Each of these elements is the subject of its own chapter later in this book, but you must start with a basic understanding of phonological awareness, phonics, vocabulary, fluency, and comprehension summarized in Figure 3.2.

Phonological Awareness. As children grow they hear many sounds. Along with music and sounds of nature and traffic, they will also encounter the sounds that are used in their home language. Children in Chile hear Spanish, and children in Japan hear Japanese.

Figure 3.2 Elements of Reading

Phonological Awareness	Noticing minimal sound units of speech
Phonics	Focusing on sound-symbol relationships in reading and spelling
Vocabulary	Recognizing words that make up language
Fluency	Developing appropriate rate, accuracy, and expression in reading
Comprehension	Understanding intended communication

Source: National Reading Panel, 2000.

These languages include sounds that differ from those heard by children in America acquiring English. Phonological awareness begins with noticing minimal sound units of speech, **phonemic awareness**, and goes on to include awareness of combinations of phonemes like **syllables** and **word families**. Phonological awareness is essential to begin to understand phoneme-grapheme correspondence—the relationship between a sound and the letters in the alphabet that represent it. It is not always easy for young children to grasp that words are made up of phonemes. When adults say words, they do not produce a series of discrete sounds; rather they fold them into one another and blend them. Most children don't struggle with hearing the difference between individual words or even the difference between syllables within words, but it is sometimes difficult for them to take the next step and segment syllables into phonemes. Recognizing phonemes is difficult for people who are learning English at any age because they have not grown up hearing the sounds of English regularly. However, if they have acquired an alphabetic language already, they understand the concept of phoneme-grapheme relationships (Lesaux, Koda, Seigel, & Shanahan, 2006).

You will be able to help children become aware of sounds as you sing songs together, read aloud to them, and recite poems and nursery rhymes. Playing with rhymes and alliterations help children notice sounds in a natural context. Such activities give them a bank of sounds from which to work as they begin the segmenting and blending required in reading and writing.

Phonics. **Phonics** stresses the sound-symbol relationships that are important in reading and spelling—especially when children are first learning to decode and later when they encounter unfamiliar words.

When some people speak about teaching reading, they may be thinking only about teaching phonics. Remember that although phonics is an important and necessary element of reading, it is only a part of a greater whole. You can teach phonics during explicit lessons, but you can also draw attention to important generalizations in the context of reading and writing together with your students.

Vocabulary.   Whereas phonics is focused on sounds that make up words, **vocabulary** is focused on the meanings of these words. Words can be officially listed in a dictionary, or they can be known or used only by a specific group of people. For example, in some parts of the country a frying pan is known as a *skillet* or a *spider*. A couch can be called a *sofa* or *davenport*, depending on where you are. All these words are part of language. Even

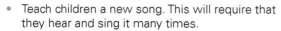

Try This for Teaching   **Songs and Sounds**

- Teach children a new song. This will require that they hear and sing it many times.
- Display a chart with song lyrics to reinforce the letter-sound relationships.
- Track the text as children sing the words.

(Gromko, 2005)

Variations for ELLs

- Try adding simple body movements or actions.
- Try using rhythm instruments such as sticks, wood blocks, or shakers.
- Each time you sing the song, highlight words within it that contain the same sound.

nonverbal forms of expression can be included as part of someone's vocabulary. You will find that knowledge of vocabulary is closely related to measures of intelligence as well as to successful reading comprehension (Nagy & Scott, 2004).

With so many words to know in any language, vocabulary acquisition can seem to be an overwhelming task. You are not responsible for teaching students every word that has ever existed. Many words are similar and share the same roots and affixes. In the context of authentic reading and writing activities, you can help students make connections. Knowing one word will help them understand the meaning of another word. When they see a word while reading, they will learn how to use the same word in their writing. Learning some words formally helps students to learn many more words informally.

A study of vocabulary is vital for students learning English because they are encountering not only many new words but words that have multiple meanings and words that can be totally misinterpreted if used in the wrong context. You may have to spend more time helping English language learners with vocabulary development than with other aspects of language (Lesaux, 2006). You can do this before, during, or after reading. You can create word collections on bulletin boards or word walls. You will be surprised how many words students will learn just in the context of having you read aloud to them or of reading on their own. In fact, reading is the single best way to develop vocabulary (Blachowicz & Fisher, 2000).

English Language Learners

Fluency.   Perhaps you have heard poor readers struggle through text that is too difficult for them. Their reading is labored as they pronounce each word with great effort. Their reading is far from fluent. **Fluency** refers to reading with appropriate rate, accuracy, and expression.

You will hear some people refer to fluency as limited to the rate or speed of someone's reading. Although speed is important, reading fluency involves more. Reading aloud to students provides a valuable model of fluency. Having children reread material with which they are already familiar and having them perform or present the reading to others are ways to practice and improve fluency.

Speaking/Listening

Comprehension.   Comprehension is the essence of reading (Durkin, 2005). **Comprehension** is understanding intended communication. Such understanding does not come by merely adding sounds to letters, grouping letters into words, and then reading those words fluently. It also depends on the background knowledge your students bring or that you can help them build. To complicate matters, comprehension is also strongly affected by the social context that surrounds the reader and the writer (Ruddell & Unrau, 2004). If one child in your class declares that a book is "dumb," others may agree without ever reading it themselves. Another student can see an off-color interpretation of text and influence others to laugh even though such an interpretation was never intended by the author. In a positive direction, a small group of children can discuss a book they are reading when one student contributes insights from his perspective and another from hers, and all are enriched by the varied background experiences that surface in the social interaction.

In the past, comprehension was addressed in classrooms primarily with a series of questions about the material being read (Pressley, Wharton-McDonald, Hampson, & Echevarria, 1998). Questions may motivate and measure comprehension, but they do not *teach* comprehension. You will need to teach specific comprehension strategies—systematic sequences of steps for understanding a text. Some of these strategies will help children draw inferences. Others will help them organize information or recognize how it has been organized. Some will simply help them monitor and become aware of their own thinking.

Traits of Writing

Some people wonder why we teach writing to children—especially when it is not emphasized in national tests. After all, the students aren't all going to become professional authors. Most are not going to be professional mathematicians either, but very few question whether we should teach mathematics. They realize it is an essential life skill, and so is writing. But the reasons to teach writing go far beyond preparing students to get jobs. Writing can enrich our lives at any age and stage. Reading provides a view of the world from the outside in—taking what is outside and putting it in. Writing is discovering what is inside and bringing it out (Liner, Kirby, & Kirby, 2003). That perspective doesn't just balance our literacy; it helps to balance our lives. When we teach writing, we are teaching thinking (Zecker, 1996). Writing is thinking made visible. It is an act of **synthesis**, taking old parts and making a new whole. When students revise and edit, they are engaged in the higher level cognitive process of **evaluation**, making informed judgments in a very personal context. Such higher-level thinking skills transfer into every other aspect of academics.

In today's global information-based economy, the demand for written communication has never been higher (Brandt, 2001). The National Commission on Writing in America's Schools and Colleges (2003) has referred to writing as a skill for the many and not just a frill for the few. Rapid development of digital technologies has impacted how, where, when, and why writing occurs (DeVoss, Cushman, & Grabill, 2005). Despite the heightened need, schools have actually seen a downturn in the amount of time spent in writing instruction—especially writing that goes beyond one draft with the expectation that students revise and edit (Gilbert & Graham, 2010). New teachers report they feel least prepared to teach writing of all the subject areas (Grisham & Wolsey, 2005).

Some teachers still equate the teaching of writing only to handwriting or the conventions of written language such as punctuation marks and spelling. Although conventions are included among the traits of quality writing, there are others that extend far beyond

> *When you teach writing you also teach thinking.*

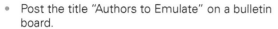 **Authors to Emulate**

- Post the title "Authors to Emulate" on a bulletin board.
- Encourage students to be on the lookout for examples of excellent writing in books they are reading or that you are reading to them.
- As they encounter a page, copy it, highlight the exemplary writing, and place it on the bulletin board.
- After you have multiple examples, introduce traits of quality writing and divide the bulletin board into labeled sections. Have students revisit the writing samples and categorize them.
- If some traits are not well represented, send students in search of writing that displays those specific straits.

Variations for ELLs

- Copy covers of books with the authors' names so that students can see the sources. This can also make the bulletin board more visually appealing.
- Add examples of student writing that fall into the different categories. This could include examples of writing done in children's first languages.
- Rather than focus on all the traits at the same time, focus on one each month and fill the board with examples of that writing trait.

Common Core
State Standards

transcription to include composition: ideas, voice, organization, word choice, sentence fluency, and presentation. These elements are identified as traits of quality writing, or **six+1 traits,** which are important regardless of the genre being addressed (Spandel, 2007). The Common Core stresses the genres of narrative, informational, and argumentative writing. Writing in these genres will be strengthened as you pay attention to the traits of quality writing summarized in Figure 3.3.

As in the section on reading elements, the elements of quality writing will each have an entire chapter devoted specifically to it later in this book, so the following discussion is only a brief overview. You can help your students become familiar with the traits in lessons, in assessments, and in writing you do together or in work you help them write on their own. You can also point out how favorite authors have used these same traits in their writing. As you do, you will be helping your students become capable of using the traits themselves to write well.

Voice. In quality writing you can hear the author's voice as you read, so writing with **voice** means writers don't try to sound like someone else. They express their ideas and feelings honestly and in their own ways. Of course, they will adapt how they write depending on their audience, but be sure to help students understand how important it is to avoid **plagiarism**, or copying someone else's work. The word *plagiarism* is derived from the Latin word for "kidnapper"—even young children can understand that this is serious.

When a fifth grader turned in his report and the teacher read, "South Carolina is a state that enjoys a delicate blend of extremes—old and the new, urban and the rural, traditional and innovative," she knew that is not how fifth graders usually express themselves. She knew that words like *delicate, blend, extremes, urban,* and *rural* were far beyond the typical word choices of her students. The youngster was probably not intending to cheat when he copied what he saw written in a book; he just needed some help learning how to write in his own voice.

Figure 3.3   Traits of Effective Writing

Voice	Expressing ideas in your own unique manner and avoiding plagiarism.
Organization	Knowing where you are taking your readers and presenting them with a path that is easy to follow.
Ideas	Sharing your main message in stimulating or uncommon ways.
Conventions	Respecting your readers enough to provide correct, accurate copy that is free from capitalization, grammar, punctuation, and spelling mistakes.
Word Choice	Using specific nouns, vibrant verbs, and rich adjectives to bring writing to life and make it memorable.
Sentence Fluency	Presenting ideas naturally as if you were speaking.
Presentation	Focusing on how your writing appears on the page considering your audience.

Source: Spandel, 2007.

Organization.   Quality writing is organized in logical ways. **Organized writing** means that the writer knows where she is taking her readers and gets there on a path that is easy to follow. The writer must gain the reader's attention, answer the reader's questions, and pull ideas together in a way that the reader will be able to remember. For a story, the organization will be different from a report, letter, or persuasive essay.

After a student wrote three pages, she wanted to read her work to her teacher. He listened as she shared information about her pet, sister, vacation, favorite school subject, best friends, and the steps for wrapping a birthday present. "Wow!" he said. "It looks like you have lots to write about. Let's zero in on one idea today and leave the others for later. Which one of these great ideas do you want to start with?" The student decided to write about her best friends, and the teacher helped her organize her thoughts into an introduction about friendship and then a few paragraphs telling about special things she had done with her friends.

When writing a persuasive piece, an author usually introduces the topic and then takes a stand supported by specific reasons. Sometimes the author can include a counterargument to make sure that the opinions of others are acknowledged, but the writing will conclude with a summary and restatement of the author's position. In informational writing, the organization can vary from comparing and contrasting to outlining a sequence of events or presenting a problem and solution. Writers have to know the structural patterns that will best help them achieve their purposes. You can help students learn these patterns by introducing them to graphic organizers in lessons and group writing experiences.

Ideas.   An **idea** is the main message the writer expresses. It is not necessarily a new thought. It is often created by putting together old thoughts in new ways or expressing common feelings in uncommon ways. Quality writing includes stimulating and important ideas and is full of rich detail. Walt Disney, who was known for his creativity and innovation, said he had lots of ideas, which he held in his head until he asked someone to write them or did so himself. Then he could start to work on them (Smith, 2001).

Students often need help recognizing an idea. One teacher asked a young teenager, "What do you have to write about?"

The teen responded, "Nothing."

The teacher asked, "What did you do this weekend?"

The young man declared, "Nothing."

The patient teacher said, "Surely something happened between the time you left school on Friday and came back on Monday!"

The teen said, "I babysat my little nephew."

The teacher said, "Tell me about it."

As the young man shared some of the humorous things his nephew had done, the teacher said, "That sounds like something to write about to me!" She helped the teen identify the literary moment (Collins, 1993). The teacher helped him see that the daily experiences he thought unimportant could be mined for fresh and original ideas that provided him with a topic for his writing.

Murray (2004) explained that some of the best ideas come not only from looking back as this student did but also from looking forward and thinking about the future. What goals, plans, and dreams does the student have? Where does he want to be in a year? in five years? in thirty? What will the world be like? These are wonderful sources of ideas for writing genres.

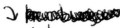

↪ ~~Introduction~~
– Intro
– Body 1
– Body 2
– Body 3
– Conclusion

English Language Learners

Struggling Learners/ RtI

Mostly means the main idea

Language Conventions

Also known as imagery and how the reader can jump into the authors thinking

Conventions. Included in the trait of **conventions** is a broad range of items: spelling, punctuation, capitalization, grammar, usage, and paragraphing. When writers want others to read their work, they are expected to conform to standards of written language. Readers expect what they read to adhere to these conventions. After they have drafted and revised their writing, authors need to carefully examine their work to be sure it contains no errors that will cause problems for their readers. You may have heard the saying "last but not least." This applies to conventions—they are not least important but they should usually be focused on last.

Word Choice. Original **word choice** is important to keep the reader's attention and interest. Word choice means using carefully selected words such as specific nouns, vibrant verbs, and rich adjectives that help bring writing to life and make it memorable. Writers find unique ways of expressing themselves instead of relying on worn out and overused phrases and expressions. In *Telling Writing*, Macrorie (1976) encouraged young writers to replace clichés such as "out of the clear blue sky," "cold shivers up my back," "racked my brain," "broke my heart," and "safe and sound" with fresh expressions: "That man is hairless as a window," "His eyes look like you picked them up from a kid's marble game, big and brown," and "All the colors outside are muted as if someone forgot to dust off the trees and grass" (p. 78).

Do you think it would be impossible to have students write with such careful and effective word choice? If so, think again. The excellent examples shared above were written by junior high school students.

Sentence Fluency. Smooth sentences allow readers to focus on what writers have written rather than being distracted by how they have written it. **Sentence fluency** means presenting ideas with a natural flow, like speaking. Writing is choppy when all the sentences are too short and bulky when they are too long.

As one teacher read over a student's paper, she realized that there was not one period for almost a page and a half. The student had combined all her thoughts with words like *and, so,* and *but.* The teacher pulled the student aside privately and complimented her on writing so much about her topic. Then she asked her to read the paper aloud and only breathe when she reached a period. The girl attempted to follow directions, but found it impossible. She got the point. No further instruction was necessary.

Presentation. Writers write differently for different audiences. Students write differently—and better—when an audience beyond the teacher will be reading what they write (Tierney & Shanahan, 1996). **Presentation** is how the writing appears on the page. It involves making choices about conventions, layout, and design, as writers consider their intended audience and share their writing in ways that will entice others to read it. Even the best students are rarely motivated to go to the effort required to write, revise, and even edit their work if it is only to be graded by the teacher. When they have an authentic audience, their motivation is heightened. Whether the audience is family, peers, or an unknown person who may read a blog or a post on the Internet, writers are better able to construct effective texts when they write and present their material with readers in mind (Baker, Rozendal, & Whitenack, 2000; Wollman-Bonilla, 2001).

One young man procrastinated fulfilling his assignment to write a personal essay. He even considered skipping it altogether until he found out the writing would be submitted to a youth writing contest being sponsored by a national magazine. The winners would receive scholarships and have their work published in the magazine. He couldn't resist.

Struggling Learners/ RtI

Try This for Teaching   **Six Traits Acronym**

- Consider using this acronym when teaching the six traits of good writing. Tell the class that these qualities of writing will give them voices in the world.

    - **V** stands for voice.
    - **O** stands for organization.
    - **I** stands for ideas.
    - **C** stands for conventions.
    - **E** stands for excellent word choice.
    - **S** stands for sentence fluency.

- Display the acronym in your room on a poster or white board.
- To include presentation, you can say these qualities of writing will help them *present* their voices to the world.

Variations for ELLs

- This acronym can be used as an easy-to-remember checklist when students confer with each other or with younger students about their writing.
- Use this acronym to create a grading rubric for assessment.

He wrote his experience, asked his mom to help him edit it, and submitted it to the contest. His teacher not only assigned him to write but to write for a real purpose and audience beyond the classroom. By the way, the boy ended up winning the contest.

Linking Reading and Writing

Elbow (1990) once explained the interconnection of reading and writing: "Reading is really 'writing' (actively creating meaning) and writing is really 'reading' (passively finding what culture and history have inscribed in our heads)" (p. 183). Most agree that the acts are reciprocal and should ideally drive each other. Just as speaking leads to listening, which leads to more speaking, reading should lead to writing, and writing should lead to more reading. Sadly, this binary relationship is often cut short. You need to take advantage of these natural connections so that your students can enjoy the active learning and improved comprehension that result (Guthrie & Wigfield, 2000).

Phonemic awareness and phonics are related with concepts about print, spelling, and handwriting. Reading fluency is connected with voice and sentence fluency in writing. Reading vocabulary is closely associated with word choice in writing, and reading comprehension is linked with organization and ideas in writing (Shanahan, 2006b).

Learners' Processes

Knowledge of what you are teaching in reading and writing is incomplete without a basic understanding of how these elements and traits can be taught. Both reading and writing involve cognitive processes that students can be taught. There may be a product that is a child's writing and a moment in time when a child is reading, but do not overlook the processes writers and readers can go through to arrive at that product or that moment in time. Similarly, listening and speaking also involve processes. When you travel you learn that arriving at the destination is not possible without the journey. You also learn that joy, satisfaction, and growth occur all along the way.

Thinking about learning how to read and write as processes makes them less intimidating to students. Presenting reading and writing as processes demystifies the literacy

Speaking/Listening

acts and breaks them down into achievable components so children can be successful. It makes the acts more personal so students take ownership and make individual decisions.

Be careful not to oversimplify these processes as a series of activities through which all children must pass at the same rate and in the precise sequence. They are not always linear. Instead you must recognize that they are recursive and interactive—flexible enough to meet the purposes of each reader and writer, listener, and speaker. No one stage is intrinsically more important than any other. Children should not be expected to go through the phases in a lockstep way. If some of the children are progressing in ways that are different from their classmates, they are not worse or better than their peers; they simply create a little differently. If some of the students double back on previous steps and occasionally (or often) combine steps, they are not wrong; they may simply be more flexible than their classmates.

You will ultimately make professional choices about when and how often to emphasize the various phases of these processes to meet the needs of your students, but in order to make such choices, you need to be familiar with the phases you can use to teach reading and writing and how they relate to one another.

Reading Process

Some people are surprised to discover that reading a selection can begin before the reader encounters printed words on the page and extend long after the book is closed. The purpose you have for having students read can determine how deliberately you focus on the various stages of the process. Some self-motivated children engage in these mental activities independently. Many others rely on adults to help them. Tompkins (2010) outlines stages in the reading process as prereading, reading, responding, exploring, and applying. This is a simplistic view of a complex endeavor, but it does provide a common instructional language and place to begin.

Prereading.   **Prereading** is getting ready to read. Sometimes it involves building background knowledge and making predictions to get the most out of the reading. Sometimes it can involve clarifying a purpose for reading and making plans and goals accordingly. **Knowledge mobilization**, which means activating the relevant schema prior to reading, often happens automatically (Keen, 2006; Tierney & Pearson, 1983). Students read the title and immediately access appropriate images in their minds. Occasionally the connection may not be so easy. Seeing the title *Stargirl* (Spinelli, 2000) could initially make readers assume the book is a science fiction thriller about space travel or a biography of a young movie star. As they read they have to draw on another schema, because this contemporary realistic fiction novel introduces them to a misfit girl in high school who is quite content to be different from others. The background knowledge of your students will vary greatly. You need to know them well enough to be able to help them access a correct schema or build it when they do not possess it.

Along with background knowledge, most readers have a clear purpose in mind before reading. They read for enjoyment or personal enrichment as well as for information. The Common Core emphasizes reader stance. Writers take a stance when presenting text. Readers must also take a stance when they interact with it.

You will need to preview text regularly to help some students determine an appropriate stance and goals. At other times students will come to you with their stance, goals, and questions already in mind, and you will need to find appropriate materials. One sixth-grade teacher experienced this when a student returned from a vacation to California and reported that he had seen the ocean liner *Queen Mary*. Another student

Common Core State Standards

said, "There is no way you could have seen that. It sank." Another student chimed in, "It was the *Titanic* that sank, not the *Queen Mary*!" Soon other students took sides, and the teacher was thrust into a spur-of-the-moment reading lesson that was completely unplanned. Students suddenly wanted to know the difference between the two ocean liners. They wanted to know who Queen Mary was and how she was related to the current royal family in England. The teacher took advantage of the curiosity that had been piqued and helped students find books in the library and information online to answer their questions.

Reading.   This stage deals with actually reading the text. It can happen orally or silently. It can happen independently if the reading material is at the student's level or together with someone else if the student needs support. During reading it is easy for students to become distracted and forget their original purpose. Maybe they become so focused on the task of decoding that they are no longer comprehending what they are reading. Maybe they worry so much about an unknown vocabulary word that they give up. Or perhaps they simply do not have the stamina and self-discipline to keep focused. You can learn a lot by watching children when they read silently or by listening to them when they read orally. You can help them succeed by finding books that match their interests.

Students reading.

Perhaps you have been reading and felt your mind drift. Sometimes you can finish entire pages only to discover that your mind has been elsewhere. You usually pause, reflect, reread, and get yourself back on track. You need to be able to notice when students drift and help them do the same.

Struggling Learners/RtI

Responding.   Students may not always respond to a text in the way you expect. Rosenblatt (2004) helped educators see that there is not just one possible interpretation of text. Just as important as what authors say to readers is what readers have to say back to the authors. A **response** includes not only what authors mean but also what authors' words mean to readers. It is more than a knee-jerk reaction of "I loved it" or "I loved it not." It is a thoughtful evaluation of the text that goes beyond summarizing to personalizing. As readers share responses, they may or may not spend much time rehashing what was in the text. Rather, they express how the words made them think and feel, and why.

After reading *Faithful Elephants* (Tsuchiya, 1997), students were saddened to learn how the zookeepers in Japan were required to kill the animals under their care during wartime because of fears that they might escape and harm people if the cages were damaged in an attack. Children's initial anger toward the zookeepers changed to anger about how unfair it is that war affects so many innocent children and animals. As they wrote their feelings in a reading log and later participated in a discussion, very few of the entries and comments had anything to do with the content or details of the book or the specifics of what happened at the Japanese zoo. The book had led children beyond itself to much larger issues.

Exploring.   Responses of readers are not set in stone. They can be shaped and educated as children explore the text in greater detail. Some people have an initial aversion to impressionistic or modern art because it doesn't look realistic. Then they take a humanities class in which they learn more about the artists and their purposes. They are helped to see symbolism and social statements that were previously beyond them. They visit a museum and encounter a piece that moves them deeply. They learn that their initial responses can change.

Similarly, a text may not be a favorite at first glance, but as students reread and examine the author's craft, they may find the text speaks to them differently. Their comprehension can be increased and their perspective broadened as they move beyond story elements to explore overarching themes. Their understanding can change completely when they go beyond identifying the main idea and begin to examine how several related ideas interact. Students can look for patterns and principles. They can find out more about the author or explore the time period in which the text was written.

Specific words and sentences may deserve attention. They may be key to unlocking meaning. They may also be excellent examples of figurative or original language. These can be breezed over or be completely overlooked in an initial reading of the text. Even if they are noticed, they can be easily forgotten if the text is not reexamined and explored carefully. Does every text deserve such in-depth treatment? Treatment often depends on the reader's initial purpose and response. Time may not permit visitors in a museum to explore each piece of art, but becoming more familiar with even a few increases general appreciation of all. The same is true of literary works.

Applying. What good is knowing something if that knowledge is not applied? You can read about the importance of wearing seatbelts and not benefit at all if you fail to use them in your own car. Learning about the health hazards of smoking does little for the person who still chooses to smoke. The reading process is incomplete until you see evidence that knowledge has been internalized, perspectives broadened, and choices improved. Being able to recognize text structure or identify the main idea of a passage in a text may not guarantee that students will be able to transfer that knowledge to real-life settings and apply it to solve problems they encounter. Education provides students with tools they need if they are to continue learning throughout their lives. Be careful not to focus so much on the tools that you overlook what the tools are meant to do. You need to be able to help students see and experience how school connects to life beyond school.

English Language Learners

One teacher read with his class about citizenship from a social studies textbook. On the pages they read a definition of the term and also several examples of people who have been exemplary citizens—one who saved a child from drowning and another who helped transform a rundown neighborhood into a better place. Still, the text was all just words until they shut the book and walked outside the school. "How can we be good citizens right here and now?" the teacher asked. Students decided they could pick up litter, weed some flowerbeds, and wash the windows of the cars in the parking lot. This citizenship took a little time, but the teacher considered it worth that investment. He said, "I saw the students go from knowing about citizenship to being good citizens."

Writing Process

Just as you can teach the reading process, you can teach the writing process. Some writers like to refer to writing as a craft (Graves, 1983; Fox, 1993). Artisans apply a good deal of individuality to the ways in which they plan, execute, polish, and perfect their work; however, they recognize that the work has to be planned before it can be carved, carved before it can be painted, and painted before it is varnished or glazed. Within the parameters of this very general process, there are many possibilities to be imagined, options to be considered, and decisions to be made. Fox (1993) put the concept of writing as a craft into perspective: "Power is being able to craft a piece of writing so effectively that its purpose is achieved. . . . Craft means being able to put . . . understandings into practice. Craft means struggling in that battlefield between the brain and the hand until the best possible draft is achieved" (p. 20). Graves (1983) describes phases of the **writing process** as prewriting, drafting, seeking a response, revising, editing, and publishing. Of course, such steps are a simple explanation of an intricate enterprise, but such language helps you communicate with others and offers you a starting point.

Prewriting.   **Prewriting** is gathering and experimenting with material before putting everything down on paper. Someone experienced in visual crafts might refer to this stage as planning, shopping, and laying out materials and tools.

A writer plans by considering reasons to write. As a teacher, you may sometimes make these decisions for your class: Everyone is going to write about an embarrassing experience, or everyone is going to write letters to the city council. At other times, you will want to let your students choose their own subjects, purpose, and audience. These decisions are important and must be considered carefully and made deliberately.

No one can make a purposeful plan for a craft without knowing what materials he or she has to work with. Ideas, experiences, opinions, details, and other materials from which writing is formed must be brought into a position where they can be examined, evaluated, and selected or set aside. The Common Core stresses the importance of children engaging in **research**—studying a topic and trying to find out more about it. This involves discovering what others have said about a topic, examining the sources' evidence and supporting ideas, and using that information to inform others.

Common Core
State Standards

When students have determined a purpose and developed ideas, they must decide how to use them. When crafting a gingerbread house, you don't start with the roof. You don't start with the decorations. The project needs a basic shape first. The same is true of crafting with opinions and ideas. If your students are telling a story, they need a definite beginning, middle, and end. That's a basic shape. If your students are writing a report of a science experiment, the basic shape will probably be hypotheses, followed by methods, followed by results. The length and complexity may vary, but the basic shape stays the same. A persuasive piece requires an opinion and a series of reasons. After gathering their materials, writers need to work out what form they will take, how they will be shaped and structured. When you or your students feel stumped, glance through the following list and consider the possibilities (see Figure 3.4). Writing can take many forms. Not only is there always something to write about but there is always a new type of writing to try. Details about each of these forms and examples can be found on the Internet or in resource books such as *Writers Express* (Sebranek, Nathan, & Kemper, 2000).

Drafting.   After a writer has gathered materials and chosen a form, it's time for **drafting**: putting the planned thoughts and ideas together and getting them down on paper. For some people this is the hardest part; for others it's the most fun. Your students' drafting styles will be different—expect variation and be prepared to give support, scaffolding, sympathy, or whatever assistance the novice writers are going to need. Children learning English may find drafting one of their greatest challenges. When

English Language
Learners

Figure 3.4 Forms of Writing

Personal			
Letters	Journals	Notes	Postcards
Anecdotes	Narratives	Autobiographies	Messages
Memoirs			

Picture Books			
ABC	Counting	Participation	Picture stories
Wordless	Engineered	Board or baby	Beginning readers
Predictable	Storyboards		

Subject/Concept			
Descriptions	How-to	News features	Pamphlets
Travelogues	Time capsules	Eyewitness accounts	Question and answer
Recipes	Profiles	Interviews	Essays
Biographies	Summaries		

Responses to Literature			
Advertisements	New covers	Letters to author	Simplified versions
Another viewpoint	Notes from characters	Prequels	Sequels
Other time periods	New settings	News articles	Meaningful quotations
Fictionalized journals	Book reviews	Imaginary interviews	Character sketches

Persuasive			
Petitions	Editorials	Dialogues	Essays

Traditional			
Fairy tales	Folk tales	Tall tales	Legends
Myths	Fables	Parodies	

Creative			
Riddles	Historical fiction	Fantasies	Science fiction
Skits	Plays	Mysteries	Songs
Bumper stickers	Slogans	Comics	Jokes
Contemporary fiction			

Poetic			
Five senses	Illustrated	Descriptive	Ballads
Limericks	Couplets	Haiku	Free verse

Poetic			
Acrostics	Cinquain	Diamante	Number
Color			

Academic			
Reports	Directions	Cause and effect	Proposals
Comparisons	Case studies	Research	Experiments
Documentaries	Surveys	Data charts	Learning logs

they are learning to speak, many experience a silent period in which they are understanding the language but are reluctant to express themselves (Haynes & Zacarian, 2010). This silent period may be mirrored in their writing development. They may be able to read and understand but resist writing.

Students writing.

Emphasize that the draft is tentative. It's experimental. It's expected to change. One teacher printed "Draft" or stamped "Work in Progress" on the paper her students used for drafting to remind them that they didn't yet have to worry about spelling, punctuation, grammar, or handwriting. Anxiety about mechanics often inhibits the flow of ideas and may restrict the kinds of words and sentences a student will attempt to use. Undue concern for neatness at this stage may prevent a student from adding information that belongs in paragraph one after she has moved into paragraph two. Regardless of how carefully writers plan, their minds have a way of coming up with ideal words for describing the accident when they are in the middle of writing about the aftermath. When the teacher downplays mechanics at this point, students are free to backtrack and change things (Pritchard & Honeycutt, 2007). They're craftspeople nailing together rough pieces of board and molding and remolding clay. Things can and should change.

Seeking a Response.   Although experienced writers consider seeking a response as part of revising, beginning writers often need to treat this as a separate step. When a draft is completed, writers often find that they are too close to their projects to be objective. Seeking a response is sharing your writing with someone who can give you a view with some distance or perspective. A young child may be surprised to learn that an outside reader doesn't necessarily know that her brother is 10 years old or that her bedroom is painted blue. A slightly older student learns that classmates want to know more about that huge cast on his leg than just "my bike fell over and I hurt my knee." Writers realize that the word or phrase that just doesn't fall into place for them comes quickly to an outsider. Think of a time when you have benefited because someone you trusted to read your writing gave you a sincere compliment, asked you a question, pointed out a need for detail, or suggested a better way of organizing your ideas. Like you, young students need an opportunity to ask someone to respond to their writing. You can provide a response to your students, but you should plan on providing a variety of response opportunities appropriate to the specific writing activities and to the needs of individual students. Sometimes a response can be provided by a partner, by a small group of peers, or by an adult volunteer.

Speaking/Listening

Revising.   **Revising** is making changes to improve the content of your writing so it will be the best it can be. Spandel (2005) pointed out, "Revision is about change, not mutilation. When your hair gets mussed, you don't shave your head" (p. 85). If you were working on a craft such as flower arranging, you wouldn't feel that you were disparaging your work if you stepped back, viewed it from a distance, and decided that a particularly vivid flower should be moved to a more central position. You would simply be changing it into something positive. Revising writing means building on strong points as well as strengthening weak areas.

If stepping back reveals that your flower arrangement is not as symmetrical as you had planned, you simply rearrange things—possibly adding, possibly eliminating—until

New Literacies

English Language
Learners

you achieve the symmetry you wanted. Writing words is the same way; you add a little more development where things seem sparse, delete a few unnecessary details, rearrange in order to bring a strong point into a more strategic position, or change to lead off with an example rather than just stating the main idea. The use of word-processing programs makes revision easier and improves the quantity and quality of student writing, especially for those who struggle (MacArthur, 2007).

With or without a computer, revision is important. After five years of working on her novel *To Kill a Mockingbird*, Harper Lee threw open her window and scattered the manuscript in the snow. A phone call to her editor calmed her down and she went outside and started revising yet again (Meltzer, 2010). When Thomas Jefferson completed his draft of the Declaration of Independence, some other members of the Continental Congress read it and suggested 87 changes. Although not all of the suggestions were followed, some words were replaced, sentences were changed, and entire paragraphs were removed. The document we have today is stronger because of the revisions that were made (Fleming, 1998).

Language Conventions

Editing.   After you have revised the content of your writing, it is time for **editing**, making sure the mechanics of writing are correct and will not distract readers from the message you are communicating. Editing is a social act of etiquette that writers complete as a favor to their audiences. Editing is the sandpaper, detailing, and varnishing stage of the process. When boards have been nailed together so they look and feel good, the craftsperson takes off the rough edges, repairs minor defects, and adds any final polish that may be appropriate. Where writing is concerned, this finish will probably include such aspects as grammar, punctuation, sentence structure, spelling, and handwriting. These transcriptional aspects must be handled if it is a public literary occasion and writing is to be shared with others. People have lost jobs because their companies were embarrassed by their poor grammar on memoranda and correspondence. But editing needs to be kept in perspective. It is a step in a longer process in which ideas, development, evaluation, and expression are paramount.

Some students are surprisingly good at discerning their own mistakes—or at least suspecting them, but they never need to complete this step alone. Professional writers turn to editors, and you should provide students with the same support before they send their writing out into the world. Students can seek help from peers, parents, siblings, and older students. These helpers may not find all the corrections that need to be made, but don't panic. When you view writing as a process, you become less concerned with improving the writing and more concerned with improving the writer. If a perfect product is the only goal, you could do all the work for the student and present a flawless paper. Such a charade does little to help anyone. The one who does the work does the learning. If you take over a piece, the child learns little. And parents are usually not interested in getting a perfect piece that was created by the teacher and just happens to have their child's name at the top of the page. They are interested in what their child is learning.

As you help children edit their own writing, let students ask for help that they need, possibly circling or underlining in advance the places where they might question the spelling of a word or the placement of a semicolon. After their questions have been asked, gently suggest your own editorial corrections—always emphasizing what has been done well and how difficult these technical matters can sometimes be.

Publishing.   **Publishing** is disseminating the students' writing to an audience beyond themselves and you, the teacher. Some lists representing the writing process end with editing; however, writers of all ages enjoy the process more and find it more meaningful if a publishing step is included. Crafts are meant to be shared. Few people would create a lovely piece of ceramic work, a skillful piece of needlepoint, or a handmade shelf and lock it away in a cupboard where no one can ever see it. There is joy in the sense of accomplishment that comes from skillful creation; but there's also joy in the presentation of one's work before an appreciative audience.

Students can create books by online publishing or by simply folding and stapling papers together. Even something as simple as using the My Story App, an electronic bookmaking tool for children (http://mystoryapp.org), and sharing with others via the Internet can give students a sense of publishing. Children's work can be displayed on a bulletin board or in the hallway outside your room, but publishing is more meaningful if students can actually get a reaction from those who read it. Class newspapers and newsletters can feature children's writing. Calendars, greeting cards, and holiday gifts can also highlight children's writing. Whole class books can be complied in a loose-leaf binder, with each child contributing a chapter, a section, or a page. Peers can be a wonderful audience for each other, but you can also find an appreciative audience among younger students, parents, and relatives, or by sending the writing to a class in another school or even in another state. Many high school or college students are willing to read children's writing and write kind notes of praise in return. Senior citizens in care centers usually enjoy reading writings done by children, and many doctors and dentists are willing to display children's writing in their waiting rooms. Remember that in public settings you need to be careful about displaying a child's full name or providing any personal information such as a school or home address.

New Literacies

Publishing does not necessarily happen with every writing project in a classroom any more than it happens with every writing project a professional writer undertakes. Most writers occasionally have times when they tire of a writing project and start another. Some work on several at the same time. In a classroom the number of publications children produce is not as important as the process they internalize. Of course, it is desirable for children to reach closure, but it does not have to happen every time.

When you teach writing, help children recognize the steps of the overall process and at the same time appreciate the individuality that the nature of crafting allows. Help students realize that just like artisans practice carpentry and ceramics and get better with time, they will improve as they practice the craft of writing.

Linking Reading and Writing

Just as the elements of reading and traits of quality writing can be interwoven, there are benefits to recognizing the interconnections between the reading and writing processes. Many view reading and writing as very similar processes that involve creating or composing meaning (Fitzgerald & Shanahan, 2000; Shanahan & Tierney, 1990; Tierney & Shanahan, 1991). Prereading and prewriting require learners to engage in similar activities. Reading and drafting align. Readers have a response to the text, and writers seek a response to their texts. Readers revisit text in an effort to monitor and

---

Try This for Teaching | **Writing Process Plus**

Although it's important to use a common language when teaching the phases of the writing process, some students find it motivating to come up with creative names that will make the phases of the writing process easier to remember and use. Here are some examples:

- Brain Drain: Getting an idea. Discover what's inside your mind and bring it out.
- Sloppy Copy: Writing the first draft. Put your ideas down on paper.
- Pair Share: Getting a response. Read your writing to someone you trust and ask for honest feedback.
- Sweet Sheet: Making revisions. Focus on improving the content of your writing.
- Goof Proof: Editing. Get help with spelling and punctuation as you prepare to share your writing with an audience.
- Glory Story: Getting published. Share your writing with others.

(Adapted from Bergenske, 1988; Carr & Lucadamo, 1991)

Variations for ELLs

Learn the names for each phase of the process in learners' first languages. Have all children in the class refer to the steps using these terms. Different first languages could be used for a month or two at a time throughout the year. For example, here are the steps in Spanish for *Los procesos de la escritura* (the writing process), as translated by ecslearningsystems.com/index.asp:

- *Antes de escribir* (prewriting) *o piénsalo* (think it)
- *El borrador* (drafting) *o escríbelo* (write it)
- *La revision* (revising) *o mejórala* (improve it)
- *La corrección* (editing) *o corrígelo* (correct it)
- *La publicación* (publishing) *o compártela* (share it)

---

explore, and writers revisit text in an effort to clarify and expand. Writers edit and publish in order to make their material more accessible, and ideally, readers receive text and apply it to their lives.

With these connections in mind, encourage your students to write like readers and read like writers (Smith, 2007). Authors write better when they write with a real audience in mind and incorporate the same qualities they appreciate when they are reading someone else's work. Readers read better when they notice what authors have done to help them compose meaning. That's why you need to teach reading and writing simultaneously. The two acts depend on and complement each other. If you leave out writing, it will damage reading instruction, and the reverse is true as well. Sending students away from schools with confidence in their ability to read but full of insecurities about writing leaves them with only some of the tools they need for a lifetime of learning. Although many students enter college as capable readers, one report reveals that 20 percent require a remedial writing class, and over half of new college students are unable to write a paper relatively free of errors (Intersegmental Committee of the Academic Senates, 2002).

Instruction

Although it is essential to understand components of literacy, such as the elements of reading and traits of writing, this information alone is not enough for teachers to be successful. Knowledge of learners' processes during reading and writing is also insufficient unless it is coupled with a clear understanding of instructional approaches and essential instructional elements that must be present within all approaches.

Approaches

Instructional approaches to teach the language arts in schools and districts are selected for a variety of reasons. Ideally, they are made considering what is best for children. Realistically, however, at times choices must also be made out of convenience or practicality. There simply may not be funding available to pursue other options. Some teachers may not be sufficiently prepared to function without a lot of guidance and direction. At times there may be political influences to consider. You need to be aware of various options and recognize the common instructional elements that should be present regardless of the approach, program, or delivery system in place. Three options include a core literacy program, workshop routines, and literature units. With the adoption of the Common Core, some districts are emphasizing self-regulated strategy development and genre writing.

Common Core
State Standards

Core Literacy Programs.   Commonly referred to as basal programs, **core literacy programs** are published comprehensive classroom literacy programs that include daily plans for teaching. There are currently three major core programs: *Reading Street* from Scott Foresman (www.pearsonschool.com/index.cfm?locator=PSZu65); *Wonders* from Macmillan McGraw-Hill (treasures.macmillanmh.com/national); and *Journeys* from Houghton Mifflin/Harcourt (www.hmheducation.com/journeys/).

Materials include stories, comprehension questions, activities, teaching strategies, worksheets, tests, and scope and sequence of specific skills. The benefits of such programs include keeping instruction unified across districts and states. These programs provide common texts classes can read together, and they outline the sequence in which skills are taught and revisited so they are presented systematically. Many beginning teachers appreciate the help and structure they provide. However, if implemented rigidly, core literacy programs may limit teachers' professionalism. Teachers committed to a lockstep sequence have fewer opportunities to meet the needs of students than those with more flexibilty. Another drawback can be a narrowing of the curriculum limited to the skills that are tested. Perhaps the biggest drawback of all is the reduction in time students spend reading. One study (Brenner & Hiebert, 2008) showed that if core programs are followed explicitly, children only read for about 18 minutes of the two hours of reading instruction.

Core literacy programs are often organized into units of instruction that focus on teaching, practicing, and assessing skills. When these skills are correlated with text that can be read as a class, teachers' manuals provide suggestions for introducing the text and the target skills, and may indicate vocabulary to introduce to the children before or during the reading. The manuals also provide questions to assess comprehension when the story is finished. Most core literacy programs expect students to revisit the text; they reread it in lower grades and review the text and examine certain parts more deeply as they gain skills and experience. In addition to whole class instruction, core programs usually provide leveled readers that can be used with small groups of students who are reading above level, at level, and below level. Specific books for ELLs may also be provided. Most programs also provide technology connections.

Core literacy programs usually emphasize reading more than writing. The programs provide a series of writing prompts related to the reading selections; the prompts elicit short responses with little expectation of revision or editing. Some teachers may be hesitant to do much with the writing component of these programs because they believe it takes time away from teaching and practicing the skills that will be tested.

In a classroom where a core literacy program is being used, you will see the whole class reading or rereading a shared text at certain times and reading leveled text in small groups at other times. In both settings you will see the teacher stressing skills as they are listed in the teachers' manual in preparation for the test. If computers are available, you may see students using them to practice skills or complete a writing assignment based on a prompt provided in the teachers' manual.

Speaking/Listening

Reading and Writing Workshops.   A reading workshop sets aside a block of time for mini-lessons by the teacher, followed by a period during which students read individually selected books, respond to them, and confer with the teacher about them. The workshop ends with a few of the children sharing what they have read.

A writing workshop is similar. The teacher begins with a mini-lesson and then provides an activity period during which students write individually, in groups, or as a class. They often respond to each other's writing or receive individual help from the teacher. During sharing time, students share their writing with their group or class. Some teachers seat students in an "author's chair," a specific chair designated for reading final drafts. Teachers may choose to share as well.

One benefit of workshops is that there is usually a strong expectation that students will choose their own books and writing topics. Such choice can be motivating to children and allows for a great deal of individualization. Another advantage is that teachers can observe students as they work and address needs when they arise. The workshop approach does not include such rigid testing deadlines, allowing teachers the freedom to spend more time focusing on learners' processes. One drawback to workshops is that many teachers have concerns about management. They may have difficulty keeping less motivated students on task while they work with individuals and small groups. Another concern of inexperienced teachers is not having a teachers' manual that provides a list of skills and suggested lesson plans. No worksheets are provided since children are expected to practice skills in their actual writing. Some educators believe that this does not provide a desired level of accountability. In the reading workshop, students may not benefit from the social context that can occur when small groups of children read and discuss the same text.

In a classroom where workshops are used, you will see a lot of students working independently on their reading or writing. The teacher meets with individuals or small groups to help them with the task at hand as well as to monitor and assess their progress. You may also see students working together in pairs or small groups without the teacher's direct supervision. The whole class meets together only for short mini-lessons and for students to take turns sharing their work with each other. If computers are available you may see students using them to read and write, but probably not to practice skills.

Literature Units.   **Literature units** use authentic literature for directed and in-depth reading instruction. Unlike the reading workshop, which typically focuses on children choosing their own books, literature units allow for students to read the same text either as a class or in small groups. Sometimes this approach uses **text sets**, collections of the same books or related books. Commonly all members of a small group read the same book at the same time, but the teacher can also provide various books written by the same author or multiple books by separate authors fitting within a genre (e.g., science fiction or historical fiction) or theme (e.g., new beginnings or communication). The teacher bases instructions to the whole class on observed needs and natural connections with the texts that are being read. The whole class may also gather to share individual or group responses.

Along with reading books together as a class, **literature discussion groups** can be used—small groups of students who meet to read and discuss the same story, poem, article, or book. Usually each group member prepares to take specific responsibilities in the upcoming discussion. The teacher facilitates the selection of reading materials and monitors each group's progress. Literature units leave little space for writing instruction. Students may keep reading logs or may be expected to write in response to the literature, but these are often single draft pieces, which may or may not be shared with others.

Strengths of this approach include the use of authentic literature and the chance for exposing children to quality literature in genres they may not choose for themselves. Because the units are completed in groups, discussion and social interaction can enrich the reading experience. Literature units lend themselves to curriculum integration, as reading material can easily be linked to topics of study in science, social studies, and even mathematics (Vacca & Vacca, 2008). One drawback of literature units is that they do not always allow skills to be addressed systematically. Some people express concern about how few books students actually read because so much time is spent elaborating on them. Another drawback is the limited focus on writing. Unless the teacher combines this approach with writing instruction, writing can be de-emphasized or left out of the curriculum.

In a classroom where literature units are being used, you will see a mixture of whole class reading and small groups. You will see the teacher instructing everyone in short lessons, but students spend most of the time reading and discussing text. When the class is divided into groups, the teacher oversees what is happening in one group at a time, but other groups may work together without the teacher's direct supervision. If computers are available you may see students using them to keep a reading log or write a response to a chapter or book. Students may share responses in small groups or with the whole class.

Self-Regulated Strategy Development.   The Common Core's emphasis on writing has sent educators in search of approaches to writing instruction that could supplement core literacy programs or literature units. **Self-regulated strategy development (SRSD)** for writing (Harris, Graham, Mason, & Friedlander, 2008) is a model for supporting students as they compose narrative, expository, and persuasive text. The focus is on skills, including the self-regulation of those skills. Thus students know not only what the skills are but when to use them appropriately. Mnemonic devices are used to help students remember steps of writing. For example, in the acronym POW, the P reminds students to pick an idea, O reminds them to organize their notes, and W means write more about it. When writing an opinion piece, students learn the acronym TREE (T = topic sentence, R = reasons, E = ending, E = examine for all parts). Students are taught these structures directly, then they are reinforced with modeling and practice.

Common Core
State Standards

Benefits of SRSD include documented improvements in students' writing test scores (Graham & Perin, 2007). In many classrooms both students and teachers enjoy the explicit direction and objectives. SRSD lends itself to whole class writing experiences that can precede group and independent practice. Since SRSD was originally developed for students with learning difficulties, one drawback can be its rigid and formulaic nature. This approach can prepare students well for writing tests, especially those graded by computers. But it may also be training children to write voiceless or passionless prose that would not move human readers. Although students may complete the writing process, there is the possibility they will see it as a recipe to follow rather than a creative experience over which they have control.

In a classroom where SRSD is being used, you will seldom see small groups. You will see the teacher in front of the class and the class working together on a shared text projected for all to see. Steps may be posted, and these steps and other skills are referred to often as the writing is produced. As children work alone, they are all working on the same project using the same steps. The teacher walks around the room monitoring progress and offering support. If computers are available you may see the teacher using one as the group composes a shared text. You may also see individuals using them as they complete their assignments or are being assessed.

Common Core State Standards

Genre Writing.   Another approach to teaching writing that addresses the Common Core is **genre writing**, which involves multiple opportunities for writing across various genres (Cope & Kalantzis, 1993; Donovan, Milewicz, & Smolkin, 2003). Like SRSD, genre writing has specific steps a teacher follows. Feez (1998) tells teachers to begin by building a context for the writing (choosing a topic or theme) and presenting a model text and looking closely at its elements. Next, the whole class writes a piece together in that genre. This is followed by children writing in that genre by themselves. This approach can be used to focus children on the three genres emphasized in the Common Core: argumentative, narrative, and informational. Skills are addressed, but only as they relate to the genre being studied.

A benefit of genre writing is the chance it gives students to learn by doing (Hyland, 2007). Students can succeed in the social context of a whole class where they might fail individually. Whole class writing provides modeling and guided practice, thus it can be an excellent context to address needs of those with learning disabilities and to differentiate instruction for those learning English. While some students work independently, teachers can assist others to complete a class or small group version of the assignment. Genre writing gives a framework and explicit outcomes that support children's learning (Swales, 1990). A workshop approach provides "students with the 'freedom' to write [and] may encourage fluency, but it does not liberate them from the constraints of grammar in constructing social meanings in public contexts" (Hyland, 2007, p. 149). Children need to learn the structures that are expected and accepted in academic and public writing.

Struggling Learners/ RtI

Drawbacks to genre writing include concerns about choice and ownership. With this teacher-directed approach, students may not gain the independence necessary to transfer the knowledge they are gaining into other writing. The task-focused instruction in genre writing may detract from applicability beyond that genre, and students may miss instruction on other skills and opportunities to explore additional writing forms. While the writing process is addressed, the main focus is on avoiding errors instead of utilizing and revising errors.

English Language Learners

In a classroom where genre writing is being used, you will see the teacher in front of the class or walking among students as they work independently. You will not see students in small groups very often. Models of the genre may be posted, and the teacher refers to these examples during whole class work and points them out to the students when they are completing their assignments. If computers are available you may see the teacher using one to help the group compose an example of the genre together. You may also see individuals using them as they complete their own example of the genre being studied. These individual pieces are usually submitted to the teacher, but you may see some students sharing them with the group as well.

Essential Elements

No matter which approach is selected in your district and school, you should make sure that your efforts in the classroom include three essential instructional elements. First, ensure time for students to learn. This instruction can include skills, strategies, concepts, and procedures. Second, allot time for students to do. They must be given opportunities to engage in the activities they are being taught so they can learn from their own experiences. Third, set aside time for students to share. They must be able to share their own writing and responses to reading. Giving students a chance to share before an audience adds authenticity to their literacy learning. It also incorporates instruction for listening and speaking that is not teacher centered. Graham, MacArthur, and Fitzgerald (2007) state that "if students are to become good writers, we need to help them become strategic, knowledgeable, and motivated writers" (p. 5). The same could be said of readers. Knowledgeable readers and writers have time to learn. Strategic readers and writers have time to do. Motivated readers and writers have time to share.

Speaking/Listening

Time to Learn.   Within the block of time allotted for literacy learning, specify time for instruction. To teach a lesson you must clarify what you are teaching and how you are going to teach it. You must also consider how students will demonstrate they have learned and what resources you may need to prepare in advance. Your resources usually include time, space, people, and materials. You might ask yourself how much time you will need, how the space will be utilized, how you will involve others, and what materials are needed. These are the most basic components of a complete lesson plan. Lesson plans can be more extensive, but sometimes simple ones can be as effective.

You can accomplish a great deal in a short amount of time by using mini-lessons. **Mini-lessons** are intense instructional sessions that usually do not go beyond 10 to 15 minutes. They focus on one specific objective. They typically address skills, strategies, concepts, and procedures. **Skills** are cognitive processes that have become or should become automatic: for example, punctuation marks or phonics generalizations. **Strategies** are cognitive processes that require attention and are completed consciously, such as comprehension strategies like identifying main ideas or visualizing. **Concepts** include ideas or abstract principles, ranging from literary genres to traits of quality writing such as voice. **Procedures** are the way to do something, usually explained in steps—such as how to share your writing with others or how to respond when others share their writing with you.

Try This for Professional Development	**Window Lesson Plan**

- Fold a piece of paper into four equal sections, resembling a window with four panes.
- Label each section: What Taught (WT), How Taught, (HT), How Evaluated (HE), and Resources (R).
- Under Resources, include time, space, people, and materials (TSPM).
- Fill in each remaining section with the details of a lesson.

Variations

- Fold the paper into four horizontal columns.
- Create a template on a word processor that can be used repeatedly.
- Try using just the abbreviations and see if you can get your lesson in as small a space as possible, like the space provided in a typical teacher's plan book.

Some lessons may extend over several days and can include a great deal of modeling. Instruction can be implicit or explicit. Some refer to **implicit instruction** as "show and tell" because the example or model is given before the explanation. Many teachers use this method when teaching concepts, patterns, and abstractions (Borich, 2006). Implicit instruction allows students to hypothesize about what is being learned. This opportunity for discovery helps students to take a little more responsibility for their own learning, generally leading to a feeling of ownership that may help students retain the information longer (Deboer, 2004).

For example, you may post two sentences on the board and ask why one has an exclamation point and the other doesn't. Students are allowed time to express their ideas. When one student finally captures the main idea—that the exclamation mark is used when the message of the sentence demands the reader's full attention—then you can validate the correct response and provide a few more examples. You can then check students' understanding by providing a few examples and nonexamples and then asking students to show you which sentences should contain an exclamation mark—with a thumbs up or thumbs down gesture—when the sentences are displayed. Perhaps you could ask for a choral response when a sentence is correct or ask students to write an example of a sentence that would need an exclamation mark. Implicit instruction is indirect and open ended so that students can learn by discovery and utilize errors.

Explicit instruction can be called "tell and show" because the explanation is provided first, followed by examples, checking, and practice. Some teachers like this approach when teaching facts, rules, and action sequences (Borich, 2006).

If you wanted to explain exclamation marks explicitly, you would gain the students' attention and then inform them of the objective—explaining to them that by the end of the lesson they will know what an exclamation point is and when to use it in their writing. Input about exclamation points would then be followed by some examples. You would finally check to make sure the students understood and allow them time to practice. Explicit instruction is direct and clear, and it helps students avoid errors.

Language learning can also involve activities that do not take the form of a lesson. Word work (Bear, Invernizzi, Templeton, & Johnston, 2011), making words (Cunningham, 2008a), and word walls (Wagstaff, 1999) are all examples of engaging activities in which students learn about language.

For example, when using the making words activity, a teacher presents students with letter cubes and asks them to pick out a letter that could be a word (*a* or *I*). Then the teacher asks students to make two-letter words (*am* or *in*). This pattern continues until the students discover the word that uses all the letters (*animal*).

Time to learn: whole class mini-lesson.

Struggling Learners/
RtI

Time to Do. In the time crunch teachers feel, they often pull back to the pattern of lessons, practice, and assessment rather than allowing children enough time to actually do what they are learning to do—read and write (Billen et al., 2011). Some people who learn a foreign language say that it helps to go to a country where that language is spoken so they can have lots of time to actually listen and speak. Some people who drive claim they learned at the wheel. Even teachers who receive years of courses in preparation for their profession usually value and implement what they learned in their field experiences most (Moore, 2003). If teachers appreciate learning to teach in actual classrooms, why do some choose to limit the time their students spend in actual reading and writing?

Effective schools allow regular blocks of time for reading and writing to, with, and by children (Mooney, 1990). Of course skills are taught, but not outside a context of authentic literacy experiences. Fox (1993) expressed concern that too many children are growing up in what she called a literacy desert because of how little reading and writing they do. She said, "We need to water the desert so that [literacy] will bloom" (p. 67).

Time to Share.   Smith (1983b) wrote, "Writing is for stories to be read, books to be published, poems to be recited, plays to be acted, songs to be sung" (p. 566). Give your students plenty of opportunities to share their work and celebrate their accomplishments. Sharing responses to reading or participating in book talks to share favorite books with their friends provides motivation and validation. Five to ten minutes a day is long enough to give a few students a chance to read what they have written or show what they have produced. Sharing might include a performance—a

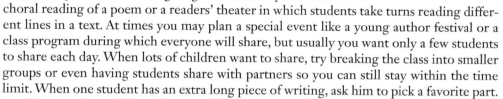
Time to do: students reading during work time.

choral reading of a poem or a readers' theater in which students take turns reading different lines in a text. At times you may plan a special event like a young author festival or a class program during which everyone will share, but usually you want only a few students to share each day. When lots of children want to share, try breaking the class into smaller groups or even having students share with partners so you can still stay within the time limit. When one student has an extra long piece of writing, ask him to pick a favorite part.

Some teachers ask for volunteers. Others assign students a specific day or have students sign up to share. You can even use sharing as a motivation for students who may not be using their time wisely. They usually want to be prepared when they present before peers, so knowing they are sharing the next day may raise their level of concern in a positive way.

Sharing time may not be the best venue to offer suggestions for improvement. Individual conferences and small groups may be a more private setting for that purpose. Sharing with the whole class is an ideal time to appreciate efforts and praise accomplishments.

Speaking/Listening

Sharing is primarily a time for the students, but occasionally children love to hear the teacher share as well. Talk about books you have read and would like to suggest to them. Tell about books you loved when you were young. Share pages of your own journal or a story you are writing. Children love to see examples of writing you did as a child or examples of writing you are doing now at various stages of completion. It brings the reading and writing processes alive when students see that you are involved.

English Language Learners

Sharing is also a time when speaking and listening are important skills. Children can learn how to present effectively and listen attentively. Those who share must speak so that they can be heard, projecting their voices and not mumbling. Those who listen must look at the one speaking and keep hands clear of distracting objects. Sharing time can offer a context in which to teach students how to compliment each other, how to receive a compliment, and how to be a courteous audience. Such an audience can help those learning English to feel safe and accepted. Providing opportunities for them to speak and listen is vital. As they feel a part of the community of readers and writers in your classroom, they may begin to feel part of the larger community beyond it.

Time to share: students presenting to peers.

Learning, doing, and sharing during a literacy block can be organized in a variety of ways. Typically, half the allotted time should be spent doing. The other half can be divided between learning and sharing. If you have one hour, plan on 30 minutes of students doing, 20 minutes of learning, and 10 minutes of sharing. Figure 3.5 shows a breakdown of literacy time.

Figure 3.5

Essential Instructional Elements

M otivation and Literacy

All of the aspects of literacy are important, but another factor must also be considered—motivation. Your goal as a teacher is not only to help children learn how to read but to encourage them to love reading. You want children to have both the *skill* and the *will* to read.

Motivation refers to the forces that arouse and direct human behavior. We know that those who devote more time to reading are better readers (Anderson, Wilson, & Fielding, 1988; Morrow, 1992). We also know that efforts to motivate struggling readers and writers can help them improve their literacy abilities (Allington, 1998; Smith-Burke, 1989). Motivation can be extrinsic or intrinsic. **Extrinsic motivation** may cause people to work on a task even if they have little interest in it because of the anticipated satisfaction they may receive. Extrinsic rewards may include grades, smiley faces, stickers, or candy. **Intrinsic motivation** comes from inside an individual. Those who are intrinsically motivated complete tasks because of the challenge, satisfaction, or pleasure that comes from the task itself.

Some educators are hesitant to endorse external motivators because they want children to be motivated from within. But motivation is multifaceted and complex. There are times when external rewards are needed until intrinsic motivation is realized. Some reading incentive programs reward children with pizza, points, or prizes depending on how much they read. Some students may read initially for the reward. As they read and discover that a book can answer their questions or make them laugh and feel good, these experiences can lead to intrinsic motivation. Students usually pass through three levels of motivation: perceived requirements, perceived expectations, and sincere desires.

Perceived Requirements

Many children begin reading and writing with a sense of perceived requirement. They want to avoid punishment or win a prize. One school librarian told of a second-grade student who was reading to obtain points that she could use to buy toys. Students were required to read books and take tests on the content in order to receive rewards. The librarian assured the child that a specific picture book he showed her had a test associated with it. The student returned after a few minutes and asked for help finding the test on the computer. Unfortunately no test was found for that book. The girl complained, "Why did I waste my time reading this book?"

Perceived Expectations

Other children read and write with perceived expectations. They feel a sense of duty. They know they should read because their teachers and parents expect it. They want to become like their parents and others whom they love and admire. They eagerly want to please the people who care most about them. Praise from adults is not a tangible reward, but children are often happy when such recognition comes and disappointed when it doesn't. One first-grade boy reread a book he brought home from school multiple times at the instruction of his teacher. He was anxious to report back to her the next day, but found a substitute in her place who did not follow up on the assignment. That evening, when the boy's father asked if he had brought home another book to read, the boy replied, "I'm not doing that until my real teacher comes back."

Sincere Desires

Reading for a prize or out of duty will never be as satisfying as reading with a sincere desire. That desire comes from seeing beyond the activity to something greater. You cannot imagine life without reading and writing. You wonder why everyone does not feel the same. You feel genuine sadness for those who are missing out. Reading and writing have stopped being ends in and of themselves; they have become means to greater ends. The librarian spoken of previously told of a time when a new shipment of books had arrived. During their lunch break, two fifth-grade girls helped him unpack some of the boxes. As they did, one commented to another, "Here's another book by Lois Lowry. I love her other books, so I want to read this one too!" In this case she was motivated by the sheer joy of reading.

Progressing Through Levels

Children who do not initially like vegetables can learn to like them. Those afraid of roller coasters can end up becoming enthusiasts. Some teacher candidates experience dramatic shifts in their own reading motivation during a children's literature class. Teachers who claim to hate writing end up loving it after participating in effective professional development. Motivation can be elevated.

Struggling Learners/ RTI

One young man described how he progressed through levels of motivation when he kept a journal:

> The only reason I started keeping a journal is because my teacher challenged me to and offered me extra credit. As other teachers spoke about the benefits of keeping a journal, they validated what I was doing and breathed new life to my efforts. I figured I owed it to my grandchildren to record my life. As I continued writing, I found my journal an ideal place to think and discover and to vent when I was upset. I realized I was not keeping it for extra credit, my teacher, or for posterity anymore, I was doing it for me because it helped me—I loved it.

Try This for Professional Development **Levels of Motivation**

- Think of something you initially didn't want to do, but later enjoyed.
- Reflect on what fostered that progress in your life.
- Consider the examples of role models (for example, a friend's hobby may become your own).
- Keep in mind how increased knowledge affected you (such as knowledge of nutrition changing eating habits).
- Competence may lead to confidence (for example, piano practice building skills that lead to increased enjoyment).

- Consider the effect of expanded perspective (such as a child viewing an immunization as painful, with adults seeing the reason for the pain).
- Share your journey with others.
- Consider how you can help children move to higher levels of motivation in their literacy learning.

Variations

- Think of something you don't do that you should. What motivation is lacking?
- Interview others about how they progressed through levels of motivation. Look for patterns and themes.

Summary

Teachers can make a positive difference. This possibility can motivate you to always teach for learning. Today the definition of good teaching includes the impact of specific teacher behaviors on the cognitive and affective behaviors of their students (Ruddell, 2008). You will have an impact in the lives of your students not only as you care about them but also as you teach with variety and clarity. Be task oriented and help students become engaged and active learners. As you help them experience a high degree of success, they will want to continue learning.

As teachers of literacy specifically, you must combine your knowledge of these key behaviors with your knowledge of the components of reading and writing. It is important for you to know the elements of reading and the traits of writing. The National Reading Panel (2000) outlined five areas that are central to the teaching of reading: phonological awareness, phonics, vocabulary, fluency, and comprehension. The traits of quality writing include the following: voice, organization, ideas, conventions, word choice, sentence fluency, and presentation (Spandel, 2007).

Knowledge of what you are teaching in reading and writing must be based on your understanding of the processes learners use as they develop literacy. Tompkins (2010) outlines stages in the reading process as prereading, reading, responding, exploring, and applying. Graves (1983) describes phases of the writing process as prewriting, drafting, seeking a response, revising, editing, and publishing. Be careful not to view all these processes as a series of activities through which every child must pass at the same rate in the same precise sequence. They are recursive and interactive. Few children go through the phases in a lockstep way.

Schools and districts choose from a broad assortment of instructional approaches for teaching the language arts. You need to be aware of these approaches. Five covered briefly in this chapter were core literacy programs, reading and writing workshops, literature units, self-regulated strategy development, and genre writing. No matter which approach or combination of approaches is selected in your district and school, you should make sure that the essential elements of instruction are present: time for learning, doing, and sharing.

Becoming familiar with levels of motivation offers a context in which you can identify where your students are and help them refine and educate their desires. You can provide the bigger picture that will inspire higher motivation. With these understandings you have a strong foundation on which to build literacy.

Self-Check

1. Discuss the meaning of learning and teaching.
2. What sets a professional teacher apart?
3. What are key behaviors of effective teaching?
4. What are the basic elements of reading?
5. What are the traits of quality writing?
6. Compare the reading and writing processes.
7. What are some of the common instructional approaches adopted by schools and districts?
8. Regardless of the approach used, what are three essential elements of instruction?

MyEducationLab™

Go to the Topics, Phonemic Awareness/Phonics, Fluency, Vocabulary, Comprehension, and Writing, in the MyEducationLab (www.myeducationlab.com) for your course, where you can:

- Find learning outcomes for Phonemic Awareness/Phonics, Fluency, Vocabulary, Comprehension, and Writing, along with the national standards that connect to these outcomes.

- Complete Assignments and Activities that can help you more deeply understand the chapter content.

- Apply and practice your understanding of the core teaching skills identified in the chapter with the Building Teaching Skills and Dispositions learning units.

- Examine challenging situations and cases presented in the IRIS Center Resources.

- Check your comprehension on the content covered in the chapter by going to the Study Plan in the Book Resources for your text. Here you will be able to take a chapter quiz, receive feedback on your answers, and then access Review, Practice, and Enrichment activities to enhance your understanding of chapter content (optional).

- Visit **A+RISE** Standards2Strategy™, an innovative and interactive online resource that offers new teachers in grades K–12 just-in-time, research-based instructional strategies that meet the linguistic needs of ELLs as they learn content, differentiate instruction for all grades and abilities, and are aligned to Common Core Elementary Language Arts Standards (for the literacy strategies) and to English language proficiency standards in WIDA, Texas, California, and Florida.

chapter 4

Emergent Literacy

Chapter Outline

ORAL LANGUAGE DEVELOPMENT
Phonology
Semantics
Syntax
Pragmatics
Schema Theory
LITERACY DEVELOPMENT
Emergent
Beginning
Fluent
AWARENESS OF SOUNDS AND LETTERS
Recognition of Language Sounds
Written Language Development
Combining Spoken and Written Language
SUMMARY

A kindergarten student was busy filling several pages in his journal with drawings and scribbles. He was working carefully and intently. When the student teacher asked for volunteers who wanted to share, the boy raised his hand enthusiastically and waved it back and forth so he would be noticed. The student teacher called on the boy and he marched confidently to the front of the room and said, "I'm going to share what I've written about my vacation." He went on tell about visiting an amusement park with his family. When he finished, the student teacher said, "That's nice, but you haven't really *written* that. But don't worry, next year in first grade you'll learn how to write." As I spoke with the student teacher after her lesson, I asked if she had ever been around a baby who was starting to talk. She said her niece was just beginning to say *mama* and *dada*. I asked her if her niece was really talking. She said, "Yes." I asked if she corrected her niece and told her to say *mother* and *father*. She said, "Of course not." Then I asked one last question, "How does that relate to the boy who wrote about the amusement park?" This student teacher began to realize that learning to write, like learning to talk, is a developmental process. Literacy development is a continuum that begins at birth and continues throughout life. This kindergartner *was* really writing—in his own way.

—Brad

Emergent literacy is the perspective that young children develop as readers and writers through a gradual process (Clay, 1979). Reading and writing need to be considered in the context of oral language development. The ability to use language to express meaning and understand messages sets humans apart from other creatures. When you receive oral language, you listen; when you receive written language, you read. When you express yourself with oral language, you speak; when you express yourself with written language, you write. It's important for you to understand how oral language develops in order to understand literacy development. With this understanding you will be able to help children increase their awareness of sounds and letters.

Oral Language Development

When children are born they do not know any language, but by the time they are five years old most are competent and confident speakers and comprehenders of their home languages. Children's acquisition of oral language varies depending on the support and interactions they have with family members and other caretakers (Hart & Risley, 1995). Children begin to have some understanding of how language works as they learn to speak. But what exactly do they know? Children understand phonology, how the sound system of our language works; semantics, how words represent meaning; syntax, how words can be arranged in the appropriate sequence to express meaning; and pragmatics, how language is used appropriately in specific situations. They also learn how to use their life experiences to create meaning, which is related to schema theory.

Phonology

Humans can make a variety of sounds with their vocal apparatus—they can sing, whistle, click, cough, and of course, they can speak. Infants are surrounded by many different sounds in their environment. Children hear the sounds of traffic, of birds chirping, of the wind blowing through trees, and of music played or sung. They also hear the sounds of people around them speaking. To acquire the ability to talk, children must be able to differentiate human speech from the multitude of other sounds around them. When they can successfully focus on speech, they begin to recognize the 44 speech sounds of English and are able to identify each specific sound as it occurs in combination with other sounds in individual words. **Phonology** is the study of speech sounds.

During their first year, children coo by producing vowel sounds. They then babble, or combine consonant and vowel sounds. By the time they are a year old, many children

Speaking/Listening

say their first word. At about 18 months they begin combining words into two-word sentences (Owens, 2011). Their efforts are generally met with great enthusiasm from adults, which encourages them to continue. After this initial success with language, children are able to play with language.

Acquisition of the sounds is essential in learning a second language, and being familiar with the sounds of one's own language assists in acquiring sounds in another. Many language minority children are able to master the sounds of the new language over a relatively short period (August & Shanahan, 2006).

English Language
Learners

Semantics

Semantics is the study of the meanings of words and sentences. When children say their first word at about 12 months of age, that word is usually a content word that is meaningful to them (*mommy*, *dada*, *cookie*). Proper and concrete nouns are often acquired first, followed by function words and abstract terms. Children develop conceptual knowledge as they acquire the ability to name those concepts. One process that is common across all aspects of oral language development is **overgeneralization**: that is, when children first understand a principle of language acquisition, they may generalize it to all situations. For example, children may learn the word *ball*. But they may overgeneralize by using that same word to name all objects that are round, including apples, oranges, and even clocks.

To know a word, one should be able to pronounce it, understand it when others use it, know its primary meaning, and be able to use it appropriately in speech. As children progress in semantic development, they must learn to deal with words that have more than one meaning. For example, many children may know the common meaning of the word *run* (to move more quickly than you walk). However, they may not be as familiar with other meanings (such as using it to describe when a car is operating, when you drive a short distance, or when you ask others to consider an idea you might have). Semantic development is crucial in early childhood and continues throughout one's life. For those learning English as another language, time must be allowed for semantic development to occur. In fact, it may take years for children to acquire the semantic sophistication to use the academic vocabulary required to be successful in school (Grabe, 2009).

English Language
Learners

Syntax

Not only must children learn to produce accurate speech sounds and string them together to produce words they must also arrange words in sequences that produce meaning. This sequencing is called **syntax**. The one-word stage begins at about 12 months, with children naming objects and asking for things, mostly with nouns and verbs. At about 18 months children begin the two-word stage, stringing two words together to express clearer meaning. When an 18-month-old child says "Daddy go," she may mean "Daddy is going now" or "I want to go with Daddy." The words used by young children are expressed together to convey meaning. Telegraphic speech follows, in which children construct short, simple sentences using content-rich words.

Like overgeneralization in semantics, overgeneralization of structure is common during syntactic development. A child may hear her parents and others say "We went to the park" and she will imitate the usage of the past tense form of the verb "to go." However, when the child understands that past tense may be marked using "-ed," she may begin to say "We wented " or "We goed." This demonstrates how the child is coming to understand how language works. This process is natural, and children benefit less from frequent adult correction than from authentic conversational interaction (Grabe, 2009).

Pragmatics

Pragmatics is the branch of linguistics that deals with the meanings and effects that come from the use of language in particular situations. This means that as children acquire language they come to understand how to use language according to their purpose and audience. Language may be used for many purposes—to explain, describe, request, demand, and so on.

Children often use an informal dialect when at home or on the playground but a more formal usage of English when in the classroom. Standard American English (SAE) is the form that is used commonly in school, in print, and on news broadcasts. Other forms or dialects of English differ in their use of phonology, semantics, and syntax. These dialects, which occur throughout the United States, include Southern American English, Chicano English, Pigeon English, and Ebonics, among others. Although these dialects may be considered by some people to be inferior forms of English, they are often just as systematic and rule-governed as SAE (Amberg & Vause, 2009).

Children of any age who learn English as another language bring benefits from their skill levels in their native language as they use the new language to make meaning. Those who are fluent in their native language bring a wealth of knowledge because they already understand many uses and structures of language, they possess substantial listening/speaking vocabularies in their first language, and they add to this a wide range of life experiences. Beyond that knowledge, they have a bank of sounds from their primary language. As they become aware of the sounds of English, they relate familiar sounds to those in their primary language. Sounds that are similar in the two languages are more quickly acquired than sounds individual to one language or the other (Peregoy & Boyle, 2008).

English Language Learners

Schema Theory

Schema theory describes how people store, access, and retrieve information in their minds to make sense of what they experience. People store information in units referred to as schemas or schemata. They use those schemata to help them understand what they experience. In the context of reading, this means that readers hold information in their minds that they use to understand words and ideas in texts. At times, even though readers have the appropriate schema, the text does not provide enough clues for them to access that information. Other times they encounter text that includes information not already in their experience. Understanding is difficult until the reader's limited schema is expanded. Occasionally, readers try to impose a schema that does not fit a text, creating a mismatch.

Insufficient Text Clues. Readers may be able to decode all of the words in a text, know the meanings of all the words, and understand the structure of the sentences they are reading, yet still not be able to fully comprehend the text if it lacks clues needed to lead them to the appropriate schema. For example, consider the following text:

> He was a gentleman. His integrity was legendary, even among his foes. How strange to be respected by those who labeled him a rebel, a traitor. This was yet another oddity accompanying the historic birth of his child, destined to change the world.

Most readers can easily decode all of the words, and they even know the meaning of each word. The sentences are structured conventionally. But many have difficulty explaining what the passage is about. But one name changes everything: George Washington. If you had seen this name before reading the text, you would have understood what was being said about the man and that the child is the country that he is considered the father of. Accessing knowledge related to the text is critical to building an understanding of what one reads in text. When students encounter insufficient text clues you will need to provide additional information.

Limited Schema. When our prior knowledge matches well with the expectations of the text, we can easily build meaning as we read. However, there are times when we have limited prior experience or knowledge of the topic we are reading about. For example, most readers cannot create the meaning that the author intended for this passage:

> The success or failure of the entire venture was in their hands. All day they had worked and hung each string meticulously. Now the efforts of the day would be rewarded at night. Of course, that would depend on whether their hands would reach. She stretched out her hand as he stretched out his. The feeling was electric to say the least. The best situation would involve less distance. But it was not lack of planning on their part. The connection they had counted on was dead. Now only their touch could bring their creation to life.

Many readers would find this passage very difficult to comprehend because they can find no related schemas in their minds. However, seeing the illustration in Figure 4.1 before reading would make the meaning clear for those familiar with hanging Christmas lights. For readers unfamiliar with this tradition, new schema would have to be built.

While this is a trick passage, there are times when readers may encounter an underdeveloped schema that prevents them from understanding a text. For example, a third-grade teacher asked a group of students to read a passage in which much of the important action took place at a beach. These students lived far from an ocean, so many of them lacked the knowledge necessary to visualize a beach. The teacher provided

Figure 4.1 Christmas Lights Schema

descriptions and photographs of beaches. She told them some of her experiences at beaches, so when the students read the passage, they were able to understand.

Mismatched Schema. Another common problem for children is when they try to apply an existing schema to a text that does not match. *Minerva Louise, the Mixed-up Hen* (Stoeke, 1991) is a picture book that illustrates this problem. The hen sees a floral pattern on a bedspread and calls it a field of flowers. She sees a tricycle and calls it a tractor. She sees logs in a fireplace and calls them a nest. When children make the same mistake, don't criticize. It usually makes them cling ever tighter to the schema they selected prematurely. Instead, acknowledge their efforts and gently present evidence that will allow them to update their schema.

Struggling Learners/ RtI

Literacy Development

All of the major aspects of oral language development are used when children acquire reading and writing skills. Semantic development in oral language relates to vocabulary knowledge in reading and writing. Syntactic development is associated with grammar issues in reading and writing. Since phonics deals with how written symbols relate to speech sounds, phonological development is related to the alphabetic code. Some refer to these three aspects of language development as the **cueing systems** in reading. Also necessary to literacy development is fluency. Readers and writers need to be able to use all of these processes quickly and accurately. All of these processes lead to acquiring comprehension of what one reads and to making one's writing comprehensible to others. Children develop as readers and writers through a developmental progression that follows three predictable stages—emergent, beginning, and fluent literacy (Chall, 1995; Juel, 1991).

Emergent

The emergent stage typically progresses from birth to kindergarten. During this period, children show an interest in reading and writing, pretend to read and write, and may be able to identify 5 to 20 words in print and write the same number of high frequency words. Many understand basic concepts about reading, like the directionality of written language and the names of the letters of the alphabet, and they are developing the ability to write letters.

In this prereading stage, children can come to realize that they are living within a literacy culture and may become aware of environmental print around them. They become excited about investigating print and books, making connections between what is around them and what is within the pages they explore.

Beginning

Children typically pass through this stage during first and second grades, but some reach it earlier and others continue in it for a longer period. At this stage most children begin to see specific relationships between oral and written language and are developing the ability to associate specific sounds with specific letters and combinations of letters. In reading

Young children writing.

they learn to use beginning, middle, and final sounds to decode. However, because children see reading as a guessing and memory task, the decoding process is deliberate; their reading is slow and often lacking in expression. They grunt and bark at the print and read each word as if it were on a separate page. Because they are "glued to print" (Chall, 1979, p. 39), they frequently point to words as they read them aloud. Most of their reading at this stage is oral, and they begin to make some self-corrections.

In writing, many progress from writing one and two sentence pieces to writing longer, better-developed compositions. They initiate a few revisions and editing corrections in their writing. Their spelling of words is often tied to the sounds they hear and becomes more conventional with practice.

Fluent

The fluent stage begins for some children in third or fourth grade and continues throughout their school years and beyond. Children at this stage can identify most words automatically and read with expression. They identify unfamiliar words using multiple cueing systems and can use various strategies to comprehend. Fluent readers are usually motivated to read independently and prefer to read silently.

Fluent writers can use the writing process to create compositions of multiple paragraphs. They spell high-frequency words conventionally and use a sophisticated vocabulary. They can apply capitalization rules and use punctuation marks to convey meaning.

Although third-graders and high schoolers can both be described as fluent readers, there are great differences in their maturity, interests, and experiences. Chall (1995) divides this stage into additional developmental phases. In third grade, children confirm their knowledge about language and develop fluent reading. They unglue themselves from print because they have created a bank of high-frequency words. They gravitate to familiar books, and many children reread the same books over and over. In this stage children increase the volume of their writing and are more willing and able to revise. They develop a sense of audience and see editing as way to reach readers.

In intermediate grades and middle school, many students realize that reading allows them to find information and answers to their questions. They expand their reading interests and are able to successfully read and write in new genres.

By high school many young people are able to read critically and understand multiple viewpoints. Their reading and writing extends well beyond school assignments to websites, social networks, and text messages. Although they have the ability to read deeply and write thoughtfully in content areas, some struggle with motivation.

College-age students usually develop a broader worldview and see how literacy connects them to that world. They are willing to read required texts because they can see benefits in learning content that goes beyond assignments. They are motivated to read and write for their own purposes.

A wareness of Sounds and Letters

Language Conventions

As children acquire their first words, they focus on meaning. Their aim is to make sense, to understand. Mechanical processes involved with sound awareness and decoding should not supersede comprehension in reading instruction. Neither should these processes be separated from understanding (Ming & Dukes, 2010). The goal is for readers to learn to decode quickly so their main attention can be focused on meaning (Cecil, 2003; Foster & Miller, 2007). After they have acquired a number of words to use in their own speech, children become aware of the sounds that make up words they already know. The Common Core stresses phonological awareness as a foundational skill. Understanding written language development and how spoken and written language are combined are also vital skills as you help children become aware of sounds and letters.

Common Core State Standards

Recognition of Language Sounds

This comprehension of the nature and function of language sounds is so important that the National Reading Panel (2000), after reviewing 100,000 studies of reading, listed sound awareness among the five most important elements in reading instruction. You must understand both phonemic and phonological awareness, as well as how they can be fostered through word play.

Phonemic Awareness.   Children delight in rhyming sounds, repeating words, and playing with sounds in their speech. As they do this, they are becoming aware that the words they can say are made of individual sounds, called **phonemes**. The phoneme is the smallest sound unit in a word, one of the 44 speech sounds that are used to create words in English. As children play with language, they develop phonemic awareness, which is the consciousness of phonemes and understanding of how they work. In order to understand and use the alphabetic system for reading and writing, they must be able to break words into those component sounds (Rohl, 2000). In becoming aware of the sounds, children begin to notice the relationship of those sounds to the letters they are accustomed to seeing on the page (Ming & Dukes, 2010).

As Rohl (2000) points out, children sometimes find it difficult to identify phonemes and attach letters to them because they hear syllables and one-syllable words as single sounds. For example, they are used to thinking of *dog* as one sound—not as a combination of three component sounds. Phonemic awareness is acquired most effectively when letters are taught in conjunction with activities involving spoken language and pictures (McGee & Richgels, 2003). Thus, if children look at a poster with a picture of a dog labeled with the segmentation /d/ /o/ /g/, possibly in conjunction with pictures and segmentation labels for /f/ /r/ /o/ /g/ and /h/ /o/ /g/ they can begin to understand that there are sounds within sounds.

English Language Learners

Phonological Awareness.   Phonemic awareness is part of the broader concept of **phonological awareness**, which expands to include larger units of speech like word families and syllables (Ehri & Nunes, 2002). When children understand that /d/ can be taken off *dog* and replaced with /h/ to form the word *hog*, they can be led to generalize further to form the word *log, jog, fog,* and *smog*. The same process can be done with *cat* (*mat, bat, rat, splat*) or *dad* (*pad, sad, mad, glad*) and other word families. Thus, children develop phonological awareness: they learn that sounds come together to form words, and some words have more than one group of sounds (syllables). For example, *jog* becomes *jogging* or *jogger*.

Phonological awareness focuses on spoken language, but it is "necessary in learning to map speech onto print" (Rivalland 2000, p. 42). Thus, by blending phonological awareness with letter knowledge, you ease children toward learning to read and write by combining spoken and written language. Some children come to kindergarten having already developed sensitivity to many of the sounds of language, whereas others must develop this awareness in school. Most children can learn what they need to know about sounds in spoken language after about 15 hours of instruction in school, building on what they have learned from being surrounded by language in their lives (National Reading Panel, 2000).

Struggling Learners/ RtI

Speaking/Listening

Word Play. You can help young children and English language learners develop phonological awareness by using activities that focus on various aspects of the sounds of language. Singing songs and enjoying poetry are ways to appreciate and play with the sounds of words. Within these contexts, you can help children focus on specific sounds and manipulate them.

Children singing with their teacher.

When playing with words and sounds, children who are beginning to read *hear* them spoken and they *say* the words—they *do not necessarily see* the letters. Their awareness begins at the oral language level, not at the written language level. You can help children develop their understanding by making activities fun instead of making them a drill. Many children love to recite nursery rhymes like "Jack be nimble, Jack be quick." They also love to sing songs like "This Land Is Your Land" and recite poetry like "Covers" from Giovanni's *The Sun Is So Quiet* (1996). All of these provide natural oral contexts to acquaint children with sounds (Taylor, 1981). To strengthen phonological awareness, teachers need only stop occasionally to call attention to specific sounds that are used effectively. Figure 4.2 shows some favorite books to use for this purpose.

When working with English language learners, you may want to find books that use both their primary language and English. For example, *Manana Iguana* (Paul, 2005)

Figure 4.2   **Children's Books for Phonological Awareness**

Cristelow, E. (2006). *Five little monkeys jumping on the bed*. Boston, MA: Clarion.

Emberley, B. (2005). *Drummer Hoff*. New York, NY: Aladdin.

Fox, M. (1998). *Tough Boris*. San Diego, CA: Harcourt.

Gag, W. (2006). *Millions of cats*. New York, NY: Puffin.

Keats, E. J. (1999). *Over in the meadow*. New York, NY: Puffin.

Lilligard, D. (2006). *Go!: Poetry in motion*. New York, NY: Knopf.

Lobel, A. (1986). *The Random House book of Mother Goose*. New York, NY: Random House.

Martin, B., Jr. (2008). *Brown bear, brown bear, what do you see?* New York, NY: Henry Holt.

Prelutsky, J., & Lobel, A. (1983). *The Random House book of poetry*. New York, NY: Random House.

Raffi. (1998). *Down by the bay: Songs to read*. New York, NY: Crown.

Shaw, N. (1997). *Sheep in a jeep*. Boston, MA: Houghton Mifflin.

Sierra, J. (2003). *Antarctic antics: A book of penguin poems*. Orlando, FL: Harcourt.

Yolen, J., & Peters, A. F. (2007). *Here's a little poem: A very first book of poetry*. Cambridge, MA: Candlewick.

Zelinksy, P. (1990). *The wheels on the bus*. New York, NY: Dutton.

and *Pio Peep!: Traditional Spanish Nursery Rhymes* (Ada, Campoy, & Shertle, 2003) are effective mixtures of Spanish and English that can be enjoyed by children from both language backgrounds, as the books encourage phonological awareness for all of them. Similar books for children are available in other languages. For example, *Dancing on Grapes* (Buonanno, 2011) is written in both English and Italian. Milet Publishing has produced bilingual books for beginners in English and German, English and Farsi, Chinese, Vietnamese, and so on (www.milet.com).

When teaching through word play, the processes in Figure 4.3 can be useful (Adams, 1992; Adams, Foorman, Lundberg, & Beeler, 2003; Yopp & Yopp, 2003). This focus on foundational skills is emphasized in the Common Core, in which children are expected to be able to rhyme, segment, blend, and substitute sounds. Specific phonological awareness processes are summarized and arranged in Figure 4.3 in order of difficulty beginning with rhyming as easiest.

English Language Learners

Common Core State Standards

Written Language Development

Semiotics refers to studying the relationship of language and other symbols to their meanings (Hodge & Kress, 1988; Saussure, 1959). Simply put, there are objects (such as apple, loyalty, and Greenland) that people agree to attach signs to. So as a society in the United States, we have agreed that the letters a-p-p-l-e arranged in that sequence name the object *apple*. A drawing of a piece of fruit could serve as a different sign for the same object. There are a number of different symbol systems—letters of the alphabet, numbers, dots and dashes (Morse code), musical notation, forms of movement, emoticons, and so on. Acquiring the ability to read and write involves coming to know how symbols represent meaning.

As children acquire understanding of speech sounds, they also explore them with their own writing. When children first attempt to write what they can say, they normally do not yet use conventional spelling or grammar. Instead, they do as they did when they learned to speak—they approximate conventional forms. For example, they might write, "it wz fne," instead of "It was funny." Although many adults may see this as wrong, those who understand the developmental nature of language realize such approximations are acceptable—and are sometimes called **invented spelling**. Invented spelling is an attempt

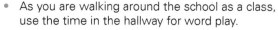

Try This for Teaching   **Word Play Around the School**

- As you are walking around the school as a class, use the time in the hallway for word play.
- As you pass a teacher's classroom and the teacher's name is Mrs. Wimmer, ask the children for a rhyming word (slimmer, glimmer).
- As you go to the lunchroom to eat tacos, ask what other words begin with /t/.
- As you go to the library or computers, ask children to segment the sounds in related words, like *book*, *screen*, and *mouse*.

- Remember to do this quietly so you do not disturb other classes.

Variations for ELLs

- Ask for translations for words around the school in children's first languages.
- From the list of phonological awareness processes in Figure 4.3, encourage ELLs to decide which process the class will use as students walk down the hall.

Figure 4.3   Phonological Awareness Processes in Order of Difficulty

Rhyming	Words sharing the same ending sounds	What word rhymes with *Matt*?
Syllable awareness	Words containing parts that each include one vowel sound and possibly one or more consonant sounds	Clap the syllables in *animal*: a ni mal
Phoneme identification	Recognizing individual sounds in spoken words by one of the following:	
	Single sound in individual word	What sound is at the beginning of *tall*?
	Same sound in more than one word	What sound is the same in *sun, soap,* and *sat*?
	Two words similar in some sounds but not others	What sound is different in *hill* and *pill*?
	A word that does not match a pattern	Which starts with a different sound: *bag, nine, bar, bike*? Which ends with a different sound: *wig, twig, dig, lift*?
	A specific sound in a familiar word	Is there a /k/ in *bike*? Is there a /p/ in *slide*?
Blending	Combining sounds to create words	What word would we have by combining /s/ /a/ /t/? What word do you hear when I say /m/ /ī/ /l/ /k/?
Phoneme segmentation	Splitting a word into sounds	What sounds do you hear in *hot*? What are the sounds in *bright*?
Phoneme counting	Counting the number of single sounds in a word	Which word has more sounds, *breakfast* or *dinner*?
Phoneme deletion	Taking one sound out of a word	What word would be left if /k/ were taken out of *cat*? What sound do you hear in *meat* that is missing in *eat*?
Phoneme substitution	Replacing a sound in a word with another	If you replaced the /ā/ in *happy* with /ō/, what would you have? If you replaced the beginning sound in *look* with /b/, what word would you have?

to spell a word based on the writer's knowledge of sounds and symbols—a temporary substitute for the conventional spelling that will come later (or sometimes be edited in a final copy). Some like to call this *temporary spelling, phonics spelling,* or *sound spelling.* Whatever term is used, children do attempt to make themselves understood by combining their knowledge of oral and written language. English language learners proceed in much the same way, although their primary language may influence their temporary spellings. With any learners, teachers and parents must encourage children's attempts instead of belittling them as they progress through five developmental stages. A developmental journal can provide a safe place for children to make progress.

English Language Learners

Developmental Stages.   As children develop greater control over writing to make meaning, they follow steps that are remarkably similar, so similar that they are frequently referred to as stages of writing development. The following sections describe the typical phases through which many children pass as they become more conventional in their writing (Bear, Invernizzi, Templeton, & Johnston, 2011; Temple, Nathan, Temple, & Burris, 1993). Examples of developmental writing phases are shown in figure 4.4.

Drawing and scribbling.   In their attempts to make meaning, children draw pictures. They also begin to make scribbles—wavy or jagged lines and letterlike shapes—that look to them like the writing others produce. They are gaining control of the pencil and understanding its use. Children also begin to understand that writing is what adults use so others can read their messages. At this point children lack a concept of written words and letter-sound correspondences.

Letter stringing.   During this phase of development, children may know the names of the letters, but have not yet connected them to sounds. Children use strings of letters, but with very limited understanding of letter-sound correspondences. They can often write the letter that begins their name, so they may use that capital letter to represent entire words. Their writing at this stage may also include numbers and other symbols, but these may be placed haphazardly on a page.

Letter name/alphabetic writing.   Children begin to understand that letters are used to represent sounds in words. Their spelling is abbreviated, with one or two letters frequently representing an entire word. Consonants are used often with vowels excluded. Letters are used for the sound or syllable that matches the letter name. For example, R = are and U = you. Children begin to sequence letters and words from left to right.

Transitional writing.   Children write a single letter or a combination of letters for the most prominent sounds they hear. For example, the word *spider* may be spelled spdr. Although the choices children make are frequently phonetically correct, they are not always conventional. Words are separated by spaces, and some of the most common words are spelled conventionally. As students progress, they use more vowels, word endings, and letter-sound correspondences to spell words.

Conventional writing.   After much experience, children use spelling conventions to write words appropriate to their grade level. They have a large store of memorized words, but may struggle with new words. That is true of writers of all ages. Very few people ever reach a point at which they can effortlessly spell all words correctly when they write (which is why spell checkers were invented).

Developmental Journal Writing.   You can help children progress through these stages by providing a safe place and a consistent time for them to experiment with written language regardless of their stage of writing. You can encourage students to use

Drawing

Scribble

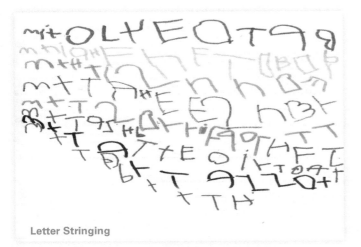

Letter Stringing

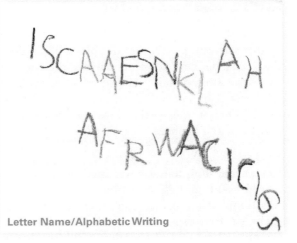

Letter Name/Alphabetic Writing

No T To HoT
LotS of CHoColata
ShaC
NoT Stir
whitneyoS GoweN
ToMac This
DoNT throwthis
AWaY

Transitional Writing

On   Halloween Night
        On   Halloween I
was   a   bride. I wore
a little make-up. My
mom put it on. I
felt domm. And the mascara
felt terrible. I felt domm.

The End

Conventional Writing

Figure 4.4   Samples of Developmental Writing Phases

a **developmental journal** in which they can draw as well as explore print. This kind of journal allows for differentiated instruction, since each child is able to work right at his or her level. Young children can begin with a single blank page without lines. Some will draw pictures, others will scribble write, and others will approximate more conventional forms of writing. You can stamp the pages with the date, file them to monitor individual progress, and ultimately bind them as a collection. If young children begin with a bound book, many will become distracted and make meaningless marks on every page. As children progress, they can write on pages that have lines for writing along with space for illustrations. Over time you can provide pages with more and more lines for writing and less space for pictures. Some educators have found developmental journal writing to be a valuable tool for responding to children's needs that appear in the RtI process.

Journal writing is an example of independent writing by students. Rather than giving children writing prompts, let them write on any topic they wish (Harwayne & Calkins, 1990). There are appropriate times for teacher-selected topics, such as when you are modeling for students or working jointly with them. But the developmental journal is the place for students to gain independence and confidence in writing, which includes the ownership that results from coming up with their own topics. A sample entry in a child's developmental journal is shown in Figure 4.5.

In developmental journals, children feel free to simply express themselves, and this freedom can be diminished if the children are expecting you to correct or fix everything. The temporary spelling they use in journal writing is for their own benefit as writers; children need to trust that these attempts are not meant to be published or displayed publicly and that they will not be criticized. When writing is ready to be shared as a final draft, you can help children revise the writing into a conventional form for the benefit of readers. A developmental journal is for the writer. If shared, developmental journal writing is read aloud by the reader or shared just with a few trusted adults.

If parents and others are uneasy about some unconventional spelling in these journals, remind them that students are not developing bad habits, but rather gaining fluency and passing through normal phases of development. When children ask how to spell a word, you can respond by saying, "Your journal will not be seen by other people right now. Just do your best." Some teachers like to have children indicate journal entries that the teacher can read and respond to, sometimes referred to as a dialogue journal. Writing positive encouragement in student journals has been shown to be effective in working with children who are experiencing difficulties and who can benefit from private teacher support (Anderson, Nelson, Richardson, Webb, & Young, 2011). Dialogue journals have been shown to be especially effective with bilingual students in improving both oral and written language (Fitzgerald & Amendum, 2007).

Struggling Learners/ RtI

English Language Learners

Figure 4.5

Sample Page from a Child's Developmental Journal

Figure 4.6

Sample Page from a
Developmental Journal
with a Teacher's
Translation

English Language
Learners

Some teachers find it useful to translate pictures or scribbles into conventional print by writing for children as they explain what they have written or drawn—just a sentence or two at the bottom of the page. This does not need to be done daily for each child or for all journal entries. A record of occasional translations can provide a model for students' later writing and also make the developmental journal more meaningful as children and parents revisit earlier pages. A sample page of a child's developmental journal showing a teacher's translation is displayed in Figure 4.6.

Combining Spoken and Written Language

Although phonological awareness is most often thought of as an oral language endeavor, children can acquire awareness of speech sounds as they learn some of the basic elements of letter-sound relationships through writing experience combined with phonics instruction (Armbruster, Lehr, & Osborn, 2001; National Reading Panel, 2000). Sometimes people confuse the terms *phonological awareness* and *phonics*; however, they do have distinct meanings. The first is concerned with awareness of speech sounds, and the second with representation of those sounds in writing. Phonological awareness prepares children for phonics instruction. The awareness of sounds plus knowledge of the letters to represent them constitute "the basis of phonics" (Ming & Dukes, 2010).

The extent to which young children are familiar with alphabet letters has been found to be "one of the strongest predictors of reading" (McGee & Richgels, 2003, p. 7; see also Beatty, 2005); but just knowing letter names is not enough. Instruction that combines written symbols with speech sounds is especially important. Many English language learners have already learned symbols in their first language that are similar to English. For example, in many of the European languages, the letter *s* usually represents /s/, as it does in English. However, many of the vowel sounds shared across these languages are represented with different letters (for example, the letter *i* represents /ē/). That is why it is important that these learners see the letters as well as hear and say the sounds they represent (Peregoy & Boyle, 2008). In order to help all learners develop the phonological understanding they need, you can use reading and writing activities as a learning context.

Picture Books.   Picture books are short illustrated texts. Many of them contain predicable patterns and deal with topics of interest to young children, making them an ideal medium for connecting specific sounds and the letters that represent them in English. Holdaway (1979) created the idea of reading from enlarged texts, which he called big books, so that all students in large groups could have access to the print. Publishers now provide many titles of books in this helpful format.

Children listening to the book *Sheep Out to Eat* (Shaw, 1992) may be able to predict that *drips* is the word in the story that rhymes with *tips*, and *crash* with *smash*. To make the prediction, students use their awareness of phonemes. Help children hear the rhyming sounds in the two words. After students are confident with the sounds, you can connect the sound to written text by highlighting the rhyming words and showing students the spelling pattern similarities. Using big books, copying sentences on chart paper, or projecting the book on a screen are all ways to display the text.

For example, after reading a phrase about a fish swimming and a frog chasing a fly in the cumulative story *Jump Frog Jump* (Kalan, 1989), ask the students if they heard words that sounded the same at the beginning. As they identify *fish*, *frog*, and *fly*, have them repeat the words aloud emphasizing the initial sound. Then display the page with that sentence and highlight the words that begin with /f/. Say the words together and point to the appropriate figures in the illustrations. With a sticky note, isolate the letter *f* at the beginning of each word in the text. Write each word on the board and ask students for other words with the same sound. Add appropriate words to the list (such as *fat*, *find*, and *four*). There are many ways to focus attention on print. Some teachers use sticky notes, frames, pointers, and colored highlighting tape.

Speaking/Listening

Language Experience Approach (LEA).   One way to explicitly show children how to connect the sounds of language with writing is to use the **language experience approach** (Ashton-Warner, 1963; Stauffer, 1970), a form of dictation in which students speak and the teacher writes. LEA is effective to use with beginning readers and writers, with English language learners, and with children who struggle with learning about letter-sound relationships at any age. These students may have many ideas they want to share but are not able to fluently record them using conventions of written language. When the teacher takes dictation from students, children are freed up to compose ideas and stories without having to be slowed down by the mechanics.

English Language Learners

In addition to providing opportunities for expression, LEA contributes to students' oral and early written language skills. Dictation helps children develop speaking and listening skills because they must listen to comments made by others. For example, if a child is listening carefully, he will know that the group is talking about their experience on the playground, and he will not chime in with "I like goldfish." Also children must speak clearly enough for the teacher to transcribe their words and must explain their points sufficiently. If the teacher asks, "What did we do on the playground?" the child must learn to answer with a complete sentence that can be transcribed, instead of just saying "played."

Struggling Learners/ RtI

Try This for Teaching   **Plastic-Covered Pages**

- Cover the text with a clear sheet of plastic or a page protector.
- Use erasable markers to circle, underline, or draw arrows as you focus on print.
- As you turn the page in the book, reposition the plastic and begin again.
- This technique is especially useful when using a big book or a document reader, when both the text and the markings can easily be seen by all.

Variations for ELLs

- Project the text on a white board and have volunteers make the marks on it.
- Pass a plastic sheet and marker to all students so they can make the same marks you make in a text shared by all as you discuss aspects of text and concepts about print.

Language Conventions

As students see their own words turned into writing, they internalize the spoken-word-to-written-word process and relationship and they relate the process to their own desire to express their experiences, knowledge, and/or feelings. While writing, the teacher demonstrates such language conventions as word boundaries and structures (Miller, 2005) and may explain how writers work out the spelling of words. When the text is completed, the teacher reads it to the students, pointing to the words as he pronounces them. Then the children read the text back, with the teacher again pointing to the words. This reading and rereading help to build students' awareness of how words come together in sentences (Nettles, 2006), as well as how the sounds and letters come together in words. Thus students learn about aspects of written language that they can transfer into their independent journal writing.

LEA consists of the following four steps, which can be adapted with many variations as teachers personalize the process.

- Focus on students' experiences. Students have an experience together (a visiting author or a sudden change in the weather) or recall an experience that they have had in common (playing in the leaves in the fall or attending a birthday party). Books they have enjoyed, technology they have explored, or the likes and dislikes of a spotlight student can also serve as topics for LEA texts (Nettles, 2006).

- Encourage students to talk. After the students have had an experience or have recalled one, ask them to talk about it. Prompts such as "What else do you remember?" or "Tell about a favorite part" can extend limited responses.

- Write what students say. As the students talk about their experience, the teacher records what the children say on paper, on the whiteboard, or on an image projected on a screen. Although it is not necessary, many teachers find it helpful to assist students in extending one-word answers into complete sentences. Some teachers smooth out grammatical errors as they write; on the other hand, writing exactly what students said can provide valuable teaching moments.

- Read together. After the children have dictated the experience and the text has been read to and by the children, you may point out to the students that when their experiences are written down, others can read their words and appreciate their experiences. Reinforce the power of text by asking visitors to the room to read what the class has composed.

Struggling Learners/ RtI

The basic LEA format can be adapted to a number of writing experiences. LEA could be used to compile the "news of the day," which might include a current events discussion, a preview of the day's activities, or accounts of what is happening in school. In addition, the content children are studying can be recorded as they talk about their learning experiences in social studies, science, or any of the content areas. You could use LEA to create how-to-do charts, record class rules, or list classroom jobs. At the end of the year, one kindergarten class used LEA to write a letter to the next year's kindergarten students, telling them what they could expect and how they could be successful.

The entire experience does not need to be recorded in one session. Students could dictate one sentence a day and watch it evolve into a short paragraph by the end of the week (Wong & Berninger, 2004). Try including one or two sentences each morning as part of

Teacher completing a Language Experience Activity (LEA) with students.

your opening-of-the-day routine. For example, you and your class could count how many days you have been in school, review the calendar, and look at the weather outside. Then you could write a few sentences as an LEA.

In reviewing the LEA text, you can remind children that print is composed of letters, words, and sentences—and that they all are related to oral language. At the letter level, show students a letter of the alphabet and ask them to find words in the text that begin with that letter. At the word level, children can match words written on separate cards with words in the text. Write words from the story on individual cards for students to group into categories, like words that begin with a specific letter, words that show action, or words that name places. At the level of sentences, children can rebuild entire sentences from the text using word cards, or they can arrange sentences in the text in sequential order. The types of extension activities you select can constitute differentiated instruction as you consider the individual needs of the students and match the activities with those needs. An example of a text produced through the LEA is shown in Figure 4.7.

> ## Our Favorite Things at School
>
> We love when our teacher reads to us. We also like to go to computers. Recess is a fun time because we play with our friends and run around. We love lunch too -- especially when we get chocolate milk.

Figure 4.7   **Example of LEA Chart**

Try This for Teaching   **Class Thank-You Note**

- Think of someone who has helped your class (such as the principal, a lunch worker, crossing guard, or custodian).
- Ask the children what they would say to thank that person if he or she were there.
- As the children talk, write on chart paper sentences using their words.
- Explain that we do not always have to thank people orally; we also can do it in writing.
- Invite all students to write their names at the bottom of the note.

- Deliver the thank-you note to the recipient.

Variations for ELLs

- Encourage children to draw a picture to accompany the note.
- If the person writes a note in return, read it to the class to reinforce the importance of authentic communication.

Summary

Many are surprised to discover that reading and writing actually begin in the context of oral language development. As children acquire oral language, they become aware of sounds (phonology) and how they are combined to make words (semantics). They also learn how words combine into sentences (syntax). Children must learn how to use language to serve different purposes (pragmatics) and learn how to access their background knowledge (schema).

Literacy acquisition is a developmental process with stages through which children progress. Emergent readers and writers turn into beginners who then become fluent. Phonological awareness cannot be overlooked as a vital element in beginning reading and writing. You can help children progress through stages of written language development within meaningful contexts such as developmental writing journals. You can use picture books and the language experience approach to combine written and spoken language. Some of your greatest satisfaction in teaching will come as you see students progress along this continuum of language and literacy development that began before they met you and will continue long after they have left your classroom.

Self-Check

1. Explain the processes of oral language that children have developed when they first come to school.

2. What is schema theory and how does it apply to reading comprehension?

3. Describe the essential elements of the beginning stage of literacy development.

4. Explain essential differences between phonemic awareness and phonological awareness.

5. How can word play help develop a child's phonological awareness?

6. Describe how you might respond to parents who are concerned that their child is just scribbling and not "really writing."

7. How much concern should you have about conventions in a developmental writing journal?

8. How can you show students how to combine spoken and written language?

MyEducationLab™

Go to the Topic, Emergent Literacy, in the MyEducationLab (www.myeducationlab.com) for your course, where you can:

- Find learning outcomes for Emergent Literacy along with the national standards that connect to these outcomes.

- Complete Assignments and Activities that can help you more deeply understand the chapter content.

- Apply and practice your understanding of the core teaching skills identified in the chapter with the Building Teaching Skills and Dispositions learning units.

- Examine challenging situations and cases presented in the IRIS Center Resources.

- Check your comprehension on the content covered in the chapter by going to the Study Plan in the Book Resources for your text. Here you will be able to take a chapter quiz, receive feedback on your answers, and then access Review, Practice, and Enrichment activities to enhance your understanding of chapter content (optional).

- Visit A+RISE Standards2Strategy™, an innovative and interactive online resource that offers new teachers in grades K–12 just-in-time, research-based instructional strategies that meet the linguistic needs of ELLs as they learn content, differentiate instruction for all grades and abilities, and are aligned to Common Core Elementary Language Arts Standards (for the literacy strategies) and to English language proficiency standards in WIDA, Texas, California, and Florida.

Beginning Reading and Writing

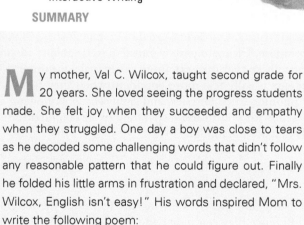

Chapter Outline

WORD IDENTIFICATION

Phonics
Word Families
Sight Words
Putting It All Together

CONVENTIONS OF WRITTEN LANGUAGE

Concepts About Print
Spelling
Handwriting
Grammar
Interactive Writing

SUMMARY

My mother, Val C. Wilcox, taught second grade for 20 years. She loved seeing the progress students made. She felt joy when they succeeded and empathy when they struggled. One day a boy was close to tears as he decoded some challenging words that didn't follow any reasonable pattern that he could figure out. Finally he folded his little arms in frustration and declared, "Mrs. Wilcox, English isn't easy!" His words inspired Mom to write the following poem:

English Isn't Easy!

English easy? No, not quite!
It can keep you up at night.
Words like *though* and *tough* and *through*,
Read like *doe* and *buff* and *dew*.
Why is *lose* spelled just like *rose*?
Yet it's said like *news* not *nose*.
That brings us to *there* and *their*.
They're just words beyond compare.
English easy? Not at all!
It can drive you up a wall.
Bite is said the same as *height*,
It's difficult to get it right.
No one wants to sound too rude,
But why do we say *sued* like *food*?
Why does *ha* sound like *hurrah*?
It should be against the law!
English easy? Sakes alive!
Yet we speak it by age five!

—Brad

English isn't easy! In fact, it is a challenge for beginning readers and writers and a monumental challenge for English language learners. But it can—and must—be mastered, and as a teacher you are a critical participant in that process.

An essential part of beginning reading and writing is developing an awareness of speech sounds and understanding relationships between spoken and written language. Contrary to popular belief, letter naming is not the beginning of reading or writing. Children acquire understanding of the world around them, experience life, and understand spoken language long before they learn their first written letter. A language- and print-rich environment is the context in which children develop an understanding the alphabetic nature of written language and build listening, speaking, reading, and writing vocabularies (Lindfors, 1991).

English Language Learners

Although not all children who come to school have a rich background in the language forms accepted by the majority, we need to recognize that all children do come to school with language—language that you can use to bridge to the conventional language of the larger society. The language children bring with them to school also gives you a lens to see into their lives. Those who are learning English as a second language bring a rich background from their first language. Listen to them communicate, and do not hesitate to speak to them because you are afraid that they will not understand.

As children begin to read and write, those processes are so interrelated that it is difficult to separate them. Some associate word identification more with reading than with writing, but in reality many children learn about phonics best as they write. Others associate spelling only with writing, but some children acquire spelling ability by reading. Help all students develop literacy by understanding its basic components: word identification and conventions of written language.

Word Identification

Phonological awareness prepares children to take their first steps in word identification, a vital part of beginning reading and writing. Our overall goal in literacy instruction is to help children comprehend and compose. Ultimately we want them to be able to identify and produce many words automatically so that they can more easily make meaning.

Common Core State Standards

In reading, teachers and students usually feel more confident when they feel competent in their knowledge about phonics, word families, and sight words. Following are discussions of these useful approaches for you to use (separately or in combination) to help your students identify words that are unfamiliar.

Phonics

Many children learn the alphabet song, but merely knowing the names of the letters is not enough. Even knowing the difference between upper and lowercase letters, which is important, does not necessarily help children decode. The **alphabetic principle**, knowing that letters represent sounds, must be internalized. The Common Core places particular emphasis on this understanding.

Phonics refers to letter-sound relationships and factors that influence those relationships. Our language uses only 26 letters to represent many sounds: for example, the letter *s* can represent /s/ in *sun*, /z/ in *as*, /sh/ in *sugar*, and /zh/ in *conclusion*. Other letters do not represent any unique sounds. The letter *c* represents /s/ in *city*, /k/ in *cake*, and /ch/ in *cello*. Because many words in English have come from other languages, phonics can seem confusing at first. However, there is enough regularity in written English to warrant teaching it. Although many words in English are not phonetically spelled, phonics is "a powerful mnemonic system that bonds the written forms of specific words to their pronunciations in memory" (Erhi & McCormick, 1998, p. 140; cited in Gunning, 2000, p. 83). If even part of a word has a regular phonetic pattern, readers use the regular pattern to trigger memory for the rest of the word (National Reading Panel, 2003).

The National Reading Panel (2000) found that children who are taught phonics learn to read more effectively than children who are not. The specificity of the Common Core standards leaves no question that these skills are essential.

Most agree that English language learners also benefit from phonics instruction when it is thoughtfully applied (Lesaux, Koda, Seigel, & Shanahan, 2006). Teachers do have to remember that these students lack the native speakers' foundation of words containing the sounds on which to build associations.

English has 21 letters that are used to represent consonant sounds and 5 letters that represent vowel sounds (*a, e, i, o*, and *u*). Note that the letters *y* and *w* can also serve as vowels (e.g., *play* and *baby*; *crow* and *flower*). All vowels represent more than one sound, including long and short vowel sounds. Some of the differences in sounds are due to pronunciation changes that occurred as the language evolved after the spelling system had been largely established. The long vowel sounds are the letter names, found in words such as the following: *maple, even, island, over,* and *useful*. The short vowel sounds, which are a little trickier, include *apple, elephant, insect, ostrich,* and *umbrella*. The most common vowel sound is the schwa. It sounds like the /ŭ/ and is represented by a backwards, upside down e (ə). Any of the five vowels can represent the schwa sound in polysyllabic words: America, sentence, pencil, oven, under.

The two main goals of phonics instruction are to acquaint students with letter-sound associations (to break the code), and to provide them with the ability to decode visually unfamiliar words. Phonics must be learned as a functional skill; that is, the ability to state phonics rules should not be confused with the ability to apply phonics knowledge. For example, knowing the terms *diphthong* or *vowel digraph* do not automatically lead to

English Language Learners

Language Conventions

Try This for Teaching   **Alphabet Name Book**

- Say the name of each student, emphasizing the initial sound. Be careful about names that start with a letter that doesn't represent the expected sound (such as Charles, Jose, or Amara). Link these names to other words that do represent the expected sound (for example, "Jose likes to jump").

- Display blank pages in the front of the room with one letter of the alphabet on each page.

- Help students find the page with the first letter of their own name and write their name on it. If several children's names start with the same letter, try working with last names or adjectives that describe the children. For example, if *J* is for *Jamie, B* can be for *Beautiful Jasmine*.

- After all names have been written, give each student a page to illustrate.

Variations for ELLs

- Select additional words that begin with the same sounds and letter patterns. For example, "Pedro can eat pancakes and pineapple" or "Hannah can hop and help."

- During shared reading, point to words in a text that begin with the same sounds as the children's names. Ask those students whose names begin with that sound to stand up or take a bow.

- In shared writing, when you write a word that has the same sound that begins a child's name, invite the child to write the letter on the chart.

proficient reading, but children should know that when they see the letters *oi* they say /oi/ and recognize that these two vowels represent one sound (diphthong), and when they see *oa* they say /o/ because there are two vowels, but they only hear one (vowel digraph).

Phonics helps with pronunciation, but not with meaning. The visually unknown words readers decode must be part of their listening/speaking vocabularies to be understood. After readers decode an unfamiliar word and pronounce it (orally or in their heads), they match it with a word in their listening/speaking vocabularies. When a match is made, readers can proceed with understanding. If readers do not already know the word, use of phonics knowledge has led them to an approximate pronunciation of an unfamiliar word, but it has not led to comprehension. Understanding letter-sound relationships is most useful to readers who have a large listening/speaking vocabulary.

Useful Generalizations. **Phonics generalizations** are statements of rules that explain why a letter or combination of letters represent individual sounds or patterns of sounds. These generalizations can be taught in a variety of ways—systematically using a scope and sequence or embedded in reading and writing experiences (Dahl, Scharer, Lawson, & Grogan, 1999) in no prescribed order.

Struggling Learners/
RTI

Teachers of students in kindergarten, first grade, and second grade will focus more attention on phonics than teachers in other grades. Some educators believe that systematic phonics instruction should be completed by the end of second grade (Anderson, Hiebert, Scott, & Wilkinson, 1984) or by the time children reach a third-grade reading level (Gunning, 2000). However, phonics instruction may be appropriate for students beyond this age or grade level when specific needs are revealed through the RtI framework.

You should have a thorough understanding of phonics and be familiar with the phonics generalizations listed in Figure 5.1. Some sources provide more than these and some fewer, but these 21 are the ones we have found most beneficial.

Surprisingly some teachers have little working knowledge of phonics generalizations. A study by Bos, Mather, Dickson, Podhajski, and Chard (2001; cited by Joshi et al., 2009) of 252 preservice teachers and 286 inservice teachers found that two-thirds of the respondents could not define phonological awareness. In addition, 53 percent of the preservice teachers and 60 percent of the practicing teachers scored below 50 percent on basic knowledge of phonics. If you do not understand phonics yourself, you may not be able to respond accurately to students' questions. You also need to know about phonics so you can identify specific needs your students have and provide appropriate instruction to meet those needs (Cunningham, 2008; Eldredge, 2003). The study by Bos et al. also showed that when teachers increased their phonics knowledge, their students increased their reading scores. You can teach students phonics generalizations in mini-lessons and revisit them often when reading or writing together as a class or in small groups.

Try This for Professional Development

Several resources are available to help you improve your basic knowledge of phonics. Some favorites include the following:

- J. Lloyd Eldredge, *Phonics for Teachers: Self-Instruction, Methods, and Activities* (2nd ed.), Prentice Hall.

Enhance Your Phonics Knowledge

- Arthur W. Heilman, *Phonics in Proper Perspective* (10th ed.), Prentice Hall.

- Roger S. Dow & G. Thomas Baer, *Self-Paced Phonics: A Text for Educators* (4th ed.), Prentice Hall.

Figure 5.1   Twenty-one Useful Phonics Generalizations

Vowel Sound Generalizations

Closed Syllable: When one vowel is in a syllable and it is not the final letter, it usually records its short sound.

add   script   con t**a**ct   p**u**b lic   **i**n dex   str**e**ngth   n**o**t

Open Syllable: When one vowel is in a syllable and it is the last letter, it usually records its long sound.

g**o**   ha l**o**   c**u** cum ber   cal c**u** late   ban j**o**   m**o** men tum

VC Final *E*: When there are two vowels in a syllable, one of which is the final *e*, and they are separated by one consonant, the long sound of the first vowel is usually recorded.

use   wh**ile**   **ace**   str**oke**   par **ade**   m**ule**   sc**ene**

VCC Final *E*: When there are two vowels in a syllable, one of which is the final *e*, and they are separated by two consonants, the short sound of the first vowel is usually recorded.

edge   p**ulse**   br**onze**   ex p**ense**   v**alve**   pr**ince**

Y Generalizations

Short *I* Sound: When *y* is in the medial position in a syllable that contains no additional vowel, it usually stands for the short *i* sound.

g**y**m   m**y**th   c**y**st   h**y**mn   s**y**s tem   g**y**p sy

Long *I* Sound: When *y* records the final sound in a one-syllable word or the final sound in a syllable of a polysyllabic word (but not the final syllable), it usually stands for the long *i* sound.

tr**y**   c**y** cle   t**y** rant   a s**y** lum   fl**y**   d**y** na mo

Long *E* Sound: When *y* records the final sound in a polysyllabic word, it usually stands for the long *e* sound.

mer r**y**   tro ph**y**   pyg m**y**   ho l**y**   au top s**y**   fan c**y**

Syllabic Division Generalizations

VCCV Pattern: When two consonants are between two vowels, a syllabic break occurs between the consonants.

bot tom   **pen cil**   **af ter**   **ad ven ture**   **ban dan** a

VCV Pattern–Long Vowel Sound: When a consonant is between two vowels, the first vowel is often in one syllable while the consonant and the vowel following are in another.

ho **tel**   pa **per**   e **lect**   si **lent**   ba **con**   o **ver**

VCV Pattern–Short Vowel Sound: When a consonant is between two vowels, the first vowel and the consonant are sometimes in one syllable and the other vowel is in the other.

man or   **en act**   **reb el**   **ben e fit**   **ed it**

-CLE Pattern: When a word ends in a consonant followed by *le*, that consonant and the *le* form the final syllable.

i **dle**   bu **gle**   thim **ble**   ar ti **cle**   am **ple**   ca pa **ble**

C and G Generalizations

C Pattern- /S/: When *c* is followed in a syllable by *e, i,* or *y,* it often stands for the soft *c* sound /s/.

cen ter   **ci** der   **cyl** in der   re **cent**   de **cide**   re **cy** cle

C Pattern- /K/: When *c* is followed by *a, o,* or *u,* it often stands for the hard *c* sound /k/.

cat   **coat**   **cup**   **ca** pa ble   **cost** ly   **cus** tom

(*continued*)

Figure 5.1 **Twenty-one Useful Phonics Generalizations** *(Continued)*

C and G Generalizations

G Pattern- /G/: When *g* is followed by *a, o,* or *u,* it often stands for the hard *g* sound /g/.

gate   **go**ne   **gu**t ter   **ga**me   a **go**   **gu**m

G Pattern- /J/: When *g* is followed in a syllable by *e, i,* or *y,* it often stands for the soft *g* sound /j/.

gem   **gi** ant   **gy**p sy   **ge**rm   en **gi**ne   **gy**m

Digraph and Diphthong Generalizations

Vowel Digraphs: Vowel digraphs consist of two vowels in the same syllable that represent the sound of one of the vowels in the digraph. Five vowel digraphs are most useful—*ai, ay, ea, ee, oa.*

m**ai**l   pl**ay**   b**ea**ch   f**ee**t   b**oa**t   m**ai**n tain   re **lay**   re p**ea**t   s**ee**d less   **oa**tmeal

Consonant Digraphs: Consonant digraphs consist of two consonants in the same syllable that represent one sound. The most regular consonant digraphs are *th, sh, ch, ph.*

wi**th**   **th**ese   **sh**ow   wi**sh**   **ch**op   **ch**ur**ch**   **ph**one   gra**ph**

Consonant Blends: Consonant clusters or blends consist of two or more consonants in the same syllable that record the sounds of all the consonants in the cluster.

fa**st**   **cl**ap   be**nd**   re ce**nt**   en a**ct**   **str**eet   **br**ake   **fl**ower

Diphthongs: Diphthongs are two vowels together in the same syllable that represent one sound. Diphthongs come in pairs—*oi* and *oy; au* and *aw; ou* and *ow.*

oil   t**oy**   c**au**ght   **aw**ful   f**ou**nd   c**ow**

Other Generalizations

R-controlled Vowel Sounds: When the letter *r* follows any of the five vowels in a syllable, the vowel sound is neither long nor short. We say that the syllable has an r-controlled vowel sound.

f**ar**   coll**ar**   f**er**n   f**ir**   f**or**   col**or**   f**ur**

Schwa Sound: The most frequent vowel sound is the schwa sound, or the short *u* sound. The schwa can be represented by any of the five vowels in polysyllabic words.

America   sen t**e**nce   an **i** mal   **o** ven   **u**n der

Instruction. For teaching phonics, two general approaches are common: synthetic and analytic. **Synthetic phonics** isolates individual sounds for teaching and then blends them to form words students can recognize. This is the approach favored by the National Reading Panel (2003) as "the most effective when introduced early" (p. 12). Dealing with words sound by sound does cause distortion, however, and thus it can sound artificial (Ehri & Nunes, 2002; Gunning, 2000). But if the teacher refers to these words/sounds as "robot talk," kindergarten or first-grade children will probably find it fun. If simple student-made robot puppets or robot badges are included, motivation can be increased. In **analytic phonics,** sounds are not isolated. Instead, you begin with a group of known words and show students the shared parts of those words, such as the letter *s* in *sun, sat,* and *so.* Many teachers like to combine the approaches, asserting that beginning readers need to highlight sounds in isolation (synthetic) but also to experience them as they function in real words (analytic) (Gunning, 2000). Either approach can incorporate both implicit (inductive) and explicit (deductive) instruction (Durkin, 2004).

Explicit instruction.   In explicit instruction a generalization is given first and then demonstrated with specific examples. When this form of direct instruction is presented with motivating, student-centered activities, it can be effective, particularly with students of varying backgrounds and ability levels (National Reading Panel, 2003). Kindergarten children have done well when instruction has been direct and explicit, and some analysts refer to this methodology as a necessity (Sonnenschein, Stapleton, & Benson, 2010). Its most distinguishing feature is that the teacher begins the lesson by announcing what sound(s) the students will be learning—and often why; then examples are provided.

> Today we will be learning about the letter *s*. *S* says ssssssssss. This is a very useful letter, because there are many important words that need ssssss. [The teacher displays on a poster, chart paper, or overhead a cartoon snake surrounded by pictures of things that start with *s*.] This is Sssally, the ssssily ssssssnake. Sally is a snob. She only likes things that start with *s*. Sally likes to wear skirts and scarves, she loves strawberries, her best friend is a snail, and she likes to go on sailboats. [As the teacher says each *s*-word, he points to a picture on the poster with the word beside it.]

After the /s/ sound—and Sally—has been appropriately introduced, the children think of additional *s* things that Sally likes, which the teacher writes on chart paper to be posted in the room. Additional practice with the new sound takes place in small group activities, during story time, at centers, or at other appropriate times during the day. Providing frequent exposure to the targets along with opportunities to practice them reinforces for the children what they are expected to learn (Justice & Kaderavek, 2004; Kaderavek & Justice, 2004).

Implicit instruction.   Implicit instruction presents examples first and asks students to generalize the sound. For example, the teacher might begin by having a few students reach into a sack and pull out items that start with *s*: sock, scissors, stapler, stamp, and so on. As the children deduce the sound, the teacher repeats it emphatically; as they say the letter, he writes it on the board. As with explicit instruction, review and practice come next, and reinforcement may be provided throughout the day. The implicit method is a little more difficult for the children, of course, and children whose language development is slow may find it particularly difficult to make the generalization (Crosbie, Holm, & Dodd, 2009); thus supplemental help or even preteaching of the letter and sound may be necessary. Implicit instruction includes six steps.

1. **Display example words.** Show students examples of words that follow the generalization being taught. For example, show the words *sat*, *in*, *end*, *on*, and *up*. These examples can easily be drawn from a story, song, or poem the students have read or will read.

2. **Read the words together.** Read the words chorally, making sure that each word is known by all of the students in the group. If the children cannot read the words yet, be sure that the words are in the students' listening/speaking vocabularies.

3. **Identify the generalization.** Ask students what they *see* that is the same in all of the example words. For example, most first-grade students should be able to notice very easily that all the sample words end in a consonant letter. Also ask them what if they *hear* that is the same as you read them. Most children will say eagerly that they have a short vowel sound. At the end of this stage of the lesson, students should be able to state the generalization: when a word ends in a consonant, the vowel sound is short. Remember that in this form of instruction, the teacher asks students to identify the generalization, even though she might need to provide some scaffolding. She does not point it out to them.

4. **Read the words again.** As children to re-read the words chorally, tell them to watch and listen carefully to the vowel sound in each word.

5. **Ask students for examples.** Ask students to provide examples of words that follow the generalization. Be sure that the students' words follow the pattern and contain the appropriate vowel sounds.

6. **Practice.** Ask students to read words in context that follow the generalization taught. A picture book, poem, song, or chant can frequently be used to allow students to use the newly learned generalization in a meaningful context.

Struggling Learners/ RtI

No matter which type of instruction is used, phonics generalizations usually tax memory, so the more multisensory the instruction can be, the better. Students benefit from variety (Adams, 1992), especially those learning English as another language. Either approach to phonics instruction does not need to take much time to be effective, even with ELLs (Lesaux & Geva, 2006).

English Language Learners

Word Families

Some English words contain similar letter patterns that can be easily recognized and spelled. These **word families** consist of a vowel sound followed by one or more consonant sounds (-am, -ack, -unk, etc.). Extensive use of word families is sometimes referred to as a third phonics teaching approach: **analogical phonics** (National Reading Panel, 2003).

Language Conventions

Adding the initial consonant sound(s) (onset) to the front of a word family pattern results in a recognizable word (*ram, sack, trunk*). Word families are sometimes referred to as *rimes* (or *analogies, chunks,* or *phonograms*). Teaching about word families has been an important part of reading instruction for many years (Smith, 2002); this is recognized as an excellent way to build reading vocabularies (Cunningham, 2008). Instruction in word families can be especially efficient for ELLs who need to expand their vocabularies quickly.

You can show students words that follow a family pattern and let them use this knowledge to decode unfamiliar words that contain the same pattern. For example, the -ill pattern is found in many words—*hill, will, fill,* and *spill.* However, not all words in the family will necessarily be in students' listening/speaking vocabularies. After students have learned the -ill pattern, they may be still be puzzled by the line in "My Country, 'Tis of Thee" that says we love "thy rocks and rills." Being able to decode the word does not teach them that the word *rill* means a small stream.

As with *rill,* if the reader does not already know the word, use of word family knowledge leads to approximate pronunciation of an unfamiliar word, but not necessarily to

Try This for Teaching   **Logo Language**

- Have children bring in items with familiar logos and brand labels such as cereal boxes and clothing labels.
- Select from these items some that exemplify the generalizations you are trying to teach.
- Use these at the beginning of your inductive lesson or as words for practice at the end of the lesson.

(Prior & Gerard, 2004)

Variations for ELLs

- Bring replicas of fast food signs, road signs, or other decorative or functional print to use in a phonics lesson.
- Create a classroom environmental print by labeling objects and areas in your classroom.
- Create a word wall or book of common words found in an environmental print that can be a reference for ELLs and others to refer to when needed.

understanding. Additional instruction and examples are needed. The 38 most common word families can be found in many locations both in print (Fry, Kress, & Fountoukidis, 2000) and online (www.enchantedlearning.com/rhymes/wordfamilies/; www.edict.biz/textanalyser/wordlists.htm).

Each of the most common word families can be taught in lessons or through word games and activities. Both approaches can be enjoyable and effective, and both can be completed in less than 10 minutes.

Instruction. Like phonics generalizations, word families can be taught using an implicit or explicit approach. The following six steps are an example of explicit instruction.

1. **Display example words.** Show students examples of words that use the same phonogram; for example, *-am* is used in *ham, jam, ram,* and *clam.* One or more of these words could come from a book or poem that students have read or will read.

2. **Read the words together.** Make sure that each word is known by all of the students in the group. If the children cannot read the words yet, be sure that the words are in the students' listening/speaking vocabularies.

3. **Explain the word family.** Point out to students the pattern they *see* in all of the example words; e.g., each word ends with the letters *am.* Also point that what they *hear* is /am/. Remember that in this form of instruction the teacher tells the students the generalization rather than asking them to identify it.

4. **Read the words again.** As you and the students re-read the words chorally, listen to the /am/ sounds and emphasize the *-am* visual pattern.

5. **Ask students for examples.** To check for understanding, ask students to provide examples of words that follow the pattern. Be sure that the words follow the pattern and contain the appropriate vowel sounds. Write the examples down and discuss whether they fit the pattern. For example, if a student volunteered the word *lamb,* point out that the word contains the same sounds but they are represented in this word with a different spelling pattern, *-amb,* so it does not fit the word family. The teacher could write the word *lamb,* showing how it fits and does not fit the pattern. Following this brief explanation, erase the word so that only words that follow the pattern are left for students to see. Consider writing these on chart paper that can be displayed for several days to remind students what they have learned.

6. **Practice.** Ask students to read words in context that follow the pattern. A picture book, poem, song, or chant can easily be used to allow students to use the newly

English Language
Learners

learned pattern in a different, meaningful context. Another way to practice is to give children letter tiles for one of the word family members (such as *h*, *a*, and *m*) and then additional tiles that can be used to create other words; *j*, *cl*, *sl*, *cr*, and so on. Students carefully read each letter as the new word is formed (Manyak, 2008).

Word Games. There are many games that help children explore words. Some can be adapted from commercial games (Balderdash from Gameworks Creations, Boggle from Parker Brothers, Scrabble from Selchow and Righter, and Scattergories and Taboo from Milton Bradley). Three favorites that focus explicitly on word families are Hink Pink (Johnson & Pearson, 1984), I'm Thinking of a Word (Wagstaff, 1999), and Making Words (Cunningham & Cunningham, 1992; Cunningham & Hall, 1994).

Hink Pink. Also sometimes called Terse Verse, Hink Pink is a word game that can be used to teach and review word families along with validating children's oral language abilities. It takes careful listening and speaking. To play, one person gives clues to lead listeners to the answer, which is a pair of rhyming words. The term *hink pink* is used if the answer is a pair of one-syllable rhyming words (most appropriate for young children, struggling children, and ELLs). You say, "What do you call an angry father? It's a hink pink." Students try to guess the answer: "mad dad." As they get more practice and experience, they can graduate to multisyllabic answers. *Hinky pinky* is used when the answer is a pair of two-syllable rhyming words, and syllables are added to *hink* and *pink* as syllables increase in the answer words. Some students may not be able to understand all of the words, so be prepared to offer brief definitions. Here are some samples followed by examples of hink pinks created by children in Figure 5.2:

- What is an obese feline? (hink pink) fat cat
- What is a wet pup? (hinky pinky) soggy doggy
- What is a productive command? (hinkety pinkety) effective directive
- What do you get from studying too hard? (hink pink) brain strain
- What do you call a finicky chicken? (hinky pinky) picky chicky
- What do you call a little scuffle? (hink pink) small brawl
- What do you call a very serious pillar? (hinky pinky) solemn column
- What do you call a little yellow bird that needs a barber? (hinky pinkety) hairy canary
- How does arithmetic homework get clean? (hink pink) math bath

---

Try This for Teaching **Hink Pink**

- Think of a pair of rhyming words.
- Describe the words using definitions or synonyms of the two words.
- Ask children to guess the rhyming words.
- The person who guesses correctly thinks of a new pair of rhyming words.
- A pair of three-syllable rhyming words is called a hinkety pinkety.

- A pair of four-syllable rhyming words is called a hinketaroo pinketaroo.

(Johnson & Pearson, 1984)

Variation for ELLs

- Consult a word family list to find rhyming words. For example, if *nail* and *jail* appear on the *-ail* list, ask, "What is a sharp prison?"

What is a hink pink for a feverish bird?

A sick chick!

What is a hinky pinky for an insane flower?

A crazy daisy!

Figure 5.2   **Sample Hink Pinks by Children**

I'm thinking of a word.   By focusing on rhymes, this game becomes especially helpful in teaching about word families, along with fostering speaking and listening abilities. In this activity one person says, "I'm thinking of a word that rhymes with _____." The others try to guess the word by asking questions, not by saying rhyming words. For example, a person could say, "I'm thinking of a word that rhymes with *bear*." Another person could ask, "Is it a fruit?" The first person replies, "No, it is not a *pear*." "Is it a female horse?" "No, it is not a *mare*." "Is it unusual?" "No, it is not *rare*." "Is it something you do with clothes?" "Yes, it is *wear*." If the person who asks the original question is stumped by one of the questioners, the questioner must reveal her word and she becomes "it." The original "it" must say the word he was thinking of and then join the ranks of the questioners—and the game goes on. Some word families that can be used with I'm Thinking of a Word include (but are not limited to) these words:

- card (answer: hard)
- cat (answer: splat)
- wear (answer: tear)
- froze (answer: nose)

Making words.   This is an activity that appeals to children of a variety of ages. In this game, the teacher provides students with letters of a word that have been scrambled using this formula: Vowels are presented first in alphabetical order, and then the consonants in alphabetical order. For example, the teacher could show these letters: *a o c s t*. Students are asked to use those letters to create words of varying length—two-letter words, three-letter words, and so forth. So students could create the following:

- Two letters: *as, at, so*
- Three letters: *cat, sat, act, cot*
- Four letters: *cots, cats, acts, taco, coat, cost*
- Five letters: *coast, coats, tacos*

Speaking/Listening

Language Conventions

Struggling Learners/ RtI

English Language Learners

Try This for Teaching   **I'm Thinking of a Word**

- One person says, "I'm thinking of a word that rhymes with _____."
- Another person thinks of a rhyming word but then asks a question without saying the word.
- The first person answers yes or no and says the rhyming word that answers the question.
- The questioner becomes the new "it" when the player is stumped.

(Wagstaff, 1999)

Variations for ELLs

- Extend the game by writing and categorizing the words that are guessed.
- Explore different spelling patterns for the sounds of the rhymes.

Sight Words

Because some words do not follow a single phonics generalization and do not contain a common word family, they must be taught as individual whole words, or **sight words**. Examples of such words are *was*, *laugh*, *said*, and *is*. The term *sight words* also refer to words that are read automatically, whether or not they follow a phonics generalization or a pattern. Automatic sight words can include **function words**, which are words that are not meaningful by themselves but that give structure to language. Examples include words like *on*, *in*, *who*, *of*, *from*, and *the*. Automatic sight words can also include **content words**, which are words that carry meaning, such as nouns, verbs, and adjectives. Examples are *week*, *forest*, *angle*, *people*, *Wednesday*, and *many*. Good readers have large sight word vocabularies.

Try This for Teaching   **Making Words**

- Show students a scrambled word.
- Ask them to create words of varying lengths using the letters in the scrambled word.
- Identify the word(s) that use all of the letters.
- See Patricia Cunningham's books for additional ideas.

(Cunningham & Cunningham, 1992)

Variations for ELLs

- Group words into word families.
- Think of new words included in that family that are not limited to the original letters.

- Sort words along multiple dimensions, both semantic and letter-sound relationships. For example, *sack* and *tack* and *pail* and *nail* can be sorted by word family, but *sack* could be grouped with *pail* (containers) and *tack* could be grouped with *nail* (sharp objects) (Cartwright, 2006).
- Have students discover the letters that will make up the scrambled word by hiding them around the room and playing warmer-colder or by giving them clues like in a treasure hunt.

High Frequency Words.   Some teachers find it useful to help children commit to memory **high frequency words** that appear most commonly in books read by children. A number of lists of high frequency words have been developed by researchers such as Edward Fry and Edward Dolch. A website that contains lists of high frequency words is www.uen.org/k-2educator/word_lists.shtml. Another good source for high frequency words is *The Reading Teacher's Book of Lists* (Fry, Kress, & Fountoukidis, 2000). Among the words that are most frequently used are: *the, on, at, this, is, by, said, do,* and *how*. Words that are less frequently used are more difficult; elements, modern, shoulder, similar, conditions, effect, and view are examples. Approximately one-third of all words in printed material are among the first 25 words on high frequency word lists. As amazing as it seems, the first 100 words on high frequency word lists make up nearly half of all written material, and the first 300 words comprise about 65 percent of all words in print. These 300 words, along with others created using suffixes like *-s, -ing, -ed, -ly,* and *-est,* provide a firm foundation for language learning (Fry, Kress, & Fountoukidis, 2000).

Instruction.   Learning sight words has been a part of reading instruction since colonial times in America. From the 1930s through the 1960s, many American children learned to read using the *Dick and Jane* series (Gray, Monroe, Artley, Arbuthnot, & Gray, 1956; Smith, 2002), which emphasized sight word instruction. Although many children can learn to read using sight word approaches, teaching children to recognize necessary sight words as part of synthetic phonics instruction have been shown to be more effective with a larger number and wider variety of children (National Reading Panel, 2003). Whatever the method, readers must never lose sight of the goal of comprehension.

Learning sight words requires memorization, so a number of multisensory experiences can be helpful (Higbee, 2001), particularly for English language learners. A lesson teaching sight words, which usually focuses on only a few words at a time, can be completed in a few minutes:

English Language
Learners

1. **Display example words.** Show students several sight words. For instance, write *science, ruler, year,* and *does* on chart paper. These words can easily be found in a book or poem that students have read or will read. They should be words that students do not know well but will frequently encounter.

2. **Read the words together.** Make sure that all of the students in the group know each word. If the children cannot read the words yet, be sure that the words are in their listening/speaking vocabularies. Discuss the meanings of the words.

3. **Highlight unique characteristics.** Enhance student learning by simultaneously involving the senses, using visual-kinesthetic as well as auditory and visual (Campbell, Helf, & Cooke, 2008) aids. Make sure students *see* the shapes and sequence of the letters in each word. Repeat the word multiple times so they can *hear* the word. Involve the tactile sense by having students trace the letters of the word; write the letters in the air; touch letters made of sandpaper, play dough, or even old carpet; or cut the letters apart and reform the word.

4. **Read the words again.** As you and the students read the words again chorally, point to the words.

5. **Ask students to use words in context.** To check for understanding, ask students to use the words in simple sentences. Be sure that the words are used appropriately; write the sentences on chart paper, a whiteboard, or using an overhead projector; and focus attention on the target words while doing so. For example, a student might give the sentence "My birthday comes once a year." The teacher can write the sentence and ask students to find the word *year* and help the teacher underline it. Consider displaying the target words for several days to remind students of the words they have learned.

6. **Practice.** Ask students to find the words in a picture book, poem, or other text you provide.

Putting It All Together

Phonics, word family, and sight word instruction should not always be segregated. You do not teach them in a particular order. Instead, you should address all three consistently throughout the year and regularly put them together. One effective way to do this is during shared reading.

Shared reading for young children requires that all in the group have access to the text so they can follow along as a leader reads fluently. You are usually the lead reader, but you can choose a child who reads with confidence for that role. The text can be a big book, individual copies of a literature anthology, charts, or texts projected on a screen. LEA texts can also become a resource for shared reading.

The level of text difficulty is not a major concern, since students do not read the text independently. Shared reading is normally done with the whole class, but it can also be done in smaller groups.

In the following example of shared reading, a first-grade teacher, Gloria, used a poem by Leland Jacobs, "First Things First" (Cecil, 1994), written on chart paper with some words covered with sticky notes. The students were seated on the floor in front of her. As they read the poem together, the teacher stopped when they came to a covered word. In the following transcription, the covered words are in brackets. Notice how Gloria uses her knowledge of all three methods—phonics generalizations, word families, and sight words—to help students with word identification. This is a short poem. You may not be able to replicate this lesson with longer text.

English Language Learners

Struggling Learners/ RtI

Try This for Teaching   **Word Hunt**

- Identify five to ten sight words that have been taught in a multisensory way.
- Provide books and other print sources that contain those words.
- Send students on a hunt for the words in these sources.
- Give points to those students who find the words fastest and to those who find the most examples.
- Give a time limit for the hunt.

- Have students mark words with sticky notes.

(Beck, McKeown, & Kucan, 2002)

Variation for ELLs

- Scaffold student learning by pairing children of differing abilities.

A comes first, then B and C,
[One] comes first, then two and three.
First things first.

[Puppy] first, and then the dog,
Tadpole first, and then the [frog].
First things first.

First the seed and then the [tree].
That's the way it had to be.
First things first!

Gloria	If I don't know this word [one], what strategy do I use? What could be under the sticky note? What would make sense?
Students	D!
Gloria	Let's read the rest of the sentence. [She pointed out that letters were the focus in the first line, but numbers were used in the second line.] What number comes before two and three?
Students	One!
Gloria	Right! Now *one* sounds like it starts with a *w*, but this is one of those words we just have to remember. [She uncovered the word.] *O-n-e* spells *one*. Let's read that line again. [As they read she pointed to the word *one*.] Let's write that on our hands. [Students wrote the letters *o-n-e* with a finger on the palm of their hands as the teacher pointed to the letters in the text.] *One* is a sight word. This is a word we just have to remember by how it looks.
Gloria	[After reading the first line of the next stanza, she paused before the covered word *puppy*.] What could this word be?
Students	Cat.
Gloria	We often hear those words together—*cat* and *dog*. If it is *cat*, what would the first letter be? [Gloria revealed the first letter, *p*.]
Students	Puppy.
Gloria	You're so smart. You figured that out so fast. "Puppy first and then the dog." How did you know the word was *puppy* and not *cat*?
Students	It starts with *p*.
Gloria	*P* says the sound /p/ just like pu-pu-puppy, or par-par-park. [Gloria quickly pointed out this phonics generalization before moving on]. "Tadpole first and then the . . . blank." What would go here?
Student	What's a tadpole?
Gloria	Before I answer that, let's look at what this word could be [pointing to the sticky note covering *frog*]. If it's going to rhyme with *dog*, it's part of the *-og* family. What other words do we know in that family?
Students	Hog. Log.
Gloria	"Tadpole is a baby . . . /f/ . . ."
Students	Frog!

Gloria	Right! "Tadpole first and then the frog, First things first." Let's read the next line together. "First the seed and then the . . ." What word goes there?
Student	Root?
Gloria	What letter would you see if it was *root*?
Students	R.
Gloria	[Revealed the letter *t* in tree] What's a /t/ word that rhymes with *be*?
Students	Tree!
Gloria	Let's read it that way and see if it makes sense.
Students	[Reading] "First the seed and then the tree."
Gloria	That's right [revealed the word *tree*]. Now let's read the whole poem.

Struggling Learners/
RtI

In this example, you can clearly see Gloria's agenda and her ability to help students use phonics, word families, and sight words to read words in the poem. But she did not stop there. Next she asked the students what they noticed about the poem. She then briefly addressed their comments. Gloria was taking her cues from her students (Smith, 1983).

Gloria	Pick any line. What do you notice?
Student	In *come* [line one], there's an *o* not a *u*.
Gloria	I'm glad you found that. *Come* is another one of those sight words that we just have to remember.
Student	There's a capital letter there [line 7, *First*].
Gloria	Why is it a capital letter?
Student	That's easy. It's the beginning of a sentence.
Student	I see *That's*.
Gloria	*That* is one of our spelling words. But why did the author add *'s*?
Student	There's more than one?
Gloria	This time, it's because he's combining two words to make a contraction. What words did he put together?
Student	*That* and *is*.
Student	There's an exclamation point [line 9].
Gloria	You've got a good eye. The author must have wanted us to read that part with excitement.
Student	*Tadpole* is a compound word [line 5].
Gloria	Correct.
Student	If you changed *t* to *d*, it'd be *dadpole* [line 5].
Gloria	That's right. You know how to replace sounds. It's good to know how to do that, but *dadpole* isn't really a word.
Student	If you moved the *b* over, you'd have *band* [line 1].
Gloria	Yes, you've made a real word. You can combine sounds too. But *band* doesn't make much sense right there.

Notice that at the end of the lesson the teacher addressed students' questions and their needs. Perhaps that's the most important point to remember about word identification. It should be driven by students' needs.

Conventions of Written Language

Along with word identification, children need to understand other aspects of written language as they make meaning of it. Young children must learn written language conventions, the accepted practices or guidelines used in written language that allow authors to communicate clearly and enable readers to understand.

Historically, written language conventions were the most important part of teaching children to read and write. As educators focused more on composition, the conventions were seen as tools to help make meaning. And now that people rely so much on electronic forms of communication, some researchers say that conventions no longer need to be taught. In the *Handbook of Research on Teaching the English Language Arts* (Flood, Lapp, Squire, & Jensen, 2003), less than one page of the book's 1,000 total pages was devoted to handwriting. However the Common Core stresses the teaching of concepts about print including mechanics, spelling, and grammar. Cursive is not directly mentioned, but handwriting instruction is assumed.

Common Core
State Standards

Spell checking programs don't catch all spelling errors, and there are writing settings where it is impossible to use technology. Serious judgments are sometimes made about a person's intellect, educational background, and potential if conventions are misused. Students' own self perceptions can be impacted as well (Schlagal, 2007).

Conventions can be taught in reading, and they can also be taught in writing. In fact, students are often more motivated to learn them in the writing context because of the personal nature of writing and their intense desire to be understood. You can begin by focusing on concepts about print, including mechanics, and then direct attention to spelling, handwriting, and grammar.

Concepts about Print

During the first phases of writing development, many children benefit when adults show them basic **print concepts** about written language such as how to identify the front and back of a book. Clay (2000) wrote *Concepts About Print*, which included directionality (that is, the left-to-right and top-to-bottom flow of words), return sweep (movement from the end of one line of print to the next line), recognition of letters, and basic end punctuation marks. All of these concepts about print are prominent in the Common Core as language and foundational skills for kindergartners and first graders. Figure 5.3 lists common concepts about print arranged in a useful order of presentation, beginning with the progression from left page to right page.

Common Core
State Standards

After students are familiar with basic print concepts, you can introduce other mechanics generalizations that help with reading and writing. When using the term *mechanics* many teachers are referring to capitalization and punctuation. The list of useful mechanics generalizations in Figure 5.4 is far from complete, but these concepts are the most basic and are listed in suggested order of presentation in mini-lessons. After each generalization is presented, you can draw attention to it when reading and writing with the whole class or in small groups.

Figure 5.3   Print Concepts

Progression of left page to right page	Differences between print and picture
Where print starts on a page	Left-to-right progression of print
Movement from the end of a line to the beginning of the next line (return sweep, top-to-bottom)	Ending punctuation marks (question mark, period, exclamation mark)
Separation of words by spaces	First and the last word on a page
Word-to-word matching (one word said for each word read)	Location of specific words
Capital and lowercase letters	Sequence of letters in a word
Location of both a first and a last letter in a word	Location of specific letters

Figure 5.4   Useful Mechanics Generalizations

Capitalization	
Pronoun I (wherever it comes in a sentence)	I ran with my friend. My friend and I have fun.
First word in a sentence	The school bell rang.
Dates and holidays	Wednesday, October 31, 2012 Halloween
Names of people	Sunhee and Tianne came to my house.
Official names of products and places	Sparkle toothpaste Wright's Department Store
End Punctuation Marks	
Period	It is starting to rain.
Question mark	Is it raining hard?
Exclamation mark	Come in from the rain!
Commas	
Dates	Tuesday, December 25, 2012
Series	I ate carrots, lettuce, and tomatoes in my salad.
Apostrophes	
Contractions	cannot, can't will not, won't they will, they'll they are, they're
Possessives	That is my sister's sweater. Mrs. Chen is the students' teacher.

Spelling

Although spelling ability proceeds along a developmental continuum and you should not be too quick to correct "errors," you can help your students progress by drawing attention to conventional spelling. These ideas are presented initially in the context of beginning reading and writing, but the same principles and suggestions can apply throughout the elementary grades.

In many schools, spelling is taught as a separate subject. Although spelling can and should be the focus of many lessons, some teachers and theorists believe that it is best taught connected with authentic reading and writing experiences (Alderman & Green, 2011); they note that spelling is not an end in itself but is a tool used to develop better readers and writers (Pinnell & Fountas, 1998).

Spelling lists have been a mainstay of spelling instruction even in the primary grades (Johnson, Langford, & Quorn, 1981). Like many activities, use of spelling lists can be effective or ineffective. You want to avoid low frequency and obscure words. Instead use high frequency words and words that follow consistent generalizations and patterns. Figure 5.5 offers eight useful spelling generalizations that can be taught in mini-lessons

Figure 5.5   **Eight Useful Spelling Generalizations**

Making Plurals of Words Ending in *y*: When you change a word that ends in *y* to a plural, change the *y* to an *i* and add *es*.

    cherry, cherries   baby, babies   county, counties   city, cities

Writing *i* Before *e*: When *i* and *e* are together in the same syllable, *i* usually precedes *e*.

    believe   thief   friend   brief   pierce   achieve

Common exceptions are when *i* and *e* follow *c*, and when the *e* and the *i* stand for the long *a* sound.

    receive   ceiling   receipt   neighbor   weigh   sleigh

Doubling Final Consonants: When a one-syllable word ends in a consonant, double the final consonant when adding a suffix.

    top, topped   swim, swimmer   get, getting

Dropping Final *e*: When a word ends with a silent *e*, delete the *e* when adding a suffix that begins with a vowel.

    use, using, useful   believe, believing, believable   surprise, surprising

Keeping the Final *e*: When a word ends with a silent *e*, keep the *e* when adding a suffix that begins with a consonant.

    use, useful   love, lovely   hope, hopeless   like, likeness

Adding a Prefix: When adding a prefix, do not change the spelling of the original word.

    move, remove   angle, triangle   spell, misspell   happy, unhappy

Keeping *e* After *v*: When a word ends with the *v* sound, write *ve* at the end.

    shave   above   effective   have   live   believe

Writing *u* After *q*: When the letter *q* is in a word, write the letter *u* just after it.

    quick   antique   equation   queen   plaque

and reinforced in authentic reading and writing experiences with the whole class or in small groups. These generalizations can guide your choice of words to include on spelling lists.

You can choose to highlight sight words or word family words, but you should also add high interest words that come from topics you are studying (Morrow, 2009), making the words responsive to what children are learning. These lists of words should be posted in prominent places in the classroom for students to use when writing and for you to refer to as these words are encountered in daily reading and writing.

Even if spelling tests are part of your language arts curriculum, do not focus too heavily on scores. Some children can score 100 percent on a spelling test but misspell the same words in their journals if you do not help them make the connections to actual writing (Gentry & Gillet, 1993). Spelling tests are best used to inform instruction rather than merely to grade students. With student learning in mind, use tests strategically. If a pretest is given, how will that change your instruction? Do posttests need to include every word from a spelling list every week? Could a sampling of words from several lists be used instead? Could students of differing abilities be held accountable for only some of the words on the list? Harward (1992) found self-corrected tests to be more effective than teacher- or peer-corrected tests when looking at retention of word spellings. His study results showed that the most effective form of self-correction came directly after each word was presented and spelled, rather than after all the words had been given. However you decide to administer and grade spelling tests, just be sure they are not becoming fillers that take time away from writing (Pritchard & Honeycutt, 2007).

Another staple of spelling instruction is the traditional spelling bee. Although this can be a motivating event to engage in once a year, it should not be a regular part of your classroom experience. Not only are the students who need the most practice eliminated first, but the entire process does not match the demands of spelling. Spelling is actually used in the context of writing, not the oral mode used in spelling bees. Usually the only time adults spell orally is when they don't want small children to know they are deciding whether or not to allow them to eat c-o-o-k-i-e-s.

Spelling study should be multisensory. Cutting paper, sorting letters, making words, playing games, chanting spellings, listening to words, and seeing word parts are all examples of engaging practice (Schlagal, 2007).

Handwriting

Like spelling, handwriting is a language tool that should be closely connected to writing rather than treated as a separate subject. Failure to develop adequate decoding skills limits comprehension; failure to develop legibility and fluency in handwriting affects content (Schlagal, 2007). Handwriting can have a positive effect on the composing abilities and confidence of young writers (Gray & Gray, 2005; Medwell & Wray, 2007). In a national survey, nine out of ten primary grade teachers reported that they teach handwriting because they realize its importance, but only 12 percent believed that they had been adequately prepared to do so when they began their careers (Graham et al., 2008).

Young children begin by forming letters in manuscript format because of the simple shapes involved—a combination of straight lines and circles. The first writing children produce may be on unlined paper. After they demonstrate sufficient dexterity (usually by first grade), teachers may find it helpful for children to begin using lined paper.

Struggling Learners/ RtI

English Language Learners

Language Conventions

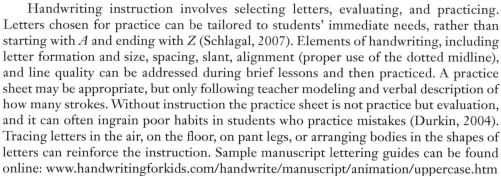

Handwriting instruction involves selecting letters, evaluating, and practicing. Letters chosen for practice can be tailored to students' immediate needs, rather than starting with *A* and ending with *Z* (Schlagal, 2007). Elements of handwriting, including letter formation and size, spacing, slant, alignment (proper use of the dotted midline), and line quality can be addressed during brief lessons and then practiced. A practice sheet may be appropriate, but only following teacher modeling and verbal description of how many strokes. Without instruction the practice sheet is not practice but evaluation, and it can often ingrain poor habits in students who practice mistakes (Durkin, 2004). Tracing letters in the air, on the floor, on pant legs, or arranging bodies in the shapes of letters can reinforce the instruction. Sample manuscript lettering guides can be found online: www.handwritingforkids.com/handwrite/manuscript/animation/uppercase.htm

The best place for practice is during actual writing. For example, children could copy a shared writing text they helped produce that is displayed on chart paper or on the whiteboard. As they copy text for which they have ownership, the practice is more meaningful than when they copy random words or phrases. This type of experience provides handwriting practice, even when final drafts are produced using word processors or Internet publishing tools. Although it is important for children to learn how to write upper- and lowercase letters, drilling these letters does not constitute the whole of writing instruction even for the youngest of children. They want to make meaning.

English Language Learners

Grammar

Grammar is the way words can be arranged to ensure understanding. It is first learned orally when acquiring language. Children can use grammar long before they can explain it (Huddelston & Pullum, 2005). When they hear a sentence, it sounds right or wrong. When they write a sentence, it looks right or wrong. This basic understanding allows students to function and communicate, but it doesn't allow them to use language as effectively as they can with additional instruction.

When you teach grammar, you help children put labels on what they already know. This helps them understand language at a heightened level and gives them greater freedom to express themselves in an influential way. Using appropriate grammar in writing and oral language shows consideration and respect for readers and listeners as well as leads to increased understanding.

Language can be divided into parts of speech. Each part is comprised of words that are used consistently in sentences as we speak and write. Some useful grammar terms are shown in Figure 5.6. These terms can strengthen your knowledge and help you teach beginners.

Figure 5.6   Useful Grammar Terms

Terms	Simple Definitions	Examples
Noun	Names a person, place, thing, or an idea	Matthew, store, sign, loyalty
Verb	Indicates action or a state of being	leap, jog, is, am
Adjective	Describes a noun	short, loud, four, blue
Adverb	Describes a verb, an adjective, or another adverb	softly, carefully, very, really
Conjunction	Connects other words	and, or, so, because
Determiner	Indicates which thing or things you are referring to	the, a, each, some, this
Preposition	Shows position or direction	on, under, by, in

Sentences are comprised of one or more words, expressing a complete thought. Orally, children recognize sentences by intonation patterns and when speakers pause to take breaths. In written language children recognize a sentence by noticing the capital letter at the beginning and a punctuation mark at the end. As children grow, they learn that sentences can be of different types. A sentence can make a statement, ask a question, or give a command. Most sentences have two basic parts: (1) a **subject**, the part of the sentence that does something or is being talked about; and (2) a **predicate**, the part of the sentence that tells about the subject and usually includes the verb. Figure 5.7 defines parts of sentences for your review and as a guide to help when you are teaching children.

Interactive Writing

English Language Learners

Interactive writing is method of instruction in which teachers and students share the pen and children take turns writing letters and words in a text composed by a group. Interactive writing is an effective way to help children understand conventions of written language. Although similar to LEA, interactive writing has a slightly different purpose. In LEA the teacher does the writing so that the story can be written quickly and other activities can follow. In interactive writing teacher and students share the pen. Both

Figure 5.7   Parts of Sentences

Terms	Simple Definitions	Examples
Subject	The part of the sentence that does something or is talked about	*Carol* teaches school.
Predicate	The part of the sentence that tells about the subject and usually includes the verb	Carol *teaches school*.
Modifier	A word that describes another word	*Her* class planned a *surprise* party.
Dependent Clause	A group of words within a sentence that also has a subject and a predicate	The children played a game *when the snow stopped falling*.
Phrase	A short group of related words within a sentence	The students wrote cards *about their teacher*.

types of instruction can closely examine letter-sound relationships, spaces between words, punctuation, and other aspects of written language as the story is written letter by letter and word by word on chart paper. When students make false steps or are unsure about a concept, you can model and explain so that the final writing is conventional. Teachers often use white correction tape to cover up miscues and allow for conventional writing to appear on the final copy (Tompkins, 2005).

Sometimes there is no need to write more than one sentence in a single interactive writing session, so like LEA it can fit naturally into your start-of-the-day routine. Also like LEA, it is an authentic context in which students are required to speak and listen with purpose. A text created using interactive writing is shown in Figure 5.8.

Interactive writing involves oral as well as written language. The teacher and students discuss each sound, word, letter, and writing convention as it is written, as well as read the product together repeatedly afterward. Students learn strategies that help them monitor their own reading (Donoghue, 2009) as well as participate in putting oral communication into writing (Combs, 2002).

When used with beginners, interactive writing results in increased understanding of letter-sound relationships. When children are asked to write a word with many sounds, you may prompt them to stretch the sounds out. You and the students say the word slowly, listening for each sound. Children are asked to write a letter for each sound they hear. In this way, each word is repeated frequently. After each sound is recorded on the chart, the word is stretched again so students can identify the next sound. Sometimes teachers use Elkonin (or sound) boxes (Elkonin, 1973) to help students hear the individual, sequential sounds in words or to show them the letter or letter combinations that are used to represent each sound.

Consider how Mamie and her students worked together in the following dialogue as they interactively wrote the sentence "The principal came to our class."

> Dear Principal,
> Thank you for coming to our class. We loved the book you read to us. Hip, hip, hooray for you today!

Figure 5.8

Sample Interactive Writing Text

Struggling Learners/ RtI

Language Conventions

Speaking/Listening

Mamie	*The.* That's a word we know. Who can come up and write *the*? [A volunteer came forward and took the marker.]
Mamie	Where's she going to start? Is she going to start at the left or in the middle?
Students	At the left! [The student put the marker in the upper-left part of the chart paper.]
Mamie	[Motioning the child to wait.] Does it start with a capital or lowercase letter?
Students	Capital. [The student wrote a capital *T.*]
Mamie	Right, because it's the beginning of a sentence. Now finish the word. [The student wrote *h* and *e* and then sat down].
Mamie	*Principal*—that's a long one. /p/ /p/ /p/. What letter does it start with?
Students	*P*!

Try This for Teaching **Elkonin Boxes**

- Draw simple squares on a page, one square for each sound in the word.
- Proceed like Hangman, but instead of providing a blank for each letter, each blank box represents a sound. (For example, to write the word *thank*, draw four boxes, one box for the sound /th/, one for /a/, one for /n/, and one for /k/).

(Elkonin, 1973)

Variations for ELLs

- Turn the activity into a game by having members of different teams fill in their own sound boxes simultaneously in relay fashion.

- When the children are familiar with this procedure, try working backwards. Instead of giving them boxes to be filled, give them a word and have them divide the word into sound boxes.
- Instead of using paper, create the boxes on the classroom floor with tape or jump ropes. Children can jump into the space as they say the appropriate sound.

Language Conventions

Mamie	Who can come up and write it? [A student came forward to take the marker and wrote a capital *p*.] Is it a capital *p*?
Students	Yes.
Mamie	Not this time, because we're not using her name. So let's put some tape over that one and try one more time. [The student wrote a lowercase *p* and sat down. As Mamie wrote the rest of the letters except the final *l*, she slowly said the sounds.] What sound do you hear at the end?
Students	/L/.
Mamie	Who can come up and write it? [A volunteer wrote the letter *l*.]
Mamie	The principal came——*came*. This one's tricky. I'll give you a clue. [She drew three boxes on the chart paper.] There's a box for every sound. A *c* goes in the first box, even though it sounds like *k*. What's the next sound you hear?
Students	/A/. [A volunteer wrote *a* in the second box.]
Mamie	The last box has two letters but only one sound. Who can come help us? [A student wrote *m*.] There's a silent letter at the end. [The student wrote the letter *e*.]
Mamie	Right, the *e* at the end makes the *a* say its own name. That's why the word is *came* and not *cam*. [Mamie finished the sentence in the same fashion.]

Interactive writing becomes a context to focus on concepts about print including mechanics. It also provides a framework for explaining and using the language tools of spelling, handwriting, and grammar.

Summary

In the song "Do-Re-Mi" from the popular musical *The Sound of Music*, Maria sings, "When you read you begin with *A-B-C*." As much as you may like the song, *A-B-C* is not the beginning of reading. You must remember the importance of a meaningful context in language development. Teaching word identification to children with limited phonological understanding is difficult and may slow their progress. You need to know useful phonics generalizations and how to teach them explicitly and implicitly. You will need to blend your phonics knowledge with word families and sight words.

Conventions of written language include concepts about print. As children develop, they must also receive instruction on spelling and handwriting. The Common Core stresses the teaching of grammar. Interactive writing is a helpful context in which to teach and practice all conventions of written language for beginners.

Is English easy? No, not quite. But you can help your students take flight! With your knowledge of beginning reading and writing, you can help your students get off to a fast start.

Self-Check

1. Since it is so confusing, why should you teach children phonics?

2. How can you teach phonics effectively to children?

3. What is a word family?

4. Explain two meanings of the term *sight word*.

5. What are concepts about print and how are they useful?

6. How can traditional spelling tests be administered more effectively?

7. What is interactive writing and how can you use it to teach children about conventions of written language?

8. Describe your role as a teacher during interactive writing.

MyEducationLab™

Go to the Topics, Phonemic Awareness/Phonics and Writing, in the **MyEducationLab** (www.myeducationlab.com) for your course, where you can:

- Find learning outcomes for Phonemic Awareness/Phonics and Writing along with the national standards that connect to these outcomes.

- Complete Assignments and Activities that can help you more deeply understand the chapter content.

- Apply and practice your understanding of the core teaching skills identified in the chapter with the Building Teaching Skills and Dispositions learning units.

- Examine challenging situations and cases presented in the IRIS Center Resources.

- Check your comprehension on the content covered in the chapter by going to the Study Plan in the Book

Resources for your text. Here you will be able to take a chapter quiz, receive feedback on your answers, and then access Review, Practice, and Enrichment activities to enhance your understanding of chapter content (optional).

- Visit **A+RISE** Standards2Strategy™, an innovative and interactive online resource that offers new teachers in grades K–12 just-in-time, research-based instructional strategies that meet the linguistic needs of ELLs as they learn content, differentiate instruction for all grades and abilities, and are aligned to Common Core Elementary Language Arts Standards (for the literacy strategies) and to English language proficiency standards in WIDA, Texas, California, and Florida.

chapter **6**

Fluency

Chapter Outline

COMPONENTS OF FLUENCY
SKILLS AND STRATEGIES
    Rate and Accuracy
    Expression
ORAL READING
    Group Reading
    Assessment
    Transition to Silent Reading
WRITTEN LANGUAGE
    Sentence Fluency
    Voice
SUMMARY

I read aloud to my third-grade students regularly, in part to model expressive oral reading for them. Among my students were several who were expressive readers. However, Allie struggled with oral reading. She read in a monotone voice and paid little attention to punctuation marks. She read as if each word were on a separate page. As I worried about how to help her read faster and with better expression, I decided to use a listening area. I set up several listening and recording stations where students could listen to recordings of children's books read by professional actors. I also encouraged them to record their own voices as they read. Students could listen to their own recordings and practice until they sounded like the models they listened to. Allie loved to take her turns and listened to books over and over again. She made recordings of her own reading. Recording her own voice and realizing that others could listen to her the way she listened to the recorded readers inspired her. Over time, her fluent reading improved, and by the end of the year her mother commented on Allie's improvement—much to Allie's delight.

—Tim

Read the following sentence aloud:

B g nn ng   r d rs   ft n   r d   w rd   b   w rd   b c s   th   l ck   fl   nc .

Did you find this difficult? After you noticed that all the vowels were missing you could read the words, but how long did it take you? Did you sound like someone talking, or were you robotically chanting? Try it one last time, and read the statement like you would say it: Beginning readers often read word by word because they lack fluency.

As young children understand that the letters they see in print represent words they know, they begin to call out the words as they discover what the print says. This slow word-by-word oral reading represents an important step in reading development. Similarly, when beginning writers learn letter formation, the spellings of common words, and basic punctuation, they can write with more fluency. The goal is for children to develop rate, accuracy, and expression in both oral and written language with an eye toward meaning (Pikulski & Chard, 2005; Rasinski, Padak, Linek, & Sturtevant, 1994). Fluency is not an isolated process; it is an aspect of literacy that helps lead to comprehension (Rasinski, 2010; Reutzel & Hollingsworth, 1993). It has been identified as one of the basic elements of reading by the National Reading Panel (2000). In order to assist children you need to know the components of literacy and how to help them turn strategies into skills in both oral and written language.

Components of Fluency

Because of the importance of automatic word identification, speed of reading has been emphasized more than other aspects of fluency. In fact, former definitions of reading fluency used to stress only speed, or **rate**, of reading. Although identifying words quickly is important, fluency is more than reading fast. Fluent readers must also read with **accuracy** by identifying words correctly and with **expression** or prosody—by reading text like it would be spoken (Rasinski, 2000). The Common Core emphasizes all three of these aspects of fluency as foundational skills. In addition, the Core stresses that readers should read with purpose and understanding. Because skilled readers spend so little time identifying each word, they are able to efficiently comprehend what they read and meet their personal needs.

You may think of teaching fluency as a series of exercises or drills. But this is not the case. Oral reading fluency is closely related to speaking and listening. Good listeners imitate what good speakers do, and good listeners and speakers become conscious of what fluent reading should sound like. As you read aloud to children, as you engage them in normal conversations and discussions, and as you help them use language to become informed and to inform others in your classroom, you are teaching fluency.

Beginning readers, struggling readers, and English language learners read text differently than proficient readers. Many of them often read slowly, working to identify the words they see in print. Since most words are unfamiliar to them, they use a number of information sources to try to identify the words: visual clues, illustration clues, and the surrounding context. They exert a great deal of effort in this decoding process and read as if each word were an isolated problem. After they have struggled to identify one word, they move on to the next. Because of the time it takes to identify each word, the reader is frequently unable to build complete meaning. But, do not be fooled by presentation alone. Some students— ELLs especially—may develop the ability to decode quickly in English and may read with

Common Core State Standards

Speaking/Listening

English Language Learners

great fluency but still not understand what they read. You can help children improve their fluency and comprehension by helping them develop both skills and stategies.

Skills and Strategies

The human mind has a limited amount of attention it can use in one time period, so when some processes become automatic, attention is freed up to focus to other things. Although the words *skills* and *strategies* are often used interchangeably, Afflerbach, Pearson, and Paris (2008) stressed crucial differences between them. Skills are processes that are completed automatically and require little attention and memory. Skills can be done almost without thinking about them, like tying a shoe or riding a bike. These tasks may be difficult at first, but when you have mastered them, you can complete them while talking to someone or thinking of something else. In reading, examples of cognitive skills include identifying letters and words, knowing about spaces between words, and understanding punctuation. Even some simple inferences can become automatic skills (Fuchs, Fuchs, Hosp, & Jenkins, 2001). Reaching an automatic level of identifying words is very important in reading development (Chall, 1995; Ehri & McCormick, 1998).

By contrast, strategies are processes readers intentionally use that require attention and memory. "Reading strategies are deliberate, goal-directed attempts to control and modify the reader's efforts to decode text, understand words, and construct meanings of text," according to Afflerbach, Pearson, and Paris (2008, p. 368). When readers have turned some strategies into automatic skills, they have attention left over to read expressively and build comprehension. This means that they can use new strategies like identifying cause-and-effect relationships, understanding the sequence of events in a passage, and clarifying meanings of unfamiliar words to create better understanding of what they read.

When children move from reliance on strategies to automatic use of skills as they read, they become skilled, fluent readers. This transition does not happen without extended practice. Consistent practice is difficult to maintain without motivation.

Rate and Accuracy

"Repeated exposures to the same words leads to improvements in fluency," noted Samuels (2003, p. 174; see also Allington, 1977, 1983a). There are many ideas for building fluency (Blevins, 2002; Kuhn & Schwanenflugel, 2008; Kuhn & Stahl, 2003). Three effective ways to help children practice increasing rate and accuracy are repeated oral reading (Samuels, 1979), neurological impress (Heckelman, 1969; Tierney & Readence, 2004), and echo reading (Tompkins, 2010). These practices help students turn reading strategies into skills (Dowhower, 1989; Eldredge, 1990; Eldredge & Quinn, 1988; O'Shea, Sindelar, & O'Shea, 1985).

Struggling Learners/ RtI

Repeated Reading. The most common approach to rate and accuracy development is the method of repeated reading. Originally developed to help children who struggle with reading, repeated reading is a simple three-step process for all students:

1. The teacher selects appropriate instructional-level texts for students. These passages, which can be narrative or informational text, should be about 200 to 250 words in length.

2. Students read the text to become familiar with it.

3. Students re-read the same passage several times quickly and with expression.

Try This for Teaching   **Repeated Reading**

- Select appropriate text.
- Let students become familiar with the text.
- Have students read the text quickly and with expression.
- Use both narrative and informational text.

(Samuels, 1979, 2003)

Variations for ELLs

- Allow students to record themselves as they read.
- Display a song or poem that children can read together chorally.

- After they become familiar with the text, ask them to read or sing it again using a different accent (such as a British accent, western or southern U.S. accent, etc.)
- Not only does this activity give you the opportunity to engage in repeated reading but it can also spark a discussion about respecting differences.
- When singing a song, try singing in opera style or rap or country and western style.
- Ask students to assume a stereotype character—read like a grandma, like someone who is angry, or like someone reading to a baby.

Although it is not essential, some students like to measure their progress by timing their readings and recording or graphing their rates (Paige, 2006). Hasbrouck and Tindal (2006) reported oral reading rates that are expected for average students in elementary grades. First graders should be reading about 20 words per minute (wpm) by February and about double that by the end of the year. Second graders should be reading about 70 wpm in the middle of the school year and 90 wpm by the end of the school year. By third grade, a student's rate should increase to about 110 wpm, reaching 125 wpm in fourth grade, 140 wpm in fifth grade, and 150 wpm in sixth grade. In general children increase their rate of reading by about 25 to 30 wpm each year over the course of their elementary school years.

Although the stress in repeated reading is on increasing rate of reading, other aspects of fluency can also be improved. By repeatedly reading the same text, students practice the same words over and over. Doing so can help them improve accuracy and automatize many high frequency words.

Repeated reading is a way to scaffold for struggling readers and for those acquiring English. As students are given multiple opportunities to read the same text, you will see them make great strides. Students have been shown to increase in rate of

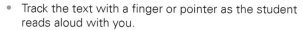

English Language Learners

Try This for Teaching   **Neurological Impress**

- Track the text with a finger or pointer as the student reads aloud with you.
- Read at a normal pace and with expression.
- If the student stops, slow down and control the pacing until he can restart.

(Heckelman, 1969; Tierney & Readence, 2004)

Variations for ELLs

- Pair two students, one designated as the lead reader, for dyad reading (Eldredge, 2005).
- Read and point while the student is silent. Track the text again as the student reads the same line.
- Have students read aloud as they listen to a recording of a book.

Echo Reading

- Select a text that is at an appropriate independent or instructional level for your students.
- Be sure that all students have access to the text (big book, projection, or individual copies).
- Read a phrase from the text aloud with appropriate rate, accuracy, and expression as you track the words.
- Immediately after you finish reading a phrase, have the students read the same words back orally.

Variations for ELLs

- Pair ELLs with more fluent partners and have them echo read.
- After an English language learner is proficient with a book, he can become the lead reader for younger children who echo him.

reading and improve decoding skills when they engage in repeated reading (Breznitz, 2006; Paige, 2011).

Neurological Impress.   Neurological impress (Heckelman, 1969; Tierney & Readence, 2004) allows a student to see the words as they are said and heard. While tracking the text with a finger or pointer, the teacher sets the pace and reads with expression so that the student can focus on saying the words quickly and accurately. The student chimes in when he can, but may follow silently at times, especially if the text is unfamiliar or is written above his instructional level. Neurological impress can help children develop rate. However, fluency varies with the difficulty level of text and with the reader's prior knowledge of the content of the passage being read. This one-on-one assistance can make a dramatic difference in reading gains, whether it is done by a teacher, an adult volunteer, or a competent peer (Eldredge, 1990; Eldredge & Quinn, 1988). Neurological impress is especially appropriate for students who are identified through RtI processes as needing additional instruction.

Struggling Learners/ RtI

English Language Learners

Echo Reading.   In echo reading children see and hear the words as you read, then they have a chance to practice immediately after. Echo reading can be done in small groups or as a whole class. You can model by reading a phrase from a text aloud, emphasizing proper rate, accuracy, and expression. After you read one phrase, the students read it back to you following your example. You can provide praise and feedback as you continue moving through the text together. To maintain continuity and interest, you will want to keep a brisk pace.

Expression

Reading rate and accuracy are two aspects of fluency, but reading with appropriate expression is frequently needed for comprehension. Reading with expression often involves reading for authentic audiences with genuine purposes. Sometimes students can lose motivation to practice skills and strategies if they feel they are re-reading text for no purpose. A sense of audience can bring new life to expressive reading practice for many children. If they know they are going to be performing for a group of parents, another class, or even for each other, children see a reason to practice. Two effective strategies that lend themselves to performance are readers' theater (Martinez, Roser, & Strecker, 1998) and puppet shows (Allington, 2001).

When students do read for an audience, identification of words becomes a skill so that students can turn their attention to expressive oral reading and using strategies to comprehend the text. As they become more skilled at identifying words, students develop better awareness of the text, and many students come to read with better expression. Zutell and Rasinski (1991) developed the Multidimensional Fluency Scale that features four dimensions of expressive reading that can be practiced and measured: expression and volume, phrasing, smoothness, and pacing.

Readers' Theater.   Readers' theater is presented like a play, but instead of memorizing and acting out parts, performers read them (Worthy & Prater, 2002) from a script. Some scripts for readers' theater are commercially produced and include parts written at different levels of difficulty (Benchmark Education Company, 2003–2005). However, students can easily create their own scripts if the teacher assigns sections of a picture book, short story, or poem to be read by individuals in a group. For example, Reader A can read the first two lines in a poem, followed by Reader B reading the next two lines, and so forth. Students can also write their own scripts. Whatever the source, students need plenty of time to practice. As they prepare to perform for an authentic audience, they feel motivated to read the text repeatedly and practice their oral reading (Millin & Rinehart, 1999; Tyler & Chard, 2000). Practice time for ELLs will be more effective if you explain some of the key words, especially **puns**, witty and humorous uses of a word or phrase with two meanings ("I wondered why the golf ball was getting bigger and bigger. Then it hit me."); **idioms**, a group of words that have a different meaning when used together from the one they would have if you considered the meaning of each word separately ("My sister is a bookworm. She is always reading a book."); and jokes.

English Language Learners

Puppet Shows.   Students can write a script with the teacher assigning parts of a story as they would in readers' theater (Rasinski & Hoffman, 2003). They can create a simple puppet theater by draping a blanket or sheet over a table and crouching behind it. Puppets do not need to be costly or elaborate. Paper drawings glued to sticks, decorated paper bags, or socks placed over hands can serve the purpose.

Struggling Learners/ RtI

When students perform puppet shows, the audience may lose interest if they cannot hear the performers well from behind the blanket. A simple solution is to allow performers to record their voices as they read the script. As they listen to the recording, they can identify problem areas and practice to improve. When they are ready, they can make a final recording of the entire script. This process allows them to practice both their speaking and listening skills. On the day of the performance, the children can play the recorded script as they move the puppets. This prior recording not only results in a louder, clearer

English Language Learners

Try This for Professional Development

Explore Expressive Reading Assessments

Compare and contrast the Multidimensional Fluency Scale (Zutell & Rasinski, 1991) with two other scales that can be used to assess fluency:

- Jerry L. Johns and Roberta L. Berglund, 2002, *Fluency: Questions, Answers, and Evidence-Based Strategies*, Kendall Hunt.

- Gay Sue Pinnell and Sheida White, 1995, *Listening to Children Read Aloud*, U.S. Department of Education (nces.ed.gov/pubs95/web/95762.asp).

Try This for Teaching ## Readers' Theater

- Locate or create a script.
- Assign parts.
- Allow plenty of time for practice.
- Perform the reading.

Variations for ELLs

- Assign several students the same part and have them read it chorally.
- Translate a short script into a different language. Have some students read a part in one language followed by the same part in a different language.

Try This for Teaching ## Books for Multiple Voices

- Use a book such as *You Read to Me, I'll Read to You* (Hoberman, 2001).
- Group students into twos or threes, assigning each group one poem to practice.
- When the groups are ready, have each group read their poem to the rest of the class.

Variations for ELLs

- Don't have all the students share on the same day you give them the assignment; instead have one or

two groups present each day over the next few weeks.

- Arrange to have students share their poem chorally over the school intercom.
- Explore other appropriate books: *Big Talk* (Fleischman, 2008); *Joyful Noise: Poems for Two Voices* (Fleischman, 2004); *Partner Poems for Building Fluency: Grades 4–6* (Rasinski, Harrison, & Fawsett, 2009).

Try This for Teaching ## Joke Books

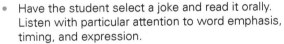

- Have the student select a joke and read it orally. Listen with particular attention to word emphasis, timing, and expression.
- Discuss both the joke and the student's delivery of the joke, identifying the source of the humor.
- Focus the student on how to use his or her voice as a tool to improve on the joke's humor.
- Point out punctuation, including question marks, commas, periods, and exclamation marks, and discuss what they contribute to the joke's meaning and humor.
- Model a proficient delivery of the joke while the student listens.
- Give students time over several days of instruction to practice their jokes in preparation for a classroom "Comedy Hour."
- Obtain good children's joke books such as *You Must be Joking!* (Brewer, 2003);

Jokelopedia: The Biggest, Best, Sillies , Joke Book Ever (Weitzman, 2006).

(Ness, 2009)

Variations for ELLs

- Use choral and echo reading to re-read the joke with the student.
- Have the student record and reflect on his or her delivery.
- Have students work with partners to tell or re-read jokes. Partners should listen and evaluate each other for their expression, timing, and word emphasis.
- Ask them to translate a joke from their first language and discuss why the translation is or is not still funny.

performance, but it can ensure less stress and more success for struggling readers and English language learners.

Oral Reading

Oral reading has had a long tradition in American schools, having been a major focus of instruction until the early 1900s. The few instructional aids for teachers included in early readers provided information about proper pronunciation and elocution (Smith, 2002). In 1908 Huey wrote about the need for silent reading capability, signaling the end of the primacy of oral reading. Although most independent reading is done silently, oral reading has purpose. In addition to the practicing and performing purposes that have already been addressed, oral reading allows us to read together in a group, and it also provides opportunities for assessment as you help students transition from oral to silent reading.

Speaking/Listening

Group Reading

When parents, teachers, and others read aloud to children, they model oral reading. Students hear appropriate rate, accuracy, and expression, which are important as they begin to practice reading orally in a group. Frequent daily practice is critical, but it should not take the form of round robin reading.

Try This for Teaching   **Puppet Shows**

- Locate or write a script.
- Create a simple theater and puppets.
- Assign parts.
- Allow time for practice.
- Present the show.

Variations for ELLs

- Record the script ahead of time.
- Prepare a puppet show as a literature response.
- Have the puppets teach a concept in one of the content areas.
- Try using shadow puppets (Peck & Virkler, 2006).

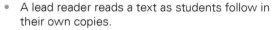

Try This for Teaching   **Fill in the Blank**

- A lead reader reads a text as students follow in their own copies.
- To ensure that all students are engaged, the lead reader can pause at certain words.
- The group fills in the blanks by reading the missing words chorally.

Variation for ELLs

- Students point to the word rather than saying it aloud.
- When the lead reader comes to dialogue, students can read the text inside the quotation marks chorally while the lead reader reads everything else.

The most common form of oral reading in elementary classrooms is traditional **round robin reading**, in which the teacher asks one student to read an unrehearsed section of text orally while the others in the group follow along silently. When that student has finished, the next student reads until all students have had their turns. The term "round robin" dates back to when crews on a ship would plan a mutiny and take turns in a circle voicing agreement with the plan so that no one was left out.

Although common, this practice is discouraged for many reasons. It is an unnatural process. Since oral reading is much slower than silent reading, round robin reading may lead to undesired silent reading habits in those who follow along. The time children spend reading in round robin fashion takes time away from other more useful teaching and practice activities. Round robin reading may give children the impression that the main purpose of reading is saying all the words right. Some children do not pay attention to the halting oral reading they hear from some of their peers. Others skim ahead to their assigned paragraph to practice for their turn. Few recall what was read or realize that comprehension is of major importance.

Instead of round robin reading, you can incorporate alternative activities within the context of **shared reading** and **guided reading** (Opitz & Rasinski, 1998). When doing shared reading with a whole class, encourage the students to silently follow along, making sure that the lead reader reads fluently. One teacher likes to begin a story or chapter by having the entire group read the first paragraph in unison (**choral reading**). This ensures that all students are engaged. Then a lead reader continues while the others follow along silently. Another teacher likes to serve as the lead reader, while the students track the text with their fingers to make sure students are following him. His students are expected to chorally read all words that are within quotation marks.

Guided reading is different because small groups of students read instructional level text with teacher assistance. A mixture of oral and silent reading is appropriate. In primary grades you can ask all of the students in your small group to read the text simultaneously. Stagger the starting times for students and encourage them to read quietly at their own pace. Some teachers call this whisper reading. Each student practices reading the entire text instead of reading only the small portion they would read in round robin reading.

When working with older students and longer texts, reading a complete book during a group meeting is not advisable. Students should be expected to read independently before the group meeting and be prepared to discuss the content. Asking them to read on their own is appropriate because the material is written at their instructional level. You can use part of the small group meeting time to have students read orally so you can assess their reading development, or you can look back over specific passages, but the focus is usually kept on comprehension and vocabulary.

Struggling Learners/
RtI

English Language
Learners

Try This for Teaching   **Fluency Phones**

- Using PVC pipe (one short length and two elbow pieces) create a telephone receiver.
- Have students read into one end so they can hear their own voice.
- You can listen to several children read simultaneously, and they will not distract each other.

- Have students whisper in the phone—they can still hear themselves surprisingly well.

Variation for ELLs

- Encourage students to listen for their own miscues as they read and refine their performance as they re-read the text.

Assessment

One of the major reasons to have children read orally is to evaluate their reading abilities. Assessment provides a window into their strengths and weaknesses that can then be addressed through instruction and practice. Assessment of an individual's reading can be accomplished during regular small group reading time. As primary or intermediate grade students individually read a common text aloud in whisper-reading fashion, you can listen in on one student at a time to evaluate progress. Then you can coach them by offering compliments and suggestions. Additionally, you may need to set aside times specifically for evaluation, especially for those who struggle. At such times you can use **running records** (Clay, 2002) or **informal reading inventories** such as the *Qualitative Reading Inventory* (Leslie & Caldwell, 2006). These are both assessment tools that involve students reading orally as the teacher listens and records errors.

Struggling Learners/ RtI

Transition to Silent Reading

Much practice and assessment in the primary grades is done orally, which is the way children first learn to read. Although they begin with oral reading, a transition to silent reading is inevitable (Kragler, 1995; Prior & Welling, 2001). After all, real-life reading is almost all silent: newspapers, magazines, or text on the computer screen. Silent reading is much faster than oral reading, and your comprehension is usually greater. Because of this efficiency, you should encourage your students to read silently after they have consolidated their understanding of letter-sound relationships. This understanding usually occurs some time in second grade.

New Literacies

Because many children do not understand at first that silent reading is possible, they can be shown what it is. Don Holdaway demonstrated a way to help young children learn the concept of silent reading by reading aloud a folktale about a woman who was returning from a shopping trip (Melser & Cowley, 1990). While walking to her home, she saw a big toe lying along the path, so she put it into her shopping bag. As she put her groceries away, she heard a voice faintly asking about its big toe. Frightened, she ran up the stairs and put the toe on the nightstand. As the voice came closer, the size of the print increased. When the voice was at her door, she hid under the covers of her bed, but said nothing. The voice grew louder and louder as it came up the stairs. When it entered her room, the woman reached from under the covers, threw the toe, and confessed that she had taken it.

As the voice left, it called out loudly that it now had its big toe back. As it moved away, the voice repeated the phrase over and over as it became fainter and fainter. In the

---

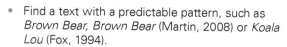
Try This for Teaching   **Turn Down the Volume**

- Find a text with a predictable pattern, such as *Brown Bear, Brown Bear* (Martin, 2008) or *Koala Lou* (Fox, 1994).

- Each time you come to the predictable section of the text, read it more quietly.

- Finally repeat the pattern without verbalizing the words—mouth the words to make sure students hear each word in their heads.

Variations for ELLs

- Provide a hand signal for each word in the pattern instead of mouthing the words.

- Engage students in an action that goes with some of the deleted words. When you get to those words, have children do the action without saying the words.

text the words grew smaller and smaller until finally, the voice could not be heard audibly and the words were gone from the book. As the words in the book became smaller, Don read them more quietly, making a hand movement for each of the words. When the words disappeared, Don continued to move his hand and asked, "What do you hear in your head? That is silent reading." In a sense, he had turned down the volume, but the children could still hear the words in their heads and began to understand what silent reading is.

Although Holdaway's demonstration of silent reading is not the efficient form that they will develop later, this is a first step in acquiring silent reading ability. You can replicate this idea of turning down the volume with other texts that have a repeated pattern.

Written Language

Rate, accuracy, and expression are concerns not only for readers, but also for writers. Children need to be able to record their ideas quickly, revise to be more expressive, and edit for accuracy. Skilled writers are not as worried about the mechanics of writing as they are about making meaning. As children become less concerned with form, they can focus more on communicating a message.

Beginning writers, struggling writers, and English language learners write differently than more proficient writers. They write very slowly, letter by letter, word by word. Because they struggle with fluency, they often feel frozen in place. They are sometimes so fixated on correctness that they frequently ask "How do you spell this word?" instead of allowing themselves to do their best and move on. Often they change what they want to say to match the limited words they know how to write correctly, instead of feeling empowered to discover and express what is truly in their minds and hearts in their own unique voices. Because they exert a great deal of effort in this encoding process, their writing is very labored and halting. You can help children improve their smoothness and personal expression in writing by focusing on sentence fluency and voice.

Sentence Fluency

Many children write with scribble marks as they begin to move through stages of writing development. The marks they make usually carry only temporary meaning, and frequently they are meaningful only for the writer himself. As children become more skilled in their ability to form letters and write words, they can begin to focus on creating sentences on their own. But, even after children are able to form letters and spell words, many still struggle to write sentences. For example, when a beginning author described his school experiences, he wrote, "I like math. I like recess. I like lunch. I like P. E." The sentences are complete, but they are choppy. Another child wrote long run-on sentences with many *ands* connecting them. "I like to eat pizza and I like ice cream and I like cookies but I don't like cooked carrots."

When children express themselves orally and hear others, the communication is fluent. It is important for you to help children realize that they can experience similar levels of fluency when they write. What we can say, we can write. Shared writing and LEA give children chances to listen as well as speak and see how such expressions are recorded in writing. As children gain more independence, they can attend to aspects of sentence fluency such as using a variety of sentence lengths and structures in their writing and using different ways to begin sentences so that their writing "invites expressive oral reading" (Spandel & Stiggins, 1997, p. 56).

Fluency can be addressed in mini-lessons and shared writing, but another natural context for instruction is when children are writing more independently. Two ways you can help students improve sentence fluency as they develop as writers are timed writing and conferencing for content.

Timed Writing.   Begin by making sure students have their pencils and writing note-books ready. Tell them that when you start the stopwatch, they should begin to write and not lift their pencils from the page until you call time. Because they do not have time to focus on conventions of writing and editing, students' writing becomes more natural and automatic. They do not have time to worry about the form; they just write their ideas, and sentences flow more smoothly, like their speaking. As weeks pass you can point out to your students that they have produced much more writing than before. You may also notice that the students compose more fluent sentences in their other classroom writing, something you can attribute to your efforts to make timed writing part of the daily classroom schedule.

English Language Learners

One opportunity to incorporate timed writing is when students are writing independently in their journals. One teacher found that, although it was useful to give students time for sustained silent journal writing, some students wasted that time by complaining "I don't know what to write about" or by writing large letters to fill the page so they could be finished. She found the quality and quantity of writing improved as she timed the students as they wrote. Timing writing for a few minutes each day also allowed her to fit writing more regularly into her busy class schedule.

At first she was discouraged when students wrote meaningless things like "This is very, very, very, very boring." But as she persisted, the students tired of such silliness and began writing more meaningfully. Having volunteers share with the rest of the class what they had written provided a positive model.

Be careful to motivate children by having them race the clock and not each other. They try to make their writing better than before, not better than someone else's writing. Teachers' concerns about timed writing usually center on students becoming too competitive. If the amount of students' writing is not recorded and tracked publicly, it can be an effective practice.

Conferencing for Content.   There are times when children's writing does not go through the entire writing process, such as when students write in a journal. There are other times when revision is essential. As you conference with individuals or small groups, be careful not to focus too quickly on conventions, which is the natural tendency for

---

Try This for Teaching   **Timed Writing**

- Make sure students have pencils and notebooks ready.
- Start timing students as they begin writing about a topic of their choice.
- Stop the writing after two to three minutes.
- Have students count the lines they wrote and measure their progress over time.

Variations for ELLs

- Display an art print to which students can respond in writing: some may list shapes they see; others may write what they think the artist is trying to communicate.
- Play music, saying, "As long as the music is playing, write. When the music stops, you may stop."

many teachers and parents. Although revision for content and editing can occur simultaneously for adults, you may find that children are more successful when they focus first on one and then on the other.

Struggling Learners/ RtI

Begin a content conference by asking the student, "What are you working on?" When she says, "I need you to edit this," ask her, "Have you made changes?" If the student has not, ask her to read what she has written and attend to content issues first. It may be helpful to close your eyes and listen as the student reads so you think about meaning and are not distracted by mechanics. If the writing is long, just attend to several paragraphs or to one page. Students can revise the organization, add details, and develop ideas. But a simple area on which to focus—especially for beginners—is sentence fluency. For example, you can ask students questions like "Can we get by without so many *ands*? Do all the sentences have to start the same? What are words we could use instead of *and then*? How could we put these two sentences together?" As they respond to these questions, students can make positive changes in their writing.

Voice

Honest voice occurs when writers are able to express their thoughts or feelings with their unique personal stamp. They do not sound like everyone else. The writing is compelling, engaging, and believable. It includes "language that literally cries out to be spoken aloud" (Spandel & Stiggins, 1997, p. 56). The reader feels that the words

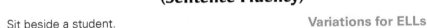

Try This for Teaching **Conferencing for Content (Sentence Fluency)**

- Sit beside a student.
- Ask "How may I help you?" or "What are you working on?"
- If the student wants editing help, tell him you want to focus on content first—don't allow yourself to be distracted by mechanics.
- Praise the sentences that flow naturally.
- Suggest separating or combining sentences as needed.

Variations for ELLs

- Students can conference with peers.
- If you have a telephone, students can call volunteers on a list who have agreed to listen to and respond to student writing.
- Ask students, "Does it sound like you're talking? Does your writing match how you would tell this to me if you just speaking?"

Try This for Professional Development **A Shift in Focus**

Preservice teacher candidates attend more to the content of their students' writing than the mechanics when they have more opportunities to work directly with individual children (Moore-Hart, 2009; Moore-Hart & Carpenter, 2009).

- Why would this be the case?

- Think about your own experience. Have you noticed a similar pattern? Why or why not?
- Why is changing focus from mechanics to content an important shift for teachers to make when working with children?

are just for him, because the author has written with a clear sense of audience. This is especially important for children who copy phrases and sentences from books and encyclopedias, not because they are trying to be dishonest, but because they have not yet found their own voice, especially when it comes to informational text, which is stressed in the Common Core.

An eighth-grade teacher who read "The British troops returned the American fire volley-for-volley" in a student paper could assume that the phrase had been lifted from a book because eighth-graders do not talk like that. Similarly, when she saw on another student's paper that "the American government has three branches (see Figure 12.3)," and knew there was no figure in the student paper, she could tell that the child was not writing in his own voice. Although you should discuss plagiarism, the intentional copying of another person's writing (from the Latin word for *kidnapper*), it is probably more helpful to show students at the same time how each of them can find and develop his or her own voice in writing.

You can begin with a shared experience in which the class works together. Then you can offer them additional opportunities to work independently. Two strategies that are helpful in teaching about voice are creating a class book and establishing a classroom post office.

Common Core State Standards

Class Books.   Rather than have every student always write her own story or book, occasionally write one together as a class. This is an effective way to scaffold for ELLs, who can have a complete writing experience and even enjoy being part of a final publication without being responsible for having to complete the project independently. Brainstorm topics as a class or present a model story to use as a pattern. Assign each student to write one or two sentences on a page. When students finish their writing, they can begin an illustration. As you move about the classroom, help students revise content and mechanics. Also make sure the writing flows from one page to another. This does not take long, since each student is responsible for only a few sentences. When you are finished editing, gather the pages and read the final product to the class. If you want students to spend more time on illustrations, try distributing pages during teacher read aloud time and let them draw as they listen. Figure 6.1 provides sample pages from class books.

English Language Learners

One third-grade teacher, Mrs. Rothstein, read aloud the picture book *In 1492* (Marzollo, 1991). It begins, "In fourteen-hundred ninety-two, Columbus sailed the ocean blue. He had three ships, and left from Spain. He sailed through sunshine, wind, and rain" (p. 1). After she finished the book and closed it, she asked, "Without looking at the book, who can tell me something you've learned?"

One student said, "Columbus sailed across the ocean." Another added, "He landed in the Bahamas and thought it was India."

As the students responded, the teacher wrote their sentences on the board in shared writing fashion. "Let's read these sentences and see if there is anything else we need to add," she said.

One girl suggested, "We need to tell when," so the teacher added the year 1492 to the end of the first sentence.

Another student said, "Columbus didn't sail alone. The book said there were 90 sailors."

The teacher revised the sentence to read "Columbus and 90 sailors sailed across the ocean in 1492." She continued with the revisions, numbered each of the eight sentences, and then assigned each student a number that corresponded to one of the sentences. "Now write a final draft of the one sentence you've been assigned and draw an illustration of it."

Sample Pages of a Class Book by First Graders

Sample Pages of a Class Book by Fourth Graders

Figure 6.1 **Examples from Three Class Books**

Sample Pages of a Class Book by Fifth Graders

Students who received number nine were assigned to create a cover with a title. Since each student wrote only one sentence, the teacher was able to move quickly around the room to help students edit while others were busy illustrating. When they were finished, she gathered the pages in order, beginning with the cover page. With a class of 24 students, three copies of the same book were produced. Mrs. Rothstein then selected one of the books to read. Finally, she held up the original picture book and said, "Jean Marzollo told the story her way, and we told it ours. It's the same story, but she used her voice and we used ours."

Struggling Learners/ RtI

Try This for Teaching   **Class Book**

- Brainstorm ideas or present a pattern book as a model.
- Assign each student to write one or two sentences, rather than the whole story.
- Help individual students revise content and mechanics while class members write and illustrate.
- Gather pages in order and read the final product to the class.
- Students complete illustrations at home or during teacher read aloud.
- One pattern for a class book can follow a song (for example, "The Twelve Days of Summer" could be patterned after "The Twelve Days of Christmas").

Variations for ELLs

- Write about a class activity like a field trip or an author visit.
- Create class books about topics in a content area (such as an ABC book about units in mathematics or science).
- Start with an open-ended question. Each page of the book is a different child's answer (for example, What is the best part about school? What is the most important thing you learned last year?).

Try This for Teaching   **Classroom Post Office**

- Distribute names of classmates and establish ground rules.
- Allow time for students to write notes.
- Deliver notes to a pocket chart, students' desks, cubbies, or another location that works in your classroom.
- Encourage students to respond to notes they have received before writing additional notes.

- Designate one student as the letter carrier for the day to deliver notes.
- The notes can require stamps (stickers) that are earned by following classroom rules.

(Pressley et al., 2003)

Variation for ELLs

- Make sure notes include three questions that the recipient can respond to.

Struggling Learners/ RtI

English Language Learners

Classroom Post Office.   Children have always passed notes in school. Maybe you can use that practice to your advantage (Pressley et al., 2003). When children write letters to the principal or to a famous author, it's important for them to edit drafts for spelling, punctuation, and appropriateness. However, personal notes to peers in a classroom are different. Peers are an informal audience. Because they know each other, they will not be critical when they see an occasional misspelled word. Note-writing provides an ideal setting in which children feel safe to write with fluency and voice. You may have to set some ground rules about not writing hurtful comments or insincere love notes. But generally children enjoy the opportunity to write notes to each other and do not abuse the privilege.

Use a pocket chart as the post office where children can get a name of a classmate and deliver a note. In this way, the teacher makes sure that names are distributed fairly and all the pockets are filled, leaving no one out. You can achieve the same goal by saying, "If someone delivers a note to your desk or cubby, you must write that person a reply before you write a note to someone else." The main thing is that students have an opportunity to write with voice, and their fluency is not bogged down by undue concern for correctness.

Summary

If students do not read fluently they do not comprehend completely.

Perhaps as you first read the above sentence you did not read it as fluently as you can if you read it again. The same is true for your students. Teaching fluency does not just deal with rate, accuracy, and expression. It is also helping students turn decoding strategies into automatic skills and providing motivation along with instruction. Oral reading allows for practice, performance, and also assessment in groups as well as individually. Avoid round robin reading and assist students to transition from oral to silent reading. Fluency is not just an issue in reading. It is important in both oral and written language. You can help students focus on sentence fluency and voice to improve the quality of their writing. As students become more fluent readers and writers, they become better meaning-makers. And, after all, that is what literacy is all about.

Self-Check

1. Describe the three aspects of fluency.

2. What are differences between skills and strategies?

3. What are some benefits of repeated oral reading in fluency instruction?

4. How can you motivate students to re-read material?

5. Explain some of the drawbacks to the traditional practice of round-robin reading.

6. List some questions you can ask your students during a writing conference focused on content and sentence fluency.

7. What do we mean by *voice* in writing?

8. How can you help students avoid plagiarism?

MyEducationLab™

Go to the Topic, Fluency, in the **MyEducationLab** (www.myeducationlab.com) for your course, where you can:

- Find learning outcomes for Fluency along with the national standards that connect to these outcomes.

- Complete Assignments and Activities that can help you more deeply understand the chapter content.

- Apply and practice your understanding of the core teaching skills identified in the chapter with the Building Teaching Skills and Dispositions learning units.

- Examine challenging situations and cases presented in the IRIS Center Resources.

- Check your comprehension on the content covered in the chapter by going to the Study Plan in the Book Resources for your text. Here you will be able to take a chapter quiz, receive feedback on your answers, and then access Review, Practice, and Enrichment activities to enhance your understanding of chapter content (optional).

- Visit **A+RISE** Standards2Strategy™, an innovative and interactive online resource that offers new teachers in grades K–12 just-in-time, research-based instructional strategies that meet the linguistic needs of ELLs as they learn content, differentiate instruction for all grades and abilities, and are aligned to Common Core Elementary Language Arts Standards (for the literacy strategies) and to English language proficiency standards in WIDA, Texas, California, and Florida.

chapter 7

Vocabulary

Chapter Outline

VOCABULARY AND READING
  Size
  Word Collections
  Guiding Principles
  Types of Words
  Instruction
VOCABULARY AND WRITING
  Word Choice
  Poetry
SUMMARY

In my preparation to become a teacher, I was told that for vocabulary instruction I just had to review the words that were identified in the teacher's manual for each story. That seemed easy enough. However, I quickly learned that I had to do more than that. Those who put the basal program together certainly didn't know the students I was teaching. I had to take charge of my vocabulary instruction. For example, one of the first stories I used from the basal took place in a large city. The author had written about walking through alleys and using tokens to ride the elevated train. My students lived in a small community and had little experience with big cities. Although the words *alley*, *token*, and *elevated train* didn't appear on the lists in the teacher's manual, I knew the students' understanding of the passage would be hindered if I didn't address them. So I showed them pictures of cities and we talked about current movies and TV shows that were set in cities. I drew diagrams on the board illustrating each word. These simple activities built or activated background knowledge that made the definitions of the words meaningful and memorable for my inexperienced students. As they read the story, these words that would have thrown up a speed bump didn't slow their understanding. As we discussed the story, it was obvious that these students understood because I didn't just follow the manual. Always remember that you are teaching students, not just words.

—Tim

In English roosters say "Cock-a-doodle-doo," but in the Czech Republic they say "Ki-ki-ri-ca." Cows say "Moo" in America, but in Holland they say "Booo." In the United States turkeys say "Gobble-gobble-gobble," but they say "Holderolderol" in Israel (Conrad, 1995). Roosters, cows, and turkeys really don't say those words, but people in different countries use different words to describe the sounds they hear animals make. **Words** are summary symbols with meanings agreed on by a society or a group. Because words are dynamic, the study of vocabulary is fascinating; however, it is not an end in and of itself. Students cannot understand what they are reading unless they know most of the words they encounter. That is why there is no better predictor of how well a student will comprehend text than his or her vocabulary knowledge (Anderson & Freebody, 1981; Armbruster, Lehr, & Osborn, 2001; Hairrell, Rupley, & Simmons, 2011; Nagy, 1988; National Reading Panel, 2000). We teach vocabulary because it contributes to comprehension. That is why vocabulary knowledge is included in the Common Core. Students must interpret words and phrases, including technical, connotative, and figurative meanings. They must analyze how specific word choices can be used to shape meaning and tone. But vocabulary is also emphasized in the standards for language. Vocabulary is not an element of reading alone; it is also important in writing.

Common Core State Standards

Vocabulary and Reading

Language can be received or expressed, and it can be oral or written. Using these ideas, we can describe the traditional **language arts** using the diagram shown in Figure 7.1. The oral, receptive language art is listening; the oral, expressive language art is speaking; the written, receptive is reading; and the written, expressive is writing (Baumann, & Kameenui, 1991).

Speaking/Listening

While receptive and expressive are useful terms that are widely accepted, they do not simply describe what we do with our thoughts. Both language modes are closely associated with generating thought and creating meaning. Many people think that when we listen or read, we passively receive meaning. But actually listeners and readers are active in creating meaning. They bring something to each text and each conversation. Similarly, some think that speaking and writing are merely expressions of thought. In reality, the acts of speaking and writing can be the creation of thought.

Viewing and presenting are also important aspects of the language arts in the context of technology and new literacies (Coiro, Knoble, Lankshear, & Leu, 2008), and the four basic language arts are essential in order to view and present. Children's vocabularies develop through rich language experiences in each of the language arts. You can help all children, including English language learners, increase the size of their vocabularies by collecting words and following some basic guiding principles when you teach them. Children can expand the repertoire of types of words they acquire and use through instruction.

New Literacies

Figure 7.1   Interrelatedness of the Language Arts

	Receptive	Expressive
Oral	Listening	Speaking
Written	Reading	Writing

Size

The size of each vocabulary will vary. Generally receptive vocabularies are larger than expressive; oral vocabularies are larger than written vocabularies. Although you can understand certain words spoken by others, you may not feel confident using those same words in your own speech. The same is true for written language: some words you can read, but you may not try to use them in your own writing (Baumann, & Kameenui, 1991; Graves, 1986; Nagy, 1988). Those acquiring a second language have similar experiences. English language learners understand much more than you may realize if you judge comprehension only on children's abilities to express themselves (Cummins, 2001).

Children develop listening and speaking vocabularies by experimenting with and responding to words. By the time they come to school, most students have already acquired more than 2,000 words in the context of their homes and communities, and some have a vocabulary of more than 25,000 words (Baumann, & Kameenui, 1991; Nagy, 1988). Some students will have smaller vocabularies than average, and others will have larger vocabularies. The difference in vocabulary size among children starting school is strongly influenced by such factors as the amount of print available at home, the value placed on literacy by caregivers, and the number and types of interactions children have with adults, siblings, and others (Blachowicz, 1985; Hart & Risley, 1995). Many children from middle-class homes develop the language that matches the expectations at most schools. Children who do not come from such home environments, including those who are learning English as a second language, also have established vocabularies, but they may not match as well with the language of school (August & Shanahan, 2006). You need to be aware of the strengths that children bring to school, including all vocabularies they have at their disposal. Instead of penalizing students because of their home backgrounds, which offer different language opportunities, you can build on whatever language background children possess and provide a rich environment for vocabulary acquisition in your classroom (Beck, McKeown, & Kucan, 2002; Peregoy & Boyle, 2008).

Of the 3,000 to 4,000 additional words children acquire each year, only one-tenth are taught in school (Anderson & Nagy, 1991). Children obviously acquire most words through informal means outside of school: by conversing with adults, being read to, and by reading a variety of texts—not just books but signs, bumper stickers, and print on the computer. Since these contexts provide so much vocabulary, some wonder if there is a need to focus on vocabulary at school (Beck, McKeown, & Kucan, 2002; Irwin, 1991). You should stress vocabulary and remember that your goal is not to teach children to memorize the 110,000 words in common use in English (Grabe, 2010). Rather your goal is to have students come to *own* some words so they can more easily acquire additional related words in indirect ways (Pearson & Johnson, 1978). At school, you are building a framework or skeleton onto which students can add related words wherever they are encountered. For example, after children have learned in school that a *submarine* is a craft that dives beneath the water, they may better understand related words they hear outside of school, such as *subterranean*, *substandard*, and *subway*. Children will not acquire as many words in their written or oral vocabularies outside of school if you do not engage them in ongoing vocabulary activities in school (Anderson & Nagy, 1991).

English language learners struggle with vocabulary more than any other aspect of reading (Graves & Watts-Taffe, 2002; Peregoy & Boyle, 2000). Because of the enormity of the task of helping children acquire so many words in a new language, many teachers feel overwhelmed and do not know where to begin. Start by enriching the literacy environment with lots of reading, discussing, and singing. Do not worry about all the words they need to know in the entire language, just begin with the words needed to understand

Struggling Learners/ RtI

English Language Learners

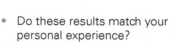

Try This for Professional Development   **Increase Affirmations**

According to Hart and Risley (2003), there is a huge difference in the number of words children hear in homes from various socioeconomic levels. In an hour children of poverty hear 72 percent fewer words that their more affluent peers. Children of poverty hear more than twice as many negative than positive comments, whereas children in homes of professionals hear six positive affirmations for each one negative comment.

- Do these results match your personal experience?
- How can you expose lower income students to more words?
- What can you do to increase the number of positive affirmations that all children hear?
- Think of a time when a teacher has complimented or ridiculed you. How did those comments affect you and your desire to learn?

the particular book or song at hand. In that context, do not limit yourself to just a few words—flood the children with vocabulary so they have a strong foundation on which to learn other words and to build comprehension (Sternberg, 1987).

Students learning English are not the only ones who need help with vocabulary. All children do. Despite this need, observations in classrooms show that explicit vocabulary instruction seldom occurs (Durkin, 1978–1979; Graves, 1986; Pressley, Wharton-McDonald, Mistretta-Hampston, & Echevarria, 1998). You can do much to help students develop their vocabularies by collecting words and explicitly teaching them following sound principles of vocabulary instruction.

Word Collections

One way to expand vocabularies is through word collections. One third-grade teacher told her students, "Some people like to collect bugs and keep them in a jar for a while to observe them more closely. But in our class, we're going to collect words." On a bulletin board, she had a large paper shaped like a jar where students could pin words they wanted to collect and examine. Some teachers use a word bank, a collection of words housed in individual student word notebooks or in recipe boxes with separate word cards. The most common way to organize a word collection is with a word wall.

A **word wall** is an alphabetical listing of selected words that is large enough for students to see from anywhere in the classroom (Allen, 1999; Cunningham & Allington, 2007). A photograph of a word wall can be found later in this chapter. Although some teachers like to use word walls to reinforce phonics generalizations and word families, many use them to teach sight words and word meanings. You can use bulletin boards, cabinet doors, or classroom walls to display words written on construction paper or cardstock. It does not really matter where the words are displayed, as long as the words are reviewed regularly and used often.

For many teachers, a permanent word wall is used to reinforce high frequency words—words that appear often in print the students read (Cunningham, 2008a). In the primary grades, these words may be among the first 300 on a high frequency word list (Fry, Kress, & Fountoukidis, 2000). In the intermediate grades, the words could come from farther down a high frequency word list. A website that contains lists of high frequency words is www.uen.org/k-2educator/word_lists.shtml. Another good source for high frequency words is *The Reading Teacher's Book of Lists* (Fry, Kress, & Fountoukidis, 2000).

Struggling Learners/ RtI

English Language Learners

Sample word wall.

English Language Learners

In addition to high frequency words, some teachers add to the word wall words from books students are reading or words that have been consistently misspelled in writing. The more connections students can make between the words on the word wall and authentic contexts, the better their comprehension will be. The word wall is a valuable tool for struggling learners because it provides a core set of words with which they are familiar.

Students are responsible for knowing each word that is added to the word wall. Tell your students to refer to the word wall if they are unsure of a word's spelling when they are writing. You also can reproduce the word wall on sheets of paper and display a copy on student desks for easier reference.

Along with a permanent word wall, some teachers create more specific, temporary collections. For example, word walls can be created to center on study in content areas—math, social studies, science, health, art, music, and PE. Another wall might focus on homographs and homophones. **Homographs** are words with different meanings that are spelled the same but pronounced differently. The word *c-o-n-t-e-n-t* can refer to the content of a movie or a feeling of contentment. *W-i-n-d* can be a breeze or a twisting motion. *T-e-a-r* can be a rip in your pants or a drop of water in the corner of your eye. **Homophones** are words with different meanings that are pronounced the same but spelled differently. Examples are *their*, *there*, and *they're*; *through* and *threw*; and *so* and *sew*. Homographs can be difficult for readers, and homophones are hard for writers.

Another category of words that can be difficult for readers, especially ELLs, are **multiple meaning words**, words that have different meanings in different contexts. An example is the word *run*, which changes meanings depending on the context: I can run to the store; there can be a run on the bank; a woman can have a run in her stocking. A word wall may feature **onomatopoeia**: words that sound like the noise they name—*buzz*, *thump*, and *snap*. Another may demonstrate **euphemisms**, words that soften harsh or distasteful language—*elderly* for *old*, or *sanitation engineer* for *garbage collector*. Figure 7.2 provides types of word walls you can consider using in your classroom.

Figure 7.2   Types of Words for Word Walls

High frequency	Appear often in print
Class books	Selected from a class book
Spelling	Studied in spelling
Content area	Used in math, social studies, science, etc.
Homographs	Different meanings, spelled the same, but pronounced differently
Homophones	Different meanings, pronounced the same, but spelled differently
Multiple meanings	Different meanings in different contexts
Onomatopoeia	Sound like the noise they name
Euphemisms	Soften harsh or distasteful language

| Try This for Teaching | **Word Wall Activities** |

- Introduce about five words each week in a meaningful context (from the spelling list or from a vocabulary lesson).
- Spell the words aloud with the students, clapping as they say each consonant and snapping fingers as they say each vowel.
- Play guessing games with the words on the wall, giving clues such as "I'm thinking of a word with one vowel that rhymes with pin" [in] or "I'm thinking of a word with two syllables and starts with o" [other].

(Herrell & Jordan, 2011)

Variations for ELLs

- Play guessing games with definitions ("I'm thinking of a word with two syllables that means *lots*" [many]).
- Hang words under letters on a clothesline strung across the room rather than posting them on a wall.
- Give students a word and ask them to make a sentence using it.

You can place these word walls in different areas of the classroom, or you can make words from content areas part of the permanent word wall. Use a color-coding scheme to show words from different subject areas; for example, write high frequency words on white cards, words from social studies on red cards, words from science on green cards, and so on. When you take down a temporary word wall, you can punch a hole in each word card and hang the words on a ring so students continue to have access to the them. This can be an effective support for those who have been identified through RtI processes as needing extra instruction.

Struggling Learners/ RtI

Guiding Principles

A variety of instructional strategies are available for teaching vocabulary, but you should be selective in the activities you use. Many teachers have gathered file cabinets full of word-find puzzles. Some computer programs have a vocabulary focus, but the quality varies. Rather than eclectically collecting from any source, you need to make your choices based on guiding principles and on knowledge of various types of vocabulary instruction (Marzano & Marzano, 1988; Stahl, 1986). Using the Four Es of vocabulary instruction— Experience, Environment, Exposure, and Engagement—you can make professional choices of instructional activities.

Experience.   Word understanding develops best when linked with life experiences. We want children to bridge from the known to the new in order for them to process words meaningfully. For example, when an American child reads the word *cricket*, he may think only of a bug and cannot understand why a crowd might be cheering at it—a race of large insets maybe? You can help by explaining, "Cricket in this book is like baseball, but it is different in these ways."

Environment.   Words are understood best in context, rather than in isolation. Children should be aware that the sentences, paragraphs, and text structure where the word is found can help them understand what the word means in a particular context. For example, a child may understand that *firm* could mean a solid surface (to step onto *firm*

English Language Learners

ground) or a company (a law *firm*). In an article about trees, *bark* will mean something very different than in a story about a dog.

Exposure. Multiple exposures to words are often necessary in order to own them. Students must have opportunities to interact with words in a variety of ways on a variety of occasions. An example is found in the way people refer to the first decade after the turn of the century. People are accustomed to the 1980s and 1990s, but how did they describe the years following 2000? Many people will not recognize the term *aughts*. It is not enough for you to acquaint students with the term—you need to repeat it and draw attention to it when students see it in literature, at school, or on the Internet. Students will then begin to notice the word on their own in conversations with adults or in dialogue on television. Finally, when referring to the decade 2000 to 2010, they began to use the word *aughts*.

Engagement. Instruction should be student-friendly and involving. For example, instead of just talking about key vocabulary words, students can dramatize or role-play. If the word is *saunter*, a student can wander across the room in a slow and meandering way. If the words are *pear* and *pair*, one student can pantomime eating a pear, while two others can stand together as a pair. Activities like this are fun, not only for those participating but also for those who are observing or perhaps guessing selected words (Herrell, 1998). This engagement is especially vital for English language learners (Jordan & Herrell, 2002).

**English Language
Learners**

As important as each guiding principle is in itself, they must be considered together. Context is helpful in many cases, but is limited in its usefulness when the surrounding words do not provide meaning or when a child's background knowledge does not match the expectations of the text (Beck, McKeown, & McCaslin, 1983; Irwin, 1991). Engagement is key to effective teaching, but children can be very engaged with practices that do not yield word understanding, such as unscrambling letters to identify words on a vocabulary list or writing those words using Morse Code.

Try This for Teaching **Vocabulary Role Play**

- Select key vocabulary words prior to reading a text.
- Write each word on a card.
- Read the text together, stopping when encountering each word.
- Pass the word card to a student who must act out the word. (For example, children could act out nouns like *statue* or *dog*; verbs like *winked* or *paraded*; and adjectives/adverbs like *leisurely* or *massive*).
- Re-read the text fluently after the words have been acted out.

(Herrell, 1998)

Variations for ELLs

- Show words to the students and ask what they know about the words.
- Sort the words into categories (such as by parts of speech or similar meanings).
- Arrange students into small groups with a set of five words for each. All groups prepare and present a skit using all their words.

Four Es Evaluation

- Observe vocabulary being taught in an elementary classroom.
- Use the Four Es (Experience, Environment, Exposure, and Engagement) to evaluate the effectiveness of the instructional activities observed.
- If the observed activities were effective, use the Four Es to explain why.

- If the activities were less than effective, consider how you could adapt them to be more effective.
- Think of other activities that could be used to teach the same vocabulary.

Types of Words

When children first come to school, a great deal of vocabulary instruction should focus on helping them match words in their listening/speaking vocabularies with their written language equivalents: that is, if children know what a cat is, you can help them see that the letters *c-a-t* represent that word in written language. This matching of known words in listening/speaking vocabularies with their unknown written equivalent occurs as a key part of vocabulary instruction for young children in primary grades. But this process is just the beginning. Along with known words, you must also use new words in vocabulary instruction, especially in intermediate grades (Graves, 1987). The Common Core stresses that students should be able to acquire and use a range of general, academic, and domain-specific words. This includes figurative language, word relationships, and nuances in word meanings.

Language Conventions

Common Core State Standards

When working with known words, you can clarify and enrich familiar meanings, or introduce new meanings (Armbruster, Lehr, & Osborn, 2001):

- Known Words

  - *Known Meanings.* Children clarify and enrich the meanings of known words. They know about *eating*, and that *gobbling, nibbling, munching,* and *devouring* are all related, but now they learn subtle distinctions among those words.

  - *New Meanings.* Children learn multiple meanings for words that are already known. Many children think of *bank* as a place where money is saved. But it can also refer to the *bank* of a river, a blood *bank*, or being able to *bank* or depend on someone.

When working with words that are new to students, you can either expand known meanings or introduce new concepts:

- New Words

  - *Known Meanings.* Children already understand a concept but learn a new word to represent it. They may know the concept of *family*, including *mom, dad, grandma, grandpa,* and *cousin*, but they may not know that *relatives, kin,* and *genealogy* are also words related to that concept.

  - *New Meanings.* When children first come to school, they may be unfamiliar with both the words and the concepts of *democracy, republic,* and *liberty*.

Word knowledge may be best understood as a continuum that ranges from unknown to acquainted to established understanding and ability to use (Armbruster, Lehr, & Osborne,

Try This for Teaching: **Fist to Five**

- When you come across a word orally or in text that may be new to yours students, ask them to show you with their fingers the level of their current understanding.

- A *fist* = I've never heard or seen the word before; *1* finger equals I know this is a word; *2* = I've heard or seen it, but don't know what it means; *3* = I recognize the word in context—It has something to do with...; *4* = I know it; *5* = I can use it in multiple contexts and language modes.

- Student familiarity with the words can help you decide how much attention to give to words.

- Reinforce the idea that word knowledge is represented by a continuum—no one can put up five fingers for every word.

(adapted from Armbruster, Lehr, & Osborn, 2001; Dale & O'Rourke, 1986)

Variations for ELLs

- If one student is very familiar with a word that is less well known to others, allow that student to explain it to the group.

- Encourage your students to initiate a fist to five rating when they come across a word they don't understand or they want to have clarified.

Struggling Learners/ RtI

English Language Learners

2001). A student may not have heard the word *paparazzi* before hearing reports of the marriage of Britain's Prince William and Kate Middleton. But when you explain that it is a word that describes intrusive reporters and photographers, the student becomes better acquainted with it. Over time he encounters the word as he reads reports of other famous people, and his understanding is better established. But it is not until he feels comfortable using the word as he speaks and writes that he has come to fully own the word. You need to meet children wherever they are on the continuum and move them along.

Another way to categorize types of words is to use the labels content, function, and academic. Content words carry the primary meaning of the text. Nouns, verbs, and adjectives are examples of content words. Function words hold ideas together in writing. Prepositions, articles, and conjunctions are some of the function words commonly found in text. **Academic words** can be content or function words (Johnson, 2009) that are related to school tasks and settings. Students will encounter and master many content and function words in causal, conversational, and social interactions yet struggle in school assignments and tests. Students may also be able to write in casual registers, such as texting or emailing, but find formal writing much more challenging. Those learning English acquire BICS capability long before CALP (Cummins, 2001; Krashen, 1996). Your classroom needs to be a place that supports CALP as well as BICS. That is why teaching academic words is important in helping students make this transition. Similarly, when students are identified through RtI processes as needing additional instruction, Johnson (2009) clarifies that the achievement gap is often a language gap. Many ELLs are missing the academic vocabulary. Lists of academic words can be found online (http://www.uefap .com/vocab/select/awl.htm) or in print (Johnson, 2009).

With so many different types of words, you may find it difficult to identify which of all the possible words deserves focus. Do you concentrate on storyline, or long words, or words that are highlighted in the text? One way to determine a manageable group of words is to ask yourself three questions that will automatically narrow your choices.

First, which will be the *hardest* words for the children in my group? If you are reading the informational book *The Children of Topaz* (Tunnell & Chilcoat, 1996) about a

Japanese-American internment camp during World War II, you will encounter words like *internment, ancestry, alien, Naturalization Act, Issei, Nisei, Executive Order, latrine, barracks,* and *flimsy.* You could focus on each of these words and many others as you read this text, but that may be too many to deal with in the time you have.

Shorten the list by asking a second question. Of these words, which are *essential* for students to understand this text? Although it would be nice for children to know the meanings of *ancestry, Naturalization Act,* and *latrine,* they are not as central to the main thrust of the book as some of the others. You might select *internment, Issei, Nisei, Executive Order, barracks,* and *flimsy,* because they are vital to understanding the experiences of the Japanese-Americans during this time. Even considering such words, you might wonder which can be dealt with briefly in the context of this particular book and which need to be considered in greater depth.

Select your vocabulary to teach by asking a third question—which of those words would be most *helpful* for students to know outside of this text? The words *Executive Order, barracks,* and *flimsy* are likely to be encountered in other settings, such as news reports, historical fiction, or conversation. Hard words are worth discussing briefly. Words that are considered to be essential to understanding a specific text are also worth discussing, but do not require much time. But words that will be found in many settings are the ones that will be most helpful to students; you need to spend the bulk of your instructional time with these words. The previous example involves reading informational text. But Cooper and Kiger (2005) suggest a similar strategy of funneling vocabulary selection in narrative text: consider which words are pivotal to understanding the storyline or plot and which of those students are most likely to encounter in other texts.

You will select many if not most of the words for your students to learn, but you should also give them opportunities to make their own choices and let them choose words they want to find out more about. **Word consciousness** refers to children's awareness of and attention to words. This word consciousness is an affective component of vocabulary instruction, as well as an effective way of engaging students. Disadvantaged students who are at high risk of school failure respond well to the element of choice and to opportunities to make personal connections to what they learn (Beck, McKeown, & Kucan, 2002; Graves & Watts-Taffe, 2002). In addition to the advantages of previewing text to find words, word consciousness is linked with listening and speaking because students are often drawn to words they have heard but do not yet understand.

Struggling Learners/
RtI

Try This for Teaching   **Word Scavenger Hunt**

- After you and/or your students have focused on some vocabulary words, increase word consciousness by having them look for use of those words in conversation and text.

- Encourage them to report back to the class when they have seen or heard the words.

- On a word wall or a poster, keep a tally of how often the words have been noticed—point out to students how often their vocabulary words are surfacing in everyday situations now that they are aware of them.

Variations for ELLs

- Keep a similar tally of how often children use the words in class or assignments.

- Ask a fellow teacher or the principal to use the words as they interact with the class or make school announcements, giving children additional opportunities to notice the words.

Instruction

After you have selected key vocabulary words, you can use strategies before, during, and after children's reading to teach them (Rupley, Logan, & Nichols, 1998–1999). Key word prediction is appropriate before reading; the five-step approach is useful during reading; and semantic mapping can be useful after reading and at other times as well.

Key Word Prediction.   Key word prediction (Nessel & Graham, 2007) is an activity that primes students for reading. Although this activity arouses curiosity and piques interest, the primary aim is to activate students' prior knowledge and improve comprehension (Blachowicz & Fisher, 2009). You should choose 7 to 12 words from a passage that students will read together as a class or in a small group. The words should relate to the topic of the passage but not give away the climax or the end of it.

Show the selected words to the students and encourage them to discuss the words and make predictions about how they will be used in the text. Next students preview the text, find the key words, and talk about how the words are used in context. If the meanings do not match students' predictions, clarify the words. When they do match, validate students' thinking. Then read the entire passage with the students, paying close attention to the key words.

One teacher used key word prediction by selecting the following words from the passage "A New Spin on Spider Silk" (*Time for Kids*, 1977): *bee, Frankenstein, jeans, Genghis Khan, genes, Kevlar, jet, pencil,* and *Natick, MA*. The teacher asked a group of sixth-graders to discuss in small groups how these nine words relate to each other and how they relate to spider silk. Groups then shared their thoughts about the meanings of the words in the passage. One student said, "This is going to be about monsters because of Frankenstein. It's going to say spiders are scary like monsters." Another said, "Genghis Khan was a warrior, but I don't get what that has to do with a jet airplane." Yet another student said, "I thought silk came from worms, not spiders."

After they had discussed the words, students surveyed the short passage, looking for the key words and highlighting them with sticky notes. They read the sentences surrounding the words and decided whether the meanings matched their predictions. The boy who mentioned Frankenstein found that the article was not about monsters, but that man can make fibers much like Dr. Frankenstein pieced together the monster. The girl who knew about Genghis Khan found that his soldiers were protected by clothing woven with spider silk, a substance so strong that a web the thickness of a pencil can stop a jet in midair. The girl who questioned the source of silk found out that a spider's web is made of a substance like silk. As students carefully read the entire text, this focus on words helped them in their understanding.

A form of key word prediction can also be used before writing. One teacher displayed a well-known art print, Winslow Homer's *Breezing Up*, showing some boys sailing. He asked his class of fifth-graders to offer words that came to mind as they viewed the painting. He listed these words on the board: *turquoise, gray, orange, sailing, evening, peaceful,* and *wind*. Drawing on these words, he asked the children to clarify their meanings by using them in sentences. For example, one girl said, "Turquoise is like Indian jewelry." Another said, "They are sailing to another land to look for buried treasure." The sentences were written on the board. With revision and editing, the following group poem resulted. Children individually wrote a final draft based on the rough draft on the board. As they did, the teacher emphasized the key words originally listed.

Dreaming with Homer

Turquoise water like Indian jewelry.
Gray sky like knitted shawl.
Orange boat like a slice of cheese.

Sailing to another land
in their minds.
Looking to find secret buried treasure
in their hearts.
Not alone on the sea, But alone
in their imaginations.

They sway between morning and evening,
quietly, peacefully.
Wind fills their sails,
and also their dreams.

Notice that both the reading and the writing examples invited a great deal of oral interaction. Children not only listened to the teacher speak, but they listened to each other. They also directed their comments to the group, not just to the teacher. This type of prediction strategy is helpful for struggling learners because the conversation provides support as they learn.

As you ask students to predict meanings of words, you can talk to them about how to use context to unlock the meanings of totally unknown words. In this way their guesses can be informed rather than haphazard. Students become actively involved in discovering word meanings by predicting instead of listening to the teacher provide them.

Speaking/Listening

Struggling Learners/
RtI

Five-Step Approach. The five-step approach (Pearson & Johnson, 1978) is useful during reading. The five steps are *see*, *discuss*, *use*, *define*, and *copy*. First, pause at a natural breaking point and return to a word in the text you have read, so students can *see* it. Next, draw on students' prior knowledge as they *discuss* what the word makes them think of or where they may have heard it before. Then encourage students to *use* the word orally in a variety of new sentences and agree on a *definition* of the word. Finally, students *copy* the word so they can look for it in any form as they continue to read.

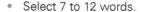 *Try This for Teaching*   **Key Word Prediction**

- Select 7 to 12 words.
- Discuss the words and have students make predictions about how they might relate to each other in the passage.
- Ask students to find the words and discuss them in context.
- Read the passage.

- Confirm predictions and clarify meanings.

(Nessel & Graham, 2007)

Variation for ELLs

- Use this strategy to initiate shared writing.

Try This for Teaching ## Contextual Redefinition

- Select one unknown word from a text that will help students' comprehension when they read.
- Create a sentence or select a sentence from the text for that word.
- Without showing students the sentence, show and pronounce the word in isolation. Invite students to tell what they think the word means and explain their rationale.
- Show students the word in the sentence. Ask them to guess the meaning of the word now presented in context.
- Explain the importance of context in determining word meaning.

- Have students check the dictionary meaning of the word if necessary.

(Readence, Bean, & Baldwin, 1998)

Variations for ELLs

- When working with ELLs, be sure the sentence context includes words that are known to them, perhaps including a synonym for the new word.
- Model thinking aloud and finding a rationale in the sentence for your guess.
- Encourage multiple students to share their guesses and rationales with each other—this affords an opportunity for students to listen to and learn from peers.

Try This for Teaching ## RIVET

- Choose five or six words that are key to understanding a text. Some words should appear at the beginning and some at the end of the text.
- Draw enough blank spaces on the board for each letter in the first word.
- Write the word on the board, writing one letter at a time and pausing to let children guess the complete word.
- After they identify the word, discuss its meaning and use it in a sentence.
- Repeat this process for the other words you selected.

- Tell students they should listen for the _ _ _ _ _ _ you read the story aloud.

(Cunningham, 2008b)

Variations for ELLs

- Have students guess the words as they are presented in Pictionary fashion.
- Let students shape the spelling of each word using clay, or for some words, have them mold the shape of the object the word identifies in clay.

A fifth-grade teacher, Angelica, used the five-step approach with a group of students who had read the first three chapters in *The Sign of the Beaver* (Speare, 1983) as part of their guided reading. When their teacher met with them, she read a passage aloud about one of the characters, Ben, who saw a rifle hanging on the wall. He admired it and touched the stock. He commented about how valuable the rifle was.

Angelica   Do you see these words—*stock*, *piece*, and *passel* [locating the words on the page]? Let's talk about what we already know about the first word—*stock*. Is it talking about stocks and bonds?

Student   No.

Angelica   Look closer at the paragraph. *Stock* refers to the rifle that Ben is touching. *Piece* is another word for the rifle.

Student	World peace?
Student	Like a time piece?
Angelica	Not exactly. It's not world peace or a time piece. Sometimes the word *piece* is used to talk about an item. So *piece* here refers to the rifle. But what is the *stock*?
Student	It must be a part of a gun.
Angelica	Yes, it's the wooden part. Can someone use stock or piece in a sentence?
Student	Dad polished the stock of his gun.
Student	We bought a new piece of furniture.
Angelica	What is a *passel*?
Student	It sounds like a parcel. Is it a package?
Angelica	Not exactly. A passel is a large collection of something. Like a herd of deer or a flock of geese.
Student	Like a school of fish.
Student	Or a pack of dogs.
Angelica	So, what would a passel of beaver be?
Student	A lot of beavers, and that's a lot of money.
Angelica	So let's define these words. In this story, *stock* is the wooden part of a gun, *piece* is another word for the gun, and *passel* is a collection of a lot of beavers. Let's read that paragraph one more time and see if it makes more sense. (One student reads the passage aloud.) Now copy these three words on your bookmark so you can remember what they look like. Let's watch for them in the coming chapters.

A form of this process can be used as you guide an individual student in his writing. One first-grader read part of an experience to her teacher: "We planted seeds and they will sprite up in the garden." The teacher pointed to the word *sprite* and said, "I'm glad you used a word besides grow, but sprite makes me think of something you drink." In their brief discussion, the teacher asked, "Are you thinking of the word *sprout*?" "Yes," the child replied, and she used the correct word as she repeated the sentence. The teacher defined the word in simple terms by explaining, "Sprout is when a seed starts to grow." The girl crossed out *sprite* and wrote *sprout* above it.

English Language
Learners

Try This for Teaching   **Five-Step Approach**

- Pause during reading.
- Return to a word already read and show it to the students.
- Discuss what students already know about the word.
- Use the word in sentences.
- Define the word.

- Have students copy the word.

(Pearson & Johnson, 1978)

Variations for ELLs

- Have students identify words they are unsure of.
- Add these words to a word wall.
- Act out the meanings of the words.

Semantic Mapping. An activity that is beneficial to students' vocabulary acquisition after reading is semantic mapping (Pearson & Johnson, 1978; Taba, 1967). Semantics refers to word meanings, so this activity focuses on mapping meanings of words. Begin by having students brainstorm many words related to the reading they have just completed. They may write the words individually, or you can write words students dictate. Then arrange the words into meaningful labeled categories. Finally, you can add words that may be new to the students, placing each word in the appropriate category.

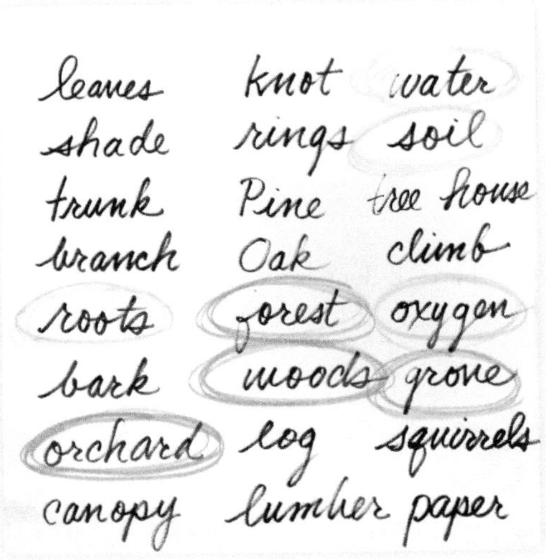

For example, after reading an article about trees, a fourth-grade teacher asked the students to write all the words they could think of related to trees in one minute. Students shared the words they had written, and the teacher wrote them on a chart. Some of the words were known by many students, such as *leaves, shade, roots,* and *bark.* Others were new to some, like *canopy, grove, knot,* and *rings,* so the teacher stopped to discuss them. When students heard words others had written, they thought of new words to add.

At this point, the teacher asked the students which words fit together. Students suggested one group that included *forest, orchard, woods,* and *grove,* with another that had *roots, water, soil,* and *oxygen.* The teacher circled the words with different colored markers (see Figure 7.3).

Next the teacher asked the students to give a label for the words in each group. "Where Trees Grow" and "Health of Trees" were the labels given for the groups mentioned. Other labels included "Products of Trees," "Types of Trees," and "Animals That Live in Trees." Finally, the teacher added some new words within the groups. Some of these new words were in the article, but were overlooked by most students. "Do you remember reading the word *demesne?* Find it on page 23. Read about that word and tell which group of words it goes with." The students placed it in the "Where Trees Grow" group because it tells about trees that grow on a well-manicured estate. Similarly, the teacher had students re-read another new word, *stomata.* Students discovered that it relates to how a tree breathes, so they put it into the "Health of Trees" category. The teacher then wrote the word *chicle* in the "Products of Trees" category and asked, "What product is *chicle* used to make?" Students read in the article about how the sap of some trees is used to make chewing gum. Figure 7.4 shows an example of a semantic map about trees.

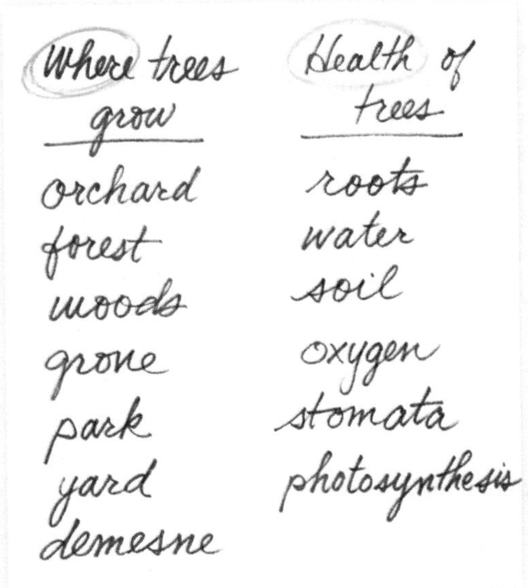

Semantic maps can be completed for many purposes. They may be used as an introduction to a unit in one of the content areas, or they can be used to develop vocabulary generally, maybe tying to a current event. If the map is made on chart paper, it can be posted in the classroom where you and your students can add words to it as you continue to study a topic.

Students can use the map to help them organize their writing about a topic. Each category could become a separate paragraph in the paper or report. Students could learn to create their own semantic maps to research a topic as they gather and organize

Figure 7.3

Semantic Mapping Chart of Related Words

Figure 7.4

Semantic Mapping with Labels and Additional Words

Try This for Teaching   **Semantic Mapping**

- Brainstorm and write down words related to the reading.
- Group the words into meaningful categories.
- Label each group of words.
- Add new words in appropriate categories.

(Pearson & Johnson, 1978; Taba, 1967)

Variations for ELLs

- Categorize the words on a graphic organizer.
- Provide a partially completed semantic map that requires students to write only some words and labels.

Try This for Teaching   **Reporting Back**

- After reading, students verbalize the steps they took to group words. (For example, they might say, "We wrote words about trees, we put them into groups, we added words from the book, we added labels for each group.")
- Have students work in pairs to practice explaining the steps using as many vocabulary words as they can.
- Each pair reports back, using many of the words. (For example, they might say, "we wrote words about trees like *roots*, *water*, *soil*, and *oxygen*, and

we put them into groups such as Where Trees Grow and Health of Trees.")

(Gibbons, 1993)

Variations for ELLs

- Use this activity across the content areas (for example, steps in using a computer, steps in completing an experiment, ways to complete an assignment).
- Encourage students to use as many vocabulary words as they can in their explanation.

information. You can also use semantic maps to assess student learning, either as a pre-assessment or as a post-unit exam. However you use them, semantic maps help students learn words in ways that follow the principles of vocabulary instruction.

Bridge from using vocabulary words in reading and writing to applying them in speaking and listening by having the students follow up any reading experience by discussing what they have read. Students learning English benefit from the support of being able to verbalize the steps they have gone through. For example, students can explain how the words were grouped.

Speaking/Listening

Vocabulary and Writing

Vocabulary development is not just about increasing the size of children's vocabularies by focusing on new and known words; it is also about helping children develop a love of language. Those with a passion for words are deliberate and selective about their own word choices as writers, and they recognize and appreciate when authors have made effective word choices, especially in poetry.

Word Choice

Word choice is selecting words that convey messages. Writers must choose words that are precise and powerful in order to make lasting impressions and create memorable images in the minds of others (Spandel & Stiggins, 1997).

Precise Language.   Precise writers are careful to choose the exact words they need to describe events or ideas. They make sure those words are accurate and that they clarify and enhance meaning. Precise words include specific nouns. For example, *Jamal* is usually a better word choice than *boy* or *nephew*. Precise words also include colorful verbs and adjectives. The sentence "The snake is on the ledge" is not as effective as "The deadly snake lurks on the ledge."

Word choice varies with the audience. **Formal language** is used in serious settings, and **informal language** is more appropriate when the tone is friendly. For example, when composing a business letter, you might write, "We respectfully request that you consider donating an item for auction. The money raised will be distributed to local charities." In an informal letter, you might communicate the same message with these words, "Hey, we sure need your help. We're trying to raise money for local charities with an auction. But we don't have anything to auction off unless you give us something people will want to buy." ELLs who acquire English in an informal setting may have difficulty making the transition to use more formal language. As children practice adapting their spoken language to various settings, they become more sensitive to the audience they are addressing in their writing.

Precise language also includes using appropriate language to avoid words that can be offensive in both speaking and writing. Most teachers have felt the discomfort of having students share writing that contains swear words, bathroom humor, or excessive violence. Similarly, it is awkward to hear children participate in a discussion and make racial slurs or sexist remarks. Once a middle school student shared his writing, which included swear words, and he thoroughly enjoyed the reaction of his peers. His teacher asked him to stop and sit down, saying, "If you want to write those words, keep it private. Some people here may not want to hear those words."

You can teach precise language as you come across examples of excellent word choice in books you are reading with students. Point out such words so your students can see the deliberate choices authors have made. However, precise language can be taught effectively in the context of authentic writing as well. Two effective strategies to help children recognize precise language in reading and writing are synonym stacking (adapted from Pearson & Johnson, 1978) and using "good" and "better" to compare examples of writing (National Urban Alliance, 2010).

English Language Learners

Synonym stacking.   A thesaurus groups together **synonyms**, words with similar meanings. Dictionaries often provide synonyms, as well as **antonyms**, words that mean the opposite. These resources, available in print or online, can be useful when teaching about precise language. Select a word from students' reading or writing and look the word up in a thesaurus. Consider the other words given and ask students to rank the words.

When a fifth-grade class used the words *pretty sunset* in a class story, the teacher encouraged them to look up the word *pretty* in a thesaurus. They found the words *attractive, beautiful, handsome, cute, gorgeous, good-looking, appealing, sweet,* and *lovely.* The teacher then asked each student to arrange the words from "least visually pleasing" to "most visually pleasing." Next, she had students work with partners to negotiate their rankings. Finally, the whole class settled on the following list: *pretty, cute, good-looking, sweet, lovely, appealing, attractive, handsome, beautiful, gorgeous.* The teacher went back to the word *pretty* in their story and

Try This for Teaching   Synonym Stacking

- Select a word from student writing.
- Look up the word in a thesaurus.
- Read a variety of options.
- Rank the words.
- Discuss which are appropriate in this context.
- Have students vote on the most precise word for the context.

(adapted from Pearson & Johnson, 1978)

Variations for ELLs

- Put the words on a visual illustration or analogy such as a thermometer or gas tank.
- Have one group use the thesaurus on the computer while another uses a book. Have a race between the two groups.
- Create a collection of precise words on chart paper or a word wall that can be used in future writing.

replaced it with each of the nine synonyms. The class discussed which words were and were not appropriate in the context. Students agreed that *cute*, *attractive*, and *handsome* were not appropriate words to describe a sunset. The students then voted on which word would make the writing more precise if they were editing the story. They settled on *gorgeous*.

Good and better.   This activity increases students' understanding of the effects of precise writing in both narrative and expository texts. Find an excellent model of precise writing in a book students are reading and create an ordinary rendering of the same sentence. For example, in the book *More Than Anything Else* (Bradby, 1995) you will find the sentence "My stomach rumbles, for we had no morning meal." You can rewrite this as the ordinary sentence "My stomach made noises because we skipped breakfast." Write both sentences on chart paper with the ordinary sentence shown first. Fold the paper so that only the ordinary sentence is shown. After you read it, say, "That's good, but it could be better." Then reveal the original, extraordinary sentence and say, "That's better!" Similar examples can be drawn from *Mufaro's Beautiful Daughters* (Steptoe, 1993) and *Charlotte's Web* (White, 2001).

When engaged in shared writing, one second-grade teacher asked, "What have we learned about wolves?" A student responded, "There used to be lots of wolves all over the place." Another student said, "There used to be lots more wolves than there are now." The teacher wrote both sentences on the board and said, "That's good, but it could be better. How can we make it better?" Some students suggested combining the sentences

Struggling Learners/ RtI

Try This for Teaching   Good and Better

- Find an excellent example of precise writing in a book.
- Create an ordinary rendering of that sentence.
- Write both sentences on chart paper, showing the ordinary sentence first.
- Say, "That's good, but it could be better."
- Reveal the original, extraordinary sentence.
- Say, "That's better!"

(National Urban Alliance, 2010)

Variations for ELLs

- Use sentences from student writing.
- After watching you, have students be the teachers by preparing an example for the class.
- Write multiple options and vote on which is preferred.
- Make revisions during shared writing using this activity.

using more specific words. The revised sentence was "The red wolf that used to number in the thousands roamed all over the southeastern United States." The teacher continued this process until they had written and revised a whole paragraph.

Powerful Language.   Skillful writers are careful to use precise words, but they also seek powerful words. Instead of using trite phrases, they use original words that convey feelings and movement. They make sure their words are vivid and impact readers' senses. For example, instead of writing "The rock felt rough like sandpaper," a powerful writer might choose a more original comparison like "The surface of the rock felt like my father's face before he shaves."

Children will see examples of powerful writing in literature. Help the students consider the opening line in *Tuck Everlasting* (Babbitt, 1975) in which the author describes a summer month as being at the top of a Ferris wheel just before it descends. Similarly, have them listen to the figurative language in the first few pages of *The Great Gilly Hopkins* (Paterson, 1978) in which a fence is described as a pen for the house and the front porch is described as its pot belly.

Powerful writing may also include dialogue that can reveal motives, feelings, and personality. It makes the reader feel present in the story instead of merely hearing about it secondhand. In the book *The Wednesday Wars* (Schmidt, 2007), Holling is a seventh-grader who becomes an actor in a community theater production of Shakespeare's *The Tempest*. Right after the performance, while still wearing his costume, Holling races to the local hardware store to get an autograph from his baseball hero. The author, Gary Schmidt, uses dialogue to show the cockiness of the baseball player and Holling's disappointment. When the boy asks for an autograph, the ballplayer asks why he is dressed up. He tells Holling he doesn't give autographs to boys who are dressed like girls. The baseball player tells the store owner that his time for signing is over and he tosses Holling's unsigned ball to the floor and walks away.

Like a melody that lingers with you after being performed, powerful language stays in your mind and heart. Perhaps one of the reasons nursery rhymes remain loved is the rhythmic cadence that is so common in them: "Jack, be nimble, Jack, be quick," "Hickory dickory dock, the mouse ran up the clock," "Hey diddle diddle, the cat and fiddle."

One of the beauties of the English language is that there are so many words that have similar meanings. This gives authors a lot of freedom and flexibility as they search for just the right word to convey their ideas. You can help your students understand that writers do not change words just for the sake of changing them—they select words purposefully. Figure 7.5 lists writing devices that can increase the power of language.

Speaking/Listening

Figure 7.5   Writing Devices for Powerful Language

Writing Device	Definition	Example
Alliteration	Repetition of the beginning consonant sound in words.	*Clever cats can climb.*
Assonance	Repetition of vowel sounds in words.	*Rain may* stop the *play today.*
Metaphor	Comparisons without using *like* or *as*.	His hands were *hammers* against the door.
Onomatopoeia	Words that sound like a noise.	The tail went *swish* as the bee *buzzed.*
Personification	Attributing human qualities to things.	The pansies *winked* from under the evergreens.
Simile	Comparisons using *like* or *as*.	Her eyes were *as* wide *as* two full moons.

Try This for Teaching   **Use Your Senses**

- Bring a variety of objects to your classroom.
- Have students take turns describing the objects using words related to their senses.
- Have the rest of the students guess the described objects.
- Encourage students to include sensory images in their writing.

Variations for ELLs

- Items could be contained in a "mystery box." If students cannot guess the object, show it and brainstorm effective clues that could have been given.
- As you read to or with your students, pause to discuss sensory phrases as you encounter them.
- Create a sensory word wall to collect such words and phrases for students to use in their own writing.

Try This for Professional Development   **Samples of Sensory Writing**

- As you read, notice when an author has used sensory images.
- Mark or copy these samples and save them in a file for future use.
- Look for samples in informational text and poetry as well as narrative.

- Expand your collection to include samples of powerful language beyond sensory images.
- Plan how you can share these samples as positive models for students.

You can help students recognize and use powerful language by incorporating these activities, such as "Use your senses" and "Throw out your first thought."

Use your senses.   Introduce multisensory activities by actually bringing in a variety of objects for students to touch without seeing them. Have students describe these objects using words related to their senses. Help them describe the objects in ways that others can guess the object by using their senses. Additionally, you can help them use their senses as they compose and revise during shared and guided writing. Ask questions such as "Could you add some sound words in your story?" or "Could you add some words about color or texture?" For example, in the picture book *Owl Moon*, Jane Yolen (1987) used all five senses in her writing. She described the feel of the cold (touch), the way the snow looked in the moonlight (sight), the smell and taste of the wool scarf, and the sound of the snow crunching as they walked.

Throw out your first thought.   A **cliché** is a trite or overused expression. You can help children avoid clichés by encouraging them to throw out their first thought. When students use a cliché in shared or guided writing, ask them to replace it with something more original. Validate improved independent writing by having students share their writing with others. If they do not want to share, you can read and praise their writing without identifying them. Students learn that the first thing that comes to their mind is often the first thing that comes to the minds of others, and they should avoid such words and phrases in their writing.

During a writing conference, a fourth-grader read what she had written: "It was as dark as night." The teacher said, "That's a description I've heard before. But it's not very original. Good writers take their first thought and throw it out. They use their second or third thought. That way they avoid sounding like everyone else." After the student made revisions, the teacher was pleased to read, "It was as dark as a secret." In another incident,

Struggling Learners/ RtI

Throw Out Your First Thought

- Identify a cliché during shared or guided writing ("It was as dark as night").
- Think of replacement words that are more original ("It was as dark as a secret").
- Share the more effective writing with others.

Variations for ELLs

- Reinforce the message of the lesson by having students put their hands to their heads as if they were grabbing a thought and throwing their arms out as if they were throwing it away.

- Create a word cemetery where students "bury" words like *said*, *good*, and *very*.
- On chart paper, write words that children brainstorm to replace worn-out words.
- ELLs can focus on cognates, words in their native language that may be close in meaning and pronunciation with words in English (such as *double*, *history*, and *title* in English and *doble*, *historia*, and *titulo* in Spanish).

sixth-grade students were describing their classroom, which had been partitioned from a larger room. One boy wrote, "Our room is a triangle." His teacher replied, "That's correct, but it's not very creative. Throw out that first thought—can you think of a new way to say that?" The teacher knew the boy understood when he wrote, "Our room is the shape of a half-eaten tuna fish sandwich." During student sharing time, the teacher asked him to share his effective writing with the class.

Poetry

Prose is the ordinary form of spoken or written language, without the structures of poetry or verse. **Poetry** is the art of vivid rhythmical and often melodic composition, written or spoken, to create beautiful, imaginative, or elevated thoughts. In simple terms, if prose is reconstituted frozen orange juice, poetry is the concentrate before the water is added. So poetry furnishes ideal examples for teaching word choice because it can be not only concise, but potent. Poems could be used daily with students. You can read a poem each day as part of your school opening or as students wait in a lunch line. Classics like Shel Silverstein's *Where the Sidewalk Ends* (1974) and Jack Prelutsky's *The New Kid on the Block* (1984) have introduced generations of children to poetry through their light, humorous verse. But they are not the only sources of poems for children. Some favorite books for children that contain both humorous and serious poetry are included in Figure 7.6.

Along with being read, poems can also be written. Some forms of poetry follow a traditional format like a couplet, a two-line verse that usually rhymes, or haiku, a three-line poem usually involving nature with five syllables in the first line, seven in the second, and five in the third. Other types of poems are less traditional. You can make a poem out of a list of what is under your bed; a definition of what is meaningful to you, like friendship; or a catalogue of your favorite things. You can write in free verse, which is not bound by traditional rhyme, form, or punctuation. Another creative format can be a telephone number poem. The first line includes the number of words that matches the first number in your phone number, and so on.

One sixth-grade teacher assigned students to write couplets in the form of epitaphs at Halloween time. Each student received the name of a faculty member and wrote a rhyme using that name. They had to be respectful, and final drafts were written on cardboard headstones that were displayed in the hallway. Examples included "Here lie the remains of our Miss Youd, she died because her class was too loud," and "Mrs. Schofield's bones lie here; when you pass, please shed a tear."

Struggling Learners/ RtI

Figure 7.6 Favorite Poetry Books

Author	Title	Publisher
de Regniers	*Sing A Song of Popcorn*	Scholastic
Dotlich	*Over in the Pink House: New Jump Rope Rhymes*	Wordsong
Giovanni	*The Sun Is So Quiet*	Henry Holt
Hoberman	*You Read to Me, I'll Read to You: Very Short Stories to Read Together*	Little Brown
Lewis	*Please Bury Me in the Library*	Harcourt
Prelutsky	*The Random House Book of Poetry*	Random House
Siebert	*Tour America: A Journey Through Poems and Art*	Chronicle
Spooner	*A Moon in Your Lunch Box*	Henry Holt
Strickland & Strickland	*Families: Poems Celebrating the African American Experience*	Wordsong
Walton	*What to Do When a Bug Climbs in Your Mouth: And Other Poems to Drive You Buggy*	Lathrop, Lee, & Shepard

Try This for Teaching **Telephone Number Poem**

- Brainstorm words that have to do with an upcoming holiday, season of the year, or some other theme.
- Write a telephone number vertically.
- Write the number of words that match the number on each line. When 0 appears, turn it into a 10.
- Revise by replacing ordinary words with more powerful ones.
- Edit the poem.
- Have students copy a final draft. Older students can copy the entire poem, while younger students can copy one line each and compile books of the poem.

(Kemper, Nathan, Elsholz, & Sebranek, 2000)

Student Examples

4 Calm, breezy starry night,
3 Welcomes tired travelers
5 As they drift to sleep.
4 Gothic city slowly becomes
2 Moonlit sky.
3 Sun falls behind
3 Mist covered mountains.
—Josh

3 Midnight has come.
6 Slight breezes float through the sky.
4 Beautiful leaves reflect moonlight
4 Sparkling like shining fairies.
5 In the magical swirling sky
3 Stars glow softly.
1 Peace.
—Sadie

Variations for ELLs

- Have the numbers stand for syllables, instead of words.
- Invite students to illustrate their poem or line.
- Create a word bank of topic-related words from which students can draw (spring = flowers, baseball, sunshine).
- Students can write their own telephone number and write their own poem.
- Try using the numbers of zip codes, addresses, birthdates, or famous dates in history instead of phone numbers.
- Use a piece of art to inspire student thinking and writing.

Summary

Words are fascinating. Have you ever heard of someone being "worth his salt?" That's because ancient Romans valued salt for its flavor and its preservative qualities. They paid their soldiers a salt allowance. *Salary* comes from the same root. Did you know that *school* comes from the Greek word that means leisure, because only those who had leisure time could afford to study? Did you know that *girl* originally meant a chatterbox (Baker, 2003), and that *boy* meant a servant or a person of low birth? (Sarnoff & Ruffins, 1981). So whether you are a boy or a girl, if you are studying vocabulary in school, you are worth your salt!

Language is a vehicle of thought. Words are used to define ourselves and make sense of the world around us. Vocabulary development involves the size of children's vocabularies and the types of words they learn. Instruction can include word collections and should be governed by four guiding principles: experience, environment, exposure, and engagement. Word choice is essential as students learn to use language in precise and powerful ways. That is why the study of words cannot be overlooked. Poetry provides an ideal genre in which to examine vocabulary and word choice.

Self-Check

1. Which of the language arts are expressive and which are receptive?

2. Since children acquire most of their vocabulary from sources beyond classroom instruction, why should you focus on teaching vocabulary?

3. Considering the variety of activities to teach vocabulary and the limited time you have in school, what guiding principles will you use to inform your choices?

4. In selecting words for vocabulary instruction, teachers often overlook academic words. Why does academic language matter?

5. When is the best time to teach vocabulary during reading instruction?

6. When children are writing, how can you help them understand when their word choice should be formal rather than informal?

7. Describe several activities you could use to teach precise language in writing.

8. Describe several activities you could use to teach powerful language in writing.

MyEducationLab™

Go to the Topic, Vocabulary, in the **MyEducationLab** (www.myeducationlab.com) for your course, where you can:

- Find learning outcomes for Vocabulary along with the national standards that connect to these outcomes.

- Complete Assignments and Activities that can help you more deeply understand the chapter content.

- Apply and practice your understanding of the core teaching skills identified in the chapter with the Building Teaching Skills and Dispositions learning units.

- Examine challenging situations and cases presented in the IRIS Center Resources.

- Check your comprehension on the content covered in the chapter by going to the Study Plan in the Book

Resources for your text. Here you will be able to take a chapter quiz, receive feedback on your answers, and then access Review, Practice, and Enrichment activities to enhance your understanding of chapter content (optional).

- Visit **A+RISE**. Standards2Strategy™, an innovative and interactive online resource that offers new teachers in grades K–12 just-in-time, research-based instructional strategies that meet the linguistic needs of ELLs as they learn content, differentiate instruction for all grades and abilities, and are aligned to Common Core Elementary Language Arts Standards (for the literacy strategies) and to English language proficiency standards in WIDA, Texas, California, and Florida.

chapter **8**

Creating Meaning

Chapter Outline

**FOUNDATIONAL MEANING-
   MAKING ABILITIES**
**CREATING MEANING THROUGH
   READING**
   Reading Comprehension
      Strategies
   Multiple Strategies
**CREATING MEANING THROUGH
   WRITING**
   Ideas
   Organization
SUMMARY

After reading the Robert Frost poem "The Road Less Taken" with my sixth-graders, I asked several questions, including "Why was Robert Frost happy that he took the road less traveled?" Several students gave predicable responses, but then one girl surprised me by saying, "Mr. Wilcox, I don't think he was happy. I think he was sad he took the road less traveled." My first inclination was to correct her, but as we reexamined the poem, we realized that the author did not write about whether he was happy or not. "All he says is that his decision 'made all the difference,'" the girl said. "Maybe he wished he had traveled with everyone else."

I thought, "How did she think of that? How come I'd never thought of it? Could my other students learn to think as this girl did?" This sixth-grader really made me reconsider the poem and also the way I was teaching comprehension. Up to that point, I had always associated comprehension with asking students questions about what they had read. Although my questions motivated thinking and good discussion resulted, I realized I was primarily testing students' thinking. I needed to teach them how to think. I began trying to identify and teach comprehension strategies. The proverbial three Rs—reading, writing, and arithmetic—are incomplete if they are not accompanied by a fourth R—reasoning.

—Brad

A bank manager placed a humorous sign in view of all employees: "Think, but don't get any ideas." Although you may not say those same words, you might sometimes be sending a similar message to your students if you are not careful. The message that is needed is "Think! Get lots of ideas, and I'll show you how."

Comprehension may seem easy to define at first—understanding what we read. However, on closer examination comprehension is a complex meaning-making process that is influenced by an author, the reader, and the contexts surrounding both (Irwin, 1991; Sweet & Snow, 2003).

Comprehension is the principal goal of reading instruction, and the ability to compose meaningful text for others is the major goal of writing instruction. Tierney and Pearson (1983) wrote, "Reading and writing [are] essentially the same processes of meaning construction" (p. 568). They are both processes that require active participation by readers and writers. Readers must identify words and construct meaning as they read. Writers must have control over basic writing mechanics like letter and word formation, and then they must learn to "read like a writer" (Smith, 1983b, p. 558) as they compose meaning. Both readers and writers use appropriate skills and strategies before, during, and after reading and writing. In order to help children to do this, you need to recognize the underlying abilities that create the foundation for making meaning.

Foundational Meaning-Making Abilities

Language Conventions

Pressley (2002) outlined five basic word-level and prior knowledge abilities that children need in order to comprehend text while reading. These abilities can be expanded to provide a foundation for composing meaning in writing as well.

First, children need to have established decoding abilities to be proficient readers (Juel, 1988) and encoding abilities to be fluent writers (Heller, 1995). Although many teachers might not immediately think of these letter-level abilities as related to making meaning, comprehension is improved when children can easily decode words. Similarly, writers can express ideas more effectively when they can produce words easily and as they eventually learn conventions of print. This alphabetic principle—understanding letter-sound relationships—is a key to unlock the door into a comfortable room where authors and readers can meet and interact.

Second, children need to have a well-developed, automatic sight word vocabulary (LaBege & Samuels, 1974; Sweet & Snow, 2003). Just knowing that letters are related to sounds is not complete. Identifying and writing words as units makes both reading and writing more efficient. The alphabetic principle may provide the key, but having a large sight word vocabulary allows students to swing the door wide and move freely about the room. Until these processes are automatic, the door is heavy and cumbersome, making the interaction between author and reader more difficult.

Third, children need to know the meanings of many words (Beck, McKeown, & Kucan, 2002). Identifying letters and sight words is important, but meaning must be attached to the words. A child can decode the word *cat* by segmenting the sounds /k/ /a/ /t/. He can even learn to identify the three letters together as a sight word. But that knowledge must be linked to the concept of cat. Similarly, visitors to Hawaii can learn to decode the Hawaiian words they see on signs, like *mahalo*, and they may see some so frequently that they become sight words. But tourists usually do not know the meanings as Hawaiians know them (*mahalo* means "thank you"). Knowing word meanings allows readers and authors to be more than tourists in the room of their interaction.

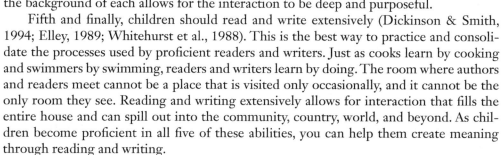

Try This for Professional Development

Many Ways to Teach Meaning Making

- When many educators think about teaching comprehension, they go quickly to strategies. The rest of this chapter is filled with strategies. But before you get to those, are there other ways to teach meaning-making?

- Look at the foundational meaning-making abilities. How have they helped you in your own reading?

- Reflect on the importance of decoding in making meaning.

- Consider the role of sight vocabulary in comprehension.

- How are vocabulary and comprehension related?

- How can you best help children build background knowledge?

- What is something you have learned (such as cooking, playing an instrument, sports)? How does the process you went through relate to literacy learning by children?

Fourth, children should relate their prior knowledge and experiences to what they read and write (Anderson & Pearson, 1984; Levin & Pressley, 1981). Some children can decode words, identify sight words, and even attach meaning to words, all without yet understanding certain texts. The child who decodes *cat*, knows it as a sight word, and may even be able to define it as a furry pet may still be confused when he reads that somebody is a "cool cat." Unless he has the prior knowledge related to this slang meaning of the word, he will struggle. No reader or author enters the shared room without bringing a lifetime of experiences. For the interaction to be more than a mere handshake, the reader and author must find common ground. Doing so may require one or both to cross the room to gain a different perspective. The experiences of each can enrich the other, and the background of each allows for the interaction to be deep and purposeful.

Fifth and finally, children should read and write extensively (Dickinson & Smith, 1994; Elley, 1989; Whitehurst et al., 1988). This is the best way to practice and consolidate the processes used by proficient readers and writers. Just as cooks learn by cooking and swimmers by swimming, readers and writers learn by doing. The room where authors and readers meet cannot be a place that is visited only occasionally, and it cannot be the only room they see. Reading and writing extensively allows for interaction that fills the entire house and can spill out into the community, country, world, and beyond. As children become proficient in all five of these abilities, you can help them create meaning through reading and writing.

Struggling Learners/ RtI

Creating Meaning through Reading

An expert is commonly viewed as someone who makes hard things look easy. What a successful basketball player does can look simple until you try it. What a dancer does looks easy until you try it. Similarly, you do things naturally as a competent reader that are difficult for a beginner. You can help children become better comprehenders by teaching them how and when to use specific reading comprehension strategies and a combination of them.

Reading Comprehension Strategies

Strategies are processes readers intentionally use that require attention and memory. "Reading strategies are deliberate, goal-directed attempts to control and modify the reader's efforts to decode text, understand words, and construct meanings of text" (Afflerbach, Pearson, & Paris, 2008, p. 368). When readers have turned word identification strategies into automatic skills, they have attention left over to build comprehension. Thus they can use new strategies like understanding cause-and-effect relationships, recognizing the sequence of events in a passage, and clarifying the meanings of unfamiliar words.

As an expert teacher, you must be able to articulate the skills and strategies you use until learners can make them second nature with practice. Comprehension strategies should be taught and modeled and then practiced and internalized by students. When children move from reliance on strategies to automatic use of skills as they read, they become expert readers. **Comprehension strategies** are "specific, learned procedures that foster active, competent, self-regulated, and intentional reading" (Trabasso & Bouchard, 2002, p. 177).

Durkin (1978–1979) reported that very little explicit comprehension instruction occurred in the many elementary classrooms where she observed. Instead, the teachers were involved with what Durkin referred to as "mentioning"; that is, those teachers brought up a topic and then assigned students to complete a worksheet on it. The worksheets that were originally intended to provide practice with a concept ended up being used for assessing what children knew and could do.

Durkin's report was followed by a decade of research on how to teach children to comprehend text (Pearson & Fielding, 1991). Unfortunately, results hauntingly similar to Durkin's were found almost 20 years later in another observational study (Pressley, Wharton-McDonald, Mistretta-Hampston, & Echevarria, 1998). Little change occurred in classroom practice. Too many teachers are still *mentioners* and *assigners* of comprehension rather than teachers of it. That is why strategies are emphasized in the Common Core State Standards (2011). You need to focus on how to teach children explicitly how to comprehend. The activities suggested throughout this chapter constitute a menu from which you can make wise selections depending on your own students' needs and experiences.

Many comprehension strategies can be taught effectively when reading and discussing with the whole class or with small groups or in mini-lessons following a gradual release of responsibility pattern, including teacher modeling, scaffolding, facilitating, and guiding student practice and participation (Kong & Pearson, 2003; Pearson & Duke, 2002). You will want to provide feedback to students as they take on greater responsibilities.

With beginners and ELLs you may act as the lead reader, relying on their listening and speaking abilities as you help them incorporate various strategies. Comprehension strategies are often divided into reader-based and text-based categories (Sweet & Snow, 2003), but it can also be helpful to place them into three different groups—organizational, inferential, and metacognitive, as shown in Figure 8.1.

Summarizing is an organizational strategy because a reader who is summarizing has to remember main points and overlook less important details. Predicting outcomes falls into the inferential category because the reader is using information that the author has provided to anticipate what might come next, which is information the author may or may not provide. Monitoring is a metacognitive strategy because a reader is thinking about his or her own thinking. Now consider each category in greater detail.

Organizational Strategies. Organizational strategies include the ability to identify the main ideas from a passage, summarize them, recognize the organizational structure of text, and recognize stance, both the author's and your own. You can use some simple but effective activities to help children apply the strategies.

Common Core State Standards

English Language Learners

Identifying Main Ideas.   Determining what is most important in text is identifying the **main idea**, and this can be very difficult for children, especially those who are learning English. As young children learn how to read, many are so focused on identifying individual words that they frequently fail to attend to the overall meaning. Identifying the main idea of a passage requires readers to attend to the organization of a text, as well as its word-level features. Children may also be confused about what is required of them, due to the number of activities that we ask students to do in the name of main idea instruction (Cunningham & Moore, 1986).

English Language
Learners

You can help children improve their ability to attend to the main ideas in a passage by stopping during your oral reading of a text and thinking aloud about what was most important in that section. You can also assist students by helping them to focus on the key events or concepts in the text. You may want to begin your instruction on main ideas by having students group words together into meaningful categories. For example, they would group *green*, *red*, and *blue* into a colors category, and they would group *pencils*, *paper*, and *glue* into a school supplies group. Later you can attend to main idea issues with larger pieces of text by asking students to group sentences that go together into a paragraph or having them identify a sentence that does not fit in a given paragraph.

Making key word notes (Nessel & Graham, 2007) is an activity that can aid comprehension when students write and talk about important words in text. Making key word notes stresses words that carry significant meaning in text. Figure 8.2 shows a sample chart that students can create before they read something at their instructional reading levels.

To replicate this chart, have students write the topic or title of the text they will read at the top of their paper. In preparation for the lesson, divide the text into four parts, with each part including at least several paragraphs. After students read the first section silently, have them write three or four words in the first section of their paper that they think will help them remember the most important information about that section. Then have pairs of students read their words to each other, explaining why they chose those

Categories	Strategies
Organizational	Identifying main ideas
	Summarizing
	Recognizing text structure
	Recognizing stance
Inferential	Predicting outcomes
	Drawing conclusions
	Making connections
	Creating mental images
	Asking/answering questions
Metacognitive	Monitoring
	Fixing up

Figure 8.1

Overview of
Comprehension
Strategies

Figure 8.2   **Key Word Notes**

Topic or Title _____
Section 1
Section 2
Section 3
Section 4
Main Idea

(Adapted from Nessel & Graham, 2007, p. 110)

words. They may change their choice of words at this point as they listen to each other and refer back to the text.

Then have the students read the next section of the text individually and again select key words. The same pairs of students again discuss their choices. Repeat this for the final two sections of the passage. After your students have read all four sections and have written key words for each, they can write individually about what they have learned in the larger fifth box.

Struggling Learners/ Rtl

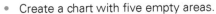

Try This for Teaching **Key Word Notes**

- Create a chart with five empty areas.
- Have students read one section of a text and write three key words in the first area.
- Repeat until the first four areas are filled.
- Direct students to write the main idea of the entire reading in the fifth area on their graphic organizers.

(Nessel & Graham, 2007)

Variations for ELLs

- Use a chart with both informational and narrative text.
- Alternate working as a small group or collaborating with a partner.
- Do a pass-along in which one student fills in one area and passes it to a neighbor who fills in the next area, and so on.

Try This for Teaching **Create a Title**

- Read a section of a text.
- Ask students to suggest a good title for that section.
- Have students generate titles.
- As a group select the title that best describes the main idea.

Variations for ELLs

- Use this activity with fables and create a moral instead of a title.
- List several titles and have the students select which one best fits a specific passage.

Try This for Teaching **Comprehension Process Motions**

- As you read a passage, hold one hand vertically and move it from right to left each time you finish a sentence that contains a detail.
- When you arrive at the main idea, hold the other hand horizontally over your vertical hand.
- Explain that as a tabletop is supported by legs, the main idea of a paragraph or text is supported by details.
- Continue to read and show with your hands how additional details fall under the main idea.

(Block, Parris, & Whiteley, 2008)

Variations for ELLs

- After you read a sentence to students, ask them if it is a table leg or a tabletop sentence. Encourage them to show you their answers with their hands.
- For similar comprehension motions related to other processes (inferring, drawing conclusions, and making predictions), refer to "CPMs: A Kinesthetic Comprehension Strategy" (Block, Parris, & Whiteley, 2008).

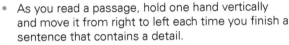

Summarizing.   The ability to **summarize** what is important in a text involves the related skills of determining what is important and organizing those ideas, events, or concepts into a coherent whole. Johnston (1983) claimed that summarizing is the most sensible way to measure comprehension because it requires individuals not only to attend to the most important features of a passage but to combine them.

Some use the terms *summarize* and *synthesize* as synonyms, but the former is actually a precursor for the latter. To summarize means to provide a cursory overview of the original author's meaning, whereas to **synthesize** means to combine that overview with information from a variety of sources to draw conclusions and create new insights. When readers are involved in this process, according to Wittrock (1981), they are engaged in generative learning.

One activity that can help children learn to summarize effectively is called read-talk-write (Nessel & Graham, 2007). After you select an appropriate text, pair your students and designate one as Student A, the other as Student B. Student A reads a portion of the text aloud to his partner. Student B then retells what she heard without looking at the text. Then both students write a one or two sentence summary of what they read and retold. At this point ask several students to read their summaries aloud to all students as examples of appropriate summaries. You can point out why the summaries are complete or explain what needs to be added to make the summaries more appropriate.

Speaking/Listening

Students then reverse roles for reading the next part of the text. Student B reads the section aloud to Student A, who then retells what he has heard. Both students write a summary. This sequence of reading, retelling, and writing continues until students have completed the entire passage. By the end of the activity, each student has produced two summaries, one oral and one written. This process frequently leads to deeper understanding. Students can also use their written summaries as a study guide to recall the content. Although this is a helpful activity to teach summarization and help students comprehend difficult text, do not overuse it. Students can burn out.

English Language Learners

Recognizing text structure.   The organization of text is called **text structure.** Knowing the structure of what one is reading helps understanding. For example, when reading a fable, a student expects animals to act like humans and watches for the moral at the end. The type of text students read determines how you need to help them go about trying to compose meaning. Three general types of text are emphasized in the Common Core: narrative, informational, and argumentative.

Common Core State Standards

Narrative.   A story, real or pretend, is called **narrative text.** Many young children come to school with a well-developed sense of narrative story structure (Blachowicz & Ogle, 2008;

| *Try This for Teaching* | **Read-Talk-Write** |

- Pair students with partners. A reads first section to B, who retells what she has heard to A.
- Have both students write a short summary.
- Share a few of the summaries and provide feedback about appropriate summaries.
- Repeat this process throughout the text.

(Nessel & Graham, 2007)

Variations for ELLs

- Have students write a summary in 10 words or less.
- Let children draw a picture before writing the summary.
- Assign partners to act out content for other students.

Try This for Teaching   **Twitter Talk**

- Introduce Tarzan. Demonstrate how Tarzan might tell his story: "Me Tarzan; plane crashed jungle; parents died; baby lived; animals raised baby."
- Introduce Jane. Demonstrate how she might tell the story: "What Tarzan is trying to tell you is that when he was a baby, he was traveling in an airplane with his parents. The plane crashed in the jungle and everyone died except for him. He survived in the jungle with the help of the wild animals."
- When people tweet, they often write like Tarzan. Challenge the class to retell a story by tweeting

(keeping the message to less than 140 characters).

- Have students go from that tweet to a more expanded form as if Jane were writing.

Variation for ELLs

- Have students read a passage and tweet a summary in oral form.

Try This for Teaching   **Best Book**

- Bring a stack of picture books into the classroom and explain that the students' job is to pick the best book.
- Tell students that since there is not time to read them all, they will have to summarize the books.
- Demonstrate summarizing by focusing on the setting, plot, and climax. Model this using one of the books.
- Have each child read one book and summarize it for a partner. The two of them decide which of their books is better.
- Group children into fours, and ask them to decide which of the two chosen books is best, based only on summaries.

- Reform into groups of eight. Continue the process until the class has settled on the best book of all.

Variations for ELLs

- Provide an authentic context by having your class of older students give some book suggestions to a kindergarten or first-grade teacher.
- Use a stopwatch, giving students a certain amount of time to summarize to be sure they are not retelling too many details of the story.
- Have children write summaries of stories they have written themselves.

Struggling Learners/ RtI

Meyer & Freedle, 1984). They have heard many stories read to them that feature story elements: characters, setting, problem, goal, events, climax, and resolution (Gordon & Braun, 1983). This is true of students who are learning English as well. Children who are experienced with stories are able to identify those that are and are not well formed. This understanding of text structure helps them build meaning as they read new stories (Reutzel, 1985).

One way to utilize and refine children's understanding of narrative text structure or teach those who do not yet have it is to use story maps. **Story maps** are visual representations of the important elements in simple stories that children read. They also help both students and teachers focus their questions and discussion on the most important parts (Pearson, 1985). In addition story maps provide a way for you to assess students' recall of important parts of a story (Johnston, 1983).

One way to use story maps is to have the whole class read an entire book in 30 minutes (Richardson, Morgan, & Fleener, 2008). One fifth-grade teacher bought two

Try This for Teaching   **Story Maps**

- Read the story.
- Construct in sequence a summary list of the setting, characters, problem, goal, major events, and resolution of the problem.
- Place the title or topic of the story at the top of the story map.
- Provide space to write the major elements of the story.
- Provide space to accommodate important details.

(Reutzel, 1985)

Variations for ELLs

- Draw dotted lines between details that are similar under each element.
- Use a chart to show major story elements.
- Try a cloze story map in which certain elements or details have been included and others are left out and must be identified and filled in by the students.

copies of the book *Knights of the Kitchen Table* (Scieszka, 1991), part of the Time Warp Trio series of books for beginning chapter book readers. This 64-page book is divided into 10 short chapters. The teacher took one of the books and stapled each chapter together as a separate unit. The other copy was used by the teacher for reference during the activity.

The teacher gave one chapter to each of 10 groups of students with the assignment to complete a story map. The groups recorded the setting information for their chapter—characters, place, and time—as well as the problems and goals they could identify and the major events that occurred in their chapter. Readers of the last chapter tried to write a resolution for the story, if they could. After each group had completed its portion of the story map, class members retold the story from beginning to end, chapter by chapter. Some ideas that were not clear in their chapter were revealed later. They also saw the progression of the story from the events before to the events following their particular chapters. Students were impressed that they read a whole book in only half an hour. Figure 8.3 shows the story map that was used with this activity.

Speaking/Listening

Informational. Although many children have a well-developed sense of story, most do not possess a corresponding sense of the structures commonly used with informational text. **Informational text**, sometimes called expository text, sets forth ideas or explains something. Such text is commonly organized in one of five ways: description, sequence,

Try This for Teaching   **A Book in 30 Minutes**

- Assign each group to read a different section of a book.
- Have groups complete a story map for their section.
- Have students retell their part of the story in correct sequence.

(Richardson, Morgan, & Fleener, 2008)

Variations for ELLs

- Introduce the process using a shorter text, such as a song with multiple verses.
- Have students reenact their parts using puppets.
- Complete story maps as a class before working in small groups.

Figure 8.3   Story Map—Read a Book in 30 Minutes

Knights of the Kitchen Table—Time Warp Trio Jon Scieszka (1991)	
Setting: Characters: Place:	Time:
Problem:	
Goal:	
Events:	
Resolution:	

comparison, cause and effect, or problem and solution (Meyer & Freedle, 1984). Children's inability to recognize text structure may be one factor in the difficulty many experience when creating meaning as they read in the content areas. Other reasons include the increased use of technical vocabulary and readers' unfamiliarity with the concepts in informational passages.

Graphic organizers provide a visual representation for what is presented in text, help children focus on what is important, and give them a way to summarize what key features they notice (Kintsch & Van Dijk, 1978; Tierney & Readence, 2004). Although graphic organizers can be used to represent any type of text, they are especially helpful with informational text. Sometimes graphic organizers are called *webs, charts, graphs, maps, clusters,* or *frames.*

Moving beyond graphic organizers, Hyerle (2004) devised Thinking Maps®, which are visual representations for eight distinct thinking processes (see Figure 8.4; Thinking Maps® is a registered trademark of Thinking Maps, Inc. and the term and images are used here with permission. Specific training is required before implementing Thinking Maps in the classroom. See www.thinkingmaps.com for more information.). The Circle Map defines in context, the Bubble Map describes, the Double-Bubble Map compares and contrasts, the Tree Map classifies, the Brace Map supports spatial reasoning, the Flow Map indicates sequences, the Multi-Flow

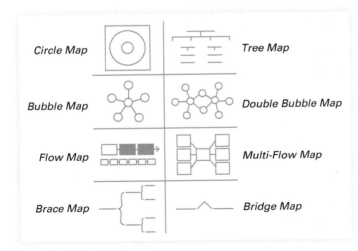

Figure 8.4

Thinking Maps
(www.thinkingmaps.
com, 2011)

Map shows cause-effect relationships, and the Bridge Map creates and explains analogies. When teachers in a school adopt and use Thinking Maps across all grade levels, the consistency is beneficial to students and teachers alike. Thinking Maps can be used in both primary and intermediate grades.

A first grade teacher in an urban school wanted to teach her students how to identify main ideas and details of a text they had read. After reading *Leon the Chameleon* (Watt, 2001), she re-read the story and created a Tree Map on chart paper with the help of her students, highlighting important information (see Figure 8.5).

After writing the title of the map, "Leon," at the top, she wrote the labels for each of the three branches of the map: "was," "turned," and "felt." After reading each page of the story, she stopped and asked students what words would fit on the map and on which branch. She made sure that only the key parts of the story were included.

After the map was completed, she modeled for the students how they could write simple sentences using words from the map. For example, she wrote, "Leon was a chameleon" and "Leon felt lonely." She then asked the students to write additional sentences using words from the Tree Map. By showing sample student sentences that were more complex, such as "Leon was different and felt embarrassed," she differentiated instruction. Students could feel success at multiple levels. Some students felt successful because these were some of the first complete sentences they had ever written. Others enjoyed the challenge of combining two ideas into one sentence. The teacher had each student write one sentence on a strip of paper that was posted on a bulletin board, together with an illustration. The students focused on what was most important in the text through use of a graphic organizer.

A sixth-grade teacher wanted his students to understand different types of clouds as they were studying weather. Before students began reading about clouds, he showed them how to create a five-branch Tree Map. Each student made a copy of the map the teacher had created on chart paper. As the students began to read a section of their science text, the teacher asked the class to pay attention to the various descriptions about clouds.

The teacher modeled for them what information to include on the map, and students completed their own maps, showing details about the major types of clouds described in the text. After they had read the entire section, the Tree Map was finished and the students had entered the most important information from the text about clouds (see Figure 8.6).

Argumentative. When authors express an opinion, debate a topic, or attempt to persuade, their writing is called **argumentative text**. This term does not mean that they are arguing or quarrelling, but rather that they are making a strong case for what they believe and are trying to convince their readers to agree with them or do what they want them to do. When dealing with this type of text, a reader's primary purpose is to evaluate critically the information that the author is presenting. The Common Core emphasizes identifying reasons authors give to support points in their text. Readers should be able to explain the evidence an author provides and make logical connections within the text to critique the author's effectiveness in reasoning. Although this can be done for narrative and informational text, it is especially suited for argumentative text.

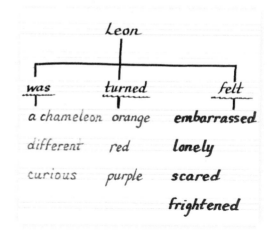

Figure 8.5

Tree Map for *Leon the Chameleon* (Watt, 2001)

Struggling Learners/ RtI

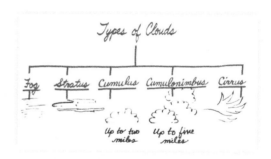

Figure 8.6

Tree Map for Types of Clouds

Try This for Teaching   **Argument Chart**

- Explain to students that every good argument has two parts: a claim and support.
- Read aloud a short persuasive text.
- Divide a chart into two columns and label one column "Claim" or "Assertion" and the other column "Support" or "Evidence."
- Ask students to identify one of the author's claims and write it on the chart.
- Ask students to identify support statements the author provides in the text. Write these on the chart.
- Highlight the support statements that are most convincing or effective.
- Have students verbally summarize the text using information from the chart.
- Have students work individually or in small groups to follow the same procedure with a new text.
- For older students, introduce a third part: opposing viewpoints or counterarguments. Although these may not be stated directly in the text, students can often express another side of the argument.

(Robb, 2002b)

Variations for ELLs

- Read a short text that expresses an opinion, like the classic *I Like You* (Warburg, 1990), in which the author provides one-sentence reasons explaining why we like people. Similarly, *The Important Book* (Brown, 1990) provides multiple reasons why something is important but then focuses on one main reason.
- Examine advertisements, both print and broadcast. Since these are primarily visual, there is less demand on student knowledge of traditional print literacy.
- Let students use the argument chart to organize their own claims and supporting points before speaking or writing about their opinions.
- Let students become familiar with the argument chart and then try using it with narrative and informational text as well as argumentation.

Common Core State Standards

Recognizing stance.   Authors of all text, whether they choose a narrative, informational, or argumentative structure, also choose a stance. The Common Core emphasizes being able to recognize an author's stance by understanding the writer's purpose: to inform, entertain, or persuade. Readers should be able to identify who is telling a story and to compare and contrast points of view. The Common Core also directs students to recognize how an author's purpose can be supported by various print and digital features (such as illustrations, graphs, and animations).

Readers also need to take a stance. Rosenblatt (2004) writes that **stance** "reflects the reader's purpose" (p. 1372). The reader needs to identify whether she is making a judgment, trying to carry away information, or enjoying the text. In addition, readers can take a sympathetic stance toward a fictional character or a politician they are reading about. They might read about the same people with a suspicious stance or a curious stance. Most people read editorials differently than they read textbooks, and websites differently than novels.

If you go into a grocery store without a list of items you need, it is easy to become distracted by displays, sale items, and free samples. You may walk out of the store with a cart full of groceries you did not need. If you can identify what you really want when you enter the store, you'll be able to reach your goal without distraction. The same is true of reading.

Struggling Learners/ RtI

Inferential Strategies.   Some comprehension strategies are organizational (identifying main ideas, summarizing, recognizing text structure and stance), whereas others involve drawing inferences to construct meaning. When authors write, they do not make everything perfectly clear. They expect readers to infer relationships among ideas in the

Try This for Teaching   **Read with Purpose**

- Before reading a text, describe for your students the author's purpose for writing the text and your purpose for reading it.

- Ask the students to fill in this blank: "When I finish reading, I should know _____," or "I should be able to do _____," or "I should be able to feel _____."

- After reading a portion of the text, pause and reflect with the students. Ask the students, "Are you achieving your purpose? Are you becoming distracted?"

- After completing the text ask, "Did you learn what you wanted to learn?"

(Robb, 2002b)

Variations for ELLs

- Look at graphs, illustrations, or charts with the students and ask if these features helped or hindered them.

- Introduce multiple accounts of the same event or several books on the same topic. Discuss whether the authors' purposes are similar.

- Introduce a narrative and an informational text about the same topic. Talk about how your stance when approaching the books may vary.

text using their own prior knowledge. Thus "any piece of information that is not explicitly stated in a text" is called an **inference** (McKoon & Ratliff, 1992, p. 440). Anderson and Pearson (1984) highlighted "the centrality of [inferences] to the overall process of comprehension" (p. 269), and Cunningham (1987) suggested that "making inferences is an integral part of all language comprehension" (p. 231). Pressley (2002) stressed the essential role of making inferences "to get the most out of text" (p. 17).

Beyond a basic definition, inferences are frequently tied to resolving causal relationships during reading (Pearson & Johnson, 1978). When readers predict outcomes before they read, they are using a form of "forward inferencing," and when they draw conclusions after reading, they are engaged in "backward inferencing" (pp. 111–113). Pressley (2002) listed many types of inferences readers make as they (1) combine their background

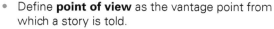

Try This for Teaching   **Point of View**

- Define **point of view** as the vantage point from which a story is told.

- Describe how different narrators might tell the same events in different ways and have students explain why.

- Provide various texts about the same event. For example, have students compare a colonist's view of the Boston Tea Party with the view of a British soldier, or they could compare a Native American's view of westward expansion with the view of a settler.

- Ask students to identify clues in the text that reveal the authors' stances.

(Lukens, 2006)

Variations for ELLs

- Use a creative option if you are unable to find texts treating the same subject from different points of view: Share one text and then have the class write about the same event from the position of one who has another point of view.

- Introduce books that tell a familiar story from different characters' points of view, such as *The True Story of the Three Little Pigs* (Scieszka, 1989) and *The Three Little Wolves and the Big Bad Pig* (Trivizas, 1997).

- Compare similar stories from different cultures, such as *Little Red Riding Hood* (Hyman, 1987) and *Lon Po Po* (Young, 1996).

knowledge and prior experiences with what the author presents in the text to make inferences, and (2) associate ideas or events in different parts of the text to make meaning.

You can show students how they make inferences as they read by asking simple questions (Richards & Anderson, 2003). Suppose you are reading the text *The Sweetest Fig* (Van Allsburg, 1993). After the main character, Monsieur Bibot, a dentist, is introduced on the first page, you can ask, "Where do you think the story takes place?" Some students may have enough French language knowledge and cultural background to recognize France or Paris as the setting. As the story progresses, Bibot mistreats his dog, Marcel, and is inconsiderate to a dental patient. When you ask students "What kind of a person is Bibot?" some may reply, "He's mean." Your follow-up question—"Did the author say that?"—will require students to infer relationships in the text as they explain how they know that Bibot is mean.

The five comprehension activities that follow involve drawing inferences in some way: predicting outcomes, drawing conclusions, making connections, creating mental images, and asking and answering questions. All five involve complex processes that you can help readers come to control as they compose meaning.

Predicting outcomes.   A **prediction** is a guess about what you think will happen in the future based on your knowledge of what has happened in the past. Sometimes teachers ask students to make predictions before they read, to heighten interest in reading a text or to focus readers' attention. Children also make predictions as they focus on what is important in text. Making predictions can help readers work through the text in purposeful, self-directed ways. You can ask students to predict what they think will happen next in a story that you read aloud to them. You'll notice that although many children are eager to offer their predictions, some do so with little thought of the text itself. Random predictions can easily lead away from the focus you want. Be sure predictions made in class discussions are not wild guesses with no supporting evidence.

Speaking/Listening

To keep students' attention on the text, you can model for them how the information you use to make predictions is logically tied to the text. For example, before you read the book *Teammates* (Golenbock, 1990) to intermediate grade students, you could tell them some of what you already know about that term. For example, you could say that the story is likely to be about sports and about people on the same team who play the sport together. When you show them the cover of the book, you can talk about the baseball uniforms the players are wearing, and you might also want to read to them the names of the players whose autographs are on the cover—those of Jackie Robinson and "Pee Wee" Reese. Children will notice that one teammate is white and the other is African American. You could briefly discuss the implications of these racial differences prior to reading the book and have the students make appropriate predictions about how these two will become teammates and what will happen to them. Such modeling is especially important for second language learners. You can also apply this method in small group settings with those who have been identified in RtI assessments as strugglers.

English Language
Learners

Drawing conclusions.   A **conclusion** is a decision that something is true, which you make after you have thought about it carefully and have considered relevant facts. The ability to draw conclusions is an extension of inferring causal relationships in text. When a reader can explain what caused an event to occur and what happened as a result, that reader is making a conclusion. Frequently the ability to draw conclusions in text requires the reader to combine information across several sentences in order to understand.

One of the Thinking Maps, the Multi-Flow Map, is a visual representation that can clearly highlight causal relationships, allowing readers to draw conclusions. In

> ### *Try This for Teaching*   **Modeling Predictions**
>
> - Choose words that describe a key concept in the text you are going to read (*friendship, prejudice, discrimination*).
> - Think aloud about possible ways the word could apply to what might happen.
> - Invite students to make predictions based on additional words or illustration clues.
>
> #### Variations for ELLs
>
> - Write the key words and hide them under students' chairs or around the room. Stress that they are easier to find with clues. Predictions must be based on clues.
>
> - Students can feel objects hidden in a mystery bag or box related to the reading, and they can predict based on the objects.
> - One benefit of making predictions is to tap into students' prior knowledge and then build bridges between the known and the new. Share personal experiences related to the reading.

the book *Officer Buckle and Gloria* (Rathmann, 1995), Officer Buckle is a police officer who presents safety rules at school assemblies. Although his presentations had been typically boring for most of his audience, they became much more lively when Gloria, a talented police dog, did things behind his back. A key event in the story was that children started liking Officer Buckle's safety speeches. A Multi-Flow Map shows the causes for children enjoying the presentations. Readers can conclude (1) that students liked the speeches because Gloria acted out what Officer Buckle was saying, and (2) that the children knew that Officer Buckle was unaware of what Gloria was doing behind his back. Two results followed from this event. Readers can conclude (1) that children wrote letters praising Officer Buckle and Gloria, and (2) that Officer Buckle and Gloria received many invitations to make safety presentations because children liked the assemblies so much. As students complete the Multi-Flow Map, they improve their ability to identify cause-and-effect relationships and draw conclusions, increasing their understanding of the text.

Struggling Learners/ RtI

Making connections.   One of the most common comprehension strategies taught in classrooms is asking students to make connections. Children make **connections** when they relate two associated ideas or concepts (Keene & Zimmermann, 2007). Readers often make connections outside the text as well as within.

Connections outside text. Keene and Zimmerman (2007) stressed three connections that readers make outside the text as they create meaning—text-to-self, text-to-world, and text-to-text connections. Text-to-self connections require students to relate what they are reading to their own life experiences ("That reminds me of a time when I was sad"). Text-to-world connections involve knowledge of information beyond personal experience ("That's just like what happened to Columbus"). In their treatment of text-to-text connections, Keene and Zimmerman asked students to think of another book they had read in the past that related to the one they were reading at the time ("The same thing happened in *The Story of Ruby Bridges*" by Robert Coles). This type of inference is closely related to the concept of intertextuality (Lenski, 1998). **Intertextuality** refers to understanding relationships that exist between different texts. The Common Core encourages students to make comparisons and contrasts across characters in familiar

Common Core State Standards

Try This for Teaching   **Reading Detectives**

- Explain what a detective is and how he or she looks for clues, sometimes using a magnifying glass, and records them in a notebook.
- Tell students that they will be "reading detectives" to find clues in the text to help them draw a conclusion.
- Read a projected text together and direct students' attention to important clues by pointing with a magnifying glass and having them make a note of these clues.
- Have students use their list of clues to draw conclusions to answer questions such as who, what, when, where, why, and how.

Variations for ELLs

- Use this activity with both narrative and informational text.
- Ask if students are familiar with the board game Clue. If so, use it as a model for drawing conclusions. If not, introduce them to the game.
- Discuss why some conclusions will be easier to draw than others.

stories, variations of the same story, different books by the same author, and texts in the same genre.

When teachers ask children to make three common connections between texts, they frequently hear comments that do not clearly relate to the texts they are reading. For example, when a cat is mentioned in a story, a student might say something like "I have a cat. Its name is Whiskers. It is black with white paws and has a long tail." Although this child has made a text-to-self connection, such a relationship may make little difference in the student's ability to understand the passage he is reading because the connections are superficial and are not related to the essential elements of the text. Making connections can enhance understanding, but the benefit depends on the depth of those connections. Make a distinction between appropriate and distracting connections using the "so what?" and "aha!" terms that Pearson and Johnson (1978) used originally to help children identify main ideas.

The Spider and the Fly (DiTerlizzi, 2002) is the classic poem about an innocent fly being coaxed into the web by the flattering words of a deceiving spider. Write connections on sticky notes and place them on the board in one of the three columns that correspond to the appropriate connection: self, world, and text. Read each connection and classify it as a "so what?" or an "aha!" connection, talking about characteristics of both types. Then invite a few connections from students. If a student says, "I saw a spider yesterday in my house," that could be classified as a "so what?" text-to-self connection because the comment does not provide information about spiders. Another child might say, "My big brother's friends are always trying to get him to do bad things." This would be an "aha!" text-to-self connection because the child is making an association with the theme of the book. Another child might say, "I know that flies lay lots of eggs," which could be classified as a "so what?" text-to-world connection. When a child says, "Some girls think they have to look like pictures in a magazine, just like the fly in the book was worried about her looks," she has made an "aha!" text-to-world connection.

To engage all students, have them write their connections on sticky notes and ask them to place each on the chart in the corresponding column. Read one of the connections, make sure it was placed in the correct category, and then ask other students to confirm the placements.

Struggling Learners/ RtI

Try This for Teaching   Venn Diagram

- Introduce the Venn diagram of overlapping circles on which students can record similarities between the two items in the shared area and differences on two outer edges.
- Read two books on a similar topic, such as *Elephants of Africa* (Gibbons, 2010b) and *Endangered Rhinoceroses* (Kalman, 2004). Label the two things being compared and contrasted in each circle (for example, elephants in one and rhinoceroses in the other).
- Record together at least three similar facts in the overlapping areas between the two labels.
- Record together at least three different facts about each label in the outer edges.
- Summarize similarities and differences based on information in the Venn diagram.

Variations for ELLs

- Complete a Venn diagram comparing two books on the same subject, recording how they were similar to and different from one another. For example, have students read *Crocodiles and Alligators* (Simon, 2001) and *Alligators and Crocodiles* (Gibbons, 2010a). Along with learning about alligators and crocodiles, students identify similarities and differences in authors' presentations of the same topic.
- Using information from the Venn diagram, students can write about what they have compared and contrasted.
- Try comparing and contrasting four items with elongated ovals that overlap like a plus sign. Similarities are recorded at the intersection of the two ovals.

Try This for Teaching   "So What?" and "Aha!" Connections

- Model ways of making connections, both during and after reading.
- Write your connections on sticky notes and categorize them into "self," "world," and "text" columns.
- Invite students to do the same.
- Divide connections in each category into "so what?" and "aha!" groups.
- Discuss the importance of "aha!" connections.

(Pearson & Johnson, 1978)

Variations for ELLs

- Model how to turn a "so what?" connection into an "aha!" connection.
- Allow students to make outrageous "so what?" connections for clear contrasts.
- Consider using other words for "so what?" You might use "interesting" or "good to know" instead of "so what?" For "aha!" you might substitute "important" or "great to know."

Connections within text. Although discussions of a text can be enriched and comprehension enhanced through reference to other related texts, many important text-to-text connections should also be made within text. Making connections within text by combining information from one part of a text with ideas from another will lead to deeper understanding. Although some within-text relationships are relatively easy to recognize, others are not—especially for children. Teaching ELLs about such within-text connections can lead to improved comprehension because all the information they need to be successful is at their fingertips, and they do not have to depend on previous reading or life experiences.

English Language Learners

One way to help children make within-text connections is to teach them about anaphoric relationships (Irwin, 1991). **Anaphora** (uh-NAH-for-uh) are words that serve as substitutes for other words in text. Examples are shown in this brief passage:

John went to the store. While <u>he</u> was <u>there</u>, <u>he</u> bought an apple, a peach, and a banana. The <u>fruit</u> tasted good.

A B C
Language Conventions

In this example the underlined words are examples of anaphora because they replace other words. Instead of repeating the name John multiple times, the author wisely chose to use the pronoun *he*. Two of the examples of anaphora are pronouns (*he* and *there*). However, not all anaphoric relationships are pronouns. The noun *fruit* replaced the three other nouns that named specific fruits. Other types of words can also serve as anaphora. For example, you might say, "Hailey is dependable. <u>So is</u> Jenn." You might read in text "<u>These</u> were the major causes of the Vietnam War" at the end of a long chapter. In such cases you need to resolve anaphoric relationships across many pages in order to understand what the author is trying to say. Figure 8.7 gives more examples of types of anaphoric relationships.

Children can be taught to make arrow and bridge connections. Arrow connections help children practice making within-text associations. You can use almost any book with connected text because authors nearly always use anaphoric relationships when they write. The book *Golem* (Wisniewski, 1996), a picture book for older children, is about the persecution of the Jewish people of Prague in the 1500s. After reading the entire book to students, you can return to it with the purpose of identifying anaphoric relationships. You can give students short excerpts from the book with strategic words italicized. Ask them to draw arrows indicating anaphoric relationships.

For example, if you underline the words *he* and *the rabbi*, students can connect them to *Rabbi Loew* with arrows. Students could draw an arrow between the words *Such a creature* and *Golem*, showing they are connected. Sometimes readers need to combine information presented on several pages to resolve anaphoric relationships. For example, understanding that Golem was created as a possible heavenly answer to protect the Jews of Prague is not possible without making connections across various parts of the book. Students could draw an arrow off the pages to show these connections.

Figure 8.7   **Types of Anaphoric Relationships**

Anaphora Type	Examples
Pronouns	Kerrie has a friend named Steve. *She* picks *him* up on the way to school. *They* ride home together, too.
Pronouns Showing Location	The team climbed to the top of Mt. Everest. Only a few people have been *there*.
Nouns	The students scheduled a meeting, but only a *few* attended. *Several* went to the beach. *Others* attended a dance. *Only the most serious* went to the meeting.
Number-related	Audrianne and James entered the building. The *former* is tall and slender. The *latter* is short and squatty. The *two* make an interesting pair.
Category and Example	The dog barked a lot. The *animal* must have seen a prowler.
Action	Someone was pounding on the door. *This* startled Tenielle.
Predicate Adjective	Hailey is dependable. *So is* Jenn.
Proverbs	Heather went to school. *So did* Eliza.

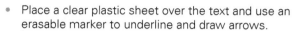

Try This for Teaching **Arrow Connections**

- Read the text, then present excerpts with example words highlighted.
- Model for students how to connect at least two words.
- Have students make connections by drawing arrows.

Variations for ELLs

- Place a clear plastic sheet over the text and use an erasable marker to underline and draw arrows.
- Draw boxes above the underlined words and have students write the related words in them.

Arrow connections are usually found across just a few sentences or paragraphs. However, authors often require readers to make connections that bridge larger sections of text—from the end of the text back to the beginning or from one chapter to a previous chapter. These bridge connections can be especially challenging if the book is being read over a longer period rather than in one sitting.

As practice in making within-text connections that go beyond a few paragraphs, have children use sticky notes as markers. In *The Sweetest Fig* (Van Allsburg, 1993), a woman gives Bibot the dentist two sweet figs as payment for pulling a tooth, and says that they are exceptional because they can make dreams come true. Nine pages later, after a series of unbelievable events, Bibot came to the realization that the woman who gave him the figs had not exaggerated. At this point, have students mark the words on this page with a sticky note. Then encourage them to go back and remind themselves of what the old woman had originally said. Tell them to put a sticky note on that page so they can refer to it later. The two sticky notes form the ends of a bridge that spans many pages and helps them comprehend the rest of the story.

Struggling Learners/ RtI

Creating mental images.   Most students have experienced the disappointment of seeing a movie made from a favorite book. They realize that the images in the movie were not the same as those created in their own minds as they read. They may not have consciously realized they were creating pictures in their minds as they read, but their disappointment in the movie was evidence that they had. When readers generate **mental imagery**, they create mental representations of physical objects or events that are not present (Gambrell & Koskinen, 2002).

Try This for Teaching **Bridge Connections**

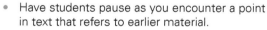

- Have students pause as you encounter a point in text that refers to earlier material.
- Mark the place with a sticky note.
- Go back through the pages until you find the referenced material.
- Mark it with a sticky note as well.
- Explain how the two sticky notes are like the ends of a bridge that spans many pages.

Variations for ELLs

- If you make several bridge connections in the same book, use different colored sticky notes for each connection.
- Write the page numbers of the related events on the sticky notes.

Teachers have long recognized the importance of using pictures, models, cultural artifacts, and video clips to facilitate comprehension. These instructional aids make it easy for students to visualize what they are reading. Proficient readers visualize without such prompts. Some use the term *visualization* instead of *mental imagery* because of the common use of the visual sense to teach children. Teachers frequently advise their students to go to the movies in their minds as they read. So when students read about a trip to the beach, each student may have a different mental picture related to a previous trip to a beach.

All five senses can be used in creating mental images. For example, when students read about a tree, they may "feel" the bark in their minds. Similarly, they may "smell" a buttery aroma in their minds when they read about going to the movies; they may "hear" the marching band playing patriotic music when they read about an Independence Day parade; and they may "taste" the cotton candy when they read about going to the fair.

Some have suggested that reading is comprised of both verbal and nonverbal imaging processes (Wittrock, 1986). In this dual coding theory, readers simultaneously use word identification and nonverbal processes to make sense of text. Sadoski and Paivio (2004) described this process with the sentence "The batter singled to center in the first." As readers begin to process the initial words in this sentence, they may use additional nonverbal information to clarify and expand their understanding. Some may "hear" the crack of the bat above the "roar" of the crowd. They may also "see" a line drive over second base. Others may "smell" hot dogs. As they create a variety of mental images while reading the words, their understanding may be expanded and deepened.

Readers' prior knowledge is often activated when they are encouraged to create a mental image of what they read. By creating mental images, readers can more easily draw inferences and make connections between the text and their prior knowledge and experience. Those who form mental images make better predictions and improve their recall of what they read. They also ask questions more directly related to what they are reading (Gambrell & Jawitz, 1993; Irwin, 1991; Oakhill & Patel, 1991; Pressley, Johnson, Symons, McGoldrick, & Kurita, 1989).

Proficient readers may have difficulty understanding how reading can occur without mental images, but some individuals do not naturally create them. Teachers can effectively teach children how to create mental images, however, and when they do, comprehension will improve (Gambrell & Jawitz, 1993).

Some simple classroom activities can be used to introduce children to the process of creating mental images. For example, have them imagine the uppercase letter *N* in their minds, mentally "drawing" a diagonal line from the upper-right side to the lower-left side, then rotating the image one-quarter turn so that they "see" an hourglass. Having children draw their mental images on paper after they read is a common activity. But you must be careful that time spent drawing does not take away from other valuable instructional activities. Also, as children grow older, many of them may become frustrated because their drawing skills are inadequate; you can introduce additional mental imagery activities that are not as dependent on their artistic skills.

Thompson (2000) suggested using pairs of words in an activity called "bee-flea." Students are shown, one at a time, two lists of 24 word pairs that name animals. On one list the word pairs name animals that are similar in size physically (flea-bee, pig-fox, and deer-cow), while the other list has word pairs naming animals that are not similar in size (quail-whale, fox-worm, and bear-frog). The teacher times students as they underline the word in each pair that names the larger of the two animals. The time required to

make decisions about size is longer when the animals named are similar in size than when they are very different because, as readers report, they created mental images of the animals in order to make their decisions about size.

Something as simple as stopping periodically and asking "What is happening in your mind now?" or "What are you aware of?" can prompt deeper processing and richer discussion. Other activities take a little more preparation and time.

Many young children are familiar with and enjoy traditional fairy tales. You should read them to young students and use them effectively in your instruction. When children are familiar with a variety of fairy tale characters, you can encourage them to create mental images as you give them clues about the identity of an unnamed fairy tale character. After giving one clue, allow students to guess the character's identity based on the mental images they have created. Continue giving clues until they know the character you are describing. For example, you can give students these clues:

English Language Learners

Speaking/Listening

> I am male.
> I have brown fur.
> My name reflects who I am.
> I left my house unlocked.
> When I returned home, I was very surprised.
> (Papa Bear, from "Goldilocks")

After each clue, allow time for discussion and prediction. Be sure to include discussion questions about what mental images students are creating. Here are some additional clues for other characters:

> I am female.
> I am a motivated worker.
> I was awakened by a prince.
> My stepmother has never liked me.
> There are many men in my life.
> (Snow White)

> I am male.
> Gold and riches are mine.
> I rarely listen to others.
> I paid dearly for worrying about what
>   others thought.
> I will never walk through the streets
>   without my clothes again!
> (Emperor)

> I am an animal.
> My species make good pets.
> I am smart and clever.
> When I am happy, I purr.
> I prefer to wear something on my feet.
> (Puss in Boots)

> I am female.
> I possess magical powers.
> I am helpful to others.
> I turned animals into humans.
> I got her to the church on time.
> (Fairy Godmother)

Asking and answering questions.   Asking questions is a common experience for nearly all people, beginning with the very young—just ask the parent of three-year-olds. They ask questions like "Why is the grass green?" "Can I get that candy bar?" and "When does mommy get home?" We usually ask questions when we do not know something we want to know, and we ask someone we think may know the answer. Most of the questions asked at home are posed by children to adults, but the reverse is true

---

Try This for Teaching   **Character Clues**

- Select a character from a familiar story.
- Create five sentences to describe the character from general to specific.
- Present one sentence at a time to students, allowing them to identify the character.
- Point out that when they successfully identified the character, it was because of the mental images they have made.

Variations for ELLs

- Replicate this strategy with other story elements, like setting.

- Involve children in making clues for others to solve.
- Read a news article to find clues about real people so students can practice creating images from an informational text.
- Give clues about familiar children's books similar to those found in *Spot the Plot* (Lewis, 2009).

Try This for Teaching   **Musical Images**

- Tell students that as you play some music they should close their eyes and see what pictures come to their minds.
- Let students listen to some vivid music.
- Discuss the mental images that came to the students' minds and the emotions on which they were based.

(Fredericks, 1986)

Variations for ELLs

- Ask students about the setting they picture in their minds when they hear the music. Have students explore other sensory images besides sight. (What is smelled in that setting? What could be touched?)
- Show students a clip from Disney's *Fantasia*, an entirely animated film consisting of musically evoked images.

Try This for Teaching   **A Play in Your Mind**

- Direct students to read a short play.
- Ask them to describe scenery, actions, costumes, and characters, all of which are not included in the text.
- Re-read the play after the discussion to enlarge their understanding.

(Fredericks, 1986)

Variations for ELLs

- Be sure children know what a play is (arrange to attend one, if possible).
- Invite a middle school or high school drama class to present a short play for your students in your classroom.

---

at school. Most questions at school are asked by teachers, and students answer questions more often than they ask them (Borich, 2006; Guszak, 1967). Traditionally, teaching comprehension has been associated with teachers asking questions (Guszak, 1967; Durkin, 1978–1979). Although teachers use questions to motivate and evaluate student thinking, you should create a classroom atmosphere that encourages students to ask their own questions as well.

Try This for Teaching   **Mind Illustrations**

- Choose a picture book and explain that you will read it without showing the pictures.
- After reading the first page, ask students to describe the illustration they see in their minds.
- Show them the illustration and make comparisons.
- Continue this throughout the book.

(McTigue, 2010)

Variations for ELLs

- After students read jokes or riddles, have them share images they created and describe an illustration that would fit.
- Show wordless picture books and have students write stories to go with them (Harvey & Goudvis, 2000). Explain that the clues revealed in the illustrations combine with pictures in our minds to create a story.
- When reading informational text that describes size, weight, length, or distance, have students create an illustration that shows the comparison between something known and something new. For example, when the text says that a Tyrannosaurus Rex's tooth is about six-and-a-half inches long, children can make a mental illustration comparing the tooth to a banana (Harvey & Goudvis, 2000).
- Instead of using a book, try storytelling to encourage students to create images in their minds.

Rosenshine, Meister, and Chapman (1996) reviewed research showing that question generation and self-questioning not only improved memory and accuracy but also led to better identification of main ideas and integration with other subject areas. Question-answer relationships present one way to learn how to transition from teacher-generated to student-generated questions. Questioning the author is another way, because you want students to be able to ask questions independently as they read.

Question-answer relationships (QAR). The question-answer relationship (QAR) taxonomy, proposed by Pearson and Johnson (1978) and extended by Raphael (1986), examines questions, responses, and the text to which they relate. Readers are told that they have two general places to go to answer questions—the text or their heads. To show the levels of relationships in the QAR, consider this short text and the questions and answers that follow.

Grandma brought out a large plate of turkey and put it on the table. Then she brought out some stuffing and green beans. We put the food on our plates next to our salads and began to eat.

In the Text

1. Right There

   Q: What was on the large plate?

   A: turkey

2. Think and Search

   Q: What food did Grandma put on the table?

   A: turkey, stuffing, green beans, and salad

In Your Head

3. Author and You

   Q: What meal was Grandma serving?

   A: dinner or Thanksgiving dinner

4. On Your Own

   Q: What do you like to eat for dinner?

   A: tacos

The QAR has four levels or types of relationships. In the first level, "Right There," the information in both the question and the answer are found within the same sentence in the text. "Think and Search" is an example of inferential thinking because, although the answer is in the text, it is not stated succinctly in one location. The reader has to combine information across several sentences. The third relationship, "Author and You," also requires inferential thinking because the reader has to use prior knowledge in conjunction with clues given by the author. In this example, the word *dinner* is not in the text, so the answer comes from the reader's head. Had the author used words like "cold cereal and milk" or "bacon and eggs," the reader may not have come to the same conclusion. The last QAR is called "On Your Own" because the reader can appropriately answer the question without making any reference to the text.

QAR is much more than a teacher-directed questioning strategy. Its real power is in helping you see what students' thinking processes are as they generate their own questions and talk about text. QAR offers both you and your students labels in a common language with which you can talk about thinking in whole class and small group discussions (Raphael & Au, 2005). For example, as students in a literature circle answer questions, they can ask each other what kind of thinking is required to answer those questions: "Is this an 'Author and You' or an 'On Your Own' question?"

English Language Learners

This is especially important as you consider the varied cultural backgrounds of your students. You may ask what you think is a good "Think and Search" question that requires processing across text. One student may use that process to answer your question, but another student may answer the question in a "Right There" way, giving only part of the answer you expected. Whether the difference is due to variety in culture, lack of ability, or desire for a quick answer, you have information to help you know what to do next. You can encourage deeper processing by showing students how to turn a "Right There" response into a "Think and Search" answer.

Questioning the author (QtA). Beck and McKeown (2006) formalized a common practice of effective readers, **questioning the author** (QtA), by which readers inquire about the content they are reading. To do so readers think beyond the words on the page and keep in mind the author's intent for the writing and his or her effectiveness at communicating it. The goal of QtA is not just to challenge or critique the author, but to evaluate the

---

Try This for Teaching   **Talking about Thinking**

- Give students a short text to read.
- Have each student write four questions about the text.
- Ask students to exchange questions with a partner and answer all four questions.
- Have them exchange papers again so that a different student reads the questions and answers and assigns the appropriate QAR and writes why.
- Ask students to pass papers back to the original author and discuss the thinking of the other students (by answering such questions as, Do you agree with the QAR assignment? Is that

the type of thinking you intended with your question?

(Raphael & Au, 2005)

Variations for ELLs

- Have three students complete this activity in front of the class. One student asks the questions orally, and the next student answers them orally. The third student assigns a label.
- Use only two categories: "In the Book" and "In Your Head."

Try This for Teaching   Questioning the Author

- Invite students to think beyond the words on the page and keep in mind the author's purpose.

- Encourage students to stop after reading a page and ask themselves one of the five basic questions of QtA.

- Have students write their responses and share them with partners or with the class.

(Beck & McKeown, 2006)

Variations for ELLs

- Roll a die to select the question, with number six being a free choice.

- Encourage students to use the five questions as a starting point and think of additional questions (such as Do I agree with the author? Is the author's evidence compelling? What did the author do to make me feel surprised?).

- Encourage students to ask similar questions as they conference about their own work and the work of peers.

- Write to authors and ask them to answer students' questions.

author's intent, craft, clarity, and organization. Did you like the text? Why? How did the author effectively reach you? Did you not like the text? Why? What could the author have done differently? Of course, many of these questions will not have definitive answers, but discussing them will improve comprehension.

The basic procedure includes five questions, which students are instructed to ask themselves regularly as they read:

1. What is the author trying to tell me?
2. Why is the author telling me that?
3. Does the author say it well?
4. How could the author have said things more effectively?
5. How would I have said it?

Metacognitive Strategies.   Have you ever read an entire page of text and then asked yourself what you just read because your mind was drifting? Have you noticed you misread a word because you realized the sentence did not make sense? These are examples of monitoring your own reading. Many struggling readers do not do what you did—they usually just keep on reading whether or not they understand.

Along with using organizational and inferential cognitive strategies, readers must monitor their understanding of what they read. This self-monitoring of one's own thinking is often referred to as **metacognition** (Brown, 1980). Metacognitive strategies include identifying problems and fixing them as you go. Such strategies are especially appropriate with students in intermediate grades and up (Haller, Child, & Walberg, 1988).

Metacognitive ability involves knowing when your reading has broken down and what steps to take to get yourself back on track. Readers use different methods to correct their course—some re-read text more slowly; others scan to find the word that tripped them up. These are examples of fix-up strategies that struggling readers need to learn.

> Struggling Learners/
> RtI

Comprehension monitoring.   Comprehension monitoring is being aware of both successes and failures in understanding text. Garner (1992) wrote, "All of us experience

Try This for Teaching   **Clicking and Clunking**

- Explain the concepts of clicking and clunking in the context of understanding text.
- Teach students hand signals to communicate both conditions.
- As students read orally or silently, stop periodically and ask them to signal a click or a clunk.

(Anderson, 1984)

Variations for ELLs

- Use analogies to make the concepts more vivid: a light bulb going on and off or an engine running smoothly or clunking.
- Have students use sticky notes to mark places in their text where they have clunked so you can discuss them together.

cognitive failure at one time or another while we attempt to comprehend. . . . What we make of this cognitive failure is critical" (p. 226).

Your purpose as a reader has a lot to do with self-monitoring. When the information is vital to you and you realize that you are not getting it, then you are motivated to take action. If information is not as important, you may take no action, even though you are aware you are missing meaning. Most readers experience both situations frequently. But teachers need to be concerned about a third possibility as well: undetected cognitive failure (Garner, 1987). This occurs when children think they are understanding what they are reading, but they really are not. How can you help students come to know that they need help, especially in dealing with sophisticated cognitive processes that are difficult to monitor? Dorthea Brande (2011) wrote, "A problem clearly stated is a problem half solved." The key is to heighten students' awareness level. Anderson (1984) said this comes "in the form of so-called clicks of comprehension or a clunk of comprehension failure. Clicks of comprehension are often accompanied by feelings of well-being, and clunks of comprehension failure are accompanied by feelings of tenseness and anxiety" (p. 496).

Explain to children that they need to pay attention to whether or not they understand what they read. For younger students, you could also provide hand signals like thumbs up when students are understanding and thumbs down when they are not. As older students read the text, urge them to reflect at the end of each paragraph or section: "Did the meaning click for me, or did it clunk?" You can gauge students' self-monitoring by asking them to signal click or clunk at given points, whether they are reading orally or silently.

Struggling Learners/ RtI

English Language Learners

Fixing up.   After a student has identified that he has not understood, he needs to be able to select an appropriate strategy to help himself. Sometimes these strategies are simple: re-reading or seeking help from knowledgeable individuals (Collins & Smith, 1980). Other clunks require more complex repair strategies to clarify understanding. Readers may have to consciously draw inferences, summarize a section of text, or assess whether they have adequate prior knowledge. Just because you can use these strategies easily, do not assume that children will know which one is best suited to help them fix up their reading problems without some direction. They need to learn how to use organizational and inferential strategies and when to use them. This instruction can happen during whole class mini-lessons, but it is also effective in small groups when children are actually in the moment of need. In either case, think-alouds can be helpful, especially for students who are struggling and those who are learning English (Baumann, Jones, & Seifert-Kessell, 1993).

> ### Try This for Teaching   **Think-Alouds**
>
> - Explain that you will stop during reading and talk about your own thinking.
> - Read a section, then verbalize several options for understanding it better.
> - Select one and model the strategy.
> - Allow students to think aloud and describe their thoughts.
> - Praise them when they do it well, and offer suggestions when they need help.
>
> (Baumann, Jones, & Seifert-Kessell, 1993)
>
> **Variations for ELLs**
>
> - Think aloud as if you are carrying on a conversation with yourself.
> - Encourage students to ask themselves questions like "I wonder what would happen if I did this strategy?"
> - Examine verbally the pros and cons of a strategy.

Begin a think-aloud session by reading part of a text aloud. Stop and explain that you are going to think aloud about how to resolve a problem so the students can see what is happening in your mind. Say, "Gosh. I just read half a page and I don't understand what's going on." Then present several options: "I could re-read this section and then go on, or I could summarize what I've read to this point. But I think I'm going to look for something that might connect to my own experience and see if that helps." Proceed to model in detail how you are making that connection. Continue modeling your thinking as you finish the passage. When students appear to understand the process, ask, "What is happening inside your head?" Allow several students to share their thinking.

Speaking/Listening

Multiple Strategies

Children learn to apply strategies best when they practice them simultaneously (National Reading Panel, 2000; Pressley, 2002; Trabasso & Bouchard, 2002). Although there is value in teaching one strategy at a time (Keene & Zimmermann, 2007), many students are able to flexibly coordinate use of several strategies at once. Children learn how to appropriately apply multiple strategies as they discuss text in teacher-led small groups.

Several multiple-strategy approaches have been used successfully with children, including transactional strategies instruction (Brown, Pressley, Van Meter, & Schuder, 1996) and concept-oriented reading instruction (Guthrie, Wigfield, & Perencevich, 2004). One of the most commonly used approaches is reciprocal teaching (Palinscar & Brown, 1984; Rosenshine & Meister, 1994).

Reciprocal teaching blends four comprehension strategies—questioning, summarizing, clarifying, and predicting. Although these can be addressed in any order, many teachers find it helpful to have students summarize and clarify before they ask questions and make predictions. Included in the procedure are teacher modeling, role-playing, practice, and feedback. When students participate, they develop important abilities to monitor their own reading. Groups typically meet for 20 to 30 minutes. Teachers lead discussions at the beginning to provide needed modeling and support. As students gain greater ability and confidence in each of the strategies, they are given more responsibility. Students may be grouped homogeneously or heterogeneously, depending on the teacher's goals. The text students read may be a selection from a basal anthology, a work of literature, or a content area text. As you differentiate instruction, you may find it useful to provide a graphic organizer for some students to use independently as they prepare for small group discussions. Figure 8.8 shows one such organizer.

Summarizing, questioning, and predicting are all strategies you know now, but clarifying may not be as familiar to you. **Clarifying** is a metacognitive strategy that involves both identifying misunderstanding and doing something about it. Children may be able to identify a word they do not know, but they may not understand what to do next. By clarifying during reciprocal teaching, teachers or peers can offer definitions or point out how comprehension problems can be resolved.

Reciprocal teaching is usually associated with experienced readers, but combining the four strategies can be helpful for beginners and for ELLs. During a read-aloud, you can stop at strategic points and have students orally summarize the text, ask questions about the content, and identify and clarify problem areas. Then you can ask students to make predictions before continuing. With struggling students, you can use wordless picture books to introduce and practice reciprocal teaching, since the story is told through illustrations. Students' lack of word identification ability does not interfere with comprehension of these texts.

English Language Learners

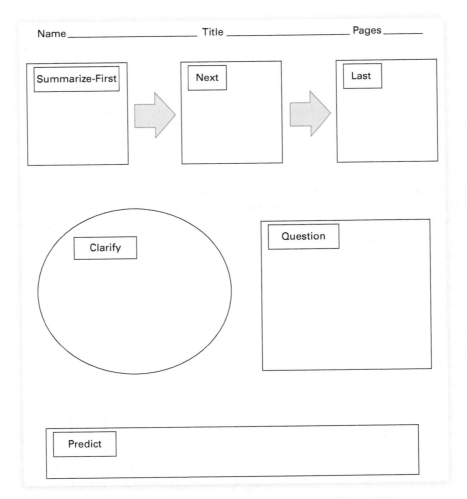

Figure 8.8 Reciprocal Teaching Graphic Organizer

Creating Meaning Through Writing

"I can't write!" is a statement that teachers often hear from frustrated students, most of whom are bemoaning their problems in punctuation, spelling, or handwriting. Teachers need to make an important distinction between composing and transcribing (Smith, 1982). **Composing** is discovering ideas and shaping and organizing them. **Transcription** is putting them on paper. One teacher told his students about a young woman who wrote beautiful stories and poems even though she had no arms or hands. She composed by dictating into a recorder. Someone else transcribed her words on paper. After hearing about this writer, one student said, "Oh, I get it! Composing is the part of writing that only I can do. Transcribing is what someone else could do for me if I didn't have any hands." Both aspects of writing are important, but too often transcription is stressed so heavily with young writers that they begin to see it as the whole of writing. In your rush to cover all the mechanics of writing, do not overlook the importance of the content. Students need to feel the excitement of finding a topic and a way to express it. These two traits of writing—ideas and organization—are how writers create meaning.

Ideas

Ideas are plans, beliefs, or possible courses of action. They are the substance of writing, but some ideas just matter more than others. Students' writing will improve as they discover ideas that are insightful and relevant, unusual and surprising. Writing should not be void of emotion. To write about meaningful ideas, authors have to be honest and brave, writing with passion (Romano, 1995). They must connect writing to their lives. Helping students make such connections may be uncomfortable—even disturbing—for educators who see a well-defined line between fill-in-the-blanks exercises and students writing about their actual experiences. But ideas worth writing about are "lifework, not deskwork" (Calkins & Harwayne, 1991, p. 7). Help students live, think, and act like writers who "live their lives differently because they write" (Calkins & Harwayne, 1991, p. 7). The act of writing encourages us to be more observant, thoughtful, sensitive, and curious. It frees us to live "wide awake lives" (Calkins & Harwayne, 1991, p. 42).

Children may think that what is happening to them is not important, but when you brainstorm with them they begin to see literary potential in the simplest of everyday occurrences. When one child commented to his mother that bird tracks in the snow looked like a quilt top, she said, "That sounds like a poem. How can we turn that thought into a poem?" The child was motivated to write his first poem, something that would

Speaking/Listening

Try This for Professional Development   **Teaching Beyond the Test**

Teachers often focus primarily on mechanics because they want their children to perform well on tests. However, some research shows that a combination of enrichment activities and explicit instruction not only improves children's attitudes but is better test preparation than a skills-only focus (Reis et al., 2007).

- Reflect on the results of the study.
- How do these results match your experience?

- How can you deal with the pressure to obtain high test results and still maintain balance in your classroom?
- Think of teachers you respect. How have they dealt with this dilemma?
- Consider your ultimate goals as a teacher. Are you teaching to the test or beyond the test?

Try This for Teaching   **Life Maps**

- Have students draw a line on paper.
- Explain that the line represents a time line of their lives.
- Have students mark significant events in the order of their occurrence.
- Conduct a conference or a small group session during which you help each student select one experience from the map to write about or to function as a springboard to additional ideas that the student can write about.

(Liner, Kirby, & Kirby, 2003)

Variations for ELLs

- Create your own life map as a model for students.
- Let children draw pictures at various points on the time line.
- Create additional maps dealing with specific themes, such as influential people, favorite pets, memorable books, or biggest blunders.
- Suggest that students draw the line in a zigzag pattern with positive events at the top and negative events below. The final product will resemble the readout from a heart monitor.

never have happened without an adult helping him see the value of his fresh and uncommon observation.

Helping students dream up bright ideas or identify literary moments is sometimes called **brainstorming**. Encourage them to keep track of their experiences and to read often. Ideas for writing can come from family, friends, and personal experiences. Teachers can also use books to help students get ideas. Three effective strategies for helping children compile writing ideas are life maps (Liner, Kirby, & Kirby, 2003), shared stories, and writers' notebooks (Calkins & Harwayne, 1991).

Life Maps.   Have students draw a line on a paper—it could be horizontal, vertical, or twisting and turning. Tell them this line represents their lives from birth right up to the present. Have them place marks on the line to indicate high points in their lives, difficult times, or memorable experiences. One child may include a move; another may choose to emphasize starting school. One child may include the date of his parents' divorce, and another may write about the first time she rode a horse. Each point on the time line can become a beginning point for writing.

Students can write about an experience or use that experience to remind them of something else that could become a piece of personal writing. For example, one student may not want to write about his parents' divorce, but recalling that difficult time may remind him of how kind his aunt was and how she brought him cookies. He may decide to write about his aunt's secret recipe, telling how the best ingredient was love, and the cookies magically made him feel better. Such experiences can also suggest ideas for other genres. Informational writing could focus on how to deal with divorce; opinion writing could explore why divorce can be positive or negative. Narrative writing could share the story of a character whose family was affected by divorce.

Shared Stories.   Calkins and Harwayne (1991) suggested gathering students together in a circle and telling them to get comfortable because the discussion may take some time. They instructed teachers to begin by sharing one of their own family memories or talking about a prized possession. Sharing in an enthusiastic way sparks students' interest, and some children will volunteer to share their own stories. You may want to make a list of key words to remind you of stories shared so children can refer back to the list as they decide what they believe is worth writing about. Stories can be about simple things like

English Language
Learners

Speaking/Listening

Try This for Teaching   **Shared Stories**

- Gather your class in a comfortable setting.
- Share a personal experience from your life.
- Invite students to share similar experiences.
- List key words to remember experiences shared— these can become a bank of ideas.

(Calkins & Harwayne, 1991)

Variations for ELLs

- Have students bring a photo from home and tell who is in the picture and what is happening.

- Consult a book like *Brown Angels* (Myers, 1996) or *The Mysteries of Harris Burdick* (Van Allsburg, 1984), in which the illustrations can prompt stories, real or imagined.
- Introduce other good beginning places like first and last, best and worst, or then and now stories or essays.
- Try starting with a quotation or a common saying (Honesty is the best policy, Don't bite off more than you can chew, More is not always better). Ask students about times when they have found that saying to be true or false in their lives.

trying out for a team or eating a new kind of food. Start talking about a time when you were really upset or explain how you got your name. Students find it almost irresistible to chime in to tell their own similar stories.

Writers' Notebooks.   Calkins and Harwayne (1991) also suggested providing each student a **writer's notebook** or having students bring one to school to record their observations and ideas. Some people like to call these daybooks. Students need to know that this is a safe place to write, where their work will not be edited, critiqued, or corrected. Because writing in the notebook is safe, ELLs can experience great success. Some may prefer to write in their first language, and you should encourage this. This is a school activity that should not make them nervous or scared. Explain that the notebook is a place where they can record whatever they want. You may start by encouraging them to think about "what if" and "why" questions: "What if animals could talk?" "What if I were magic?" "Why do I feel happy at home?" and "Why do I like school?" Topics should not drive the notebook beyond some introductory activities. As children are given opportunities to share, they will naturally give ideas to each other. When students say they have

English Language Learners

Try This for Teaching   **Writers' Notebooks**

- Provide a notebook for each student.
- Clarify that the writing in the notebook is personal and will not be corrected or evaluated.
- Provide time for students to write.
- Provide time for volunteers to share their writing.

(Calkins & Harwayne, 1991)

Variations for ELLs

- Encourage students to make lists (such as things under my bed or favorite foods).

- Have students write a "how-to" piece (such as how to make a taco, how to tie your shoes, how to send a text message).
- Try writing definitions (for example, What is the real meaning of courage? or What qualities do real friends possess?).
- Take students on a walk around the schoolyard. Tell them they must remain completely silent. The only "talking" allowed is with their pencil, recording what they see, hear, touch, or experience.

nothing to write about, encourage them to open their notebooks and begin writing. Ideas will come once they start moving their pencils. The notebook will become a seedbed for ideas that will later go through the entire writing process.

Organization

In addition to coming up with ideas, a writer needs to shape them. One teacher emphasizes the importance of organization in writing by drawing an analogy to something familiar to his students—a hamburger. He says, "A hamburger has meat, lettuce, tomatoes, pickles, and a bun, and the order they come in makes a big difference. You could put the lettuce and the tomato outside the bun. It might even taste the same, but it will be tricky to get your hands around it." The same is true for writing. Organized writing allows readers to hold onto ideas and manage them through logical sequencing and well-controlled pacing. The order, structure, and presentation of the writing make a difference. Disorganized writing, like a disorganized hamburger, can fall apart easily. Organized writing presents ideas in a smooth, clear, and reasonable way. Successful authors know where they are taking their readers and guide them effectively. Their path is easy to follow.

The picture word inductive model (Calhoun, 1999) is a simple way to help children organize writing. Although it was designed for younger readers and writers, the same process could be adapted as an introduction to organization at any grade level. Following the model, one teacher displayed a picture of a typical autumn scene including a scarecrow, haystacks, and pumpkins at the front of the room. As children entered the classroom, they were met with written instructions to see how many objects they could recognize and name in the picture.

As the children named objects (barn, fence, and scarecrow), the teacher wrote the words on cards and then pasted them around the picture, drawing arrows from the words to the corresponding objects in the picture. She had the students read the words again, and with the support of the picture, all students were very successful in matching the words with their corresponding images.

On the following day she reviewed the words surrounding the picture and asked children to identify several words that were related to one another. She then had the children create a sentence using the related words, requiring them to remain true to the picture. She recorded the sentences and praised the students for being able to write complete sentences.

On the next day she showed the students how those sentences made a paragraph and praised them for already knowing how to write a paragraph at such a young age. She followed the same process over the next week, creating additional words, sentences, and paragraphs about the same picture.

English Language Learners

With older students, you could work on revising paragraphs after your students had constructed them, focusing particularly on ideas and organization. Pictures could be given to small groups or individuals, challenging them to go through the process. After this experience, the students could lead younger students through the process, acting as coaches.

The people who make hamburgers at a restaurant consider who the hamburger is for and what types of burgers their restaurant is famous for as they put the sandwiches together. When authors make choices about organizing their writing, the same two factors influence them—audience and forms of writing. As they keep these in mind, they will be able to create a product that is inviting, interesting, and satisfying.

Audience.   A writer's **audience** is made up of the people who read or listen to his or her writing. Students write primarily for themselves or for a small circle of family and friends, but there are times when they also must write for a more formal audience, such

Try This for Teaching   **Picture Word Inductive Model**

- Display a picture and ask students to identify items.
- Write words that children volunteer and post them on cards around the picture.
- Create sentences based on the words.
- Organize the sentences into a meaningful paragraph.

(Calhoun, 1999)

Variations for ELLs

- Give pictures to individuals or small groups.
- Revise paragraphs as students complete the writing process.
- Let older students lead younger students through this organizational process, acting as teachers or coaches.

---

as when they write letters to a business or are writing for a magazine. Formal audiences can motivate students to do their best because children's writing is influenced by their intended readers (Britton, Burgess, Martin, McLeod, & Rosen, 1975). Children benefit from recognizing a variety of different audiences and having authentic experiences writing for them. Two useful activities to help your students define different audiences are creating new titles and writing to pen pals (Teale & Gambrell, 2007).

Create a new title.   Choose a picture book with limited text, like *Tough Boris* (Fox, 1998), so you can read it quickly to students. After reading, discuss how the title would need to be changed to appeal to a variety of audiences. Give students some possible audiences to consider, and let them create new titles for the book. For example, ask, "How could we change *Tough Boris* if the audience were cowboys, university professors, or doctors?" For cowboys, the title might read, *Bucking Bronco Boris Rides Again*. University professors might respond to a title such as *Pirates Are Not Always the Bad Guys: The Dangers of Stereotyping*. And doctors might be interested in reading *A Case Study in the Effects of Anger on Stress Levels*.

Pen pals.   A student teacher was observed teaching the format of a friendly letter. After her instruction, she told the students, "Let's pretend to write a letter." As she reflected on the lesson, she realized it would have been better for her students to practice the format by writing actual letters instead of pretend letters. Authentic learning experiences are especially meaningful when you are teaching about a sense of audience. Some teachers have been successful in creating a real audience by providing pen pals for their students. These can be other students in a neighboring school or college students who are preparing to become teachers.

English Language Learners

Try This for Teaching   **Create a Title**

- Choose a picture book with limited text.
- Read it to your students.
- Discuss a variety of possible audiences.
- Create new titles for the book that would appeal to the different audiences.

Variations for ELLs

- Have students change the title to appeal to characters in the book, including both heroes and villains.
- Have students create titles for different grade levels. Survey students at your school to see if these titles appeal to them.

Pen Pals

- Arrange with a colleague to exchange letters with students in your class.
- Have your class write the first letters.
- Revise and edit the letters.
- Review the letters to be sure only first names are given and no contact information is included.
- Send the letters to your colleague, including the date on which you expect the responses.
- When responses come, allow time for sharing.
- Have your students write back quickly while enthusiasm is high.

Variations for ELLs

- Consider using technology as a communication tool.
- Approach senior citizens as possible pen pals.
- Contact international schools in foreign countries (www.epals.com/).
- Send copies of final drafts of children's writing or artwork and ask for a response.
- Find out if students have friends or family living elsewhere with whom they could correspond.

New Literacies

Make contact with another teacher or a professor. Ask if he or she is willing to provide pen pals for your students. Have your students write first. Gather their letters and send them in one envelope to your colleague, rather than assuming students will send them on their own. Instruct students to sign only their first names and to provide their school address as the only contact information. Suggest a reasonable deadline so the letters are not overlooked. When you receive replies from the pen pals, allow students time to share their letters. Have your students write back quickly while enthusiasm is high and while they have their audience (their specific pen pal) in mind. If computers are available, this activity is a natural technology connection. Students can email or write on a class blog or a wiki. The communication is not limited to personal letters—students can share stories, essays, and reports with pen pals.

Forms of Writing. The audience children write to often influences the writing form they select. However, their purposes as authors also shape their decision. Are they writing to inform, entertain, or persuade (Brewer, 1980)? Typically, **genres of writing** can be categorized as poetry or prose. Prose includes fictional and informational text (Tunnell & Jacobs, 2007). *Genre* is a French word that means "type" or "kind." Within those genres, the forms of writing are as open-ended as creativity allows. **Forms of writing** include different types of poetry (limericks and haiku), different types of stories (mysteries and fables), and different types of informational text (essays and directions). Students can choose to write in forms that range from bumper stickers, riddles, and recipes to cartoons, advertising slogans, and song lyrics. There are entire books available that explain different forms of writing, and many resources are available to teachers of younger and older students (Kemper, Nathan, Elsholz, & Sebranek 2000; Rothstein, Rothstein, & Lauber, 2006). Three forms that children find appealing are stories (Beers, 2002; Rothstein, Rothstein, & Lauber, 2006), memoirs (Calkins & Harwayne, 1991), and class newspapers.

Common Core State Standards

Stories. The Common Core uses personal writing as a springboard to other forms, including narrative text. Writing that tells a story, real or imaginary, is referred to as narrative text. Students are expected to write stories that include events, show the order of the events, and indicate reactions. Authors often describe characters and

Figure 8.9   Story Elements

Characters	People in a story
Setting	Place or surroundings where a story takes place
Problem	Situation that is unsatisfactory or needs to be resolved
Goal	Plan the characters have to solve the problem
Events	Sequence which unfolds over time
Climax	Turning point in the sequence of events—high point in the action
Resolution	Final solution (or failure to find a solution) for the problem

(Gordon & Braun, 1983)

settings and then present a problem that usually is resolved after a series of events. To keep readers' interest, writers use specific details, realistic dialogue, and intriguing action.

Since many children come to school with a well-developed sense of story, narrative text is a comfortable genre for them to write. However, they still need instruction to learn how to make their stories compelling by describing the appearance and habits of realistic characters, by presenting problems with which readers can relate, and by describing settings so that readers feel they are there. Students also learn to pace their stories to create tension and suspense.

When planning a story, students can focus on story elements. The same story maps they use in reading can guide their writing. Even kindergartners have been shown to improve the complexity of their writing in this way (Watanabe & Hall-Kenyon, 2011). Figure 8.9 outlines the major elements of a story.

When the actual writing begins, students need to understand that it will require multiple drafts so they can worry about grammar, punctuation, and spelling toward the end of the process. Some students also find it helpful to write within a framework.

A **writing frame** is a structure or a textual outline that gives students a starting point. Beers (2002) suggested using the words *somebody, wants, but, so* as a technique for summarizing text, but these words can also be adapted as a frame for writing a story. Tell students that the five fingers on their hand can remind them of five key words to guide them in writing a story—*who, wants, but, then, finally*. Have the students list a variety of characters that the story could be about (a teacher, Superman, or a chicken). When writing a class story, have students vote on which character to write about. Then ask, "What does our character want?" Let them formulate a list (money, fame, or a home). Next, create a list of possibilities under the "but" column. What is keeping the character from his or her goal? (fear, big bad wolf, always busy, or the boss). Continue the pattern for the "then" and "finally" categories. Use this as a frame to build the story. As the story develops, students need not feel bound to their original choices when they make revisions and edit. However, this writing frame gives them a starting place.

Memoirs.   The Common Core refers to memoirs as a form of narrative text. A **memoir** is not a biography or autobiography. Rather, it is a collection of meaningful and significant memories of an individual's life tied together with a unifying theme. Calkins and Harwayne (1991) pointed out that a memoir allows writers to not only gather several

Struggling Learners/
RtI

Language Conventions

English Language
Learners

Common Core
State Standards

Try This for Teaching   # Writing Frames

- Tell students five key words to structure a story—*who, wants, but, then, finally.*
- List options for each category.
- Select from among the options and have students start the story as a group.
- Revise and edit as the story develops.

(Beers, 2002)

Variations for ELLs

- List six options under each category. Have students roll a die with the number determining which of the six options they will use.
- Use a picture book as a model or pattern to follow. Encourage students to imitate the form without copying the content.

- After writing a group story, have individuals write their own stories, choosing among the options on the board or choosing their own options for each key word.
- Use story elements as a similar writing frame (character, setting, problem, goal, events, resolution).
- Structure a story using the retelling strategy called STORE (adapted from Bos & Vaughn, 1998):

    - **S** etting   Who, What, When, Where
    - **T** rouble   What is the trouble?
    - **O** rder of Action   What happened to deal with the trouble? (correct/logical order)
    - **R** esolution   What was the outcome (resolution) for each action?
    - **E** nd   What happened in the end?

Try This for Teaching   # Memoir

- Explain that a memoir is a collection of significant memories and experiences.
- Help students select an image or symbol to represent themselves.
- Determine experiences that can be linked together using that symbol.
- Assist students as they write meaningful memories and tie them together with a uniting theme.
- Revise and edit during the writing process.

(Calkins & Harwayne, 1991)

Variations for ELLs

- Use phrases from a quotation or poem instead of a visual symbol. For example, the Scout Oath begins "On my honor"; students can write about what that means to them and then write about the next phrase and the next.
- You could also share examples of short memoirs such as *When I Was Young in the Mountains* (Rylant, 1993) or *When I Was Little: A Four-Year-Old's Memoir of Her Youth* (Curtis, 1995).
- Encourage students to think of different rooms in their home or apartment and have them write a vivid memory for each room.

personal narratives together but also to celebrate the themes and deeper meanings found within them.

Have your students select an image or symbol that represents themselves (examples might include a lighthouse, flower, house, or animal). Determine how different experiences have shaped their lives. For example, if a girl chooses a flower to symbolize her life, the stem and leaves may represent her family. One of the petals is how she got her name, another is a favorite book she read as a child, and yet another represents when she began school. To create a memoir, students may begin with the image and write memories, or they may begin with a collection of personal writing and look for the theme or image to emerge. Either way, a memoir is more than a life sketch. A memoir focuses on the high points and most significant events and ties them together without trying to include all the details between the events.

> *Try This for Teaching*   **Class Newspapers**

- Obtain some newspapers that students can read regularly.
- Identify the parts of the paper you want to include in your class project.
- Determine the types of stories and issues that will be interesting to your audience.
- Assign specific tasks to individuals or small groups.
- Revise and edit stories and articles.
- Publish and distribute the newspaper to the class or school.

- Create a magazine patterned after *Time*, *Newsweek*, or *People*.
- Write a newspaper or magazine set in the past, in the future, or in another country.

Variations for ELLs

- Create a literary magazine, sharing student poems and stories rather than news items.
- Write letters to the editor of the newspapers you have been reading.

Class newspapers.   Students usually love to report on what is happening in their own classroom, school, and community. Most students have the curiosity and interest in people and events to be able to create an interesting newspaper. Their writing focuses on real events and real people, but it needs to be unusual enough to be newsworthy. Most children can do well with three types of stories: news articles, human-interest stories, and opinions and editorials. But do not overlook other parts of a newspaper that can be fun for children to write: comic strips, political cartoons, want ads, advertisements, and even advice columns. You may need to do some instruction on how to interview, find news stories, write headlines (titles), and create leads (introductions). Some of the best learning can take place as students immerse themselves in newspapers and model their writing on what they read. Many newspapers are willing to deliver copies to classrooms at low cost if they know the newspapers will be used. Older newspapers are readily available without cost.

Students can also access newspapers on the Internet. If the student-made newspaper is distributed around the grade level or the school or is posted on the school website, motivation to write increases, and students feel pride in participating in a meaningful project. Class newspapers provide a way for students to work in teams and cooperative groups as they accomplish their tasks. Computer programs are available that allow you to present the material in actual newspaper format.

New Literacies

Summary

“Think, but don't get any ideas.” That humorous message was posted at a bank. Compare it with a sign posted in one teacher's classroom: “My job is to teach you *how* to think, not just *what* to think.” This teacher invites students to go on a comprehension journey well beyond traditional memorization and fact recall.

Comprehension may be difficult to define, but it can be taught effectively if we remember there are essential foundational skills that cannot be overlooked: established decoding abilities; a well-developed, automatic sight word vocabulary; established understanding of the meanings for many words; appropriate prior knowledge; and opportunities for wide reading and writing.

As children read to make meaning, comprehension strategies can be identified and taught explicitly—organizational, inferential, and metacognitive. You do not want to merely measure comprehension when you can teach it.

Although most people connect comprehension only with reading, meaning can also be created through writing.

Children need freedom to explore a variety of ideas and organize them for specific audiences using many possible forms, including stories, memoirs, and class newspapers.

In both reading and writing our message needs to be "Think and get lots of ideas."

Self-Check

1. Why is comprehension difficult to define?

2. What are essential foundational skills of reading comprehension?

3. Why are organization comprehension strategies important?

4. Name some inferential comprehension strategies.

5. What does the term *metacognitive* mean?

6. How can you help children discover their own ideas to write about?

7. Why is organization important in writing?

8. How can you provide a real audience for your students' writing?

MyEducationLab™

Go to the Topic, Comprehension, in the MyEducationLab (www.myeducationlab.com) for your course, where you can:

- Find learning outcomes for Comprehension along with the national standards that connect to these outcomes.

- Complete Assignments and Activities that can help you more deeply understand the chapter content.

- Apply and practice your understanding of the core teaching skills identified in the chapter with the Building Teaching Skills and Dispositions learning units.

- Examine challenging situations and cases presented in the IRIS Center Resources.

- Check your comprehension on the content covered in the chapter by going to the Study Plan in the Book

Resources for your text. Here you will be able to take a chapter quiz, receive feedback on your answers, and then access Review, Practice, and Enrichment activities to enhance your understanding of chapter content (optional).

- Visit **A+RISE** Standards2Strategy™, an innovative and interactive online resource that offers new teachers in grades K–12 just-in-time, research-based instructional strategies that meet the linguistic needs of ELLs as they learn content, differentiate instruction for all grades and abilities, and are aligned to Common Core Elementary Language Arts Standards (for the literacy strategies) and to English language proficiency standards in WIDA, Texas, California, and Florida.

chapter 9

Integrating Literacy with Content Areas

Chapter Outline

READING IN CONTENT AREAS
  Expository Text Structure
  Expository Text Features
  Study Strategies
  Study Guides
WRITING IN CONTENT AREAS
  Writing without Revision
  Writing with Revision
  Expository Text
  Argumentative Writing
SUMMARY

I was invited to assist with some efforts to improve literacy levels at a middle school where students were struggling. In my first meeting with the principal, she listed all the serious challenges facing these students and teachers. She thanked me for being willing to help and gave me a schedule of when I would be meeting with the English teachers. I said, "This is great, but when do I meet with the whole faculty?" She replied, "Since we are only focusing on literacy, I didn't think the other teachers really needed to be involved." I had only been there a short time, but I could already see one thing that needed to change: the perception that literacy is only the job of the English teachers in middle school or the primary grade teachers in elementary school. *Every* teacher is a teacher of literacy, no matter the content area. I spent the next few visits at the school helping the principal and faculty members see the value of integrating literacy with content areas. It was exciting to see these educators begin to take learning and teaching to a whole new level in their school.

—Brad

Reading and writing are referred to as basics in education. For that reason some see them as completely separate subjects from **content areas** such as science, mathematics, social studies, art, music, and health. In reality, reading and writing are inseparable from content. You cannot read without reading about content, whether literature or informational text. You cannot write without writing content. Others see reading and writing as precursors to content learning: "First you learn to read and then you read to learn." It's a clever saying, but in reality we are always learning to read better and always reading to learn more. Integrating literacy with content areas allows you to interactively improve literacy and content area learning (Bosse & Faulconer, 2008; Jones & Thomas, 2006).

For example, Guthrie, Wigfield, and Perencevich (2004) reported that third-graders who read an expository text about one of the concepts from their science lesson during their reading instruction showed higher interest in what they read, engaged more fully with the text, processed the material more deeply, gained richer conceptual understanding, and built background knowledge that improved their comprehension of narrative texts read later. Similarly, Applebee and Langer (2006) analyzed results of the National Assessment of Educational Progress writing assessment, along with other sources, across a decade and reported that students who frequently wrote a paragraph or more in content areas achieved higher writing scores. Thus integration of literacy with content areas is not just efficient use of classroom time, it strengthens learning in both areas. All teachers need to know the basic components of reading and writing, and ways to integrate them with content area instruction.

Reading in Content Areas

When reading content area material, readers' purposes are usually efferent. This means they want to locate, organize, and utilize information. Informational or expository text explains information about the natural and social world, and it uses particular text structures and features to accomplish that purpose. Readers rarely read it as they do narrative or poetic text. Think of how you read a newspaper or navigate a website. You usually don't start at the beginning and read through every word of every article and advertisement. You choose sections to read and disregard others. You click on certain options and bypass others. You read headlines until one catches your interest and you want to know more. Then you read the article or parts of the article until you are satisfied.

New Literacies

Children will do the same with most informational books, but they are not exposed to informational text as often as they are to other genres—especially in primary grades. One study examined first-grade classrooms and reported that expository texts were being used for an average of only 3.6 minutes a day (Duke, 2000). Teachers must do more to engage and develop children's natural curiosity and interest in the world around them by connecting them with more informational books. Figure 9.1 lists some favorites, including some that are easy to read and some picture books. Along with introducing children to more informational books, you can help them succeed in content area reading by familiarizing them with expository text structure and features, providing them with study strategies, and helping them use study guides.

Expository Text Structure

Children are not usually as familiar with expository text as they are with narrative because informational books are not read aloud to them as often (Jacobs, Morrison, & Swinyard, 2000). But with a little instruction they begin to recognize expository text

Figure 9.1   Favorite Informational Texts for Children

Altman, Joyce (2001)	*Lunch at the Zoo: What Zoo Animals Eat and Why*
Ambrose, Stephen (2001)	*The Good Fight: How World War II Was Won*
Armstrong, Jennifer (1998)	*Shipwreck at the Bottom of the World*
Blackwood, Gary (2008)	*The Great Race: The Amazing Round-the-World Auto Race of 1908*
Burleigh, Robert (1991)	*Flight: The Journey of Charles Lindbergh*
Cobb, Vicki, & Kathy Darling (1980)	*Bet You Can't: Science Impossibilities to Fool You*
Crowe, Chris (2003)	*Getting Away with Murder: The True Story of the Emmett Till Case*
Friedman, Russell (2010)	*The War to End All Wars: World War I*
Fritz, Jean (1987)	*Shh! We're Writing the Constitution*
Hopkinson, Deborah (2006)	*Sky Boys: How They Built the Empire State Building*
Jenkins, Steve (2004)	*Actual Size*
Jones, Charlotte Foltz (1996)	*Accidents May Happen: Fifty Inventions Discovered by Mistake*
Macaulay, David (2003)	*Mosque*
Nelson, Kadir (2008)	*We Are the Ship: The Story of the Negro League Baseball*
Simon, Seymour (2006)	*Emergency Vehicles*
Singer, Marilyn (2008)	*Eggs*
Stanley, Jerry (1992)	*Children of the Dustbowl*
Tunnel, Michael O. (2010)	*Candy Bomber: The Story of the Berlin Airlift's "Chocolate Pilot"*
Walker, Sally M. (2005)	*Secrets of a Civil War Submarine*

structure (Moss, 2004). Authors of informational text can be creative, and their writing can take a variety of forms. Sometimes they use multiple structures within one article or book. Nevertheless, informational text usually falls into one of five general categories: description, sequence, comparison, cause and effect, and problem and solution (Tompkins, 2010).

Description.   **Descriptive text** explains a topic or idea by giving details about its characteristics and attributes. Authors describe features of the topic and illustrate it with examples. A few signal words that children can watch for are *such as, including, is like, for example*, and *for instance*. *We're Sailing Down the Nile* (Krebs, 2008) is an example of descriptive text because the author takes readers on a journey through Egypt explaining statues, temples, tombs, mummies, and, of course, the legendary Sphinx and Great Pyramid.

Reference books such as dictionaries are a type of descriptive text because they provide definitions and backgrounds of words. However, these can seem overwhelming for children unless you first introduce them to simplified versions or content-specific reference books like *Math Dictionary: The Easy, Simple Fun Guide to Help Math Phobics Become Math Lovers* (Monroe, 2006).

Sequence.   When authors list items or give a chronological or numerical order, they are writing **sequential text**. Sometimes this is obvious, and other times an order may only be implied. Words that are prevalent in sequential text include the following: *first, second, third, next, then, now, previously, finally,* and *since.* In *First the Egg,* Seeger (2007) shows sequence by using simple die-cuts to transform a seed into a flower, a tadpole into a frog, and a caterpillar into a butterfly.

Comparison.   Authors create **comparison text** when they compare and contrast information by explaining how something is alike or different from something else. Such texts may present events, concepts, theories, or people. They usually include some of the following words: *however, on the other hand, nevertheless, but, similarly, although, also, just like, either,* and *likewise.* A book that provides a good example of comparison text is *The Frogs and Toads of North America* (Elliott, Gerhardt, & Davidson, 2009), in which the authors compare and contrast the identification, behavior, and calls of frogs and toads.

Cause and Effect.   **Cause-and-effect text** attributes a result or an effect to one or more specific causes related to events, people, or ideas. Authors often signal cause-effect with words like *because, therefore, reasons, consequently, hence, due to, thus,* and *as a result. Causes and Effects of the American Civil War* (O'Muhr, 2009) is an example of a cause-and-effect text that analyses in simple ways what led up to and resulted from this milestone in American history.

Problem and Solution.   Writing that describes how a problem or multiple problems were solved can be categorized as **problem-and-solution text**. Sometimes authors write about problems of the past and their solutions. Sometimes they present possible solutions to current problems. Signal words for children to notice include *dilemma, so that, if/then, puzzle, crisis, setback, difficulty, challenge, resolution, answer,* and *key.* In *Confessions of a Former Bully* (Ludwig, 2010), the author addresses the problem of bullying and offers solutions. On a less serious note, Stevens (2008) addresses real problems and solutions for pet owners from a creative viewpoint in *Help Me, Mr. Mutt!: Expert Answers for Dogs with People Problems.*

Expository Text Features

Besides familiarizing your students with the structure of informational texts, you will need to help them understand and use the text features they will encounter in content area material. Structure is like the floor plan of a house. Features are the fixtures and furnishings within the house. Along with knowing where a bathroom is, you need to know what a shower is and how to use one. You may be able to recognize the dining room, but your use of it will be enhanced if you know how to sit at the table and use a place setting. Text features can be categorized as print features, organizational aids, and graphic aids.

Print Features.   **Print features** are aspects of text that guide readers and expand their understanding. Common print features are defined in Figure 9.2. Not all informational books and websites include every feature. Some may include only a few, but the more familiar children are with all of them, the more comfortable they feel with expository text. For example, a table of contents gives the topics that will be covered and the order in which they come. Websites often organize content with a menu. Like a table of contents or menu, an index also lists the topics found within the book, but gives them in

New Literacies

Figure 9.2   **Print Features and Definitions**

Print Feature	Definition
Table of Contents	List of topics at the beginning of a book arranged in the order of appearance
Menu	Electronic table of contents
Index	List of topics at the end of a book arranged in alphabetical order
Glossary	Alphabetical listing of words used in a book, including their definitions
Pronunciation Guide	Respellings of words to help readers say them correctly
Preface	Explanation that precedes the main body of a text
Appendix	Additional clarification and details that follow a main text
Illustrations	Drawing or photographs that accompany a text

alphabetical order and provides page numbers where each can be found. Some informational text comes with a glossary where words are defined. This is different from a dictionary because it deals only with terms that are used in the book or on the website. The glossary sometimes includes a pronunciation guide to inform readers how to say difficult words. When working at a computer, you can sometimes click on the word in question in a pronunciation guide and a voice will pronounce it so you can hear it.

Information or explanation that precedes the main body of the text is called a preface, and additional clarification and details that follow the main text appear in an appendix. Illustrations, usually found throughout the text, can consist of drawings and photographs of actual people, places, or things. They can also be enlargements and magnifications of things that can't easily be seen.

Organizational Aids.   Many expository texts include **organizational aids** to help readers locate important information quickly. Figure 9.3 lists some of the most common organizational aids. Italics, bold type, or colored print draw attention to words that might be new to your students and need explanation. Words highlighted on a website often

New Literacies

Figure 9.3   **Organizational Aids and Definitions**

Organizational Aid	Definition
Bullets	Column of dots followed by brief snippets of information
Title	Brief designation of what will be presented
Heading/subheading	Short phrases that serve as titles for particular sections
Caption	Brief explanation that appears next to an illustration
Sidebar	Summary of or new information related to a topic
Marginal note	Definition, explanation, or guide for making personal connections found in the margins of text

provide a link to another site that will provide more information about that concept or idea. Some authors use bullets, a column of dots followed by brief snippets of information, to isolate a series of points. Bulleted lists stand out more than the points would if they were included as sentences within a paragraph.

Unlike narrative text in which titles of books and chapters are meant to intrigue and sometimes generate questions, titles in expository text usually let you know accurately what the text is going to cover. Authors can still be creative, but the titles let readers know what to expect. Similarly, headings and subheadings are brief statements that act as titles for particular sections. Children can get an overview of the entire book just by scanning the headings and looking through some of the captions, which are brief explanations associated with illustrations, graphs, and charts. Some books, magazines, and websites include sidebars and marginal notes that can provide definitions, summaries of information, or even new information related to the topic. Occasionally, these features may encourage children to make connections between what they are reading and other books, the real world, and their own life experiences.

Graphic Aids.   Sometimes authors include **graphic aids** that present information visually so it is easy to comprehend (see Figure 9.4). Tables summarize a lot of information and present it visually so it is easy to comprehend. Diagrams and graphs are visual representations of difficult concepts and ideas. Figures can include drawings or photographs, but some figures also present additional text—lists or samples of what is being presented by the authors—that is spotlighted to call attention to the information it provides.

Maps are valuable aids that help children visualize locations and comprehend distances and directions. Many websites offer virtual tours that make maps come to life. Another graphic aid that helps children is a timeline, which places events and people in chronological order so that children can connect new information to what they already know.

New Literacies

Study Strategies

Most college students can tell you their personal strategies. One student said, "I highlight important parts in the reading with a yellow highlighter." Another said, "I take notes during lectures and also during the reading." These are effective strategies for them. One young woman said, "I have to have music or the TV going in the background. Believe it or not, that helps me. I can't concentrate if it is too quiet." This may not be the best

---

Try This for Teaching   **Textbook Scavenger Hunt**

- Introduce children to the features of a textbook by sending them on a scavenger hunt.
- Preview a book and locate features you want students to pay attention to.
- Create clues that will direct students to appropriate page numbers. You can give students clues orally or in writing.
- Have them report their findings.

- Teach a mini-lesson on any features that are unfamiliar to the students.

(Lenski, Caskey, Johns, & Wham, 2007)

Variations for ELLs

- Children can create a scavenger hunt for each other.
- Include multiple texts and have students move from station to station to find either the same features in different texts or examples of different features.

Figure 9.4   **Graphic Aids and Definitions**

Graphic Aid	Definition
Table	Graphic summary of information
Diagram/graph	Visual representation of difficult concept
Figure	Drawing, photograph, or list or sample that represents content
Map	Representation of locations and directions
Time line	Chronological listing

strategy for most people, but it seems to work for this student. In time children who lack the experience of these college students will also find strategies that work for them, but they need a place to begin. Three study strategies that are especially helpful for beginners are SQ3R, mnemonic devices, and KWL.

SQ3R.   This strategy was first developed during World War II to help military personnel learn complex material quickly. In the years since, it has been widely used for older students. SQ3R can be used with guidance in groups or independently to engage effectively with informational text (Robinson, 1970). The S stands for survey. Children first look over the material they are going to read, examining headings, photographs, captions, and graphs. As they become familiar with what the text will cover, they are led to question—the Q stands for question. Based on their survey of the material, children decide what they want to know. If questions are provided at the back of a chapter or on a study guide, those questions may direct their search for answers in their reading. The three Rs stand for read, recite, and review. Children read the material independently if it is at their level or with assistance if it is above their level. Rather than reading everything, they read to find answers to questions, sometimes skimming over some parts of the text that do not apply to the questions asked.

Struggling Learners/ RtI

Skimming, originally the term for gathering the cream from the top of a fresh bucket of milk, has been used by readers to mean gathering main ideas and overlooking the details. They capture the essence of the text without reading all the words, paying close attention to headings and to the first three sentences in paragraphs as they look for only main ideas. In SQ3R children skim to locate the part of the text that may answer each question. Then they slow the pace and read to find the answer they seek. Some educators are afraid that by teaching skimming they are encouraging children to develop a bad habit or discouraging them from ever reading in greater depth. On the contrary, skimming is a necessary skill because students have to deal with the mountains of information available to them in this digital age (Collins & Halverson, 2009). Skimming is similar to scanning. **Scanning** is visually searching over a page to locate a specific date, key word, or answer.

In SQ3R, after students have skimmed or scanned and found the answer to their question, they should recite it to someone—a knowledgeable peer or adult—who can make sure they have the correct response. Then children need to review those answers so the information can be remembered for a test and can be useful in their lives.

After introducing this strategy to children, one student teacher confessed, "It didn't work the way I thought it would. I had to make some alterations." She was preparing to read a section from the science text about endangered animals. "I asked them to survey the text and they did. The colorful illustrations and photographs grabbed their attention. Then I asked if they had any questions and no one did. They didn't want to know anything. They were content to just look at the pictures."

Then the student teacher asked, "What would a teacher ask on a test?" Slowly, the questions started to come: What does the word *endangered* mean? Which animals are endangered and why? "That gave us enough to start with, and we began reading to find those answers," she said. After the students began reading, they started to have more questions of their own. Whether the questions were their own or were questions they assumed a teacher might ask, the children still were able to read with greater purpose. Other educators have made similar adaptations; for example, in the study strategy SQW3R (Learning Centre, 2011), the *W* stands for "write notes" as you read, recite, and review. In SQ4R (Forsythe & Forsythe, 1993), the fourth *R* stands for "reflect."

Struggling Learners/ RtI

Mnemonic Devices.   Learning techniques that aid memory are called **mnemonic** (new-monik; the initial *m* is silent) **devices**. The word seems strange until you realize it was derived from the name Mnemosyne, the goddess of memory in Greek mythology. You can help students remember what they learn and experience a high success rate on tests by employing a few of these devices, which make associations between items that are hard to remember and items students already remember easily. Some devices are as simple as putting words into a familiar song tune (Bintz, 2010). Many children learn the names of the letters of the alphabet by singing them to the tune of "Twinkle, Twinkle Little Star." Stories or poems can be useful. Some children remember the states by making up a story about Ida who was hoeing (Idaho) her mountain (Montana) and along came someone who asked her why (Wyoming), adding other states as the story continues. Others remember how many days in each month with this little poem: "Thirty days hath September/April, June, and November." Higbee (2001) suggested several other mnemonic devices that children can manage easily: letters, physical spaces, and peg lists.

Letters.   Many children studying music learn the notes on the lines of the treble clef by reciting "Every good boy does fine." The first letter of each word names the note.

Children studying geography remember the names of the Great Lakes by spelling the word *homes* (**H**uron, **O**ntario, **M**ichigan, **E**rie, **S**uperior). The names of the letters are ingrained in children's memories, so you can use them to help your students remember new items.

Physical spaces.   Some things don't change—the structure of bodies or the rooms in houses. You can help students use this stable knowledge to remember new material. Children can remember the amendments in the Bill of Rights by associating them with parts of their body, starting from their feet and working up to their heads. For example, they can remember that the first amendment grants freedom of religion (People using their *feet* to walk in or out of any church they desire). The second amendment grants the right to bear arms (Picture a pistol strapped to a cowboy's *leg*). The third amendment means people can't be forced to house or feed soldiers (Pat your *stomach* as you think about feeding soldiers).

Children can also use the rooms in their houses or apartments, starting with their front doors. Students picture the front door with a religious symbol on it for the first amendment. Mentally they open the door and stand in the entryway and imagine a gun hanging on the wall for the second amendment. Next they enter the living room and picture a soldier sitting there eating food for the third amendment. The more unusual the image, the easier it will be to remember.

Peg lists.   Numbers are ingrained in children's memories, so you can use the shape or sound of the number to remember lists of items. For example, if children use their imaginations, the number *1* looks like a candle, and *2* looks like a swan. Turn *3* on its side, and it looks like part of a clover, and *4* looks like a chair. If you are teaching the names of the presidents of the United States in order, associate a candle with Washington (who is going to wash a ton of candles) and swan with Adams (a swan with an enormous Adam's apple). If three reminds children of a clover, they can associate that with Jefferson (Jeff and his son are picking lucky clovers).

Another peg list uses words that rhyme with numbers (1-thumb, 2-shoe, 3-tree) and helps children make associations with those rhymes. Washington—He is washing his thumb. Adams—Adam is leaving the Garden of Eden and needs shoes. Jefferson—Jeff is climbing a tree to find his son. If the items on your list go beyond 10, associate 11 with 1 [After Washington washes his thumb he is going to poke (Polk) someone with it], 12 with 2, 13 with 3, and so forth. When you reach 21, link it to 11 and to 1 [After Washington washes his thumb he is going to poke (Polk) Arthur in the chest (Chester A. Arthur)]. It may sound strange—even silly—but perhaps that is why children enjoy making and remembering these associations. Figure 9.5 shows two peg lists, one based on the shape of the digits and another on rhyming words.

English Language Learners

Rhyming Words	Shapes
1-thumb	1-candle
2-shoe	2-swan
3-tree	3-clover
4-door	4-chair
5-hive	5-hook
6-sticks	6-yo-yo
7-heaven	7-arrow
8-gate	8-hour glass
9-spine	9-balloon
10-hen	10-bat and ball

Figure 9.5

Number Peg Lists to Aid Children's Memories

(adapted from Higbee, 2001)

KWL.   KWL is a study strategy in which readers assess what they know about a topic and determine what they want to find out before reading expository text. After reading, they determine what they learned. The letters stand for three questions: What do I **KNOW**? What do I **WANT** to find out? What have I **LEARNED**? The strategy was developed by Ogle (1986), who wanted to focus teachers on students'

English Language Learners

prior knowledge (backgrounds and interests) and help students become more active learners.

A fifth-grade teacher planned to read *Golden Gate Bridge: Now That's Big* (Riggs, 2009) with his students. He began the KWL strategy by asking, "What do we know about the Golden Gate Bridge?"

One child said, "It's red."

Another responded, "It's a suspension bridge."

Another said, "It's really tall."

The teacher wrote these and other students' responses on the board in a column labeled "What We Know." He then asked, "What do we want to learn?" and got a less than enthusiastic response. The teacher heightened interest by drawing into question what they claimed to know. He created a little disequilibrium by going back to the original list and asking questions. He pointed to the word *red* and asked, "Really? Are you sure?"

Some of the students said, "Yes."

The teacher said, "If it is red, why did they choose that color?"

Next he pointed to the words *suspension bridge* and asked, "Are you sure?"

The students were silent. They were not so confident now.

The teacher said, "You are right about it being tall, but how tall?"

Suddenly the students had questions—not necessarily new ones, but questions about what they had been so sure they knew. They were suddenly eager to get their hands on the book.

As they read, one student said, "Ah ha! I knew it was a suspension bridge. I knew it!" The teacher wrote it in the column labeled, "What We Learned." The students were amazed to find out that the floor of the bridge is 220 feet (67 meters) above the water. "That's over 20 stories!" called out one of the students. The teacher wrote it down. They found out the red color they were so sure about is actually more of a rusty color called *international orange* and crews are constantly repainting the bridge to keep it from rusting. The teacher wrote this down. The study strategy worked because the teacher made sure the students had genuine questions and a high level of interest in finding out the answers before he opened the book.

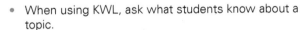

Try This for Teaching　**Are You Sure?**

- When using KWL, ask what students know about a topic.
- List their responses.
- Create disequilibrium by questioning what students claim to know.
- Ask questions to raise interest, such as "Are you sure?"
- Ask clarifying questions, such as "How tall is tall?" or "Was anyone else involved?"
- This should lead to some genuine questions to which students want answers.
- Read to confirm what they claimed to know or to extend their original responses.

Variations for ELLs

- KWL Plus (Carr & Ogle, 1987) is an activity that suggests having students summarize and organize their findings rather than just leaving a random list of what was learned.
- KWHL (Wills, 1995) is an adaptation in which the question "How do I find out?" is added to help students identify and use multiple resources to locate answers.
- KWWL (Bryan, 1998) is a version of the study strategy that adds a fourth column to indicate "where to find the information."

Try This for Professional Development   **Reversing the Trend**

A disappointing trend has been noted, especially in urban schools, for teachers to move away from use of texts in content areas because students can't or won't read them (Balfanz & Byrnes, 2006; Balfanz, Herzog, & MacIver, 2007).

- Determine why this trend is a problem.
- Consider alternatives to support students as they read in content areas.

- Reflect on how teachers helped or didn't help you as you were assigned to read content area material.
- Select a topic and search for simplified or alternative texts on that topic.

Study Guides

Along with knowing expository text structures and features and being equipped with some useful study strategies, children also benefit from **study guides**, which are created by teachers in advance to focus children's attention on the main points of the reading and make sure they have captured the essence of the material (Manzo, Manzo, & Thomas, 2009). The reading level of many informational texts may be above the ability of some class members, so assigning a class to read a chapter independently is rarely an effective option. However, reading every chapter in the textbook together as a class becomes burdensome and time consuming. A study guide is a bridge to student independence. It allows you to offer the help you might have provided if you had been reading together, but allows the child to work alone or with a partner.

Struggling Learners/ RtI

A study guide is not a worksheet. Worksheets are usually developed to be used as practice or assessment after the reading or lesson. Study guides can be used *during* the reading. They also can be used to hold students accountable, but that is not their main purpose. They are meant to offer the assistance children need to be successful with reading tasks that would ordinarily be too difficult. There are many different types of study guides, but four guides that are especially useful are graphic organizers, anticipation guides, Internet inquiries, and games.

Graphic Organizers.   Graphic organizers are visual ways of organizing information. Some call them concept maps, mind maps, or relationship charts. Whatever term is applied, they guide students through reading material (or lectures, DVDs, or websites) and help them compress all the information they receive into a simple-to-remember graphic display. There are many "one-size-fits-all" organizers that can be printed from sites on the Internet, but the more personalized an organizer is to your students and to the specific reading they are doing, the more useful it will be—right down to page numbers you want them to turn to and illustrations you want them to examine.

Keep the organizer simple and focused on main ideas and key vocabulary. Rather than just leaving blank space for the whole answer, try leaving one blank for each letter. If the main heading is Revolutionary War, print

$$_ {}_ v _ {}_ _ {}_ _ {}_ i _ {}_ _ {}_ _ {}_ _ {}_ y\, W _ {}_ _ {}$$

at the top of the page. The number of words and letters gives children enough clues to make sure they write the correct answer. If the whole space is left blank, they may write something totally different and miss the main point.

Don't just use the organizer as a place to record main headings and facts. Leave space for students to write. Add comparisons with your own classroom or community to keep students interested and to make the material more meaningful. For example, if the text reports that about 400 American soldiers died in the Battle of Bunker Hill, you can write, "How many American soldiers died at Bunker Hill?" and leave a space for students to write the answer. Then add a comment such as, "That is about half the number of students in our school!" If the text says that American colonists felt the taxes they had to pay were unfair, you could help children personalize that information by asking, "When have you ever felt like something is unfair?" and leave a space for a short response. When preparing a graphic organizer, ask yourself not only what main points you want the children to carry away from the reading or what words you want them to define but also what asides you would make and what additional information you would provide to bring the text to life if you were reading it together as a class. You can incorporate some of that into your graphic organizer. Internet sites such as www.teachnology.com/web_tools/graphic_org/ offer examples of organizers you can use as a pattern and tools to generate your own. Figure 9.6 shows several teacher-made graphic organizers.

Struggling Learners/ Rtl

Anticipation Guides.   An **anticipation guide** is a list of statements related to the topic of the text the students will be reading. Ideally, the list should be more than a true/false test that students can pass without completing the reading. Anticipation guides should not only assess what students already know, but also challenge some of those beliefs (Duffelmeyer, 1994).

Before they read, ask students if they agree or disagree with each of the statements on the list. You may want to ask older students to explain why. The purpose of this study guide is to activate students' prior knowledge, raise some questions in their minds,

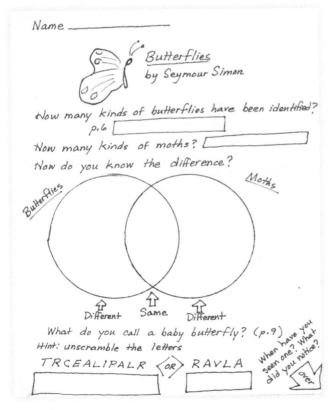

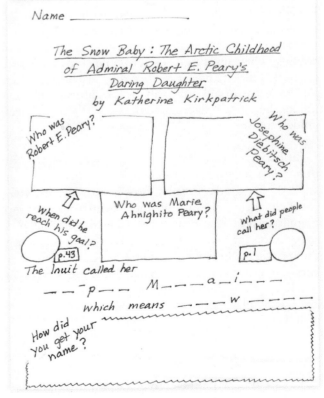

Figure 9.6

Teacher-made Graphic Organizers for *Butterflies* (Simon, 2011) and *The Snow Baby* (Kirkpatrick, 2007)

Try This for Teaching   **Create Your Own Graphic Organizers**

- Create your own graphic organizer rather than over relying on ready-made patterns from the Internet.
- Preview the reading and decide what main points you want students to take away.
- Draw circles or squares on a paper to correspond to these points and leave blanks that students can fill in so they record the correct headings in the correct spaces.
- Add spaces focused on key vocabulary and other important points.
- Make comparisons between information in the text and your class, school, and community.

- Leave space for students to write personal responses as well as note information from the text.
- Check to make sure students used the organizers correctly.

Variations for ELLs

- Use the organizer as a frame for writing about what the students learned together as a class or independently.
- Allow students who need extra assistance to complete the organizer with a buddy.

and help provide purpose for reading. This may be to answer questions, to confirm their previous belief, or to cause them to revise their perceptions based on the information provided by the author. As with graphic organizers, some anticipation guides come ready-made for specific texts. You can adapt what has been done or create your own.

To use an anticipation guide, pass it out to children before they read and have them mark whether they agree or disagree with the statements. They can work independently, with partners, or even in small groups. Discuss their responses as a class and then turn

Speaking/Listening

Figure 9.7   Teacher-made Anticipation Guide

Anticipation Guide

DIRECTIONS: Before reading the text, read each statement below and mark your response in the *agree* or *disagree* column. Be ready to explain your choices. Then read "A Letter to My Daughter" (Joyner, 2011) and return to the list after reading.

Before Reading			After Reading	
Agree	Disagree		Agree	Disagree
☐	☐	Mary, Florence Griffith Joyner's (Flo Jo's) daughter, started running track at a young age.	☐	☐
☐	☐	Flo Jo's family was a greater priority to her than athletics.	☐	☐
☐	☐	Even though Florence never met her grandfather, he had an impact on her.	☐	☐
☐	☐	Flo Jo thought it was her duty to make sure her daughter became a superstar.	☐	☐
☐	☐	Children are too young to choose what they should pursue.	☐	☐
☐	☐	Being with family is more important than reaching a goal.	☐	☐
☐	☐	A reward like a gold medal is worth any sacrifice.	☐	☐

Create Your Own Anticipation Guide

- Preview the text the children will read.
- Write statements rather than questions about the main points.
- Focus on points in the text that may challenge common conceptions.
- Include statements that are both general and specific.
- Provide space for students to record whether they agree or disagree with each statement.

- Include simple directions.

(Duffelmeyer, 1994)

Variations for ELLs

- Have students mark the statements as true or false.
- Ask students to supply reasons to support their beliefs or to alter their decisions.

---

them to the reading. After they have read the text, encourage students to go back to the anticipation guide and respond again to indicate whether or not they agree with the statements. Older students can write down ideas from the text that support their initial reaction or made them change their minds. This could lead naturally to another class discussion.

Figure 9.7 is an example of a teacher-made anticipation guide for use with "A Letter to My Daughter," by Olympic gold medalist Florence Griffith Joyner (2011).

New Literacies

Internet Inquiries. More than 75 percent of American homes now have access to the Internet, making it a source of information for many students—and the primary source for most (Eagleton & Dobler, 2007). The amount of information available to students on the Internet is mind boggling. Search engines such as Google enable instant access to billions of pages. That is too much information for anyone to deal with—especially children who find that much of it is written well above their reading levels. They need guidance as they read on the Internet.

Internet inquiry projects focus students on questions with many possible answers, including real-world problems that are unsolved. The students pursue answers to these questions with resources on the Internet. Some educators distinguish between a project, which is more student-directed, and a WebQuest, which is more teacher-directed (Leu, Leu, & Coiro, 2004). In either category, teachers carefully structure the inquiry so it

Internet Inquiry

- Ensure that students have the Internet research skills needed to complete the project.
- Make sure questions have multiple and/or competing answers.
- Plan so that Internet inquiry projects can be completed in a reasonable amount of time.
- Provide students with a list of websites to explore that you have previewed and know are appropriate for young audiences.

- Help students to organize and present findings.

Variations for ELLs

- If using primary documents, make sure students can analyze them in meaningful ways (Barton, 2001; Moss & Young, 2010).
- Collaborate in groups. This could include other classes outside of your school or area that you can work with using the Internet.

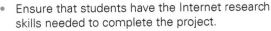

is manageable. For example, you can limit materials students will access to ensure that less time is spent locating appropriate material and more time is spent processing it. Teachers help students locate primary and secondary sources and other data (Dodge, 1995; Molebash & Dodge, 2003).

Your students could choose to inquire about which mode of public transportation is the safest or what events led to the vote being extended to women and 18-year-olds. Prepare an introduction to gain their attention and then clarify how they should locate and organize information. You also need to explain how their findings would be presented and evaluated. Will students persuade others to their point of view or simply present a possible answer or solution for others to consider? Will their findings be shared orally, presented as a PowerPoint presentation, or written? Will the work be evaluated by you, peers, or others?

Students working at computer stations.

Next you need to explain and model the process they should use on the Internet. Sites that can help you get started are located at www.epals.com/ and webquest.sdsu.edu. Remind students that they are not just learning about a particular topic; rather, they are learning how to locate, organize, and present information using the Internet. Although these projects require a significant amount of research and preparation by the teacher, the skills students develop will serve them far beyond that one project. Explore the possibilities of enriching the inquires with Google Maps (maps.google.com/).

New Literacies

Games. Although they are not conventional study guides, simple games can motivate children to complete content area reading. Jeopardy-style review games with questions that test the students' knowledge of the material can be fun after reading. However, the main purpose of a study guide is to help children *during* reading. Some children may not be initially interested in the topics they are expected to read about, but they usually are interested in games. Choose simple games that take little preparation: Tic-Tac-Toe, Hangman, Dots and Boxes, Blockhead, or Bingo. The games don't have to be related to the topic at all. You simply use the game as a way to motivate students to read. For example, when students are

---

Try This for Professional Development

WebQuests Across the Grades

- Using webquest.sdsu.edu, look at sample WebQuests at various grade levels.

  - Grades K–2 example: "Please Help Our Ocean Animals" (informational text)

  - Grades 3–5 example: "All About Me" (personal narrative)

  - Grade 4 example: "Rhyme Time Circus" (poetry)

  - Grades 5–6 example: "Wanted: Wild West Outlaws" (personal narrative)

- Grades 6–8 example: "Fat Facts" (persuasive argument)

- What changes do you notice from grade level to grade level?

- What adaptations would you make if you were going to do something similar?

- How would you accommodate ELLs and strugglers?

Struggling Learners/
RtI

reading about the California Gold Rush in a social studies text, you might challenge them with "Let's play Tic-Tac-Toe. I place my X here, and you need to earn your chance to place an O by telling me what a boomtown was." Children then read the text as a class or in groups with lead readers. They may just skim the material individually until they find the answer. The answer gives them an O to place in the game. You place your next X, and then send the children in search of at least two countries from which people moved to California during the Gold Rush. You can ask questions that go beyond the facts presented in the text. Then, after students have completed reading a section of the text, you can synthesize and apply information as well: "What if gold had never been discovered in California? How would the history of our country be different?" "What economic forces today motivate people to move?" When students have responded in writing and/or discussed the question sufficiently, they earn their next O and the chance to place it on the board. After the game begins, children who cared little about the Gold Rush when you began may be willing to read intently from their social studies book.

The use of games is not limited to times you read the text together as a class. If children are using another study guide, such as a graphic organizer, you can use the game to help them stay on task. For example, if you are playing Bingo, inform them that you will not play until everyone is working quietly. When students follow directions, compliment their hard work by calling one or two Bingo numbers, "B-7 and N-49." Some teachers express concern that games may result in management problems, but usually they offer

---

Try This for Teaching   **Survivor Whiteboard Game**

- Use this simple game to motivate students during content area reading.

- Draw connecting circles on the board—a few more than the number of students in the class.

- Have students pick a circle and claim it by placing their initials in the circle.

- Indicate a starting place with an arrow.

- Tell students that you will eliminate circles as they read and answer questions in order to see who survives.

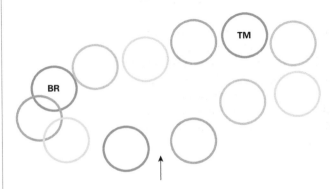

- Ask students a question related to the reading. Call on a student to answer the question. If she

answers correctly, she rolls a die, which determines whose circles will be eliminated. If she answers incorrectly, go to another student.

- For example, if the student rolls a three, start at the arrow and cross out every third circle until you get back to the arrow. Finish counting past the arrow if needed. Turn 1 into 11 and 2 into 12 so the game is not over too quickly.

- Repeat the process of reading, answering questions, and eliminating circles until there is one survivor left.

- When students' circles are eliminated, they still are allowed to read and answer questions to see who survives.

- Unlike other games, there is no strategy involved. Students can't count ahead or put their initials in a better place. The outcome is random, so the focus remains on the content the students are reading rather than on the game itself.

- You can include your initials in one of the circles or add the initials of the principal and a few other teachers. Students delight in seeing those circles eliminated.

- Use both dice instead of only one to generate larger numbers and make the game last longer.

Figure 9.8   **Simple Games That Can Be Adapted for Classroom Use**

Battle Ship	Dots and Boxes	Blockhead	Mission Cube	Racko
Break Out	Mind Reader	Pick Up Sticks	Tic-Tac-Toe	Mad Libs
Hangman	Potato People	Jenga	Tail on the Donkey	Mazes
Concentration	Miniature Golf	Pictionary	Shell Game	Puzzles
Connect Four	Steal the Bacon	Lights All	Hot Potato	Fruit Basket

children motivation to stay engaged and in control in order to continue playing the game. If things get out of hand, you can stop the game.

If you are not sure how to play Tic-Tac-Toe, Bingo, or other simple games, search on the Internet for "Bingo rules" or "How to play Tic-Tac-Toe," and you will be led to websites that give you the information you need. In some cases you will need to simplify or adapt the rules for classroom use. Playing the game exactly as it should be played is not your end goal; the game is only a means of guiding students through expository material that can sometimes be challenging for them.

Students can play games against each other, or they can play you. No additional rewards need to be offered beyond the satisfaction of winning, and games don't have to be finished at one set time. They can be put on hold and continued over several days if the reading will require that much time. Figure 9.8 provides a list of simple games that can be adapted easily for classroom use. Electronic versions of several of these games—with directions—are available at the following website: www.teach-nology.com/web_tools/games/.

Writing in Content Areas

In addition to reading, children are also expected to write in content areas. The Common Core (2011) emphasizes informational writing, yet this is the genre that new teachers feel least qualified to teach (Grisham & Wolsey, 2011). Some teachers think that writing in content areas takes too much time (Newell, Koukis, & Boster, 2007), but "writing is how students connect the dots in their knowledge" (National Commission on Writing, 2003, p. 3). Content area writing allows them to initiate, respond to, and explore new thinking as well as to demonstrate what they have learned.

Writing can be integrated with the content areas on two levels. You can easily incorporate the first level, writing without revision, into any content area instruction. The second level of integration, writing with revision, may take more time, but it enables you to connect the writing process more fully with content area instruction. Circumstances determine which level is appropriate. You will need to be familiar with various forms of expository text and with argumentative writing as well. Although argumentation is not always related to content area study, it can be used effectively as you deal with issues in science, social studies, art, mathematics, and other content areas.

Common Core
State Standards

Writing without Revision

Writing without requiring revision is a simple, efficient way to help students think their way into content area topics. Often the focus of writing is on helping the student internalize or explore content rather than on the mechanics of the writing, such as spelling.

Three effective approaches for writing without revision in content areas are learning logs, think-write-show, and note taking/note making.

Learning Logs.

Learning logs are notebooks in which students reflect on readings, lessons, or class experiences in response to teacher questions or writing prompts. One teacher calls them "think pads." At the beginning of your lesson, give students a prompt and ask them to write briefly on that topic. This activity is designed to encourage students to focus their minds and make sense of the content material. Learning logs are different from journals in which students write about whatever they wish. Learning logs have been used successfully across all content areas (Audet, Hickman, & Dobrynina, 1996; McIntosh & Draper, 2001).

English Language
Learners

One fifth-grade teacher typically used learning logs in social studies to review previously learned material. On one occasion, she posted the prompt, "What did we learn about reading a map?" Most students wrote at least a half-page filled with explanations and examples.

While studying the westward migration of the United States, one student wrote the following:

> Most people came west for land and gold, but others came for freedom. The United States was supposed to be free, but there were some who were persecuted so much they had to leave the land of the free to really be free.

He then gave examples of several groups that migrated west. This student's teacher found that the quality of the learning logs improved as students shared their work: "When

Figure 9.9   **General Writing Prompts That Can Be Adapted to Specific Content Areas**

Write a personal response to a statement or quote.

Identify main points of a reading.

Write a newspaper headline summarizing a passage.

Write a note to a child explaining the concept in simple terms.

Draw a graphic representation illustrating the point of a passage.

Write about a possible application of the topic in the real world.

Describe the importance of one or two words in a passage.

Write about a topic from another perspective.

Suggest a solution to a topic-related problem.

Compare two different ideas presented.

Outline a lesson or a presentation you might give.

Write about a personal experience that relates to the topic.

Write a short poem or new words to a song using ideas from the reading.

Write an advertisement related to the topic.

Create an imaginary dialogue between two or more people discussing the topic.

Write about a person related to the topic you would like to meet.

(adapted from Wright, 2002)

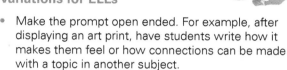

> *Try This for Teaching* **Learning Logs**
>
> - Make sure students have a notebook or a section in their notes designated as a learning log.
> - Write a prompt focused on material learned recently or on the topic to be discussed that day.
> - Allow time for students to write.
> - Occasionally ask a few volunteers to share their entries.
>
> **Variations for ELLs**
>
> - Make the prompt open ended. For example, after displaying an art print, have students write how it makes them feel or how connections can be made with a topic in another subject.
> - Play a piece of music and have students write a reflection about their feelings or make connections to other content areas.

I found a student whose log showed that he really understood, I used it as an example for others to follow." Along with discovering that learning logs could be an effective way to introduce or close a lesson, the teacher also observed that the quality of student discussion during lessons was richer when students were expected to write. Figure 9.9 provides some general prompts that can be adapted to specific content areas.

Speaking/Listening

Think-Write-Share. When teachers ask questions, they may count on having at least one or two students with raised hands. Think-write-share is an activity that requires all students to write a response to a teacher-posed question before some are asked to share (Silver, Strong, & Perini, 2008).

One fourth-grade teacher often tried to involve everyone by allowing think time and expecting students to write before sharing. For one think-write-share activity in mathematics, she asked, "What is an equivalent fraction?" She gave the class a few minutes to think and then asked them to write their responses before she called on students to share, using a document camera. In reflecting on the use of this strategy, the teacher made the following comments:

> I assumed that everyone understood [what an equivalent fraction is], because we've done it for a while. However, as we shared, I soon realized that some of my students thought that equivalent fractions were [only] fractions that were the same, for example, 1/4 = 1/4.

To address this misconception, the teacher strategically selected students to share, based on the thinking she had seen demonstrated. She chose kids who were getting it wrong, kids who were getting it a little, and those who knew it well. The think-write-share activity heightened student engagement in writing. Students were held accountable for their own understanding in content areas (Wilcox & Monroe, 2011). Figure 9.10 shows an example of an intermediate grade student who completed a think-write-share activity about fractions.

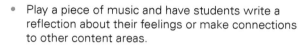

Figure 9.10

Student Example of Think-Write-Share

Try This for Teaching   **Think-Write-Share**

- Ask students a question.
- Allow time for them to think about possible answers.
- Before anyone responds, give all students a chance to write a response to the question.
- Call on students to share their written responses.

Variations for ELLs

- Think-write-pair-share (Nessel & Graham, 2007) is an adaptation in which students share with partners and have a chance to revise their responses before sharing with the whole class.
- For complex questions, suggest students write down a few key words from which they can formulate oral responses.

- After the students have written their responses, have them pass their writing from student to student and then write responses to what has already been written.
- Students can hold up green, red, or yellow papers to show they agree, disagree, or are unsure about a response.
- Try letting students wad up the paper on which they have written a response and then throw it across the room to someone else like a snowball. Have everyone unfold papers, read answers, write another response, wad up the paper, and repeat the process several more times.

Note Taking/Note Making.   Students may be accustomed to taking notes, but you can ask them to *make* notes as well. Making notes consists of annotating, paraphrasing, and synthesizing the content of their reading or lesson. Along with listing the main points, students can write their own reflections and insights (Robb, 2002). This process has also been referred to as creating a double-entry journal (Daniels & Zemelman, 2004).

One fifth-grade teacher used the strategy of note taking/note making in science to explore several moon formation theories. She asked her students to fold their papers in half vertically. Then she directed students to outline the three main theories about how the moon came to be on the left side of the paper: (1) It was formed at the same time as the Earth; (2) It broke away from the Earth but remained trapped by its gravity; (3) It was floating through space and was caught by Earth's gravity. On the right side of the paper, students wrote their own reactions and observations. One student wrote, "Even though the moon seems close, it is really very far away. I think that is cool." Another wrote, "It's weird to think that the moon could have started as a piece of the Earth. I wonder how something that big could have gotten broken off without leaving a hole." The same student went on to create his own analogy: "I guess it is like putting a spoon in and getting a big bite of cereal. That bite is gone, but the bowl still looks full. No one can tell you took a bite." Note making encourages students to make connections between new concepts and previously learned material as well as with their personal experience. Figure 9.11 shows a student example of note taking/note making.

English Language Learners

Writing with Revision

As engaging as writing without revision may be, there are times when students need to complete the writing process. If children are never required to write more that a quick response or a personal opinion with no expectation of revision, they are not learning to think deeply about topics and refine their thinking. The writing process requires brainstorming, synthesizing, and evaluating. As you integrate the entire writing process with content area studies, your students can improve their writing and extend their content area thinking (Whitin & Whitin, 2000).

Not all writing assignments need to be completed individually. Ideas and meaning are often constructed and refined through group interactions (Newell, Koukis, & Boster, 2007). Children need not only to learn content material but also to find ways to communicate it to others. Two ways to have children do this without teaching them all individually are to complete a shared writing together as a class and to have children work in small groups.

Shared Writing. With shared writing the class completes the writing process together. The teacher or a student volunteer writes on a chart or at the board while the class decides what should be written and how (Ministry of Education, 1994; Tompkins & Collom, 2004). Wilcox and Monroe (2011) described how a third-grade teacher used shared writing with her students to review what they learned in their geometry unit. Using chart paper, the teacher recorded a student-generated word bank that included *face, edge, vertex, congruent figures, polygons*, and other content-related terms. On subsequent sheets, the teacher used a black marker to record in sentences what the students shared about their learning. Next she guided them to suggest revisions and additions to their shared writing, recording those suggestions in a different color. Some changes had to do with word choice ("learning *about* geometry" became "learning *and exploring* geometry"), and other changes related to geometry concepts. In the shared writing, the class had listed 3-D shapes—*spheres, cones, cubes, cylinders*, and so on—and had given real-life examples. During revision

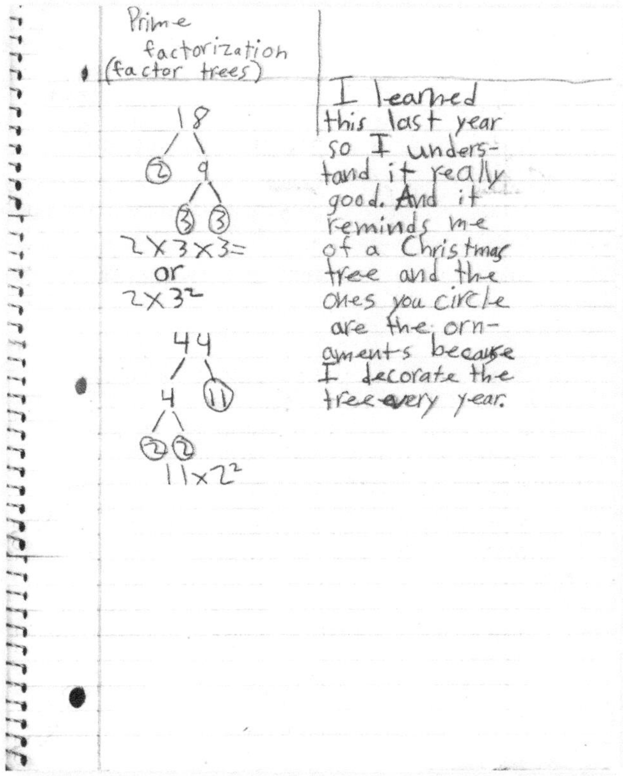

Figure 9.11

Sample Student Note Taking/Note Making

Try This for Teaching **Collaborative Book**

- Write a collaborative book about a concept being learned in a content area. For example, students could write a book that they title *Florence Nightingale: The Lady with the Lamp* or *Believe It Or Not, Earthquakes Happen All the Time*.

- Provide a sense of audience by informing older students that they are writing this book for children in younger grades. Then the picture book format does not seem so elementary to them.

- Begin with a shared writing, complete with revisions and editing, on chart paper or at the board.

- Number the sentences and assign each student a numbered part to write as a final draft for a page in the class book.

- Move from student to student to edit papers. This requires little time because each child is only completing a sentence or two.

- Encourage students to fill the remainder of their papers with visual representations or illustrations for the specific sentences they have written.

- When students are finished, gather the pages in sequence and add a cover with a title.

Variations for ELLs

- When the shared writing has only a few sentences, create multiple copies of the same book.

- As you edit, have students finish their pictures. When editing is finished, encourage them to illustrate during your read-aloud time.

Struggling Learners/
RtI

they went beyond visualization to include attributes: "Some 3-D figures will have vertexes (corners), edges, and faces." Students then suggested three titles and voted on which they liked best. Figure 9.12 shows another example of shared writing.

Small Groups.   Before assigning students to write a report or essay individually, you can group them to complete small parts of a class project. For example, you might inform the students that they will be writing a class report on Germany. Since your focus at this point is on organizing and presenting information rather than locating it, provide basic information that is short and simple. Even some children's informational books may provide too much information for this activity. Choose instead a source such as the *World Book Student Discovery Encyclopedia* (2000), in which the information on Germany is summarized on four pages using large print and the article is written at about a third-grade reading level.

Read the three-paragraph introduction and use shared writing to summarize it into one paragraph. Then divide the children into five groups—since there are five headings in the article. Pass the first group a copy of the section about the land in Germany. Give the other groups the sections on people, resources and products, history, and facts about Germany. Designate a lead reader and writer in each group to help the students summarize the material into one or two short paragraphs. As the groups complete their rough drafts, work with one group at a time to help them revise and edit their work. Other groups can be working on illustrations when they have finished their writing and are waiting for your assistance. After you have helped a group to revise and edit their section, make a copy of that version for each group member and instruct all to complete a final draft of the paper. This can be done in nice handwriting or at the computer. Each child is responsible for turning in a final draft of the section that he or she helped to write, revise, and edit in

Cardinals are Cool!
~~Cardinals~~
~~Learning About Cardinals~~

In our third grade we have been learning about birds. ~~Our~~ One of our favorites is the Cardinal. ~~The~~ Cardinals are found ~~in the East.~~ throughout the eastern half of North America. When they are grown they are 7 to 9 inches long. Cardinals are bright ~~and~~ red ~~and~~ with gray on their backs. They have black feathers around their eyes and ~~mouths~~ bills. They eat seeds, ~~They eat~~ grain, and worms, ~~They eat~~ and beetles. They ~~sound~~ make have a cheerful song that sounds like a flute. They ~~sound happy.~~ are songbirds

Figure 9.12

Example of Shared
Writing in Science

Try This for Teaching	**Put It in Your Own Words**

- Help children avoid copying from textbooks, encyclopedias, or websites by having them answer simple questions as they begin writing.
- Assign each student one of the following question words: who, what, when, where, why, how.
- Read material from the textbook or another source.
- Have students listen for answers to their assigned question, such as "Who was Napoleon?" "What did he do?" "When did he live?"
- Ask students to answer their questions in a complete sentence or two.

- Write the sentences on the board or a chart as they are given.
- Revise the sentences into a coherent paragraph.
- Explain that this is how you "put it in your own words" rather than copying.

Variations for ELLs

- Students can work with partners or in small groups.
- Students can provide brief answers that can be expanded by you or the class.

a small group. When all your students have finished their final drafts, gather one from each group and add a copy of the class-created introduction and a cover; copies of this class book on Germany can be placed in the classroom library or the school library, or they can be given to younger classes for their reading centers.

Completing this form of collaborative report allows students to experience the benefits of cooperative learning and the safety of a support group around them as they learn—both essentials for ELLs. It also makes the workload manageable for the teacher. Rather than having 30 complete reports from 30 children who may all need your assistance, each group is only doing one section of a complete report. Furthermore, rather than having about six papers per group to work with, the teacher only helps to revise and edit one page for each group, which is copied and becomes the rough draft used by all the students. When the activity is finished, the teacher has edited only one report, and yet all the students have learned the content-area material and benefited from experiencing the entire writing process together in preparation for more independent assignments later.

English Language Learners

Other forms of expository writing could also be completed using small groups. For example, for a class persuasive essay, you can complete the first paragraph together in a shared writing, settling on the argument you are making and the reasons you will give. Then the groups can each write more about one of the reasons. Perhaps one group could explore a counter argument, and another group could write a conclusion.

In addition to exploring different forms of expository writing, you can also explore different genres using small groups. Try using the sections of a newspaper or a magazine as a pattern for producing expository text. When one class was studying ancient Rome, their teacher divided them into writing groups. Some groups were asked to create headlines and articles that would have appeared in a newspaper in ancient Rome. One group worked on a sports section, and another group wrote want ads. Still another group wrote about entertainment, and a final group created a few advertisements that highlighted products that would have appealed to Roman families in those days. When all the groups put their sections together, they had created a newspaper much like the one shown in the book *The Roman News* (Langley & De Souza, 1997).

Expository Text

You need to know how to integrate content area instruction with writing, both with and without revision. In addition, you need to understand various forms that are used when writing expository text. Authors use expository text structures and features as they write books, instructions, essays, reports, memos, applications, manuals, case studies, and other things. Many genres are explained and explored specifically in resources such as *Writers Express* (Sebranek, Nathan, Kemper, & Krevzke, 2000).

The purpose of expository text is usually to convey information accurately or to explain concepts, ideas, or steps in a process. But it can also include elements of the narrative and opinion genres. For example, expository writing may include stories and personal anecdotes to introduce or support the information, or it may include reasons for its importance. Key words associated with

Student conducting an interview with an author.

expository writing include *types, components, size, function, definitions, names, differentiation,* and *analysis*. Expository writing describes the when, where, why, and how of people, places, and things.

Most children are anxious and motivated to express ideas and share what they have learned with others. However, without guidance these ideas often come out in a random jumble of disconnected expressions. With instruction and direction, children are able to organize and group their ideas into coherent formats. They learn how to focus on one topic and incorporate only relevant examples, facts, and details into their writing (Common Core State Standards, 2011).

Common Core State Standards

As children produce writing focused on informing or explaining, they draw on what they know or can learn from both primary and secondary resources. A **primary source** is material that has been recorded firsthand by participants or in-person observations. An interview, journal entry, participant description, or account of an eyewitness might qualify as a primary source. Technology tools make it easier to access primary sources. For example, interviews can be done with people across the world through Skype. A **secondary source** contains information that was originally presented elsewhere. Examples include articles from an encyclopedia and books written about a topic by those who are reporting the knowledge or experience of others. As children gain experience, they must learn to judge the reliability and validity of their sources and to avoid copying the words that others have written.

New Literacies

The most common genre of expository writing in elementary school is a report. Another can be an alphabet book.

Reports.   Children write reports about animals, countries, states, or famous people. Topics may also include books they have read, the curriculum they study, extracurricular activities they observe or participate in, or projects or experiments they create. Whatever the content, well-written reports demonstrate not only understanding but also mastery of skills and processes involved in producing them—everything from researching and following directions to revising, editing, and completing work on schedule. Typically teachers assign report topics, but there is great value in allowing students to pursue their own interests. In 1984 Macrorie coined the term *I-Search* and explained, "Contrary to most school research papers, the I-Search comes out of a student's life and answers a need in it" (p. ii). Although such an ideal level of personal inquiry may not be manageable in every

---

Try This for Teaching   **Put Yourself in the Writing**

- One way to help children avoid plagiarism and use their own words when writing expository text is to encourage them to add their own thoughts.

- Along with writing about the topic, they must write connections between the topic and their own experiences.

- If the book the child has read includes information about the Alamo, a child might write, "I remember going there with my dad," making a personal experience connection.

- Another student could write, "I saw a movie about the Alamo." This is a vicarious experience connection.

- Another student might write, "The Alamo is about standing up for what you believe, and I do that when I say no to drugs." This is a personal application connection.

- When you review student writing and it sounds like it was cut and pasted, tell the child you don't see him in the writing and ask for revisions.

Variation for ELLs

- Along with connections, students can write about how the informational text connects with their interests or talents (for example, how is what you read about the Alamo like playing soccer or practicing the piano?).

classroom, you can always look for opportunities to offer children choice. They may all have to complete a state report, but they can select a state with which they have personal contact or experience. They may be assigned to report on a planet, but they can select the one about which they are most curious.

Children can succeed in writing reports when you provide clear guidelines. Communicate exactly what the assignment entails before they begin gathering information or writing. Consider the age of the children when you determine appropriate length requirements and formatting instructions. Provide examples for children to follow, such as those given by Sebranek, Nathan, Kemper, and Krevzke (2000). Reports typically include four sections: an introduction to the topic (beginning), main points and details (middle), a summary of the ideas or a look to the future (end), and a list of materials and sources used to write the report (bibliography). Figure 9.13 provides a few more details about each of these sections.

Along with clear expectations and examples, you will need to determine a suitable schedule for the work that will allow all children to receive the assistance they need before the due date or publishing deadline. Remember that you have to plan time for researching as well as completing the writing process. Be sure to consider what else is going on in the classroom and school at that time. You need to be able to help children within the time set aside for that purpose without having to reschedule other classes or push aside other curriculum. Children work best within a predictable schedule and regular routine. If you are expecting parents to help, don't assume their children will inform them. You must communicate the details of the assignment and the due date.

Students research their topics by reading a combination of print and online materials. Make sure they are using credible sources so their reports are accurate. Study guides and strategies may help students remember and organize what they learn. Original research can be conducted as they complete experiments or projects. Remind students about the importance of avoiding plagiarism by using their own original wording, citing material used, and adding their own personal thoughts, insights, and experiences.

When the actual writing begins, students need to understand that a good report requires multiple drafts. They will compose a rough draft and then revise it based on feedback they receive from you and others. They don't need to worry about grammar,

New Literacies

Figure 9.13   **Four Sections of a Classroom Report**

Beginning	Start with an introduction that will get your readers' attention and hook them so they want to keep reading. It may be a personal experience or story about the topic, an interesting quotation or fascinating fact, or a question that makes the readers curious about the topic.
Middle	Give your main points and some details about each. You could share lots of information, but limit yourself to only the best ideas and most interesting details. Arrange the main points in an order that makes sense.
Ending	Finish by reviewing the main points you have covered and reminding readers of the introduction. If you began with a personal experience, you may want to mention it again. If you began with a question, you may want to restate it or ask one that is similar. You can also help your readers look to the future. Explain what is going to happen next or where they can get more information.
Bibliography	List the materials and sources you used to write your report. These can include books, encyclopedias, films, interviews, websites, etc. Young children can simply list authors and titles. As children get older they can be expected to add more information such as place of publication, publisher's name, and copyright date.

(adapted from Sebranek, Nathan, Kemper, & Krevzke, 2000)

Language Conventions

punctuation, and spelling until they have all their ideas down and are sure the report flows well. Assure them they never have to make those corrections alone. Everyone does better when a fresh set of eyes or a word-processing program can highlight errors that need to be taken care of. Students will take more pride in their work and feel more motivation if they know they will be sharing their writing with others or that their report will be read by someone besides the teacher.

Alphabet Books.   One fifth-grade teacher helps her students create alphabet books to develop content area vocabulary. She assigns students letters of the alphabet and sends them on a search for new and complex words in their textbook, notes, a thesaurus, or a dictionary. She assigns students to use each word in a meaningful sentence, draw an appropriate representation, or write a real-world connection. The teacher explains, "Because the format of an alphabet book requires brevity, I can readily respond to what students have written individually in short conferences, offering both compliments and suggestions for improvement. I can discuss their content knowledge and their writing in the same conference."

Students then revise and edit as they prepare a final draft for publication. Alphabet books not only introduce students to a delightful genre but they allow students to experience every phase of the writing process. At the same time, they help students develop vocabulary essential for thinking in the assigned content areas. The format invites the use of meaningful communication through words, graphic representations, and symbols. Figure 9.14 shows three sample pages of an ABC book integrating writing with mathematics.

Try This for Teaching   **Class ABC Books**

- Consider the topic you are currently teaching in mathematics, science, or another content area.

- Assign students letters of the alphabet and have them search for vocabulary words important to the topic that begin with that letter. For example, if the content area is geometry, words such as *symmetry, reflection,* and *transformation* will probably emerge as students search. If you are focusing on the metric system, then students will find words like *meter, gram,* and *liter* to be important vocabulary.

- If students have trouble finding words for some letters, encourage them to be creative: For example, *J* is for "just about everywhere—that's where we see geometry," or *Z* is for "zinc, which can be measured with metric units of mass."

- Assign students to use each word in a meaningful sentence, draw an appropriate representation, or write a real-world connection. They might also write their own definitions.

- Because each student is assigned only one or two letters with one page per letter, you can quickly help students revise and edit. Look for accuracy in thinking about content area

material as well as clarity and use of writing conventions.

- Bind the pages into a class book, add a cover, and share your publication with another class.

- For a little more of a challenge, follow the pattern set forth in creative ABC books such as *Q is for Duck* (Elting & Folsom, 1980) (Q is for duck because a duck quacks), *Tomorrow's Alphabet* (Shannon, 1996) (A is for seed, tomorrow's apple), or *Antics* (Hepworth, 1992) (all words contain the word *ant,* such as antique, brilliant, chant, deviant, etc.).

- Encourage students to write about their word or topic using as much alliteration as possible and to draw pictures that include multiple items beginning with that letter. *Animalia* (Base, 1996) is a good pattern to follow for this.

(Wilcox & Monroe, 2011)

Variations for ELLs

- Introduce a variety of ABC books to the class, including *Navajo ABC* (Tapahonso & Schick, 1995), *A is for America* (Scillian, 2001), and *An Edible Alphabet* (Christensen, 1994)

- Students can work with partners to create a page.

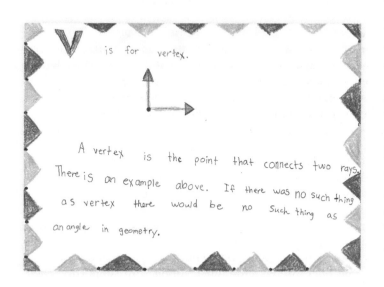

V is for vertex.

A vertex is the point that connects two rays. There is an example above. If there was no such thing as vertex there would be no such thing as an angle in geometry.

T is for Tons

By Shelby

Tons are a weight of something. It can be the weight of cars, elephants, or whales, etc... Tons are 2,000 pounds and you would usually use tons for something big.

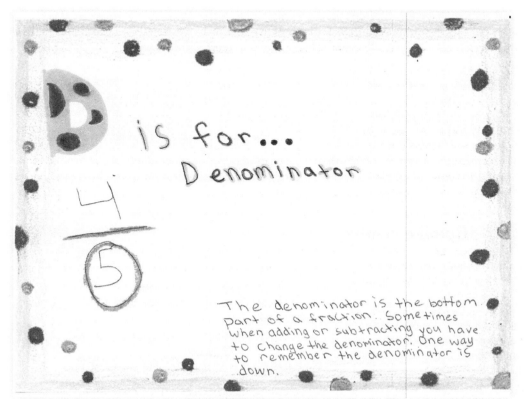

D is for... Denominator

$\dfrac{4}{5}$

The denominator is the bottom part of a fraction. Sometimes when adding or subtracting you have to change the denominator. One way to remember the denominator is down.

Figure 9.14

Sample Student-created ABC Book Pages Integrating Writing and Mathematics

Argumentative Writing

Just because argumentative writing is included in this discussion about content area study does not mean that its use is limited to it. Any writing that is presented in an attempt to change the point of view of a reader or motivate the reader to action is called argumentative writing. As authors try to convince readers to accept their ideas, conclusions, or proposals, they often include information, explanations, stories, and personal examples, appearing at first to be like narrative or expository writing. But argumentative writing is different because it assumes that the reader does not accept what the writer considers to be truth or the best possible way. Expository or narrative writing assumes agreement on the basics (Common Core State Standards, 2011). Key words associated with argumentative writing include *best, better, only, accept, evaluation, reason, logic, evidence, results, conclusion, consequences, worth, defense, judgment, answer, scientific,* and *authority.*

Common Core State Standards

Many children come to school quite convinced that their views, ideas, and conceptions are correct and that everyone who does not share them is wrong. However, the only support they may offer for their adamant opinions is "I said so" or "That's just the way it is." The only way they know to strengthen that argument is to speak louder, repeat the words over and over, or accompany them with name calling.

Fortunately, with guidance and instruction, these students can learn to support their positions in more reasonable and logical ways. They will learn to provide evidence, definitions, reasons, and examples to support their assertions. They also learn that the evidence and examples they use must be relevant and substantial. Along with supporting their ideas, children can be taught to consider opposing ideas and to acknowledge the reasons others may have for different points of view.

The most common genre in argumentative writing in elementary school is a persuasive paper. Another activity that can be challenging and enjoyable is writing advertisements.

Persuasive Papers.   Students are sometimes required to write persuasive essays, letters, or editorials, forms many states use in assessments. Sometimes the topics are silly, such as writing Santa to persuade him that his elves need vacations. At other times the topics are serious and politically involved and may include gun control, health care, and presidential elections. Teachers must be sensitive and tactful when these kinds of topics are used because students often just parrot what they have heard parents or other adults say. It may be more useful to write about topics that have more immediate application to the lives of children

---

Try This for Teaching   **Opinion Writing**

- *Argument* is a word that may be misunderstood by young children. Try calling it opinion writing or persuasive writing.

- Teach them to support an opinion by adding the word *because*. If a child writes "I like animals," have her add *because*. If another student says, "This music (or this electronic game) is the best," have him add *because*.

- The evidence young children include in their writing may be based on personal experience or other sources ("My mom says," "I read it in a book," or "I tried it myself").

Variation for ELLs

- As children gain experience, they can be asked to add more than one *because*.

- Use *why* questions to encourage students to include supporting reasons.

- Practice argumentative writing in your shared writing with the students before they are expected to do it independently.

and about which they have their own opinions: Should students be expected to help with school lunch duty? Should certain parts of the playground be off limits for younger students? Should rewards be given in school for good behavior? Whatever the topic, a well-written persuasive essay shows a student's ability to reason, see other points of view, and present evidence that may potentially influence others. It also shows that the student is mastering all of the elements of the writing process, from brainstorming to publishing, for a specific audience.

Communicating clear guidelines can help children succeed in writing persuasive essays. They need to know the details, including length and formatting requirements. Examples can make a difference. Share samples of outstanding children's essays that have received high scores. Show them that although the authors of these essays may have shown great creativity and originality, they have done so within a framework that readers have come to expect in persuasive essays.

Robb (2002) outlines four sections that should be included in a persuasive piece: (1) an introduction that includes the author's viewpoint or opinion; (2) support that includes at least three reasons and details; (3) acknowledgement of the opposing viewpoint; and (4) a conclusion. The introduction captures the readers' attention and then explains clearly the viewpoint or opinions of the author. The support section provides at least three reasons to help convince readers why they should accept the viewpoint of the author. Next the author presents an opposing viewpoint and demonstrates why it is insufficient. Not all argumentative writing has this pro-con feature, so if children are primed to look for it in what they read, they will not always find it. Still, writing an opposing opinion is beneficial for students. Finally, a conclusion allows the author to return to the stated opinion and supporting reasons, ensuring that these are the final points that will linger in the readers' minds. Figure 9.15 gives a few more details about each of these sections.

Along with clear expectations and examples, you will also need to determine a suitable schedule. Remember that you have to plan time for assisting the children throughout the writing process. Many parents are willing to help at home, but they don't want to find out about the assignment the day before it is due. You will also need to be sensitive when children express opinions different from those of their parents.

When the actual writing begins, students need to understand that they will need to make several drafts. Rather than focusing too quickly on grammar, punctuation, and spelling, emphasize the reasoning and thinking they will use to form their persuasive argument.

Struggling Learners/RtI

Language Conventions

Figure 9.15 **Four Sections of a Persuasive Essay**

Introduction	Capture the readers' attention with a personal experience, quote, or question. Follow this with a clear statement of a strong opinion.
Support	Provide at least three reasons that will convince readers they should accept your opinion. Each reason should be followed by details or examples. If you take information from other sources, you must give credit by providing reference information.
Opposing Viewpoint	Show you understand the thoughts and feelings of those who may not share your viewpoint opinion by stating fairly their viewpoint. Follow this with an explanation why such thinking may be insufficient or unacceptable.
Conclusion	You may want to tie back to the introduction so there is a sense of closure, but your last words should be a restatement of your opinion and a brief summary of the reasons you have given in support of it.

(adapted from Robb, 2002)

Futuristic Planet

Come visit the moon! Take your loved ones on an amazing Space moonwalk!! Also Come on into our most Popular restaurant and order our "to die for" Specials with an "out of this world" drink it is Called the Rocky Road Shake. You Can also take a ride around the Solar-System in a extremly fast rocket! Spend a relaxing day in our luxurious Spa! So come on over and have some fun on the moon!!

The read PHaraOH's Secret

If you read The PHaraOHS Secret you will Be in a Differant Place, like you've Been sucked into the Book. Titles and front pictures can Be BaD, But that Doesn't mean the Book's BaD. If you like Egypt then you'll love this Book. May your Secrets stay Secrets.

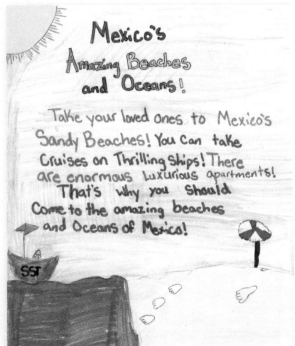

Mexico's Amazing Beaches and Oceans!

Take your loved ones to Mexico's Sandy Beaches! You can take Cruises on Thrilling Ships! There are enormous Luxurious apartments! That's why you Should Come to the amazing beaches and Oceans of Mexico!

Baby Cat.

MEOW MEOW Meow Meow Meow meow meow MEOW MEOW MEOW MEOW MEOW MEOW Meow

This cat is A boy, that needs A home. He is well behaved, Potty trained, and Loves to snuggle! He has Black + White Poke-A-Dots + Cute little Whiskers! He is Just ADORABLE!

Figure 9.16

Sample Fifth-Grade Advertisements

> **Try This for Teaching** **Create Travel Brochures**
>
> - Have students practice persuasive techniques by creating travel brochures.
> - Have each student select a location (city, state, country, etc.).
> - Encourage students to create a list of appealing attributes of that place.
> - Select an appropriate persuasion technique—logic, emotions, or relationships of trust.
> - Write a text using that persuasion technique and combine it with graphics.
> - Revise to include descriptive and sensory language (cascading waterfalls, brilliant sunsets, and shimmering pool).
> - Have students present their brochures to the class or to another grade level.
>
> - Students could vote on which brochures were most successful.
>
> (adapted from Fink, 2011)
>
> **Variations for ELLs**
>
> - Beside geography, connect with other content areas; for example, students could make brochures about visiting another planet, an internal body system, or another period of time or historical event.
> - Make a brochure to promote the setting of a story, even if it is imaginary, such as Hogwarts or Fablehaven.

Premature evaluation of mechanics will short-circuit the process and discourage risk taking, thus stunting creativity and the exploration of ideas (Pritchard & Honeycutt, 2007).

Advertisements.   Children are bombarded by argumentative writing in the form of advertisements. Businesses use various persuasion techniques to appeal to their senses and emotions and to convince them that their lives are incomplete without this or that product. Since students are so familiar with commercials, you can use them as a context for identifying persuasive techniques that students can use and fallacies they need to be aware of.

Sometimes advertisements appeal to your mind with logical reasoning (the sale ends Friday, so hurry!) and results of research (research proves that this product combats allergies). Other advertisements appeal to your emotions with sentimentality (donate money to help poor lost animals) or by evoking fear (vote for so-and-so or gang violence will proliferate). Still other advertisements appeal to your sense of trust (Joe Touchdown uses these shoes).

Have children choose a product or service to promote and help them create a printed advertisement, a radio spot, or a TV commercial. Connect the activity to school by having them promote a book, school lunch, or an afterschool program. Graphic organizers can be helpful as students prepare their advertisements. You could also begin with a word bank focusing on persuasive words they could use, such as *best, better, guaranteed, maximum, new, strong, improved*, and *ultra* (see Figure 9.16 for examples).

English Language Learners

Summary

Teaching literacy is the responsibility of every teacher. Integrating reading and writing with content areas is not just efficient use of classroom time, it is also a multifaceted opportunity to improve both literacy and content area learning. Readers don't read expository text like they read narrative or poetic writing—cover to cover or start to finish. They read it for information they want or need.

You can help children succeed with expository text by introducing them to informational books that match their interests. You can also familiarize them with expository text structure and features and help them study both expository and argumentative texts with effective strategies and guides.

Children are expected to write as well as read in the content areas. The Common Core (2011) emphasizes expository writing and argumentative writing. There are two levels of integrating writing with the content areas: writing without revision and writing with revision. Each level can be appropriate depending on the circumstances, and neither needs to take too much time or become too much of a burden for you. It is important for you to know some writing activities in both of these genres.

Self-Check

1. What are benefits of integrating literacy with content areas?

2. What is expository text, and what are some of the structures and features it typically includes?

3. Why is it necessary to teach study strategies?

4. What are study guides and why are they useful for students?

5. Explain several ways that students can write without revision in content areas.

6. How are expository writing and argumentative writing similar and different?

7. Since the term *argument* can be easily misunderstood by young children, what other terms can be used and how can it be taught?

8. List four main sections of a persuasive essay and give the purpose of each.

MyEducationLab™

Go to the Topic, Reading and Writing in the Content Areas, in the **MyEducationLab** (www.myeducationlab.com) for your course, where you can:

- Find learning outcomes for Reading and Writing in the Content Areas, along with the national standards that connect to these outcomes.

- Apply and practice your understanding of the core teaching skills identified in the chapter with the Building Teaching Skills and Dispositions learning units.

- Examine challenging situations and cases presented in the IRIS Center Resources.

- Check your comprehension on the content covered in the chapter by going to the Study Plan in the Book Resources for your text. Here you will be able to take a chapter quiz, receive feedback on your answers, and then access Review, Practice, and Enrichment activities to enhance your understanding of chapter content (optional).

- Visit **A+RISE** Standards2Strategy™, an innovative and interactive online resource that offers new teachers in grades K–12 just-in-time, research-based instructional strategies that meet the linguistic needs of ELLs as they learn content, differentiate instruction for all grades and abilities, and are aligned to Common Core Elementary Language Arts standards (for the literacy strategies) and to English language proficiency standards in WIDA, Texas, California, and Florida.

chapter 10

Assessing for Learning

Chapter Outline

TYPES OF ASSESSMENT
  Summative
  Formative
  Performance-Based
READING ASSESSMENT
  Individual Methods
  Student-Text Matching
WRITING ASSESSMENT
  Large-Scale
  Classroom
INFORMING INSTRUCTION
SUMMARY

As a third-grade teacher, I was required to administer a national standardized test each year. These tests were completed so late in the school year that the results were not available until the following fall when school began again, so the results were not helpful to me in planning instruction to meet students' needs. However, I still reviewed them. I noticed that some of my exceptional readers did not receive the high scores that I expected, and other students' scores were higher than I had anticipated. I resolved to pay closer attention not just to my instruction but also to the test-taking strategies of my

students in the coming year. The next spring I watched the students' behavior carefully as they completed the tests. The student who struggled the most in my class with reading finished the test very quickly. Two of my students who had comprehended the best were not able to complete the reading test in the allotted time. One student created a zigzag pattern as he completed the bubble answer sheet. I wrote notes about what I observed.

The next fall when the scores were given to us, I took out my notes. The poor reader who was quick to finish the test and the student who made a visual pattern with his responses had scored higher than I had expected, but the students who had not completed the test had scored lower. I learned that test scores do not always represent students' true abilities. I also learned that some students put forth little effort, and I needed to help them take testing more seriously. Finally, I learned that although standardized tests have a place, they are not the best way to measure individual student ability or to identify student needs.

—Tim

When most people think about assessment in a school setting, they think of letter grades, such as *A*, *B*, and *F*. Although grading is accepted and expected in our culture, it is not the only reason to assess. Assessment is an integral part of education that serves many purposes and addresses the needs of a variety of stakeholders. The general public wants information about how groups of students are performing so they can judge the effectiveness of schools and districts. School administrators need group scores to assist in evaluating the curriculum, programs, materials, and teachers. Parents are stakeholders who are most interested in the progress their children are making, as well as the effectiveness of specific schools. Teachers care for many of these reasons, but they want specific information about the abilities and needs of their students so they can provide appropriate expectations, instruction, and learning experiences. Other important stakeholders who are, ironically, sometimes overlooked are the students themselves. They deserve to know their strengths and struggles for improvement (Johnston & Costello, 2005). To serve the needs and interests of everyone who has a stake in the education of young people, you need to be familiar with a variety of assessment types in both reading and writing.

Types of Assessment

Assessments can be quantitative or qualitative. **Quantitative assessments** emphasize a numerical score obtained from tests or ratings. **Qualitative assessments** include more depth of information through interviews and observations. Both types of assessment are important.

Whether quantitative or qualitative data are used, summative assessment helps educators make judgments and decisions about individuals and groups of students. Formative assessment permits teachers to address specific needs of individual students. Performance-based assessment stresses what an individual student knows and can do, as well as how that knowledge and competence change over time. You need to be familiar with all of these types of assessments, because each has an important role in the education enterprise.

Summative

Summative assessment is the process of evaluating (and grading) the learning of students at a specific point in time. Usually summative assessments occur after students have been taught a body of content to evaluate the extent of understanding. Summative assessments are used in assigning students to groups or tracks, deciding who will receive special assistance, and making decisions about graduation. Such assessment can take the form of both norm-referenced and criterion-referenced tests.

Norm-Referenced.   When **norm-referenced tests** are used, scores for individuals and groups are compared with the average score obtained from a sample of the target population. For example, instead of obtaining an average score for the entire population of third-graders in the United States, a representative sample of third-grade students is tested and raw scores that others earn from the test are compared with the average score of the sample group. When a large number of students take a well-constructed test, the result is a normal distribution of scores. The middle score represents the mean or average score in that distribution, and half of the students' scores are above and half are below that average.

Common ways to describe results of a standardized test are percentiles, stanines, and grade equivalent scores. **Percentile scores** represent the relative position or rank of each raw score among the scores in the norm group. A child who receives the percentile score 75 has a specific raw score higher than 75 percent of the raw scores obtained by students in the sample group. Another way to describe how raw scores lie on a normal distribution is with stanine scores. A **stanine score** is a specific nine-point scale used for normalized test scores, with 1–3 below average, 4–6 average, and 7–9 above average. If a child receives a stanine of 8, her raw score was well above average. A grade equivalent score is a converted score that attempts to predict how well a student would perform on a test. For example, if a third-grader obtains a grade equivalent score of 5.2, his raw score is about the same score that a student in the second month of fifth grade would receive if he had taken the same test. A grade equivalent score does not mean that this third-grader possesses the same skills and abilities as a fifth-grader, or that he should be promoted to fifth grade. This score indicates nothing about a

Children taking tests.

child's social, physical, or emotional maturity. Grade equivalent scores are only derived scores, so you should be cautious in using them and help parents and others understand their limitations.

Criterion-Referenced.   Whereas norm-referenced tests compare scores to mean scores obtained by norm groups, **criterion-referenced tests** compare individual raw scores with a specific standard or expectation. For example, if you determine that students who can answer 80 percent of test items correctly know enough about the subject, then you can easily determine which have met that standard or criterion. Students are compared with expectations, not with others' scores. There are times when standardized tests are used as criterion-referenced tests, such as when a specific cut score is expected for a student to gain admission to a graduate program at a university. Many teacher-made tests are criterion-referenced tests, but so are most statewide assessments. You can use results of both of these types of tests to identify which students are mastering concepts and which are struggling and need your help.

Although both norm- and criterion-referenced tests can be used as large-scale assessments to reveal trends among groups of student, standardized tests were never meant to provide all the information needed about individual students. The International Reading Association (1999) issued a position paper about literacy assessment that included several fundamental proposals. One proposal was that educational entities should implement large-scale assessments on a sampling basis instead of requiring a test score from all students. Thus instead of testing all third-graders in a school district, only a sample of third-grade students need to be tested in order to obtain an accurate picture of how third-graders in general are performing in that district. The IRA paper also opposed school-by-school, district-by-district comparisons using standardized test scores reported for individual students, classes, or schools. Instead, educators are encouraged to use authentic tests, texts, and tasks that reveal change over time for individual students. Such assessment is more formative.

Formative

Formative assessment is testing that is part of the developmental or ongoing teaching/learning process; students should receive feedback from these types of tests, as should other stakeholders. Such assessment is used to give teachers specific information about student needs. Teachers can use a variety of formative assessment procedures to obtain such data. Two widely used approaches are response to intervention (RtI) (International Reading Association, 2010; National Association of State Directors of Special Education and Council of Administrators of Special Education, 2006) and assessment for learning (Black, Harrison, Lee, Marshall, & Wiliam, 2003).

Struggling Learners/ RtI

Try This for Professional Development	**Prep for Praxis**

(www.ets.org/praxis/prepare/materials/5031)

One test that you might have to take as a teacher candidate is the Praxis II. This is a norm-referenced test, but it is also used as a criterion-referenced test because a cutoff score is frequently used. The purpose of this text is not primarily to prepare you for the Reading and Language Arts subtest of the Praxis; however, you will find the information you are learning to be helpful when you take the test. The following topics are covered in the Praxis and are explained in the chapters listed:

- Chapter 2—Support of second language learners
- Chapter 3—Traits of writing and writing process
- Chapter 4—Language acquisition; concepts about print; phonological awareness; literacy development; syntax, semantics, phonology; stages of early writing

- Chapter 5—Phonics; word analysis; grammar; sentence types, sentence structure
- Chapter 6—Oral reading fluency; puppetry; readers' theater
- Chapter 7—Poetry; meanings of words; figurative language; root words and affixes
- Chapter 8—Comprehension; literature/narrative text; comprehension strategies; organizing writing; graphic organizers
- Chapter 9—Informational text structures; graphic organizers; persuasive text
- Chapter 14—Journaling
- Icons throughout this text focus on speaking, listening, and new literacies, and the information they highlight can be helpful to you as you prepare for the Praxis also.

Response to Intervention (RtI).   Response to intervention is a multilevel intervention system that provides early, systematic assistance to children who are having difficulty learning. It includes a set of procedures to identify students who may need special services because they are not responding well to the regular instruction that is being provided for them (Batsche et al., 2005). Working with other professionals in your school or school district, you identify students with low learning outcomes, provide appropriate instruction, monitor their progress, adjust the intensity and nature of the instruction depending on the students' responsiveness, and identify students with learning disabilities (Hawken, Vincent, & Schumann, 2008). Three tiers of RtI define the scope of the model:

1. Effective core reading instruction for all students in a classroom with screening to identify those who need more specialized help

2. Supplementary instruction for a small group of about 15 percent of the students to provide early intervention

3. Intensive intervention that provides individualization for about 5 percent of students

RtI consists of five key elements. First, professionals assess students to identify those who need closer attention and to identify specific needs of those students. Second, teachers provide tiered instruction that increases in intensity and difficulty. Third, teachers use instructional tasks that have been shown to be effective. Fourth, teachers closely monitor students' ongoing progress. Fifth, teachers make informed decisions regarding the next steps to take for individual students (Fuchs & Fuchs, 2006).

Struggling Learners/ RtI

One common set of tools used to assess students in literacy, called DIBELS (Dynamic Indicators of Basic Early Literacy Skills), consists of a series of seven one-minute measures administered one-on-one by a teacher to a student. The student reads lists of words and performs other timed tasks administered by the teacher to discern the child's overall early literacy capabilities (Good, Gruba, & Kaminski, 2001). The subtests of DIBELS include measures of initial sounds fluency, letter naming fluency, phoneme segmentation fluency, nonsense word fluency, oral reading fluency, retelling fluency, and word use fluency.

New versions of DIBELS are being developed (dibels.uoregon.edu/). For example, DIBELS Next no longer tests for word use fluency. Retelling fluency has been replaced with a test called Daze, a comprehension measure for intermediate grade students in which they choose from given words to fill in blanks in passages. Additional changes are the inclusion of checklists of common response patterns and new scores available on some measures.

Use of DIBELS has become widespread; almost two million students are tested nationally each year using these assessment tools. The DIBELS test is appealing because it has earned a reputation for being scientific, it is easy to administer, it has close ties to federal and state assessment requirements, and it is a low-cost alternative.

Still, many have criticized these tests. Goodman (2006) explained that the content of DIBELS has become a blueprint for publishers, district officials, and teachers in creating a narrow curriculum in which the items on the DIBELS tests are taught at the expense of other areas, such as writing, oral language, content knowledge, and discussion. Others complain that the focus of the tests is really on three areas of reading—phonological awareness, phonics, and fluency, while vocabulary and comprehension are downplayed. Another concern is that the DIBELS oral reading fluency subtest scores do not predict how well students will score on comprehensive measures of reading (Seay, 2006). Pearson (2006), who has built a reputation for taking positions characterized as centrist, has stated, "I have decided to join that group . . . convinced that DIBELS is the worst thing to happen to the teaching of reading since the development of flash cards" (p. v).

DIBELS can be replaced with other tools that will help you make informed judgments about students' needs and abilities. Dorn and Soffos (2012) recommend use of a set of assessments that provide pre- and post-assessments, diagnostic surveys, and progress-monitoring devices. These tools can give you useful information to identify children who need extra help and to determine if your instructional assistance is effective.

Try This for Professional Development

- Visit the RtI website at www.rti4success.org/.
- Examine the tools recommended for progress monitoring, screening, and instructional intervention.
- Select one in each area and view the samples provided online. For example, the Test of Early

Review of RtI Assessments

Literacy has samples at www.aimsweb.com/measures-2/test-of-early-literacy-cbm/.

- Describe strengths and weaknesses of these measures.

English Language Learners

Assessment for Learning.   Assessment for learning (Black & Wiliam, 2006; Black, Harrison, Lee, Marshall, & Wiliam, 2002) is a formative assessment comprised of three general phases: first, establishing where the students are in their learning; next, identifying where they are going; and last, determining what needs to be done to get them there. Also central to this model is the responsibility of the students in each phase to become self-regulated learners.

As you implement assessment for learning principles, you will provide feedback to students and chart their progress by how they are doing compared with their learning goals, not compared to their peers. You will encourage students' involvement in their own learning and collaborate with other teachers to design and refine teacher-made assessment.

Everything students do—such as conversing in groups, completing seatwork, answering and asking questions, working on projects, handing in homework assignments, even sitting silently and looking confused—is a potential source of information about how much they understand (Leahy, Lyon, Thompson, & Wiliam, 2005, p. 19).

Assessment for learning is not a specific set of tests, but rather a philosophy that teachers adopt that determines their choice of testing materials. Teachers who adopt this perspective have reported that they spend less time grading student work, enjoy their out-of-class preparation time more, and find their classroom instruction less exhausting to them and more engaging to students (Black & Wiliam, 2009). Teachers who have used this approach also have reported that they have changed the testing culture of their classrooms by helping students feel safe to take risks (Organisation for Economic Co-operation and Development, 2005).

Assessment for learning and RtI are similar in that both encourage screening students, providing quality instruction, and carrying out ongoing assessments to be sure students are making progress. However, the assessment for learning model may be more comprehensive, allowing for use of a variety of assessment tools. It is also less prescriptive.

Performance-Based

Heavy stress on assessment in schools can narrow instruction because some teachers will only teach what is tested (Goodman, 2006). Thus some researchers argue that we should carefully design assessment tools that are consistent with the kind of learning we really desire (Cohen & Spillane, 1992; O'Day & Smith, 1993). The purpose of **performance-based assessment**, commonly called authentic assessment, is to measure students' academic achievement by evaluating their performance in hands-on tasks. Instead of having students complete assessments separate from the tasks they completed to learn the content, teachers assess student understanding by evaluating their performance on ongoing literacy tasks such as completing projects, reports, and presentations.

When performances are used to measure student learning and growth, many teachers create **rubrics**, which are guidelines for rating student performances. Rubrics outline the characteristics of the work required for the various levels of performance; the

English Language Learners

rating on each characteristic provides students with detailed information about how well they performed. Having the rubric in advance gives students specific expectations as they begin their learning task, so they can focus on process, product, attitude, effort, or a combination of these. In reading and writing, items on the rubric should be broad enough to go beyond decoding and written conventions. Three general types of performance-based assessments that can be measured with rubrics are performances, portfolios, and projects.

Speaking/Listening

Performances.   Performances can be traditional presentations at the front of the class, but they can also include any work that is completed and shared with others (such as written text and artwork). A performance does not have to happen in front of a large group; one student reading aloud to the teacher is a type of performance. Regardless of the performance type, students should be given the expectations when the assignment is made. They should be familiar with all aspects of the assignment and have opportunities to discuss any unclear issues with the teacher. Many times the discussion of the expectations includes a review of the rubric that will be used for evaluation.

One teacher divided her class into groups to practice performing readers' theater. She asked other teachers in the school if they would be willing to allow one of her groups to perform for each class. Prior to the presentations, she had the groups present to each other, and she filled out a simple rubric giving feedback to each group. On the rubric were such expectations as "readers spoke loudly enough for all to hear," "readers spoke with expression," and "students read at a natural pace." Next to each expectation was a scale from 1 to 5, with 5 representing "Excellent." Groups used the feedback as they practiced before performing in front of other classes.

A group of students presenting as a performance assessment.

Portfolios.   Portfolios are used in many professions to collect typical or exemplary samples of performance. Stockbrokers might refer to a client's portfolio; artists and models may create a portfolio to display their work for a job interview; advertisers, publishers, and salespeople may display portfolios at business meetings. The central purpose of a **portfolio** is to collect and display an assortment of materials that have been gathered or produced (Farr, 1990; Olson, 1991). The language arts portfolio can be used as a means to document students' literacy development at levels not possible by other assessments.

In a school setting, portfolios can be used to assess student learning or to provide insight into instructional steps that should be taken next. In most cases students should play a central role in creating their portfolios. They should be involved in self-reflection and critical thinking as they take responsibility for their learning by deciding what to include and exclude from their portfolios. They should be able to justify their choices. Simply giving parents a file folder full of student work you have collected does not qualify as creating a portfolio for their child. Portfolios require student choice and rationale. Portfolios can provide a more authentic and detailed way to show student progress as well as to showcase excellence. As you use portfolios, be sure you communicate their purpose clearly to students (Valencia, 1998).

A teacher saved writing that students had done at various stages of completion. Before parent-teacher conferences, he had students go through the collection and select pieces to represent their learning to their parents. Each child completed a slip of paper that was stapled to the work: "I chose this because _____." One child wrote, "I chose this because it represents my best work." Another wrote, "I chose this because it shows how many revisions I made."

English Language Learners

Projects.   Projects may be completed by individuals, by pairs of students, or by small groups. Less common is a project that is completed by the entire class. Projects can take many forms: traditional library research, Internet research, scientific experiments, and so on. Whether or not projects result in presentations, they can be assessed using rubrics.

In response to a book read in a small group, students created posters to advertise their book to others. The scoring rubric that the teacher developed was given to students early. It informed students that the poster must include their opinion about the book, a sample of the author's writing, descriptions of characters and the setting, and ways the book related to their lives. As the posters were turned in, the teacher awarded points in each of those areas. Students could quickly see what they had done well and where they needed to improve next time.

Try This for Professional Development   Create Your Own Rubric

- Consider the elements of the performance, portfolio, or project you want to assess.
- Create a matrix of columns and rows like a Tic-Tac-Toe game.
- List key expectations in the column on the left side of the paper.
- Place a number scale in the top row (such as 1–5, 1–10, 1–20).
- Under each number, write a short description of what that number represents (for example, 1 = incomplete, 3 = acceptable, 5 = exceptional).
- Leave a space for comments.

- If the sum of the numbers will be used to assign grades, include that information as well (90–100 points = A; 80–89 = B).

Variations

- Create the grading rubric as a class, using input from your students.
- Have students evaluate themselves using the rubric.
- Find existing rubrics online that you can use as examples or that can be adapted for your purposes.

Reading Assessment

Children's reading abilities can be assessed using multiple tools and for multiple purposes. Assessment tools for younger children will generally be different than those created for older students. But some measures are appropriate for all, and you should be familiar with a variety of them. In addition to assessing children, assessment in reading also involves determining the difficulty of reading material so that children can sometimes be matched with books that are at appropriate levels for them.

Individual Methods

Some measures of young children's reading abilities focus on foundational skills like phonological awareness, print concepts, and phonics knowledge. Assessments are available to determine children's abilities in several aspects of phonological awareness. Tests of rhyming, segmenting, and blending can be given to young children to gain a sense of their understanding as well as foundational skills in oral language (Invernizzi, Meier, & Juel, 2003; Torgeson & Bryant, 2004; Yopp, 1995).

Clay (2002) developed *An Observation Survey of Early Literacy Achievement*, a series of assessments for young children focused on such foundational skills as book handling, print directionality (left-to-right, top-to-bottom progression), and basic letter-sound understanding. These assessments can help teachers locate and describe children's literacy strengths and needs. Although you can compare your students' scores with scores from a norm group, you'll experience greater value from these assessment tools by using them to examine the specific needs and abilities of individual children.

The Names Test (Cunningham, 1990) provides a fast and simple way to assess phonics understanding for students in grades three through six. Students are asked to read a list of 25 names (for example, Chester Wright, Grace Brewster, and Bernard Pendergraph) to see if they can apply their phonics knowledge to read these names. Mather, Sammons, and Schwartz (2006) published an adaptation of the test for children in grades one and two. The names on this test are shorter and simpler (Rob Hap, Kate Tide, and Beck Daw).

You may find it helpful to observe children as they engage in various literacy activities to build a clear picture of children as literacy learners. To be an effective "kid watcher" (Goodman, 1978), you should be aware of both children's literacy development and their growth and progression. For observations to be effective, be systematic in making them. Make sure that you observe all children in your class by setting up a regular schedule of observations, and make note of what you observe so you can refer to your notes when planning instruction and preparing for parent conferences.

These individual measures of student learning are a few of many tools from which you can choose. However, two more that you should master are running records and informal reading inventories.

Running Records. A **running record** is an individually administered reading assessment in which the teacher listens to a child read a short passage orally and records **miscues** (any departure from the text during oral reading) (Goodman, 1979). Teachers can use running records to determine what cueing systems (structure, meaning, and visual) students use, identify individual children's reading levels, understand their word identification abilities, assess their rate of oral reading, and document progress (Clay, 2000b). All you need to take a running record is a text, a child, and a piece of paper and pencil.

To begin, choose a passage that approximates the student's independent reading level. Ask the child to read aloud as you observe and record her reading performance. Sit next to the student so that you can see the text and the student's finger and eye movements as she reads the text. As the student reads, mark each word on the paper by using the appropriate running record symbols. Place a check mark to represent each word that the child reads correctly. If the student reads something incorrectly, write what she said above the correct word. If the student is reading too fast for you to keep up, ask her to pause until you catch up. Intervene as little as possible while the student is reading. If the student becomes stuck and is unable to continue, wait 5 to 10 seconds, then provide the word. If the student seems confused, give an explanation to clear up the confusion and then say, "try again" or "keep going."

Figure 10.1   **Reading Miscues and Marking Symbols for the Sentence, "The horse ran fast."**

Miscue	Recording Direction	Example
No miscue	Write a check mark for all words read correctly.	horse ✔
Substitution	Draw a line, writing above it what the student said and below the word in the text.	house / horse
Omission	Write the word from the text that the child did not read and write a dash above it.	– / fast
Insertion	Write the word that was not in the text that the child said.	– / really
Self-correction	Write the letters *sc* when the reader corrects a miscue.	house *sc* / horse
Repetition	Draw a line over the word a reader repeats with the letter *R* following.	ℛ / fast
Punctuation ignored	Draw a line through any punctuation mark the reader does not seem to note.	fast/

As you take a running record, note the types of miscues the child makes: substitution (*house* instead of *horse*); mispronunciation (*pacific* instead of *specific*); omission (*the cat*, instead of *the old cat*). Each time a student makes a miscue, record it. Each time the student reads a word correctly, write a check mark to keep your place in text. Figure 10.1 shows various miscues with common symbols used to record them using the sample sentence "The horse ran fast."

The official marking system for running records is detailed and precise. By taking time to become familiar with the marks and being consistent in using them, you and others can look back at any running record to see exactly how the child read.

After children read the text, you can analyze their miscues. Clay suggested that you examine each miscue and decide what information the reader used when that miscue was made: meaning (M), structure (S), or visual (V) information. The MSV approach examines miscues according to the major information sources children develop during the oral language acquisition process, referred to as the cueing systems. When readers do not use the appropriate cueing system at the appropriate time, their comprehension will suffer. By tracking the way children utilize the cueing systems, you are better able to help them improve their reading as well as document their progress.

Your ability to take accurate running records and to interpret the results of running records takes both time and practice. Do not be discouraged as

Teacher completing a running record.

you begin. Start by just paying conscious attention to when children read correctly and when they do not.

One major purpose of running records is to identify the reader's independent, instructional, and frustrational reading levels so that appropriate matches can be made with texts. At his **independent reading level** the reader can read almost all of the words of a text accurately and quickly and can comprehend most of what is read. At the **instructional reading level** the reader is able to identify words and comprehend the passage with support from the teacher. Texts at the **frustrational level** are too difficult for the student even with teacher support (see Figure 10.2).

Informal Reading Inventories. An **informal reading inventory** (IRI) is an individually administered assessment of a student's reading abilities, during which a student reads a series of predetermined, increasingly difficult passages. An IRI, like a running record, involves the child reading and the teacher listening, but the IRI takes longer and is more comprehensive. Another major difference is that specific passages are provided for the student to read with an IRI, whereas any passage can be used in a running record. As the child reads passages in order of difficulty, you can easily move the child into more difficult or easier reading as needed. Another difference is that IRIs usually include features that are not included in running records: word lists the child reads first in order to give a general indication of the level on which to begin, and questions to help you assess comprehension after reading.

To begin, have the child read a word list that will be easy for him—usually a list of words two grade levels below his actual level. Have him continue to read lists of words until he misses at least five words on a single list. Select the passage that corresponds to that list, which will probably be at the student's independent reading level. Because these words also appear in the passages, you can see if the child can read the same words both in isolation and in context.

Explain to the child that he will read that passage aloud as you observe and make notes about his reading. Sit next to the student so that you can see the text and the student's finger and eye movements as he reads. Record the miscues on a teacher copy of the text. Unlike running records, the IRI does not record any marks for the words the student reads correctly. Intervene as little as possible.

Following the reading, tell the child that you will ask some questions about the passage he just read. Ask the student the questions and record his responses, which will enable you to assess his level of understanding for that passage. Resist the urge to ask students to support their answers when using an IRI. However, keep in mind when teaching comprehension that the Common Core stresses the importance of students reading text closely enough that they can use the text to support their statements.

Using both the word identification and the comprehension data provided by the IRI, you can determine whether the passage was at the student's independent, instructional, or frustrational level. Figure 10.2 defines these levels.

Common Core
State Standards

Figure 10.2 Definitions of Reading Levels

	Word Identification	Comprehension
Independent	95–100%	90%
Instructional	90–95%	75–89%
Frustrational	less than 90%	less than 75%

In addition to assessing a student's reading level, the IRI can provide rich information about the individual's instructional needs. Most IRIs also offer a way to conduct a miscue analysis for each passage, providing greater insight into the student's abilities. Information from the word list, the miscues, and the responses to the comprehension questions will give you insight into areas of both strength and need. Some IRIs provide ways to assess background knowledge prior to the reading and offer students the option to retell the content of the reading instead of answering questions.

Some assessment tools are similar to IRIs. The Developmental Reading Assessment (Beaver, 2006) and the Fountas and Pinnell Benchmark Assessment System (2007) are assessment tools that also require students to read aloud passages of various levels as the teacher records miscues and subsequently to answer comprehension questions. If you are comfortable using an IRI, you will be able to quickly learn how to use similar tools.

Student-Text Matching

Children feel successful when they read materials that closely match their reading abilities. However, this matching is not as easy as it might seem. One part of the equation is to find out how well the child can read by using running records and IRIs. The other part is to determine how difficult a text is to read. The two most common approaches to identifying the reading level have been to use readability formulas and text level processes. Cloze procedures, once used for that purpose, are now used more for instruction. The Common Core emphasizes considering a range of text complexity when matching students to text.

Struggling Learners/ RtI

Readability Formulas.   **Readability formulas** are quantitative methods that estimate the reading demands of a text; most use measures of word and sentence length. Generally a text that contains short words and short sentences will be easier to understand than a text with longer words and longer sentences. A third factor used in some readability formulas is word familiarity. A passage that contains more high frequency words will be easier to understand than one that includes more rare words. Readability formulas examine samples from a text and determine the word length, sentence length, and number of high frequency words to arrive at an estimate of the difficulty of a passage.

Readability formulas have been used for many years by publishers, teachers, and others. Common readability formulas include the Fry (1968), Flesch-Kincaid (Flesch, 1948), and Dale-Chall (Chall & Dale, 1995).

Although they are helpful, readability formulas consider only two or three factors that may affect how difficult a book may be for a student to comprehend. Other factors like syntactic complexity of the text, the number of abstract concepts, and the overall concept load should also be taken into account to determine the difficulty of a passage.

Many agree that although readability formulas have a place, they provide only a general indication of the difficulty level of a passage. You should also take into account the interest and maturity of the reader and the purpose for reading. For example, a readability formula may grade a book about the Holocaust at the second-grade level, but that does not mean that most second-graders are ready for the topic. Always consider readability results with common sense. Three systems can help you: The Lexile framework, ATOS, and text levels.

Lexile framework.   A recent development in readability formulas has been the Lexile framework (Stenner, 1996), which uses a form of the Flesch-Kincaid formula. This method provides a way to evaluate both readers and texts using the same scoring scale. For example, a child reading with a 520 Lexile score should read books with a 520 score. Some states are providing lists of books for students to read based on their Lexile scores. The Lexile framework website (www.lexile.com/fab/) provides a useful tool for finding the reading level for many children's books.

Advantage/TASA Open Standard (ATOS).   The ATOS system was developed for Renaissance Learning, the company that created the Accelerated Reader Program (Milone, 2009), in conjunction with Touchstone Applied Science Associates (TASA). ATOS, available online, is similar to other readability formulas in that it measures word length, sentence length, and word difficulty (average grade level of the words in the book). A major difference is that instead of sampling from a book, ATOS scans the entire book to derive its score. As with Lexile, you can find the reading level of thousands of books by accessing their website (www.arbookfind.com/default.aspx) and entering the titles of books you are interested in leveling.

New Literacies

Text levels.   Instead of using quantitative methods to determine the reading difficulty level of texts, some **researchers** have recommended using qualitative approaches, which involve informed judgments of readers. Text leveling involves determining the relative position or rank of a book on a scale. Although text leveling has become popular recently (Fountas & Pinnell, 1996), it has been recommended for many years (Chall, Bissex, Conard, & Harris-Sharples, 1996; Singer, 1975).

To level texts you can work with a group of teachers to examine characteristics of specific books and arrange a book collection in a gradient from easier to more difficult. You can describe the features of the texts to justify the groupings that you make (such as size of print and number of illustrations). Those written descriptions can guide future text leveling. You may want to begin with a few anchor books with levels already accepted. You can compare new books with those exemplar books to make leveling decisions. Your leveling decisions are based on text characteristics as well as your knowledge of how students respond to the books.

Many leveling systems have been used. The Reading Recovery program (Clay, 1993), an early intervention program for struggling first-graders, has adopted a leveling system that arranges books in difficulty levels labeled from 1 to 20. The Fountas and Pinnell (1999) system labels the levels from A to Z. A color-wheel leveling system used in New Zealand assigns colors to the different levels (Ministry of Education, 1996). It is common practice for publishers to level books that they provide for teachers, but teachers sometimes face a problem in determining how to arrange books that have been leveled by different sources into a single coherent collection. Various conversion charts are available online to assist in comparing leveling labels across systems (for example, the PDF file at title1.spps.org/uploads/TEXT_CORRELATION_CHART.pdf provides a way to compare different text leveling systems). Figure 10.3 shows an easy-to-use comparison chart.

Cloze Procedure.   IRIs estimate a child's reading level, and text leveling systems provide the level of a text. One approach that has been developed to match the two levels appropriately is the cloze procedure (Taylor, 1953). The **cloze procedure** removes selected words from a text and asks students to replace them. To create a cloze test, select a passage of about 100 to 150 words. Leave the first and the last sentences intact, and

Struggling Learners/ RtI

Figure 10.3   Text Leveling Conversion Chart

Grade	Fountas & Pinnell	Reading Recovery	Color Wheel	Lexile Framework
K	A	A, B	Starters 1	
K–1	B	1, 2	Starters 2	100–149
K–1	C	3, 4	Red	150–199
1	D	5, 6	Red/Yellow	200–249
1	E	7, 6	Yellow	
1	F	9, 10	Blue	250–299
1	G	12	Blue/Green	
1–2	H	14	Green	300–349
1–2	I	16	Orange	
2	J	18	Turquoise	350–399
2	K	18	Purple	400–449
2–3	L	20	Gold	450–499
2–3	M	20	Gold	
3	N	22	Silver	500–549
3–4	O	24	Silver	550–599
3–4	P	24	Emerald	600–649
4	Q	26	Emerald/Ruby	650–699
4	R	26	Ruby	700–749
4–5	S	26	Ruby	750–799
4–5	T	26	Ruby	
5	U	28	Sapphire	800–849
5–6	V	28	Sapphire	850–899
5–6	W	28	Sapphire	
6–8	X	30		900–949
6–8	Y	30		950–999
7–8	Z	32, 34		1000–1049

then delete every fifth word, leaving a blank line for each. Students read the passage and fill in each blank with a word that they think fits. Scoring is by exact replacement—if the student writes the exact word that was deleted from the text, that item is counted as correct. If the student leaves a blank or writes a word other than the word that was deleted, even if it is a close synonym, the item is scored as incorrect. Final judgments are then made to determine how appropriate this text is for each student tested. If a student completes 60 percent or more of the blanks correctly, the passage is considered to be at an independent level for that student. If fewer than 40 percent of the words are exact replacements, the text is frustrational. When between 40 percent and 60 percent of the words supplied by the student are exact replacements, the text is considered to be instructional.

Some have criticized the use of cloze tests to match students to texts (Bernhardt & Kamil, 1995; Shanahan, Kamil, & Tobin, 1982), arguing that readers completing a cloze test bring each individual sentence to closure instead of examining the entire text to judge which word should be written. Because of such drawbacks, many educators do not recommend using the cloze procedure to match students to text. Instead, it is recommended as an effective tool for instruction (Bernhardt & Kamil, 1995; Shanahan, Kamil, & Tobin, 1982).

Instead of deleting every fifth word in a passage, be selective in what you leave out. For example, you could delete all of the adjectives in a short passage and discuss with your students what kinds of words are missing and what would be effective words to fill in the blanks. You could also use what is called the maze procedure (Guthrie, Seifert, Burnham, & Caplan, 1974), which provides choices of words to complete the blanks instead of requiring children to come up with their own. A number of publications for teachers provide cloze and maze activities for students (Moore, 2005).

Common Core State Standards

Range of Text Complexity. The Common Core calls for attention to issues of **text complexity** by recommending a three-part model for examining texts, which includes considering qualitative, quantitative, and reader and task considerations. This approach uses a variety of information sources to determine which texts are appropriate for students.

Qualitative. Qualitative dimensions of text complexity include attention to aspects of text that are best measured by a reader, including "levels of meaning or purpose; structure; language conventionality and clarity; and knowledge demands" (National Governors Association Center for Best Practices & Council of Chief State School Officers, 2010, Appendix A, p. 4).

Quantitative. The quantitative aspect of text complexity refers to issues such as "word length or frequency, sentence length, and text cohesion" (National Governors Association Center for Best Practices & Council of Chief State School Officers, 2010, Appendix A, p. 4). A group of researchers are developing an online tool to assist in measuring a number of text cohesion variables (Coh-Metrix, 2011). When this tool is available, it will likely add information that will be used to quantitatively measure text difficulty.

Reader and task considerations. Reader and task issues should also be considered in establishing the difficulty level of texts. Individuals must determine how aspects of specific texts, tasks, and readers match up in relation to the qualitative and quantitative results. This three-part model for determining the difficulty level of texts holds promise for avoiding reliance on a single measure.

Writing Assessment

Like reading assessment, writing assessment serves many audiences and can be used for a variety purposes: to provide information about groups of students, to identify strengths and needs of individual students, and to determine grades, to name just a few reasons for assessing the writing skills of students (Tompkins, 2012). Some large-scale writing assessments gather data at the school district, state, or national level. Other assessments are for the classroom. Both are important and serve specific needs.

Large-Scale

Assessments that measure the writing abilities of large groups of students are being used by states and school districts, but usually only at specific grade levels. For example, students in grades four, eight, and eleven may be asked to respond in writing to a prompt related to a genre of writing that is included in the state standards. The students have limited time to plan and write their composition either by hand or on a word processor.

For such assessments, you will probably know well in advance which genre of writing students will need to use, but the specific prompt is not revealed ahead of the test administration. Teach your students to read the prompt carefully. If the genre is unknown, you can help students learn to identify the genre by the words used in the prompt. For example, if the prompt uses words such as *convince*, *persuade*, or *argue*, the writing genre is probably persuasive. But if key words in the prompt are *explain*, *inform*, or *describe*, the genre is likely to be informational. Prompts that use words like *story*, *experience*, or *account* usually expect students to write a narrative. With the widespread use of the Common Core, these three writing genres will be used often in the prompts.

You will want to use some instructional time preparing your students to write in a specific genre. If the genre is informational writing, prepare your students to write using an organizational plan to fit that genre. The same holds true for narrative and persuasive writing. Use of graphic organizers to plan the structure of the writing will help the students organize their compositions properly.

Student writing on large-scale tests is scored by individual raters or by software programs that have been written to score writing. Be sure you are aware of the scoring criteria that will be used to evaluate student writing so you can prepare your class well.

Common Core State Standards

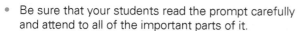 *Try This for Teaching*   **Attend to Genre Prompts**

- Be sure that your students read the prompt carefully and attend to all of the important parts of it.

- If the prompt asks for the students' opinions, teach them to explicitly state what they believe.

- If the prompt includes a requirement to provide reasons for a position, be sure students know how to include multiple reasons.

- If the prompt requires a story, make sure the students can include essential story map information (setting, characters, problem, goal, events, and resolution).

Variations for ELLs

- Read the prompt orally to students.

- Make sure you have defined words that are critical to understanding the task (such as *opinion*, *position*, *reasons*, and *story*).

Some states or districts will provide sample writing prompts and scoring procedures so you can simulate the test. Take advantage of these opportunities so you can give your students adequate preparation. However, the time spent preparing your students for a large-scale test should be limited. Do not be tempted to spend too much time preparing. Test preparation is not ideal writing instruction, but learning how to take a test is also important to know. There is no better way to prepare for any writing assessment than to write regularly.

Classroom

More important than large-scale writing assessment is the writing evaluation you do in your own classroom. Most of this assessment is informal and will directly serve your needs as you help your students improve as writers. You can use classroom-based assessments to evaluate writing for a variety of purposes and a range of audiences in an array of settings (National Council of Teachers of English, 2009). As you work with your students, you will assess to provide them with ongoing assistance as well as to judge student writing.

Ongoing Assistance.   Because students are involved in a process of writing that occurs over time, you will want to assess not only their writing products but also ways they proceed through the process of creating their final products. As you provide ongoing assistance, you will be involved in observing and making anecdotal notes, conferencing with students, and using checklists or rubrics.

Observing and making anecdotal notes.   In keeping with the "kid-watching" practices discussed previously for reading assessment, you will want to observe individuals closely as they work during writing instruction. Watch for those who seem to naturally use their time productively, as well as those who get off to a slow start. Take notice of those who seem to have a flair for giving positive or especially helpful feedback to peers. Pay attention to students who are particularly adept at organizing their writing or who are skilled at editing. Some students may keep a very detailed and useful writer's notebook, while others are able to describe realistic characters. Some may be able to write persuasive essays that are compelling, and others may be able to explain or describe things effectively. You should expect such differences among your students, and you can promote and encourage development of strengths by allowing students to become helpers or assistant teachers in their ability areas.

Struggling Learners/ RtI

As you observe your students, be sure to make **anecdotal notes** that record your impressions for future reference. You may want to use a notebook with a tab for each student. Some teachers prefer to carry a clipboard with blank paper to record observations. Some teachers target specific students each day to ensure that all receive equal attention. Others set aside time each day to record notes on the computer. Whatever practice works for you, take time to regularly watch students as they work, record your observations, and use that information in your planning and teaching.

Speaking/Listening

Conferencing with students.   Take time to regularly visit with students about their writing in a teacher-student **conference**. Very informal spontaneous conferences can be used to monitor children's work. When you see something that arouses your curiosity, use the moment to talk to the student about what you are seeing. In addition, plan to have regular conferences with all of your students, discussing concerns you have noticed during

Try This for Teaching   **"Fix It"**

- In the fall of the school year, collect a writing sample from each student in your class and store a photocopy of each sample in a file.
- At parent-teacher conference time, give students the copy of their earlier work and ask them to fix it.
- Encourage students to use the knowledge they have gained about writing to improve their writing in another draft of what they did at the beginning of the year. They may be able to make improvements in the organization, word choice, punctuation, and spelling of their writing.

(Klein, 1996)

Variations for ELLs

- Have students work together in small groups to fix their writing, one paper at a time.
- Allow students to share their "before" and "after" writing with the class or with parents.
- Display the "before" and "after" writing to parents and ask them to comment on the progress they see.

an observation or following up from a previous conference. At these sessions students can share their writing or talk about plans they have for current or future writing. Conferences progress from an instructional focus to an assessment focus when you ask questions to encourage reflection, such as "How is your writing going?" "What do you plan to do next?" "What part of your writing sounds really good to you?" "What's not going well?"

Students can maintain writing folders where they store works in progress, ideas for future writing, prewriting plans, rubrics, and checklists. As you conference with students, review what they have in their folders. Use these products to review their progress as writers. Is there evidence of prewriting? Has the student revised his or her writing? How has the student implemented the skills taught in mini-lessons? As you review students' writing folders, you will be able to identify needs that can be addressed in whole class or small group lessons.

Using checklists.   You might want to create a checklist that identifies the major aspects of the writing process so you can evaluate how the students are using it and document their progress. You can also make a checklist that focuses on the traits of quality writing, assessing students' abilities in specific areas like organizing or editing their work. These checklists can be helpful reminders to students of the steps they need to follow and guidelines they need to check. But do not just look at the checklists without also reviewing the writing—at times writers check off items on a list while there are still revisions or edits that need to be made in the text.

English Language Learners

Judging Student Writing.   Because evaluating students' writing can be challenging and time-consuming, many teachers reduce the number of writing projects that are graded to a few for each grading term. If you have to submit a grade for writing on a report card, let these few graded pieces represent the writing rather than assessing and averaging all the projects to generate a grade.

When students have turned in these papers, you have to decide how to grade them. Perhaps the easiest way to grade student writing is to mark spelling, punctuation, and grammar. But doing this emphasizes to the least important parts of writing and decreases attention to more important features like content, organization, and voice. When you assess student writing, it is a good idea to have specific criteria in mind. Two major types of writing assessment are holistic and analytic.

AUTHORS: A Quality Writing Checklist

Help students stay focused on content rather than mechanics by providing the following checklist to be used during peer conferences, teacher conferences, and student revising:

- **A** = Audience. Make sure everything is appropriate for the intended readers.
- **U** = Unique and surprising ideas. Search for ideas that are fresh and uncommon.
- **T** = Titles. Make a good first impression and invite readers to read on.
- **H** = Honest voice. Express your own thoughts rather than trying to sound like everyone else.
- **O** = Organization. Present ideas in smooth, clear, and reasonable ways.

- **R** = Rich detail. Choose vivid words that appeal to the senses.
- **S** = Sentences. Vary the length and structure of sentences in order to keep the interest of your readers.

(Wilcox, 1996)

Variations for ELLs

- Create a similar checklist that focuses on the process of writing.
- Create a checklist that reminds students what to look for when editing for mechanics or elements of a specific genre.

Holistic.   **Holistic scoring** involves assigning a single overall score to represent the piece. When using this general impression scoring method, you can read the papers once and then sort them into piles that represent stronger to weaker papers. Another way to use holistic scoring is to identify a paper that exemplifies each of the categories—strong, developing, and weak. You can use these as anchor papers to compare to those papers you haven't read yet. Through making comparisons, you can classify each paper into one of the categories and assign a grade.

Analytic.   When using **analytic scoring** methods, you assign scores to specific aspects of a paper so that strengths and weaknesses can be identified. To use this form of assessment, you must first identify the characteristics of writing you want to evaluate. The Hunter College Reading/Writing Center has identified five characteristics for evaluating student writing: focus, development, unity, coherence, and correctness (Hunter College, 1999). Anderson (2005) described four characteristics: structure, details, voice, and conventions. Perhaps the most commonly used list of writing qualities for public schools is the six traits of writing (Spandel, 2008). The original six traits were ideas, organization, voice, word choice, sentence fluency, and conventions. Another trait, presentation, was added later. This trait focuses on how the writing actually appears on the page. Because it is in widespread use, many educators are familiar with the six traits in analytic scoring.

After you have selected the characteristics of quality writing you plan to use to assess student writing, you need to create a scoring guide or rubric to indicate a range of performance for each trait. For example, you could use a five-point scale to show how the writer of a paper might be scored on the trait of *ideas*. The scale could show progression from *experimenting* to *emerging* to *developing* to *capable* and finally to *experienced*. Descriptions for each of the stages explain expectations, and specific papers are judged against the criteria listed. The Education Northwest website provides a wealth of information about the six traits, including scoring rubrics for each trait, sample papers at each developmental level for various grades, and examples you can use for scoring practice (educationnorthwest.org/traits).

Try This for Teaching   **Publishing Deadlines**

- Explain that in the world of publishing, authors have to meet deadlines.

- Tell your class that rather than turning in everything for feedback and a grade, they will have to choose one piece to submit on the publishing deadline.

- Complete a rubric or enlist the help of others to do so for these pieces.

- Let the final score for that last piece cover the entire grading period.

- The number of deadlines for the year can depend on various factors, but a good starting place is to think of the grade level you teach. First grade may have one publishing deadline in the spring. Second grade may have two, one in the fall and one in the spring. Sixth grade will have six, three in the fall and three in the spring.

Variations for ELLs

- Consider reducing the number of publishing deadlines for ELLs.

- Accept partially completed work at the deadline.

- Assign a partner or mentor to work with ELLs who need extra support in reaching the publishing deadline.

Don't try to use a rubric for everything that children do. You may want to have publishing deadlines, specific dates on which students will turn in something for you to assess. One child might have a dozen pieces of writing from which she must choose one. Another child will be lucky to have one to turn in. Either way, on the publishing deadline, each child submits only one sample of his or her writing to be reviewed with a rubric.

Informing Instruction

Although it is important to know different types of assessment and a variety of ways to evaluate reading and writing, assessment is not an end in itself. You must use the results of any measure to inform and improve teaching and learning. Tests can help you determine students' achievement levels, document progress, and identify strengths and weaknesses. But the tests themselves don't change any of those things. Simply putting a thermometer in a child's mouth over and over doesn't change his body temperature. You need to read the thermometer and use that information to do something to bring the temperature down. It's the same with testing and teaching. Testing children over and over will do little to improve their proficiency. Instruction and intervention are what make the difference.

For example, if you complete an IRI with a student and find that she has difficulty identifying words accurately, you could use Elkonin boxes to help students isolate individual sounds. You could prepare a lesson that focuses on onset-rime awareness or vowel sounds and spelling patterns. During shared or guided reading you could highlight consonant sounds in unfamiliar words.

If you find that the child cannot identify words automatically, you should consider using echo reading or repeated readings to increase sight word rate. You could pay close attention to what the student is reading during independent reading and make sure he is following the lead reader during whole class shared reading. When a student has difficulty comprehending, you could describe your comprehension processes as you think aloud during oral reading. You could build a relevant knowledge base for the student before asking her to read. Encourage the child to use mental images as she reads. You could use reciprocal teaching to help the child become more independent in using comprehension processes.

Struggling Learners/ RtI

In writing you may have a conference with a student and find that she is struggling with content-focused issues such as ideas and organization. You could help the student limit the number of ideas she is going to include in her project. You could provide a pattern for her writing using a structure that is already developed. Perhaps a graphic organizer could be a useful tool for this student. If you find a student struggles with issues of mechanics, you could teach a mini-lesson reviewing basics like capital letters at the beginning of sentences and punctuation marks at the end. You could look for words that are consistently misspelled and include them on her spelling list. Pair the student with a more experienced writer and have them look in a book to see how other authors have used the conventions of writing to better communicate with their readers.

When you use assessment data to inform instruction, you are acting professionally. You are recognizing needs and meeting them. There is not always a clear-cut answer or a definitive resource that can give a solution to every problem. This is where your knowledge base and experience must be used to make and reflect upon decisions. If you go to a doctor complaining about a stomachache, you would be disappointed if the doctor said, "Let me check my doctor's manual. Oh, it looks like today is headache day." You might say, "But I have a stomachache." A professional doctor won't say, "We don't do stomachaches until February." Similarly, if a doctor prescribes something for your stomach and it doesn't work, she is not going to say, "Well, I did what the manual said to do, so if it didn't work it's your problem." Instead, she is likely to say, "Let's see what else we can try to solve this problem." Professional teachers must do the same. Teachers' manuals can be helpful resources, but you are the one who knows the needs of your students and must make wise judgments to meet those needs. Assessments can provide important data, but you are the one who must use that information to inform and improve teaching and learning.

English Language Learners

Summary

A ssessment is a vital part of literacy teaching. It serves many purposes for various audiences, from the teacher who wants to improve her teaching and her students' learning to a state superintendent of instruction who wants to know how well fourth-graders throughout the state can write. The need for information determines which assessment tool will be most helpful.

Two general methods of assessment are summative and formative. Decisions about students and programs are usually made using summative assessment. Both norm-referenced and criterion-referenced tests can be used to provide relevant data. Formative assessment uses measures to monitor progress over time and to identify areas of need. Three examples of formative approaches to assessment include RtI, assessment for learning, and performance-based assessment.

Reading assessment can be done using summative tests, but usually teachers use more informal means to determine student strengths and areas of need. Young children's reading abilities can be assessed using tools included in Clay's book *An Observation Survey of Early Literacy Achievement* (2002), as well as a variety of other phonological awareness and phonics measures. One of the best ways to evaluate students' ongoing reading abilities is to listen to them read to you individually, using running records or informal reading inventory techniques to assess their progress.

One major purpose of reading assessment is to match students with appropriate reading material. Readability formulas have long been used to determine the difficulty level of written text, and new approaches to readability including Lexile and ATOS systems have been developed. The Common Core emphasizes using a multi-prong approach including qualitative, quantitative, and reader/task considerations to determine the fitness of text for students.

Writing assessment must meet the needs and desires of many stakeholders. Large-scale assessments usually involve students writing to a specific prompt. Teachers help prepare students for these tests by showing them how to address the entire prompt, how to organize their writing, and how to attend to all of the expectations on the scoring rubric that will be used to evaluate their writing.

Writing assessments that are most important for you in your classroom are those that allow you to monitor student growth and needs as you observe students writing and record anecdotal notes. Individual and small group conferences can also be a source of information about students' writing abilities. Checklists that relate to various aspects of the writing process can be one way to provide opportunities for students to evaluate their own progress. When assessing student writing, you can use either a holistic approach, which assigns a single overall score to represent the piece, or an analytic approach, which involves evaluating specific aspects of a paper. Assessment is much more that assigning letter grades. As you explore its many aspects and purposes, you will see why it is essential for literacy instruction.

Self-Check

1. Describe what is meant by the term *summative assessment*.

2. Explain how norm-referenced and criterion-referenced tests are similar to and different from one another.

3. List some options for conducting formative assessments.

4. Describe the method commonly used to assess performances of students on presentations or projects.

5. Describe two common informal assessments that are used to evaluate student oral reading.

6. What methods have been used to estimate the difficulty level of reading materials?

7. Describe the general process used to assess writing in large-scale assessments.

8. Explain the differences between holistic and analytic scoring of writing.

MyEducationLab™

Go to the Topic, Assessment, in the MyEducationLab (www .myeducationlab.com) for your course, where you can:

- Find learning outcomes for Assessment, along with the national standards that connect to these outcomes.

- Complete Assignments and Activities that can help you more deeply understand the chapter content.

- Apply and practice your understanding of the core teaching skills identified in the chapter with the Building Teaching Skills and Dispositions learning units.

- Examine challenging situations and cases presented in the IRIS Center Resources.

- Check your comprehension on the content covered in the chapter by going to the Study Plan in the Book

Resources for your text. Here you will be able to take a chapter quiz, receive feedback on your answers, and then access Review, Practice, and Enrichment activities to enhance your understanding of chapter content (optional).

- Visit A+RISE Standards2Strategy™, an innovative and interactive online resource that offers new teachers in grades K–12 just-in-time, research-based instructional strategies that meet the linguistic needs of ELLs as they learn content, differentiate instruction for all grades and abilities, and are aligned to Common Core Elementary Language Arts Standards (for the literacy strategies) and to English language proficiency standards in WIDA, Texas, California, and Florida.

chapter 11

Reading and Writing to Children

Chapter Outline

READING TO CHILDREN
    Importance of Reading Aloud
    Read-Aloud Techniques
    Book Selection
WRITING TO CHILDREN
    Methods
    Models
SUMMARY

As a child I loved recess as much as anyone. But in fourth grade I started looking forward to the bell that signaled the end of lunch recess. I knew the minute I got back to the classroom Mr. Rogers would read to us. He would sit on a big overstuffed chair and read aloud *Pippi Longstocking* and *Where the Red Fern Grows*, among others. I loved getting lost in those books. When I grew up and became a teacher myself, one of the first things I did was to move a big, overstuffed chair into my classroom and pick out some great books to read aloud to my sixth-grade class after lunch recess. Sometimes I gathered them on the rug around me. Sometimes they sat at their desks and drew as I read. Either way, I knew they were enjoying the books because when I would get to the end of a chapter the children would say, "You *can't* stop there!" or "Please, just read a few more pages!" My favorite day was when a boy hurried into the classroom and said, "I thought recess was *never* going end. I have been dying to find out what is going to happen in the book." Looking back, there are many things I would do differently in my first year now that I have more experience and education. But I wouldn't change the reading aloud I did. Mr. Rogers did it right. So did my parents. And so did I in my own classroom.

—Brad

To, With, and By
Val C. Wilcox

After lunch
We sit
On the rug
Feeling the rhythm
Of our teacher's rocking chair,
Catching cadences of language,
Seeing pictures in our minds.
She reads to us.
She loves books.

After recess
We sit
In a circle
Feeling comfortable with
Arms on cool tabletop,
Weaving words into meaning,
Seeing pictures on the pages.
We read with each other.
We love books.

After science
I sit
At the back of the room
Feeling snug in my
Bean-bag-and-pillow nest—
A wizard making magic with 26 letters,
Seeing pictures behind each word.
I read by myself.
I love books.

This poem illustrates the gradual release of responsibility that is ideal in all learning. Think of when you learned to drive a car. First you needed to see someone driving. If you had never seen anyone drive a car before, you wouldn't feel motivated to drive yourself. Next, you needed somebody to tell you how to drive—how to fasten the seatbelt and how to turn on the ignition. The person teaching you probably had you sit beside him or her. Maybe you got to turn the steering wheel as your teacher drove around an empty parking lot. Later, you switched places and you sat in the driver's seat and your teacher gave you guidance as you drove. Then, you were ready to go out on the road with a learner's permit. After many hours of practice, the essentials of driving became more automatic to you. You came to the point where driving became second nature. You became so confident that you could listen to the radio or carry on a conversation while you were driving, things you could never have done when you were a beginner. Driving allowed you freedom to reach destinations that were impossible before. Your world was enlarged, and you were better able to serve others.

A similar gradual release of responsibility happened when you learned to read and write (Kong & Pearson, 2003; Mooney, 1990; Pearson & Gallagher, 1983). As your parents or teachers read to you, you enjoyed the books. You began to see how reading could be beneficial to you. Maybe they pointed out some words and illustrations. Soon you began to focus on the text as they read. You might have chimed in with words and phrases that became familiar. Soon you began to choose books that you could read while someone listened to you, offering assistance with difficult words and helping you to understand. Finally, you needed time with books—maybe it was in a library, or with a flashlight under your covers, or in a treehouse. Wherever it was, as you read on your own, you gained fluency and confidence, and your world was expanded. Suddenly you realized that books could take you places and offer insights impossible to encounter in any other way. You came across more new words that you would never have heard by engaging in conversations, by watching TV, or by playing electronic games. You gained power over time itself as you controlled the rate at which you processed information, and with that power you were in a position to be of service to others.

Whether driving, reading, or writing, it all starts with a role model—a vision of what you, too, can achieve. Booker T. Washington grew up in slavery, not allowed to learn to read:

> I had no schooling whatever while I was a slave. Though I remember on several occasions, I went as far as the schoolhouse door with one of my young mistresses to carry her books. The picture of several dozen boys and girls in a schoolroom engaged in study made a deep impression upon me, and I had the feeling that to get into a schoolhouse and study in this way would be about the same as getting into paradise. (Washington, 1901, p. 4)

After the Civil War, Booker and his family were freed, but opportunities were still limited for them. He worked in a salt mine with his stepfather and brother. Then one day, he saw a black man reading a newspaper aloud. This model gave him hope that he would also one day be able to read (Bradby, 1995).

Some children have the advantage of seeing many models of literacy from the day they are born. But for some children, you may be the most effective model they experience. That is why it is essential that you do not neglect reading and writing to the children you teach.

Reading to Children

Some believe that reading aloud is not a productive use of school time because it does not address specific skills that may appear on an upcoming test, because it takes time from explicit instruction, or because in today's electronic world, information can be obtained more efficiently online. However, it has been emphasized for decades that "the single most important activity for building the knowledge required for eventual success in reading is reading aloud to children" (Anderson, Hiebert, Scott, & Wilkinson, 1985, p. 23).

Many teachers have learned from experience the benefits of reading aloud, even though some advantages may not show up immediately. One elementary school teacher crossed paths with a former student 25 years later. The student, now an adult with a family of her own, said, "I don't remember everything you taught me, but I remember you reading to us. I will never forget that. Those books are still some of my favorites and I now read them to my children." For you to one day have this same kind of experience as a teacher, you need to appreciate the importance of reading aloud, learn how to do it effectively, and choose books that will impact your students.

Try This for Teaching **Read-Aloud Memories**

- Share with your class a memory of someone reading aloud to you.
- Invite students to share their own memories.
- Instruct them to listen to how reading aloud has been a part of the literacy learning and motivation for others.

Variations for ELLs

- Share memories as partners or in small groups.
- Compile a list of favorite book titles from the memories.
- Write thank-you notes to teachers, parents, and grandparents who read aloud.

Importance of Reading Aloud

The purpose of literature and education is not limited to passing tests or gaining access to information. It is to provide meaning and direction for our lives. Trelease (2006) reminded us that it is through literature that we can connect with the human heart, and C. S. Lewis (1961) has written that lifelong readers seldom realize how much they owe to authors. He said that by reading great literature he was able to find himself and rise above himself.

Beyond offering the broadened perspective and purpose that literature brings, **read alouds**— adults reading texts to children—provide four additional advantages: stronger motivation, greater vocabulary, more exposure to concepts about language and print, and increased attention span.

A teacher reading aloud to her class.

Motivation. Some people believe that motivation is as essential an element in learning to read as the alphabet (Gambrell, 1996; Guthrie, 1996). Reading aloud is motivating because it stimulates creativity and imagination within each individual listener, but it also leads to connections with others. Reading is relational—it allows you to build relationships with authors and characters. Many will read a book just because they like the author's work, or they will read a sequel because they want to have more experiences with characters they have come to know. In addition, reading allows you to build relationships with others who have read the same books. With technology today, you can share book titles and experiences you have had with books through social networking sites (such as Good Reads, www.goodreads.com). Suddenly through sharing books, you find you have something in common with people all around the world. The same thing can happen in classrooms. Sharing books together offers a rich and unifying source for laughter and tears in a school setting that might otherwise be emotionally flat (Goodlad, 1984). In addition to bonding with others who have read the same book, young children also bond with the person who reads the book to them. They may enjoy the once-upon-a-time story they hear, but they may also enjoy the once-upon-a-dad or once-upon-a-mom experience that is part of being read to. This shared warmth can also occur in classrooms as teachers read to children.

Struggling Learners/ RtI

An educational literacy consultant working in an urban city noticed a tough sixth-grader standing alone at recess. His dress and appearance evidenced that he came from a difficult background and was facing an unsure future. The consultant approached him and started a conversation by asking, "Do you like to read?" In his street-smart voice, the boy replied, "I didn't used to but I do now." "So what's your favorite book?" Without a pause, the hardened young man responded, "*Little Women*." This was *not* a title the consultant had expected to hear. It turns out the boy's teacher loved Louisa May Alcott's book and was reading it to her class. Her enthusiasm was contagious. Clearly, the boy identified with the characters and events in the book, but the read-aloud experience also gave him a connection to the rest of the class and a bond with his teacher that motivated him to enjoy reading, and to actually admit it.

English Language Learners

Vocabulary. Children expand their vocabulary more through exposure to language than through explicit teaching. Furthermore, that exposure is far greater in reading—either through teacher read-alouds or student independent reading—than through oral language (Brett, Rothlein, & Hurley, 1996; Nagy & Anderson, 1984; Sternberg, 1987). Hayes and Ahrens (1988) documented that for every 1,000 words in typical children's books, the number of rare words is about 31, compared to 17 rare words per 1,000 in adult conversations, and 2 rare words per 1,000 on educational TV programs. Just reading a newspaper or magazines can expose a reader to as many 68 rare words per 1,000. Those who are learning English benefit greatly from the increased exposure to vocabulary that they receive when you read aloud to them.

As children experience the world around them, listen to conversations, and watch TV and movies, they are exposed to myriad emotions, concepts, and actions, but have few opportunities to hear the words that label such things. Children rarely hear words like *saunter* on television, for example. If somebody saunters or walks at an easy, slow pace on TV, children see the action, but don't hear the word describing it. This is one reason why reading aloud is so valuable—children can be flooded with words in a secure, comfortable setting.

Struggling Learners/ RtI

Language and Print Concepts. Fox (1993) and a colleague taught a small group of intermediate grade students. They had only limited time with them each week. These teachers found the children so hungry for a good book that they abandoned their other

---

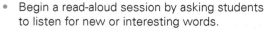

Try This for Teaching **Where Else Do You Hear These Words?**

- Begin a read-aloud session by asking students to listen for new or interesting words.

- As you read, have students create their own lists of words.

- Create a compilation of 3 to 5 words for the whole class.

- Assign students to keep the list with them for a few days as they watch TV, listen to conversations, and engage in their own reading.

- Have students keep a running tally of how often they encounter a word on the list.

- After several days, have students report their findings. Point out that we learn new and interesting words more from reading than in other ways.

Variations for ELLs

- Small groups could have distinct lists, and each group could report its findings.

- Have students create graphs of their findings.

plans and read *The Indian in the Cupboard* (1980) to the children. Later, when the principal heard that they had only read aloud to the children, he asked, "Is that all? You mean you didn't teach them *anything*?" They replied, "No we didn't. But don't worry: *The Indian in the Cupboard* did" (p. 112).

When you read aloud to children, you are team teaching. You are bringing into your classroom some of the greatest masters of language in the world, and together you are exposing children to concepts about print and the rhythm of language.

Since the difficulty level of reading material is not as important during read-aloud time as it is during other reading experiences, you can expose children to books that they could never read on their own. Doing so can challenge their minds and stretch their abilities and interests. When children are read to often, they gain a sense of story that helps them as they learn to read and write themselves (Stein & Glenn, 1979; Sweet & Snow, 2003). Young children are also exposed to many concepts about printed language (Clay, 2002): the directions of written language—left-to-right, top-to-bottom, front-to-back—capital letters, punctuation marks, and word-to-word-matching.

Language Conventions

Attention Span. In a busy classroom it is easy to run out of time for reading aloud unless it has become a regular pattern. Some teachers like to set aside the same time every day, such as right after recess or just before going home. Others like to use it as a transition activity when children return from PE or computer lab. Regardless of when you choose, reading aloud should occur daily. Be careful to avoid making reading aloud a reward that children must earn by obeying or completing work. Instead, consider reading aloud a vital part of your comprehensive literacy instruction.

Reading aloud to children regularly and re-reading favorite books increase children's attention spans (Lewman, 1999). One second-grade teacher said, "I can always tell which children have been read aloud to and which ones haven't, just by their attention spans." As children listen to stories and books, they learn to sit still and focus their minds for longer and longer periods. Some educators (Boushey & Moser, 2006) call this **reading stamina**, or the ability to read for long periods without getting distracted or distracting others.

Speaking/Listening

When the second-grade teacher mentioned previously began reading longer chapter books without illustrations, she read for about the same amount of time it takes to read a picture book. Slowly she stretched that time out until children were content to listen for 15 to 20 minutes at a time. She said, "My favorite words to hear are 'You've got to keep reading!' Then I know I have them hooked."

Children who grow up with fast action on TV and special effects in movies and electronic games may need practice receiving information in a different form, at a

---

Try This for Professional Development | **Information for Parents**

- Considering motivation, vocabulary, language and print concepts, and attention span, prepare information for parents about the importance of reading aloud.
- Prepare a series of short articles that could be included in a school or classroom newsletter.
- Prepare a presentation that you could give at a gathering of parents. Choose a book to read aloud

to parents that emphasizes the importance of reading to children (examples include *The Wretched Stone*, by Chris Van Allsburg, 1991; *It's a Book*, by Lane Smith; and *A Bedtime Story*, by Mem Fox, 1996).

slower pace. This requires regular practice and effort, but they soon find that the action and effects they create with their minds are just as satisfying, if not more so. Children are often disappointed in movies made from books if they have read the book first.

Read-Aloud Techniques

Reading aloud to children does not always happen effectively without advance planning. Teachers should do the oral reading themselves. Children will have chances to read orally when you are working with them. You will need to become familiar with the book you want to read and think through options of how to best share it with children. You will want to consider using various forms of expression, how to show the accompanying illustrations, and when to stop and ask questions.

Expression.   As you read orally to children, you model for them appropriate oral reading practices. When children hear you read, they should think, "This is what good reading sounds like." You need to read at an appropriate pace, read all of the words correctly and clearly, and read with natural intonation. Use a loud voice with effective expression, maybe even use different inflections for different characters. Group the words into meaningful phrases so the children can better understand what the author has written. As you read smoothly, children will enjoy listening to the text, but you can engage them further as you hold the book so your voice is not blocked, and so that children can see your face. Maintain eye contact with your students without losing your place in the book.

As you begin reading aloud to children, you may need to practice reading the text orally beforehand. You are probably used to reading silently. It may have been a long time since you "performed" a text for others. Pay attention to the parts of the text that are particularly difficult or strange for you. Maybe the author uses expressions that are outdated or do not match your dialect. There may be some words that you do not use naturally in your speech. Whatever the potential obstacles, practicing trouble spots beforehand usually makes the oral reading more beneficial to the listeners. If you feel like your own oral reading lacks expression, try playing a book on CD during read-aloud time. Not only will students enjoy the professional reader, but you can learn techniques for oral reading.

Speaking/Listening

Try This for Teaching	**Recorded Books**

- Find a recording of a favorite book.
- Play it during your read-aloud time.
- Don't leave the children unattended. Rather, listen to the book together.
- Ask the children what the reader does to make the story easy to listen to.
- Try to incorporate the same expressive style as you read aloud and encourage children to do the same.

Variations for ELLs

- Have students record themselves reading a book while they practice expressive reading.
- Share these recordings with other classes or donate them with a copy of the book to a homeless shelter or crisis center.

Illustrations.   Picture books are structured so that, in most cases, the illustrations and written text are interdependent. When reading picture books aloud to groups of children, you will need to make important decisions about how to show the illustrations. Some teachers like to show the illustrations as they read; others read the text on one page then show the illustrations. Both methods can be appropriate and effective.

Beck and McKeown (2001) found that when the illustrations and the text matched very closely, many children used the pictures rather than the text to make meaning. When the illustrations are so supportive, you may want to show them after reading a page of text so the students do not learn to attend only to the pictures. Additionally, when illustrations depict only part of the action on a page, many children recall only what was illustrated, and their overall comprehension of the story can be diminished or sidetracked because the illustrations have overpowered the language of the story. Be aware of the role of the illustrations in the books you read aloud and make your oral reading plans accordingly. Technology makes it possible to project enlargements of illustrations to the whole class instead of relying only on the book itself, which may not always be seen clearly by all. Just be sure that the technology does not break up the story's flow or distract the listeners. Illustrations provide a much needed support for those learning English and for strugglers who are less motivated than many of their peers.

Struggling Learners/
RtI

Questions.   In their years before coming to school, reading aloud for some children involved caregivers reading the words alone without any interjections. For others, parents may have stopped occasionally to ask questions that were relevant to what they were reading, such as "Where is the sun?" "Why did the dog stop?" or "How will they get home?" (Gregory & Morrison, 1998; Martin & Reutzel, 1999). Asking questions like these frequently results in conversations about the story that lead to improved comprehension. This is the case with older as well as younger children (Pressley & Forrest-Pressley, 1985). Fisher, Flood, Lapp, and Frey (2004) found that expert teachers in their study focused on both efferent and aesthetic questions. Their efferent questions allowed students to focus on information and details in the text. Their aesthetic questions helped bring the text to life and encouraged students to make connections between the text and their own lives. You can ask questions before reading to direct the listening and thinking. You can also ask questions during and after the reading to summarize and make predictions. Such intentional or interactive read aloud sessions can be instructional.

English Language
Learners

Try This for Teaching   **Lines, Between the Lines, and Beyond the Lines**

- During a read-aloud session, pause to ask questions.
- Try some literal questions (reading the lines).
- Ask some interpretive questions (reading between the lines).
- Explore some critical and creative questions (reading beyond the lines).
- Do not attempt to do all three types of questions each time you pause.

Variations for ELLs

- Encourage students to come up with questions in each of these categories, as well as to answer them.
- After you ask a question, have the students explain which category the question comes from before they answer it.

(Smith, 1969)

As beneficial as such questions can be, do not permit them to unnecessarily interrupt the flow of the story. Think of how annoying it would be if you were viewing a movie that was interrupted every two minutes so the audience could discuss the setting or define some words. On the other hand, think of how you might benefit if you could stop a movie part way through to discuss what had happened so far so you could make better predictions about what could happen next. When you stop the flow of reading a book, follow the Goldilocks principle: not too many or too few interruptions, but just the right number. Make sure the interruptions are enhancing, not interfering with comprehension.

Do not feel obligated to always integrate read-aloud material with content area objectives and curriculum. Even literacy objectives such as word identification techniques or comprehension strategies may be best taught during other reading experiences and not during read-aloud. "If literature in the classroom is to be effective teachers must learn to trust the book to do its own teaching" (Silvey, 1989, p. 550). Reading aloud needs to be done primarily for children's enrichment and enjoyment. Any interjections should be made with those ends in mind.

Speaking/Listening

Book Selection

Along with understanding the value of reading aloud and improving your read-aloud techniques, it is also important to select appropriate reading material. Always choose books you like and know well. These titles can come from your own reading experience or that of trusted associates. In addition, you may find that award-winning books such as Newbery or Caldecott winners or books that have received notice in some other way (such as the International Reading Association's Teachers' Choices, California Young Reader Medal, National Book Award, various state children's choice awards) can provide a variety of quality book choices. Figure 11.1 provides a list of some children's book

Figure 11.1 **Children's Book Awards**

Award	Description
Randolph Caldecott Medal	To the illustrator of the most distinguished American picture book.
John Newbery Medal	To the author of the book judged to have made the most distinguished contribution to children's literature.
Coretta Scott King Award	Recognizes the creative work of black authors and illustrators.
Boston Globe–Horn Book Award	Given to authors and illustrators for outstanding fiction and non-fiction.
Orbis Pictus Award	For outstanding nonfiction books for children.
Pura Belpré Award	Recognizes the creative work of Latino/Latina authors and illustrators.
Scott O'Dell Award	To the author of a distinguished work of historical fiction for children.
Edgar Allen Poe Award	Best juvenile novel in mystery, crime, and suspense.

awards. Other favorite resources include *Books Kids Will Sit Still For: A Read-Aloud Guide* (Freeman, 2006) and the website of books recommended by the New York City Public Library (kids.nypl.org/reading/recommended.cfm). When choosing books to read aloud, be sure to select from narrative, informational, and poetic texts. Choosing books from these genres will appeal to a broad cross-section of students and expand their interests and knowledge.

You also want to make sure you start reading aloud to students right on the first day. Figure 11.2 includes some favorite first-of-the-year read alouds. Some of these books are sure to get you off on the right foot. The grade level on the list does not refer to readability of the book or curriculum, but rather to the age of children who will respond well to the content. Some of the books are narrative, some informational, and some include poetry. You will find traditional and modern fantasy, as well as realistic fiction (both historical and contemporary). Some are picture books and others are chapter books.

Even if a book has won an award, or is one of your favorites, do not be afraid to put it down if students become bored with it. Tell them, "If you really want to finish this one, do it during your silent, sustained reading time." This decision models the power students have to choose different books when certain ones don't please them. Similarly, don't feel bound to read parts that might make you or some of your students uncomfortable. Jacobs and Tunnell (2004) remind us that books should be windows to the world rather than

Figure 11.2   Favorite First-of-the-Year Read Alouds

Grade Level	Author	Date	Title
Kindergarten	Paul O. Zelinsky	2000	*The Wheels on the Bus*
	Simms Taback	2007	*There Was an Old Lady Who Swallowed a Fly*
First grade	Marjorie Barker	1989	*Magical Hands*
	John Steptoe	2003	*Mufaro's Beautiful Daughters*
Second grade	Barbara Cooney	1982	*Miss Rumphius*
	Colleen Stanley Bare	1994	*Never Kiss an Alligator!*
Third grade	Seymour Simon	2002	*Animals Nobody Loves*
	Gerald McDermott	2004	*Arrow to the Sun*
Fourth grade	Patricia MacLachlan	1999	*All the Places to Love*
	Patricia Polacco	2001	*Thank You, Mr. Falker*
Fifth grade	Russell Freedman	1998	*Kids at Work*
	Alexander Key	2006	*The Forgotten Door*
Sixth grade	Richard Peck	2005	*The Teacher's Funeral*
	Gary D. Schmidt	2007	*The Wednesday Wars*
Middle school	Mildred Taylor	2004	*Wait Till Helen Comes*
	Mary Downing Hahn	2008	*Roll of Thunder, Hear, My Cry*

mirrors that reflect back our own values and standards. One of the greatest benefits of books is the opportunity they grant us to peek into the lives, cultures, and experiences of people who are different from us and to understand and learn from those differences. Still, when reading aloud to the whole class, be sensitive. Reading *Are You There God? It's Me, Margaret* (Blume, 2010) may get awkward when issues dealing with maturation surface. Swear words may be part of the vocabulary of some people, but you may try softening them as you read. In *View from the Cherry Tree* (Roberts, 1994), the cat is called S.O.B. One teacher decided to substitute the name Sam each time she came to the pet's name and by so doing avoided ruffling the feathers of some parents and administrators. Another teacher read *A Day No Pigs Would Die* (Peck, 1994), but chose to skip over a few controversial pages about mating animals. He found that this did not dilute the powerful messages of the book for the children.

Narrative.   When a story is told, it is called narrative text. Narrative text includes the genres of fantasy and realistic fiction, and these genres include fables, mysteries, science fiction, animal stories, and more. The formats of these works can include picture books, beginning chapter books, and novels. Some classic examples of narrative read-alouds come from the National Education Association's Top 100 Books for Children (www.nea.org/grants/13154.htm): *Charlotte's Web*, by E. B. White; *Where the Wild Things Are*, by Maurice Sendak; *Green Eggs and Ham*, by Dr. Seuss; *Because of Winn Dixie*, by Kate DiCamillo; *The Little House*, by Virginia Lee Burton; and *The Polar Express*, by Chris Van Allsburg. The Common Core emphasizes narrative writing especially in the primary grades. Students will be able to meet the expectation to write narrative text better if you consistently read narrative texts aloud to them.

Speaking/Listening

Common Core
State Standards

Informational.   The genre of informational text includes biographies as well as expository text about everything from history and space to music, sports, and cooking. Children are fascinated by things around them and wonder about how things work. Yet teachers seldom use informational books as read-alouds (Duke, 2000), despite the fact that boys often prefer informational text to narrative (Yopp & Yopp, 2006). The Common Core places emphasis on expository or informational text and suggests that for grades 3 to 8, this genre should represent 35 percent of a student's writing. Students will be unprepared to write informational text well unless they are exposed regularly to this type of text. Some teachers say the reason they do not read more informational text is because of length. You can deal with this challenge by reading only the captions of illustrations or diagrams or stringing headings together over several pages of text. Many informational texts, such as *In the Next Three Seconds* (Morgan, 1997), *Accidents May Happen* (Jones, 1996), and *Material World* (Menzel, 1994), are not meant to be read from cover to cover. Instead, you can choose to read aloud any sections you want to read in any sequence you choose.

Some informational books you can read to your class successfully include *Shipwreck at the Bottom of the World*, by Jennifer Armstrong; *Bet You Can't*, by Vicki Cobb and Kathy Darling; *Lincoln: A Photobiography*, by Russell Freedman; *You Want Women to Vote, Lizzie Stanton?* by Jean Fritz; *How to Talk to Your Dog*, by Jean Craighead George; and *How Much Is a Million?* by David Schwartz.

Poetic.   Poems are concise expressions of thoughts and feelings. Many children express enjoyment of poetry and have a natural affinity for nursery rhymes, jump-rope jingles, and songs. But, like informational text, poetry is often neglected in read-aloud

Try This for Teaching **Caption Read-Alouds**

- When informational text becomes too detailed or complicated for your students, try reading aloud only the captions of illustrations.
- As you encounter a picture, point to it as you read the caption.
- Continue this pattern as you move from picture to picture.
- Fill in some background information between pictures.
- Invite children who are interested in learning more about this topic to look

at the book in more detail during inde[pendent] reading time.

(Mooney & Young, 2006)

Variations for ELLs

- Alternate between reading portions of the text and captions. This may take some advance preparation.
- Read headings and subheadings, expounding on them to provide continuity.

experiences. Some favorite books of poetry include *You Read to Me, I'll Read to You*, by Mary Ann Hoberman; *Random House Book of Poetry for Children*, compiled by Jack Prelutsky; *Celebrations*, by Myra Livingston; *Lizards, Frogs, and Polliwogs*, by Douglas Florian; and *Where the Sidewalk Ends*, by Shel Silverstein.

Writing to Children

Teachers often read to children much more than they write to children, even though writing to students has many of the same rewards. Students benefit from a positive role model and feel motivated. Writing to students can expose them to written vocabulary and other aspects of print.

Have you ever received a note from a child thanking you or giving you a compliment? Did you save that note because it meant so much to you? Many teachers do, but how many write back? If a child's note to you is so important that you saved it, don't you think that a note from you will have a similar impact in a child's life? One second-grade teacher sent a thank-you note to her student through the mail for a gift he had given her. The little boy was so excited to receive an envelope addressed to him that he carried it around, showing it to everyone. He called his grandparents to let them know the exciting news. He posted it beside his bed where he could see it morning and night. What else received such a place of honor all year? He didn't post his spelling tests, worksheets, or standardized test scores. He posted a note from his teacher. This child's response is not unique. Salcedo (2009) found that diverse language learners in her study had similar reactions—the value they place on written communications from teachers is extremely high. As you write to your students, consider various methods and models.

English Language Learners

Methods

There are many ways for you to write to children. Perhaps remembering to do it consistently is the most difficult hurdle to overcome. Five effective methods are personal notes, morning messages, instructions, classroom labels, and dialogue journals.

Personal Notes.   Teachers often spend a lot of time offering children words of validation and praise—"Thanks for lining up quietly," and "Good job on remembering your homework." Why not make some of these literacy occasions? By writing these comments, we not only make our praise more meaningful but we also model writing for real purposes. Notes can be as simple as one sentence on a sticky note placed on a student's desk, or they could be longer messages on colorful stationary that you distribute at the end of the day. To be sure some children are not left out, keep a list of your students on your desk. Each time you write a note, put a check next to the student's name, and you can quickly make sure notes are being evenly distributed.

Struggling Learners/ RtI

Try This for Teaching   **Notes for Everyone**

- Keep a list of all student names nearby.
- Each time you write a note, put a check next to the student's name.
- Make sure students are not overlooked.
- When everyone has received a note, start a new list.

Variations for ELLs

- Address an envelope to every student in your class. Write several notes each week until the pile is empty.
- Link your note writing with the children's birthdays so everyone gets at least one note.

One principal would notice when students' artwork or writing was displayed in the hallway. She would write a note to the class, complimenting them on their hard work, and then she stapled the note to the bulletin board. Not only was the class excited to receive a note from the principal, but all the other classes that walked down the hall also saw the note. This leader got a lot of mileage out of one simple note. With today's technology, you can write notes to children through email. One benefit of electronic messages is that the majority of your letter can remain the same for all students and then personalized comments can be added for each. The Common Core emphasizes the use of technology in student writing. By sending students emails and inviting them to reply, you are attending to this expectation.

New Literacies

Morning Messages.   Along with writing notes to individuals, you can write a personal note to the entire class. Teachers sometimes refer to this as a morning message (Payne & Schulman, 1999). Morning messages, frequently written on chart paper or on the whiteboard, can be used to begin the day with a positive, friendly tone.

In the form of a friendly letter, the messages can contain things that are happening that day. They can also include high frequency words or punctuation marks you happen to be stressing at the time. But most children are more motivated to read the message if it reflects the teacher's personality and is not just a review of conventions. You could include references to events that are happening in the community (the big soccer game on Friday), upcoming holidays (traditions being celebrated on Cinco de Mayo), children's birthdays (personal wishes), or a joke or riddle. One teacher described the morning message as a low-tech Facebook post or blog.

A B C

Language Conventions

Usually you will write the message before the school day begins. At times, you will read the message to the students, but at other times you can let the students read the message on their own without drawing any special attention to it. Some teachers have found it helpful to combine this modeled writing with shared reading activities (www .cliontheweb.org/content/message-time-plus). You can begin this practice on the first day of school. In a morning message, you could describe yourself and give the reasons why you became a teacher. For example, you could write something similar to this:

> *Dear Class,*
>
> *My name is Mr. Wilcox. I love pizza and peanut M&Ms, but I'm trying hard to learn to like salads. I love listening to music in my car, and I usually keep the volume turned way up. I'm looking forward to teaching you this year. Teaching is my passion. I love feeling like I can make a difference in the world. We're going to have a great year!*
>
> *Love, Mr. Wilcox*

Occasionally, you may write the message as the students observe. When you think aloud as you write, you can call attention to skills you have taught, such as directionality of written language, letter names, sentences, and so on.

Another way to create morning messages is to use a computer and a projector. When creating digital morning messages (Labbo, 2005), you can write the message on your computer with the message projected on the screen for all to see. The students can see the letters and words being written in sequence with conventional spelling and punctuation being modeled. With certain software programs, such as Kid Pix, you can highlight sections of the text and students can hear a voice synthesizer saying the words as they view them. A printed copy of the message could be sent home with students for them to share with family members. Since the message is a model, it may not be an appropriate time to deliberately make intentional spelling or punctuation mistakes, but you could leave blanks to be filled in.

Instructions.   Personal notes and morning messages usually do not include instructions to students. However, giving directions can also be a time to write to students. Instead of saying "Line up for lunch," try writing those words on the board and complimenting students as they follow the written direction.

Speaking/Listening

Language Conventions

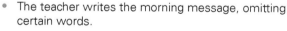

Try This for Teaching   **Fill-in-the-Blank Morning Message**

- The teacher writes the morning message, omitting certain words.
- The teacher reads the entire message as if all the words were there.
- During the second reading, the children identify the missing words and the teacher writes them in the blanks.

(Tompkins, 2010)

Variations for ELLs

- Write the missing words on cards and display them so that students can choose the right word for each blank.
- After completing the chart, re-read the message, counting the sentences or circling high-frequency words.
- Think of different words (such as synonyms, rhyming words, or antonyms) to replace those in the blanks.
- Read the message chorally.

One fifth-grade teacher takes advantage of a change in the schedule to write to students. When the children arrive in the morning, they see chart paper hanging in the doorway. On the paper the students read, "Today there will be an assembly, so we will do math first thing." The teacher also often includes instructions for getting the materials they will need for specific lessons. The teacher explained, "At first, I thought I was just saving myself the trouble of repeating my instructions 39 times. Now I understand that by writing, I'm sending two messages: one message about math and an additional message about one of the purposes about writing."

When writing instructions, messages, and notes, try doing so in cursive. Students do not see cursive in books or on computer screens. Many of their parents do not write in cursive. No wonder they balk at the cursive and complain, "Does it *have* to be in cursive?" They rarely see it modeled. Some students believe that cursive, like shorthand, is no longer useful in our technological society, but they will still encounter it enough that they need to be able to read it. Even in the primary grades, if you write instructions in cursive, the children can practice decoding it within the context of your writing.

English Language Learners

Labels in a classroom.

Classroom Labels. One of the simplest ways to write to children is to label items and locations around your classroom (e.g., *window, door, sink, conference corner,* and *author's chair*). Some see this strategy as effective only in the early primary grades. But it can be effective across all grade levels, especially considering the needs of English language learners. Some teachers create labels in different languages: *chair/silla* (Spanish); *desk/tisch* (German). You could also create synonym labels: *closet/storage, clock/timepiece, screen/monitor.* Other teachers like to go beyond simply naming things and write phrases and sentences: "This is the north side of our classroom" "The calendar tells us what date it is" "The flag is a symbol of our country." One

---

Try This for Teaching   **Reading Around the Room**

- Label items and areas in the classroom.
- Individually, in small groups, or as a class, assign students to read labels.
- Use a pointer or have students use a pointer to focus attention on specific labels.

(Isbell, 1995)

Variations for ELLs

- Extend the reading to material found on charts, posters, and bulletin boards.
- As they read the words, have students write them on paper.
- Alphabetize the words they write.
- Find parts of words (e.g., word families, vowels, words that start the same).

second-grade teacher hung an empty frame in front of the window. Below the frame she wrote, "Our changing picture of the world."

These labels could be commercially produced, printed from a computer, or handwritten in manuscript or cursive script. As you change labels regularly, students' attention will be drawn to them. You can also direct attention to them by asking students to read around the room.

English Language Learners

Dialogue Journals. Unlike personal notes, morning messages, instructions, and labels, dialogue journals are usually written in response to something students have written first. Students can write in their journals or notebooks daily.

Occasionally you can read what students have written and write something back. This takes a little extra effort, but it pays off, especially for students who are struggling. Many teachers have found this to be a useful intervention for children identified through RtI procedures. Gambrell (1985) reminded that this is not a time to correct children's grammatical or spelling errors, but instead it is a time to encourage their writing by commenting on what they have written ("I'm glad you like your dog. My family likes dogs, too.") and asking questions to invite response ("Do you keep your dog inside the house or outside? Where do you walk your dog?").

Struggling Learners/ RtI

Staton (1987) suggested that you should write less than your students and that you should avoid nonspecific comments like "interesting" or "good beginning." Your comments need to relate directly to the content of the child's writing and not necessarily to the organization or word choice. In addition to asking students questions, encourage them to ask you questions to carry on the conversation. However, dialogue journals are different from pen pal letters in that the responder is not a peer, but rather a teacher. You are not just providing an audience for the writer but are modeling writing. Bode (1989) emphasized that this modeling is most powerful when the dialogue is a private communication between you and each student. That personal context makes the experience extremely meaningful.

Teachers' major complaint about using dialogue journals is that they are time consuming. Do not feel obligated to write to each student each day. Some teachers gather journals from one table each week or pick a few journals randomly for response. As long as your writing to children is consistent throughout the year, all children will benefit from this interaction even if is does not occur daily.

Try This for Teaching **Dialogue Journals**

- Have students write a journal entry on a topic of their choice.
- Respond to the content of a child's entry.
- Do not correct spelling or grammar or make comments about organization or word choice.
- Repeat this dialogue as often as possible.

(Gambrell, 1985)

Variations for ELLs

- Limit the number of journals in which you respond by gathering from only one table each week, or select a few journals randomly. This gives you more time to respond regularly to students who may need extra encouragement.
- Designate a place in your classroom where students can drop off their journals for response.

Models

Writing to children is one way to provide a model, but there are others as well. You can invite authors to visit your school or classroom, share your own writing with children at various stages of completion, or examine an author's craft as you share an example of quality literature.

Author Visits.   "The benefits of visiting with an author . . . in person often last a lifetime. Once people see and hear [an author], their view of books enters a different sphere and is never quite the same again" (Jacobs & Tunnell, 2004, p. 355). You might look for the opportunity to invite a published author to your school or district. If you do, children are fascinated to hear how authors find ideas, create their rough drafts, and make many revisions. They love seeing work at various stages of completion and asking questions about the author's books, characters, or writing habits. An author's visit puts a face on the writing, and seeing that real people create books demystifies the writing process and helps students realize that they are also authors.

New Literacies

If a personal visit is not feasible, check out the websites of favorite authors or play a segment of a DVD on which an author shares his or her experiences and suggestions (e.g., Kidz Investigate Series, 2005). Provide some background about authors by using short biographies (e.g., Kovacs & Preller, 1999; Krull, 1994). Arrange for a long-distance visit by phone or have students Skype authors or write emails to them. Send letters in care of publishers' addresses found on websites or on the copyright pages of their books.

Teacher Modeling.   Although it would be wonderful to invite a published author to visit your classroom, such visits may be costly and hard to arrange. Children can learn similar lessons if you are willing to share your writing with them. Share a story

---

Try This for Professional Development   **Successful Author Visits**

- Plan ahead. Author visits usually cost money.
- Contact an author's appearance coordinator at the publisher's office.
- Coordinate with the publisher (you may need to order books, make transportation and lodging reservations, and request publicity materials).
- Ask about the author's personal preferences (such as audio-visual equipment requests, physical arrangements, and dietary restrictions).
- Prepare the audience (make them familiar with the author's books and brainstorm questions to ask).
- After the visit, have students write thank-you notes and review what they have learned from the visit.

(Jacobs & Tunnell, 2004)

Variations

- Although you may be able to contact some authors directly through their websites, others need to be contacted through their publishers.
- Some authors are willing to talk to parents as well as to children.
- Some may be prepared to conduct professional in-service sessions for teachers and in-class demonstration lessons.

you wrote when you were in elementary school or share a page from your journal or family blog. Show children the rough draft of one of your college papers and then the final draft. Show them a shopping list or a note you wrote. Try writing a personal essay or a poem just for your class. The Common Core emphasizes that one-third of children's writing should be argumentative, and yet children are rarely exposed to persuasive arguments during read-alouds. Your model in this genre can be especially valuable. For example, write a persuasive essay to your class about why they should be at school on time or why they should wash their hands before eating. Not only will you be reviewing important points that you would be making anyway but you will be doing it in writing and children will be exposed to the format of a well-formed persuasive essay.

Common Core
State Standards

After you share your writing, you can even ask for feedback from students. Some teachers feel nervous about sharing their own writing. In some cases they may not believe that it is as polished as a professional writer's work might be, but remember that you are working with elementary children. Anything you produce will be above their capabilities and will seem wonderful to them.

Author's Craft.   Another way to bring authors into your classroom is by examining books and discussing the **author's craft** (Raphael et al., 1992). Holdaway (1984) suggested that part of modeling writing for children includes sharing outstanding examples of poems, songs, and prose with children. As you do, you can examine together how the author successfully touched your emotions and created images in your mind: "How did the author make us feel surprised in this part of the story?" or "What did the author do to make us laugh here?" Look at the plot, characters and story elements. After looking at informational text, ask students, "What evidence did the author provide that convinced you to agree with him?" In all texts, locate examples of similes, metaphors, and other figurative and sensory language. Point out powerful phrases that communicate in an especially effective way. Fox (1993) wrote about how listening to books being read aloud helps her as an author: "The music, the word choice, the feelings, the flow of the structure, the new ideas, the fresh thoughts—all these and more are banked in my writing checking account whenever I am fortunate enough to be read to" (p. 70). When author Gerald N. Lund was asked, "How did you learn to write so well?" he said, "I learned to write from the best writing teachers in the world—books" (personal communication, April, 2010).

Team-teaching with books and their authors can open the door for children to be successful—especially those learning English. In the book *Wonderous Words*, Ray (2010) encourages young writers to imitate form but not substance. In other words, students can follow the format or pattern that an author has established in a mentor text and then fill in their own ideas with their own words.

English Language
Learners

One fifth-grade teacher read *Names for Snow* by Judi K. Beach (2003) and encouraged students to pay close attention to the author's craft. Students discovered that the author posed a question and then provided multiple answers that were full of figurative language and rich detail. She compared snow to a sleeping kitten and then to delicate lace.

Following this pattern, a student who had recently moved from South America wrote, "What is grass? We call it a rug when we walk barefoot." An English learner from Africa wrote, "What is rain? We call it life when ground is dry. We call it tears from heaven when people are mean to one another."

Summary

Some adults' fondest memories of elementary school include being read to by their teachers. That is why it is surprising to them when others call this practice a waste of time. Contrary to what some people may believe, reading aloud provides a model that is a vital part of the gradual release of responsibility in the learning process. Reading to children is an essential part of literacy instruction because it provides stronger motivation, larger vocabulary, wider exposure to concepts about language and print, and increased attention span. Despite these benefits, reading aloud can be painful rather than pleasurable if you do not read with expression, share illustrations, and interact with children by occasionally asking appropriate questions. Wise teachers select books carefully and include informational and poetic texts along with narrative.

Some adults can remember a compliment or an expression of confidence that was given to them by an elementary teacher. When such words are written, they are often kept and treasured over many years. Writing to children is important in literacy instruction because it can provide a powerful model. Along with personal notes, you can write morning messages, instructions, classroom labels, and dialogue journal conversations.

Author visits can also be memorable for children, but if those are not feasible, you can share some of your own writing at various stages of completion. You can also examine the author's craft with your class when you read a piece of quality writing. As you team-teach with authors of books, you can invite students to imitate form without copying substance. This allows all students to experience a high success rate.

Self-Check

1. What is meant by a gradual release of responsibility?

2. What are some benefits of reading aloud to children?

3. Why should you select books from a variety of genres?

4. What ways can be used to write to children?

5. What is the main goal of a morning message?

6. How can you use dialogue journals without feeling overwhelmed?

7. How can an author's visit benefit your students?

8. How can discussions about an author's craft help children with their writing?

MyEducationLab™

Go to the Topics, Vocabulary, Writing, and Organization and Management, in the **MyEducationLab** (www.myeducation lab.com) for your course, where you can:

- Find learning outcomes for Vocabulary, Writing, and Organization and Management, along with the national standards that connect to these outcomes.

- Complete Assignments and Activities that can help you more deeply understand the chapter content.

- Apply and practice your understanding of the core teaching skills identified in the chapter with the Building Teaching Skills and Dispositions learning units.

- Examine challenging situations and cases presented in the IRIS Center Resources.

- Check your comprehension of the content covered in the chapter by going to the Study Plan in the Book

Resources for your text. Here you will be able to take a chapter quiz, receive feedback on your answers, and then access Review, Practice, and Enrichment activities to enhance your understanding of chapter content (optional).

- Visit **A+RISE** Standards2Strategy™, an innovative and interactive online resource that offers new teachers in grades K–12 just-in-time, research-based instructional strategies that meet the linguistic needs of ELLs as they learn content, differentiate instruction for all grades and abilities, and are aligned to Common Core Elementary Language Arts Standards (for the literacy strategies) and to English language proficiency standards in WIDA, Texas, California, and Florida.

Reading and Writing with Children—Whole Class

Chapter Outline

**READING WITH CHILDREN—
WHOLE CLASS**
Shared Reading within Various
Instructional Approaches
Reading Process
**WRITING WITH CHILDREN—
WHOLE CLASS**
Shared Writing within Various
Instructional Approaches
Writing Process
SUMMARY

My sixth-graders were reading Anne Frank's *The Diary of a Young Girl* (1952) and were having a hard time getting into the book. Some teachers had warned that it might be a little too ambitious of me to introduce that book. I had read it myself when I was older. But I loved the book and wanted my students to experience its haunting and life-changing power. I decided I needed to do more to help bring the book to life for them. I built background knowledge by showing them pictures of Jewish children their age in pre–World War II Germany who were forced to wear the Star of David on their clothes. I read firsthand accounts of the prejudice and discrimination these children faced. On the day we read about Anne's family going into hiding, I made arrangements with the school custodian to lead us into the basement of the school where we read together by flashlight and then discussed how the Frank family must have felt. My efforts had the desired effect. Instead of being bored, the children could not get enough of the book. They began to read related material about World War II and they researched what happened to the people in the book. We were all better off for sharing the reading experience as a class.

—Brad

When you are learning to drive a car, the example of your teacher is essential to motivate you and to release responsibility gradually to you. But a responsible teacher does not just give you keys to the car and wish you luck. Although independent practice is an important step in the learning process, it must be preceded by shared experiences when you and your teacher are in the car together. Your teacher begins by sitting in the driver's seat while you are in the passenger's seat. Your teacher will point out how she is shifting gears or pushing on the brake. She shows you how to turn on the lights and windshield wipers. You have sat in cars for years as a passenger, but you have never before paid such close attention to what the driver is doing. You will be more prepared to sit in the driver's seat yourself after having watched what your teacher does there.

The same is true when students learn to read and write. Learners will gain confidence as you talk them through the reading process and the writing process. When you read a text together with your class, you are in the driver's seat and students are watching you closely. When you write together as a class, your students are in the zone of proximal development (Vygotsky, 1962). They are able to do something *with* you that they might not be able to do on their own. As they succeed with your help, their ability increases, and later they can work more independently.

Occasionally you may hear stories about someone who made it through the entire school system—including college—without knowing how to read and write. One such student was John Corcoran, who manipulated his way through school by avoiding participation and guessing on all the tests (Corcoran, 1994). He slipped by and even graduated from high school, though he could not read a word of his diploma or write a thank-you note to one of his teachers. How did that happen? How did he go to school year after year and never have a teacher recognize his deficiency? Surely they were not so uncaring or apathetic that they would knowingly send him ill equipped into the world without trying to help. More likely, his teachers were not aware of the problem. Perhaps this was because John was a good faker. But maybe it was at least partly because the teachers had allowed themselves to be assigners of reading and writing and graders of tests without actually ever *sharing* the reading and writing process together with their students. Had John's teachers simply read and written with him, he could not have slipped by unnoticed as he did.

Struggling Learners/
RtI

Reading with Children—Whole Class

Written text can be compared to a stream of refreshing water. Too many people pass it by, rarely stopping to drink. Others take an occasional sip. Some drink deeply from the stream and return often to quench their thirst. Reading with children is a way to help your whole class feel the satisfaction of taking a long, cool drink. Holdaway (1979) described **shared reading** as reading text together that may be too difficult for many in the class to read independently.

Shared Reading within Various Instructional Approaches

Sharing the reading process with the whole class is a vital part of the gradual release of responsibility from teacher to student, but it must also connect with essential instructional elements of learning, doing, and sharing in a variety of ways. Some districts require teachers to use a basal program. Others expect workshop routines to be followed. Still others organize reading instruction into literature units, and then there are those who work out a combination of several approaches. Whole class reading experiences should be included within all of these approaches to reading instruction. Begin your planning by using standards or curriculum guides that provide aims, goals, and objectives. But remember that your general plans must be sensitive to student needs, regardless of the instructional approach you take.

English Language Learners

Core Literacy Programs.

Core literacy programs, commonly called basals, usually organize instruction into weekly units that emphasize skills to be taught, practiced, and tested in conjunction with several readings meant to be completed as a class. There are currently three major core programs: *Reading Street* by Pearson Scott Foresman (www.pearsonschool.com/index.cfm?locator=PSZu65); *Treasures* by Macmillan McGraw-Hill (treasures.macmillanmh.com/national) soon to be renamed *Wonders*; and *Journeys* by Houghton Mifflin/Harcourt (www.hmheducation.com/journeys/).

Teachers' manuals provide guidance that is not included in the student texts. These instructions sometimes offer suggestions for introducing the text and the target skills within the text. They may highlight difficult vocabulary that you should address before or during the reading. Manuals may also provide questions to help you plan and lead discussions when the reading is finished. The expectation of most basal programs is that you

A whole class reading together.

will take time throughout the week to read and re-read the offerings in the student text together as a class.

Assigning the students to read the text independently is not an appropriate option because the students in your class will be at a variety of reading levels. Repeated readings allow students to practice fluency, but these should be oral reading experiences rather than silent ones. One of the benefits of a basal program is that multiple copies of the text are available so students can follow along as lead readers help them through. Some teachers are hesitant to take much time to explore and apply the text after reading it, perhaps because of time constraints imposed by the list of skills their students must master. Don't forget that skills are best taught in meaningful contexts, however. Taking time to read and respond to a story or article provides a rich context in which skills make sense and can transfer beyond Friday's test. Sharing responses to readings with each other provides motivation as well as depth.

Reading Workshop.

A reading workshop usually focuses on students choosing their own texts, reading them at their own pace, and responding individually during a sharing time (Dorn & Soffos, 2005). Skill instruction usually takes place in whole class or small group mini-lessons. A mini-lesson takes about 10 to 15 minutes and provides the area of focus for the workshop. Although some independent practice by students may be appropriate, in a workshop the practice usually occurs during reading. Teachers follow up on the mini-lessons during one-on-one conferences during which students are held accountable. During work time teachers meet individually with students, monitoring and discussing their reading, helping them with difficulties or questions they are having, and encouraging them to reflect on their growth and progress as readers (Atwell, 2007).

Students respond to questions such as "What's going well?" "What's not going so well?" "What goals do you have for the future?" During a sharing time, students share with the class what they are reading independently, along with their individual responses. Some educators might claim that there is no place for whole class reading experiences within traditional workshop routines. However, other educators have adapted these structures to include whole class and small group work along with independent reading.

During work time you can tell the students that they will need to put their own reading on hold temporarily while you read something together as a class. In workshop settings it is best to use shorter texts for whole class reading. Select texts that can be introduced, read, and responded to in one or two sittings. Poems and songs are ideal, and news stories can also be effective—especially when they deal with current events. You can hand out copies of these short texts to everyone or project the text on a screen.

Struggling Learners/ RtI

One fourth-grade teacher would conference with her students during a reading workshop. When she found that a student was struggling to comprehend a particular passage, chapter, or section, she would ask permission to share the situation with the whole class. With the student's consent, on the following day she would gather the class to read the text together. As part of introducing the text to the class, the student would summarize the text to that point. The teacher would then present the problem. Sometimes there was a problem with decoding. Other times vocabulary was holding up the reader. Following the pattern of a newspaper advice column, the teacher would ask, "So what advice would you give the reader in this situation?" Other students then volunteered solutions and suggestions for the student as the class read and responded to the text together. This procedure allowed students to take turns in the roles of advice givers and advice receivers. Thus all students could continue to read independently in the workshop while still benefiting from some whole class reading and discussion.

English Language Learners

Literature Units.   In literature units teachers guide students as they read a single book or several books about the same topic, in the same genre, or by the same author. Sometimes literature units involve use of text sets, collections of the books related to the same topic (Opitz, 1998). Many text sets include materials at different levels to help English learners and struggling readers (Robb, 2002a). As with other instructional approaches, the teacher makes use of mini-lessons to address skills. Time is also allowed for sharing responses and listening to book talks from individuals and groups. Units can

---

Try This for Teaching   **Share Your Advice**

- As you conference with students about their reading, watch for situations that would present good dilemmas for the class to resolve together.

- Ask for the student's permission to share the dilemma with his or her help.

- Gather the class and invite the student to share some background of the book.

- Provide access to the text by projecting it and read it together, highlighting the problem.

- In advice column form, ask class members what solutions they can offer.

Variations for ELLs

- Watch for incidents in which one student surprises you by comprehending difficult text well. Highlight the positive with the whole class in a shared reading experience. Instead of asking for suggestions for solving a problem, elicit praise for what the student did well.

- Present the struggle or victory anonymously. Have students give advice without knowing to whom the advice is being given.

feature whole class discussions of a single novel or they can be organized to study a theme through reading a variety of texts.

Whole class novel.   Some educators caution against reading novels or nonfiction books together as a class (Fisher & Ivey, 2007) because of concerns that different reading levels are not addressed, that reading the books takes too long, and that reading together is a teacher-centered rather than student-centered or standards-based process. Although it is difficult to select a book that will interest and challenge everyone, novel study exposes students to significant pieces of work they might never choose on their own and also provides a common context for instruction. It takes time to finish an entire book together, but it doesn't have to take too long. Keep a crisp pace.

Dragging a classroom novel on and on for half a year, analyzing each detail along the way, can discourage further reading instead of motivating it. The power of teaching literature units is that children have the opportunity to be immersed in literature not extraneous material.

Be careful not to micromanage to the point that you are actually pulling students away from the reading. Three guidelines may help you. First, spend more time reading than introducing and responding. Building background knowledge and encouraging literature responses must be balanced with actual reading. If any one part of the reading process overpowers the others, you run the risk of losing the interest of some students. Every chapter does not need an introduction, and every paragraph does not need a discussion. Second, variety makes a difference for students. If you use the same vocabulary strategy over and over or have the students re-read every chapter for fluency practice, students will tire quickly. Continually try something new. Third, be judicious in assigning worksheets and reading guides. Used sparingly, such supplements can be useful to help students move through the text effectively. However, some teachers use packets of supplemental materials and activities for specific novels that are thicker than the books themselves. Character name crossword puzzles and word finds may not help children share the reading process. Before assigning work in addition to the reading itself, ask yourself why. If the answer is that the assignment can enrich the students' shared reading experience, then proceed. If the answer is only that it will keep students busy, think again.

Thematic study.   Pappas, Kiefer, and Levstik (2005) encouraged use of **thematic units**, organized instruction around a central concept or theme. Themes can be broad concepts such as "journeys," "discoveries," or "courage," or they can focus on a particular type of literature (animal stories or mysteries) or books by a particular author (such as Walter Dean Myers or Lois Lowry) or books about a specific time period (the Civil War). Teachers usually spend a little time introducing the theme and then proceed with the reading as a group. Texts can be books, but they can also include related materials found in magazines and online sources. Many of the readings will be completed as a class, but other reading can be done in small groups as long as a lead reader is assigned to each group. Allow time for students to read individually and in small groups with leveled texts, but be sure to include whole class shared experiences as well.

English Language
Learners

New Literacies

Reading Process

In any instructional approach, shared reading helps students see that decoding a few words here and there is not nearly as satisfying as experiencing the entire reading process. Tompkins (2010) identified the reading process as including activities before, during, and after reading. You can assist your students before reading by activating their background knowledge and encouraging them to come to the text with questions they want to answer. You can help them during the reading by clarifying the meanings of unknown words or phrases. After the reading, you can help students to explore the text for hidden patterns or meaningful symbols. You can help them apply what they are learning to their own lives and guide them to become aware of their own responses to the text.

Before Reading.   "Open your books to page 72. Read the story and answer the questions at the end." As often as words like these have been spoken by teachers, they have done little to meaningfully prepare students for reading. You didn't go through an entire teacher preparation program at a university to say "Open your books to page 72." You can extend a much more enticing invitation to your students by preparing them for the reading experience. Increase their understanding by building background knowledge in a schema orientation. Help them feel motivated with an attitude orientation. Focus them on what they will encounter during the upcoming reading with an activity orientation. You won't use all three orientations each time. In fact, you should rarely introduce text the same way. You must know your students well enough to understand their needs and then choose from a variety of options and ideas available to meet those needs.

Schema.   *Schema* is a word used to describe our flexible and growing mental frameworks. If children are already familiar with the content to be read, your task might be to activate the background knowledge they already have. If they are not at all familiar with the topic, you may have to build background knowledge so they can understand the text.

Suppose you plan to read *The Story of the Olympics* (Lacey, 2008) as a class. Your students may have watched television coverage of part of an Olympics opening ceremony, or they may have seen an athlete awarded a medal. They might recognize the interlocking rings of the Olympic symbol, or they might be familiar with the tradition of the running of the torch. Before you read with the class, remind them of what they already know. The same students may be unfamiliar with other aspects of the Olympics; for example, you may need to explain the difference between the summer and winter games. The term *skeleton* might conjure up thoughts of Halloween rather than sledding, so you could play a video of the skeleton event to show students that the familiar word also refers to an athlete sliding face first down an icy track at incredible speeds. To your students, *curling* might be associated only with hair or gift wrap. You could show them how the sport of curling involves athletes sliding a weight across the ice without letting it go too far or fall too short; perhaps they could practice this skill by sliding a penny across a tabletop without letting it fall off. By activating or building background knowledge, you prepare your students to read and comprehend the text successfully. You spark questions they would never have if they were reading without assistance.

English Language Learners

Struggling Learners/ RtI

Attitude.   Help students feel motivated to read the text. Sometimes students are already familiar with the content or context of the text you plan to read together, and because they think they already know everything they may complain, "This is so boring," or "This is dumb," without giving the book a chance. You can increase students' enthusiasm by introducing the text with activities designed to improve their attitudes. When preparing to read about the Olympics, for example, try playing the theme music from the last

Try This for Teaching   Realia

- **Realia** is a term for real things or concrete objects that can be used to build background knowledge.
- Identify vocabulary in a passage that might be unfamiliar to your students.
- Gather objects that relate to those words and concepts (e.g., household items, clothing, tools, crafts).
- Before and during reading, allow students to see, hear, smell, and handle objects.
- Compare and contrast the objects with those described in the text.
- Keep the objects close by for future use.

(Herrell & Jordan, 2011)

Variations for ELLs

- Consider field trips as possible times to experience realia.
- Try to gather items from various ethnic groups (e.g., piñatas, chopsticks, and woks).
- Ask children to bring realia to share (e.g., animals and plants).
- Put the objects in a bag so students cannot see them. Have them touch the objects to see if they can guess them before seeing them.
- Let children see multiple objects displayed for 30 seconds. Then cover them and ask the children to remember and describe them.

Olympics, with students marching around the room to the music and waving flags from different countries. Plan a simple competition like tossing wadded up paper into the wastepaper basket and then placing a gold, silver, and bronze paper medal around the winners' necks. Giving students a small taste of what characters or people in the book are experiencing can prove to be exciting for them and can help them approach the text with increased desire to read it well.

Activity.   Help your students prepare for reading by focusing them on specifics they will encounter in the text: "As you read this book about the Olympics, see if you can identify the country where the Olympics first began," or "The author is going to give you three reasons the Olympics are worthwhile; see if you can come up with any more reasons that the author has not given."

English Language Learners

Try This for Teaching   Role Play

- Identify key vocabulary in a text that children will read.
- During a shared reading, stop when the key words are encountered and act out the words.
- Connect the words to past experiences by creating a card for each word and asking students when they have seen the words used.
- Sort the cards into groups (e.g., similar meanings, the same part of speech).
- Divide the class into small groups, giving each group four or five words.
- Have each group create a scene or skit using their words.

- Let each group practice and perform its scene. Have the rest of the class identify the words that were performed.

(Herrell, 1998)

Variations for ELLs

- Discuss multiple-meaning words and have the group perform a skit using alternative meanings.
- Give each group the same word and have them perform different skits around the same word.
- Display word cards on posters or word walls.

Try This for Teaching **Verify and Clarify**

- Prepare for reading by asking students what they already know about the topic.
- Record responses so all can see.
- Invite students to read the text to verify and clarify their original thinking.
- After the reading, revisit the facts on the board to determine which ones were accurate and which ones need to be revised.

Variations for ELLs

- If answers are not provided in the text, ask students where they could turn to learn more.
- Discuss the qualifications of the author and publisher of the text and compare other sources, deciding whether to trust or distrust the information given.
- Have children write at least one of the responses they want to verify or clarify as they read. Encourage them to revise that sentence appropriately after reading. Perhaps they could write it as a newspaper headline.

Struggling Learners/ Rtl

One eighth-grade teacher found she could focus her students on the text by asking what they thought they knew about the subject. As students responded, she listed key words for each response on the board. She then asked them to read the text in order to verify or clarify what they knew.

During Reading.   As you share the reading process with your students you will find it helpful to prepare them before reading a text or a selection from a text. You will also find it important to actually read the text together as a class. There are many ways to do this, but some are more effective than others. Some practices are common in classrooms despite research that shows they are counterproductive (Ash, Kuhn, & Walpole, 2009). Two examples of counterproductive methods are using round-robin reading and assigning individuals to finish class reading independently. Perhaps they are just traditional classroom activities, or maybe they are easy for teachers to use. Whatever the reason for their popularity, you can find positive alternatives for ineffective practices by providing access to print and appointing lead readers.

Round-robin reading.   The practice of assigning one student to read the first paragraph, the next student to read the next paragraph, and so forth is commonly called round-robin reading. As you read something in a small group of adults or even in a family, this can seem like an efficient way to share the reading load. However, the practice has drawbacks—especially when working with children (Rasinski, 2006). It creates high anxiety for the ones reading because you are putting them in the uncomfortable position of performing before peers without any time to prepare or practice. Even the best readers don't want to risk possible embarrassment. Round-robin reading rarely engages other students in the classroom because those in the immediate lineup are usually counting paragraphs so they can preview the text they will have to read, while those across the room are daydreaming because they know the teacher will never get to them. This all leads to poor comprehension. The nervous reader has not been paying attention beyond his or her paragraph. Others are rehearsing rather than listening. And the rest of the class is bored because the readers are usually far from fluent or loud enough to hear. Teachers ask, "So what did we just read?" No one responds. Then the teacher starts the whole process again as if doing more of what is not working is going to solve to the problem.

A popular variation to round-robin reading, called popcorn reading, has the reader or teacher call on any class member randomly to pick up where the reader left off. Popcorn reading raises the anxiety for everyone in the class because anyone could be called on at any time. Although this may lead to greater engagement—because no one knows who will be next—it still does little to focus attention on the text and improve comprehension. Students are often reading word by word instead of looking at phrases and watching the meaning of the entire text unfold. Their primary concern is usually where the class is in the text rather than what is being communicated by the text. Some children delight in catching a peer who has lost his place rather than catching on to the meaning of the text.

Assigned reading.   After reading the first part of a chapter or story together, teachers commonly say, "Now finish this on your own." Even if you give time in class for students to complete the assignment, they may not have interest in finishing the material because they did not select it themselves. A greater concern is that the material is often above the instructional reading levels of many of the students, so finishing independently becomes overly burdensome and those students may give up before they finish. Some children might pretend to be reading and even turn pages to keep up appearances, but they are not reading or comprehending. If the teacher tries to return to the reading or topic later, a discussion or response activity is impossible because of the holes left in the students' comprehension.

Students need time to read by themselves, but silent reading is usually most effective with leveled or self-selected material. Reading together as a class should be completed together. The goal of whole class reading is not to have every student read orally; whole class reading is an opportunity to share the process by providing students access to the text and the example of a fluent lead reader so they can all focus on comprehension rather than just decoding.

Access to print.   Sharing the reading process with children is complete if they can see the text as it is read (Holdaway, 1979). Individual copies of the text for all the children is nice, but far from essential. Several children can share a book, text can be projected on a screen or displayed on charts, or big books can be used so all students can see the enlarged pictures and text. Regardless of how text is provided, your goal is to keep students' eyes on it (Depree & Iversen, 1996).

Some teachers do this with a pointer when text is displayed in front of the group. Think of the pointer as a conductor's baton: If the conductor is skillful, the musicians know when to stop, when to go, and what tempo to maintain. But don't just wave a stick across a chart or the page of a big book. Instead, use your pointer deliberately to emphasize words, keep an even pace, and highlight punctuation marks or letters.

Language Conventions

Some teachers keep students focused on text by making a game of it. Try reading several sentences and then suddenly stopping. Students take the cue to fill in the blank and read the next word chorally. Be careful you do not do this so often that it distracts from the flow of the text. Similarly, try setting a timer while you read and students follow along. No one knows when the timer is going to ring. When it does, praise the students who are able to put their fingers on the paragraph where you are reading. When you are reading a longer text together and heads start to go down on desks or students start to gaze out the window, try some choral or echo reading for a paragraph or two. In choral

Back-and-Forth Reading

- Preview the text and make sure there are pages that contain a lot of dialogue using quotation marks.

- Explain that you are going to read all the text that is outside quotation marks as the students follow along. When you come to text inside quotation marks, the students will read it chorally.

- Demonstrate and practice until students understand their role.

- Proceed with the reading as a class, but only for a few pages. Students will enjoy this back-and-forth reading, but not if it is overused or goes on too long.

Variations for ELLs

- If expository text does not contain a lot of quotation marks, have students follow as you read the bulk of the text but encourage them to chorally read the headings or the bold words. You could also try having them read the captions of pictures as you come to them.

- If you come to a dialogue between two or three characters, divide the class into two or three groups and assign each group a character to read chorally.

Struggling Learners/ RtI

English Language Learners

reading everyone reads the text aloud together. In echo reading children listen to you read a phrase, sentence, or group of sentences and then re-read the same text right after you. Don't let these strategies go on too long. Your goal with these activities is simply to get everyone sitting up again, refocused on the text.

Lead readers. Along with access to the print, whole class reading experiences should provide your students with access to a **lead reader**—someone who can read fluently in order to avoid distracting from the meaning of the text. Text difficulty becomes an issue when students are being asked to read in small groups or independently, but it is not a great concern in shared reading experiences if you or someone in your class can be a lead reader. Some students read well and are confident before their peers. Begin by asking for volunteers. If a child is willing to read but not quite up to the task, don't be afraid to step in. Just say, "Thanks for your help. I'll take it from here," and keep reading yourself. Other students may be able but unwilling. Try giving them advance notice and time to practice and prepare; for example, you might tell a student, "I would like to call on you to be a lead reader as we move on to Chapter 3. Please look it over tonight and let me know tomorrow if you feel comfortable helping out." When dealing with short texts, you might want to provide the whole class time to read silently to themselves and then ask for a volunteer. If no one volunteers, you can take the role of lead reader and proceed.

Another way to provide access to a lead reader is by dividing the class into pairs or threesomes for buddy reading. This is most effective when you assign the companionships deliberately rather than just randomly pairing students with the person next to them or letting them choose friends as partners. Ideally, you want weaker readers paired with stronger readers who can take the lead. The goal

Students reading together.

of buddy reading is not necessarily to take turns, since weaker readers may not be able to pull their weight. Lead readers can read the entire selection as their partners follow along. This practice does not have the disadvantages of round-robin reading or independent completion. However, it does create management concerns if everyone is doing it at the same time. The classroom may become too noisy, and there may not be space for the partnerships to spread out. It could become difficult for you to monitor what is happening and make sure the time is being used well by all the students. Consider buddy reading as an option for some students rather than for all. It is especially appropriate practice for students who are identified through RtI processes as needing more instruction.

Struggling Learners/ RtI

One type of buddy reading that has been shown to help students make great gains quickly is dyad reading, during which weaker readers are given one-on-one assistance by the teacher, an adult volunteer, a cross-age tutor, or a competent peer (Eldredge, 1990; Eldredge & Quinn, 1988). Sometimes called shadow reading or copycat reading, dyad reading consists of the lead reader tracking the text with a finger as the weaker reader reads along as best he can. The lead reader reads at a normal pace and with normal expression. The weaker reader may follow silently at times when he encounters difficult words and phrases, but the goal is for her to read orally along with her partner. If the weaker reader drops out completely, the lead reader must slow down until they can read together again. For best results these partnerships must read together consistently—either daily or several times a week. When students who are learning English are placed in pairs for dyad reading, they make impressive gains (Almaguer, 2005).

English Language Learners

After Reading.   When you are sharing the reading process with the whole class, students learn that they are not finished when they get to the end of the story or chapter. Reading is not just about what authors and text offer the reader but also about what the reader offers in return. Rosenblatt (1978) focused educators on the importance of reader response. One child may read a story about snow and like it because she enjoys skiing. Another may have a negative response to the story because his family once drove through a severe snowstorm and the experience scared him. Still another may have never seen snow except in movies. Asking children to identify settings, characters, and the climax may help with comprehension, but it does not allow for a response. Similarly, fact-recall questions such as "What was the color of the sweater worn by the main character's aunt at the family party?" or "What was the third word in the fourth paragraph on the sixth

---

Try This for Teaching   **Dyad Reading**

- Pair two students, one designated as the lead reader, for regularly scheduled reading times.
- Encourage the lead reader to read at a normal pace and with expression and to track the text with his finger so the weaker reader can follow.
- Instruct the weaker reader to shadow or copy the lead reader.
- If the weaker reader stops, instruct the lead reader to slow down and control the pacing until the weaker reader gets started again.

(Eldredge, 2005)

Variations for ELLs

- Have both students read along as they listen to a recording of a book. The lead reader still tracks the text with a finger so the weaker reader doesn't become lost.
- After practicing dyad reading with a competent lead reader, offer the weaker reader the opportunity to be a lead reader for a younger student on a simpler text.

A class having a discussion.

Common Core
State Standards

English Language
Learners

page?" are much too specific and detailed to encourage the higher-level thinking required for a response. You can encourage both immediate and deliberate responses by planning experiences that mirror incidents in the book and by integrating reading, writing, and the arts.

Immediate responses.   Children have the right to their opinions. They can give a book thumbs up or thumbs down, but they must learn how to substantiate and support those opinions with evidence. Don't settle for "This is a lousy book because I hated it." You have to help students express their opinions with clarity as well as passion. The Common Core emphasizes this ability, and response to shared reading becomes an excellent context in which to teach and practice it. Discussions are one way to guide students in expressing immediate responses, and also to offer them the chance to change their minds as they hear the thoughts of others.

Through observation of discussions at school, we know that the most common interaction is the IRE pattern—Initiate, Response, and Evaluation (Mehan, 1979). The teacher asks a question, a student responds, and the teacher evaluates the response. What the teacher does next can encourage or limit further student discussion. The teacher frequently acknowledges the student response and then asks a new question. Following is an example.

Teacher   Who went to the store?

Student   Mom.

Teacher   Right. What did she buy there?

Such questions don't always encourage discussion or response. You want to invite students to talk to you and to one another about what they are reading or studying. One way to do this is to ask **open-ended questions**, those that have several possible appropriate answers. "Who was the first U.S. president?" is a closed question with one correct answer. "Who was the most effective president?" is an open-ended question. When you ask such questions, be prepared to accept a variety of reasonable responses, some of which you may not have anticipated. When students are responding to open-ended questions, be careful not to praise responses; praise leads to conformity. If you ask for the name of the first U.S. president and a child answers "Washington," you can appropriately respond with "Good answer!" "Way to go!" or "Excellent!" However, such praise after an open-ended question will limit the thinking that goes on. If you ask for the name of the most effective president and someone responds "Lincoln," be careful not to praise. If you say "Good answer!" or "Excellent!" children will assume Lincoln was the correct response and might be unwilling to explore additional answers that could be equally defensible. In such moments, try responding with a simple "Thank you." It acknowledges the response without passing a value judgment.

Another way to encourage discussion through questioning is to use appropriate **wait times,** pauses during questioning to allow for more thoughtful responses and greater interaction (Rowe, 1986). Two types of wait times can encourage discussion. First, after you ask a question, wait for at least three to five seconds before saying anything more. Allowing time for students to think before they answer can result in longer and more topic-related responses. A second type of wait time occurs after a student has responded. Wait for another three to five seconds before you say anything. This extra wait time may encourage the student to expand on his ideas or permit another student to respond before you do.

A third way to promote discussion is to ask leveled questions, which require students to engage in cognitive processing at a variety of levels. Some have categorized questions into hierarchies (Bloom, 1956; Sanders, 1966; Smith & Barrett, 1979) that rank question types from the lowest cognitive levels to the highest. Unfortunately, about two-thirds of the questions teachers ask are at low (literal) levels, such as "Who?" or "What?" (Guszak, 1967). You need to ask students higher-level questions such as "How?" "Why?" "What if?" to help them relate the material to their own lives (Strong, Silver, & Perini, 2007).

Many types of questioning activities have been suggested. One that has survived the test of time is the six Ws (Rosenshine, Meister, & Chapman, 1996)—who, what, when, where, why, and how (with the *w* at the end of the word). The teacher begins by asking questions beginning with *who, what, when,* and *where.* These don't always have to be closed questions, but the answers are usually facts. Don't stop there. Broaden the discussion by asking more open-ended *why* and *how* questions. Strong, Silver, and Perini (2007) suggested adding two more *w* questions, a *what if* question and a *we* question: "What if the story had a different setting?" and "What can we learn from this?" Three ways to improve discussions are eight Ws, student survey, and the answering game.

Speaking/Listening

Eight Ws. After reading the folk tale *The Little Red Hen* (Pinkney, 2006), you can ask the following questions: "*Who* greeted the sun with a cheery good morning?" "*What* did the little red hen decide to bake?" "*When* did she ask the other animals to help?" "*Where* did she plant the seeds?" "*Why* did she not want to share the bread?" "*How* did the animals avoid helping?" "*What if* the animals had helped from the beginning?" "What can *we* learn from this?" "How does it relate to us?"

Student survey. After a child answers a question orally, see what the rest of the students think of their classmate's answer: "How many agree with her?" or "Raise your hand if you think this is a good idea." If, in response to a fact question, the only hands that shoot

English Language Learners

Eight Ws

- After reading, ask questions related to important parts of the text using *who, what, when, where, why,* and *how.*
- Ask *what if* questions to encourage synthesis.
- Ask *we* questions to stimulate application and evaluation.

(Rosenshine, Meister, & Chapman, 1996)

Variations for ELLs

- Use a die or a spinner to randomly select the type of question for students to answer (1 = who, 2 = what, etc.).

- After students are familiar with answering these questions, some can generate questions using the same key words for others to answer, and then students can switch roles, so the questioners become the ones giving the answers.
- Use the same questions to help students justify their responses: *Who* says? *What* evidence do you have? *When* did you change your mind? *Where* did you find that in the text? *Why* are you so sure? *How* can you prove that? *What if* other evidence were presented? *When* has someone agreed or disagreed with you?

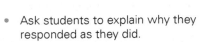

Try This for Teaching **Student Survey**

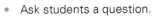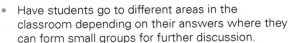

- Ask students a question.
- After one student responds, ask others to raise their hands if they agree or disagree.
- Ask additional questions ("How many think that's a good idea?" "Who has had similar experiences?")

- Ask students to explain why they responded as they did.
- Have students go to different areas in the classroom depending on their answers where they can form small groups for further discussion.

Variations for ELLs

- Have students graph the numbers of each type of response.

---

up belong to the same students who always participate, ask the students to discuss their responses quietly with their neighbors. When two talk, four become engaged; the four can quickly become eight, and so on, until the entire class is involved. Try proposing several answers to a particular question. Then have the students select their favorites by standing up for the first option, staying seated for the second, and sitting on the floor for the third.

Struggling Learners/ RtI

Answering game. Try dividing your students into groups and set out one less object (beanbag, ball, or spoon) than members in the group. After you present a question and they have been given time to think, give them a signal and tell all the children to grab one of the objects. The student who is left without an object must answer the question or formulate a question for others to answer.

Deliberate responses. Immediate responses may not always show the depth and higher-level thinking that teachers desire. In addition to the immediate responses that can be expressed and supported in a discussion, help students make more deliberate responses by planning experiences that mirror incidents in the book and by integrating reading, writing, and the arts.

Try This for Teaching **Answering Game**

- Divide your students into groups.
- Set out one less object than members in the group.
- Present a question and give students time to think.
- Give a signal for each child to grab an object.
- The one without an object responds to the question or formulates a question for others to answer.

(King, 2008)

Variations for ELLs

- Throw out a beanbag along with a question. Let students toss it around like a hot potato until you call stop. The one holding the beanbag must answer the question.
- Write questions on paper and put them inside balloons in place of beanbags.
- Hide a simple prize under one of three cups. By answering questions, students earn the right to guess where the prize is.

Mirror experiences. Follow up the reading with experiences that mirror what happened in the text. If you are reading about how plants grow, plant and water some seeds. If you are reading about running, take the class to the playground to run a short race. If you are reading about square dancing, try doing it. Few things elicit a response like actually experiencing what characters in the book experienced. You will appreciate the hardships of the Pilgrims more after you sit in a roped-off space approximately the actual size of the Mayflower.

"Message in a Starry Sky" (Baslaw-Finger, 1993) tells the story of a Jewish family in France that goes into hiding when the Nazis invade. Knowing how difficult it will be for his daughter, Mottle, the father of the family helps her make a memory bottle. He pretends to take an imaginary object off a shelf and tells her they must put into it the smells and sights most precious to them. He makes her walk barefoot across a lawn and asks her to remember how it feels. He has her smell different kinds of flowers, close her eyes, and recall the fragrances. Mottle concentrates on the color of the sky and the feel of the breeze. The father then tells her to put a cork in her imaginary bottle. The author describes how discouraged she became staying in the basement and how her father would encourage her to take a piece of blue sky or the smell of a rose out of her memory bottle. This made her feel better.

A mirror experience would be to have children make their own memory bottles. They could walk barefoot through the grass and remember how it feels. They could smell a flower and look at the sky and create their own imaginary bottles.

Curriculum integration. Of course, it may not always be possible to do such a follow-up activity for every text that is read. If you read about a lighthouse, you may not be able to visit one. If you read about a lion, you wouldn't want to bring one to the classroom even if you could. Even making a memory bottle may not be practical in your classroom. However, you can always write, draw, role-play, sing, act, or dance about such things (Cowan & Albers, 2006; Wilhelm, 2002). Students could write about what they would place in their own memory bottles and why. Or they could draw what they would place in their memory bottles. You might have them role play or act out what Mottle and her father did. They could even represent the experience with creative movement put to music. Such integration allows students to be creative and explore artistically in connection with what they are reading together as a class (Cornett, 2006).

Many publications offer literature response ideas to teachers (Yopp & Yopp, 2009). Be careful and selective as you consider what you would like your students to do. Some response activities are time-consuming and require investments in resources by children and their parents. If reading the text together takes half an hour and the response activity takes days, you may want to reconsider. If a project requires a lot of effort, such as making paper dolls of the main characters complete with multiple wardrobes, you may want to ask yourself how much of a true response is being elicited. Is the activity promoting a response or taking the place of one? Remember it is not necessary to respond to everything that is read together as a class. Your goal is to help students share the reading process, and that doesn't always require a deliberate or visual response. Such activities are a lot like seasonings in a soup. A few sprinkled in at just the right moment can enhance the flavor of the soup and make the meal especially memorable. Dumping in tins of seasonings can actually ruin the soup so no one wants to eat it. Some favorite ways to help children respond to what they read together as a class are listed in Figure 12.1.

Figure 12.1   Teachers' Favorite Literature Responses

Create an ABC book.
Write a letter to an author.
Write a part of the story from another point of view.
Plan a party for the characters in a book (e.g., invitations, food, games, and gifts).
Write a brief alternate ending.
Gather five artifacts that relate to the story.
Ask and answer "If . . . then" questions (e.g., If the main character had been a girl, then . . .).
Nominate the book for an award or write a book review and post it online.
Create a simple board game (e.g., Candy Land, Chutes and Ladders, or Clue).
Select a color, a piece of music, or a work of art to represent a book.

For additional ideas consult Manning and Manning (1996) and Nicholson-Nelson (1999).

Writing with Children—Whole Class

Before students catch the vision of writing individually, they must work alongside knowledgeable writers. In **shared writing** the teacher works with a class of children in writing a collective (shared) text (Ministry of Education, 1994). Mooney (2006b) wrote, "The teacher's role in shared writing is to make the act of writing accessible to every student. In shared writing the teacher 'talks through' how a text is composed and refined" (p. 28). Boscolo and Gelati (2007) stated that in collaborative writing ideas are generated and texts are written and revised as a group in order to obtain a common product. Along with instructional benefits, students can experience

---

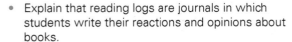 *Try This for Teaching*   **Reading Logs**

- Explain that reading logs are journals in which students write their reactions and opinions about books.
- After reading, encourage students to write reflections, memorable quotes, interesting words, or notes about characters.
- Allow time for students to share their entries with partners or in a group.
- Create the log to reflect the theme of the book (such as a cloth-covered diary about pioneers or a foil-covered space log).

(Hancock, 2007)

Variations for ELLs

- Try having students create a simulated journal in which they write as if they were one of the characters.
- Assign some topics or questions for all as well as allowing free writing.
- Have students keep a reading log on the computer. You could give your email address and have them send you reading log entries or set up a class blog where students could take turns adding entries.

increased motivation. Boscolo and Gelati wrote, "We view collaborative writing as an essential element for leading students to appreciate and enjoy writing as a process and product" (p. 219).

Shared Writing Within Various Instructional Approaches

Sharing the writing process with the whole class is a vital part of the gradual release of responsibility. Teachers are working with students, and students are learning by doing—both essential elements of effective literacy instruction. Shared writing can be incorporated into whatever instructional approaches are being used by your district, whether these are core literacy programs, writing workshops, or some combination of both. With the adoption of the Common Core, some districts are emphasizing self-regulated strategy development and genre writing. Whole class writing experiences not only can but should be used within both of these.

Common Core
State Standards

Core Literacy Programs.   Core literacy programs are usually focused more on reading than writing. Most contain a writing prompt with each unit, but some evidence suggests that teachers often overlook this component (Billen et al., 2011). Even when the prompt is assigned, the writing is usually completed in one draft—rarely revised, edited, or published for an audience beyond the teacher. Some teachers may be hesitant to do much with the writing component of core literacy programs because they believe it takes time away from teaching and practicing the skills for which students and teachers are held responsible. But remember that skills are best taught in a meaningful context, and writing can provide a meaningful context just as reading can—especially when you are writing about the prompt as a class and you can emphasize the specific skills being taught and tested in the particular basal unit. Taking time to write together as a class provides a rich context in which the skill instruction makes sense. The expectation of the basal program might be that students complete the writing prompt independently, but occasionally you can share the writing experience together as a step toward that independence. What students do as a class today they will be able to do better independently tomorrow.

Writing Workshop.   A writing workshop is usually strongly focused on students choosing their own topics and working on their own projects, which when completed can be shared at a designated time with the entire class. Skill instruction usually takes place in mini-lessons and during one-on-one conferences with the teacher. During work time teachers meet individually with students, monitoring and discussing their writing, helping them with difficulties they are having, and encouraging them to reflect on their growth and progress as young authors. Some might claim that there is no place for whole class writing experiences in the workshop routines. Yet shared writing can be included successfully.

During work time you can tell the students to put their own writing away for a while as you do some class writing together. This breaks up the routine and adds variety. Switching between group and independent writing can provide a new perspective for all. Grouping does not need to take long. Many whole class writing experiences can work the entire writing process into 30 to 40 minutes or extend it over the course of several days.

Self-Regulated Strategy Development.   Self-regulated strategy development (SRSD) for writing (Harris, Graham, Mason, & Friedlander, 2008) is a model for supporting students as they compose narrative, expository, and persuasive text. They develop

Struggling Learners/
RtI

self-regulation skills as they monitor their own writing while they apply specific steps and strategies to complete an assignment (Pritchard & Honeycutt, 2007). Mnemonic devices are used to remember steps or formulas for writing a story or essay. When writing a report, for example, children can be told to start with a question to gain the attention of the readers. Then they are told to introduce the topic of their report, followed by three details of interest, which are then explained in subsequent paragraphs. They are instructed to end the report with a conclusion that summarizes the topics of all the paragraphs again and ties back into the introduction. Since SRSD was originally developed for students with learning difficulties, some teachers may see this approach as being too formulaic in nature. However, SRSD is an appealing choice in many classrooms because it has been shown to improve student test scores (Graham & Perin, 2007). Some teachers and students seem to respond well to a prescribed approach. SRSD lends itself to whole class writing experiences because specific patterns and strategies require explicit instruction and modeling before any small group or independent practice.

Genre Writing. Writing instruction should include exposure to various contexts and across various genres (Donovan, Milewicz, & Smolkin, 2003). Like SRSD, genre writing introduces the specific elements of a particular genre and teaches them explicitly. Then the whole class writes an entire piece together in that genre before the children use the genre for their own individual pieces.

The Common Core emphasizes writing beyond personal narrative, including argumentative writing, in which students must present evidence for their opinions. Young children may follow the phrase "I like soccer" with the word *because*, giving specific reasons supporting the statement they have made (I can make goals, and everybody cheers for me). Older students are expected to provide evidence for their claims beyond their own opinions or feelings. They will need to find sources to cite. For example, "Doctors warn that childhood obesity is a serious problem" should be developed with dangers that real doctors have pointed out. As with SRSD, genre writing naturally connects with shared writing in that the specific features of a genre need to be introduced and illustrated for children as an article, story, essay, or poem is constructed as a class.

Whole class writing not only provides modeling and guided practice but may facilitate differentiated instruction that is helpful to those who struggle with writing skills and with learning English. As some students work independently, you can work with others to complete a small group version of the assignment. In this way all students will have successfully written in the genre, but some will have done it in groups rather than alone.

Writing Process

Graves (2003) described the phases of the writing process as prewriting, drafting, seeking a response, revising, editing, and publishing. Despite decades of focus on effective writing instruction, many teachers may not be fully implementing this process, or they may be using it in ineffective ways. Applebee and Langer (2006) reported that, although process-oriented writing has dominated teacher vocabulary for many years, it is still unclear what teachers mean by this term and how it is implemented in their classrooms. Some teachers implement process writing in a rigid, formulaic fashion that does not reflect how writing naturally occurs (Petraglia, 1999). Other teachers do not model for their students, provide time for student sharing, or allow for choice of topics (Kara-Soteriou & Kaufman, 2002).

Perhaps one of the reasons for these problems is that teachers do not see themselves as writers (Emig, 1971). They feel awkward when they are required to teach something that they don't do themselves. Think how difficult it would be to teach someone to drive if you did not know how or lacked confidence. If you feel less than confident in your own writing abilities, the good news is that you do not need to be Emily Dickinson or Robert Frost in order to teach writing well. You simply have to recognize the role that writing plays in your own life and be willing to share with children the processes you go through. Perhaps you keep a journal or blog. Perhaps you email, text, post comments on friends' Facebook pages, or have reviewed a book on line. Surely you have written messages in greeting cards or made out a shopping list. In your preparation to become a teacher, you have written lesson plans and assignments for school. In each case you went through a process—sometimes more deliberately and extensively than at other times—but a process nonetheless.

A whole class writing together.

Another problem may be that teachers feel overwhelmed with the demands of teaching so many subjects. They don't think there is time to teach writing. Time management is a challenge in school. Every year teachers are required to do more without being given any additional time. The good news is that by sharing the writing experience, you can go through the entire writing process with groups of students in much less time than you would need to help them individually.

In addition, working as a group allows you to treat writing as a social event that does not always have to take place in isolation (McCutchen, 2006). Shared writing allows you to teach the writing process through modeling, support, and practice (Tyner, 2004). As students experience and internalize the entire writing process, they gain confidence and are prepared to work more independently. You can assist your students before writing, during writing, and after writing.

Struggling Learners/ RtI

Before Writing.   An important part of students' independent writing is coming up with their own topics. But when the students are working together as a class, prompts and teacher-assigned topics are appropriate. Most students don't wake up in the morning with a strong desire to write a state or country report. You can help students pay close attention to the prompts and to plan and develop their ideas in advance of writing.

Prompts and assignments.   Whole class writing gives students a safe place to stretch outside their comfort zones and explore topics they might not choose independently. But some level of choice is still important. Students may need to write a report on an animal, but they can select which animal. Even when prompts become narrow and specific, choice should still be offered. The teacher who says, "Today we are going to write a persuasive essay encouraging people to pick up litter" may be met with less student enthusiasm than "In our class essay should we persuade people to pick up litter, participate in recycling, or is there another way we can convince them they could help the environment?" A list of several possible prompts can provide some choice and also be a springboard for additional ideas that you and the class may not have even considered. Figure 12.2 offers a list of ideas that can be a starting point for you and your class.

Try This for Teaching   **Artistic Prompts**

- Display an art print.
- Brainstorm a variety of possible topics (shapes and colors used, the story the picture tells, artist's motivation, the mood the picture evokes).
- Select one of the topics and write about it together as a class.
- Revise, edit, and publish the work.

(adapted from Greenberg, 2008)

Variations for ELLs

- Play a piece of music and brainstorm together.

- Divide children into smaller writing groups based on their interest in the various topics that have been brainstormed together.
- Create a word bank by asking "What words come to your mind when you see this (or listen to this)?" List the words the class generates and use the list as a basis for more ideas.
- Try using Storybird.com. A variety of illustration options are provided that can prompt simple text. Final stories can be shared on the site or through email and Facebook.

Figure 12.2   **A List of Possible Topics for Class Writing**

Future	Tree houses	Choices	Scares	Basements
Blunders	Acting	Souvenirs	Interviews	Walks
Being alone	Beauty	Websites	Restaurants	Photos
Lessons learned	Balloons	Inventions	Senior citizens	Recess
Music	Baby sitters	Intended professions	Embarrassment	Keys
Health	Integrity	Pain	Hospitals	Holidays
Accomplishment	Mountains	After school	Mornings	Homework
Three wishes	Rain forests	Hairstyles	Talents	Dancing
Worry	Heroes	Honesty	Memories	Darkness
Teams	Clubs	Space	Art	Water
Building	Tears	Machines	Full life	Helping
Junk	Best friends	Sports	Freedom	Snow
Exercise	Dreams	Creatures	Money	Beaches
Pollution	Bullies	Wheelchairs	Foolishness	Mom
Cruelty	Moving	Rings	Being lost	Dad
Odd Jobs	Vacations	Summer games	Goals	Rockets
Energy sources	Sisters	Electricity	How to	Bike riding
Reading	Skills	Donuts	Discoveries	Service
Stores	Beliefs	Lessons	Open minds	Gifts
Singers	Bouquets	Individuality	Adults	Challenges
Clothes	Uncomfortable clothes	Board games	Rules	Toys
Attics	Faith	Swimming	Love	Trust
Cartoons	Laws	Knowledge	Greed	Brothers
Forts	Something unbelievable	Seasons	Pet peeves	Bedtime
Planets	Winning	Grandparents	Hard work	Jokes
Glasses	Anger	Libraries	Fund raisers	Oceans
Museums	Courage	Circuses	Cabins	Future

Advance Planning.   After you have provided your class with a prompt or settled on an assignment, you must help students pay close attention to what is being asked of them and plan their writing purposefully. Students who plan and develop their ideas in advance of writing have been shown to perform better on writing assessments than those who don't (Applebee & Langer, 2006). It may seem simple and obvious to read a prompt twice, paying special attention to the length and elements required, but many adults as well as children don't do this. Editors of research journals reject many articles before even examining the content because the authors haven't conformed to the listed publication requirements, including number of pages, style guidelines, and appropriateness for the journal audience.

One sixth-grade teacher prepared his students for tests by teaching them how to read prompts thoroughly. He said, "I always felt like I was throwing my students to the lions, so I decided to use the letters in that word to help them be better prepared." The first letter in the word *LIONS*, L, stands for length. Students should ask, "How long should the writing be? Is longer better, or am I expected to limit my comments?" I stands for inspection. Students should consider who is going to be evaluating their writing so they know what tone they should take. O reminds students to consider the organization of their writing. Many prompts will suggest an organization; if the prompt calls for the pros and cons of an issue, for example, students need to be sure to treat both sides—one side is only 50 percent of the assignment. N stands for numbers. Students need to notice if the prompt includes a number ("What are the three causes of . . ." or "List the four ways to . . ."). If a certain number of items is expected, students should write about that number of items in their responses. S is for support. Students must find support beyond their own opinions.

Struggling Learners/ RtI

When your students are aware of what is being asked of them, you need to show them how to jot down a simple outline or list some ideas they don't want to lose. When working as a class, you may want to break into small brainstorming groups for a few minutes and then have each group share ideas for the whole class to vote on.

Sometimes students may struggle to give you a response to a general question such as "What shall we write about?" or even "What shall we write about volcanoes?" These questions may be too broad. Try narrowing your request by asking for one

---

Try This for Teaching   **Hunting for LIONS**

Explain to students that when they encounter writing prompts, whether on tests or as part of other assignments, they need to first hunt for details about what is expected. Each letter in the word *LIONS* reminds them of a question to consider.

- L is for length. How long should it be?
- I is for inspection. Who will be evaluating the writing? What are audience members looking for?
- O is for organization. Does the prompt suggest certain organizational expectations?

- N stands for numbers. Are there numbers included in the prompt that should show up in the writing?
- S stands for support. What evidence will I offer to support my claims and answers?

Variation for ELLs

- ELLs sometimes feel an added temptation to lift material from written sources. Remind children that cutting and pasting responses from the Internet or plagiarizing other students' work is not acceptable. They can ask themselves, "Am I lyin'?"

| *Try This for Teaching* | **Word Banks** |

- Ask students to provide words associated with your writing topic.
- List the words where all can see them.
- Organize the words into groups.
- Use the words as you construct a class sentence, paragraph, essay, poem, or story.
- All words do not have to be used in the writing. The word bank is just a place to begin.

(Rothstein, Rothstein, & Lauber, 2006)

Variations for ELLs

- Have each student write an appropriate word on a strip of paper and then tape the strips at the front of the room, discarding or thinking of synonyms for duplicates.
- When you have a long enough list, assign each child a word to be expanded into a sentence. Children can illustrate their sentences as you go from child to child to help them revise and edit. Finished papers can be bound together into a class picture book or organized into paragraphs.

English Language Learners

word. Anyone can give you one word, and once you have one word from several children you have created a **word bank**—a list of words your students help you compile on any given subject (Rothstein, Rothstein, & Lauber, 2006). When you are doing a class writing project, ask students to think of words associated with the topic you have settled on by asking questions such as "What words describe summertime?" or "What words do you think of when I say 'Panama Canal'?" As students provide words, you can list and display them where all can see. The list becomes a seedbed for sentences and paragraphs, or even an outline for an entire essay. Words on similar subjects can be grouped, and words that don't end up fitting can be crossed out. A word bank gives you and the students a starting place—something with which to begin building and planning.

During Writing. Some teachers call a first draft a "sloppy copy" because they know that neatness should not be a major concern at this point. Students shouldn't be overly concerned with handwriting, spelling, and punctuation. Instead they should concentrate on getting their ideas down on paper where they can begin to work with them.

When beloved children's author Dr. Seuss passed away, he had the beginnings of his next book down on paper. It was only a rough draft, but publishers invited Jack Prelutsky and Lane Smith to help Dr. Seuss finish his last project, which was titled *Hooray for Diffendoofer Day* (Seuss, Prelutsky, & Smith, 1998). When the book was printed, the publishers included some samples of Dr. Seuss's rough drafts in the back of the book so children can see what writing looks like when it first begins. Children can see how Dr. Seuss was crossing out words and sentences, playing with rhymes and experimenting with alternate word choices. They can feel validated as they recognize that Dr. Seuss's first draft doesn't look all that different from some of their own rough drafts.

Struggling Learners/ RtI

To much student laughter and enthusiasm, one teacher calls a rough draft "writing in its underwear." He says, "When we take our writing out in public we need to finish getting it all dressed up, but it starts in its underwear." As well as showing children examples of rough drafts, you must also help them create drafts as a class. As with reading, when you share the writing process as a whole class experience, you need to provide access to print and to the example of lead writers.

Access to print.   Access to print can be provided as lead writers work on chart paper, whiteboards, smart boards, or as they project what they are writing on a paper or at the computer. It doesn't really matter how, as long as everyone can see and follow along.

The easiest way to share the writing process as a class is to take **dictation**, the lead writer writing while others are speaking. When you act as the lead writer, don't be overly concerned about making sense of everything immediately, since one child's comment may not blend with another's. You can smooth things out later as you revise together. When taking dictation, you don't have to write everything word for word. When writing about favorite foods, one child might say, "Apples." You can write a complete sentence: *Apples are wonderful.* Another child might say, "I like bananas." You can change the words so they represent the whole class: *We like bananas.*

With younger children and those learning English, include print conventions as you take dictation; for example, you might say, "I am putting a capital letter here because it is the beginning of a sentence." Such comments can provide helpful reminders or important instruction within the context of a shared writing experience. Children in the lower grades benefit from a focus on letter sounds, punctuation marks, and concepts of print such as directionality and return sweep. For intermediate grades it is more appropriate to focus on word choice ("Is there a better word we could use than *said*?"), sentence fluency ("What are some ways to begin besides *we*?"), and spelling ("Is *sincerely* spelled with an *-ely* or just an *-ly* at the end?"). Such additions are not a mini-lesson as such; you are simply drawing attention to what you as an experienced writer do as you write.

Lead writers.   **Lead writers** can decide to accept the suggestions offered by others during dictation, or they can make choices independent of the group. You may act as the lead writer—especially as you begin using shared writing in your classroom. However, as students are ready, you can make the experience more interactive by sharing the pen with one student or several. Invite volunteers to help with encoding. You may ask them to make one of the letters or invite them to write a word or a sentence. In spelling you may ask them to fill in blanks on a chart or vote on which of various options is correct.

One second-grade teacher engaged students by asking them to write a word with their fingers in the air as she wrote it on the chart paper. Sometimes she would ask them to fingerprint the word on their hands or laps. (She called these actions the original

Speaking/Listening

Language Conventions

Try This for Teaching   **Spelling in Context**

- Focus on generated spelling in shared writing experiences by leaving blanks for letters and having students volunteer to come fill in the blanks [e.g., Yesterday we had a __ __ __ __ __ __ __ __ __ __ __ [frustrating] experience.

- Focus on recognizing correct spelling in shared writing experiences by providing several options and having children select the correct one [It was a sad day for (our, are, hour) class. We (didn't, did'nt) (know, no, now) what to (due, do, doo, dew).]

- Add words that students were unable to spell correctly to a word wall or list of bonus spelling words so students will see them again.

Variations for ELLs

- When you come to a word that you have already studied as a class or included on your word wall, draw special attention to the word by having the whole class spell it orally as you write it or by inviting a volunteer to come to the front and write the word.

- When students want to use a difficult word in the shared writing (one that may even stump you), turn to a dictionary and look it up together. Shared writing is an ideal time to incorporate a dictionary or thesaurus because of the scaffolded nature of the experience.

> **Try This for Teaching** **Individual Whiteboards**
>
> - Create small slate boards by having a large section of Masonite cut into manageable pieces.
> - Place a dry erase marker and a rag for erasing into individual packets that can be distributed and gathered efficiently.
> - Have students write letters, words, and punctuation marks that you encounter together in whole class writing.
> - Give a signal indicating that it is time to lift the boards and show them to you so you can check for understanding and hold students accountable.
> - Try having students help a partner before giving the signal for all to show their work.
>
> **Variations for ELLs**
>
> - Use individual boards during mathematics, social studies, and science. Be careful not to overuse them; you don't want children to lose interest and motivation.
> - Distribute only a few slate boards to students who are designated as being in the "hot seat." As several children try to complete the required task, they reveal their attempts to the class to vote on which they like best or to see which one comes closest to what the teacher wrote on the big board. The slates are then passed to new students. This saves time in distributing to the whole class.

Struggling Learners/ RtI

English Language Learners

handheld devices and laptops.) She also gave all the children in her class the opportunity to become more engaged in shared writing by passing out individual whiteboards. As she came to a tricky word in front of the class, she would encourage them to try to write the word on their whiteboards. After she revealed the correct spelling, she had students write the word correctly on their individual boards and show her. When she came to the end of the sentence she would say, "Write on your whiteboard the punctuation mark I need to put right here."

If you share the writing process with the class on a regular basis, the sessions do not need to be long. For example, you could do one or two sentences as part of the opening of the day in your classroom. This way the students do not become bored with the process by trying to do too much in one sitting. By the end of the week, you will usually complete an entire chart paper or a finished paragraph that can then be revised, edited, and published.

The interactive work done on slate boards can become more permanent when it is done on paper. When each child works on his or her own piece of paper, the papers can be saved, compiled, and bound into a class book. Students can answer the same question or complete a sentence in a variety of ways, illustrate their responses, and compile them into a class picture book. Use open-ended questions or sentences for completion, such as "How did you feel on the first day of school?" "One thing I won't forget about this year is . . ." "What advice would you give students entering our grade next year?" Responses should be short so that children understand that each page is part of a class project and not an assignment to be completed independently.

Students can also work in small groups to complete a class project, such as a group persuasive essay. One fifth-grade teacher assigned her class into groups, designating a lead writer in each one. Before they met as groups, she helped the class decide on an opinion and three main reasons. For example, a prompt that asked for reasons why people should or should not vote elicited these three reasons from students: people should vote because it is a responsibility, it can lead to change, and it gives you a voice. Then she assigned the first group to write an introduction that included the opinion "People should vote." Other groups were assigned to write about each of the reasons. Another group wrote a counterargument (some people say that one vote doesn't matter), and the final group wrote a summary and conclusion. When all the sections of the essay were put together, the class had completed an entire persuasive piece. The next time, the teacher would make sure that the groups all were assigned different sections to write. By the time the teacher conducted this whole class writing experience multiple times, the students understood the various components of the persuasive essay and felt more confident completing one on their own.

Shared writing can also happen as students work in pairs. As peers work with each other or with cross-age tutors, most children can have the opportunity of being the lead writer in a shared experience. Tutors often benefit as much or more than tutees (Paquette, 2009).

After Writing.   By completing whole class projects, children can experience the entire writing process quickly and efficiently without the experience becoming unduly tedious for them or burdensome for you. You do not have to respond to each individual student, nor do you have to help each one revise and edit because you do these things once for the whole class or for each group. Because the students are completing small parts of a class project rather than working on their own, each child's contribution is manageable. Of course, whole class writing does not take the place of individual writing, but it is a vital part in the gradual release of responsibility as children prepare to succeed on their own.

English Language
Learners

Responding and revising.   When the draft is produced, whether it is a teacher-generated chart, student-generated individual pages of a class book, or group-generated paragraphs of a class essay, the shared writing process is not yet completed. You can also revise, edit, and publish as a class.

If teachers are not careful, they might communicate to students that having to make changes in their writing means they are poor writers or they didn't do it "right" the first time. As you share the entire writing process with the class, including making revisions, they will begin to see that change doesn't equal mistake. They learn that revision is not only a necessary step but a healthy and valuable process. One teacher told his students that writing is like playing basketball. "You don't take one shot and then say, 'I'm done!'" he told his class. "You shoot and then you shoot again and again. A game is more than one shot, and writing is more than one draft. Good basketball players are not the ones who don't make a lot of shots, but the ones who do." Your students can benefit a great deal as they watch how you work on revising a piece of writing you have done together.

Before going out in public, people usually look at a reflection of themselves in a mirror. The image helps them see whether they need to straighten their hair or brush lint off their coats. Writers usually re-read their first drafts themselves, but they also read them to others who act as mirrors and show them which parts may need adjusting. Children can be taught to give and receive feedback appropriately. Most people are thankful for a mirror, as it may show them something that could be potentially embarrassing. Similarly, most writers appreciate honest feedback from trusted colleagues, family members, or friends. They can also take the role of providing feedback to others. Authors ultimately decide whether or not to take the advice offered by others. The words *author* and *authority* have the same roots. When it comes to your own writing, you are the ultimate authority. But receiving and accepting feedback is part of the process. Students benefit by reflecting on the procedure they went through in their writing: what they did or didn't include and why.

Encourage students to ask for and give specific compliments and suggestions. Feedback is most helpful when it goes beyond general comments like "That was really good," or "I didn't like it too much." Such comments leave writers with few specific directions for making positive changes. You can set a minimum standard for responding by

Speaking/Listening

Try This for Teaching — Four Ps of Reflection

Help students reflect on their own writing or the writing of others by asking questions centered on four words starting with the letter *P*:

- **Procedure:** What happened? What did you do? Why did you do it? When did you come up with the idea? How did you develop it?
- **Praise:** What went well? What parts clearly stand out as being effective? What caused us to listen closely? What parts elicited a positive response from the group?
- **Polish:** What didn't go so well? What parts were misunderstood? When did the others lose interest?

- **Plan:** What are you going to do now? What needs to be left out? What needs to be added in? Who can help?

Variations for ELLs

- Write responses in each category—especially the final part about a plan—so that feedback is not quickly forgotten.
- Add another P—**Positive**. Make sure that feedback always keeps a positive tone.

Try This for Professional Development — Reflect on Your Teaching

Use these same steps (Procedure, Praise, Polish, and Plan) as you reflect on your own work as a teacher.

- What are you doing?
- What are you doing well?

- What is not going as well as you would like?
- What specific actions can you take to make improvements?

Struggling Learners/ RtI

calling for one "heart" (a compliment) and one "wish" (a suggestion). Another idea is to have students give one "I liked" (compliment), one "I thought" (suggestion), and one "I wondered" (question). This by no means should be the extent of the feedback, but it provides children a place to begin.

When feedback starts falling into a predictable pattern as the group works together, try focusing children on additional qualities of effective writing. These can be introduced in mini-lessons, of course, but they can also be reviewed during whole class writing experiences. For example, after finishing a group-constructed paragraph at the board, one teacher has a student roll a die. The six numbers correspond to the six traits of effective writing (Spandel, 2007): specifically, 1 = voice, 2 = organization, 3 = ideas, 4 = conventions, 5 = word choice, and 6 = sentence fluency. The number on the die directs the focus of the class during revision. If the student rolls a 3, the teacher asks, "Are there any ideas we can leave out or related ideas we can include?" If the student rolls a 6, the teacher says, "Do our sentences have enough variety? Are there any that are too long that need to be divided? Are there any too short that can be combined?"

Speaking/Listening

Providing a checklist or posting a list where everyone can it see reminds students of a variety of elements of writing to consider. When most of their compliments and suggestions are focused on mechanics such as spelling and capitalization, try helping responders focus on content by providing a checklist that does not include mechanics at all.

Another way to help students revise is to involve physical movement. If students have completed single pages of a class book by expanding on an assigned word or providing their own answer to a class question, you can have them read their sentences and then group and regroup them to improve the organization. There may be some sentences that stand out as natural beginnings or endings. Have students stand and read their contributions. Then ask other children to be editors and help you rearrange the students and their sentences into a better order. After the bodies are in the desired order, be sure to have students number their pages so you don't forget the correct order.

Editing and publishing. When you edit and publish together as a class, you mirror the actual writing process of published authors. Few authors edit their own work. By working together as a class, children learn that writing is not always a solitary endeavor. On the contrary, many researchers claim individuals learn best "within a social context that shapes and constrains new understandings" (Newell, Koukis, & Boster, 2007, p. 76).

Because of your age, experience, and education, you are the senior editor for student work. However, this role doesn't need to be overwhelming. In shared writing you are only editing once for the whole class or once for each small group. During a whole class writing experience, individual students may not have produced more than a sentence or two; thus, you can edit in a short amount of time. For example, after you edit one draft at the front of the class, assign students to copy a final draft. You have edited only one draft but have covered the whole class.

Struggling Learners/ RtI

When students are working in smaller groups, they are still producing only one paper per group. Gather the group around you so they can all see the text. Edit through the paper continually, asking students questions about their choices or explaining why you are making changes. Make photocopies of the edited sheet and distribute them to each member of the group, instructing each to produce a final draft. You have edited only one draft, and yet each member of the group has had the experience of being edited and can be held responsible for completing the final draft.

English Language Learners

Group publishing ideas do not need to take a lot of time. The simplest approach is for you to make a final version of the rough draft that you have created, revised, and edited together. Then display the rough draft and the final version side by side, labeling one "Our Sloppy Copy" and the other "Our Glory Story." You may want to invite the students to all sign their names on the final draft because they are joint authors. Figure 12.3 shows an example of a rough draft and a final draft of shared writing displayed side by side.

Language Conventions

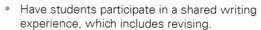
Try This for Teaching **Interactive Editing**

- Have students participate in a shared writing experience, which includes revising.
- Explain that it is time to edit the piece and ask for volunteers to help.
- Have volunteers correct spelling, punctuation, and grammar.
- Explain or have students explain their changes.
- If students make a change that is incorrect or unnecessary, make the correction a learning experience for the entire class, but avoid embarrassing the individual.

(Swartz, 2001)

Variations for ELLs

- You can deliberately include some mistakes in the text for students to find and correct.
- Increase student engagement by having all students create their own versions of the text, making the needed changes before verifying the corrections with the whole class. If the text is long, you may want to do this for only a few of the sentences and then complete the rest together.
- Assign certain students to be the "spelling police" and others to be the "punctuation police" or "grammar police." It is sometimes helpful to have students looking for only one specific kind of mistake rather than trying to find everything at once.

Try This for Professional Development   **Adapting Instruction**

Return to the *Try This* boxes in this chapter that are focused on intermediate grade children:

- Share Your Advice
- Verify and Clarify
- Back-and-Forth Reading
- Eight Ws
- Answering Game
- Reading Logs
- Artistic Prompts
- Hunting for LIONS
- Four Ps of Reflection
- Interactive Editing
- Consider how these could be adapted for use in primary grades.
- Choose one activity and develop a plan to use it with younger children.

Return to the *Try This* boxes in this chapter that are focused on primary grade children:

- Realia
- Role Play
- Dyad Reading
- Student Survey
- Word Banks
- Focus on Spelling
- Individual Whiteboards
- Consider how these could be adapted for use in intermediate grades.
- Choose one activity and develop a plan to use it with older children.

Another way to publish class projects is to have each child write an individual final draft of the group rough draft. This could be on one page, or it could be sentence by sentence on multiple pages, creating a simple picture book. Older students usually do not feel such a picture book is beneath them if they are told that it will be shared with younger children. Sentence one is copied onto the first page, sentence two on the second, and so forth. Illustrations can be added when the writing has been completed and double-checked by the teacher. As some students illustrate their books, you are free to help others who may have been identified by RtI as needing additional assistance. When all children have completed the writing, you can have students finish illustrations while listening to you read a book aloud after lunch or when recess has been moved indoors by stormy weather. If the shared writing has only six sentences, you can assign the first six children one sentence each and then assign the seventh child to come up with a title and a cover. Follow the same pattern with the next seven children and so forth. The class will end up with multiple copies of the book to place in the reading center or to present to other classes or audiences beyond the school.

Figure 12.3

A Rough Draft and Final Draft of Shared Writing Displayed Together

Summary

Some students slip through the entire school system without being able to read or write well. Often what they have missed is the experiences of the teacher reading and writing with the students. When this happens, not only do students miss being held accountable, they miss the instruction and motivation they need.

Shared reading and writing can be incorporated within various instructional approaches even when it is not called for specifically; it can enrich basal programs as well as a reading or writing workshop. Whole class reading can be incorporated with literature units, and whole class writing is a natural fit for both self-regulated strategy development and genre writing. Remember that what children can't do independently today, they can often do with help. And what they can do with help today, they can often do independently tomorrow.

Whole class experiences allow you to share the reading and writing processes with your students. You can orient them before reading and provide access to print and a lead reader during reading. After reading you can help students articulate immediate responses and also elevate deliberate responses by exploring and applying what they are reading.

In writing you can help focus students on prompts and assignments, teaching them to plan in advance of writing. You can provide access to print and lead writers as work is completed on chart paper, whiteboards, smart boards, or text projection in a variety of other ways. After writing you can respond and revise together and also edit and publish as a group.

Self-Check

1. What is the zone of proximal development and how does it relate to whole class reading and writing experiences?

2. How do whole class reading and writing experiences fit within a core literacy program?

3. Discuss three different ways you can orient or prepare your students before reading.

4. Detail two elements that facilitate effective whole class reading.

5. List two ways by which students can respond to text more deliberately than with class discussions.

6. When so much is said about allowing children to select their own topics for writing, how are prompts and writing assignments justified?

7. What is being missed if teachers and students complete only one draft of a whole class writing experience?

8. List a few ways you can publish whole class writing.

MyEducationLab™

Go to the Topics, Comprehension, Writing, and Organization and Management, in the MyEducationLab (www.myeducationlab.com) for your course, where you can:

- Find learning outcomes for Comprehension, Writing, and Organization and Management, along with the national standards that connect to these outcomes.

- Complete Assignments and Activities that can help you more deeply understand the chapter content.

- Apply and practice your understanding of the core teaching skills identified in the chapter with the Building Teaching Skills and Dispositions learning units.

- Examine challenging situations and cases presented in the IRIS Center Resources.

- Check your comprehension on the content covered in the chapter by going to the Study Plan in the Book Resources for your text. Here you will be able to take a chapter quiz, receive feedback on your answers, and then access Review, Practice, and Enrichment activities to enhance your understanding of chapter content (optional).

- Visit **A+RISE** Standards2Strategy™, an innovative and interactive online resource that offers new teachers in grades K–12 just-in-time, research-based instructional strategies that meet the linguistic needs of ELLs as they learn content, differentiate instruction for all grades and abilities, and are aligned to Common Core Elementary Language Arts Standards (for the literacy strategies) and to English language proficiency standards in WIDA, Texas, California, and Florida.

Reading and Writing with Children—Small Groups

Chapter Outline

**READING WITH CHILDREN—
SMALL GROUPS**
Core Literacy Programs
Reading Workshop
Literature Discussion Groups
**WRITING WITH CHILDREN—
SMALL GROUPS**
Core Literacy Programs
Writing Workshop
Formula Writing
SUMMARY

My wife and I had the opportunity several years ago to direct a university study abroad program in Auckland, New Zealand. This program, which was designed for elementary teacher candidates, included courses and field experiences to help them prepare to become teachers. New Zealand was selected as the location because of its long and successful tradition of effective literacy instruction in schools (Ministry of Education, 1996; 2002). Our university students spent extended time in local primary schools working with teachers and children. We all noticed many similarities and differences between the classrooms in Auckland and the ones we were familiar with in the United States. The subject matter taught was similar, and educators in both countries were facing an influx of students learning English. One difference we noticed was the amount of work done in small groups, one of the hallmarks of instruction in New Zealand primary schools. New Zealand teachers grouped their students for most subject areas—reading, mathematics, and writing, including spelling. They carefully observed students as they worked with them in small groups. They noted who was struggling and who was excelling, and they gave effective feedback. The groups were not permanent; students were flexibly moved from group to group throughout the school day and over the four months we were there. My wife and I knew our teacher candidates would be better for having experienced such effective small group instruction firsthand.

—Tim

Sitting in the passenger seat when your teacher is driving is not enough to make you a driver even if your teacher has carefully described each step in detail and warned you of all the possible pitfalls. Observing is helpful, but you still need the opportunity to take your place behind the wheel with your teacher sitting in the passenger seat. As you drive, your teacher reminds you of what you have learned and guides you along. You hear reassuring compliments and gentle suggestions. Of course, you are probably not doing this in the middle of a busy freeway. Your teacher has helped you select a safe place where you can practice and perfect your driving ability. The advice may be ideas you have heard before, but suddenly they take on more meaning because you are receiving them right when you are in the act.

As children develop their reading and writing abilities, they must frequently get behind the wheel while you sit in the passenger seat. They will gain confidence as you coach them through the learning processes while they are actually in the acts of reading and writing. Some of the most meaningful teaching you will do is when you are conferencing with students. The right piece of advice at just the right moment can make a major difference.

One of the reasons classrooms can be such valuable environments for learning is that many diverse people have been brought together in a group. Class members are able to learn much from each other. Some interaction occurs in whole class settings, but more personal, focused collaboration can occur in small groups or in pairs. Positive group interactions can affect academic achievement and social development (Battistich, Solomon, & Delucchi, 1993). People understand the world better by experiencing it through others' perspectives as well as their own.

In small groups children have more opportunities to share, question, discuss, explain, and present than in larger settings. Taylor, Pearson, Clark, and Walpole (2000) found that effective teachers used a variety of groupings during the school day. These authors specified that the most effective literacy teachers spent more time each day in small group instruction than in whole class work. Some small groups may meet only once; others may meet for several weeks. An example of a long-term grouping are reading groups that are frequently formed to enable students with similar abilities to read and discuss text together. You may find it useful in your classroom to set up writing groups so that a small number of writers can meet together to share their work. Some groups are formed based on students' abilities, and others are focused on interests or needs. Small groups are usually created to heighten students' participation and also to permit teachers to more closely identify needs and monitor progress.

Reading with Children— Small Groups

Reading skills have been taught to children in small groups for years. During **small group reading** students read and discuss a common text with or without teacher support. When children read texts of appropriate difficulty levels some have called this **guided reading** (Fountas & Pinnell, 1996) or classified it as a form of differentiated instruction (Tomlinson & McTighe, 2006). You will need to know how to organize and facilitate small group reading in order to coach children throughout the reading process in both primary and intermediate grades.

Struggling Learners/ RtI

District leaders across the country have some degree of independence as they select instructional approaches; the same privilege is sometimes granted to teachers at individual schools. Some select a core program; others teach literacy within workshop routines or organize reading instruction into literature discussion groups. Some teachers and principals will use an eclectic approach and garner what they consider the best of several approaches. Small group instruction can be used effectively within all of these types of instruction.

Core Literacy Programs

Core literacy programs, sometimes called basals, are comprehensive sets of materials for literacy instruction that contain readings for the whole class and for small groups, teachers' manuals, practice materials, and assessment tools. Core programs include a scope and sequence of skills that are developed throughout the program. At each grade level materials are organized into units of instruction focused on predetermined skills. The programs generally provide **anthologies**, texts with many selections from which the whole class reads together, and leveled books for small group instruction. Each program is different, but most include texts written for children at three different levels: below grade level, on grade level, and above grade level. Most programs also provide small texts specifically for ELLs, as well as audio and video materials and online support.

English Language Learners

Teachers' manuals provide guidance for introducing selections and working with small groups assigned to read them, often including literacy activities you can use with children. Most core programs assume that you will divide the class into groups and use the leveled readers during group time. Because the difficulty levels of these texts generally match the reading abilities of the students, assigning students to read them independently is an appropriate option in most cases.

One benefit of a core program is that copies of these leveled texts come with the materials. As small groups of students read their leveled texts, you are guided to help students explore and apply what they have read. Because of a strong focus on assessment in core programs, you will be expected to teach those skills that will be tested.

Another benefit is that these programs are comprehensive—they include reading, writing, spelling, and content area literacy components. Many new teachers appreciate the directions provided, which often guide their preparation time.

Some more experienced teachers find core materials somewhat confining. They feel that their creativity may be diminished and that they will have difficulty addressing the needs of individual students if required to adhere to such a regimented program. Despite these concerns, teacher-led small groups in core literacy programs can provide an excellent context in which skill instruction is successful for many students.

Primary Grade Groups.   Literacy instruction looks different in primary and intermediate grades. These differences may not be easily seen when teachers work with the whole class, but they become very apparent as teachers organize, work with, and facilitate small groups.

Organizing.   It is one thing to write or speak of small groups and leveled text and another to organize such groups. Teachers have frequently assigned students to groups based on their abilities, grouping them by similar levels of intelligence or achievement. For reading, children's abilities are usually assessed using measures such as running records or informal reading inventories. You can use that information, together with estimates of text difficulty, to match students with appropriate texts.

In the past, ability groups have been relatively permanent—students who were assigned to lower groups remained in those groups throughout the school year and sometimes across school years. This practice has been shown to have serious consequences for the children emotionally, socially, and academically (Allington, 1983b; Hiebert, 1983). In more recent years, grouping practices have changed to avoid these drawbacks and disadvantages. You will closely monitor student progress and make more changes in group membership. This flexible grouping practice allows you to regroup children as they progress and their abilities change, and children do not miss anything as they move from group to group because skills are taught to the whole class and then practiced and reinforced as children read leveled books. If a few children are moved to different groups, they simply practice in different books. As children become older, groups usually include the same members. However, these groups are temporary in that they should be used only during teacher-led small groups and not for the entire reading block or school day (Ford & Opitz, 2008).

You should meet with each small group regularly, at least twice each week and in some cases daily with those students who struggle. The group meetings usually last at least 10 to 15 minutes, and since you will likely meet with three groups each day, you will need to devote from 30 to 45 minutes daily to small group reading instruction as a minimum.

Struggling Learners/ RtI

Working.   Since primary grade reading selections are often very short, with little text, they are usually read in their entirety during a single session. In the primary grades a typical small group reading session includes several common steps: preparing students to read the selection, reading the text individually, discussing the content of the text, teaching specific skills, and assessing students' needs (Fountas & Pinnell, 1996).

Before reading. Before children read a passage, you should prepare them to be successful in understanding it. One way to introduce a book to new readers is to engage in a picture walk. Talk about differences between words and illustrations in books, and tell students that you will first focus only on the pictures. As you page through the book, discuss what the children notice in the pictures and invite them to make predictions. Alternatively you may want to focus children's attention on specific words that you think may be difficult for young readers to identify, as well as words they may not know well. Help them use their prior knowledge about language and about the topic of the book to prepare them to read.

During reading. Reading in the primary grades is often done orally because beginning readers find it difficult to read silently until they reach a fluent level. In a small group setting, all of the students should have the opportunity to read all of the words in the text while you observe each of them. This is in contrast to round-robin reading in which each student reads only a portion of the text while the others in the group follow along silently. To allow multiple children to read aloud simultaneously, encourage them to whisper read, or to read in very quiet voices. Avoid turning it into a choral reading by starting your students reading the text at different times. By staggering their starts, you can give each student the opportunity to read the entire text independently. If some students finish reading before others, have them simply begin again. Beginning readers are often overwhelmed with the task of working out the pronunciations of words, so you generally will not ask students to do more with text during reading than just decode the words.

English Language Learners

A teacher listening during a small group session.

As students are reading, lean close to individuals in turn and listen carefully while also looking at the text. You may choose to support and prompt the reader, or this could be an ideal time to take a running record as a formative assessment. Make note of any needs that surface, and share praise or suggestions. If a child struggles significantly, you can help, but be aware that the difficulty may signal that the student needs to be in another group with reading material he can handle. This is not a time for mini-lessons or excessive teacher talking. You are listening, supporting, and settling on specifics you can coach them on after reading or later address in a whole class mini-lesson.

After reading. Compliment the children on the good things they were doing as they read and offer a few suggestions for improvement. Even if only one child struggled with a particular problem, you can still make the suggestion to the whole group. You will be tempted to spend time helping students identify individual words they missed. However, remember that reading is comprehending—reading is not occurring unless the reader is understanding what was read.

The discussion and most other activities relevant to a text read should occur during the same lesson. Because you will try to fit the before, during, and after activities into one session, you will find that you often have little time for extensive after-reading activities. In addition to some coaching, try to revisit what you did before the students read. For example, talk about the predictions the students made, discuss the major events of the story, and talk about the characters. In addition, return to the vocabulary words that you highlighted before they read. You will not have time to do all of these things after reading each selection, but be sure your attention is frequently on comprehension.

Facilitating. Working with small groups is a challenge if other students are interrupting you or disrupting the class by misbehaving. While you work with small reading groups, the other students need to be engaged in independent or small group activities that do not require your immediate supervision or assistance. Most core literacy programs provide ideas for developmentally appropriate centers or workstations.

Workstations encourage students to take responsibility for their own learning. They can focus on mathematics, science, and other subjects, but they can and should also include literacy experiences. Typical primary grade centers are included in Figure 13.1.

Often your lowest groups include students who also struggle with behavior issues. Having them together the entire time, especially when they are not under your direct supervision, can present problems. Although it is beneficial for children to be homogeneously grouped as you lead them in small group reading, they do not need to spend the entire reading block in these groups. Ability grouping is not necessary for children to successfully write in their journals, re-read old favorites, or write notes in the class post office. By grouping children heterogeneously for workstations, you can make sure there is a strong leader in each group helping to keep the others on task and to be a model. These group leaders can also help things run smoothly by encouraging students to clean up

Struggling Learners/ RtI

Figure 13.1   Typical Primary Grade Workstations

Activity	Description
Journal writing	Write or draw in journals on any topic with an eye toward reading entries during a later sharing time.
Reading the room	Walk around the classroom with a pointer and read signs, posters, bulletin boards, etc.
Sustained silent reading	Read self-selected material individually.
Old favorites	Re-read books that have been read previously (e.g., leveled books, big books, read-alouds).
Alphabet	Use magnet letters, felt letters, or cut out paper letters to create words, alphabetize lists, compare upper and lowercase letters, sort vowels and consonants, etc.
Word wall	Copy words from the word wall, rhyme words, find words with similar spelling patterns, etc.
Listening center	Follow along in a book while listening with headphones to a recording of it.
Post office	Write notes and letters to classmates and deliver them.
Independent practice	Complete a practice sheet that utilizes a skill taught during a mini-lesson (e.g., handwriting, spelling, or phonics).

when it is time. If students are expected to complete some tasks with buddies, you may pair struggling students with peers who can offer support.

If students are on a timed rotation from center to center, do not make small group reading with you one of those stations. If the students are rotating independent of you, call students from different places in the room to read with you. This frees you to take as much or as little time as you need with reading groups or choose to work one-on-one with those who need special attention. This freedom also allows you to walk around the room occasionally and make sure that all children are engaged at their various workstations before you call for another reading group. Don't be concerned that children will miss out on an activity when they are called to work with you. If you use the same workstations over an extended period, students will experience them all sooner or later.

Students working at a station without teacher supervision.

Intermediate Grade Groups.   Literacy instruction is different in the intermediate grades than in primary grades, especially as teachers organize, work with, and facilitate small groups.

Organizing.   If you are following a core literacy program in the intermediate grades, you will typically use a form of IRI to assess children for placement in small reading groups. You will meet with each small group regularly, spending more time with strugglers. Because students are reading longer and more complex texts, group meetings may last from about 15 to 30 minutes (Ford & Opitz, 2008). You will be able to meet with only two or three groups each day. However, older students are more able to work independently than younger children, and they should have the stamina to read for more extended periods. Most of their reading can occur outside the actual group meeting times because they are in leveled text.

Working.   In intermediate grades, a typical small group reading session is composed of several common steps: preparing students to read the selection, teaching specific skills, practicing those skills, discussing and responding to the reading, and assessing students' needs. A major difference in the upper grades is that the students do not read the entire text while they are with you.

Before reading. Because students may spend several days reading the text, you will probably not always include before-reading activities when you introduce a new section of the text. Instead, you will frequently begin sessions by reviewing what students have read thus far in the book. If students have completed a written response to their reading, you will want to review what they have prepared before turning attention to something else. For example, if you have been mapping the major events of a story, continue with that process through your reading of new parts of the text. If you have been examining the cause-and-effect relationships in a piece of informational text, review what you have focused on so far and prepare students to pay attention to the same relationships in subsequent text segments. Don't get so caught up in small tasks that you overlook the main idea the author was expressing.

During reading. In intermediate grades, students' reading is almost always silent. Students usually spend their time in small group reading sessions discussing what they have read and describing the strategies you are attending to, rather than reading the bulk of the text. Similarly, they don't stay as a group in another part of the room and read the text together. Since the reading material matches students' abilities, most of the reading students do can be completed individually. Along with reading independently, students usually complete tasks you assign during the small group session. For instance, you could ask students to respond in writing to what they read. The students then bring these written responses to the group meeting when you discuss the text together. This is not to say that you never listen to students read. On the contrary, take time to listen to, support, and prompt struggling students as they read small portions of the text orally, and to informally assess and coach them, offering praise and direction. You can even meet individually with struggling students just before or just after meeting with the entire group.

Struggling Learners/ RtI

After reading. When students meet with their classmates and teacher in small groups, they refer to any independent written responses as they contribute to the discussion. At times you may ask them to attend to specific comprehension strategies, vocabulary words, literary elements, written language conventions, or other particular elements in post-reading discussions as suggested by the teachers' manual.

Language Conventions

Facilitating.   Working with small groups in intermediate grades assumes that students spend most of their time reading leveled text independently or working on other activities when they have finished reading. These are done in preparation for small group sessions with you. Most core literacy programs provide ideas for activities students can complete independently, with a partner, or occasionally in small groups.

In addition, you can provide a list of other appropriate tasks that will keep all students engaged while you work with small groups. Examples include writing in journals, reading books of their choice, and completing work in mathematics, social studies, or other content areas.

Try This for Teaching   **Exploring Newspapers**

- One independent task students can complete after they have finished their reading and associated assignments is to explore newspapers.
- Local newspapers are often generous in providing copies, or you can use old issues. If computers are available, students can explore online news sites.
- Along with reading stories that may interest them, have students search for specific kinds of words (such as multisyllabic words, descriptive words, or unknown words).
- Encourage students to alphabetize headlines or sort stories into categories (fact or editorial, nature or manmade, local or national, and positive or negative).

Variations for ELLs

- If you have enough copies of newspapers, have students cut out items as they find and sort articles.
- Students can write their own article following a pattern found in the newspaper.
- Students can draw their own political cartoon, comic strip, or advertisement.
- Students can conduct their own poll about a current school issue and report it during a sharing time.

Reading Workshop

A reading workshop is a block of time set aside for reading instruction that usually begins with a whole class mini-lesson by the teacher; is followed by a work period in which students read individually selected books at their levels, respond to those books, or confer with the teacher; and ends with a sharing session (Atwell, 1998). Reading workshops also sometimes include small group instructional sessions that may take the form of guided reading or literature discussions (Dorn & Soffos, 2005). Student choice of books to read is strongly emphasized and students usually read at their own pace. They may choose to respond to a text in a way that can be presented to the group during sharing time (Dorn & Soffos, 2005). Specific skills are emphasized, but rather than being prescribed in a teachers' manual, they are identified by teachers in response to problems and questions they encounter as they conference with students. The amount of time spent in the activity period can vary from class to class depending on the age and reading stamina of the children.

Some educators might claim that there is no place for small group reading experiences within the workshop routines. On the contrary, some teachers have found that adding small group work gives the workshop variety and enables an efficient use of time (Dorn & Soffos, 2005; Hornsby, Parry, & Sukarna, 1992). In small groups the teacher is able to coach more children at the same time and touch base with all children more often. One benefit of the workshop approach is it does not require sets of books for the class or small groups. Children can find books in their classroom library, the school library,

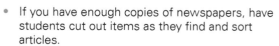

Speaking/Listening

or public libraries, or they can bring them from home. If students are unsure about the level of a text, they can find it on the websites www.lexile.com or www.renlearn.com/ar/overview/ATOS/.

Organizing. In a reading workshop, students may be grouped according to reading ability, but you can also confer with students individually. You assess students to identify levels and monitor progress. In traditional workshops, children are grouped for short periods to study specific skills or literary elements using whatever books they are reading.

Working. During the reading workshop, you are guiding students through the reading process by helping them before, during, and after their reading. For example, you may teach a whole class mini-lesson about how characters are revealed in text—through narrator comments, by what characters say, by what others say about the characters, by actions involving the characters, and so on (Lukens, 2006). Students read their books, examining how the characters are revealed, and meet in a small group to discuss character development. The difficulty levels of the books students are reading or the reading abilities of the students are not as important as what each student brings to the discussion about character development in his or her book.

Language Conventions

Before reading. Present a whole class mini-lesson on a comprehension strategy, a literary element, a phonics generalization, or another appropriate topic. When you meet regularly with children, you will recognize needs that you should address. These must be general enough that they can apply across many texts and even genres.

Struggling Learners/RtI

During reading. Reading in workshop activity time is usually silent until students meet with you. As you conference with children, you can listen to them read wherever they are in the text and coach, support, and prompt them. You will not have time for individual lessons on phonics, vocabulary, fluency, or comprehension. Instead you should remind them of what has been taught in previous lessons to the class and also gather ideas for upcoming lessons that could be helpful. You may want to spend a little more time with struggling readers or English language learners than with students who are already at

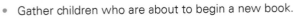

Try This for Teaching   **Preparing to Read**

- Gather children who are about to begin a new book.
- Ask them why they selected their books.
- Encourage them to share what background knowledge they may or may not have about the topic, genre, or author. Suggest resources that might help them learn more before they begin.
- Ask them to make predictions or formulate questions based on the title.
- Have them scan the first few pages or the first chapter to see if there are unfamiliar words you

could discuss as a group before they all begin.

Variations for ELLs

- Ask students what goals they have for reading this new book based on previous reading.
- Ask "How can I help you?" or "What expectations do you have of me?" This encourages students to be self-directed in their learning.

grade level or above, although they also deserve their individual time with you so you can coach and encourage them. All children benefit from having their strengths recognized and from being shown how to improve.

After reading.   You do not need to wait until several children have finished their books to gather them together in small groups. At any point you can bring groups of children to you and ask general questions to help them reflect on their reading: "How is it going?" "What page are you on?" "Did your predictions come true?" "How were you surprised?" "Have you found the answers to your questions?" "Have you encountered any especially descriptive phrases?" "How have our class mini-lessons helped you?"

One of the benefits of using groups is that you are not tempted to spend all your time helping individuals decode words. If decoding is discussed, it must be discussed in a way that is general enough to apply to all group members. Similarly, because the students are not all using the same text, the discussion must go beyond recalling the events of the story or facts presented in an article. As you focus on comprehension strategies, it must be in a way that can be applied to a variety of texts.

English Language
Learners

Facilitating.   Working with individuals or small groups in a workshop requires that other students are mature and self-directed enough to remain on task during the activity time. Rather than creating workstations or task lists for them, you should expect students to be reading or responding independently throughout the workshop time. Taking this responsibility has benefits for those who can handle it, but those who lack such reading stamina may need to be eased in by beginning with shorter periods and gradually lengthening the work time. Some teachers break up the activity time into small periods by doing it before and after a recess or a specialty class like computers, or they have one short session in the morning, one closer to lunch, and one in the afternoon.

Literature Discussion Groups

Literature discussion groups are small temporary groups of students who read and discuss the same story, poem, article, or book. The texts can be narrative, informational, or persuasive. Each member prepares a response to the reading that may include specific responsibilities for the upcoming discussion. The teacher facilitates the selection of reading materials and monitors each group's progress. Literature discussion groups are sometimes called book clubs or literature circles (Daniels, 2002; Probst, 1991; Raphael,

---

Try This for Teaching   **Language Arts Workshop**

- Rather than having students work on either their reading or writing during activity time, integrate the subjects.

- If students tire of reading, they can work on their writing, and vice versa, while you hold conferences with individuals or small groups.

- During your conferences, hold students accountable for progressing in both areas.

- You can teach mini-lessons on both reading and writing topics during the workshop.

- Use sharing time to highlight both what students have read and what they have written.

(Frey & Fisher, 2005)

Variation for ELLs

- Include ample listening and speaking opportunities during lessons, conferences, and sharing.

Florio-Ruane, & George, 2001). They encourage reader response to text, as advocated by Rosenblatt (1991).

In literature discussion groups, students can meet with the teacher or they can meet without adult supervision. In either case the group decides how much text they will read. Students in the intermediate grades often read longer texts than primary grade children, so they read segments of the text independently with a specific role assignment given to each student to prepare for the group discussion. Many times literature discussion groups are teacher led at the beginning of the school year and later may become student directed. Also the assignments given to the students at the beginning of the year are often more specific than at the middle and end of the school year (Daniels, 2002). Young (2006) warned, "During guided instruction too many teachers keep students dependent upon them. . . . Effective teachers only provide support when needed, while less effective teachers control the students' reading" (p. 180).

Speaking/Listening

Organizing. When you form literature groups, in addition to identifying students' reading abilities, you can consider two other criteria: students' expressed choices of texts and teacher concerns about possible student behavior. Some teachers select books representing a range of difficulty levels and prepare a book talk for each. Students write down their first three choices among the books. Teachers use that information along with students' reading abilities to make grouping decisions. You probably want to make sure that certain students who distract each other are not in the same group and that students who can support one another are together so they can do so. All three criteria are helpful in creating successful groups.

Working. During literature discussion groups you are guiding students through the reading process. Help them before, during, and after their reading.

Before reading. Because each group is reading a book in common, you can build background knowledge in preparation for reading. Although in primary grades this might

---

Try This for Teaching **Voting for Books**

- Help students make an independent choice of a book rather than being influenced by others.
- Write brief summaries of the books to be used and give each student a copy.
- Have students read the summaries and number their top three choices (in private).
- Formulate groups using this information in combination with what you know about students' reading abilities and maturity. Make sure that struggling readers are paired with a partner who can give them support.
- If students complain about not getting their first choice, remind them that they got one of their first three choices and tell them that they can always read the desired book during their sustained silent reading time.

- You are not limited to including only books you have read. Try books that are recommended but new to you.

Variation for ELLs

- Students can vote for a book to read, but they can also vote after reading on how much they liked it and if they would recommend it to others.
- To use discussion groups, you will need multiple copies of the same book. You will also need various titles representing a range of reading levels. Collecting that many books may seem overwhelming to an individual teacher, but grade-level teams or entire school faculties can pool resources to create a leveled book library that can be shared.

only be done once because the text is so short, in intermediate grades you might build background before each chapter.

At the beginning of the school year, you will need to introduce children to various roles they can play when they respond to what they are reading. Daniels (2002) suggests seven possible roles from which you and your students can choose. Figure 13.2 shows each role with its accompanying responsibility. Be sure that all students have the opportunity to play different roles throughout the year and even within the same book. In more student-directed groups, you may want to add a role called *leader* to guide the group and hold other students responsible for contributing to the discussion.

During reading.   Reading in literature discussion groups is usually silent in the intermediate grades unless you assign some buddies to read the text together. Students work on their role assignments independently in preparation for the next group meeting.

After reading.   When you meet with each group, have students report on their role assignments. You may want to start with the summarizer, since what that student says provides the foundation for the discussion. One benefit of using roles is that everyone is expected to contribute. A drawback is that the reporting takes a lot of time.

Struggling Learners/ RtI

English Language Learners

Figure 13.2   Roles and Responsibilities for Literature Discussion Groups

Role	Responsibility
Summarizer	Write a short summary of the reading assignment. Be prepared to talk to the group about the major ideas and events in the reading.
Connector	Find ways to show how the text the group is reading is associated with other texts, events, and experiences. The connections may be personal or may relate to knowledge or experiences the group may have. Be sure the connections will enhance understanding of the text.
Artist	Create a visual depiction of any part of the text: characters, setting, events, problems, solutions, causes, effects, etc. After showing the picture to group members, discuss how it relates to the content of the text.
Investigator	Locate background information on a topic related to the text. This could include information about the book itself (e.g., locations, characters, events, or concepts), about the author (e.g., experiences or other writings), about related historical information (e.g., time period, key figures), about other related concepts (e.g., pictures, objects, art, or music).
Highlighter	Find and mark parts of the reading assignment that are memorable for some reason: interesting, vivid, crucial, or entertaining. Read these aloud during the discussion and talk about how they make the writing more meaningful.
Word Master	Identify words in the reading assignment that are key to understanding the text, as well as words that may be used in unusual ways, words that are unfamiliar, or words that stand out in some way. Be prepared to discuss meanings of the words and share the words with others.
Locator	Show where events in the book occurred and their sequence by creating a map and tracking events. Be prepared to share the events with others.

(adapted from Daniels, 2002)

A student presenting to the class about his book.

Try randomly selecting a few students to report each time instead of having all students report. In this way everyone is prepared, but the discussion will not go on for too long.

An alternative to role assignments is to use a reciprocal teaching approach in which students summarize what they have read, clarify words and concepts, ask each other questions about the text, and make predictions (Palincsar & Brown, 1986). Ultimately your goal is to have students read and comprehend a book. Whatever helps you reach that goal is worth pursuing.

Facilitating.   While you work with one literature discussion group, the other students are reading and working on their assignments in preparation for their next meetings with you. If students in intermediate grades

---

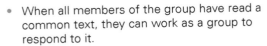

Try This for Teaching   **Group Responses**

- When all members of the group have read a common text, they can work as a group to respond to it.
- As they are reading and discussing the book, let students know that their group will be responsible to present their book to the others in class.
- Provide many different options to choose from: create a picture book, draw a mural, write riddles about your characters, make a story quilt, or develop an advertisement based on the book.

- Each group presents their group respo[...] class.

(Barchers, 1988)

Variations for ELLs

- Make presentations to younger classes or to parents.
- Consider a response that involves a performance. For example, you might have students present a skit of a scene from the book, wearing costumes or using props to represent characters.

Try This for Professional Development   **Instructional Moves During Small Groups**

- Frey and Fisher (2010) identified a four-part process that expert teachers use to scaffold student understanding during small group work: (1) questioning to check for understanding; (2) prompting cognitive and metacognitive thinking; (3) cueing students' attention; and (4) providing direct explanations and modeling.
- Are you using elaboration, clarification, and divergent questions?
- Are you prompting for background knowledge, process or procedural knowledge, or reflective knowledge?

- Are you using visual, verbal, or gestural cues?
- Are you using think-alouds, allowing students to see your cognitive processes as a proficient reader?
- Reflect on strengths you have in each of these four areas.
- Set a goal to improve or try something new in at least one area.

need additional tasks to engage them, they take multiple role assignments, read another book for enjoyment, or write independently in their journals. Fast finishers can become peer-tutors to assist other students who may not be so quick to complete their preparations.

English Language Learners

Writing with Children—Small Groups

Sometimes teachers shy away from having their students write because they visualize mountains of student papers that they are responsible for reading, editing, and grading outside of class, or they imagine themselves sitting at their desks during class time helping one student revise a paper while 26 others wait in line. It doesn't have to be so difficult. Educators rarely teach reading one-on-one with every student as others wait in line. Teachers guide small groups through the reading process; similarly, you can guide small groups through the writing process. Mooney (2006a) claimed, "Guided writing warrants as much attention as guided reading" (p. 108). After observing classrooms in which children have been successful in writing, researchers attributed improvement to "the interaction of writers with teachers and peers during conferences and small group work" (Gere & Abbott, 1985, pp. 34–35).

Some administrators in districts and schools have expectations about how writing should be taught. Others may allow you to select from various instructional approaches. You need to know how to organize, work with, and facilitate small group writing in both primary and intermediate grades whether you use a core literacy program, a workshop approach, or formula writing.

Core Literacy Programs

Core literacy programs are comprehensive in that they integrate writing and reading instruction. Units include materials for both whole class and small group reading and writing prompts focused on the same topic. For example, if students are reading about health-care workers in a story or a nonfiction article about hospitals, they might be asked to write an informational article about emergency rooms or people who work at hospitals. Different skills needed to write the article are addressed each week as students complete the unit of instruction. Each program is a little different, but without direction for organizing the class, the writing expectations can be overwhelming. Many teachers ask students to complete only one draft, and others disregard the prompts completely. Instead, you can use the same groups formed for guided reading for guided writing as well. By working with only a few students at a time, you can assist individuals as they successfully complete the writing process.

Primary Grade Groups.   Even casual observers recognize a difference between what goes on in primary and intermediate grades during writing instruction. These differences may not be apparent during whole class activities, but they become more evident as teachers organize, work with, and facilitate small groups.

Organizing.   You have divided your class into at least three groups for reading, and you can use the same organization for writing. As you already meet with each small group regularly, you can devote some of this time to coaching reading and some to coaching writing.

Working.   In the primary grades a typical small group writing session focuses on completing the writing process in five days. The teachers' manuals provide some suggested writing activities for each day. For example, on the first day you might discuss the topic for the writing and help children formulate questions about it. On day two you will guide them through a prewriting activity, like locating appropriate sources and information. On the third day students write a first draft focusing on a particular skill, like using precise words. On day four you will help the children revise and edit what they have written, using proofreading marks. On the fifth day, you will evaluate students' writing, and they will have the opportunity to share it with the group or class.

The suggestions contained in teachers' manuals are sequential, but children in your classroom may not be prepared to go through the writing process in such a rigid manner. Some may not be ready to move forward on the given day. You may not have time to help each student, even in small groups, especially when students are all revising and editing on the same day. You may have to make some adaptations before, during, and after writing.

Struggling Learners/ RtI

Before writing. Perhaps discussing the topic and brainstorming questions can be completed as a group rather than by having each child formulate his or her own questions. You could also do any outlining or planning as a group.

English Language Learners

During writing. Maybe you could write the first few sentences as a group on a chart. Young students could then be expected to add one or two individual sentences to extend the group writing. Another adaptation is to have one student in a group complete the process suggested in the teachers' manual under the guidance of the rest of the group. Peers can help the writer brainstorm. They can offer suggestions for revision and can help edit the piece as it nears completion. The next week another member of the group is the writer while the others serve as helpers. Young writers are often so overwhelmed with transcription that writing turns into "how-do-you-spell" sessions. Keep the focus on the message by taking dictation as the students speak. This frees them to be thinking more about composition. As they gain confidence, you can release the responsibility for transcription to them. As students make progress in writing, be sure to praise effort and attitude as well as achievement. Direct your coaching and suggestions to the group rather than always singling out individuals.

A teacher writing with a small group.

After writing. If you are only revising and editing a few sentences for each child or one paper for the entire group, then the task is more feasible and children have still experienced the entire process. Instead of having everyone present his or her ideas each Friday, you could select only one or two students to share each time.

Facilitating. Working with small groups will only be effective if other children are engaged in meaningful activities that do not require your immediate help. Most core literacy programs provide ideas for developmentally appropriate centers or workstations.

The discussion of writing skills and the draft that is started during group time does not all have to be completed during the group meetings. Related tasks can be assigned to be completed at a workstation or independently at the students' desks. You may assign some activities to be completed with buddies, pairing struggling students with peers who can offer support. As students are engaged at workstations, you have time to work one-on-one with those who need special attention or to begin working with another group.

Intermediate Grade Groups.   Primary and intermediate grade writing instruction differs. These differences are not just in the content, but also in how teachers organize, work with, and facilitate small groups.

Organizing.   If you are following a core literacy program in the intermediate grades, you will meet for reading with each small group. Use the same groups for writing. You may not be able to meet with each group daily, but because older students can work independently, you don't need to. Much of their writing can occur outside the actual group meeting times.

Working.   Typically students in intermediate grades are expected to write on a daily prompt tied to the whole class reading. In addition, the teachers' manual suggests that students prewrite, draft, revise, and publish weekly. Although these tasks are not assigned to a particular day, there are skills that you are expected to encourage students to use in their writing, such as including details.

Before writing. After your small group has read about animals, for example, discuss experiences group members have had with animals. Each child chooses one experience to write about. Show the students how they can plan their writing by outlining the details of their experience.

During writing. Students use their outline to write about their experience. For students who struggle, perhaps the assignment could be completed in partnerships. Remind students that this is a draft and that spelling and punctuation can be addressed later.

Struggling Learners/ RtI

English Language Learners

After writing. Before students revise, focus on a skill such as deleting unimportant details or avoiding run-on sentences. With these skills in mind, students revise and edit their writing with peers and then share their writing with the group. Keep in mind that although the majority of the students can work independently, you may need to supervise some individuals or partnerships more closely than others.

Facilitating.   Working with small groups in intermediate grades assumes that the others can work independently. Most core literacy programs provide ideas for activities students can complete independently, with a partner, or occasionally in small groups. But most often intermediate grade students are expected to be reading and writing in preparation for their own group meetings as you are working with one group at a time.

Writing Workshop

Like a reading workshop, a writing workshop consists of instructional strategies in a well-organized framework, usually beginning with a whole class mini-lesson by the teacher and continuing with a work period in which students write. They choose their own subjects and often their own forms of writing, and they move through the process individually

Students showing where they are in the writing process by using clothespins.

rather than as a group. The workshop ends with a sharing session (Atwell, 1998). Specific skills instruction is generated by needs that have surfaced as teachers confer with students. In intermediate grades more time is devoted to independent work than in primary grades, as children are more mature and have developed more writing stamina.

Teachers often associate workshops with one-on-one conferences, but they can also work with small groups of children who are on the same phase of the writing process. One group can brainstorm together while another may respond to one another's writing. These groups do not need to be based on ability level; they are temporary and may not meet for more than a short period.

Organizing. In a writing workshop, a "state of the class time" typically follows a mini-lesson. At this time the students can inform the teacher about what aspect of the process they will focus on that day. Some teachers use a chart or poster showing different phases of the writing process and have students place their nametag under the appropriate label.

Working. As you implement a writing workshop, you are guiding students through the writing process. You may meet in writing conferences with small groups before, during, and after writing. A writing conference is a short conversation between at least two people about a student's writing. It is not a mini-lesson and doesn't involve a formal plan. You may not even know what you need to say until you sit down next to some children and ask, "How can I help you?" As you sense needs, you can meet them.

In a conference you take off your instructor's hat and put on a coach's cap, becoming a consultant rather than a manager or a critic. You are still teaching, but you are teaching in response to what is going right or wrong in the moment rather than relying on a teacher's manual. A sports coach watches the team practice or play and then huddles the members together and gives some pointers before sending them back onto the field. Similarly, a drama coach doesn't always show up at a rehearsal with a lesson

---

Try This for Teaching | **Clothespin Organization**

- In order to keep track of where individual students are in the writing process, write their names on clothespins.
- Before beginning work time, have a few students come up and clip their clothespin onto posters or banners that are labeled with the phases of the writing process to show what they are working on.
- You can quickly see which students are progressing and which are stuck.
- Use the clothespins to organize children into small groups or partners and identify individuals who may need your help.

Variations for ELLs

- To make the experience more tactile use an actual clothesline partitioned off with writing process labels for students to clip on their clothespins.
- Label the writing process on visuals representing animals. Each animal could have a tail made out of rope or ribbon onto which students could clip their clothespins.
- Label the steps of the process on metal cookie sheets and put students' names on magnets that can be moved from sheet to sheet.

plan. After watching the rehearsal she gathers the cast and says, "You need to get into your characters more. Gestures need to be more natural. Get more conviction into your lines." Then the actors go back to the stage. As you guide children in their writing, you huddle with a small group and give them pointers wherever they happen to be in the process. After examining classrooms in which the writing process was taught, Gere and Abbott (1985) concluded that the success of the approach was dependent on the interaction of writers with teachers and peers during conferences and small group work.

Calkins (1986) said, "Our first job in a conference, then, is to be a person not just a teacher. It is to enjoy, to care, and to respond" (p. 118). For students, your role as nurturer is much more important than your role as instructor. Be approachable and friendly, acknowledging the writer's strengths in order to build trust. Remember praise, polish, and plan. Give some compliments about what is going well, offer a few suggestions for improvement, and help students set some specific goals so they walk away from your conference with a plan in mind.

A teacher conferencing with a student.

Struggling Learners/RtI

Before writing.   If you notice that some students are having a hard time getting started with their writing, get them together to help. Ask what they have written recently. After they respond, ask if they want to continue with that piece or if they want to try a new topic.

One third-grade teacher, Ms. Horowitz, asked a student, "What is something that you do when you are not at school?"

Felipe answered, "Soccer."

"When you think of the word *soccer*, what comes to mind?" asked Ms. Horowitz.

Felipe responded, "My friends, Javier and Hugo."

"When you think about Javier, what do you think of?"

"He's funny," answered Felipe.

Help the child realize that he has landed on something he can write about, a funny experience that happened with Javier. You can follow a similar process with another student in the group. As one person speaks, ideas in others' minds are often sparked.

Sometimes you may want to ask students to bring their journals to the group to share a favorite part with the others. Then ask children to elaborate and write more about the topic of the chosen entry. You could brainstorm with the group a list of possible ways to expand the topic and give the students a copy of the list to keep in their writing folders.

English Language Learners

During writing.   Many children can work independently when drafting, but you may need to give special attention to those who struggle. In some cases you may need to take dictation as the child expresses himself orally. At other times, pass the pen or pencil back and forth, allowing a child who is learning English to write the words she knows while you write the rest. As a group, you might compose several sentences together to get started, with you acting as scribe, and then let the students continue composing more of the piece at their seats.

Struggling Learners/RtI

English Language Learners

Try This for Teaching | Journals to Projects

- After children have been in the pattern of writing in their journals on topics of their own choice, ask them to identify favorite entries.

- When they have selected one to work on further, guide the writing by asking them to expand that entry on another paper.

- Guide the process with questions. For example, if the child has written "I like animals," ask why. The child might respond, "Because animals are fun to play with."

- Help the child write that answer down.

- Continue questioning. "Are all animals fun to play with?"

- When the child responds, encourage her to write what she said.

- Continue this process until the child has expanded sufficiently on the original idea.

- In subsequent meetings, help the child revise, edit, and share the writing.

- For more experienced students, you could present various genre options—what started as a journal entry could become a personal narrative, an informational piece, or a poem.

(Calkins & Harwayne,. 1991)

Variation for ELLs

- With ELLs and struggling students you can share the pen and write the child's answers together. In some cases, you may need to begin by simply taking dictation.

After writing. After students have written a draft, you can help them by giving them feedback so they can revise. You are also going to help them edit as they prepare to publish a final draft.

When working in small groups, ask some members to be your helpers as you respond to one student or edit with another. Peers can offer compliments and suggestions just as you do. A student helper or two can provide extra sets of eyes when editing to help catch mistakes that need to be corrected. If one student has a lengthy piece, each member of the group can edit one page and complete the task in a short time. You need to give peer tutors

Try This for Teaching | WRITE: Conferencing Tips

- Use this acronym to remember what to do during a writing conference and to help peers or adult volunteers as they conference with students.

  - **W** is for Watch. Watch for content before mechanics. Content is the cake; mechanics is the frosting. Bake the cake before you worry about frosting it.

  - **R** is for Respect. Respect the author's paper and ownership. As often as possible, allow the student to make changes on the paper. Allow the student to choose which suggestions to implement.

  - **I** is for Involve. Involve the author by asking lots of questions: Why did you do this? What other reason could you

give for that? How did you de
A conference is a time for listening, not just talking.

  - **T** is for Teach. Conferences are an effective time to explain the reasons behind the changes you are asking the author to make, but don't make a lesson out of every little thing. Just focus on a few items. As you see glaring needs, you may consider teaching a mini-lesson on those topics to the whole class.

  - **E** is for Encourage. Stay positive. No one gets mad at a seed for not being a flower. You just recognize the potential and nurture the growth.

(Wilcox, 1994)

and helpers specific guidelines and preparation. Without them, students are usually reluctant to critique each other or unable to offer significant help (DiPardo & Freedman, 1988).

You might be concerned that the students are not going to find all the errors. Don't worry. Unless you are preparing the manuscript for an official publication that is going to be displayed before the whole school, remind yourself that you are focusing on a process as well as a product. The process will transfer even when the student doesn't remember what the writing was about. When editing, you and a peer helper may catch all the mistakes, but there is no guarantee that the young author will not make more as he or she prepares a final draft. Remember that you are improving the writing only as a means of improving the writer. When you display less than perfect writing in the classroom or send it home include a disclaimer such as, "This represents our best efforts at this time of the year," or "You may still find some errors but we've made great improvement."

In place of conferencing with students, many teachers traditionally have taken writing home, revised and edited it, and passed back the corrected papers to their students. As entrenched as this practice has become in many schools, it is not the most effective way to teach writing (Hillocks, 1986). Carnicelli (1980) found that oral communication in conferences led to better understanding and improved writing over written feedback.

The one who does the work does the learning. If you are editing dozens of papers you are learning a lot, but your students are not. It is better to give feedback and ask students to make the changes. If you correct papers, many students can feel like they have lost ownership of the writing, and they lose motivation. It also makes the communication one-sided: You are sending messages to students but do not hear their reasoning, thoughts, and ideas in return.

A student once wrote, "DUM, DUM, DUM, DUM, etc." at the top of his paper and then began a story. Had the teacher been editing the paper at home, she would have crossed out the words immediately. Because the teacher was conferencing, she asked, "What is this?" The child then hummed the theme music to the TV series *Dragnet*. The teacher laughed and explained how the student could write it so that readers would know that it was a song. A clever idea would have been lost and that child might have been left discouraged instead of validated had the teacher not been open to two-way communication in a conference.

Speaking/Listening

When correcting papers at home, teachers easily become frustrated and tired. You may unintentionally begin to be quite abrupt and sharp in your comments: "Where is your thesis statement?" "Cliché, cliché, cliché!" or "Put it in your own words!" These comments can be discouraging to young writers who were hoping you would notice what they did well or may not yet know how to fix the problems you have highlighted. When sitting side by side with a small group of children, it is easier to maintain a positive tone and address the needs that surface.

Try This for Professional Development   **Visit the Writing Center**

- Most colleges and universities have a writing center where tutors work one-on-one with writers.
- Take a piece of your writing to a writing center and meet with a tutor.
- Pay close attention to what the tutor does or does not do to make you feel comfortable and help you.
- Set goals for your own conferencing with children based on this experience.

Variations

- If no writing center is available, arrange to conference with one of your professors or a colleague.
- Save your rough draft and revised drafts to show your future students as you discuss the writing process.

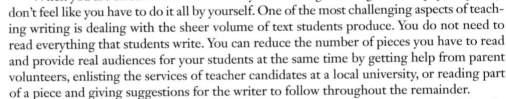

Try This for Professional Development   **Enlisting Readers**

- Contact a teacher at a local middle school or high school.
- Make arrangements to send your students' writing to that teacher to share with her class. This can be facilitated through the Internet. Papers could be sent electronically. Revisions or editing suggestions could be made using a Track Changes feature.
- Make sure that names do not appear on the papers.
- Clarify your expectations: Do you want feedback on content, editing for conventions, or both?
- The other teacher can pass one paper to each student for a response.
- After the papers have been collected, the teacher can return them to you by email, district mail, or in

a self-addressed, stamped envelope you provide.

- Remind your students that these readers have provided feedback to help them. The readers may not have fixed every mistake, and the writers don't have to accept every suggestion.

Variations

- Contact a nearby college or university teacher preparation program and enlist help from students in literacy courses.
- Include a rubric with the writing and have the older readers grade the students.

Speaking/Listening

New Literacies

Struggling Learners/ RtI

When you are under a time crunch and you need to get through a lot of papers quickly, don't feel like you have to do it all by yourself. One of the most challenging aspects of teaching writing is dealing with the sheer volume of text students produce. You do not need to read everything that students write. You can reduce the number of pieces you have to read and provide real audiences for your students at the same time by getting help from parent volunteers, enlisting the services of teacher candidates at a local university, or reading part of a piece and giving suggestions for the writer to follow throughout the remainder.

As students finish the process of writing, they expect to share their writing with others. Arrange for a sharing time in which they share with peers. You can also share with other classes or post student writing on a class blog. Nothing motivates writing like sharing. Professional basketball players have a large and paying audience, but most people who play basketball don't get a big paycheck or the chance to play in a large arena. Still, they enjoy the sport. Most people are content to play with a group of friends or even one-on-one. The same is true for writers. Some professional writers are read by millions, but most don't have to have such a large audience; they just need a real one.

Facilitating.   Sometimes teachers panic when they hear the term *writing workshop* because they think of it as a loosely structured time in which children are wandering wherever they want in the classroom or working in groups underneath desks while lying on pillows. They think of it as a noisy free for all. That does not have to be the case. Conferencing with small groups can only happen when the rest of the class is working productively and quietly on their writing. Generally students write, revise, or produce a final draft without assistance. If they get stuck and you can't work with them immediately, they can work on another project or draw an illustration as they wait.

Most classrooms have four corners, and some teachers have found it useful to limit the conferencing to those corners of the room (Lensmire, 1994), leaving a quiet workspace in the center of the room for most of the class. You can conduct conferences in one corner. Peers or cross-age tutors can work effectively in two more. Paquette (2009) found that

---

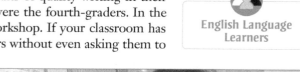

Try This for Teaching · Final Draft Workstation

- Complete a class shared writing on chart paper.
- Cut the first sentence off the shared writing and place it at a workstation.
- As children rotate to this station, expect them to copy a final draft of the sentence you composed, revised, and edited together as a class.
- After they finish the sentence, children may draw an illustration for it.
- Do this same activity on successive days with the other sentences from the shared writing chart.

- By the end of the week, add a cover, and all the children have completed their own books to take home.
- More advanced students could write larger chunks of the chart in one sitting.

Variation for ELLs

- Children could write their own additional sentences on the same topic in their native languages to also be included in their books.

---

when fourth-graders helped second-graders incorporate traits of quality writing in their work, both benefited, but the ones who learned the most were the fourth-graders. In the last corner, try incorporating phone conferences in your workshop. If your classroom has phone access, you can enlist the assistance of adult volunteers without even asking them to come to school. You may be able to find volunteers who speak the home languages of students who are learning English.

Since volunteers do not need to come to school and will only get called at an expected time, speakers of children's first languages can be encouraged to help so that phone conferences can be conducted in the child's first language.

One way to facilitate effective writing groups is to have students maintain writing folders in which they store works in progress, ideas for future writing, prewriting plans, rubrics, and checklists. As you conference with students, review what they have in their folders to monitor their progress as writers. Is there evidence of prewriting? Has the student revised his or her writing? How have the students implemented the skills taught in mini-lessons? As you review students' writing folders, you will be able to identify needs that can be addressed in whole class or small groups.

English Language Learners

A student conferencing about her writing by telephone in a classroom.

Formula Writing

Formula writing, providing children specifc steps of structures to follow, began as a strategy for struggling learners. Teachers were once advised to use it judiciously, but now it is being advocated as beneficial for all. Miller (2006) wrote, "As students progress through the elementary grades, the tension between a focus on product and a focus on process intensifies. . . . An increasingly popular response to this 'pressure to produce' is the use of

Struggling Learners/ RtI

Try This for Teaching　**Phone Conferences**

- Enlist the help of adult volunteers who can conference without even coming to school.
- Make a list of phone numbers for moms, dads, grandparents, or friends who have said they would be willing to take a call at a certain time of day.
- Have students sign up for a turn to make calls.
- Instruct children to call someone on the list, introduce themselves, and ask if the adult has time to listen. If the answer is no or if the call goes to an answering machine, the child can call another number on the list.
- Have the child read her writing (or a favorite part if it is lengthy) to the adult.
- Tell the adults to give at least one compliment and ask at least one question. Because the adults can't see the paper the questions are usually content focused—as they should be.
- Coach the child to thank the volunteer, say goodbye, and let the next child on the sign-up list know it is his or her turn.
- Have the writer return to her desk and make revisions based on the feedback.

Variations for ELLs

- Calling a volunteer can be a reward for positive behavior ("Whitney, thanks for using your time wisely. Go sign up for a phone conference.").
- Students can write thank-you notes to the volunteers who helped them.

writing frames and formulas" (p. 74). Helping children follow formulas in their writing can lead to test success (De La Paz, 2007), but often leaves writers creating lifeless prose with little sensitivity to audience.

Common Core State Standards

Because the Common Core emphasizes only specific genres of writing (narrative, informational, and argumentative), personal and poetic writing are left to individual teacher discretion. This strong focus on genres has led to instructional approaches in which children are taught formulas for specific genres. If you use these approaches, you should still allow time for sharing, but the bulk of your time will be spent in mini-lessons explaining and modeling the formulas. You will then need to help students practice individually, as a class, or in small groups.

Two of the most common approaches are self-regulated strategy development for writing (SRSD) (Harris, Graham, Mason, & Friedlander, 2008) and genre writing (Donovan, Milewicz, & Smolkin, 2003). SRSD gives specific steps for students to follow when writing. The students memorize the steps and regulate their implementation as they complete assignments. Similarly, in genre writing specific elements of a particular genre are taught explicitly and followed by students.

English Language Learners

Organizing.　Most of your instruction and modeling will be done with the whole class, so groups are usually organized only as children practice or need specific help. Groups do not need to be based on students' abilities, and they do not need to be long term. One way to organize groups is to have a checkout problem at the end of your whole class lesson. After you introduce a formula or a genre element, ask children to write it down or demonstrate mastery in another way. Move from child to child checking for understanding of the formula. Those who are correct can continue with their writing independently. Those who need more help can be invited to meet with you for additional instruction and modeling in a small group.

Another way to organize groups is to monitor children as they write. Those who are not catching on can be invited to meet with you in a corner of the room where you can help them take the next steps. Revising and editing groups can operate much like in writing workshops. The major difference is that instead of working on their own projects, they are all writing in the same genre, following the same formula.

Working.   In formula writing the steps of explicit instruction are followed. You introduce the formula, model how to use it, and practice by writing together as a class. Gradually, students take responsibility for creating their own pieces following the same formula. Small groups can provide an effective step between whole class and individual work.

Before writing.   With a small group, reinforce what you have taught and modeled to the whole class. You will only meet with children before writing if they have not understood how to use the formula. Try to determine what it is they do not understand. Many children just need a little clarification, some additional modeling, and time for guided practice. The opportunity to follow the formula in the safety of a group before having to do it independently helps.

Struggling Learners/
RtI

During writing.   For the students who cannot draft independently, you may need to offer to take dictation. If the child can verbalize, you can transcribe for him on paper or using a keyboard. For example, if you have taught students that an introduction to an essay should include a question to catch the reader's attention, help the child formulate such a question orally and then write or type it in front of him and read it together. You could allow the child to write or type those words in the question that he knows. As a group, you might compose one sentence together at the beginning of each section the formula calls for. Then have students finish the sections independently or with partners.

English Language
Learners

After writing.   After children have produced a draft, you will help them revise and edit, just as you would in other instructional approaches. Group conferencing will help students proceed. While conferencing in a writing workshop is quite open-ended, conferencing when using the formula approach involves more checking for understanding and making sure students have successfully followed the plan.

Facilitating.   Some teachers enjoy the structure and clear expectations of formula writing. Even during work time children know exactly what to do next, and you can monitor individuals within small groups. You may want to provide several additional tasks that children can work on when they finish their writing or get stuck so they can continue to work productively while waiting for help instead of sitting with hands raised for long periods. The conferencing corners used in a writing workshop could also work well during independent practice time because they create a division between places where students must be quiet and places where students can talk together. If it is too difficult for you to monitor three corners in addition to your own, reduce the number of corners until the noise level is acceptable. Tell children that you add corners when they show that they can use them responsibly.

Summary

Working in small groups has benefits not available in either whole class or individual settings. Small groups give children a safe environment to take risks. They may say things in a small group that they would not say in front of the whole class. Thus you need to know how to use small groups as you read and write with children.

Various instructional approaches are used in literacy classrooms, including core programs, reading/writing workshops, literature discussion groups, and formula writing. Although all of these approaches should include lesson time, work time, and sharing time, the unique expectations of each approach are quite different. You will need to organize groups, work with groups, and facilitate groups differently, depending on the approach you select or are expected to use in your school. As you work with small groups, there are things you can do before, during, and after reading and writing to ensure that children are experiencing both processes completely.

Self-Check

1. Describe the reading materials that are available in core literacy programs.

2. What are some appropriate workstations or centers for primary grades?

3. How do you facilitate small groups in intermediate grades without using centers?

4. Describe a reading or writing workshop.

5. What criteria can you use to create literature discussion groups?

6. What are some of the roles children can play in literature discussion groups?

7. What are some benefits of writing conferences?

8. What is the major difference between conferencing in a writing workshop and conferencing when using formula writing?

MyEducationLab™

Go to the Topics, Comprehension, Writing, and Organization and Management in the **MyEducationLab** (www.myeducationlab.com) for your course, where you can:

- Find learning outcomes for Comprehension, Writing, and Organization and Management along with the national standards that connect to these outcomes.

- Complete Assignments and Activities that can help you more deeply understand the chapter content.

- Apply and practice your understanding of the core teaching skills identified in the chapter with the Building Teaching Skills and Dispositions learning units.

- Examine challenging situations and cases presented in the IRIS Center Resources.

- Check your comprehension on the content covered in the chapter by going to the Study Plan in the Book

Resources for your text. Here you will be able to take a chapter quiz, receive feedback on your answers, and then access Review, Practice, and Enrichment activities to enhance your understanding of chapter content (optional).

- Visit **A+RISE** Standards2Strategy™, an innovative and interactive online resource that offers new teachers in grades K–12 just-in-time, research-based instructional strategies that meet the linguistic needs of ELLs as they learn content, differentiate instruction for all grades and abilities, and are aligned to Common Core Elementary Language Arts Standards (for the literacy strategies) and to English language proficiency standards in WIDA, Texas, California, and Florida.

Reading and Writing by Children

Chapter Outline

READING BY CHILDREN
Classroom Libraries
Teacher Support and
Encouragement
WRITING BY CHILDREN
Journals
Technology
SUMMARY

A s a sixth-grade teacher, I always had my students write in their journals when they first got to school. If they came 15 minutes early or five minutes late, they knew exactly what they needed to do when they sat down at their desks. It made for a nice transition at the start of the school day, but it also gave the students a safe place where they could express their thoughts and feelings without being overly concerned about mechanics. I remember seeing great progress in their fluency, competence, and motivation, but I wondered if my students saw similar value in the daily routine. Were they just jumping a required hoop? Imagine my satisfaction when many years later I received a note from one of my former students, Sarah, who wrote, "Believe it or not, I've been in the process of typing up my sixth-grade journal as part of my life history, and I had to thank you. That was a wonderful thing you did with our class. The journal forced me to write something every day, and it has been interesting to see the progression of my writing during that year. Looking back, I think it was that sixth-grade journal that gave me confidence and made me enthusiastic about continuing writing even after I left your class."

—Brad

When you are learning to drive a car, you need a model. Then you need to have someone show you how and guide you as you make your first attempts. But you also need time when you can just get in the car and drive. Many hours of practice build your confidence and capability. Similarly, when learning to read and write, children need instruction and modeling followed by periods of consistent practice when they are reading and writing by themselves in order to reach their potential. This constitutes the end of the gradual release of responsibility because the student has taken ownership for her own literacy and is less dependent on help from teachers and others (Pearson & Gallagher, 1983). Cunningham and Allington (2007) found that schools with high-achieving students scheduled more time for independent reading and writing than other schools. The Common Core stresses the importance of children reading narrative and informational texts of steadily increasing complexity. Students are also expected to write to accomplish their own purposes.

Common Core State Standards

Reading by Children

The volume of independent silent reading children do in school is significantly related to reading achievement (Cunningham & Stanovich, 1996). It impacts comprehension, vocabulary, spelling, writing style, oral language, control of grammar, and fluency (Allington, 2001; Krashen, 2004). The highest achievers in classrooms are likely to read 200 times as many minutes as the lowest achievers, and the frequency with which children read in and out of school depends significantly on the priority the teacher gives to independent reading (Anderson, Wilson, & Fielding, 1988).

Since publication of the *Report of the National Reading Panel* in 2000 (National Reading Panel), some educators have questioned the value of using school time for independent reading (Hiebert & Reutzel, 2010). But others continue to support the practice (Krashen, 2001; Pressley, Dolezal, Roehrig, & Hilden, 2002; Wu & Samuels, 2004). Some claim that independent reading is best done at home (Shanahan, 2006a). Although such would be the ideal, researchers have found that only 2 percent of free time is spent reading—less than an average of 10 minutes a day for most children. Many do not read outside of school at all (Fielding, Wilson, & Anderson, 1984). Using school time for independent reading seems justified, not just to reach academic goals but also to motivate students. No practice affects reading attitudes more than independent reading (Yoon, 2002). Neuroscientists have shown that the emotional response of fear occurs at the cellular level (Campeau et al., 1991), "therefore, a student's dislike of reading can occur instantly and become permanent from the brain's chemical point of view" (Block & Parris, 2008, p. 122). Kandel (2006) argued that educators need to reduce students' fear of making mistakes in reading by creating an emotionally risk-free environment. Allowing time for independent reading in school is one way to create such an environment.

Illiteracy, or not being able to read and write, is a huge and heartbreaking problem, but so is **aliteracy**, which is being able to read and write but choosing not to do so. Almost half of all Americans ages 15 to 24 do not read any books for pleasure (National Endowment for the Arts, 2007). You may have seen this bumper sticker: "If you can read this, thank a teacher." Perhaps it is time to produce a new bumper sticker that says: "If you WANT to read this, thank a teacher who did it right."

Many teachers and administrators allow time in school for independent reading and refer to this practice as **sustained silent reading (SSR)**. Some educators make a distinction between independent reading (more structured and teacher guided) and SSR (less

English Language Learners

structured and student controlled) (Buly, 2006). However, most teachers use these terms synonymously, as they are used here.

Struggling Learners/ Rtl

SSR includes a set daily time when each student reads self-selected material. Some teachers say SSR stands for self-selected reading. (One teacher says it just stands for sit down, shut up, and read). Regardless of the term, the goal is to allow students time to read by themselves, select their own material, and simply enjoy their reading without reports or records (Hunt, 1970). You can make sure that time is being used wisely by creating and using classroom libraries, providing teacher support and encouragement, sharing book talks, and using motivation and incentive programs thoughtfully.

Not only does SSR allow children to practice, but it also offers them the opportunity to develop a love of reading and see themselves as readers (Gardiner, 2005). One middle school teacher spoke of his students' independent reading: "It has been such a joy for me to see students stop tolerating books and actually begin to like them. In some cases I'm seeing love affairs begin between kids and books" (Jensen, 2001, p. 34).

Classroom Libraries

A large, varied, and regularly refreshed collection of books in the classroom is critical in improving children's reading performance and motivation. Students with immediate access to books in their classrooms read as much as 60 percent more than students lacking such access (Neuman, 1999). Making books available is especially important when you are working with students from low-income neighborhoods where it is not as common to have books available in homes and in the community (Neuman & Celano, 2001).

If you want a child to swim, you don't invite him to a pool that has an inch of cold water at the bottom. You fill the pool! If you provide warm and inviting water, most children can't resist jumping in. It's the same with books. One father took his children to the library and let them choose stacks and stacks of books. The librarian said, "Your children won't be able to read all of these before they're due." The father responded, "They don't

Children in a classroom library looking for books.

Struggling Learners/
RtI

have to read them all. I'm just putting water in the pool." The shocked librarian replied, "You better not put these books in the pool." Of course the father had no intention of putting books in a pool. He wanted the books to *become* the pool his children could not resist entering. Mem Fox (1996) wrote about having "books here, books there, books and stories everywhere" (p. 3). When this occurs, children usually pick them up. To provide this immediate access to books, you need to create a classroom library and then use it effectively.

Creating a Classroom Library. A classroom library should consist of a variety of books from different genres representing various ethnic and cultural backgrounds. You should also have materials representing a wide range of reading levels included in your collection (Reutzel & Fawson, 2002). Magazines, newspapers, and books written by student authors from your own class can be popular items. Effective libraries include a reading center and/or various nooks and crannies where children can spread out and be comfortable as they read. You may wonder how you can afford to build a classroom library with limited financial resources. Experienced teachers suggest promoting book orders, inviting gift books, collecting used books, and using online resources, as well as creating affordable reading centers.

Book orders. Promote the book order offers you receive from publishers like Scholastic, Arrow, Lucky, and See-Saw. The programs provide fliers from which children and parents can order low-cost books. In return for distributing the fliers and collecting orders, the publishers give teachers points they can redeem for free books. One teacher stimulated interest in the orders by sending an additional note home indicating the books she felt were best. She highlighted quality children's literature and found that parents and students trusted her opinions. The increased orders allowed her enough points to literally fill shelves in her classroom with books. She said, "When I get the books for free, I don't feel as protective of them. I can put them out where the kids have access to them." You do not have to apologize for encouraging parents to buy books, because the number of books in a home has been shown to be a significant predictor of academic achievement (National Endowment for the Arts, 2007).

Gift books. Teachers regularly celebrate holidays and the birthdays of their students. Make books part of the celebration. On such occasions, invite children to bring a book that can be given to the whole class. It can be used or new. One teacher personalizes the gift book by placing a picture of the birthday student in the front of the book and encourages the child to write a note telling why he or she chose that book to donate to the class library. On some holidays students traditionally give teachers gifts. As a result, most teachers have more mugs, pens, and tree ornaments than they can use. Spread the word that instead of candy or collectibles, you want books for the classroom library. In this way, the generosity of a few can be enjoyed by everyone.

Used books. Garage sales and thrift stores can be a rich source of books. With a little investment of your time, you will be surprised at the treasures you can pick up. You may even be able to find inexpensive books on eBay, Amazon, or other online sources (www. bookcloseouts.com). In many cases, those selling used books charge very little when they find out you are a teacher. The condition of the book does not have to be perfect to make it useful in your class. Subscriptions to current magazines and newspapers can be costly, but you can usually find outdated materials for very little. Elementary school children

Try This for Teaching   **Book Exchanges**

- Ask all children to bring a book from home to give away.
- Exchange the books by use of a drawing or secret pals.
- Be sure to review expectations of saying "thank you" and being courteous.
- Let the children take their "new" books home.

(Chayet, 1994)

Variations for ELLs

- Be prepared with books for children who are unable to bring their own or who forget.

- Assure children that books can be used or new. You may want to use the words "well-loved" instead of "used." Remind students that books can be in another language for those who speak more than one.
- Have students talk about their books and why they chose to bring them to heighten interest and excitement.

are not as concerned about the date of the publication as they are about the content of the illustrations, photographs, and articles. Similarly, many older coffee-table books and encyclopedia volumes can be purchased quite reasonably.

Online resources.   Many reading materials are available online for you to use with your students. Some classic children's books (*Alice in Wonderland, Treasure Island,* and *The Jungle Book,* for example) are available free through Project Gutenberg (www.gutenberg .org/wiki/Children's_Literature_Bookshelf). Some popular children's magazines can also be accessed online (e.g., kids.nationalgeographic.com/kids/). Additional resources have been developed especially for English learners. At www.rong-chang.com/kids.htm, children can access stories, songs, and games at a range of language levels.

New Literacies

English Language Learners

Reading centers.   Make sure your reading center is comfortable and well lit. Some teachers like to include carpet squares, beanbag chairs, or tossed pillows. But none of these materials need to be brand new. Occasionally, business owners are willing to donate

Try This for Teaching   **Just What the Doctor Ordered**

- Approach local doctors, dentists, and other professionals.
- Ask if they would be willing to donate outdated magazines and books from their waiting rooms.
- Have students write thank-you notes to show their appreciation.
- You may also want to name the donors in a school newsletter or on a school website.
- Have students write letters to local doctors and dentists requesting donations.
- Enlist a parent volunteer to spearhead this effort.

- Ask restaurants for old menus and travel agencies for outdated travel brochures (Chayet, 1994).

Variations for ELLs

- Work in groups rather than individually to complete the above tasks.
- You may also ask if they will display students' writing in waiting rooms. Be sure full names and photos of children are not included.

Children using online resources.

A classroom reading center.

such items; it never hurts to ask. If you do need to purchase something, be sure to ask for an educator discount. One teacher added a rocking chair that she found at a rummage sale. Another included an old bathtub she and her colleague cleaned up after finding it discarded. Plants can be an inexpensive way to enhance the tone of your reading center by making it appear less institutional and more home-like. A reading center can be used as a workstation for a small group of students engaged in SSR or when the rest of the class is involved in other tasks and activities. If the whole class is doing SSR at the same time, perhaps the opportunity to use the reading center can be rotated from row to row or table to table. Using the reading center can also be a reward for students who are working hard at a different time of the day.

Using a Classroom Library. After you have created a classroom library, you must also insure it is being used effectively. It is painful to see class-rooms with shelves of books that are rarely read. Make sure this does not happen in your classroom by providing a set reading time, displaying books, allowing for student choice, simplifying the check-out system, and avoiding required reports.

Regular time. One father and mother felt very successful when their oldest daughter fol-lowed their example and became an avid reader. Then along came their son who, despite the same example, was uninterested in reading. They filled his room with books, both narrative and informa-tional. They regularly read aloud to him, which he enjoyed, but he still had absolutely no interest in reading on his own. The parents considered pay-ing him for reading books since he was always motivated to earn money, but they knew that this motivation would probably not last long. Finally, they determined to send this third-grader to bed a little early. He complained, "But I'm not tired." "Then read," his father responded. "But I don't want to read," came the boy's answer. "Then sleep," the father replied. When the choice was play or read, reading lost. When the choice was watch TV or read, reading lost. But when the choice was sleep or read, reading occasionally won. Because of the regular time set aside for reading, it wasn't long before Dr. Seuss, the Berenstain Bears, and Mrs. Pigglewiggle worked their magic and the boy began to enjoy reading on his own.

In a similar way, you must provide a regular time—15 to 20 minutes—at school that is dedicated just to reading. If reading becomes a fast-finisher assignment, the ones who need the practice the most usually miss it. Make SSR part of the regular classroom rou-tine so that children know that at a certain time of day everyone reads. In upper grades it

| *Try This for Teaching* | **Readers in a Box** |

- Approach someone at a local furniture store and ask for large discarded boxes (such as those from refrigerators, freezers, or TVs).
- Paint and decorate the boxes to look like cars or homes, or just paint them with bright colors.
- Place the boxes in your reading center and allow students to sit inside them to read during SSR.
- Remind students to be careful because the boxes are not extremely sturdy.
- Link several boxes together to create a larger area.

- Put some cushions or pillows on the floor inside to make boxes more comfortable.

Variations for ELLs

- Ask students to help decorate the boxes. Consider international themes.
- Encourage ELLs to record themselves or read aloud quietly while sitting in the box. The cardboard walls help them avoid distractions and assure privacy.

can be a transition when the class returns from the computer lab or PE. In lower grades it might be a learning center to which some students rotate while the teacher works with small groups. The time of day matters little as long as it is regular, students can count on it, and everyone participates.

Book displays.   Along with time set aside for reading, students need to see books displayed. One teacher questioned, "Why is it that I can go into a library and walk out without a book, but I can't go into a bookstore without buying one?" Her answer was the book covers. In libraries she saw a lot of spines of books that did not call to her, but in bookstores she saw a lot of covers that did. She said, "I determined right then that I was going to make my classroom library more like a bookstore!"

Display book covers by turning books sideways on shelves, but also by spreading books on tables. It is not uncommon to see bulletin boards in elementary classrooms featuring such slogans as "Got hooked on books!" or "Read to succeed!" Rather than stapling book jackets around these words, put out actual books that children can pick, peruse, and carry to their desks. Book jackets can make a nice display, but the covers of real books can encourage reading.

English Language
Learners

| *Try This for Teaching* | **Rain Gutter Display** |

- Use the space under the whiteboard to display book covers.
- Locate a section of rain gutter that will fit in that space.
- Hang the gutter on the chalk tray or attach it to the wall.
- Display books that are inviting to your students.
- Paint the rain gutter a bright color.
- Use a length of wood molding instead of a rain gutter.
- If you lack the skills to mount this, enlist the help of a custodian, parent, or Boy Scout looking for a service project.

Variations for ELLs

- Display books from a variety of reading levels.
- Display books based on the interests of ELLs students.
- Include some books written in the students' first languages, if possible.
- Encourage students to talk about the books they finish and display them for others to read.

Struggling Learners/
RtI

Common Core
State Standards

Student choice.   When reading to and with students, you have more control over the titles. However, when students are reading by themselves, you should allow a lot of freedom for individual choice. One child may be re-reading the same book for the third time. Another might bring a comic book or graphic novel from home. Still another may be looking at a book about motorcycles that is way above his independent reading level because he loves the topic. During SSR don't be overly concerned about what the students are reading. Just be grateful they are enjoying books.

In discussion of text complexity, the Common Core stresses three factors that can help with text selection: quantitative, qualitative, and reader/task considerations. These are especially important when reading with children as a whole class or in small groups. During independent reading, these factors can be helpful to guide students toward appropriate text. However, self-selection of text according to student interests has been shown to have a more powerful impact on comprehension and recall than the readability of the text (Anderson, Hiebert, Scott, & Wilkinson, 1985). Reutzel and Cooter (1992) explained that practices such as self-selected reading "allow students to choose topics they find interesting and pleasurable. Choice promotes independence in learning, one of the ultimate goals of education" (p. 10). Your students may not be able to choose whether or not to read during SSR, but they should have a choice of what they are reading. Almost all young readers, regardless of age or gender, agree that their favorite books have been the ones they chose themselves (Lee, 2007; Scholastic, 2010). Walt Disney said that at one point or another everyone has been influenced by a book. In his case it was a book he chose on cartoon animation, which he discovered in a Kansas City library (Smith, 2001).

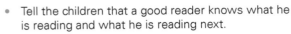

Try This for Teaching   **Two Books Are Better Than One**

- Tell the children that a good reader knows what he is reading and what he is reading next.
- Encourage them to always have two books at their desks.
- If they finish or tire of one book during SSR, they can turn to the next without disturbing others.
- Keep books in a bag or other container if you use tables instead of desks. Pockets can be

created that hang on the backs of classroom chairs.

Variations for ELLs

- With ELLs, you may encourage them to select three or four simpler books at a time.
- One book could be from the school library and one from the classroom library.

Simplified checkout.   Obviously students must be held accountable for books they borrow from a classroom library, but not to the point that checkout systems become complicated. Your classroom library is available only to your students. You know them; thus you have an advantage. You may need to actually write down the titles of books that are borrowed by some students, whereas you can give others more leeway. Similarly, you know that some books you have are more valuable than others. There may be some that you will not lend without a record. Others can be lent out more freely. If you do not allow students to take classroom books outside the classroom, you stand a better chance of not having books disappear. One teacher hung a chart paper on the wall and asked students to record their name, the date, and the titles of whatever books they took to their desks. Because the chart was big and visible to all, the children helped monitor each other. Students reminded each other to sign up if someone forgot. "This probably would not have happened had I tried to have cards in the back of the books or some sort of filing system that was not so easily accessed," this teacher recalled.

Alternative book reports.   One of the benefits of SSR is the motivation it can provide. You don't want to hurt that by requiring reading logs or reports for every book. Traditional book reports focusing on plot, characters, setting, and theme have done little to foster a love of reading through the years. They continue to be used because many teachers demand tangible evidence the child has read the book. However, students discover they can write such reports without having read the books, so the assignment usually does little to reach the goals of either teachers or students (Tunnell, Jacobs, Young, & Bryan, 2012).

Responses to literature and reading logs are helpful and appropriate when you read with students, but when they are reading independently such practices can sometimes block the very windows you are attempting to open for them. Similarly, keeping records of books completed or evaluating students on their participation can reduce the benefits of SSR (Pilgreen, 2000). When students are reading by themselves, you need to give them space just to enjoy the books. Adults don't have to do book reports on books they read for pleasure. They may share their excitement and passion for a book with friends and family, but they usually don't do that in the form of a report.

Teacher Support and Encouragement

Don't expect students to take SSR time seriously if you use the time to put up a bulletin board, grade papers, or leave the room to run an errand. Recreational reading may be an independent activity, but children need to be held accountable for using that time wisely. This can be done if the teacher models reading, interacts with students, and creates a lending library.

Teacher Modeling.   Applegate and Applegate (2004) reported that the reading habits of teachers significantly affected student engagement, achievement, and motivation in reading. Although most teachers value reading, only about half read for pleasure daily. But teachers who read more than 30 minutes per day use a greater number of recommended literacy practices in their teaching (McKool & Gespass, 2009; Morrison, Jacobs, & Swinyard, 1999). Children should not be expected to do what you do not do. Be sure you are reading yourself and occasionally let students see you reading, especially books they may have suggested to you. Regularly share insights and titles from your personal reading.

Speaking/Listening

One way to do this is through **book talks**, "brief teasers that teachers give to introduce students to particular books and interest them in reading" (Tompkins, 2010, p. 429). Like previews for upcoming films in a theater, book talks can create interest and motivation. One middle school teacher recalled, "I remember the day I showed a book [I was reading]. After I read a few samples, there was almost a riot when everyone in the class thought that he or she ought to be first to read it" (Jensen, 2001, p. 33). A book talk can include reading a few pages and giving a little background without revealing too much of the plot. Include your own personal response to the book and ask a few cliffhanger questions like "Will Rob be able to catch the murderer before he gets caught himself?" or "What can fly faster—a crow or a bat?"

Try This for Teaching **Book Talks**

- Show the book.
- Summarize it without giving away the ending.
- Read a short excerpt aloud to hook students' interest.
- Pass the book off to an interested reader or place it in the classroom library.
- Give your own personal response to the book.
- Introduce several books at once and make them available to students in a basket.
- Introduce books as a text set; for example, choose books that revolve around a similar theme, such as

Harriet Tubman and the Underground Railroad (Gambrell & Almasi, 1996).

- Ask some cliffhanger questions.

(Moss & Young, 2010)

Variations for ELLs

- Encourage students to use similar steps as they give book talks about what they are reading during SSR.
- Allow students to ask ELLs questions about their books. They must answer without giving away the ending.

English Language Learners

Interacting with Students. One way to help keep children on task during SSR is to interact with them. Sit next to a child and listen to him read. Ask about the book: why he decided to read it, and what page he expects to be on by the end of the week. Check back to see if he has reached his goal. The practice of having brief conferences is especially effective for students who are not always self-motivated. Kelley and Clausen-Grace (2008) have introduced R5, in which students read and relax, but then reflect, respond, and even rap about what they are reading. Bryan, Fawson, and Reutzel (2003) demonstrated that when teachers monitored students using short discussions and brief accountability conferences during SSR, the students actually spent their time reading.

Struggling Learners/ RtI

Lending Libraries. SSR has been shown to increase out-of-class leisure reading for some students (Chua, 2008). Others struggle making this transfer. One way you can help is by establishing a **lending library**. The defining feature of a lending library is that books children borrow are at an independent level for them. These books do not necessarily need to be read during SSR time. Some children feel embarrassed by reading books that are below the level of their peers. Although they may be willing to read them at home, they might not have access to leveled material there. Try sending books home with just a few students who need extra practice. Hold children accountable to return the books and then supply them with new ones. The exchange of books can happen during SSR time. The success children feel as they complete books and progress to higher levels may increase their motivation to keep reading, not to mention the value of building home-school connections that support and actually increase children's reading achievement and motivation at school (Morrow & Young, 1997; Sonnenschein & Schmidt, 2000).

Teacher interacting with student during SSR time.

Try This for Teaching   ## Scaffolded Silent Reading (ScSR)

- Identify students who have difficulty maintaining attention during SSR.
- Become familiar with their interests and abilities.
- Help them find an appropriate independent level text.
- Monitor them periodically by asking them questions about the text and encouraging them to continue reading.
- Hold them accountable by having them respond to you or to their peers.

(Reutzel, Jones, Fawson, & Smith, 2008)

Variations for ELLs

- Ask the students to read parts of the book orally to you.
- Have the students practice fluency by re-reading a part of the text three to five times with feedback from you.

Incentive Programs.   Read to earn a pizza. Read to get your name in a drawing for a bicycle. Read enough books to have a basketball player visit your school. Read so that your principal will shave his head, eat a worm, or kiss a pig. These are all incentives that schools use with results highlighted in newspaper articles or on TV news broadcasts. Although such incentives can be fun and entertaining, you need to consider carefully the potential benefits and risks of **incentive programs** before you employ them as a regular practice in your classroom. In some cases external rewards have been shown to actually hinder internal motivation (Fawson & Moore, 1999).

Extrinsic motivation is doing something (such as reading) in order to obtain recognition and rewards or to avoid a punishment. Goals focus on compliance and competition. You may see the amount of reading skyrocket momentarily but dwindle in the long term, doing little to encourage lifelong reading (Sweet & Guthrie, 1996). Intrinsic motivation refers to goals (such as reading an interesting book) that come from inside the reader, generated by personal hobbies and experiences. Students read because they are curious, they want to be involved and challenged, or they just want to enjoy themselves (Guthrie et al., 2009).

If you choose to become involved in incentive programs, it is better to track amount of time rather than number of pages or books (Fawson & Moore, 1999). It is also better to tally the total amount of time across a group rather than to showcase individual successes and failures. Gambrell and Marinak (2009) also suggested that if you want children to value books, then you should give them books or other literacy-related materials as

Struggling Learners/ RtI

Try This for Teaching   ## Lending Library

- Identify students who read at especially low levels.
- Tell the students that they may read anything they like during SSR time in class but that you want to lend them books written at their level to read at home.
- Clarify expectations that the books be taken care of and be returned on time.
- Establish a set time when students can discreetly return books and receive new ones.

Variations for ELLs

- Talk to the students about the books they have read.
- Encourage students to read the books aloud to parents or siblings.
- Have the students read the books to younger students at school.

Try This for Teaching — Genre Wheel

- Draw a circle on a piece of paper and divide it into sections like a pie.
- In each section, list a different genre of literature.
- For younger children, start with large sections divided into story, information, and poem.
- For older children, use smaller sections including autobiography, historical fiction, fantasy, folktales, mysteries, sports, and so on.
- Encourage children to read from a variety of genres and track the amount of time they spend in each.
- For every 30 minutes spent in a genre, have students mark off a section of the chart with a sticker or a star.
- Have students keep the individual wheels in their desks so they are private.

- Create a genre wheel for the class, tracking time spent in various genres.
- Use this class wheel to encourage wide writing as well as reading.

(Cope & Kalantzis, 1993)

Variations for ELLs

- Give each child a passport rather than a wheel. They can get stamps on their passport for "visiting" multicultural genres.
- Rather than genres, encourage students to visit literature from different countries or read authors from different cultures. Track this on a class map.

rewards instead of food or skateboards. Encourage wide reading across genres to stretch students out of their comfort zones.

Although many incentive programs are teacher generated, some are commercially sponsored and adopted by a school or a district (such as Accelerated Reader). These programs usually require students to read books and pass tests about their content on the computer. Books are leveled, and more points are given for longer and more difficult books. These programs often focus on principles of external rather than internal motivation, so be careful not to let them become too influential in your overall literacy efforts. One concern is that students' reading may be limited only to the books on the program's list. Another is that the test items used to evaluate students' knowledge of what they have read may focus on unimportant or trivial points in the book. Professors of children's literature have taken some of the tests for books they have read dozens of times and have not passed. They could not figure out what some of the questions were asking. Similarly, authors like Susan Fletcher and Roland Smith have taken the tests for their own books and only scored 80 percent (Tunnell, Jacobs, Young, & Bryan, 2012).

Whether the program is teacher made or commercial, such incentives are too often an attempt to make up for weak reading programs. If teachers are reading to and with students and allowing students to read by themselves, students see reading as a worthwhile act that is rewarding and empowering in and of itself. If teachers allow students time to read, write, and share along with their lessons, there is usually little need to supplement those authentic literacy activities.

Writing by Children

Just as children need time to read by themselves, they need time for independent writing. Graves (1996) has said that children must not merely be taught to write, but must come to love to write and need to write throughout their lives. He wrote, "If they do not see themselves as writers, chances are they won't use writing in their adult lives . . . to think, to clarify matters for themselves, to rediscover a sunset, to write letters to the editor" (p. 26). What do lifetime writers look like? Graves said they see the purpose of writing; they initiate writing, discover their voice, and can work well independently. Writing definitely prepares students to make a living in the future, and it also gives them the means to make a life.

Check yourself against these standards. Are you a lifelong writer? Many teachers see themselves as readers, but not as writers (Bowie, 1996). You do not have to be a published author to teach writing to children, but you need to be engaged in regular writing experiences (Morgan, 2010; Whitney, 2008). You can become and encourage students to become lifelong writers by using journals and technology.

Journals

Some teachers like to use such terms as *writer's notebook*, *daybook*, or *diary* to describe the place where students complete sustained silent writing. Journals do not have to be expensive or fancy. Children are content with a few bound pages or a simple notebook covered with contact paper. Diehn (2010) gives ideas on how children can make and bind their own journals.

Journals are excellent places for students to develop consistency, style, flow, and rhythm in their writing. Although they provide valuable practice, journals are a far cry from practice workbooks. Journals enable students to record the events of their lives for future generations. However, this is not their primary purpose either, since journals can be lost or destroyed. Journals provide an ideal environment in which to become a perfect place to think, feel, discover, and dream. Smith (1981) taught,

> Thoughts are created in the act of writing. [It is a myth that] you must have something to say in order to write. Reality: You often need to write in order to have anything to say. (p. 793)

Journal writing is validating; it reinforces the idea that each person is important. Each individual's experiences and feelings are valuable and worth recording. When we write our deepest feelings, we are better for having forced ourselves to face, organize, and express them. Calkins and Harwayne (1991) wrote, "We cannot give youngsters rich lives. But we can give them the lens to appreciate the richness that is already there in their lives" (p. 35). Most students find a journal inviting because it is a protected and unstructured place where they can afford to take a risk, experiment with ideas, and even make a mistake (Lickteig, 1981). This is especially important for English learners who have been shown to improve their writing skills if given the opportunity to write without feeling rushed within a safe environment (Foulger & Jimenez-Silvia, 2007). The pages of a journal invite students to share themselves—their real selves. Journals are safe places where conventions and mechanics are deemphasized and where personal hopes and dreams take center stage.

English Language Learners

On Saturday, June 20, 1942, a young Jewish girl, Anne Frank (1952), wrote the following in her journal:

> I haven't written for a few days, because I wanted first of all to think about my diary. It's an odd idea for someone like me to keep a diary; not only because I have never done so before, but because it seems that neither I—nor for that matter anyone else—will be interested in the unbosomings of a thirteen-year-old schoolgirl. Still, what does it matter? I want to write, but more than that. I want to bring out all the kinds of things that lie buried deep in my heart. (p. 2)

Child writing in her journal.

English Language
Learners

Anne never lived to know that she was wrong—many have eagerly read what she had written in her journal. But even if the journal had never been discovered or published, it still would have been worthwhile just for Anne's sake. Journals can be successful for your students if you reserve a set time of day for writing in them and if you allow choice of topic.

Regular Time.   Many students in the United States learn the Pledge of Allegiance. Teachers do not spend a lot of time on it and rarely discuss it, but students are successful with it because in most classrooms it happens every day. Even children learning English may not be able to say a lot of things, but they can say the Pledge of Allegiance. This is the pattern we need to follow with journal writing. Make your motto "A little bit every day is better than a lot in May." You can make journal writing a transition as children return from recess, or it can be an activity completed by some students while you work with others in small groups. When it happens matters less than that it happens consistently. You can't say, "If you finish your math, pull out your journal." The students who need the journal the most will never be given the time to write.

Most journal writing should happen at school, but students can also write at home. You can encourage children to keep a journal in both locations. Although much has been written about involving parents in supporting their children as readers (e.g., www.reading .org/InformationFor/Parents.aspx), much less information has been provided for supporting children's writing (Clay, 1987). Farris (1987) introduced the idea of bridging home and school through independent reading and writing.

Choice of Topic.   One of the most influential experiences that improves preservice teachers' attitudes and perceptions about writing is the opportunity to choose their

---

Try This for Teaching   **Traveling Tales**

(Reutzel & Fawson, 1990)

- Stock a backpack with an assortment of writing materials (construction paper, crayons, markers, notebooks).
- Write a letter to parents explaining the purpose and particulars of the writing expectation.
- Send the backpack and letter home with a different child each night.
- Alone or with the help of a parent, the child brainstorms a topic to write about and drafts a page to take back to school.
- At school have the child share her experience and her writing.

- Encourage other students to respond.

Variations for ELLs

- Send a stuffed animal home with the backpack. Students can write about the adventures of the stuffed animal as it goes from house to house and family to family.
- The writing does not always need to be personal narrative. Students could write lists, cards, poetry, descriptions, or opinions.
- If possible, have the parent letter translated into the first language of the home.

own topics (Morgan, 2010). The same privilege you desire is also sought by children. Fletcher (1996) compared a journal to a ditch that gathers all kinds of unexpected little critters. He wrote, "If you dig it, they will come. You'll be amazed by what you catch there" (p. 2). A journal is a place for independent writing. Assigned topics may be useful when working with students in whole class or small group writing experiences, but when students are writing by themselves, they should come up with their topics independently. If teachers constantly provide topics and prompts because they feel children are not ready to choose their own, when do children get ready to choose? Calkins (1983) called this cycle "writer's welfare." If you are always there with a topic, when does the student learn to take responsibility? One teacher told her fifth-graders, "I prefer that you choose your own topics, but if you really can't think of anything, come to me individually and I will give you a topic." Only three students in her class of almost 30 did *not* come and ask her for a topic. She realized she was making it too easy for them.

Another drawback with teacher-generated topics is that students view writing as an assignment that they can finish quickly. They hurriedly dash off several sentences in response to the prompt and declare, "I'm done!" By not offering a prompt, you are expecting them to be more thoughtful. They are not "done" until journal time is over.

Teach a few mini-lessons focused on what to write about. Students can create lists of ideas that might be worth pursuing individually or as a class. In the book *I'm in Charge of Celebrations* (Baylor, 1986), a girl says she knows when something is worth recording in her journal because her heart pounds and she feels like she is having to catch her breath. Sharing such examples with children helps them identify literary moments. But when all the lessons are taught, lists are made, and books read, it is up to the child to make the choice about what will go in his or her journal.

You will find that asking one or two children to share will often prime the pump for others better than anything else. One story always leads to another. If one child reads from her journal, "We went to Disneyland," there are usually other students anxious to share similar experiences. Rather than letting everyone share orally, tell the students to jot down three key words that will remind them of what they are thinking so they can write about it later. Similarly, if one student tells about a dream or a nightmare, have other students write three words about their own dreams or nightmares. Follow a similar pattern as children share about birthday celebrations, books they are reading, kind acts they have observed, or a most prized possession. For young children and those just learning English, three words may constitute an entire journal entry.

One danger with letting children write whatever they please is that they may write inappropriate or offensive entries. Rather than talking about right and wrong or good and bad, focus instead on "public" and "private." For example, you might say, "If you want to write about stuff like that, do it in private but not in public." Most teachers do not have time or even desire to read each child's journal entry every day. As long as children are using their journal time wisely and pages are getting filled, you do not have to be overly concerned about content. If you do choose to read journals, assure the children that their privacy will be respected. They can turn down the corner of a page or mark it in some way to let you know this writing is private. However, when children choose to share journal entries with you, in small groups, or with the whole class, their writing becomes public. They must be sensitive to their audience. When a child shares writing that includes violent, sexual, or abusive language, you need to ask him to sit down, and you may plan to preview what he wishes to share in the future. Before sending a journal home with students, include a disclaimer that says something like this: *This journal was not edited for content or conventions. It represents your child's thinking and private writing.*

English Language Learners

Speaking/Listening

Struggling Learners/ RtI

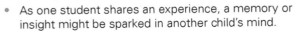

Try This for Teaching   **Three-Word Journal**

- As one student shares an experience, a memory or insight might be sparked in another child's mind.

- At such a moment, rather than have all students share orally, instruct them to write three words that capture what they are thinking.

- When writing in their journals, they may choose to expand on those three words and write about what they were thinking in more detail.

- When a child comes to tattle, tell him to go write at least three words about it in his journal, and you will read them there.

(Wright, 2010)

Variations for ELLs

- As a teacher, you could share your own journal entries to spark ideas.

- You could also share your three words after someone else has shared an idea.

- Use this technique in content areas by having students record three words that summarize a lesson, a video presentation, or a reading experience.

Try This for Professional Development   **Taking a Stand?**

Some teachers may want to implement SSR or journals but are discouraged to do so by principals or fellow teachers. Hall (2009) found in her study that 88 percent of preservice teachers indicated they were willing to compromise what they knew to be good literacy instruction in order to fit in with their future colleagues. When torn between their own beliefs and what was expected by their schools or districts, many yielded to the expectations of others.

- Consider the reasons that explain such findings.
- Reflect on the implications of these choices.
- What are some possible ways to handle such conflicts of interests?

Technology

New Literacies

Scholastic (2010) reported that 41 percent of parents surveyed are concerned that the time their children spend with electronic or digital devices negatively affects their literacy development. Although technology may be a stumbling block for some students, it can be a stepping stone for others, especially when it comes to independent writing. When you consider emails, blogs, tweets, Facebook, and text messaging, the writing possibilities are endless. Students are highly motivated to use the computer, Internet, iPads, smart phones, and other electronic devices. Extend this natural motivation by making such tools a part of learning at school. Some claim that writing in an online learning environment gives students more time to focus on a topic, shape ideas, and modify and refine their writing than they would have in traditional classroom settings (Peterson & Slotta, 2009). Such writing offers reluctant and otherwise disengaged students this opportunity to find a voice and feel successful, which they rarely do in more traditional school assignments (Levine, 2012).

In many elementary schools, teachers focus on basic skills such as keyboarding and using spell-checking software. But with this skill focus, the potential of the computer to enhance independent writing and provide a real audience has gone untapped. Prensky (2010) advised that teachers are sometimes hesitant to do more with computers because they feel inadequate, claiming that students know more than the teachers do. Although

English Language
Learners

Try This for Teaching   **Emails and Attachments**

- Teach students how to use online features to communicate with others.
- Have students begin by sending emails and attachments to you.
- Expand the audience to include peers, family members, and other trusted adults.
- Encourage students to improve the quality of their emails by proofreading and using online tools such as spell-check before sending messages.
- Stress the importance of composing at the computer.
- Remind students to be cautious about revealing

personal information online and to send email only to people they know.

(Valmont, 2003)

Variations for ELLs

- Introduce emoticons (;-}) or words in parentheses (ha ha!). Find a list at messenger.msn.com/Resource/Emoticons.aspx
- Teach children how to scan their own drawings or class work and share it as an attachment.
- Have older students work as computer buddies with younger students as they complete these tasks.

---

this is a real concern, resources are available that can help you (Richardson, 2010). Besides, it can be healthy for children to see that the teacher does not have to be the expert in all things and that learning is a socially constructed experience through which we can learn from one another. Some teachers have created class websites, others have created class blogs, and others have encouraged their students to make their own podcasts. If that feels overwhelming, a good place to begin is with sending emails and email attachments. Students can write to other students (sometimes called e-pals or web-pals), family members, and other adults as well as to you. Remember that if you are using this as independent writing, the receiver of the messages should be someone who will be understanding and tolerant of young students' initial attempts. If you plan to write to authors, political figures, or even the principal, that is best done *with* students so that their writing can be edited.

New Literacies

Summary

We learn to swim by swimming, and we learn to drive by driving. We learn to read and write by actually reading and writing. You must never become so focused on preparing students to be literate that you fail to let them be literate. One study showed that during 90 minutes of reading instruction, students actually read for only 18 minutes (Brenner, Tompkins, & Riley, 2007). Think of your own experience in preparing to become a teacher. Of course, there is a place for instruction in methods classes, but you also learn a great deal from observing models of good teaching, and most teachers are quick to recognize that they learn best when they are actually in real classrooms with real children. Sustained silent reading gives children the chance to really read with real books.

You can encourage SSR by using classroom libraries, providing teacher support and encouragement, sharing book talks, and using incentive programs thoughtfully. Just as children need the opportunity to read by themselves, they need chances to write by themselves. This independent writing can be done in journals and by using technology.

As students work independently, teachers sometimes feel like they are not teaching because they are not talking, directing, or standing in front. Don't be misled. As you allow time for your students to do and to share, occasionally taking your place as a coach and a guide, your students will gain confidence and their learning will improve both inside and outside of school.

Self-Check

1. What is the value of sustained silent reading?

2. How can you create a classroom library inexpensively?

3. Why is student choice so important in independent reading?

4. What is a book talk?

5. What are some concerns that have been raised about incentive programs?

6. Identify benefits of writing in a personal journal.

7. What should you do if children write something inappropriate in their journals?

8. How can you promote independent writing using technology?

MyEducationLab™

Go to the Topics, Comprehension, Writing, Organization and Management, and Media/Digital Literacy, in the MyEducationLab (www.myeducationlab.com) for your course, where you can:

- Find learning outcomes for Comprehension, Writing, Organization and Management, and Media/Digital Literacy, along with the national standards that connect to these outcomes.

- Complete Assignments and Activities that can help you more deeply understand the chapter content.

- Apply and practice your understanding of the core teaching skills identified in the chapter with the Building Teaching Skills and Dispositions learning units.

- Examine challenging situations and cases presented in the IRIS Center Resources.

- Check your comprehension on the content covered in the chapter by going to the Study Plan in the Book Resources for your text. Here you will be able to take a chapter quiz, receive feedback on your answers, and then access Review, Practice, and Enrichment activities to enhance your understanding of chapter content (optional).

- Visit **A+RISE** Standards2Strategy™, an innovative and interactive online resource that offers new teachers in grades K–12 just-in-time, research-based instructional strategies that meet the linguistic needs of ELLs as they learn content, differentiate instruction for all grades and abilities, and are aligned to Common Core Elementary Language Arts Standards (for the literacy strategies) and to English language proficiency standards in WIDA, Texas, California, and Florida.

Glossary

Academic words content or function words that are related to school subjects, tasks, and settings.

Accuracy identifying words correctly when reading.

Achievement gap disparity in scores on achievement tests among groups of students from different cultures, races/ethnicities, and income levels.

Aesthetic stance approaching text by paying attention to feelings, images, and emotions that are evoked by the text.

Aliteracy choosing not to read or write, although capable of doing so.

Alphabetic principle the concept that written letters represent speech sounds.

Analogical phonics an approach to phonics instruction in which word families are used to show letter/sound relationships.

Analytic phonics an approach to phonics instruction in which known words are presented first so that generalizations about sounds can be derived from them.

Analytic scoring a form of writing assessment in which scores are assigned to specific aspects of a paper so that strengths and weaknesses can be identified.

Anaphora words that serve as substitutes for other words in text.

Anecdotal notes a form of classroom assessment in which an observer records impressions for future reference.

Anthology a text associated with core literacy programs with many selections from which the whole class reads together.

Antonyms words that mean the opposite of one another.

Argumentative text a writing genre in which writers try to convince others to accept their arguments, agree with their facts, share their values, or adopt their way of thinking.

Audience individuals who have varying interests and expectations who read a particular piece of writing.

Author's craft how an author successfully touches readers' emotions and creates images in their minds.

Basic interpersonal communication skills (BICS) the ability of second language learners to converse in casual conversation and carry out many functions of everyday life using simple oral language.

Behaviorist movement the study of observed human behaviors.

Book talks brief introductions that teachers or students give to books in order to interest others in reading them.

Bottom-up theory a linear model of reading that proceeds from perceiving letters to understanding sentences.

Brainstorming method for generating creative ideas and solutions through informal group discussion.

Cause-and-effect text an expository text structure that attributes a result or an effect to one or more specific causes related to events, people, or ideas.

Choral reading a type of oral reading in which an entire group reads a text in unison.

Clarifying a metacognitive strategy that involves both identifying misunderstanding and taking action to correct it.

Clarity teacher behavior ensuring that presentations, expectations, and instructions are easy to understand and simple to follow.

Cliché a trite or overused expression.

Cloze procedure a test for measuring reading ability in which words are deleted from a passage and the reader is required to fill in the blanks.

Cognitive academic language proficiency (CALP) those language abilities required for second language learners to succeed with the demands of academic learning in schools.

Common Core State Standards expectations for English/Language Arts learning that are similar in almost all U.S. states.

Comparison text an expository text structure that compares and contrasts information by explaining how something is alike or different from something else.

Compensation when one information source in the reading process is weaker; the strengths of the others can make up the difference.

Composing discovering ideas and shaping and organizing them in order to make meaning.

Comprehension understanding intended communication; a complex meaning-making process that is influenced by an author, the reader, and the contexts surrounding both.

Comprehension strategies procedures that can be taught to encourage engaged and proficient reading controlled by the reader.

Concept an idea or abstract principle.

Conclusion a decision that something is true, which you make after careful thought and consideration of relevant facts.

Conference a one-on-one conversation between a teacher and student or between peers about a student's literacy.

Connections relating two associated ideas or concepts outside or within text.

Constructivist movement a theory of knowledge that humans create understanding and meaning based on their experiences and ideas.

Content areas subject areas apart from the language arts such as science, mathematics, social studies, art, music, and health.

Content words words that carry meaning, like nouns, verbs, and adjectives.

Conventions the accepted practices or guidelines used in written language that allow authors to communicate clearly and enable readers to understand.

Core literacy programs published comprehensive classroom literacy programs that include daily plans for teaching; also called basals.

Criterion-referenced test a type of evaluation in which individual raw scores are compared with a specific standard or expectation.

Critical stance approaching text by evaluating authors' words and analyzing the support given for their positions.

Cueing systems aspects of oral language development that relate to literacy development (phonics, semantics, and syntax).

Cultural capital the knowledge, accomplishments, and qualifications that an individual has within a given social circle.

Culture the network of practices, beliefs, values, customs, ideas, attitudes, language, and ceremonies unique to a specific group of people.

Descriptive text an expository text structure that explains a topic or an idea by giving details about its characteristics and attributes.

Developmental journal a personal journal in which children can draw as well as explore print.

Dictation the process in which a lead writer writes exactly what someone says or reads.

Drafting putting prepared thoughts and ideas together and getting them on paper.

Eclectic instruction emphasizing both alphabetic and whole word methods.

Editing making sure the mechanics of writing are correct and will not distract readers from the message.

Efferent stance approaching text by focusing on the meaning or information in a text.

Elements of reading five areas central to the teaching of reading as outlined by the National Reading Panel.

Elocution speaking clearly with a conventional accent.

Emergent literacy the perspective that young children develop as readers and writers through a gradual process.

Engagement students' on-task behavior and involvement.

English language learners (ELLs) those who acquire the English language in addition to their first language.

Euphemism a word that softens harsh or distasteful language, such as *elderly* for *old* or *sanitation engineer* for *garbage collector*.

Evaluation (as a higher-level cognitive process) making informed judgments.

Explicit instruction a "tell and show" method of teaching in which the explanation is provided first, followed by examples, checking, and practice.

Expository text a type of writing that informs, describes, explains, or defines the author's subject.

Expression (prosody) reading orally with appropriate volume, pacing, smoothness, and phrasing.

Extrinsic motivation external forces that cause people to work on a task even if they have little interest in it because of the anticipated reward they may receive.

Fluency reading with appropriate rate, accuracy, and expression while maintaining comprehension.

Formal language the type of expression used in serious settings.

Formative assessment evaluating students as part of the developmental or ongoing teaching/learning process.

Forms of writing different types of poetry (such as limericks and haiku), different types of stories (such as mysteries and fables), and different types of informational text (such as essays and directions).

Formula writing providing children with specific steps or structures to follow.

Frustrational reading level a student reads fewer than 90 percent of the words correctly and finds it difficult to understand the text.

Function words words that are not meaningful by themselves but give structure to language.

Genre writing multiple opportunities for writing across various genres following model texts.

Genres of writing writing that is categorized as poetry or prose, which includes fictional and informational text.

Grade equivalent score a converted score from a standardized test that attempts to predict how well a student would perform on a test.

Gradual release of responsibility a model of instruction that includes reading and writing to, with, and by students.

Grammar the way words can be arranged to make meaning.

Graphic aids visual elements in text that summarize the information, making it easy to comprehend (such as tables, diagrams, and maps).

Graphic organizers visual representations (webs, charts, graphs, maps, clusters, or frames) for information presented in text that help students make sense of what they are reading.

Guided reading a type of small group reading instruction in which students read text appropriate to their level with teacher assistance.

High frequency words words that appear most commonly in books read by children.

Holistic scoring a form of assessment that involves assigning a single overall score to represent a piece of writing.

Homographs words with different meanings that are spelled the same but pronounced differently (read, read).

Homophones words with different meanings that are pronounced the same but spelled differently (their, they're, there).

Hornbook a small paddle with a sheet of paper placed beneath a thin piece of clear horn from an animal used in the past to teach beginning reading.

Idea (in writing) the author's main message that includes plans, beliefs, or possible courses of action.

Idiom a group of words that have a different meaning when used together from the one they would have if you considered the meaning of each word separately.

Illiteracy the inability to read and write.

Implicit instruction a "show and tell" method of teaching in which an example or model is given before the explanation.

Incentive programs use of external and unrelated rewards to motivate literacy.

Independent reading level ability to read the vast majority of the words accurately, comprehend the text, and independently solve problems while reading.

Inference ideas not directly expressed in text.

Informal language the type of expression used in friendly settings.

Informal reading inventory an assessment tool that involves students reading orally as teachers listen, record errors, and check for comprehension.

Informational text text that is written to set forth ideas or explain (also called expository text).

Initial teaching alphabet (ITA) an English language writing system with 44 symbols that match exactly with 44 speech sounds.

Instructional reading level ability to read 90–94 percent of the words accurately but may need assistance or guidance.

Interactive theory a theory of information processing that proposes the notion of parallel processing—multiple information sources used simultaneously to create meaning.

Interactive writing teachers and students take turns writing letters and words in a text composed together.

International Reading Association Standards guidelines developed by a professional organization that outline the content of literacy instruction.

Intertextuality understanding relationships that exist between different texts.

Intrinsic motivation internal forces that cause people to work on a task because of the challenge, satisfaction, or pleasure that comes from the task itself.

Invented spelling an attempt to spell a word based on the writer's knowledge of sounds and symbols (also known as temporary spelling, phonics spelling, or sound spelling).

Knowledge mobilization activating relevant schema prior to reading.

Language arts listening, speaking, reading, and writing; viewing and presenting.

Language experience approach (LEA) a form of dictation in which students speak and the teacher writes, based on a shared or common experience.

Lead reader someone who can read aloud fluently while others follow in the text.

Lead writer someone who writes during a shared writing experience and can decide to accept or respect the suggestions offered by others.

Learning disability an auditory, visual, neurological, or perceptual disability that interferes with a child's ability to learn.

Learning log a journal or notebook in which students reflect on readings, lessons, class experiences, or learning.

Lending library a collection of books that children borrow that are at an independent level for them.

Literature discussion groups small temporary groups of students who meet with or without a teacher to read and discuss the same story, poem, article, or book (also called literature circles, book clubs).

Literature units authentic literature used for directed and in-depth reading instruction.

Main idea the most important thought in text.

Mechanics a convention of writing that deals primarily with capitalization and punctuation.

Memoir narrative written from the personal experiences of an author.

Mental imagery (visualization) mental representations of physical objects or events that are not present.

Metacognition readers monitoring their understanding of what they read by thinking about their own thinking.

Mini-lessons intense instructional sessions that usually do not go beyond 10 to 15 minutes.

Miscues any departure from the text that a reader makes during oral reading.

Mnemonic devices learning techniques that aid memory.

Motivation the forces that arouse and direct human behavior.

Multiple meaning words words that have different meanings in different contexts (e.g., run).

Narrative text a story, real or pretend.

New literacies new forms of literacy made possible by digital technology developments.

Norm-referenced test a type of evaluation in which scores for individuals and groups are compared with the average score obtained from a sample of the target population.

Onomatopoeia words that sound like the noise they name (buzz, thump, and snap).

Open-ended questions questions that have several possible appropriate answers.

Organizational aids text elements that help readers quickly locate important information, such as headings, bullets, and captions.

Organized writing presenting ideas in smooth, clear, and reasonable ways.

Overgeneralization understanding a principle of language acquisition and then generalizing it to other settings where it does not apply.

Percentile score a score from a standardized test that tells what percentage of scores are at or below a given raw score.

Performance-based assessment the process of measuring students' achievement by evaluating their performance with hands-on tasks (also called authentic assessment).

Phoneme the smallest sound unit in a word.

Phonemic awareness noticing minimal sound units of speech.

Phonics sound-symbol relationships and factors that influence them that are important in reading and spelling.

Phonics generalizations statements of rules that explain why a letter or combination of letters represents individual sounds or patterns of sounds.

Phonological awareness noticing both minimal units of speech sounds and combinations of those sounds into larger units.

Phonology the sound system of language.

Plagiarism intentionally copying someone else's work without permission or failing to give credit for using someone's ideas.

Poetry the art of vivid, rhythmical, and often melodic composition, written or spoken, to create beautiful, imaginative, or elevated thoughts.

Point of view standpoint from which a speaker or writer relates a narrative or presents information.

Portfolio an assessment in which a student collects and displays assorted materials that have been gathered or produced.

Poverty meager amounts of earned income opportunities and access to benefits.

Pragmatics how language is used appropriately in specific situations.

Predicate the part of the sentence that tells about the subject and usually includes the verb.

Prediction a guess about what will happen in the future based on knowledge of what has happened in the past.

Prereading getting ready to read by building background knowledge, making predictions, clarifying a purpose, and making plans and goals.

Presentation (in writing) how the writing appears on the page for others to access.

Prewriting gathering and experimenting with ideas and materials before drafting a piece of writing.

Primary source material that has been recorded firsthand by participants or in-person observations.

Primer an instructional tool for teaching reading to emerging and beginning readers.

Print concepts basic features of written language such as identifying the front and back of a book, directionality, and spoken and written language matching.

Print features aspects of text that guide readers and expand their understanding (such as a table of contents, index, and glossary).

Problem-and-solution text an expository text structure that describes how a problem or multiple problems can be solved.

Procedures the way of doing something, usually explained in steps.

Prose the ordinary form of spoken or written language, without the structures of poetry or verse.

Publishing disseminating writing to an audience.

Pun a witty and humorous use of a word or phrase with two meanings.

Qualitative assessment a type of evaluation in which in-depth information is provided through interviews and observations.

Quantitative assessment a type of evaluation that emphasizes numerical scores obtained from tests or ratings.

Question-answer relationships (QAR)　a taxonomy that examines questions, answers, and the text to which they relate.

Questioning the author (QtA)　a process in which readers deliberately inquire about the content they read, keeping in mind the author's intent and effectiveness.

Rate　the speed of reading.

Readability formula　a quantitative method used to estimate the reading demands of a text.

Read-alouds　reading text to others.

Reading stamina　the ability to read for long periods without becoming distracted or distracting others.

Realia　actual concrete objects that can be used to build background knowledge.

Reciprocal teaching　a classroom activity in which a teacher and students take turns leading a discussion using four cognitive strategies: summarizing, question asking, clarifying, and predicting.

Research　studying a topic and trying to find out more about it.

Response　a thoughtful evaluation of text that goes beyond summarizing to personalizing.

Response to intervention (RtI)　teachers making decisions based on data, including screening students to identify needs, organizing classrooms to allow for differentiated instruction, and monitoring progress.

Revising　making changes to improve the content and presentation of thoughts or writing.

Round-robin reading　a type of oral reading in which the teacher asks students to take turns orally reading unrehearsed sections of text while others in the group follow along silently.

Rubrics　guidelines for rating student performances.

Running record　an assessment tool that involves students reading orally as the teacher listens and records errors.

Rural　a small community that is at least five miles from an urbanized center.

Scanning　a type of reading in which the reader searches visually over a page to locate a specific date, key word, or answer.

Schema theory　how people store, access, and retrieve information in their minds to make sense of what they experience; an attempt to understand our flexible and growing mental frameworks.

Secondary source　information that was originally presented elsewhere shared by someone reporting the knowledge and experience of others.

Self-regulated strategy development　a model for supporting students as they compose narrative, expository, and persuasive text.

Semantics　how words represent meaning.

Semiotics　the study of relationships between language and other symbols to their meanings.

Sentence　one or more words that express a complete thought.

Sentence fluency　(in writing) presenting ideas with a natural flow.

Sequential text　an expository text structure that lists items or gives a chronological or numerical order.

Shared reading　a type of oral reading in which the whole class follows in the text while a lead reader reads.

Shared writing　a process in which teachers and students work together to write a collective text.

Sheltered instruction　teachers adjusting how much they teach vocabulary, connect content to students' prior knowledge, and use visuals and real objects to help English learners acquire the content of the curriculum while learning English.

Sight words　(1) words that are read automatically, whether or not they follow a phonics generalization or a pattern; (2) words that do not follow a single phonics generalization, do not contain a common word family, and must be taught as individual whole words.

Silent period　the time when learners do not speak much as they acquire a second language.

6 + 1 Traits　an analytical model for assessing and teaching specific aspects of writing.

Skills　cognitive processes that have become or should become automatic.

Skimming　a type of reading to quickly gather main ideas by overlooking details.

Small group reading　an activity in which students read and discuss a common text with or without teacher support.

Stance　personal attitudes, feelings, or positions of a reader or writer.

Stanine score　a specific nine-point scale used to represent raw scores for a standardized test.

Story maps　visual representations of the important elements in simple stories.

Strategies　cognitive processes that require attention and are completed consciously.

Study guides　aids created by teachers in advance to focus children on the main points of the reading and make sure they have captured the essence of the material.

Subject　the part of the sentence that does something or is being talked about.

Success rate　controlling the level of difficulty at which material is presented so that learners can experience success.

Summarize　using the related skills of determining what is important and organizing ideas, events, or concepts in order to compose a brief statement about the reading.

Summative assessment the process of evaluating (and grading) the learning of students at a specific point in time.

Sustained silent reading (SSR) a designated daily time when each student reads self-selected material without or with limited teacher involvement (also known as self-selected reading or independent reading).

Syllable a unit of spoken language that is larger than a speech sound and consists of one or more vowel sounds alone or of a combination of vowel and consonant sounds.

Synonyms words with similar meanings.

Syntax how words can be arranged in appropriate sequences to express meaning.

Synthesis the process of taking old parts and making a new whole.

Synthesize combining information from a variety of sources to draw conclusions and create new insights.

Synthetic phonics an approach to phonics instruction in which each sound in a word is segmented and then blended to pronounce the word.

Task orientation being goal oriented and achievement oriented.

Text complexity a three-part model for examining texts proposed by the Common Core that includes quantitative data, qualitative information, and reader and task considerations.

Text leveling a method of determining the relative position or rank of a book on a scale.

Text sets collections of the same books or related books for literacy instruction.

Text structure the organization of the writing in a text to meet different purposes.

Thematic units organized instruction around a central concept or theme (such as journeys, discoveries, or courage).

Title I a federal program that provides financial assistance to school districts with high percentages of students from low-income families.

Top-down theory a linear model of reading that begins with meaning-making processes such as using semantic and syntactic information and only later employs visual information like association of letters and sounds.

Transcription making a written record of dictated material.

Urban describing a community with a population of over 250,000.

Variety variability and flexibility during teaching.

Vocabulary understanding the meanings of words.

Voice expressing ideas and feelings honestly and in personal ways.

Wait time pauses during questioning to allow for more thoughtful responses and greater interaction, both after asking a question and after a student responds.

Word bank a list of words compiled by children and teachers on any given subject.

Word choice (in writing) using carefully selected words such as specific nouns, vibrant verbs, and rich adjectives.

Word consciousness children's awareness of and attention to words.

Word family a vowel sound followed by one or more consonant sounds creating a consistent pattern (also referred to as a rime, analogy, chunk, or phonogram).

Word wall an alphabetical listing of selected words that is large enough for students to see from anywhere in the classroom.

Words summary symbols with meanings agreed on by a society or group.

Workshop format an instructional format in which students learn reading or writing skills and strategies while engaged in authentic literacy activities with opportunities to share their experience with others.

Writer's notebook a place for writers to record their observations and ideas (also called a daybook, diary, or journal).

Writing frame a structure or a textual outline that gives students a starting point for their writing.

Writing process writing a text by prewriting, drafting, seeking a response, revising, editing, and publishing.

References

Ada, A. F., Campoy, F. I., & Shertle, A. (2003). *Pio peep!: Traditional Spanish nursery rhymes*. New York, NY: Rayo.

Adams, M. J. (1992). *Beginning reading: Thinking and learning about print*. Cambridge, MA: MIT Press.

Adams, M. J., Foorman, B., Lundberg, I., & Beeler, T. (2003). *Phonemic awareness in young children: A classroom curriculum*. Baltimore, MD: Brookes.

Afflerbach, P., Pearson, P. D., & Paris, S. G. (2008). Clarifying differences between reading skills and reading strategies. *The Reading Teacher, 61*, 364–373.

Alderman, G. L., & Green, S. K. (2011). Fostering lifelong spellers through meaningful experiences. *The Reading Teacher, 64*, 599–605.

Alexander, K. L., Entwisle, D. R., & Olson, L. S. (2011). Schools, achievement, and inequality: A seasonal perspective. *Educational Evaluation and Policy Analysis, 23*, 171–191.

Allen, J. (1999). *Words, words, words: Teaching vocabulary in grade 4–12*. Portland, ME: Stenhouse.

Allington, R. L. (1977). If they don't read much, how they ever gonna get good? *Journal of Reading, 21*, 57–61.

Allington, R. L. (1983a). Fluency: The neglected reading goal. *The Reading Teacher, 36*, 556–561.

Allington, R. L. (1983b). The reading instruction provided readers of differing reading ability. *Elementary School Journal, 83*, 255–265.

Allington, R. L. (1998). *Teaching struggling readers: Articles from The Reading Teacher*. Newark, DE: International Reading Association.

Allington, R. L. (2001). *What really matters for struggling readers: Designing research based programs*. New York, NY: Addison Wesley Longman.

Allington, R. L. (2002a). *Big brother and the national reading curriculum: How ideology trumped evidence*. Portsmouth, NH: Heinemann.

Allington, R. L. (2002b). What I've learned about effective reading instruction from a decade of studying exemplary elementary classroom teachers. *Phi Delta Kappan, 83*, 740–747.

Almaguer, I. (2005). Effects of dyad reading instruction on the reading achievement of Hispanic third-grade English language learners. *Bilingual Research Journal, 29*, 509–526.

Amberg, J. S., & Vause, D. J. (2009). *American English: History, structure, and usage*. Cambridge, England: Cambridge University Press.

Anderson, C. (2005). *Assessing writers*. Portsmouth, NH: Heinemann.

Anderson, D. H., Nelson, J. P., Richardson, M. J., Webb, N., & Young, E. L. (2011). Using dialogue journals to strengthen the student-teacher relationship: A comparative case study. *College Student Journal, 45*(2), 269–287.

Anderson, R. C., & Freebody, P. (1981). Vocabulary knowledge. In J. Guthrie (Ed.), *Comprehension and teaching: Research reviews* (pp. 77–117). Newark, DE: International Reading Association.

Anderson, R. C., & Nagy, W. E. (1991). Word meanings. In R. Barr, M. L. Kamil, P. Mosenthal, & P. D. Pearson (Eds.), *Handbook of reading research* (Vol. 2, pp. 690–724). Mahwah, NJ: Lawrence Erlbaum.

Anderson, R. C., & Pearson, P. D. (1984). A schema-theoretic view of basic processes in reading. In P. D. Pearson, R. Barr, M. L. Kamil, & P. Mosenthal (Eds.), *Handbook of reading research* (pp. 255–291). New York, NY: Longman.

Anderson, R. C., Hiebert, E. H., Scott, J. A., & Wilkinson, I. A. G. (1985). *Becoming a nation of readers: The report of the Commission on Reading*. Washington, DC: National Institute of Education.

Anderson, R. C., Wilson, P. T., & Fielding, L. G. (1988). Growth in reading and how children spend their time outside of school. *Reading Research Quarterly, 23*, 285–303.

Anderson, T. H. (1984). Study strategies and adjunct aids. In R. J. Spiro, B. C. Bruce, & W. F. Brewer (Eds.), *Theoretical issues in reading comprehension: Perspectives from cognitive psychology, linguistics, artificial intelligence, and education* (pp. 483–502). Hillsdale, NJ: Lawrence Erlbaum.

Applebee, A. N., & Langer, J. A. (2006). *The state of writing instruction in America's schools: What existing data tell us*. Albany, NY: State University of New York Center on English Learning & Achievement.

Applegate, A. J., & Applegate, M. D. (2004). The rater effect: Reading habits and attitudes of preservice teachers. *The Reading Teacher, 57*, 554–563.

Armbruster, B. B, Lehr, F., & Osborn, J. (2001). *Put reading first: The research building blocks for teaching children to read*. Washington, DC: National Institute for Literacy.

Ash, G. W., Kuhn, M. R., & Walpole, S. (2009). Analyzing inconsistencies in practice: Teachers' continued use of round robin reading. *Reading and Writing Quarterly, 25*, 87–103.

Ashton-Warner, S. (1963). *Teacher*. New York, NY: Touchstone.

Atwell, N. (1987). *In the middle: Writing, reading and learning with adolescents*. Portsmouth, NH: Heinemann.

Atwell, N. (1998). *In the middle: New understandings about reading and writing with adolescents* (2nd ed.). Upper Montclair, NJ: Boynton/Cook.

Atwell, N. (2007). *The reading zone: How to help kids become skilled, passionate, habitual, critical readers*. New York, NY: Scholastic Teaching Resources.

Au, K. H. (2000). Literacy instruction for young children of diverse backgrounds. In D. S. Strickland & L. M. Morrow (Eds.), *Beginning reading and writing* (pp. 35–45). New York, NY: Teachers College Press.

Au, K. H. (2006). *Multicultural issues and literacy achievement*, Mahwah, NJ: Erlbaum.

Au, K. H., Hirata, S. Y., & Raphael, T. E. (2005). Improving literacy achievement through standards. *California Reader, 39*(1), 5–10.

Audet, R. H., Hickman, P., & Dobrynina, G. (1996). Learning logs: A classroom practice for enhancing scientific sense making. *Journal of Research in Science Teaching, 33*(2), 205–222.

August, D., & Shanahan, T. (Eds.). (2006). *Developing literacy in second-language learners: Report of the National Literacy Panel on Language-Minority Children and Youth*. Mahwah, NJ: Lawrence Erlbaum.

Babbitt, N. (1975). *Tuck everlasting*. New York, NY: Farrar, Strauss, & Giroux.

Baker, E. A., Rozendal, M. S., & Whitenack, J. W. (2000). Audience awareness in a technology-rich elementary classroom. *Journal of Literacy Research, 32*, 395–419.

Baker, R. (2003). *In a word: 750 words and their fascinating stories and origins*. Petersborough, NH: Cobblestone.

Balfanz, R., & Byrnes, V. (2006). Closing the mathematics achievement gap in high poverty middle schools: Enablers and constraints. *Journal of Education for Students Placed at Risk, 11*, 143–159.

Balfanz, R., Herzog, L., & MacIver, D. J. (2007). Preventing student disengagement and keeping students on the graduation path in urban middle-grades schools: Early identification and effective interventions. *Educational Psychologist, 42*(4), 223–235.

Banks, L. R. (1980). *The Indian in the Cupboard*. Garden City, NY: Doubleday.

Barchers, S. (1988, October). 75 ways to share a book. *Learning, 33*.

Barton, K. C. (2001). A picture's worth: Analyzing historical photographs in the elementary grades. *Social Education, 65*(5), 278–283.

Base, G. (1996). *Animalia*. New York, NY: Harry N. Abrams.

Baslaw-Finger, A. (1993, November). Message in a starry sky. *Reader's Digest*, 137–141.

Batsche, G., Elliot, J., Graden, J. L., Grimes, J., Kovaleski, J. F., Prasse, D., ... Tilly, W. D. (2005). *Response to intervention: Policy considerations and implementation*. Alexandria, VA: National Association of State Directors of Special Education.

Battistich, V., Solomon, D., & Delucchi, K. (1993). Interaction processes and student outcomes in cooperative learning groups. *Elementary School Journal, 94*(1), 19–32.

Baumann, J. F., & Kameenui, E. J. (1991). Research on vocabulary instruction: Ode to Voltaire. In J. Flood, J. M. Jensen, D. Lapp, & J. R. Squire (Eds.), *Handbook of research on teaching the English language arts* (pp. 604–631). New York, NY: Macmillan.

Baumann, J. F., Jones, L. A., & Seifert-Kessell, N. (1993). Using think-alouds to enhance children's comprehension monitoring abilities. *The Reading Teacher, 47*, 184–193.

Baylor, B. (1986). *I'm in charge of celebrations*. New York, NY: Macmillan.

Beach, J. K. (2003). *Names for snow*. New York, NY: Hyperion.

Bear, D. R., Invernizzi, M., Templeton, S. R., & Johnston, F. R. (2011). *Words their way: Word study for phonics, vocabulary, and spelling instruction* (5th ed.). Boston, MA: Allyn & Bacon.

Beaver, J. (2006). *The developmental reading assessment* (2nd ed.). Lebanon, IN: Pearson.

Beck, I. L., & McKeown, M. G. (2001). Text talk: Capturing the benefits of read-aloud experiences for young children. *The Reading Teacher, 55*, 10–20.

Beck, I. L., & McKeown, M. G. (2006). *Improving comprehension with questioning the author: A fresh and expanded view of a powerful approach*. New York, NY: Scholastic.

Beck, I. L., McKeown, M. G., & Kucan, L. (2002). *Bringing words to life: Robust vocabulary instruction*. New York, NY: Guilford.

Beck, I. L., McKeown, M. G., & McCaslin, E. S. (1983). Vocabulary development: Not all contexts are created equal. *The Elementary School Journal, 83*(3), 177–181.

Beck, I. L., Perfetti, C. A., & McKeown, M. G. (1982). Effects of long-term vocabulary instruction on lexical access and reading comprehension. *Journal of Educational Psychology, 74*, 506–521.

Beers, K. (2002). *When kids can't read: What teachers can do; A guide for teachers 6–12*. Portsmouth, NH: Heinemann.

Benchmark Education Company. (2003–2005). Retrieved from www.benchmarkeducation.com

Bergenske, M. D. (1988). Sloppy copy to glory story. *The Reading Teacher, 41*(4), 489–490.

Bernhardt, E. B., & Kamil, M. L. (1995). Interpreting relationships between L1 and L2 reading: Consolidating the linguistic threshold and the linguistic interdependence hypotheses. *Applied Linguistics, 16*, 15–34.

Biancarosa, G., & Snow, C. E. (2004). *Reading next: A vision for action and research for middle and high school literacy*. Washington, DC: Alliance for Excellent Education.

Billen, M. T., Wilcox, B., Bahr, D., Shumway, J., Korth, B., Yates, E., ... Pierce, L. E. (2011). Instruction and physical environments that support process writing in elementary classrooms. In T. G. Morrison, S. Szabo, L. Marin, & M. L. Boggs (Eds.). Literacy promises. In *Yearbook of the Association of Literacy Educators and Researchers* (Vol. 33, pp. 101–116). Commerce, TX: Texas A & M University-Commerce Press.

Bintz, W. P. (2010). Singing across the curriculum. *The Reading Teacher, 63*, 683–686.

Blachowicz, C., & Fisher, P. J. (2009). *Teaching vocabulary in all classrooms* (4th ed.). Boston, MA: Allyn & Bacon.

Blachowicz, C., & Ogle, D. (2008). *Reading comprehension: Strategies for independent learners* (2nd ed.). New York, NY: Guilford.

Blachowicz, C. Z. (1985). Vocabulary development and reading: From research to instruction. *The Reading Teacher, 38*, 876–881.

Blachowicz, C. Z., & Fisher, P. (2000). Vocabulary instruction. In M. L. Kamil, P. B. Mosenthal, P. D. Pearson, & R. Barr (Eds.), *Handbook of reading research* (Vol. 3, pp. 503–523). Mahwah, NJ: Lawrence Erlbaum.

Black, P., & Wiliam, D. (2006). Developing a theory of formative assessment. In J. Gardner (Ed.), *Assessment and learning* (pp. 81–100). London, England: Sage.

Black, P., & Wiliam, D. (2009). Developing the theory of formative assessment. *Educational Assessment, Evaluation and Accountability, 21*, 5–31.

Black, P., Harrison, C., Lee, C., Marshall, B., & Wiliam, D. (2002). *Working inside the black box: Assessment for learning in the classroom*. London, England: GL Assessment.

Black, P., Harrison, C., Lee, C., Marshall, B., & Wiliam, D. (2003). *Assessment for learning: Putting it into practice*. Berkshire, England: Open University Press.

Blevins, W. (2002). *Building fluency: Lessons and strategies for reading success*. New York, NY: Scholastic.

Block, C. C., & Parris, S. R. (Eds.). (2008). *Comprehension instruction: Research-based best practices* (2nd ed.). New York, NY: Guilford.

Block, C. C., Parris, S. R., & Whiteley, C. S. (2008). CPMs: A kinesthetic comprehension strategy. *The Reading Teacher, 61*, 460–470.

Bloom, B. S. (1956). *Taxonomy of educational objectives*. New York, NY: David McKay.

Bloomfield, L. (1942). Linguistics and reading. *Elementary English Review, 19*, 125–130, 183–186.

Blume, J. (2010). *Are you there God? It's me, Margaret*. New York, NY: Delacorte.

Bode, B. A. (1989). Dialogue journal writing. *The Reading Teacher, 42*, 568–571.

Bond, G. L., & Dykstra, R. (1967). The cooperative research program in first grade reading instruction. *Reading Research Quarterly, 2*(4), 5–142.

Borich, G. D. (2006). *Effective teaching methods* (6th ed.). Upper Saddle River, NJ: Pearson Merrill Prentice Hall.

Bos, C., Mather, N., Dickson, S., Podhajski, B., & Chard, D. (2001). Perceptions and knowledge of preservice and inservice educators about early reading instruction. *Annals of Dyslexia, 51*, 97–120.

Bos, C. S., & Vaughn, S. (1998). *Strategies for teaching students with learning and behavior problems*. Boston, MA: Allyn & Bacon.

Boscolo, P., & Gelati, C. (2007). Best practices in promoting motivation for writing. In S. Graham, C. A. MacArthur, & J. Fitzgerald (Eds.), *Best practices in writing instruction* (pp. 202–221). New York, NY: Gilford Press.

Bosse, M. J., & Faulconer, J. (2008). Learning and assessing mathematics through reading and writing. *School Science and Mathematics, 108*, 8–19.

Boushey, G., & Moser, J. (2006). *The daily five*. Portland, ME: Stenhouse.

Boushey, G., & Moser, J. (2009). *The CAFÉ book: Engaging all students in daily literary assessment and instruction*. Portland, ME: Stenhouse.

Bowie, R. (1996). *Future teachers' perceptions of themselves as writers and teachers of writing: Implications for teacher education programs*. Paper presented at the annual meeting of the College Reading Association, Charleston, SC.

Bradby, M. (1995). *More than anything else*. New York, NY: Scholastic/Orchard.

Brande, D. (2011). *Dorthea Brande quotes*. Retrieved from www .brainyquote.com/quotes/authors/d/dorthea_brande.html

Brandt, D. (2001). *Literacy in American lives*. New York, NY: Cambridge University Press.

Brenner, D., & Hiebert, E. (2008). *The impact of professional development focusing on time spent reading on teaching practices in third grade classrooms*. Presentation at the 58th Annual Meeting of the National Reading Conference, Orlando, FL.

Brenner, D., Tompkins, R., & Riley, M. (2007, November). *If I follow the teacher's manual, isn't that enough? Analyzing opportunity to read afforded by three core programs*. Paper presented at the 57th National Reading Conference. Austin, TX.

Brett, A., Rothlein, L., & Hurley, M. (1996). Vocabulary acquisition from listening to stories and explanations of target words. *The Elementary School Journal, 96*, 415–422.

Brewer, P. (2003). *You must be joking!: Lots of cool jokes, plus 17½ tips for remembering, telling, and making up your own jokes*. Battle Creek, MI: Cricket.

Brewer, W. F. (1980). Literacy theory, rhetoric, and stylistics: Implications for psychology. In R. J. Spiro, B. C. Bruce, & W. F. Brewer (Eds.), *Theoretical issues in reading comprehension: Perspectives from cognitive psychology, linguistics, artificial intelligence, and education* (pp. 221–239). Hillsdale, NJ: Lawrence Erlbaum.

Breznitz, Z. (2006). *Fluency in reading: Synchronization of processes*. Mahwah, NJ: Lawrence Erlbaum.

Britton, J., Burgess, T., Martin, N., McLeod, A., & Rosen, H. (1975). *The development of writing abilities (11–18)*. London, England: Schools Council Publications.

Brophy, J., & Good, T. (1986). Teacher behavior and student achievement. In M. C. Wittrock (Ed.), *Handbook of research on teaching* (3rd ed., pp. 328–375). New York, NY: Macmillan.

Brown, A. L. (1980). Metacognitive development and reading. In R. J. Spiro, B. C. Bruce, & W. F. Brewer (Eds.), *Theoretical issues in reading comprehension: Perspectives from cognitive psychology, linguistics, artificial intelligence, and education* (pp. 453–482). Hillsdale, NJ: Lawrence Erlbaum.

Brown, M. W. (1990). *The important book*. New York, NY: HarperCollins.

Brown, R., Pressley, M., Van Meter, P., & Schuder, T. (1996). A quasi-experimental validation of transactional strategies instruction with low-achieving second-grade readers. *Journal of Educational Psychology, 88*, 18–37.

Bryan, G., Fawson, P. C., & Reutzel, D. R. (2003). Sustained silent reading: Exploring the value of literature discussion with three non-engaged readers. *Reading Research and Instruction 43*(1), 47–73.

Bryan, J. (1998). K-W-W-L: Questioning the known. *The Reading Teacher, 51*, 618–620.

Buchanan, C. D. (1966). *Programmed prereader*. St. Louis, MO: Sullivan Associates.

Buly, M. R. (2006). Independent reading. In M. E. Mooney & T. A. Young (Eds.), *Caught in the spell of writing and reading* (pp. 123–154). Katonah, NY: Richard C. Owen.

Buonanno, G. P. (2011). *Dancing on grapes*. Honesdale, PA: Boyds Mills.

Calhoun, E. F. (1999). *Teaching beginning reading and writing with the picture word inductive model*. Washington, DC: Association of Supervision and Curriculum Development.

Calkins, L. M. (1983). *Lessons from a child*. Portsmouth, NH: Heinemann.

Calkins, L. M. (1986). *The art of teaching writing*. Portsmouth, NH: Heinemann.

Calkins, L. M., & Harwayne, S. (1991). *Living between the lines*. Portsmouth, NH: Heinemann.

Cambourne, B. (1988). *The whole story: Natural learning and the acquisition of literacy in the classroom*. Acukland, New Zealand: Ashton Scholastic.

Campbell, M. L., Helf, S. H., & Cooke, N. L. (2008). Effects of adding multisensory components to a supplemental reading program on the decoding skills of treatment resisters. *Education and Treatment of Children, 31*(3), 267–295.

Campeau, S., Hayward, M. D., Hope, B. T., Rosen, J. B., Nestler, E. J., & Davis, M. (1991). Induction of the *c-fos* proto-oncogene in rat amygdala during unconditioned and conditioned fear. *Brain Research, 565*, 349–352.

Carnicelli, T. A. (1980). The writing conference: A one-to-one conversation. In T. Donovan & B. W. McClelland (Eds.), *Eight approaches to teaching comprehension* (pp. 101–131). Urbana, IL: National Council of Teachers of English.

Carr, D., & Lucadamo, E. (1991). Writing process plus. *Learning 91, 20*(2), 16.

Carr, E., & Ogle, D. (1987). KWL Plus: A strategy for comprehension and summarization. *Journal of Reading, 30*(7), 626–631.

Cartwright, K. B. (2006). Fostering flexibility and comprehension in elementary students. *The Reading Teacher, 59*, 628–634.

Cecil, N. L. (1994). *For the love of language: Poetry for every learner*. Winnipeg, MB, Canada: Peguis.

Cecil, N. L. (2003). *Striking a balance: Best practices for early literacy* (2nd ed.). Scottsdale, AZ: Holcomb Hathaway.

Chall, J. S. (1967). *Learning to read: The great debate*. New York, NY: McGraw-Hill.

Chall, J. S. (1979). The great debate: Ten years later, with a modest proposal for reading stages. In L. B. Resnick & P. A. Weaver (Eds.), *Theory and practice of early reading* (Vol. 1, pp. 29–55). Hillsdale, NJ: Erlbaum.

Chall, J., Bissex, G., Conard, S., & Harris-Sharples, S. (1996). *Qualitative assessment of text difficulty: A practical guide for teachers and writers*. Cambridge, MA: Brookline.

Chall, J. S. (1995). *Stages of reading development*. Florence, KY: Wadsworth.

Chall, J. S., & Dale, E. (1995). *Readability revisited: The new Dale-Chall readability formula*. Cambridge, MA: Brookline.

Chayet, B. (1994). 20 penny-pinching ways to double your classroom library. *Instructor, 4*, 51–53.

Chomsky, N. (1965). *Aspects of the theory of syntax*. Cambridge, MA: MIT Press.

Christensen, B. (1994). *An edible alphabet*. New York, NY: Dial.

Chua, S. P. (2008). The effects of the sustained silent reading program on cultivating students' habits and attitudes in reading books for leisure. *The Clearing House, 81*, 180–184.

Clark, D. C., & Cutler, B. R. (1990). *Teaching: An introduction*. San Diego, CA: Harcourt Brace.

Clay, M. (1987). *Writing begins at home*. Portsmouth, NH: Heinemann.

Clay, M. M. (1979). *Reading: The patterning of complex behavior* (2nd ed.). Auckland, New Zealand: Heinemann Educational Books.

Clay, M. M. (1993). *Reading recovery: A guidebook for teachers in training*. Portsmouth, NH: Heinemann.

Clay, M. M. (2000a). *Concepts about print: What have children learned about the way we print language?* Portsmouth, NH: Heinemann.

Clay, M. M. (2000b). *Running records for classroom teachers*. Portsmouth, NH: Heinemann.

Clay, M. M. (2002). *An observation survey of early literacy achievement* (2nd ed.). Portsmouth, NH: Heinemann.

Cohen, D. K., & Spillane, J. P. (1992). Policy and practice: The relations between governance and instruction. In G. Grant (Ed.), *Review of research in education* (Vol. 18, pp. 3–50). Washington, DC: American Educational Research Association.

Coh-Metrix. (2011). Coh-Metrix. Retrieved from cohmetrix.memphis.edu/cohmetrixpr/index.html

Coiro, J., Knobel, M., Lankshear, C., & Leu, D. J. (Eds.). (2008). *Handbook of research on new literacies*. New York, NY: Routledge.

Coles, R. (1995). *The story of Ruby Bridges*. New York, NY: Scholastic.

Collins, A., & Halverson, R. (2009). *Rethinking education in the age of technology: The digital revolution and schooling in America*. New York, NY: Teachers College Press.

Collins, A., & Smith, E. (1980). *Teaching the process of reading comprehension* (Tech. Rep. No. 182). Urbana-Champaign, IL: University of Illinois at Urbana-Champaign, Center for the Study of Reading.

Collins, N. D., (1993). Three kinds of writing that preserve the past. *Teaching Pre K–8, 24*(1), 72.

Combs, M. (2002). *Readers and writers in primary grades: A balanced and integrated approach* (2nd ed.). Upper Saddle River, NJ: Merrill Prentice Hall.

Common Core State Standards. (2011). *Common core state standards initiative*. Retrieved from www.corestandards.org.

Connell, R. W. (1994). Poverty and education. *Harvard Educational Review, 64*(2), 125–149.

Conrad, P. (1995). *Animal lingo*. New York, NY: HarperCollins.

Cooper, E. J. (2004). The pursuit of equity and excellence in educational opportunity. In D. Lapp, C. C. Block, E. J. Cooper, J. Flood, N. Roser, & J. V. Tinajero (Eds.), *Teaching all the children: Strategies for developing literacy in an urban setting* (pp. 12–30). New York, NY: Guilford.

Cooper, J. D., & Kiger, N. D. (2005). *Literacy: Helping children construct meaning* (6th ed.). Beverly, MA: Wadsworth.

Cope, B., & Kalantzis, M. (Eds.). (1993). *The powers of literacy: A genre approach to teaching writing*. London, England: Falmer Press.

Corcoran, J. (1994). *The teacher who couldn't read*. Colorado Springs, CO: Focus on the Family.

Cornett, C. E. (2006). Center stage: Arts-based read-alouds. *The Reading Teacher, 60*, 234–240.

Cowan, K., & Albers, P. (2006). Semiotic representations: Building complex literacy practices through the arts. *The Reading Teacher, 60*, 124–137.

Crosbie, S., Holm, A., & Dodd, B. (2009). Cognitive flexibility in children with and without speech disorder. *Child Language Teaching and Therapy, 25*(2), 250–270. doi: 10.1177/0265659009102990

Cummins, J. (2008). BICS and CALP: Empirical and theoretical status of the distinction. In B. Street & N. H. Hornberger (Eds.), *Encyclopedia of Language and Education* (2nd ed.): Vol. 2. *Literacy* (pp. 71–83). New York, NY: Springer Science + Business Media.

Cummins, J. P. (2001). *Language, power, and pedagogy: Bilingual children in the crossfire*. Avon, England: Multilingual Matters Limited.

Cunningham, A. E., & Stanovich, K. E (1996). What reading does for the mind. *Journal of Direct Instruction, 1*(2), 137–149.

Cunningham, J. W. (1987). Toward a pedagogy of inferential comprehension and creative response. In R. J. Tierney, P. J. Anders, & J. N. Mitchell (Eds.), *Understanding readers' understanding: Theory and practice* (pp. 229–253). Hillsdale, NJ: Lawrence Erlbaum.

Cunningham, J. W., & Moore, D. W. (1986). The confused world of main idea. In J. F. Baumann (Ed.), *Teaching main idea comprehension* (pp. 1–17). Newark, DE: International Reading Association.

Cunningham, P. (1990). The names test: A quick assessment of decoding ability. *The Reading Teacher, 44*, 124–129.

Cunningham, P. M. (2008a). *Phonics they use: Words for reading and writing* (5th ed.). Boston, MA: Allyn & Bacon.

Cunningham, P. M. (2008b). *What really matters in vocabulary*. Boston, MA: Allyn & Bacon.

Cunningham, P. M., & Allington, R. L. (2007). *Classrooms that work: They can all read and write* (4th ed.). Boston, MA: Pearson.

Cunningham, P. M., & Cunningham, J. W. (1992). Making words: Enhancing the invented spelling-decoding connection. *The Reading Teacher, 46*, 106–115.

Cunningham, P. M., & Hall, D. P. (1994). *Making words: Multilevel, hands-on developmentally appropriate spelling and phonics activities*. Parsippany, NJ: Good Apple.

Curtis, J. L. (1995). *When I was little: A four-year-old's memoir of her youth*. New York, NY: Harper Collins.

Dahl, K. L., Scharer, P. L., Lawson, L. L., & Grogan, P. R. (1999). Phonics instruction and student achievement in whole language first-grade classrooms. *Reading Research Quarterly, 34*, 312–341.

Dale, E., & O'Rourke, J. (1986). *Vocabulary building*. Columbus, OH: Zaner Bloser.

Daniels, H. (2002). *Literature circles*. Portland, ME: Stenhouse.

Daniels, H., & Zemelman, S. (2004). *Subject matter: Every teacher's guide to content-area reading*. Portsmouth, NH: Heinemann.

De Carlo, J. E. (1995). *Perspectives in whole language*. Boston, MA: Allyn & Bacon.

De La Paz, S. (2007). Managing cognitive demands for writing: Comparing the effects of instructional components in strategy instruction. *Reading and Writing Research Quarterly, 23*, 249–266.

Deboer, G. E. (2004). Historical perspectives on inquiry teaching in schools. *Scientific Inquiry and Nature of Science, 25*, 17–35.

DeGroot, A. (2010). *Reading the past: Preservice teachers' reflections on their literacy histories*. Presentation at annual meeting of the Association of Literacy Educators and Researchers, Omaha, NE.

Depree, H., & Iversen, S. (1996). *Early literacy in the classroom: A new standard for young readers*. Bothell, WA: Wright Group.

DeVoss, D., Cushman, E., & Grabill, J. (2005). The infrastructure of composing: The when of new-media writing. *College Composition and Communication, 57*, 14–44.

Dewey, J. (1916). *Democracy and education*. Old Tappan, NJ: Macmillan.

Dickinson, D. K., & Smith, M. W. (1994). Long-term effects of preschool teachers' book readings on low-income children's vocabulary and story comprehension. *Reading Research Quarterly, 29*, 104–122.

Diederich, P. (1974). *Measuring growth in English*. Urbana, IL: National Council of Teachers of English.

Diehn, G. (2010). *Live & learn: Real life journals: Designing & using handmade books*. Asheville, NC: Lark.

DiPardo, A. P., & Freedman, S. W. (1988). Peer response groups in the writing classroom: Theoretic foundations and new directions. *Review of Educational Research, 58*, 119–149.

DiTerlizzi, T. (2002). *The spider and the fly*. New York, NY: Simon & Schuster.

Dodge, B. (1995). WebQuests: A technique for Internet-based learning. *Distance Educator, 1*(2), 10–13.

Donoghue, R. M. (2009). *Language arts: Integrating skills for classroom teaching*. Thousand Oaks, CA: Sage.

Donovan, C. A., Milewicz, E. J., & Smolkin, L. B. (2003). Beyond the single text: Young children's interest in reading and writing for multiple purposes. *YC Young Children, 58*, 30–36.

Dorn, L. J., & Soffos, C. (2005). *Teaching for deep comprehension: A reading workshop approach*. Portland, ME: Stenhouse.

Dorn, L. J., & Soffos, C. (2012). *Interventions that work: A comprehensive intervention model for preventing reading failure in grades K–3*. Boston, MA: Pearson.

Dow, R. S., & Baer, G. T. (2006). *Self-paced phonics: A text for educators* (4th ed.). New York, NY: Prentice Hall.

Dowhower, S. L. (1989). Repeated reading: Research into practice. *The Reading Teacher, 42*, 502–507.

Duff, P. (2005). ESL in secondary school: Programs, problematics, and possibilities. In E. Hinkel (Ed.), *Handbook of research in second language teaching and learning* (pp. 45–63). Mahwah, NJ: Lawrence Erlbaum.

Duffelmeyer, F. (1994). Effective anticipation guide statements for learning from expository prose. *Journal of Reading, 37*, 452–455.

Duke, N. K. (2000). 3.6 minutes per day: The scarcity of informational texts in first grade. *Reading Research Quarterly, 35*(2), 202–224.

Durkin, D. (1978–1979). What classroom observations reveal about reading comprehension instruction. *Reading Research Quarterly, 14*, 481–533.

Durkin, D. (2005). *Teaching them to read* (6th ed.). Boston, MA: Allyn & Bacon.

Eagleton, M. B., & Dobler, E. (2007). *Reading the Web: Strategies for Internet inquiry.* New York, NY: Guilford Press.

Echevarria, J., Vogt, M., & Short, D. J. (2008). *Making content comprehensible for English learners: The SIOP model.* Boston, MA: Pearson.

Education Northwest. (2011). *6 + 1 trait writing.* Retrieved from educationnorthwest.org/traits

Ehri, L. C., & McCormick, S. (1998). Phases of word learning: Implications for instruction with delayed and disabled readers. *Reading and Writing Quarterly: Overcoming Learning Disabilities, 14*, 135–163.

Ehri, L. C., & Nunes, S. R. (2002). The role of phonemic awareness in learning to read. In A. E. Farstrup & S. J. Samuels (Eds.), *What research has to say about reading instruction* (3rd ed., pp. 110–139). Newark, DE: International Reading Association.

Elbow, P. (1973). *Writing without teachers.* New York, NY: Oxford University Press.

Elbow, P. (1990). *What is English?* New York, NY: The Modern Language Association of America.

Eldredge, J. L. (1990). Increasing the performance of poor readers in the third grade with a group-assisted strategy. *Journal of Educational Research, 84*, 69–77.

Eldredge, J. L. (2003). *Phonics for teachers: Self-instruction, methods, and activities* (2nd ed.). Upper Saddle River, NJ: Merrill Prentice Hall.

Eldredge, J. L. (2005). *Teaching decoding: Why and how* (2nd ed.). Upper Saddle River, NJ: Pearson Merrill Prentice Hall.

Eldredge, J. L., & Quinn, D. W. (1988). Increasing reading performance of low-achieving second graders by using dyad reading groups. *Journal of Educational Research, 82*, 40–46.

Elkonin, D. B. (1973). Reading in the U.S.S.R. In D. Downing (Ed.), *Comparative reading* (pp. 551–579). New York, NY: Macmillan.

Elley, W. B. (1989). Vocabulary acquisition from listening to stories. *Reading Research Quarterly, 24*, 174–187.

Elliot, L., Gerhardt, C., & Davidson, C. (2009). *The frogs and toads of North America: A comprehensive guide to their identification, behavior, and calls.* Boston, MA: Mariner.

Elting, M., & Folsom, M. (1980). *Q is for duck.* New York, NY: Clarion.

Emig, J. (1971). *The composing process of twelfth graders* (Research report #13). Champaign, IL: National Council of Teachers of English.

Engelmann, S., & Bruner, E. C. (1988). *Reading mastery I.* Chicago, IL: Science Research Associates.

Farr, R. (1990). Setting directions for language arts portfolios. *Educational Leadership, 48*(3), 103.

Farris, P. (1987). Promoting family reading through magazine packs. *The Reading Teacher, 40*, 825–826.

Fawson, P. C., & Moore, S. A. (1999). Reading incentive programs: Beliefs and practices. *Reading Psychology, 20*, 325–340.

Feez, S. (1998). *Text-based syllabus design.* Sydney, Australia: McQuarie University/AMES.

Fielding, L. G., Wilson, P. T., & Anderson, R. C. (1984). A new focus on free reading: The role of trade books in reading instruction. In T. E. Raphael & R. E. Reynolds (Eds.), *The contexts of school-based literacy* (pp. 149–162). New York, NY: Random House.

Fink, L. S. (2011). Travel brochures: Highlighting the setting of a story. Retrieved from www.readwritethink.org/classroom-resources/lesson-plans/travel-brochures-highlighting-setting-961.html

Fisher, C., Filby, N., Marliave, R., Cahen, L., Dishaw, M., More, J., & Berliner, D. (1978). *Teaching behaviors, academic learning time and student achievement. Final Report of Phase III-B, Beginning Teacher Evaluation Study* (Tech. Rep. No V-1). San Francisco, CA: Far West Laboratory for Educational Research and Development.

Fisher, D., & Ivey, G. (2007). Farewell to *A Farewell to Arms*: Deemphasizing the whole-class novel. *Phi Delta Kappan, 88*, 494–497.

Fisher, D., Flood, J., Lapp, D., and Frey, N. (2004). Interactive read-alouds: Is there a common set of implementation practices? *The Reading Teacher, 58*, 8–17.

Fitzgerald, J., & Amendum, S. (2007). What is sound writing instruction for multilingual learners? In S. Graham, C. A. MacArthur, & J. Fitzgerald (Eds.), *Best practices in writing instruction* (pp. 289–307). New York, NY: Guilford.

Fitzgerald, J., & Shanahan, T. (2000). Reading and writing relations and their development. *Educational Psychologist, 35*(1), 39–50.

Fleischman, P. (2004). *Joyful noise: Poems for two voices.* New York, NY: HarperCollins.

Fleischman, P. (2008). *Big talk: Poems for four voices.* Somerville, MA: Candlewick.

Fleming, C. (1998). *The hatmaker's sign: A story of Benjamin Franklin.* New York, NY: Orchard.

Flesch, R. (1955). *Why Johnny can't read: And what you can do about it.* New York, NY: Harper.

Flesch, R. F. (1948). A new readability yardstick. *Journal of Applied Psychology, 32*, 221–233.

Fletcher, J., Coulter, W. A., Reschly, D. J., & Vaughn, S. (2004). Alternative approaches to the definition and identification of learning disabilities: Some questions and answers. *Annals of Dyslexia, 54*, 304–331.

Fletcher, R. (1996). *A writer's notebook.* New York, NY: HarperCollins.

Flood, J., & Anders, P. (2005). *Literacy development of students in urban schools: Research and policy.* Newark, DE: International Reading Association.

Flood, J., Lapp, D., Squire, J. R., & Jensen, J. M. (Eds.). (2003). *Handbook of research on teaching the English language arts.* Mahwah, NJ: Erlbaum.

Ford, M. P., & Opitz, M. F. (2008). A national survey of guided reading practices: What we can learn from primary teachers. *Literacy Research and Instruction, 47*(4), 309–331.

Forsyth, P. D., & Forsyth, G. A. (1993). *Study guide to accompany Understanding Children* (2nd ed.). Mountain View, CA: Mayfield.

Foster, W. A., & Miller, M. (2007). Development of the literacy achievement gap: A longitudinal study of kindergarten through third grade. *Language, Speech and Hearing Services in Schools, 38*, 173–181.

Foulger, T. S., & Jimenez-Silva, M. (2007). Enhancing the writing development of English language learners: Teacher perceptions of common technology in project-based learning. *Journal of Research in Childhood Education, 22*(2), 109–124.

Fountas, I., & Pinnell, G. S. (1996). *Guided reading: Good first teaching for all.* Portsmouth, NH: Heinemann.

Fountas, I., & Pinnell, G. S. (2007). *Benchmark assessment system* (2nd ed.). Portsmouth, NH: Heinemann.

Fox, M. (1993). *Radical reflections: Passionate opinions on teaching, learning, and living.* San Diego, CA: Harcourt Brace.

Fox, M. (1994). *Koala Lou.* Boston, MA: Sandpiper.

Fox, M. (1996). *A bedtime story.* Greenvale, NY: Mondo.

Fox, M. (1998). *Tough Boris.* San Diego, CA: Harcourt Brace.

Frank, A. (1952). *Anne Frank: The diary of a young girl.* New York, NY: Random House.

Fredericks, A. D. (1986). Mental imagery activities to improve comprehension. *The Reading Teacher, 40*, 78–81.

Freedom Writers. (1999). *The freedom writers diary: How a teacher and 150 teens used writing to change themselves and the world around them.* New York, NY: Broadway.

Freeman, J. (2006). *Books kids will sit still for 3: A read-aloud guide.* Santa Barbara, CA: Libraries Unlimited.

Frey, N., & Fisher, D. (2005). *Language arts workshop: Purposeful reading and writing instruction.* Upper Saddle River, NJ: Prentice Hall.

Frey, N., & Fisher, D. (2010). Identifying instructional moves during guided learning. *The Reading Teacher, 64,* 84–95.

Fries, C. C. (1963). *Linguistics and reading.* New York, NY: Rinehart & Winston.

Fry, E. (1968). A readability formula that saves time. *Journal of Reading, 11,* 587.

Fry, E. B., Kress, J. E., & Fountoukidis, D. L. (2000). *The reading teacher's book of lists* (4th ed.). Paramus, NJ: Prentice Hall.

Fuchs, D., & Fuchs, L. S. (2006). Introduction to response to intervention: What, why, and how valid is it? *Reading Research Quarterly, 41,* 93–99.

Fuchs, L. S., Fuchs, D., Hosp, M. K., & Jenkins, J. R. (2001). Oral reading fluency as an indicator of reading competence: A theoretical, empirical, and historical analysis. *Scientific Studies of Reading, 5*(3), 239–256.

Gag, W. (2006). *Millions of cats.* New York, NY: Puffin.

Gage, N. (2004). *A Place for us: A Greek immigrant boy's odyssey to a new country and an unknown father.* Worcester, MA: Chandler House.

Gagne, R. M. (1985). *The conditions of learning and theory of instruction.* New York, NY: Holt, Rinehart, & Winston.

Gambrell, L. B. (1985). Dialogue journals: Reading-writing interaction. *The Reading Teacher, 38,* 512–515.

Gambrell, L. B. (1996). Creating classroom cultures that foster reading motivation. *The Reading Teacher, 50,* 14–25.

Gambrell, L. B., & Almasi, J. F. (Eds.). (1996). *Lively discussions! Fostering engaged reading.* Newark, DE: International Reading Association.

Gambrell, L. B., & Jawitz, P. B. (1993). Mental imagery, text illustrations, and children's story comprehension and recall. *Reading Research Quarterly, 28,* 265–273.

Gambrell, L. B., & Koskinen, P. S. (2002). Imagery: A strategy for enhancing comprehension. In C. C. Block & M. Pressley (Eds.), *Comprehension instruction: Research-based best practices* (pp. 305–318). New York, NY: Guilford.

Gambrell, L. B., & Marinak, B. A. (2009). *Classroom practices that support reading motivation: Findings from recent investigations.* Paper presented at the 54th annual convention of the International Reading Association, Minneapolis, MN.

Gardiner, S. (2005). *Building students' literacy through SSR.* Alexandria, VA: Association for Supervision and Curriculum Development.

Garner, R. (1987). *Metacognition and reading comprehension.* Norwood, NJ: Ablex.

Garner, R. (1992). Self-regulated learning, strategy shifts, and shared expertise: Reactions to Palincsar and Klenk. *Journal of Learning Disabilities, 25,* 226–229.

Gentry, J. R., & Gillet, J. W. (1993). *Teaching kids to spell.* Portsmouth, NH: Heinemann.

Gere, A., & Abbott, R. D. (1985). Talking about writing: The language of writing groups. *Research in the Teaching of English, 19,* 362–385.

Gibbons, G. (2010a). *Alligators and crocodiles.* New York, NY: Holiday House.

Gibbons, G. (2010b). *Elephants of Africa.* New York, NY: Holiday House.

Gibbons, P. (1993). *Learning to learn in a second language.* Portsmouth NH: Heinemann.

Gilbert, J., & Graham, S. (2010). Teaching writing to elementary students in grades 4–6: A national survey. *The Elementary School Journal, 110,* 494–517.

Giovanni, N. (1996). *The sun is so quiet.* New York, NY: Henry Holt.

Golenbock, P. (1990). *Teammates.* San Diego, CA: Gulliver.

Gonzales, N., Moll, L., & Amanti, C. (2005). *Funds of knowledge: Theorizing practices in households and classrooms.* Mahwah, NJ: Lawrence Erlbaum.

Good, R. H., Gruba, J., & Kaminski, R. A. (2001). Best practices in using Dynamic Indicators of Basic Early Literacy Skills (DIBELS) in an outcome-driven model. In A. Thomas & J. Grimes (Eds.), *Best practices in school psychology IV* (pp. 679–700). Washington, DC: National Association of School Psychologists.

Goodlad, J. (1984). *A place called school: Prospects for the future.* New York, NY: McGraw-Hill.

Goodman, K. S. (1967). Reading: A psycholinguistic guessing game. In H. Singer & R. B. Ruddell (Eds.), *Theoretical models and processes of reading* (2nd ed., pp. 497–508). Newark, DE: International Reading Association.

Goodman, K. S. (1979). Miscues: Windows on the reading process. In K. S. Goodman (Ed.), *Miscue analysis* (pp. 3–14). Urbana, IL: Clearinghouse on Reading and Communication Skills.

Goodman, K. S. (Ed.). (2006). *The truth about DIBELS: What it is—What it does.* Portsmouth, NH: Heinemann.

Goodman, Y. M. (1978). Kid watching: An alternative to testing. *The National Elementary Principal, 57,* 41–45.

Gordon, C. J., & Braun, C. (1983). Using story schema as an aid to reading and writing. *The Reading Teacher, 37,* 116–121.

Gough, P. B. (1972). One second of reading. In J. F. Kavanagh & I. G. Mattingly (Eds.), *Language by ear and by eye* (pp. 331–358). Cambridge, MA: MIT Press.

Grabe, W. (2009). *Reading in a second language: Moving from theory to practice.* New York, NY: Cambridge University Press.

Graham, S., & Perin, D. (2007). A meta-analysis of writing instruction for adolescent students. *Journal of Educational Psychology, 99,* 445–476.

Graham, S., Harris, K. R., Mason, L., Fink-Chorzempa, B., Moran, S., & Saddler, B. (2008). How do primary grade teachers teach handwriting? A national survey. *Reading and Writing: An Interdisciplinary Journal, 21*(1–2), 49–69.

Graham, S., MacArthur, C. A., & Fitzgerald, J. (Eds.). (2007). *Best practices in writing instruction.* New York, NY: Guildford.

Graves, D. H. (1983). *Writing: Teachers and children at work.* Portsmouth, NH: Heinemann.

Graves, D. H. (1996). Spot the lifetime writers. *Instructor, 105*(7), 26–27.

Graves, M. F. (1986). Vocabulary learning and instruction. In E. Z. Rothkopf (Ed.), *Review of research in education* (Vol. 13, pp. 49–89). Washington, DC: American Educational Research Association.

Graves, M. F. (1987). Roles of instruction in fostering vocabulary development. In M. G. McKeown & M. E. Curtis (Eds.), *The nature of vocabulary acquisition* (pp. 165–184). Hillsdale, NJ: Erlbaum.

Graves, M. F., & Watts-Taffe, S. N. (2002). The place of word consciousness in a research-based vocabulary program. In A. E. Farstrup & S. J. Samuels (Eds.), *What research has to say about reading instruction* (3rd ed., pp. 140–165). Newark, DE: International Reading Association.

Gray, D., & Gray, K. (2005). What happened to penmanship? *Middle Ground, 8*(4), 29.

Gray, W. S. (1927). *The curriculum foundation program.* Chicago, IL: Scott, Foresman.

Gray, W. S., Monroe, M., Artley, A. S., Arbuthnot, M. H., & Gray, L. (1956). *Guidebook to accompany the three pre-primers.* Chicago, IL: Scott Foresman.

Greenberg, J. (2008). *Side by side: New poems inspired by art from around the world.* New York, NY: Abrams.

Gregory, L. P., & Morrison, T. G. (1998). Lap reading for young at-risk children: Introducing families to books. *Early Childhood Education Journal, 26,* 67–77.

Grisham, D. L., & Wolsey, T. D. (2005). Assessing writing: Comparing the responses of 8th graders, preservice teachers and experienced teachers in a graduate reading program. *Reading and Writing Quarterly, 21*(4), 315–330.

Grisham, D. L., & Wolsey, T. D. (2011). Writing instruction for teacher candidates: Strengthening a weak curricular area. *Literacy Research and Instruction, 50,* 348–364.

Gromko, J. E. (2005). The effect of music instruction on phonemic awareness in beginning readers. *Journal of Research in Music Education, 53*(3), 199–209.

Gunning, T. G. (2000). *Creating literacy instruction for all children* (3rd ed.). Boston: Allyn & Bacon.

Guszak, F. J. (1967). Teacher questioning and reading. *The Reading Teacher, 21,* 227–234.

Guthrie, J. T. (1996). Educational contexts for engagement in literacy. *The Reading Teacher, 49,* 432–445.

Guthrie, J. T., & Wigfield, A. (2000). Engagement and motivation in reading. In M. Kamil & P. Mosenthal (Eds.), *Handbook of reading research* (Vol. 3, pp. 403–422). Mahwah, NJ: Lawrence Erlbaum.

Guthrie, J. T., McRae, A., Coddington, C. S., Kluda, S. L., Wigfield, A., & Barosa, P. (2009). Impacts of comprehensive reading instruction on diverse outcomes of low- and high-achieving readers. *Journal of Learning Disabilities, 42*(3), 195–214.

Guthrie, J. T., Seifert, M., Burnham, N. A., & Caplan, R. I. (1974). The maze technique to assess, monitor reading comprehension. *The Reading Teacher, 28,* 161–168.

Guthrie, J. T., Wigfield, A., & Perencevich, K. C. (2004). *Motivating reading comprehension: Concept-oriented reading instruction.* Mahwah, NJ: Lawrence Erlbaum.

Hairrell, A., Rupley, W., & Simmons, D. (2011). The state of vocabulary research. *Literacy Research and Instruction, 50,* 1–19.

Hall, L. A. (2009). "A necessary part of good teaching": Using book clubs to develop preservice teachers' visions of self. *Literacy Research and Instruction, 48,* 1–20.

Hallahan, D. P., & Kauffman, J. M. (2000). *Exceptional learners: Introduction to special education.* Boston, MA: Allyn & Bacon.

Haller, E. P., Child, D. A., & Walberg, H. J. (1988). Can comprehension be taught? A quantitative synthesis of "metacognitive" studies. *Educational Researcher, 17,* 5–8.

Hancock, M. K. (2007). *A celebration of literature and response* (3rd ed.). Upper Saddle River, NJ: Prentice Hall.

Harris, K. R., Graham, S., Mason, L. H., & Friedlander, B. (2008). *Powerful writing strategies for all students.* Baltimore, MD: Brookes.

Hart, B., & Risley, T. R. (1995). *Meaningful differences in the everyday experience of young American children.* Baltimore, MD: Brookes.

Hart, B., & Risley, T. R. (2003). The early catastrophe: The 30 million word gap by age 3. *American Educator, 27*(1), 4–9.

Harvey, S., & Goudvis, A. (2000). *Strategies that work: Teaching comprehension to enhance understanding.* York, ME: Stenhouse.

Harward, S. V. (1992). *The effectiveness of four self-corrected test methods on spelling achievement of fourth-grade students.* Unpublished master's thesis, Brigham Young University, Provo, UT.

Harwayne, S., & Calkins, L. (1990). *Living between the lines.* Portsmouth, NH: Heinemann.

Hasbrouck, J., & Tindal, G. A. (2006). Oral reading fluency norms: A valuable assessment tool for reading teachers. *The Reading Teacher, 59,* 636–644.

Hawken, L. S., Vincent, C. G., & Schumann, J. (2008). Response to intervention for social behavior: Challenges and opportunities. *Journal of Emotional and Behavioral Disorders, 16*(4), 213–225.

Hayes, D. P., & Ahrens, M. (1988). Vocabulary simplification for children: A special case of "motherese." *Journal of Child Language, 15,* 395–410.

Haynes, J., & Zacarian, D. (2010). *Teaching English language learners: Across the content areas.* Alexandria, VA: Association for Supervision and Curriculum Development.

Heartman, C. F. (1727). *The New England primer.* Boston, MA: S. Kneeland and T. Green.

Heckelman, R. G. (1969). A neurological-impress method of remedial-reading instruction. *Academic Therapy Quarterly, 4,* 277–282.

Heller, M. F. (1995). *Reading-writing connections: From theory to practice* (2nd ed.). White Plains, NY: Longman.

Hepworth, C. (1992). *Antics!* New York, NY: Putnam.

Herrell, A. L. (1998). *Exemplary practices in teaching English language learners.* Fresno, CA: California State University, Fresno.

Herrell, A., & Jordan, M. (2011). *Fifty strategies for teaching English language learners* (4th ed.). Boston, MA: Allyn & Bacon.

Hickam, H. (2000). *October sky.* New York, NY: Dell.

Hiebert, E. H. (1983). An examination of ability grouping for reading instruction. *Reading Research Quarterly, 18,* 231–255.

Hiebert, E. H., & Reutzel, D. R. (2010). *Revisiting silent reading: New directions for teachers and researchers.* Newark, DE: International Reading Association.

Higbee, K. L. (2001). *Your memory: How it works and how to improve it* (2nd ed.). Cambridge, MA: DaCapo Press.

Hill, L. C. (2009). *Harlem stomp!: A cultural history of the Harlem Renaissance.* New York, NY: Little, Brown Books for Young Readers.

Hillocks, G. (1986). *Research on written composition: New directions for teaching.* Urbana, IL: ERIC Clearinghouse on Reading and Communication Skills.

Hoberman, M. A. (2001). *You read to me, I'll read to you: Very short stories to read together.* Boston, MA: Little, Brown.

Hodge, R., & Kress, G. R. (1988). *Social semiotics.* Cambridge, England: Polity Press.

Holdaway, D. (1979). *The foundations of literacy.* Sydney, Australia: Ashton Scholastic.

Holdaway, D. (1984). *Stability and change in literacy learning.* Portsmouth, NH: Heinemann.

Hornsby, D., Parry, J., & Sukarna, D. (1992). *Teach on: Teaching strategies for reading and writing workshops.* Portsmouth, NH: Heinemann.

Huddelston, R., & Pullum, G. K. (2005). *A student's introduction to English grammar.* Cambridge, England: Cambridge University Press.

Huey, E. B. (1908). *The psychology and pedagogy of reading.* Cambridge, MA: MIT Press.

Hunt, L. C. (1970). The effect of self-selection, interest, and motivation upon independent, instructional, and frustrational levels. *The Reading Teacher, 24,* 146–151, 158.

Hunter College. (1999). *Five important qualities of good writing.* Retrieved from rwc.hunter.cuny.edu/reading-writing/on-line/quality.html

Hyerle, D. (2004). *Student success with thinking maps: School-based research, results, and models for achievement using visual tools.* Thousand Oaks, CA: Corwin.

Hyerle, D. (2011). *What are thinking maps and how do they work?* Retrieved from www.thinkingmaps.com/products.php

Hyland, K. (2007). Genre pedagogy: Language, literacy and L2 writing instruction. *Journal of Second Language Writing, 16*(3), 148–164.

Hyman, T. S. (1987). *Little red riding hood.* New York, NY: Holiday House.

International Reading Association. (1999). *High-stakes assessment in reading: A position statement by the International Reading Association.* Retrieved from www.reading.org/General/AboutIRA/Position-Statements/HighStakesPosition.aspx

International Reading Association. (2010). *Response to intervention: Guiding principles for educators from the International Reading Association.* Newark, DE: International Reading Association.

Intersegmental Committee of the Academic Senates. (2002). *A statement of competencies of students entering California's public colleges and universities.* Sacramento. CA: Intersegmental Committee of the Academic Senates.

Invernizzi, M., Meier, J. D., & Juel, C. (2003). *Phonological awareness literacy screening system (PALS).* Charlottesville, VA: University of Virginia Press.

Irwin, J. W. (1991). *Teaching reading comprehension processes* (2nd ed.). Englewood Cliffs, NJ: Prentice Hall.

Isbell, R. (1995). *The complete learning center book: An illustrated guide for 32 different early childhood learning centers.* Beltsville, MD: Gryphon House.

Jackson, Y. (2001). Reversing underachievement in urban students: Pedagogy of confidence. In A. Costa (Ed.), *Developing minds: A resource book for teaching thinking* (3rd ed., pp. 222–228) . Alexandria, VA: Association for Supervision and Curriculum Development.

Jacob, B. A., & Lefgren, L. (2007). What do parents value in education? An empirical investigation of parents' revealed preferences for teachers. *The Quarterly Journal of Economics, 122*(4), 1603–1637.

Jacob, B. A., Lefgren, L., & Sims, D. P. (2010). The persistence of teacher-induced learning. *Journal of Human Resources, 45*(4), 915–943.

Jacobs, J. S., & Tunnell, M. O. (2004). *Children's literature, briefly* (3rd ed.). Upper Saddle River, NJ: Pearson Merrill Prentice Hall.

Jacobs, J. S., Morrison, T. G., & Swinyard, W. R. (2000). Reading aloud to students: A national probability study of classroom practices of elementary school teachers. *Reading Psychology, 21,* 171–193.

Jensen, R. (2001). Creating classroom libraries students really use. *The Utah Journal of Reading and Literacy, 6*(1), 32–34.

Johnson, D. D., & Pearson, P. D. (1984). *Teaching reading vocabulary.* New York, NY: Holt, Rinehart, & Winston.

Johnson, E. R. (2009). *Academic language! Academic literacy!* Thousand Oaks, CA: Corwin.

Johnson, T. D., Langford, K. G., & Quorn, K. C. (1981). Characteristics of an effective spelling program. *Language Arts, 58,* 581–588.

Johnston, P., & Costello, P. (2005, April–May-June). Principles for literacy assessment. *Reading Research Quarterly, 40,* 256–267.

Johnston, P. H. (1983). *Reading comprehension assessment: A cognitive basis.* Newark, DE: International Reading Association.

Jones, C. F. (1996). *Accidents may happen: Fifty inventions discovered by accident.* New York, NY: Delacorte.

Jones, R. C., & Thomas, T. G. (2006). Leave no discipline behind. *Reading Teacher, 60,* 58–64.

Jordan, M., & Herrell, A. (2002). Building comprehension bridges: A multiple strategies approach. *California Reader, 35*(4), 14–19.

Joshi, R. M., Binks, E., Hougen, M., Dahlgren, M. E., Ocker-Dean, E., & Smith, D. L. (2009). Why elementary teachers might be inadequately prepared to teach reading. *Journal of Learning Disabilities, 42*(5), 392–402. doi: 10.1177/0022219409338736

Joyner, F. G. (2011). *A letter to my daughter.* Retrieved from sportales.com/running/a-letter-to-my-daughter/

Juel, C. (1988). Learning to read and write: A longitudinal study of fifty-four children from first through fourth grade. *Journal of Educational Psychology, 80,* 437–447.

Juel, C. (1991). Beginning reading. In R. Barr, M. L. Kamil, P. Mosenthal, & P. D. Pearson (Eds.), *Handbook of reading research* (Vol. 2, pp. 759–788). New York, NY: Longman.

Justice, L. M., & Kaderavek, J. N. (2004). Embedded-explicit emergent literacy intervention I: Background and description of approach. *Language, Speech, and Hearing Services in Schools, 35*(3), 201–211.

Kaderavek, J. N., & Justice, L. M. (2004). Embedded-emergent literacy intervention II: Goal selection and implementation in the early childhood classroom. *Language, Speech, and Hearing Services in Schools, 35*(3), 212–228.

Kalan, R. (1989). *Jump, frog, jump.* New York, NY: HarperCollins.

Kalman, B. (2004). *Endangered rhinoceroses.* New York, NY: Crabtree.

Kandel, E. R. (2006). *In search of memory: The emergence of a new science of mind.* New York, NY: Norton.

Kara-Soteriou, J., & Kaufman, D. (2002). Writing in the elementary school: The missing pieces. *The New England Reading Association Journal, 38*(3), 25–33.

Keen, P. (2006). Knowledge mobilization: The challenge for information professionals. In C. Khoo & D. Singh (Eds.), *Proceedings of the Asia-Pacific conference on library and information education and practice.* (pp. 1–9). Singapore: Nanyang Technological University.

Keene, E. O., & Zimmermann, S. (2007). *Mosaic of thought: The power of comprehension strategy instruction* (2nd ed.). Portsmouth, NH: Heinemann.

Kelley, M. J., & Clausen-Grace, N. (2008). *R5 in your classroom: A guide to differentiating independent reading and developing avid readers.* Newark, DE: International Reading Association.

Kemper, D., Nathan, R., Elsholz, C., & Sebranek, P. (2000). *Writers express.* Wilmington, MA: Great Source.

Kidz Investigate Series. (2005). *Interview with award-winning author Carl Sommer* (DVD). Dover, DE: Digital Cornerstone.

King, B. (2008). *The pocket guide to games.* Salt Lake City, UT: Gibbs Smith.

Kintsch, W., & Van Dijk, T. A. (1978). Toward a model of text comprehension and production. *Psychological Review, 85,* 363–394.

Kirkpatrick, K. (2007). *The snow baby: The arctic childhood of Admiral Robert E. Peary's daring daughter.* New York, NY: Holiday House.

Klein, A. (1996, January–February.). 6 ways to assess writing. *Instructor,* 44–46.

Kong, A., & Pearson, P. D. (2003). The road to participation: The construction of a literacy practice in a learning community of linguistically diverse learners. *Research in the Teaching of English, 38,* 85–124.

Korbin, J. E. (1992). Introduction: Child poverty in the United States. *American Behavioral Scientist, 35,* 213–219.

Kovacs, D., & Preller, J. (1999). *Meet the authors and illustrators: Volume 2* (Grades K–6). New York, NY: Scholastic.

Kozol, J. (2006). *The shame of the nation: The restoration of apartheid schooling in America.* New York, NY: Broadway.

Kragler, S. (1995). The transition from oral to silent reading. *Reading Psychology, 16,* 395–408.

Krashen, S. (2001). More smoke and mirrors: A critique of the National Reading Panel report on fluency. *Phi Delta Kappan, 83*(2), 119–123.

Krashen, S. D. (1996). *The natural approach: Language acquisition in the classroom.* Northumberland, England: Bloodaxe Books.

Krashen, S. D. (2004). *The power of reading: Insights from the research.* Englewood, CO: Libraries Unlimited.

Krashen, S. D., & Terrell, T. (1983). *The natural approach: Language acquisition in the classroom.* New York, NY: Pergamon.

Krathwohl, J. R. (1989). Attitudes and affect in learning and instruction. *Educational Media International, 26*(2), 85–100.

Krebs, L. (2008). *We're sailing down the Nile.* Cambridge, MA: Barefoot Books.

Krull, K. (1994). *Lives of the writers: Comedies, tragedies (and what the neighbors thought).* New York, NY: Harcourt.

Kuhn, M. R., & Schwanenflugel, P. (Eds.) (2008). *Fluency in the classroom.* New York, NY: Guilford.

Kuhn, M. R., & Stahl, S. A. (2003). Fluency: A review of developmental and remedial practices. *Journal of Educational Psychology, 95,* 3–21.

Labbo, L. D. (2005). From morning message to digital morning message: Moving from the tried and true to the new. *The Reading Teacher, 58,* 782–785.

LaBerge, D., & Samuels, S. J. (1974). Toward a theory of automatic information processing in reading. *Cognitive Psychology, 6*, 293–323.

Lacey, M. (2008). *The story of the Olympics*. London, England: Usborne.

Langley, A., & De Souza, P. (1997). *The Roman news: The greatest newspaper in civilization*. Cambridge, MA: Candlewick.

Leahy, S., Lyon, C., Thompson, M., & Wiliam, D. (2005). Classroom assessment: Minute by minute, day by day. *Educational Leadership, 63*(3), 19–24.

Learning Centre. (2011). *Reading for understanding: The SQW3R method of study*. Retrieved from www.lc.unsw.edu.au/onlib/sqw3r.html

Learning Disabilities Association of America. (2011). *Types of learning disabilities*. Retrieved from www.ldanatl.org/aboutld/teachers/understanding/types.asp

Lee, S. (2007). Revelations from three consecutive studies on extensive reading. *RELC Journal, 38*(2), 150–170.

Lenski, S. D. (1998). Intertextual intentions: Making connections across texts. *Clearing House, 72*, 74–80.

Lenski, S. D., Caskey, M. M., Johns, J. L., & Wham, M. A. (2007). *Reading and learning strategies: Middle grades through high school* (3rd ed.). Dubuque, IA: Kendall/Hunt.

Lensmire, T. J. (1994). Writing workshop as carnival: Reflections on an alternative learning environment. *Harvard Educational Review, 64*(4), 371–391.

Lesaux, N., Koda, K., Seigel, L., & Shanahan, T. (2006). Development of literacy. In D. August & T. Shanahan (Eds.), *Developing literacy in second-language learners* (pp. 75–122). Mahwah, NJ: Lawrence Erlbaum.

Lesaux, N. K., & Geva, E. (2006). Synthesis: Development of literacy in language-minority students. In D. August & T. Shanahan (Eds.), *Developing literacy in second-language learners* (pp. 53–74). Mahwah, NJ: Lawrence Erlbaum.

Leslie, L., & Caldwell, J. (2006). *Qualitative reading inventory-4*. Boston, MA: Pearson Education.

Leu, D. J., Jr., Leu, D. D. & Coiro, J. (2004). *Teaching with the Internet: New literacies for new times* (4th ed.). Norwood, MA: Christopher-Gordon.

Levin, J. R., & Pressley, M. (1981). Improving children's prose comprehension: Selected strategies that seem to succeed. In C. M. Santa & B. L. Hayes (Eds.), *Children's prose comprehension: Research and practice* (pp. 44–71). Newark, DE: International Reading Association.

Levine, D. U. (2000). National Urban Alliance professional development model for improving achievement in the context of effective schools research. *Journal of Negro Education, 69*, 305–322.

Levine, M. (2012). *Technology outside of the formal classroom*. Presentation at the Early Education and Technology for Children Conference, Salt Lake City, UT.

Lewis, C. S. (1961). *An experiment in criticism*. Cambridge, England: Cambridge University Press.

Lewis, J. P. (2009). *Spot the plot*. San Francisco, CA: Chronicle.

Lewman, B. (1999). Read it again! How rereading—and rereading— stories heightens children's literacy. *Children and Families, 8*, 12–15.

Lickteig, M. J. (1981). Research-based recommendations for teachers of writing. *Language Arts, 58*, 44–50.

Lindfors, J. W. (1991). *Children's language and learning* (2nd ed.). Englewood Cliffs, NJ: Prentice Hall.

Liner, T., Kirby, D. L., & Kirby, D. (2003). *Inside out: Strategies for teaching writing* (3rd ed.). Portsmouth, NH: Heinemann.

Lippman, L., Burns, S., & McArthur, E. (1996). *Urban schools: The challenge of location and poverty*. Washington, DC: U.S. Department of Education Office of Educational Research and Improvement.

Ludwig, T. (2010). *Confessions of a former bully*. Berkeley, CA: Tricycle Press.

Lukens, R. J. (2006). *A critical handbook of children's literature* (8th ed.). Boston, MA: Allyn & Bacon.

MacArthur, C. A. (2007). Best practices in teaching evaluation and revision. In S. Graham, C. A. MacArthur, & J. Fitzgerald (Eds.), *Best practices in writing instruction* (pp. 141–162). New York, NY: Guilford.

Macrorie, K. (1976). *Telling writing*. Portsmouth, NH: Boynton Cook.

Macrorie, K. (1984). *Searching writing*. Upper Montclair, NJ: Boynton Cook.

Mann, A. (2001). *Phonics and vocabulary building guidebook*. New York, NY: Intensified Accelerated Systems.

Manning, M., & Manning, G. (1996, October). 58 literature responses. *Teaching, K8*, 100–101.

Manyak, P. C. (2008). Phonemes in use: Multiple activities for a critical process. *The Reading Teacher, 62*(8), 659–662. doi: 10.1598/RT.61.88

Manzo, U. C., Manzo, A. V., & Thomas, M. M. (2009). *Content area literacy: A framework for reading-based instruction* (5th ed.). New York, NY: Wiley.

Martin, B., Jr. (2008). *Brown bear, brown bear, what do you see?* New York, NY: Henry Holt.

Martin, L. E., & Reutzel, D. R. (1999). Sharing books: Examining how and why mothers deviate from the print. *Reading Research and Instruction, 39*, 39–70.

Martinez, M., Roser, N. L., & Strecker, S. (1998). "I never thought I could be a star": A reader's theatre ticket to fluency. *The Reading Teacher, 52*, 326–334.

Marzano, R. J. (2004). *Building background knowledge for academic achievement: Research on what works in schools*. Washington, DC: Association for Supervision and Curriculum Development.

Marzano, R. J., & Marzano, J. S. (1988). *A cluster approach to elementary vocabulary instruction*. Newark, DE: International Reading Association.

Marzollo, J. (1991). *In 1492*. New York, NY: Scholastic.

Mather, N., Sammons, J., & Schwartz, J. (2006). Adaptations of the Names Test: Easy-to-use phonics assessments. *The Reading Teacher, 60*(2), 114–122.

Mazurkiewicz, A. J., & Tanyzer, H. J. (1966). *Workbook to accompany book 5*. New York, NY: Initial Teaching Alphabet Publications.

McCutchen, D. (2006). Cognitive factors in the development of children's writing. In C. A. MacArthur, S. Graham, & J. Fitzgerald (Eds.), *Handbook of writing research* (pp. 115–130). New York, NY: Gilford Press.

McGee, L. M., & Richgels, D. J. (2003). *Designing early literacy programs: Strategies for at-risk preschool and kindergarten children*. New York, NY: Guilford.

McGuffey, W. H. (1866). *McGuffey's new first eclectic reader*. Cincinnati, OH: Van Antwerp, Bragg and Company.

McIntosh, M. E., & Draper, R. J. (2001). Using learning logs in mathematics: Writing to learn. *Mathematics Teacher, 94*, 554–555.

McKay, D. O. (1934). The opportunities of the class teacher. *The Relief Society Magazine, 21*, 721–724.

McKool, S. S., & Gespass, S. (2009). Does Johnny's reading teacher love to read? How teachers' personal reading habits affect instructional practices. *Literacy Research and Instruction, 48*, 264–276.

McKoon, G., & Ratcliff, R. (1992). Inference during reading. *Psychological Review, 99*(3), 440–466.

McLaughlin, M., & DeVoogd, G. (2004). Critical literacy as comprehension: Expanding reader response. *Journal of Adolescent and Adult Literacy, 48*, 52–62.

McTigue, E. M. (2010). Teaching young readers imagery in storytelling: What color is the monkey? *The Reading Teacher, 64*, 53–56.

Medoff, M. (1987, February). In praise of teachers. *Reader's Digest,* 69–73.

Medwell, J., & Wray, D. (2007). Handwriting: What do we know and what do we need to know? *Literacy, 41*(1), 10–15.

Mehan, H. (1979). *Learning lessons.* Cambridge, MA: Harvard University Press.

Melser, J., & Cowley, J. (1990). *The big toe.* Bothell, WA: The Wright Group.

Meltzer, B. (2010). *Heroes for my son.* New York, NY: HarperCollins.

Menzel, P. (1994). *Material world: A global family portrait.* San Francisco, CA: Sierra Club Books.

Meyer, B. J. F., & Freedle, R. O. (1984). Effects of discourse type on recall. *American Educational Research Journal, 21*, 121–143.

Miller, J. (2006). Shared writing. In M. E. Mooney & T. A. Young (Eds.), *Caught in the spell of writing and reading* (pp. 61–76). Katonah, NY: Richard C. Owen.

Miller, W. H. (2005). *Improving early literacy: Strategies and activities for struggling students (K–3).* San Francisco, CA: Jossey Bass.

Millin, S. K., & Rinehart, S. D. (1999). Some of the benefits of readers' theater participation for second grade Title I students. *Reading Research and Instruction, 39*(1), 71–88.

Milone, M. (2009). *The development of ATOS: The Renaissance readability formula.* Wisconsin Rapids, WI: Renaissance Learning.

Ming, K., & Dukes, C. (2010). Gimme five: Creating a comprehensive reading lesson with all the essential elements. *Teaching Exceptional Children, 42*(3), 22–28.

Ministry of Education. (1994). *Dancing with the pen.* Wellington, New Zealand: Learning Media.

Ministry of Education. (1996). *The learner as a reader: Developing reading programmes.* Wellington, New Zealand: Learning Media.

Ministry of Education. (2002). *Guided reading: Years 1–4.* Wellington, New Zealand: Learning Media.

Molebash, P., & Dodge, B. (2003). Kickstarting inquiry with WebQuests and Web inquiry projects. *Social Education, 67*, 158–162.

Monroe, E. E. (2006). *Math dictionary: The easy, simple fun guide to help math phobics become math lovers.* Honesdale, PA: Boyds Mills.

Montgomery, E., Bauer, W. W., & Gray, W. S. (1948). *Happy days with our friends.* Chicago, IL: Scott Foresman.

Mooney, M. E. (1990). *Reading to, with, and by children.* Katonah, NY: Richard C. Owen.

Mooney, M. E. (2006a). Guiding writers to independence. In M. E. Mooney & T. A. Young (Eds.), *Caught in the spell of writing and reading* (pp. 103–119). Katonah, NY: Richard C. Owen.

Mooney, M. E. (2006b). Writing for and with students. In M. E. Mooney, & T. A. Young (Eds.). *Caught in the spell of writing and reading* (pp. 21–40). Katonah, NY: Richard C. Owen.

Mooney, M. E., & Young, T. A. (2006). *Caught in the spell of writing and reading.* Katonah, NY: Richard C. Owen.

Moore, G. (2005). *Contemporary cloze, grades 3–5.* Jacksonville, FL: World Teachers Press.

Moore, R. (2003). Reexamining the field experiences of preservice teachers. *Journal of Teacher Education, 54*, 31–42.

Moore-Hart, M. A. (2009). *Teaching writing in diverse classrooms, K–8: Enhancing writing through literature, real-life experiences, and technology.* New York, NY: Prentice Hall.

Moore-Hart, M. A., & Carpenter, R. (2009). *Improving preservice teachers' attitudes toward writing: A comparison of two university courses.* Paper presented at the annual meeting of the National Reading Conference, Albuquerque, NM.

Morgan, D. N. (2010). Preservice teachers as writers. *Literacy Research and Instruction, 49*, 352–365.

Morgan, R. (1997). *In the next three seconds.* New York, NY: Lodestar.

Morrison, T. G., Jacobs, J. S., & Swinyard, W. R. (1999) Do teachers who read personally use recommended practices in their classrooms? *Reading Research and Instruction, 38*, 81–100.

Morrow, L. M. (1992). The impact of a literature-based program on literacy achievement, use of literature, and attitudes of children from minority backgrounds. *Reading Research Quarterly, 27*, 250–275.

Morrow, L. M. (2009). *Literacy development in the early years: Helping children read and write* (6th ed.). Boston, MA: Pearson.

Morrow, L. M., & Young, J. (1997). Parent, teacher, and child participation in a collaborative family literacy program: The effects of attitude, motivation, and literacy achievement. *Journal of Educational Psychology, 89*, 736–742.

Moss, B. (2004). Teach expository text structure through information trade book retellings. *The Reading Teacher, 57*, 710–718.

Moss, B., & Young, T. A. (2010). *Creating lifelong readers through independent reading.* Newark, DE: International Reading Association.

Mraz, M., & Rasinski, T. V. (2007). Summer reading loss. *The Reading Teacher, 60*, 784–789.

Murray, D. M. (1968). *A writer teaches writing.* Boston, MA: Houghton Mifflin.

Murray, D. M. (2004). *Write to learn* (8th ed.). Florence, KY: Wadsworth.

Myers, W. D. (1996). *Brown angels: An album of pictures and verse.* New York, NY: HarperCollins.

Nagy, W. E. (1988). *Teaching vocabulary to improve comprehension.* Urbana, IL: National Council of Teachers of English.

Nagy, W. E., & Anderson, R. C. (1984). How many words are there in printed school English? *Reading Research Quarterly, 19*, 304–330.

Nagy, W. E., & Scott, J. A. (2004). Vocabulary processes. In R. B. Ruddell & N. J. Unrau (Eds.), *Theoretical models and processes of reading* (5th ed., pp. 574–593). Newark, DE: International Reading Association.

National Assessment of Educational Progress. (2005). *Reading: The nation's report card.* Retrieved from nces.ed.gov/nationsreportcard/reading

National Association of State Directors of Special Education and Council of Administrators of Special Education. (2006, May). *Response to Intervention: NASDE and CASE white paper on RtI.* Alexandria, VA: Authors. Retrieved from www.nasdse.org/Portals/0/Documents/Download%20Publications/RtIAnAdministratorsPerspective1-06.pdf.

National Center for Educational Statistics. (2011a). *English language leaner needs.* Retrieved from nces.ed.gov/pubs2010/2010015/indicator2_8.asp

National Center for Educational Statistics. (2011b). *Rural education in America.* Retrieved from nces.ed.gov/surveys/ruraled/page2.asp

National Center on Response to Intervention. (2011). *The essential components of RTI.* Retrieved from www.rti4success.org

National Commission on Writing in America's Schools and Colleges. (2003). *The neglected "R": The need for a writing revolution.* Mt. Vernon, IL: College Entrance Examination Board.

National Council of Teachers of English. (2009). *Writing assessment: A position statement.* Retrieved from www.ncte.org/cccc/resources/positions/writingassessment.

National Endowment for the Arts. (2007). *To read or not to read: A question of national consequence.* Washington, DC: National Endowment for the Arts.

National Governors Association Center for Best Practices, and Council of Chief State School Officers. (2010). *State standards adoption states.* Retrieved from www.corestandards.org/in-the-states

National Reading Panel. (2000). *Report of the National Reading Panel: Teaching children to read.* Washington, DC: National Institute of Child Health and Human Development.

National Reading Panel. (2003). *Put reading first: Kindergarten through grade 3* (2nd ed.). Retrieved from www.nifi.gov/partnershipforreading

National Urban Alliance. (2010). *Good and better.* Retrieved from www.madzander.com/nua_stratbank.html

Ness, M. (2009). Laughing through rereadings: Using joke books to build fluency. *The Reading Teacher, 62*(8), 691–694.

Nessel, D. D., & Graham, J. M. (2007). *Thinking strategies for student achievement: Improving learning across the curriculum, K–12* (2nd ed.). Thousand Oaks, CA: Corwin.

Nettles, D. H. (2006). *Toolkit for teachers of literacy.* Boston, MA: Pearson Education.

Neuman, S. B. (1999). Books make a difference: A study of access to literacy. *Reading Research Quarterly, 34*(3), 286–311.

Neuman, S. B., & Celano, D. (2001). Access to print in low-income and middle-income communities: An ecological study of four neighborhoods. *Reading Research Quarterly, 36*(1), 8–26.

Newell, G. E., Koukis, S., & Boster, S. (2007). Best practices in developing across the curriculum program in the secondary school. In S. Graham, C. A. MacArthur, & J. Fitzgerald (Eds.), *Best practices in writing instruction* (pp. 74–98). New York, NY: Guilford.

Nicholson-Nelson, K. (1999, October). Let 100 flowers bloom. *Scholastic Instructor,* 32–35.

No Child Left Behind Act. (2001). Pub. L., No. 107-110, 115 Stat. 1425.

Nobles, W. W. (1990). The infusion of African and African American content: A question of content and intent. In A. G. Hilliard, L. Payton-Stewart, & L. O. Williams (Eds.), *Proceedings of the First National Conference* (pp. 4–28). Chicago, IL: Third World Press.

North, S. M. (1987). *The making of knowledge in composition: Portrait of an emerging field.* Upper Montclair, NJ: Boynton/Cook.

O'Day, J. A., & Smith, M. S. (1993). Systemic school reform and educational opportunity. In S. Fuhrman (Ed.), *Designing coherent educational policy: Improving the system* (pp. 250–311). San Francisco, CA: Jossey-Bass.

O'Muhr, G. O. (2009). *Causes and effects of the American Civil War.* New York, NY: Rosen.

O'Shea, L. J., Sindelar, P. T., & O'Shea, D J. (1985). The effects of repeated readings and attentional cues on reading fluency and comprehension. *Journal of Reading Behavior, 17,* 19–142.

Oakhill, J., & Patel, S. (1991). Can imagery training help children who have comprehension problems? *Journal of Research in Reading, 14,* 106–115.

Ogle, D. (1986). K-W-L: A teaching model that develops active reading of expository text. *The Reading Teacher, 39,* 564–570.

Olson, M. W. (1991). Portfolios: Education tools. *Reading Psychology, 12*(1), 73–80.

Opitz, M. F. (1998). Text sets: One way to flex your grouping—in first grade, too! *The Reading Teacher, 51,* 622–624.

Opitz, M. F., & Rasinski, T. V. (1998). *Good-bye round robin reading: 25 effective oral reading strategies.* Portsmouth, NH: Heinemann.

Organisation for Economic Co-operation and Development. (2005). *Formative assessment: Improving learning in secondary classrooms.* Paris, France: Centre for Educational Research and Innovation.

Ortiz, S. O. (2004). Learning disabilities: A primer for parents about identification. In A. S. Canter, L. Z. Paige, M. D. Roth, I. Romero, & S. A. Carroll, (Eds.), *Helping children at home and school II: Handouts for families and educators* (pp. S8-117–S8-119). Bethesda, MD: National Association of School Psychologists.

Osguthorpe, R. T., & Osguthorpe, L. S. (2009). *Choose to learn: Teaching for success every day.* Thousand Oaks, CA: Corwin.

Owens, R. E. (2011). *Language development: An introduction* (8th ed.). Boston, MA: Allyn & Bacon.

Paige, D. D. (2006). Increasing fluency in disabled middle school readers: Repeated reading utilizing above grade level reading passages. *Reading Horizons, 46*(3), 167–181.

Paige, D. D. (2011). Testing the acceleration hypothesis: Fluency outcomes utilizing still—versus accelerated—text in sixth-grade students with reading disabilities. *Literacy Research and Instruction, 50,* 1–19.

Palincsar, A. S., & Brown, A. L. (1984). Reciprocal teaching of comprehension-fostering and comprehension-monitoring activities. *Cognition and Instruction, 2,* 117–175.

Palincsar, A. S., & Brown, A. L. (1986). Interactive teaching to promote independent learning from text. *The Reading Teacher, 39,* 771–777.

Pappas, C. C., Kiefer, B. Z., & Levstik, L. S. (2005). *An integrated language perspective in the elementary school: An action approach* (4th ed.). Boston, MA: Allyn & Bacon.

Paquette, K. (2009). Integrating the 6 + 1 writing traits model with cross-age tutoring: An investigation of elementary students' writing development. *Literacy Research and Instruction, 48*(1), 28–38.

Paterson, K. (1978). *The Great Gilly Hopkins.* New York, NY: Avon.

Paul, A. W. (2005). *Manana Iguana.* New York, NY: Holiday House.

Payne, C. D., & Schulman, M. B. (1999). *Getting the most out of morning message and other shared writing lessons.* New York, NY: Scholastic.

Pearson, P. D. (1985). Changing the face of reading comprehension instruction. *The Reading Teacher, 38,* 724–737.

Pearson, P. D. (2006). Foreword. In K. S. Goodman (Ed.), *The truth about DIBELS: What it is—What it does* (pp. v–xix). Portsmouth, NH: Heinemann.

Pearson, P. D., & Duke, N. (2002). Effective practices for developing reading comprehension. In A. E. Farstrup & S. J. Samuels (Eds.), *What research has to say about reading instruction* (3rd ed., pp. 205–242). Newark, DE: International Reading Association.

Pearson, P. D., & Fielding, L. (1991). Comprehension instruction. In R. Barr, M. L. Kamil, P. B. Mosenthal, & P. D. Pearson (Eds.), *Handbook of reading research,* (Vol. 2, pp. 815–860). New York, NY: Longman.

Pearson, P. D., & Gallagher, M. (1983). The instruction of reading comprehension. *Contemporary Educational Psychology, 8,* 317–344.

Pearson, P. D., & Johnson, D. D. (1978). *Teaching reading comprehension.* New York, NY: Holt, Rinehart, & Winston.

Peck, R. N. (1994). *A day no pigs would die.* New York, NY: Laurel Leaf.

Peck, S. M., & Virkler, A. J. (2006). Reading in the shadows: Extending literacy skills through shadow-puppet theater. *The Reading Teacher, 59,* 786–795.

Peregoy, S. F., & Boyle, O. F. (2008). *Reading, writing, and learning in ESL: A resource book for teaching K–12 English learners* (5th ed.). Boston, MA: Pearson.

Persky, H. R., Daane, M. C., & Jin, Y. (2003). *The nation's report card: Writing 2002.* (NCES 2003-529). U.S. Department of Education, Institute of Education Services, National Center for Education Statistics. Washington, DC: Government Printing Office.

Peterson, S., & Slotta, J. (2009). Saying yes to online learning: A first time experience teaching an online graduate course in literacy education. *Literacy Research and Instruction, 48,* 1–17.

Petraglia, J. (1999). Is there life after process: The role of social scientism in a changing discipline. In T. Kent (Ed.), *Post-process theory: Beyond the writing process paradigm* (pp. 49–65). Carbondale, IL: Southern Illinois University Press.

Petroski, H. (1990). *The pencil: A history of design and circumstance.* New York, NY: Alfred A. Knopf.

Piaget, J. (1926). *The language and thought of the child.* London, England: Routledge & K. Paul.

Piaget, J. (1969). *The psychology of intelligence.* Patterson, NJ: Littlefield, Adams.

Pikulski, J. J., & Chard, D. J. (2005). Fluency: Bridge between decoding and reading comprehension. *The Reading Teacher, 58,* 510–519.

Pilgreen, J. L. (2000). *The SSR handbook: How to organize and manage a sustained silent reading program.* Portsmouth, NH: Boynton/Cook/Heinemann.

Pinkney, J. (2006). *The little red hen.* New York, NY: Dial.

Pinnell, G. S., & Fountas, I. C. (1998). *Word matters: Teaching phonics and spelling in reading/writing classrooms.* Portsmouth, NH: Heinemann.

Polacco, P. (2001). *Thank you, Mr. Falker.* New York, NY: Philomel.

Prelutsky, J. (1984). *The new kid on the block.* New York, NY: Greenwillow.

Prensky, M. (2010). *Teaching digital natives: Partnering for real learning.* Thousand Oaks, CA: Corwin.

Pressley, M. (2002). Comprehension strategies instruction. In C. C. Block & M. Pressley (Eds.), *Comprehension instruction: Research-based best practices* (pp. 11–27). New York, NY: Guilford.

Pressley, M., & Forrest-Pressley, D. (1985). Questions and children's cognitive processing. In A. C. G. B. Black (Ed.), *The psychology of questions* (pp. 277–296). Hillsdale, NJ: Erlbaum.

Pressley, M., Dolezal, S., Roehrig, A. D., & Hilden, K. (2002). Why the National Reading Panel's recommendations are not enough. In R. Allington (Ed.), *Big brother and the national reading curriculum: How ideology trumped evidence* (pp. 75–89). Portsmouth, NH: Heinemann.

Pressley, M., Dolezal-Kersey, S. E., Bogaert, L. R., Mohan, L., Roehrig, A. D., & Warzon, K. B. (2003). *Motivating primary-grade students.* New York, NY: Guilford.

Pressley, M., Gaskins, I. W., Solic, K., & Collins, S. (2006). A portrait of Benchmark School: How a school produces high achievement in students who previously failed. *Journal of Educational Psychology, 98*(2), 282–306.

Pressley, M., Johnson, C. J., Symons, S., McGoldrick, J. A., & Kurita, J. A. (1989). Strategies that improve children's memory and comprehension. *Elementary School Journal, 90,* 3–32.

Pressley, M., Wharton-McDonald, R., Mistretta-Hampston, J. M., & Echevarria, M. (1998). The nature of literacy instruction in ten grade 4/5 classrooms in upstate New York. *Scientific Studies of Reading, 2,* 159–194.

Prior, J., & Gerard, M. R. (2004). *Environmental print in the classroom: Meaningful connections for learning to read.* Newark, DE: International Reading Association.

Prior, S. M., & Welling, K. A. (2001). "Read in your head": A Vygotskian analysis of the transition from oral to silent reading. *Reading Psychology, 22,* 1–15.

Pritchard, R. J., & Honeycutt, R. L. (2007). Best practices in implementing a process approach to teaching writing. In S. Graham, C. A. MacArthur, & J. Fitzgerald (Eds.), *Best practices in writing instruction* (pp. 28–49). New York, NY: Guilford.

Probst, R. (1991). Response to literature. In J. Flood, J. Jensen, D. Lapp, & J. Squire (Eds.), *Handbook of research in the teaching of the English language arts* (pp. 655–663). New York, NY: Macmillan.

Raphael, T. E. (1986). Teaching question answer relationships, revisited. *The Reading Teacher, 39,* 516–522.

Raphael, T. E., & Au, K. H. (2005). QAR: Enhancing comprehension and test taking across grades and content areas. *The Reading Teacher, 59,* 206–221.

Raphael, T. E., Florio-Ruane, S., & George, M. (2001). Book club plus: A conceptual framework to organize literacy instruction. *Language Arts, 79*(2), 159–168.

Raphael, T. E., McMahon, S. I., Goatley, V. J., Boyd, F. B., Pardo, L. S., & Woodman, D. A. (1992). Research directions: Literature and discussion in the reading program. *Language Arts, 69,* 54–61.

Rasinski, T. V. (2000). Speed does matter in reading. *The Reading Teacher, 54,* 146–151.

Rasinski, T. V. (2006). A brief history of reading fluency. In S. J. Samuels & A. E. Farstrup (Eds.), *What research has to say about fluency instruction* (pp. 4–22). Newark, DE: International Reading Association.

Rasinski, T. V. (2010). *The fluent reader: Oral reading strategies for building word recognition, fluency, and comprehension* (2nd ed.). New York, NY: Scholastic.

Rasinski, T. V., Harrison, D., & Fawsett, G. (2009). *Partner poems for building fluency: Grades 4–6; 40 engaging poems for two voices with motivating activities that help students improve their fluency and comprehension.* New York, NY: Scholastic Teaching Resources.

Rasinski, T. V., & Hoffman, J. V. (2003). Oral reading in the school curriculum. *Reading Research Quarterly, 38,* 510–522.

Rasinski, T. V., Padak, N., Linek, W., & Sturtevant, E. (1994). Effects of fluency development on urban second-grade readers. *Journal of Educational Research, 87*(3), 158–165.

Rathmann, P. (1995). *Officer Buckle and Gloria.* New York, NY: Scholastic.

Ray, K. W. (2010). *Wondrous words: Writers and writing in the elementary classroom.* Urbana, IL: National Council of Teachers of English.

Readence, J. E., Bean, T. W., & Baldwin, R. S. (1998). *Content area literacy: An integrated approach* (6th ed.). Dubuque, IA: Kendall/Hunt.

Reis, S. M., McCoach, D. B., Coyne, M., Schreiber, F. J., Eckert, R. D., & Gubbins, E. J. (2007). Using planned enrichment strategies with direct instruction to improve reading fluency, comprehension, and attitude toward reading: An evidence-based study. *The Elementary School Journal, 108*(1), 3–23.

Reutzel, D. R. (1985). Story maps improve comprehension. *The Reading Teacher, 38,* 400–411.

Reutzel, D. R., & Cooter, R. B. (1992). *Teaching children to read: From basals to books.* New York, NY: Merrill.

Reutzel, D. R., & Fawson, P. C. (1990). Traveling tales: Connecting parents and children through writing. *The Reading Teacher, 44,* 222–227.

Reutzel, D. R., & Fawson, P. C. (2002). *Your classroom library: New ways to give it more teaching power.* New York, NY: Scholastic.

Reutzel, D. R., & Hollingsworth, P. M. (1993). Effects of fluency training on second graders' reading comprehension. *Journal of Educational Research, 86*(6), 325–331.

Reutzel, D., Jones, C. D., Fawson, P. C., & Smith, J. A. (2008). Scaffolded silent reading: A complement to guided repeated oral reading that works! *The Reading Teacher, 62,* 194–207.

Richards, J. C., & Anderson, N. A. (2003). How do you know? A strategy to help emergent readers make inferences. *The Reading Teacher, 57,* 290–293.

Richardson, J. S., Morgan, R. F., & Fleener, C. (2008). *Reading to learn in the content areas.* Beverly, MA: Wadsworth.

Richardson, W. (2010). *Blogs, wikis, podcasts, and other powerful Web tools for classrooms.* Thousand Oaks, CA: Corwin.

Riggs, K. (2009). *Golden Gate Bridge: Now that's big.* Surrey, England: Creative Education.

Rivallend, J. (2000). Linking literacy learning across different contexts. In C. Barratt-Pugh & M. Rohl (Eds.), *Literacy learning in the early years* (pp. 27–56). Philadelphia, PA: Open University Press.

Robb, L. (2002a). Multiple texts: Multiple opportunities for teaching and learning. *Voices from the Middle, 9*(4), 28–32.

Robb, L. (2002b). *Readers' handbook: A student guide for reading and learning.* Wilmington, MA: Great Source.

Roberts, W. D. (1994). *The view from the cherry tree.* New York, NY: Aladdin.

Robinson, F. P. (1970). *Effective study.* New York, NY: Harper & Row.

Rogers, C. (1969). *Freedom to learn.* Columbus, OH: Merrill.

Rohl, M. (2000). Learning about words, sounds and letters. In C. Barratt-Pugh & M. Rohl (Eds.), *Literacy learning in the early years* (pp. 57–80). Philadelphia, PA: Open University Press.

Romano, T. (1995). *Writing with passion: Life stories, multiple genres.* Portsmouth, NH: Heinemann.

Rosenblatt, L. (1991). Literary theory. In J. Flood, J. Jensen, D. Lapp, & J. Squire (Eds.), *Handbook of research in the teaching of the English language arts* (pp. 57–62). New York, NY: Macmillan.

Rosenblatt, L. M. (1978). *The reader, the text, the poem: The transactional theory of the literary work.* Carbondale, IL: Southern Illinois University Press.

Rosenblatt, L. M. (2004). The transactional theory of reading and writing. In R. B. Ruddell & N. J. Unrau (Eds.), *Theoretical models and processes of reading* (5th ed., pp. 1363–1398). Newark, DE: International Reading Association.

Rosenshine, B., & Meister, C. (1994). Reciprocal teaching: A review of the research. *Review of Educational Research, 64,* 479–530.

Rosenshine, B., Meister, C., & Chapman, S. (1996). Teaching students to generate questions: A review of the intervention studies. *Review of Educational Research, 66,* 181–221.

Rothstein, A. S., Rothstein, E. B., & Lauber, G. (2006). *Writing as learning: A content-based approach* (2nd ed.). Thousand Oaks, CA: Corwin.

Rowe, M. B. (1986). Wait time: Slowing down may be a way of speeding up! *Journal of Teacher Education, 37,* 43–50.

Ruddell, R. B. (2008). *How to teach reading to elementary and middle school students: Practical ideas from highly effective teachers.* Boston, MA: Allyn & Bacon.

Ruddell, R. B., & Unrau, N. J. (2004). Reading as a meaning-construction process: The reader, the text, and the teacher. In R. B. Ruddell & N. J. Unrau (Eds.), *Theoretical models and processes of reading* (5th ed., pp. 1462–1521). Newark, DE: International Reading Association.

Rumelhart, D. E. (1976). Toward an interactive model of reading. In S. Dornic (Ed.), *Attention and performance, VI.* Hillsdale, NJ: Lawrence Erlbaum.

Rupley, W. H., Logan, J. W., & Nichols, W. D. (1998–99). Vocabulary instruction in a balanced reading program. *The Reading Teacher, 52,* 336–346.

Rylant, C. (1993). *When I was young in the mountains.* New York, NY: Puffin.

Sadoski, M., & Paivio, A. (2004). A dual coding theoretical model of reading. In R. B. Ruddell & N. J. Unrau (Eds.), *Theoretical models and processes of reading* (5th ed., pp. 1329–1362). Newark, DE: International Reading Association.

Salcedo, J. B. (2009). Inviting students and teachers to connect. *Language Arts, 86,* 440–448.

Samuels, S. J. (1979). The method of repeated readings. *The Reading Teacher, 32,* 403–408.

Samuels, S. J. (2003). Reading fluency: Its development and assessment. In A. E. Farstrup & S. J. Samuels (Eds.), *What research has to say about reading instruction* (3rd ed., pp. 166–183). Newark, DE: International Reading Association.

Sanders, N. M. (1966). *Classroom questions: What kinds?* New York, NY: Harper & Row.

Sarnoff, J., & Ruffins, R. (1981). *Words: A book about the origins of everyday words and phrases.* New York, NY: Charles Scribners' Sons.

Saussure, F. (1959). *Course in general linguistics.* New York, NY: Philosophical Library.

Scardamalia, M., & Bereiter, C. (2006). Knowledge building: Theory, pedagogy, and technology. In R. K. Sawyer (Ed.), *The Cambridge handbook of the learning sciences* (pp. 97–118). London, England: Cambridge University Press.

Schafft, K., & Jackson, A. Y. (2010). *Rural education for the twenty-first century: Identity, place, and community in a globalizing world.* University Park, PA: Penn State University Press.

Schlagal, B. (2007). Best practices in spelling and handwriting. In S. Graham, C. A. MacArthur, & J. Fitzgerald (Eds.), *Best practices in writing instruction* (pp. 179–201). New York, NY: Guilford.

Schmidt, G. D. (2007). *The Wednesday wars.* New York, NY: Clarion.

Schneider, R. B., & Barone, D. (1997). Cross-age tutoring. *Childhood Education, 73*(3), 136–144.

Scholastic. (2010). *2010 kids and family reading report.* Retrieved from mediaroom.scholastic.com/research

Scieszka, J. (1989). *The true story of the three little pigs.* New York, NY: Viking.

Scieszka, J. (1991). *Knights of the kitchen table.* New York, NY: Viking.

Scillian, D. (2001). *A is for America.* Chelsea, MI: Sleeping Bear.

Seay, S. (2006). How DIBELS failed Alabama: A research report. In K. S. Goodman (Ed.), *The truth about DIBELS: What it is—What it does* (pp. 60–65). Portsmouth, NH: Heinemann.

Seeger, L. V. (2007). *First the egg.* New York, NY: Roaring Brook Press.

Seuss, D., Prelutsky, J., & Smith, L. (1998). *Hooray for diffendoofer day!* New York, NY: Knopf.

Shanahan, T. (2006a). Does he really think kids shouldn't read? *Reading Today, 23*(6), 12.

Shanahan, T. (2006b). Relations among oral language, reading, and writing development. In C. A. McArthur, S. Graham, & J. Fitzgerald (Eds.), *Handbook of writing research* (pp. 171–183). New York, NY: Guilford.

Shanahan, T., & Tierney, R. J. (1990). Reading-writing relationships: Three perspectives. In J. Zutell & S. McCormick (Eds.), *Literacy theory and research: Analyses from multiple paradigms* (Thirty-ninth Yearbook of the National Reading Conference, pp. 13–34). Chicago, IL: National Reading Conference.

Shanahan, T., Kamil, M. L., & Tobin, A. W. (1982). Cloze as a measure of intersentential comprehension. *Reading Research Quarterly, 17,* 229–255.

Shannon, G. (1996). *Tomorrow's alphabet.* New York, NY: Greenwillow.

Shaw, N. (1992). *Sheep out to eat.* New York, NY: Trumpet.

Silver, H. F., Strong, R. W., & Perini, M. J. (2008). *The strategic teacher: Selecting the right research-based strategy for every lesson.* New York, NY: Prentice Hall.

Silverstein, S. (1974). *Where the sidewalk ends.* New York, NY: Harper.

Silvey, A. (1989, September-October). Editorial: The basalization of trade books. *The Horn Book,* 549–550.

Simon, S. (2001). *Crocodiles & alligators.* New York, NY: HarperCollins.

Simon, S. (2011). *Butterflies.* New York, NY: Collins.

Singer, H. (1975). The Seer technique: A non-computational procedure for quickly estimating readability level. *Journal of Literacy Research, 7,* 255–267.

Skinner, B. F. (1954). The science of learning and the art of teaching. *Harvard Educational Review, 24,* 86–97.

Skinner, B. F. (1974). *About behaviorism.* New York, NY: Random House.

Smith, D. (2001). *The quotable Walt Disney.* New York, NY: Disney Enterprises.

Smith, F. (1971). *Understanding reading: A psycholinguistic analysis of reading and learning to read.* New York, NY: Holt, Rinehart & Winston.

Smith, F. (1981). Myths of writing. *Language Arts, 58,* 792–798.

Smith, F. (1982). *Writing and the writer.* New York, NY: Holt, Rinehart, & Winston.

Smith, F. (1983a). *Essays into literacy: Selected papers and some afterthoughts.* Portsmouth, NH: Heinemann.

Smith, F. (1983b). Reading like a writer. *Language Arts, 60*(5), 558–567.

Smith, F. (2007). *Reading: FAQ.* New York, NY: Teachers College Press.

Smith, L. (2010). *It's a book.* New York, NY: Roaring Book.

Smith, N. B. (1969). The many faces of reading comprehension. *The Reading Teacher, 23*(3), 249–259, 291.

Smith, N. B. (2002). *American reading instruction* (Special ed.). Newark, DE: International Reading Association.

Smith, R. J., & Barrett, T. C. (1979). *Teaching reading in the middle grades.* Reading, MA: Addison Wesley.

Smith-Burke, T. M. (1989). Political and economic dimensions of literacy: Challenges for the 1990s. In S. McCormick & J. Zutell (Eds.), *Cognitive and social perspectives for literacy research and instruction* (pp. 1–18). Chicago, IL: National Reading Conference.

Snow, C. E., Barnes, W. S., Chandler, J., Goodman, I. F., & Hemphill, L. (1991). *Unfulfilled expectations: Home and school influences on literacy.* Cambridge, MA: Harvard University Press.

Sonnenschein, S., & Schmidt, D. (2000). Fostering home and community connections to support children's reading. In L. Baker, M. J. Dreher, & J. T. Guthrie (Eds.), *Engaging young readers: Promoting achievement and motivation* (pp. 264–284). New York, NY: Guilford.

Sonnenschein, S., Stapleton, L. M., & Benson, A. (2010). The relation between the type and amount of instruction and growth in children's reading competencies. *American Educational Research Journal, 47*(2), 358–389. doi: 10.3102/0002831209349215

Spandel, V., & Stiggins, R. J. (1997). *Creating writers: Linking writing assessment and instruction* (2nd ed.). New York, NY: Longman.

Spandel, V. (2005). *The 9 rights of every writer: A guide for teachers.* Portsmouth, NH: Heinemann.

Spandel, V. (2007). *Creating young writers: Using the six traits to enrich the writing process in primary classrooms* (2nd ed.). Boston, MA: Allyn & Bacon.

Spandel, V. (2008). *Creating writers through 6-trait writing assessment and instruction* (5th ed.). Boston, MA: Allyn & Bacon.

Spandel, V., & Stiggins, R. J. (1997). *Creating writers: Linking writing assessment and instruction* (2nd ed.). New York, NY: Longman.

Speare, E. G. (1983). *The sign of the beaver.* New York, NY: Dell.

Spinelli, J. (2000). *Stargirl.* New York, NY: Alfred A. Knopf.

Stahl, S. A. (1986). Three principles of effective vocabulary instruction. *Journal of Reading, 29,* 662–668.

Stanovich, K. O. (1984). Toward an interactive-compensatory model of individual differences in the development of reading fluency. *Reading Research Quarterly, 16,* 32–71.

Staton, J. (1987). The power of responding in dialogue journals. In T. Fulwiler (Ed.), *The journal book* (pp. 47–63). Portsmouth, NH: Boynton/Cook.

Stauffer, R. G. (1970). *The language-experience approach to the teaching of reading.* New York, NY: Harper & Row.

Stein, N., & Glenn, C. F. (1979). An analysis of story comprehension in elementary school children. In R. O. Freedle (Ed.), *New directions in discourse processing*: Vol. 2. *Advances in discourse processes* (pp. 53–120). Norwood, NJ: Ablex.

Stenner, A. J. (1996). *Measuring reading comprehension with the Lexile framework.* Durham, NC: MetaMetrics.

Steptoe, J. (1993). *Mufaro's beautiful daughters.* New York, NY: HarperTrophy.

Sternberg, R. J. (1987). Most vocabulary is learned from context. In M. G. McKeown & M. E. Curtis (Eds.), *The nature of vocabulary acquisition* (pp. 89–105). Hillsdale, NJ: Elrbaum.

Stevens, J. (2008). *Help me, Mr. Mutt!: Expert answers for dogs with people problems.* Boston, MA: Harcourt.

Stoeke, J. M. (1991). *Minerva Louise, the mixed-up hen.* New York, NY: Scholastic.

Strong, R. W., Silver, H. F., & Perini, M. J. (2007). *Reading for academic success, grades 2–6: Differentiated strategies for struggling, average, and advanced readers.* Thousand Oaks, CA: Corwin.

Sullivan, A. (2001). Cultural capital and educational attainment. *Sociology, 35,* 893–912.

Swales, J. (1990). *Genre analysis.* Cambridge, England: Cambridge University Press.

Swartz, S. (2001). *Interactive writing and interactive editing.* Carlsbad, CA: Dominie.

Sweet, A. P., & Guthrie, J. T. (1996). How children's motivations relate to literacy development and instruction. *The Reading Teacher, 49,* 660–662.

Sweet, A. P., & Snow, C. E. (2003). *Rethinking reading comprehension.* New York, NY: Guilford.

Taba, H. (1967). *Teacher's handbook for elementary social studies.* Reading, MA: Addison-Wesley.

Tapahonso, L., & Schick, E. (1995). *Navajo ABC.* New York, NY: Simon & Schuster.

Taylor, B. M., Pearson, P. D., Clark, K., & Walpole, S. (2000). Effective schools and accomplished teachers: Lessons about primary-grade reading instruction in low-income schools. *The Elementary School Journal, 101,* 121–165.

Taylor, B. M., Pearson, P. D., Peterson, D. P., & Rodriguez, M. C. (2003). Reading growth in high-poverty classrooms: The influence of teacher practices that encourage cognitive engagement in literacy learning. *The Elementary School Journal, 104,* 3–28.

Taylor, B. M., Pearson, P. D., Peterson, D. P., & Rodriguez, M. C. (2005). The CIERA School Change Framework: An evidence-based approach to professional development and school reading improvement. *Reading Research Quarterly, 40,* 40–69.

Taylor, G. C. (1981). ERIC/RCS report: Music in language arts instruction. *Language Arts, 58,* 363–368.

Taylor, W. (1953). "Cloze procedure": A new tool for measuring readability. *Journalism Quarterly, 30,* 415–433.

Teale, W. H., & Gambrell, L. B. (2007). Raising urban students' literacy achievement by engaging in authentic, challenging work. *The Reading Teacher, 60,* 728–739.

Temple, C., Nathan, R., Temple, F., & Burris, N. A. (1993). *The beginnings of writing* (3rd ed.). Boston, MA: Allyn & Bacon.

Thompson, W. B. (2000). Is a bee bigger than a flea? A classroom mental imagery activity. *Teaching of Psychology, 27,* 212–215.

Tierney, R. J., & Pearson, P. D. (1983). Toward a composing model of reading. *Language Arts, 60*(5), 568–580.

Tierney, R. J., & Readence, J. E. (2004). *Reading strategies and practices: A compendium* (6th ed.). Boston, MA: Allyn & Bacon.

Tierney, R. J., & Shanahan, T. (1996). Research on the reading-writing relationship: Interactions, transactions, and outcomes. In R. Barr, M. L. Kamil, P. Mosenthal, & P. D. Pearson (Eds.), *Handbook of reading research* (Vol. 2, pp. 246–280). Mahwah, NJ: Erlbaum.

Tierney, R. J., & Thome, C. (2006). Is DIBELS leading us down the wrong path? In K. S. Goodman (Ed.), *The truth about DIBELS: What it is—What it does* (pp. 50–59). Portsmouth, NH: Heinemann.

Time for Kids. (1977, October.). A new spin on spider silk. *Time for Kids World Report Edition, 3*(7).

Tomlinson, C. A., & McTighe, J. (2006). *Integrating differentiated instruction and understanding by design: Connecting content and kids.* Washington, DC: Association for Supervision and Curriculum Development.

Tompkins, G. E. (2005). *Language arts: Patterns of practice* (6th ed.). Upper Saddle River, NJ: Pearson Prentice Hall.

Tompkins, G. E. (2010). *Literacy for the 21st century: A balanced approach* (5th ed.). Boston, MA: Allyn & Bacon.

Tompkins, G. E. (2012). *Teaching writing: Balancing process and product* (6th ed.). Boston, MA: Pearson.

Tompkins, G. E., & Collom, S. (Eds.). (2004). *Sharing the pen: Interactive writing with young children.* Upper Saddle River, NJ: Merrill/Prentice Hall.

Torgeson, J. K., & Bryant, B. R. (2004). *Test of phonological awareness* (2nd ed.). East Moline, IL: LinguiSystems.

Trabasso, T., & Bouchard, E. (2002). Teaching readers how to comprehend text strategically. In C. C. Block & M. Pressley (Eds.), *Comprehension instruction: Research-based best practices* (pp. 176–200). New York, NY: Guilford.

Trelease, J. (2006). *The read-aloud handbook* (6th ed.). New York, NY: Penguin.

Trivizas, E. (1997). *The three little wolves and the big bad pig.* New York, NY: Margaret K. McElderry.

Tsuchiya, Y. (1997). *Faithful elephants: A true story of animals, people, and war.* Boston, MA: Sandpiper.

Tunnell, M. O., & Chilcoat, G. W. (1996). *The children of Topaz: The story of a Japanese-American internment camp.* New York, NY: Holiday House.

Tunnell, M. O., & Jacobs, J. S. (2007). *Children's literature, briefly* (4th ed.). Upper Saddle River, NJ: Prentice Hall.

Tunnell, M. O., Jacobs, J. S., Young, T. A., & Bryan, G. W. (2012). *Children's literature, briefly* (5th ed.). Boston, MA: Pearson.

Tyler, B., & Chard, D. J. (2000). Using readers' theatre to foster fluency in struggling readers: A twist on the repeated reading strategy. *Reading and Writing Quarterly, 16*, 163–168.

Tyner, B. (2004). *Small-group reading instruction: A differentiated teaching model for beginning and struggling readers.* Newark, DE: International Reading Association.

USDA Economic Research Service. (2011). *Rural education at a glance.* Retrieved from www.ers.usda.gov/publications/rdrr98/rdrr98_lowres.pdf

Vacca, R. T., & Vacca, J. L. (2008). *Content area reading: Literacy and learning across the curriculum* (9th ed.). Boston, MA: Allyn & Bacon.

Valencia, S. W. (1998) *Literacy portfolios in action.* Beverly, MA: Wadsworth.

Valmont, W. J. (2003). *Technology for literacy teaching and learning.* Boston, MA: Houghton Mifflin.

Van Allsburg, C. (1984). *The mysteries of Harris Burdick.* Boston, MA: Houghton Mifflin.

Van Allsburg, C. (1991). *The wretched stone.* Boston, MA: Houghton Mifflin.

Van Allsburg, C. (1993). *The sweetest fig.* Boston, MA: Houghton Mifflin.

Vygotsky, L. S. (1962). *Thought and language.* Cambridge, MA: MIT Press.

Vygotsky, L. S. (1978). *Mind in society.* Cambridge, MA: Harvard University Press.

Wagstaff, J. (1999). *Teaching reading and writing with word walls (Grades K–3).* Bethesda, MD: Teaching Strategies.

Warburg, S. S. (1990). *I like you.* New York, NY: Houghton Mifflin.

Washington, B. T. (1901). *Up from slavery: An autobiography.* Danvers, MA: Doubleday.

Watanabe, L. M., & Hall-Kenyon, K. M. (2011). Improving young children's writing: The influence of story structure on kindergartners' writing complexity. *Literacy Research and Instruction, 50,* 272–293.

Watt, M. (2001). *Leon the chameleon.* Tonawanda, NY: Kids Can Press.

Webster, N. (1798). *The American spelling book.* Boston, MA: Isaiah Thomas and Ebenezer Andrews.

Weitzman, I. (2006). *Jokelopedia: The biggest, best, silliest, dumbest joke book ever.* New York, NY: Workman.

White, E. B. (2001). *Charlotte's web.* New York, NY: HarperCollins.

White, S. (1995). *Listening to children read.* Washington, DC: U.S. Department of Education. Retrieved from: nces.ed.gov/pubs95/web/95762.asp

Whitehurst, G. J., Falco, F. L., Lonigan, C. J., Fischel, J. E., DeBaryshe, B. D., Vladez-Menchaca, M. C., & Caulfield, M. (1988). Accelerating language development through picture book reading. *Developmental Psychology, 24,* 552–559.

Whitin, D. J., & Whitin, P. (2000). Exploring mathematics through talking and writing. In M. Burke and F. R. Curcio (Eds.), *Learning mathematics for a new century. 2000 Yearbook;* Reston, VA: National Council of Teachers of Mathematics.

Whitney, A. (2008). Teacher transformation in the National Writing Project. *Research in the Teaching of English, 43,* 144–187.

Wilcox, B. (1994). Conferencing tips. *The Writing Lab Newsletter, 18* (8), 13.

Wilcox, B. (1996). Helping peer tutors. *Writing Teacher, 9*(3), 31.

Wilcox, B., & Monroe, E. E. (2011). Integrating writing and mathematics. *Reading Teacher, 64,* 521–529.

Wilhelm, J. D. (2002). *Action strategies for deepening comprehension: Role plays, text structure tableaux, talking statues, and other enrichment techniques that engage students with text.* New York, NY: Scholastic Professional Books.

Wills, C. (1995). Voice of inquiry: Possibilities and perspectives. *Childhood Education, 71,* 261–265.

Wisniewski, D. (1996). *Golem.* New York, NY: Clarion.

Witherell, C. S., & Erickson, V. L. (1978). Teacher education as adult development. *Theory into Practice, 17,* 229–238.

Wittrock, M. C. (1981). Reading comprehension. In F. J. Pirozollo & M. C. Wittrock (Eds.), *Neuropsychological and cognitive processes in reading.* New York, NY: Academic Press.

Wittrock, M. C. (1986). Students' thought processes. In M. C. Wittrock (Ed.), *Handbook of research on teaching* (3rd ed., pp. 297–314). New York, NY: Macmillan.

Wollman-Bonilla, J. E. (2001). Can first-grade writers demonstrate audience awareness? *Reading Research Quarterly, 36*(2), 184–201.

Wong, B. Y. L., & Berninger, V. W. (2004). Cognitive processes of teachers in implementing composition research in elementary, middle, and high school classrooms. In C. A. Stone, E. R. Silliman, B. J. Ehren, & K. Apel (Eds.), *Handbook of language and literacy: Development and disorders* (pp. 600–624). New York, NY: Guilford.

World Book Student Discovery Encyclopedia (2000). Chicago, IL: World Book.

Worthy, J., & Prater, K. (2002). "I thought about it all night": Reader's theatre for reading fluency and motivation. *The Reading Teacher, 56,* 294–297.

Wright, D. A. (2002). Using writing to enhance learning: Practical ideas for classroom use. *The Religious Educator, 3*(3), 115–121.

Wright, R. A. (2010). *The 3 word journal.* Austin, TX: National Family Institute.

Wu, Y., & Samuels, S. J. (2004). *How the amount of time spent on independent reading affects reading achievement: A response to the National Reading Panel.* Paper presented at the 49th annual convention of the International Reading Association, Reno, NV. Retrieved from www.tc.umn.edu/~samue001/web%20pdf/time_spent_on_reading.pdf

Wyne, M., & Stuck, G. (1982). Time and learning: Implications for the classroom teacher. *Elementary School Journal, 83,* 67–75.

Yolen, J. (1987). *Owl moon.* New York, NY: Philomel.

Yoon, J. C. (2002). Three decades of sustained silent reading: A meta-analytic review of the effects of SSR on attitude toward reading. *Reading Improvement, 39*(4), 186–195.

Yopp, H. (1995). The Yopp-Singer test of phoneme segmentation. *The Reading Teacher, 49,* 20–29.

Yopp, H. K., & Yopp, R. H. (2003). *Oo-pples and boo-noo-noos: Songs and activities for phonemic awareness.* New York, NY: Harcourt School.

Yopp, R. H., & Yopp, H. K. (2006). Informational texts as read-alouds at school and home. *Journal of Literacy Research, 38,* 37–51.

Yopp, R. H., & Yopp, H. K. (2009). *Literature-based reading activities* (5th ed.). Boston, MA: Allyn & Bacon.

Yopp, H. K., & Yopp, R. H. (2010). *Purposeful play for early childhood phonological awareness.* Huntington Beach, CA: Shell Educational Publishing.

Young, E. (1996). *Lon Po Po.* New York, NY: Puffin.

Young, T. A. (2006). Weaving the magic together: Threads of student success and engagement. In M. E. Mooney & T. A. Young (Eds.), *Caught in the spell of writing and reading* (pp. 175–189). Katonah, NY: Richard C. Owen.

Zecker, L. B. (1996). Early development in written language: Children's emergent knowledge of genre-specific characteristics. *Reading and Writing, 8,* 5–25.

Zutell, J., & Rasinski, T. (1991). Training teachers to attend to their students' oral reading fluency. *Theory into Practice, 30,* 211–217.

Name Index

Abbott, R. D., 303, 307
Ada, A. F., 73
Adams, M. J., 73, 90
Afflerbach, P., 110, 152
Ahrens, M., 246
Albers, P., 275
Alcott, L. M., 246
Alderman, G. L., 101
Alexander, K. L., 23
Allen, J., 129
Allington, R. L., 7, 31, 60, 110, 112, 129, 293, 316
Almaguer, L., 271
Almasi, J. F., 324
Amanti, C., 16
Amberg, J. S., 67
Amendum, S., 77
Anders, P., 25
Anderson, C., 238
Anderson, D. H., 77
Anderson, N. A., 162
Anderson, R. C., 60, 127, 128, 151, 161, 244, 246, 316, 322
Anderson, T. H., 174
Applebee, A. N., 8, 188, 278, 281
Applegate, A. J., 323
Applegate, M. D., 323
Arbuthnot, M. H., 95
Armbruster, B. B., 78, 127, 133–134
Armstrong, J., 252
Artley, A. S., 95
Ash, G. W., 268
Ashton-Warner, S., 79
Atwell, N., 7, 263, 297, 306
Au, K. H., 16, 24, 172
Audet, R. H., 204
August, D., 66, 128

Babbitt, N., 143
Baer, G. T., 86
Bahr, D., 58, 277
Baker, E. A., 42
Baker, R., 148
Baldwin, R. S., 138
Balfanz, R., 197
Barchers, S., 302
Barnes, W. S., 23
Barone, D., 35
Barosa, P., 325
Barrett, T. C., 273
Barton, K. C., 200
Baruch, D. W., 4
Base, G., 212
Baslaw-Finger, A., 275
Batsche, G., 223
Battistich, V., 291
Baumann, J. F., 127, 128, 174, 175
Baylor, B., 329
Beach, J. K., 259
Bean, T. W., 138
Bear, D. R., 58, 75
Beaver, J., 231
Beck, I. L., 96, 128, 132, 135, 150, 172, 173, 249
Beeler, T., 73
Beers, K., 182–184
Benchmark Education Company, 113

Benson, A., 89
Bereiter, C., 32
Bergenske, M. D., 52
Berglund, R. L., 113
Berliner, D., 34
Bernhardt, E. B., 234
Berninger, V. W., 80
Biancarosa, G., 36
Billen, M. T., 58, 277
Binks, E., 86
Bintz, W. P., 194
Bissex, G., 232
Blachowicz, C., 38, 128, 136, 155–156
Black, P., 222, 224, 225
Blevins, W., 110
Block, C. C., 154, 316
Bloom, B. S., 273
Bloomfield, L., 4
Blume, J., 252
Bode, B. A., 257
Bogaert, L. R., 124
Bond, G,. L., 6
Borich, G. D., 33, 34, 58, 170
Bos, C. S., 86, 184
Boscolo, P., 276–277
Bosse, M. J., 188
Boster, S., 203, 207, 287
Bouchard, E., 152, 175
Boushey, G., 225, 247
Bowie, R., 327
Boyd, F. B., 259
Boyle, O. F., 67, 78, 128
Bradby, M., 143, 244
Brande, D., 174
Brandt, D., 8, 39
Braun, C., 156, 183
Brenner, D., 53, 331
Brett, A., 246
Brewer, P., 114
Breznitz, Z., 112
Britton, J., 181
Brophy, J., 34
Brown, A. L., 173, 175, 302
Brown, M. W., 160
Brown, R., 175
Bruner, E. C., 5
Bryan, G. W., 323, 324, 326
Bryan, J., 196
Bryant, B. R., 228
Buchanan, C. D., 5
Buly, M. R., 317
Buonanno, G. P., 73
Burgess, T., 181
Burnham, N. A., 234
Burns, S., 24
Burris, N. A., 75

Cahen, L., 34
Caldwell, J., 117
Calhoun, D. F., 180, 181
Calkins, L. M., 7, 77, 177–179, 182–184, 307, 308, 327, 329
Cambourne, B., 6–7
Campbell, M. L., 95
Campeau, S., 316
Campoy, F. I., 73

Caplan, R. I., 234
Carnicelli, T. A., 309
Carpenter, R., 120
Carr, D., 52
Carr, E., 196
Cartwright, K. B., 94
Caskey, M. M., 192
Caulfield, M., 151
Cecil, N. L., 70, 96
Celano, D., 317
Chall, J., 6, 69, 70, 110, 231, 232
Chandler, J., 23
Chapman, S., 171, 273
Chard, D. J., 86, 109, 113, 117
Chayet, B., 319
Chilcoat, G. W., 134
Child, D. A., 173
Chomsky, N., 6, 10
Christensen, B., 212
Chua, S. P., 324
Clark, D. C., 31
Clark, K., 24, 291
Clausen-Grace, N., 324
Clay, M. M., 65, 99, 117, 228, 229, 232, 240, 247, 328
Cobb, V., 252
Coddington, C. S., 325
Cohen, D. K., 225
Coh-Metrix, 234
Coiro, J., 8, 127, 200
Coles, R., 163
Collins, A., 174, 193
Collins, N. D., 41
Collom, S., 207
Combs, M., 105
Common Core Standards, 8, 40, 44, 47, 53, 55, 56, 73, 84, 85, 99, 103, 109, 121, 127, 133, 152, 159, 160, 163, 182, 183, 203, 210, 214, 218, 230, 231, 234, 240, 252, 254, 259, 272, 277, 278, 312, 316, 322
Conard, S., 232
Connell, R. W., 23
Conrad, P., 127
Cooke, N. L., 95
Cooper, E. J., 24
Cooper, J. D., 135
Cooter, R. B., 322
Cope, B., 56, 326
Corcoran, J., 262
Cornett, C. E., 275
Costello, B., 220
Coulter, W. A., 26
Cowan, K., 275
Cowley, J., 117
Coyne, M., 177
Crosbie, S., 89
Cummins, J. P., 21, 128, 134
Cunningham, A. E., 316
Cunningham, J. W., 92, 94, 153, 161
Cunningham, P., 228
Cunningham, P. M., 58, 86, 90, 92, 94, 129, 138, 316
Curtis, J. L., 184
Cushman, E., 39
Cutler, B. R., 31

Dahl, K. L., 86
Dahlgren, M. E., 86
Dale, E., 134, 231
Daniels, H., 206, 299–301
Darling, K., 252
Davidson, C., 190
Davis, M., 316
De Baryshe, B. D., 151
Deboer, G. E., 58
De Carlo, J. E., 7
DeGroot, A., 28
De La Paz, S., 312
Delucchi, K., 291
Depree, H., 269
De Souza, P., 209
DeVoogd, G., 11
DeVoss, D., 39
Dewey, J., 4, 5
DiCamillo, K., 252
Dickinson, D. K., 151
Dickinson, E., 279
Dickson, S., 86
Diederich, P., 7
Diehn, G., 327
DiPardo, A. P., 309
Dishaw, M., 34
Disney, W., 41, 322
DiTerlizzi, T., 164
Dixon, J., 5
Dobler, E., 200
Dobrynina, G., 204
Dodd, B., 89
Dodge, B., 201
Dolch, E., 95
Dolezal, S., 316
Dolezal-Kersey, S. E., 124
Donoghue, R. M., 105
Donovan, C. A., 56, 278, 312
Dorn, L. J., 224, 263, 297
Dow, R. S., 86
Dowhower, S. L., 110
Draper, R. J., 204
Duff, P., 21
Duffelmeyer, F., 198, 200
Duke, N. K., 152, 188, 252
Dukes, C., 70, 71, 78
Durkin, D., 38, 129, 152, 170
Dykstra, R., 6

Eagleton, M. B., 200
Echevarria, J., 20, 21
Echevarria, M., 38, 129, 152
Eckert, R. D., 177
Education Northwest, 7, 238
Ehri, L. C., 71, 85, 88, 110
Elbow, P., 7, 43
Eldredge, J. L., 86, 110–112, 271
Elkonin, D. B., 105, 106
Elley, W. B., 151
Elliot, J., 223
Elliott, L., 190
Elsholz, C., 147, 182, 222
Elting, M., 7, 278
Emig, J., 7, 278
Engelmann, S., 5
Entwisle, D. R., 23
Erickson, V. L., 31

Falco, F. L., 151
Farr, R., 226
Farris, P., 328
Faulconer, J., 188
Fawsett, G., 114
Fawson, P. C., 318, 324, 325, 328
Feez, S., 56
Fielding, L. G., 60, 152, 316
Filby, N., 34
Fink, L. S., 217
Fink-Chorzempa, B., 102
Fischel, J. E., 151
Fisher, C., 34
Fisher, D., 249, 265, 299, 302
Fisher, P. J., 38, 136
Fitzgerald, J., 51, 57, 77
Fleener, C., 156, 157
Fleischman, P., 114
Fleming, C., 50
Flesch, R. F., 4, 231
Fletcher, J., 26
Fletcher, R., 329
Fletcher, S., 326
Flood, J., 25, 99, 249
Florian, D., 253
Florio-Ruane, S., 299–300
Folsom, M., 212
Foorman, B., 73
Ford, M. P., 293, 296
Forrest-Pressley, D., 249
Forsythe, G. A., 194
Forsythe, P. D., 194
Foster, W. A., 70
Foulger, T. S., 327
Fountas, I. C., 101, 113, 231, 232, 291, 293
Fountoukidis, D. L., 91, 95, 129
Fox, M., 46–47, 59, 117, 181, 246, 247, 259, 318
Frank, A., 261, 327–328
Fredericks, A. D., 170
Freebody, P., 127
Freedle, R. O., 155–156, 158
Freedman, R., 252
Freedman, S. W., 309
The Freedom Writers, 25
Freeman, J., 251
Frey, N., 249, 299, 302
Friedlander, B., 55, 277, 312
Fries, C. C., 4
Fritz, J., 252
Frost, R., 149, 279
Fry, E. B., 91, 95, 129, 231
Fuchs, D., 110, 223
Fuchs, L. S., 110, 223

Gage, N., 32
Gagne, R. M., 32
Gallagher, M., 243, 316
Gambrell, L. B., 24, 167, 168, 181, 245, 257, 324, 325
Gardiner, S., 317
Garner, R., 173, 174
Gelati, C., 276–277
Gentry, J. R., 102
George, J. C., 252
George, M., 299–300
Gerard, M. R., 90
Gere, A., 303, 307
Gerhardt, C., 190
Gespass, S., 323
Geva, E., 90
Gibbons, G., 141, 165

Gilbert, J., 8, 39
Gillet, J. W., 102
Giovani, N., 72
Glenn, C. F., 247
Goatley, V. J., 259
Golenbock, P., 162
Gonzales, N., 16
Good, R. H., 223
Good, T., 34
Goodlad, J., 31, 245
Goodman, I. F., 23
Goodman, K. S., 10, 27, 224, 225, 228
Goodman, Y. M., 228
Gordon, C. J., 156, 183
Goudvis, A., 171
Gough, P. B., 9
Grabe, W., 20, 66
Grabill, J., 39
Graden, J. L., 223
Graham, J. M., 136, 137, 153–155, 206
Graham, S., 8, 39, 55, 57, 102, 277, 278, 312
Graves, D. H., 7, 46–47, 62, 278, 326–327
Graves, M. F., 128, 129, 133, 135
Gray, D., 102
Gray, K., 102
Gray, L., 95
Gray, W. S., 4, 95
Green, S. K., 101
Greenberg, J., 280
Gregory, L. P., 249
Grimes, J., 223
Grisham, D. L., 39, 203
Grogan, P. R., 86
Gromko, J. E., 37
Gruba, J., 223
Gruwell, E., 25
Gubbins, E. J., 177
Gunning, T. G., 85, 86, 88
Guszak, F. J., 170, 273
Guthrie, J. T., 43, 175, 188, 234, 245, 325

Hairrell, A., 127
Hall, D. P., 92
Hall, L. A., 330
Hallahan, D. P., 26, 92
Haller, E. P., 173
Hall-Kenyon, K. M., 183
Halverson, R., 193
Hampson, J. M., 38
Hancock, M. K., 276
Harris, K. R., 55, 102, 277, 312
Harrison, C., 222, 224
Harrison, D., 114
Harris-Sharples, S., 232
Hart, B., 65, 128, 129
Harvey, S., 171
Harward, S. V., 102
Harwayne, S., 77, 177–179, 182–184, 308, 327
Hasbrouck, J., 111
Hawken, L. S., 223
Hayes, D. P., 246
Haynes, J., 20, 21, 47
Hayward, M. D., 316
Heartman, C. F., 3
Heckelman, R. G., 110–112
Heilman, A. W., 86
Helf, S. H., 95

Heller, M. F., 150
Hemphill, L., 23
Hepworth, C., 212
Herrell, A. L., 21–23, 131, 132, 267
Herzog, L., 197
Hickam, H., 26
Hickman, P., 204
Hiebert, E. H., 244, 293, 316, 322
Higbee, K. L., 95, 194, 195
Hilden, K., 316
Hill, L. C., 17
Hillocks, G., 309
Hirata, S. Y., 24
Hoberman, M. A., 114, 253
Hodge, R., 73
Hoffman, J. V., 113
Holdaway, D., 78, 117, 118, 259, 262, 269
Hollingsworth, P. M., 109
Holm, A., 89
Homer, W., 136
Honeycutt, R. L., 49, 102, 217, 278
Hope, B. T., 316
Hornsby, D., 297
Hosp, M. K., 110
Hougen, M., 86
Huddelston, R., 103
Huey, E. B., 1, 4, 9, 115, 119
Hunt, L. C., 317
Hunter College, 238
Hurley, M., 246
Hyerle, D., 158
Hyland, K., 56
Hyman, T. S., 161

International Reading Association, 222, 250
Intersegmental Committee of the Academic Senates, 52
Invernizzi, M., 58, 75, 228
Irwin, J. W., 128, 132, 150, 165, 168
Isbell, R., 256
Iversen, S., 269
Ivey, G., 265

Jackson, A. Y., 25
Jackson, Y., 16
Jacob, B. A., 33
Jacobs, J. S., 182, 188, 251, 258, 323, 326
Jacobs, L., 96
Jawitz, P. B., 168
Jenkins, J. R., 110
Jensen, J. M., 99
Jensen, R., 317, 323
Jimenez-Silva, M., 327
Johns, J. L., 113, 192
Johnson, C. J., 168
Johnson, D. D., 28, 92, 128, 137, 139–143, 161, 164, 165, 171
Johnson, E. R., 134
Johnson, T. D., 101
Johnston, F. R., 58, 75
Johnston, P., 220
Johnston, P. H., 155, 156
Jones, C. D., 325
Jones, C. F., 252
Jones, L. A., 174, 175
Jones, R. C., 188
Jordan, M., 21–23, 131, 132, 267
Joshi, R. M., 86
Joyner, F. G., 199, 200

Juel, C., 69, 150, 228
Justice, L. M., 89

Kaderavek, J. N., 89
Kalan, R., 79
Kalantzis, M., 56, 326
Kalman, B., 165
Kameenui, E. J., 127, 128
Kamil, M. L., 234
Kaminski, R. A., 223
Kandel, E. R., 316
Kara-Soteriou, J., 278
Kauffman, J. M., 26
Kaufman, D., 278
Keen, P., 44
Keene, E. O., 163, 175
Kelley, M. J., 324
Kemper, D., 147, 182, 222
Kiefer, B. Z., 265
Kiger, N. D., 135
King, B., 274
Kintsch, W., 158
Kirby, D. L., 39, 178
Kirkpatrick, K., 198
Klein, A., 237
Kluda, S. L., 325
Knobel, M., 8, 127
Koda, K., 37, 85
Kong, A., 152, 243
Korbin, J. E., 23
Korth, B., 58, 277
Koskinen, P. S., 167
Koukis, S., 203, 207, 287
Kovacs, D., 258
Kovaleski, J. F., 223
Kozol, J., 23
Kragler, S., 117
Krashen, S. D., 20, 134, 316
Krathwohl, J. R., 32
Krebs, L., 189
Kress, G. R., 73
Kress, J. E., 91, 95, 129
Krull, K., 258
Kucan, L., 96, 128, 135, 150
Kuhn, M. R., 110, 268
Kurita, J. A., 168

Labbo, L. D., 255
LaBerge, D., 9, 150
Lacey, M., 266
Langer, J. A., 8, 188, 278, 281
Langford, K. G., 101
Langley, A., 209
Lankshear, C., 8, 127
Lapp, D., 99, 249
Lauber, G., 182, 282
Lawson, L. L., 86
Leahy, S., 225
Learning Center, 194
Learning Disabilities Association of America, 26
Lee, C., 222, 224
Lee, S., 322
Lefgren, L., 33
Lehr, F., 78, 127, 133–134
Lenski, S. D., 163, 192
Lensmire, T. J., 310
Lesaux, N. K., 37, 38, 85, 90
Leslie, L., 117
Leu, D. D., 200
Leu, D. J., Jr., 8, 127, 200
Levin, J. R., 151
Levine, D. U., 16

Levine, M., 330
Levstik, L. S., 265
Lewis, C. S., 245
Lewis, J. P., 170
Lewman, B., 247
Lickteig, M. J., 327
Lindfors, J. W., 84
Linek, W., 109
Liner, T., 39, 178
Lippman, L., 24
Livingston, M., 253
Logan, J. W., 136
Lonigan, C. J., 151
Lowry, L., 61, 265
Lucadamo, E., 52
Ludwig, T., 190
Lukens, R. J., 161, 298
Lund, G. N., 259
Lundberg, I., 73
Lyon, C., 225

MacArthur, C. A., 50, 57
MacIver, D. J., 197
Macrorie, K., 42, 210
Mann, A., 19
Manning, G., 276
Manning, M., 276
Manyak, P. C., 92
Manzo, A. V., 197
Manzo, U.C., 197
Marinak, B. A., 325
Marliave, R., 34
Marshall, B., 222, 224
Martin, B., Jr., 112, 117
Martin, L. E., 249
Martin, N., 181
Martinez, M., 112
Marzano, J. S., 131
Marzano, R. J., 28, 131
Marzollo, J., 121, 123
Mason, L., 102
Mason, L. H., 55, 277, 312
Mather, N., 86, 228
Mazurkiewicz, A. J., 5
McArthur, E., 24
McCoach, D. B., 177
McCormick, S., 85, 110, 113
McCutchen, D., 279
McGee, L. M., 71, 78
McGoldrick, J. A., 168
McGuffey, W. H., 3
McIntosh, M. E., 204
McKay, D. O., 32
McKeown, M. G., 96, 128, 132, 135, 150, 172, 173, 249
McKool, S. S., 323
McKoon, G., 161
McLaughlin, M., 11
McLeod, A., 181
McMahon, S. I., 259
McRae, A., 325
McTighe, J., 291
McTigue, E. M., 171
Medoff, M., 32
Medwell, J., 102
Mehan, H., 272
Meier, J. D., 228
Meister, C., 171, 175, 273
Melser, J., 117
Meltzer, B., 50
Menzel, P., 252
Meyer, B.J.F., 155–156, 158

Milewicz, E. J., 56, 278, 312
Miller, J., 311
Miller, M., 70
Miller, W. H., 80
Millin, S. K., 113
Milone, M., 232
Ming, K., 70, 71, 78
Mistretta-Hampston, J. M., 129, 152
Mohan, L., 124
Molebash,k P., 201
Moll, L., 16
Monroe, E. E., 189, 205, 207, 212
Monroe, M., 95
Montgomery, E., 4
Mooney, M. E., 59, 243, 253, 276, 303
Moore, D. W., 153
Moore, G., 234
Moore, R., 58
Moore, S. A., 325
Moore-Hart, M. A., 120
Moran, S., 102
More, J., 34
Morgan, D. N., 327, 328–329
Morgan, R., 252
Morgan, R. F., 156, 157
Morrison, T. G., 188, 249, 323
Morrow, L. M., 60, 102, 324
Moser, J., 225, 247
Moss, B., 188–189, 200, 324
Mraz, M., 24
Murray, D. M., 7, 41
Myers, W. D., 19, 179, 265

Nagy, W. E., 38, 127, 128, 246
Nathan, R., 75, 147, 182, 222
National Assessment of Educational Progress, 23, 188
National Association of State Directors of Special Education and Council of Administrators of Special Education, 222
National Center for Educational Statistics, 20, 24, 25
National Center on Response to Intervention, 26
National Commission on Writing in America's Schools and Colleges, 8, 39, 203
National Council of Teachers of English, 236
National Education Association, 252
National Endowment for the Arts, 316, 318
National Governors Association Center for Best Practices, and Council of Chief State School Officers, 234
National Reading Panel, 7, 27, 36, 62, 71, 78, 85, 88–90, 95, 112, 127, 175, 316, 317
National Urban Alliance, 142, 144
Nelson, J. P., 77
Ness, M., 114
Nessel, D. D., 136, 137, 153–155, 206
Nestler, E. J., 316
Nettles, D. H., 80
Neuman, S. B., 317
Newell, G. E., 203, 207, 287
Nichols, W. D., 136

Nicholson-Nelson, K., 276
Nobles, W. W., 15
North, S. M., 4
Nunes, S. R., 71, 88

Oakhill, J., 168
Ocker-Dean, E., 86
O'Day, J. A., 225
Ogle, D., 155–156, 195–196
Olson, L. S., 23
Olson, M. W., 226
O'Muhr, G. O,., 190
Opitz, M. F., 116, 264, 293, 296
Organisation for Economic Co-operation and Development, 225
O'Rourke, J., 134
Ortiz, S. O., 27
Osborn, J., 78, 127, 133–134
Osguthorpe, R. T., 33
Osguthorpe L. S., 33
O'Shea, D. J., 110
O'Shea, L. J., 110
Owens, R. E., 66

Padak, N., 109
Paige, D. D., 111, 112
Paivio, A., 168
Palincsar, A. S., 175, 302
Pappas, C. C., 265
Paquette, K., 285, 310–311
Pardo, L. S., 259
Paris, S. G., 110, 152
Parris, S. R., 154, 316
Parry, J., 297
Patel, S., 168
Paterson, K., 143
Paul, A. W., 73
Payne, C. D., 254
Pearson, P. D., 24, 28, 44, 92, 110, 128, 137, 139–143, 150–152, 156, 161, 164, 165, 171, 224, 243, 291, 316
Peck, R. N., 252
Peck, S. M., 115
Peregoy, S. F., 67, 78, 128
Perencevich, K. C., 175, 188
Perin, D., 55, 278
Perini, M. J., 205, 273
Peterson, D. P., 24
Peterson, S., 330
Petraglia, J., 278
Petroski, H., 5
Piaget, J., 5, 7, 11
Pierce, L. E., 58, 277
Pikulski, J. J., 109
Pilgreen, J. L., 323
Pinkney, J., 273
Pinnell, G. S., 101, 113, 231, 232, 291, 293
Podhajski, B., 86
Polacco, P., 32
Prasse, D., 223
Prater, K., 113
Preller, J., 258
Prelutsky, J., 146, 253, 282
Prensky, M., 330
Pressley, M., 38, 124, 129, 150–152, 161, 168, 175, 249, 316
Prior, J., 90
Prior, S. M., 117
Pritchard, R. J., 49, 102, 217, 278

Probst, R., 299–300
Pullum, G. K., 103

Quinn, D. W., 110, 112, 271
Quorn, K. C., 101

Raphael, T. E., 24, 171, 172, 259, 299–300
Rasinski, T. V., 24, 109, 113, 114, 116, 268
Ratcliff, R., 161
Rathmann, P., 163
Ray, K. W., 259
Readence, J. E., 110–112, 138, 158
Reis, S. M., 177
Reschly, D. J., 26
Reutzel, D. R., 109, 156, 157, 249, 316, 318, 322, 324, 325, 328
Richards, J. C., 162
Richardson, J. S., 156, 157
Richardson, M. J., 77
Richardson, W., 9, 331
Richgels, D. J., 71, 78
Riggs, K., 196
Riley, M., 331
Rinehart, S. D., 113
Risley, T. R., 65, 128, 129
Rivalland, J., 71
Robb, L., 160, 161, 206, 215, 264
Roberts, W. D., 252
Robinson, F. P., 193, 194
Rodriguez, M. C., 24
Roehrig, A. D., 124, 316
Rogers, C., 7
Rohl, M., 71
Romano, T., 177
Rosen, H., 181
Rosen, J. B., 316
Rosenblatt, L. M., 11, 45, 160, 271
Rosenshine, B., 171, 175, 273
Roser, N. L., 112
Rothlein, L., 246
Rothstein, A. S., 182, 282
Rothstein, E. B., 182, 282
Rowe, M. B., 272
Rozendal, M. S., 42
Ruddell, R. B., 33, 38, 62
Ruffins, R., 148
Rumelhart, D. E., 10
Rupley, W., 127
Rupley, W. H., 136
Rylant, C., 184

Saddler, B., 102
Sadoski, M., 168
Salcedo, J. B., 253
Sammons, J., 228
Samuels, S. J., 9, 110, 111, 150, 316
Sanders, N. M., 273
Sarnoff, J., 148
Saussure, F., 73
Say, A., 19
Scardamalia, M., 32
Schafft, K., 25
Scharer, P. L., 86
Schick, E., 212
Schlagal, B., 99, 102, 103
Schmidt, D., 324
Schmidt, G. D., 144
Schneider, R. B., 35
Scholastic, 322, 330
Schreiber, F. J., 177

Schuder, T., 175
Schulman, M. B., 254
Schumann, J., 223
Schwanenflugel, P., 110
Schwartz, D., 252
Schwartz, J., 228
Scieszka, J., 157
Scillian, D., 212
Scott, J. A., 38, 244, 322
Seay, S., 224
Sebranek, P., 147, 182, 222
Seeger, L. V., 190
Seifert, M., 234
Seifert-Kessell, N., 174, 175
Seigel, L., 37, 85
Sendak, M., 252
Seuss, D., 252, 282
Shanahan, T., 37, 42, 43, 51, 66, 85, 128, 234, 316
Shannon, G., 212
Shaw, N., 79
Shertle, A., 73
Short, D. J., 20, 21
Shumway, J., 58, 277
Silver, H. F., 205, 273
Silverstein, S., 146, 253
Silvey, A., 250
Simmons, D., 127
Simon, S., 165, 198
Sindelar, P. T., 110
Singer, H., 232
Skinner, B. F., 4, 11
Slotta, J., 330
Smith, D., 41, 322
Smith, D. L., 86
Smith, E., 174
Smith, F., 10, 11, 52, 59, 98, 150, 177, 327
Smith, J. A., 325
Smith, L., 247, 282
Smith, M. S., 225
Smith, M. W., 151
Smith, N. B., 2, 90, 95, 115, 249
Smith, R. J., 273, 326
Smith-Burke, T. M., 60
Smolkin, L. B., 56, 278, 312
Snow, C. E., 23, 36, 150, 152, 247
Soffos, C., 224, 263, 297
Solomon, D., 291
Sonnenschein, S., 89, 324

Spandel, V., 40, 49, 62, 118, 120, 142, 238
Speare, E. G., 138
Spillane, J. P., 225
Spinelli, J., 44
Squire, J. R., 99
Stahl, S. A., 110, 131
Stanovich, K. E., 10, 316
Stapleton, L. M., 89
Staton, J., 257
Stauffer, R. G., 79
Stein, N., 247
Stenner, A. J., 232
Steptoe, J., 143
Sternberg, R. J., 129, 246
Stevens, J., 190
Stiggins, R. J., 118, 120, 142
Stoeke, J. M., 69
Strecker, S., 112
Strong, R. W., 205, 273
Stuck, G., 36
Sturtevant, E., 109
Sukarna, D., 297
Sullivan, A., 16
Swales, J., 56
Swartz, S., 287
Sweet, A. P., 150, 152, 247, 325
Swinyard, W. R., 188, 323
Symons, S., 168

Taba, H., 140, 141
Tanyzer, H. J., 5
Tapahonso, L., 212
Taylor, B. M., 24, 291
Taylor, G. C., 72
Taylor, W., 232
Teale, W. H., 24, 181
Temple, C., 75
Temple, F., 75
Templeton, S. R., 58, 75
Terrell, T., 20
Thomas, M. M., 197
Thomas, T. G., 188
Thome, C., 27
Thompson, M., 225
Thompson, W. B., 168
Tierney, R. J., 27, 42, 44, 51, 110–112, 150, 158
Tilly, W. D., 223
Tindal, G. A., 111

Tobin, A. W., 234
Tomlinson, C. A., 291
Tompkins, G. E., 44, 62, 105, 110, 189, 207, 235, 255, 265–266, 323
Tompkins, R., 331
Torgeson, J. K., 228
Touchstone Applied Science Associates (TASA), 232
Trabasso, T., 152, 175
Trelease, J., 245
Trivias, E., 161
Tsuchiya, Y., 45
Tunnell, M. O., 134, 182, 251, 258, 323, 326
Tyler, B., 113
Tyner, B., 279

Unrau, N. J., 38
U.S. Department of Education, 113
USDA Economic Research Service, 24

Vacca, J. L., 55
Vacca, R. T., 55
Valencia, S. W., 227
Valmont, W. J., 331
Van Allsburg, C., 162, 167, 179, 247, 252
Van Dijk, T. A., 158
Van Meter, P., 175
Vaughn, S., 26, 184
Vause, D. J., 67
Vincent, C. G., 223
Virkler, A. J., 115
Vladez-Menchaca, M. C., 151
Vogt, M., 20, 21
Vygotsky, L. S., 7, 11, 262

Wagstaff, J., 58, 92, 94
Walberg, H. J., 173
Walpole, S., 24, 268, 291
Warburg, S. S., 160
Warzon, K. B., 124
Washington, B. T., 32, 244
Watanabe, L. M., 183
Watt, M., 159
Watts-Taffe, S. N., 128, 135
Webb, N., 77
Webster, N., 3
Weitzman, I., 114

Welling, K. A., 117
Wham, M. A., 192
Wharton-McDonald, R., 38, 129, 152
White, E. B., 143, 252
White, S., 113
Whitehurst, G. J., 151
Whiteley, C. S., 154
Whitenack, J. W., 42
Whitin, D. J., 206
Whitin, P., 206
Whitney, A., 327
Wigfield, A., 43, 175, 188, 325
Wilcox, B., 58, 205, 207, 212, 238, 277, 308
Wilcox, V. C., 83
Wilhelm, J. D., 275
Wiliam, D., 222, 224, 225
Wilkinson, I. A. G., 244, 322
Wills, C., 196
Wilson, P. T., 60, 316
Wisniewski, D., 166
Witherell, C. S., 31
Wittrock, M. C., 155, 168
Wollman-Bonilla, J. E., 42
Wolsey, T. D., 39, 203
Wong, B. Y. L., 80
Woodman, D. A., 259
Worthy, J., 113
Wray, D., 102
Wright, D. A., 204
Wright, R. A., 330
Wu, Y., 316
Wyne, M., 36

Yates, E., 58, 277
Yolen, J., 144
Yoon, J. C., 316
Yopp, H. K., 28, 73, 228, 252, 275
Yopp, R. H., 28, 73, 252, 275
Young, E., 161
Young, E. L., 77
Young, J., 324
Young, T. A., 200, 253, 300, 323, 324, 326

Zacarian, D., 20, 21, 47
Zecker, L. B., 39
Zemelman, S., 206
Zimmermann, S., 163, 175
Zutell, J., 113

Subject Index

Academic words, 134
Access to print
    shared reading and, 269–270
    shared writing and, 283
Accuracy in reading, 109, 110–112
Achievement gap, 16
Acquisition of vocabulary, 128
Advanced fluency stage of second language
    acquisition, 21
Advance planning for shared writing, 281–282
Advantage/TASA Open Standard (ATOS)
    system, 232
Aesthetic stance, 11
After reading activities
    literature discussion groups, 301–302
    reading workshops, 299
    shared reading, 271–276
    small group sessions, 294, 296
After writing activities
    formula writing, 313
    intermediate grade writing groups, 305
    primary grade writing groups, 304
    shared writing, 285–288
    writing workshops, 308–310
Aliteracy, 316
Alphabet books, 212–213
Alphabetic principle, 84
Analogical phonics (word families), 90–94
Analytic phonics, 88
Analytic scoring methods, 238
Anaphora, 165–166
Anecdotal notes, 236
Answering game, 274
Anthologies, 292
Anticipation guides, 198–200
Antonyms, 142
Applying stage of reading process, 46
Argumentative text
    advertisements, 216, 217
    description of, 159–160
    persuasive papers, 214–215, 217
Arrow connections, 166–167
Assessment
    abilities and, 219–220
    as informing instruction, 239–240
    of oral reading, 117
    of reading, 227–234
    role of, 220
    types of, 220–227
    of writing, 235–239
Assessment for learning philosophy, 224–225
Assignments
    for shared reading, 269
    for shared writing, 279–280
ATOS (Advantage/TASA Open Standard)
    system, 232
Attention span and reading aloud, 247–248
Attitude in shared reading, 266–267
Audience for writing, 180–182
Author's craft, examining and discussing, 259
Author visits, 258
Awards for children's books, 250
Awareness of sounds and letters
    combining spoken and written language,
        78–81
    overview of, 70–71
    recognition of language sounds, 71–73
    written language development, 73–78

Basals. See core literacy programs
Basic interpersonal communication skills (BICS),
    21, 134
Bee-flea activity, 168–169
Before reading activities
    literature discussion groups, 300–301
    reading workshops, 298
    shared reading, 266–268
    small group sessions, 293, 296
Before writing activities
    formula writing, 313
    intermediate grade writing groups, 305
    primary grade writing groups, 304
    shared writing, 279–280
    writing workshops, 307
Beginning stage of literacy development, 69–70,
    84. See also word identification
Beginning stage of writing. See conventions of
    written language
Behaviorist movement, 4
BICS (basic interpersonal communication skills),
    21, 134
Book order offers, promoting, 318
Books. See also text
    awards for, 250
    class books, 121–123
    for classroom libraries, 318–320
    for dealing with disabilities, 27
    displaying, 321
    for high frequency words, 95, 129
    informational texts, 189, 190
    joke books, 114
    multicultural, 17–19
    for multiple voices, 114
    for phonological awareness, 72–73
    picture books, 78–79
    for poetry, 146, 147
    for powerful language, 143, 144
    for precise writing, 143
    for reading aloud, 250–253
    Time Warp Trio series, 157
Book talks, 323–324
Bottom-up theory, 9–10
Brainstorming, 178
Bridge connections, 166–167
Buddy reading, 270–271

CALP (cognitive academic language proficiency),
    21, 134
Cause-and-effect text, 190
Chall, Jeanne, *Learning to Read: The Great
    Debate*, 6
Checking out books from classroom libraries,
    322–323
Checklists for writing process, 237
Children
    fresh perspectives of, 14
    reading to, 244–253
    writing to, 253–259
Choice
    of material for sustained silent
        reading, 322
    of topic for journal writing, 328–329
Choral reading, 116, 269–270
Clarifying strategy, 176
Clarity in teaching, 34
Class books, 121–123
Class newspapers, 185

Classroom libraries
    creating, 318–320
    importance of, 317–318
    lending libraries, 324, 325
    using, 320–323
Classroom post office, 124
Classroom writing assessment, 236–239
Clichés, 144
Cloze procedure, 232, 234
Cognitive academic language proficiency (CALP),
    21, 134
Cognitive processes
    overview of, 43–44
    in reading, 44–46
    in writing, 46–47, 49–51
Collaborative writing, 208–209
Common Core State Standards
    components of fluency and, 109
    comprehension strategies and, 152
    genre writing and, 56, 312
    informational writing and, 203
    overview of, 8
    phonics and, 84
    self-regulated strategy development and, 55
    shared writing and, 277, 278
    text complexity and, 234, 322
    text structure and, 155
    vocabulary and, 133
Comparison text, 190
Composition, 177
Comprehension. See also meaning construction
    description of, 38–39
    as goal of reading instruction, 150
Comprehension monitoring, 173–174
Comprehension strategies, definition of, 152
Computer technology and literacy development,
    330–331
Concepts, definition of, 57
Concepts about print
    description of, 99–100
    reading aloud and, 246–247
Conclusions, drawing, 162–163
Conferences about writing, 236–237, 310–311
Conferencing for content, 119–120
Connections, making, 163–167
Constructivist movement, 6
Content areas
    argumentative writing in, 214–217
    definition of, 188
    expository text features, 190–192
    expository text structure, 188–190, 209–213
    general writing prompts for adaptation
        to, 204
    reading in, 188
    study guides, 197–203
    study strategies, 192–197
    writing in, 203
    writing without revision in, 203–207
    writing with revision in, 207–209
Content words, 94
Conventions in effective writing, 42
Conventions of written language
    concepts about print, 99–100
    grammar, 103–104
    handwriting, 102–103
    interactive writing, 104–106
    overview of, 99
    spelling, 101–102

Core literacy programs
  description of, 53–54
  shared reading within, 263
  shared writing within, 277
  small group reading instruction within, 292–297
  small group writing instruction within, 303–305
Criterion-referenced tests, 221–222
Critical stance, 11
Cross-age tutoring, 35
Cueing systems, 69
Cultural capital, 16
Culture, 15–19
CultureGrams web site, 16–17
Curriculum integration, 275
Cursive writing, 103, 256

Decoding abilities, 150
Deliberate responses to reading, 274–276
Descriptive text, 189
Developmental journal writing, 75, 77–78
Dialogue journals, 257
Diaries. *See* journal writing
The Diary of a Young Girl (Frank), 261
DIBELS (Dynamic Indicators of Basic Early Literacy Skills), 223–224
Dick and Jane series readers, 4, 95
Dictation, taking, 283
Discussion, encouraging, 272–273
DISTAR program, 5
Drafting stage of writing process, 47, 49, 282, 288
Drawing conclusions, 162–163
During reading activities
  literature discussion groups, 301
  reading workshops, 298–299
  shared reading, 268–271
  small group sessions, 293–294, 296
During writing activities
  formula writing, 313
  intermediate grade writing groups, 305
  primary grade writing groups, 304
  shared writing, 282–285
  writing workshops, 307
Dyad reading, 271
Dynamic Indicators of Basic Early Literacy Skills (DIBELS), 223–224

Early production stage of second language acquisition, 20
Echo reading, 112, 269–270
Editing stage of writing process, 50, 287
Efferent stance, 11
Eight Ws, 273
Elementary and Secondary Education Act, Title I, 23
Elements of reading. *See* reading, elements of
ELLs. *See* English language learners
Elocution, 4
Emergent literacy
  combining spoken and written language, 78–81
  definition of, 65, 69
  oral language development, 65–69
  recognition of language sounds, 71–73
  written language development, 73–78
Engagement of students, 35, 132
English language learners (ELLs)
  fluency of, 109–110
  focus on teaching of, 8
  multiple meaning words and, 130
  readers' theater and, 113

second language acquisition and, 20–21
special services for, 21–22
vocabulary and, 128–129
Environment and vocabulary, 131–132
Euphemisms, 130
Evaluation process in writing, 39
Experience, linking words with, 131
Explicit instruction
  definition of, 58
  in phonics, 89
  in word families, 91–92
Exploring stage of reading process, 45–46
Expository text
  description of, 157–159
  reading and features of, 190–192
  reading and structure of, 188–190
  writing and, 209–213
Exposure to words, 132
Expression, reading with, 109, 112–115, 248
Expressive vocabularies, 127, 128
Extrinsic motivation, 60

Facilitating
  formula writing, 313
  intermediate grade reading groups, 296–297
  intermediate grade writing groups, 305
  literature discussion groups, 302–303
  primary grade reading groups, 294–295
  primary grade writing groups, 304–305
  reading workshops, 299
  writing workshops, 310–311
Fairy tales, 169
First Grade Studies, 6
First thoughts, throwing out, 144–146
Five-step approach to vocabulary instruction, 137–139
Fluency in reading
  components of, 109–110
  description of, 38
  expression and, 112–115
  rate, accuracy, and, 110–112
Fluency in written language
  sentence fluency, 42, 118–120
  voice, 120–124
Fluent stage of literacy development, 70
Formal language, 142
Formative assessment, 222–225
Forms of writing
  memoirs, 183–184
  newspapers, 185
  stories, 182–183
Formula writing, 311–313
Four Es of vocabulary instruction, 131–133
Frost, Robert, "The Road Less Taken," 149
Frustrational levels, 230
Function words, 94
Funds of knowledge, 16

Games as study guides, 201–203
Generalizations
  mechanics, 99, 100
  phonics, 86–88
  spelling, 101
Genres of writing, 182
Genre writing
  description of, 56
  shared writing within, 278
Gift books, 318
Gradual release of responsibility, 243–244, 316
Grammar, 103–104
Graphic aids in expository text, 192, 193
Graphic organizers, 158–159, 197–198

Group reading, 115–116
Gruwell, Erin, *The Freedom Writers Diary*, 25
Guided reading, 116, 292
Guided writing, 303

Handwriting, 99, 102–103
Hickam, Homer, *October Sky*, 26
High frequency words, 95, 129
Hink Pink word game, 92–93
History of literacy instruction
  colonial period, 2–3
  early American history, 3–4
  early 1900s, 4–5
  late 1900s, 6–7
  2000s, 7–8
Holistic scoring methods, 238
Homographs, 130
Homophones, 130
Hooray for Diffendoofer Day (Seuss, Prelutsky, & Smith), 282
Hornbooks, 2
Huey, Edmund Burke, *The Psychology and Pedagogy of Reading*, 1

Ideas in effective writing, 41, 177–180
Idioms, 113
Illiteracy, 316
Illustrations and reading aloud, 249
Immediate fluency stage of second language acquisition, 21
Immediate responses to reading, 272–274
Implementing
  formula writing, 313
  intermediate grade reading groups, 296
  intermediate grade writing groups, 305
  literature discussion groups, 300–302
  primary grade reading groups, 293–294
  primary grade writing groups, 303–304
  reading workshops, 298–299
  writing workshops, 306–310
Implicit instruction
  definition of, 58
  in phonics, 89–90
"I'm thinking of a word" game, 93, 94
Incentive programs, 325–326
Independent reading
  levels of, 230
  volume of, and reading achievement, 316–317
Individual methods of reading assessment, 228–231
Inferential strategies
  asking and answering questions, 169–173
  creating mental images, 167–169
  drawing conclusions, 162–163
  making connections, 163–167
  overview of, 160–162
  predicting outcomes, 162
Informal language, 142
Informal reading inventories, 117, 230–231
Informational text
  description of, 157–159
  reading aloud, 252
  reading and features of, 190–192
  reading and structure of, 188–190
  writing and, 209–213
Initial teaching alphabet, 5
Initiate, Response, and Evaluation (IRE), 272
Input category of learning disability, 26
Instruction, essential elements of
  overview of, 57
  time to do, 58–59
  time to learn, 57–58
  time to share, 59–60

Instructional approaches. *See also* small group instruction
  assessment as informing, 239–240
  core literacy programs, 53–54
  genre writing, 56
  literature units, 55–56
  overview of, 53
  phonics, 88–90
  reading and writing workshops, 54
  self-regulated strategy development, 55–56
  shared reading within, 262–265
  shared writing within, 277–278
  sight words, 95–96
  for vocabulary, 131–133, 136–141
  word families, 91–92
Instructional support for language minorities, 22
Instructions, writing to students, 255–256
Interaction during sustained silent reading, 324
Interactive theory, 10–11
Interactive writing, 104–106
Intermediate grade groups
  reading, 295–297
  writing, 305
Internet inquiry projects, 200–201
Intertextuality, 163–164
Intrinsic motivation, 60
Invented spelling, 73–74
IRE (Initiate, Response, and Evaluation), 272
I-Search, 210

Jacobs, Leland, "First Things First," 96
Jefferson, Thomas, Declaration of Independence, 50
Journal writing
  benefits of, 315
  choice of topics for, 328–329
  description of, 327–328
  developmental, 75, 77–78
  dialogue journals, 257
  providing time for, 328
Judging student writing, 237–239

Key behaviors of effective teaching, 33–36
Keyboarding, 7
Key word notes, 153–154
Key word prediction, 136–137
Knowledge, funds of, 16. *See also* prior knowledge
Knowledge mobilization, 44
Known words, 133
KWL study strategy, 195–196

Labels in classrooms, 256–257
Language arts, 127
Language development. *See* oral language development; written language development
Language experience approach (LEA)
  description of, 79–81
  interactive writing compared to, 104–105
Language minorities
  school assistance, 21–22
  second language acquisition, 20–21
Languages children bring to school, 84
Language sounds, recognition of, 71–73
Large-scale writing assessment, 235–236
LEA. *See* language experience approach
Lead readers, 270–271
Lead writers, 283–285
Learning, definition of, 32–33
Learning disabilities, 26–28
Learning logs, 204–205
Lee, Harper, *To Kill a Mockingbird*, 50

Lending libraries, 324, 325
Letters, awareness of
  combining spoken and written language, 78–81
  overview of, 70–71
  recognition of language sounds, 71–73
  written language development, 73–78
Letters as mnemonic devices, 194–195
Levels of motivation, 60–61
Lexile framework, 232
Libraries in classrooms
  creating, 318–320
  importance of, 317–318
  lending libraries, 324, 325
  using, 320–323
Life maps, 178
Limited schema, 68–69
LIONS approach, 281
Literacy development
  beginning stage, 69–70
  as continuum, 64–65
  emergent stage, 65, 69
  fluent stage, 70
  overview of, 69
Literature discussion groups
  description of, 55
  implementing, 299–303
  roles and responsibilities for, 301
Literature units
  description of, 54–55
  shared reading within, 264–265

Main ideas, identifying, 153–154
Making words activity, 93–94
Marking system for running records, 229
McGuffey's readers, 3–4
Meaning construction
  foundational meaning-making abilities, 150–151
  ideas, 177–180
  inferential strategies, 160–173
  metacognitive strategies, 173–175
  multiple strategies, 175–176
  organizational strategies, 152–160
  reading comprehension strategies, 151–153
  through writing, 177–185
Mechanics generalizations, 99, 100
Memoirs, writing, 183–184
Memory category of learning disability, 26
Mental images, creating, 167–169
"Message in a Starry Sky" (Baslaw-Finger), 275
Metacognitive strategies, 173–175
Mini-lessons, 57
Minimal pairs contrast approach, 4–5
Mirror experiences, 275
Mismatched schema, 69
Mnemonic devices, 194–195
Modeling
  reading, 323
  writing, 258–259
Morning messages, 254–255
Motivation, 60–61, 245–246
MSV approach to running records, 229
Multicultural books, 17–19
Multi-Flow Maps, 162–163
Multiple meaning words, 130
Multisensory activities, 144

Names Test, 228
Narrative text
  description of, 155–157
  reading aloud, 252

Neurological impress, 112
The New England Primer, 3
Newspapers for class, 185
New words, 133
Norm-referenced tests, 221, 222
Note taking/note making, 206
Novels for shared reading, 265

An Observation Survey of Early Literacy Achievement (Clay), 228
Ongoing assistance with writing, 236–237
Online reading resources, 319
Onomatopoeia, 130
Oral language development
  overview of, 65–67
  schema theory, 67–69
Oral reading. *See also* fluency in reading
  assessment of, 117
  group reading, 115–116
  transition to silent reading, 117–118
Organizational aids in expository text, 191–192
Organizational strategies
  identifying main ideas, 153–154
  overview of, 152
  recognizing stance, 160
  recognizing text structure, 155–160
  summarizing, 155
Organization category of learning disability, 26
Organization in writing
  audience, 180–182
  forms of writing, 182–185
  as trait, 41
Organizing
  formula writing, 312–313
  intermediate grade reading groups, 295–296
  intermediate grade writing groups, 305
  literature discussion groups, 300
  primary grade reading groups, 292–293
  primary grade writing groups, 303
  reading workshops, 298
  writing workshops, 306
Outcomes, predicting, 162
Output category of learning disability, 26
Outside of school reading and writing, 8–9
Overgeneralization, 66

Peg lists, 195
Pen pals, 181–182
Perceived expectation motivation, 60–61
Perceived requirement motivation, 60
Percentile scores, 221
Performance-based assessment, 225–227
Personal notes to students, 254
Persuasive papers, writing, 214–215, 217
Phonemes, 71
Phonemic awareness, 37, 71
Phonics
  analogical (word families), 90–94
  description of, 37, 84–85
  generalizations, 86–88
  goals of instruction in, 85–86
  instructional approaches to, 88–90
  phonological awareness compared to, 78
Phonological awareness
  description of, 36–37, 71
  learning disability and, 27–28
  phonics compared to, 78
  processes of, in order of difficulty, 74
Phonology, 65–66
Physical spaces as mnemonic devices, 195
Picture books, 78–79
Picture word inductive model, 180

A Place Called School (Goodlad), 31
Plagiarism, 40
Poetry
    reading aloud, 252–253
    writing, 146–147
Popcorn reading, 269
Portfolios, 226–227
Poverty, 23–24
Powerful language, 143–146
Pragmatics, 66
Precise language, 142–143
Predicates, definition of, 104
Predicting outcomes, 162
Pre-production stage of second language
    acquisition, 20
Prereading stage of reading process, 44–45
Presentation in effective writing, 42–43
Prewriting stage of writing process, 47
Primary grade groups
    reading, 292–295
    writing, 303–305
Primary sources, 210
Primers, 3
Print, access to
    shared reading and, 269–270
    shared writing and, 283
Print concepts
    description of, 99–100
    reading aloud and, 246–247
Print features of expository text, 190–191
Prior knowledge
    comprehension and, 151
    inference and, 161–162
    mental imagery and, 168
Problem-and-solution text, 190
Procedures, definition of, 57
Programmed reading, 5
Projects, assessment of, 227
Prompts for shared writing, 279–280
Prose, 146
Publishing stage of writing process, 51, 287–288
Puns, 113
Puppet shows, 113, 115

QAR (question-answer relationships), 171–172
QtA (questioning the author), 172–173
Qualitative assessment, 220
Qualitative dimensions of text complexity, 234
Quantitative assessment, 220
Quantitative dimensions of text complexity, 234
Question-answer relationships (QAR), 171–172
Questioning the author (QtA), 172–173
Questions
    asking and answering, 169–173
    leveled, 273
    open-ended, 272
    reading aloud and, 249–250

Rate of oral reading, 110–112
Readability formulas, 231–232
Reader dimensions of text complexity, 234
Readers' theater, 113
Reading. *See also* oral reading; reading, elements
    of; reading aloud; shared reading;
    vocabulary and reading
    accuracy in, 109, 110–112
    assessment of, 227–234
    to children, 244–253
    cognitive processes in, 44–46
    in content areas, 188
    with expression, 109, 112–115, 248
    incentive programs for, 325–326

linking with writing, 43, 51–52
small group instruction in, 292–303
teacher interaction during, 324
teacher modeling of, 323
Reading, elements of
    comprehension, 38–39, 150
    fluency, 38
    overview of, 36
    phonics, 37, 78, 84–94
    phonological awareness, 27–28, 36–37, 71,
        74, 78
    vocabulary, 28, 37–38, 142–147, 246
Reading aloud
    book selection for, 250–253
    expression and, 248
    illustrations and, 249
    importance of, 245–248
    overview of, 244
    questions and, 249–250
Reading centers, 319–320
Reading mastery program, 5
Reading stage of reading process, 45
Reading stamina, 247
Receptive vocabularies, 127, 128
Reciprocal teaching, 175–176
Repeated reading, 110–112
The Report of the National Reading Panel, 7–8, 316
Reports
    sections of, 211
    writing, 208–212
Responding stage
    of reading process, 45
    of writing process, 285–287
Revising stage of writing process, 49–50, 285–287
Revision, writing with
    overview of, 206–207
    shared writing, 207–208
    small groups, 208–209
Revision, writing without
    learning logs, 204–205
    note taking/note making, 206
    overview of, 203–204
    think-write-share, 205–206
Rough drafts, 282
Round robin reading, 115–116, 268–269
RtI (response to intervention), 8, 26–28, 223–224
Rubrics, 225–226
Running records, 117, 228–230
Rural education, 25–26

Scanning, 193
Schema in shared reading, 266
Schema theory, 67–69
School assistance for language minorities, 21–22
Secondary sources, 210
Second language acquisition, 20–21
Seeking response stage of writing process, 49
Self-regulated strategy development (SRSD)
    description of, 55–56, 312
    shared writing within, 277–278
Semantic mapping, 140–141
Semantics, 66
Semiotics, 73
Senses, using in writing, 144
Sentence fluency, 42, 118–120
Sentences, definition and parts of, 104
Sequential text, 190
Shared reading
    fluency and, 116
    within instructional approaches, 262–265
    process of, 265–276
    word identification and, 96–99

Shared stories, 178–179
Shared writing
    within instructional approaches, 277–278
    overview of, 276–277
    process of, 278–288
    writing with revision, 207–208
Sharing work, opportunities for, 59–60
Sheltered instruction, 22
Sight words, 94–96, 150
Silent period, 20
Silent reading. *See also* sustained silent reading
    independent, volume of, and reading
        achievement, 316–317
    transition from oral reading to, 117–118
Sincere desire motivation, 61
Six+1 traits of effective writing. *See* writing,
    traits of
Skills, definition of, 57, 110
Skimming, 193
Small group instruction
    core literacy programs, 292–297, 303–305
    formula writing, 311–313
    literature discussion groups, 299–303
    in New Zealand, 290
    overview of, 291
    reading workshops, 297–299
    writing workshops, 305–311
Small groups, writing in, 208–209
Sounds, language, recognition of, 71–73. *See also*
    awareness of sounds and letters
Speech emergence stage of second language
    acquisition, 20
Spelling, 101–102
Spelling bees, 102
SQ3R study strategy, 193–194
SRSD. *See* self-regulated strategy development
SSR. *See* sustained silent reading
Stance, recognizing, 160
Stanine scores, 221
Stories, writing, 182–183
Story maps, 156–157
Strategies. *See also* inferential strategies;
    organizational strategies
    comprehension, definition of, 152
    definition of, 110, 151
    metacognitive, 173–175
    study, 192–196
Student choice
    of material for sustained silent reading, 322
    of topic for journal writing, 328–329
Student surveys, 273–274
Student-text matching, 231–234
Study guides
    anticipation guides, 198–200
    games, 201–203
    graphic organizers, 197–198
    Internet inquiries, 200–201
    overview of, 197
Study strategies
    KWL, 195–196
    mnemonic devices, 194–195
    overview of, 192–193
    SQ3R, 193–194
Subjects, definition of, 104
Success rate, 35–36
Summarizing, 155
Summative assessment, 220–222
Sustained silent reading (SSR)
    choice of materials for, 322
    description of, 316–317
    interaction during, 324
    motivation and, 323
    providing time for, 320

Synonym stacking, 142–143
Syntax, 66
Synthesis/synthesizing, 39, 155
Synthetic approach to phonics, 5, 88

Task orientation in teaching, 34–35
Teaching
    definition of, 32–33
    impact of, 32–36
    key behaviors of effective, 33–36
Technology and literacy development,
    330–331
Tests of spelling, 102
Text. *See also* books; text structure
    complexity of, 234, 322
    making connections outside, 163–164
    making connections within, 165–167
    types of, 189–190
    visualization of, 168
Text clues, insufficient, 68
Text leveling, 232, 233
Text structure
    argumentative, 159–160, 214–217
    informational, 157–159, 188–192,
        209–213, 252
    narrative, 155–157
Thematic units of study, 265
Theories of literacy
    bottom-up, 9–10
    interactive, 10–11
    top-down, 10
Think-alouds, 174–175
Thinking Maps, 158–159, 162–163
Think-write-share activity, 205–206
Time, providing in classrooms
    for doing, 58–59
    for learning, 57–58
    for reading, 320–321
    for sharing, 59–60
    for writing, 328
Timed writing, 119
Title I, Elementary and Secondary Education
    Act, 23
Titles, creating new, 181
"To, With, and By" (Wilcox), 243
Top-down theory, 10
Topic for journal writing, choice of, 328–329
Tracking books read by students, 323
Traits of effective writing. *See* writing, traits of
Transcription, 177
Tree Maps, 158, 159

Tutoring, cross-age, 35
Types of words, 133–135

Urban education, 24–25
Used books, 318–319

Variety in teaching, 34
Visualization of text, 168
Vocabulary. *See also* words
    description of, 37–38
    development of, and learning
        disability, 28
    poetry, 146–147
    reading aloud and, 246
    word choice in writing, 142–146
    writing and, 142–147
Vocabulary and reading
    guiding principles, 131–133
    instructional approaches, 136–141
    overview of, 127
    size of vocabularies, 128
    types of words, 133–135
    word collections, 129–131
Voice
    in effective writing, 40
    in fluency in written language, 120–124

Wait times, 272–273
Webster, Noah, *American Spelling Book*, 3
Whole class reading. *See* shared reading
Whole class writing. *See* shared writing
Whole language movement, 6–7
Whole word approach to reading
    instruction, 4
Wilcox, Val C., 83
Word banks, 282
Word choice in effective writing
    powerful language, 143–146
    precise language, 142–143
    as trait, 42
Word collections/walls, 129–131
Word consciousness, 135
Word families, 90–94
Word games, 92–94
Word identification
    phonics, 84–90
    shared reading, 96–99
    sight words, 94–96, 150
    word families, 90–94
Word play, 72

Words. *See also* word choice in effective writing;
        word identification
    definition of, 127
    exposure to, 132
    function, 94
    high frequency, 95, 129
    types of, 133–135
Worksheets, study guides compared to, 197
Workshop format
    for reading instruction, 54, 297–299
    shared reading within, 263–264
    shared writing within, 277
    for writing instruction, 7, 54, 305–311
Writers' notebooks, 179–180
Writing. *See also* journal writing; shared writing;
        writing, traits of; writing instruction
    assessment of, 235–239
    audience for, 180–182
    cognitive processes in, 46–47, 49–51
    in content areas, 203
    cursive, 103, 256
    forms of, 48
    independent, 230, 326–327
    meaning construction through, 177–185
    with revision, 206–209
    small group instruction in, 303–313
    technology, 330–331
    vocabulary and, 142–147
    without revision, 203–206
Writing, traits of
    conventions, 42
    ideas, 41
    organization, 41, 180–185
    overview of, 39–40
    presentation, 42–43
    sentence fluency, 42, 118–120
    voice, 40, 120–124
    word choice, 42, 142–146
Writing frames, 183
Writing instruction
    genres of writing, 8
    history of, 3–5, 7
    linking reading with, 43, 51–52
    workshop format for, 7, 54
Written language development. *See also* fluency in
        written language
    conventions of written language, 99–104
    journal writing, 75, 77–78
    overview of, 73–74
    stages of, 75, 76

Text Credits

Chapter 1   **Figure 1.1:** Sample Hornbook. Reprinted by permission of Brigham Young University.

Figure 1.2: New England Primer. Reprinted by permission of Brigham Young University.

Figure 1.3: McGuffey's Reader. Reprinted by permission of Brigham Young University.

Figure 1.4: Image of Dick and Jane Reader. Text and Illustration on p.19 from *Happy Days with Our Friends* by Elizabeth Montgomery, W. W. Bauer, and William S. Gray, illustrated by Ruth Steed, Copyright © 1948, by Scott Foresman and company, © renewed 1974. Reprinted by permission of Pearson Education, Inc.

Chapter 2   p. 15, Letter from First Grade Teacher. Reprinted by permission of the author.

Chapter 3   **Figure 3.1:** Effective Teaching Methods. Borich, Gary D., *Effective Teaching Methods with Bridges Activity Book*, 5th Ed., © 2004. Reprinted and electronically reproduced by permission of Pearson Education, Inc., Upper Saddle River, New Jersey.

Figure 3.3: Traits of Effective Writing. Spandel, Vicki, *Creating Young Writers: Using the Six Traits to Enrich Writing Process in Primary Classrooms*, 2nd Ed., © 2008. Reprinted and electronically reproduced by permission of Pearson Education, Inc., Upper Saddle River, New Jersey.

p. 61, Journal Entry. Reprinted by permission of the author.

Chapter 4   **Figure 4.1** Christmas Lights Drawing by Steve Morrison. Not previously published. Printed by permission of the author.

Figure 4.4: Samples of Developmental Writing Phases. Reprinted by permission of the rights holders.

Figure 4.5: Sample Page from a Child's Developmental Journal. Reprinted by permission of the rights holder.

Figure 4.6: Sample Page from a Developmental Journal with a Teacher's Translation. Reprinted by permission of the rights holder.

Chapter 5   p. 83, English Isn't Easy! Reprinted by permission of the author.

Figure 5.2 Sample Hink Pinks by Children. Reprinted by permission of the rights holders.

Figure 5.3 Concepts about Print. Reprinted by permission of Pearson New Zealand and the Marie Clay Trust.

Chapter 6   **Figure 6.1** Class Book by First, Fourth, and Fifth Graders. Reprinted by permission of the rights holders.

Chapter 7   p. 143, More than Anything Else quote. From *More than Anything Else* by Marie Bradly. Scholastic Inc./Orchard Books. Copyright © 1995 by Marie Bradley. Used by permission.

p. 147, Student Sample Telephone Number Poems. Reprinted by permission of the rights holders.

Chapter 9   **Figure 9.10:** Sample Think-Write-Share. Reprinted by permission of the rights holder.

Figure 9.11: Samples of Student Note Taking. Reprinted by permission of the rights holder.

Figure 9.14: ABC Book. Reprinted by permission of the rights holders.

Figure 9.16: Student-Made Ads. Reprinted by permission of the rights holders.

Chapter 11   p. 243, To, With, and By. Reprinted by permission of the author.

Chapter 13   **Figure 13.2:** Roles and Responsibilities for Literature Discussion Groups. Adapted from *Literature Circles* by Harvey Daniels, copyright © 2002, used by permission of Stenhouse Publishers.

Chapter 14   p. 315, Note to Mr. Wilcox. Reprinted by permission of the author.

Photo Credits

p. 8, © Rob/Fotolia LLC; p. 23, David Grossman/Alamy; p. 24, © Alex Segre/Alamy; p. 25, © MauMar70/Fotolia LLC; p. 27, © Darrin Henry/Fotolia LLC; p. 32, © World History Archive/Alamy; p. 35, nyul/Fotolia LLC; p. 45, © Monkey Business/Fotolia LLC; p. 59 top, © Jacek Chabraszewski/ Fotolia LLC; p. 69, © Prod. Numérik/Fotolia LLC; p. 201, © Monkey Business/Fotolia LLC; p. 272, © Monkey Business/ Fotolia LLC; p. 304, © iofoto/Fotolia LLC; p. 307, © Monkey Business/Fotolia LLC; p. 320, © Isaiah Love/Fotolia LLC; p. 336, © Monkey Business/Fotolia LLC; p. 340, © El.onore H/Fotolia LLC; pp. 16, 22, 49, 58, 59 bottom, 72, 80, 130, 209, 221, 226, 256, 263, 270, 279, 288, 294, 295, 302, 306, 311, 317, 320 bottom., courtesy of authors.

IRA Standards, 2010

IRA Standards, 2010	Element Number and Description	Where it is covered in *Developing Literacy: Reading and Writing To, With, and By Children*
Standard 1 **Foundational Knowledge** Candidates understand the theoretical and evidence-based foundations of reading and writing processes and instruction.	**Element 1.1** Candidates understand major theories and empirical research that describe the cognitive, linguistic, motivational, and sociocultural foundations of reading and writing development, processes, and components, including word recognition, language comprehension, strategic knowledge, and reading–writing connections.	**Chapters 1, 2, 3, 4, 6, 7, 8**
	Element 1.2 Candidates understand the historically shared knowledge of the profession and changes over time in the perceptions of reading and writing development, processes, and components.	**Chapters 1, 2, 3**
	Element 1.3 Candidates understand the role of professional judgment and practical knowledge for improving all students' reading development and achievement.	**Chapters 3, 10, 11, 12, 13, 14**
Standard 2 **Curriculum and Instruction** Candidates use instructional approaches, materials, and an integrated, comprehensive, balanced curriculum to support student learning in reading and writing.	**Element 2.1** Candidates use foundational knowledge to design or implement an integrated, comprehensive, and balanced curriculum.	**Chapters 1, 2, 3, 11, 12, 13, 14** *"Try This for Teaching" boxes throughout*
	Element 2.2 Candidates use appropriate and varied instructional approaches, including those that develop word recognition, language comprehension, strategic knowledge, and reading–writing connections.	**Chapters 4, 5, 6, 7, 8, 9, 11, 12, 13, 14** *"Try This for Teaching" boxes throughout*
	Element 2.3 Candidates use a wide range of texts (e.g., narrative, expository, and poetry) from traditional print, digital, and online resources.	**Chapters 3, 4, 7, 8, 9, 11, 12, 13** *"Try This for Teaching" boxes throughout*
Standard 3 **Assessment and Evaluation** Candidates use a variety of assessment tools and practices to plan and evaluate effective reading and writing instruction.	**Element 3.1** Candidates understand types of assessments and their purposes, strengths, and limitations.	**Chapters 2, 6, 10**
	Element 3.2 Candidates select, develop, administer, and interpret assessments, both traditional print and electronic, for specific purposes.	**Chapters 2, 6, 10** *Struggling Learners marginal icons throughout*
	Element 3.3 Candidates use assessment information to plan and evaluate instruction.	**Chapters 10, 11, 12, 13, 14**
	Element 3.4 Candidates communicate assessment results and implications to a variety of audiences.	**Chapter 10**